Informatik aktuell

Herausgeber: W. Brauer
im Auftrag der Gesellschaft für Informatik (GI)

Springer
*Berlin
Heidelberg
New York
Barcelona
Budapest
Hongkong
London
Mailand
Paris
Santa Clara
Singapur
Tokio*

Martina Zitterbart (Hrsg.)

Kommunikation in Verteilten Systemen

GI/ITG-Fachtagung
Braunschweig, 19.–21. Februar 1997

Springer

Herausgeber

Martina Zitterbart
Technische Universität Braunschweig
Institut für Betriebssysteme und Rechnerverbund
Bültenweg 74/75, D-38106 Braunschweig

Programmausschuß

Sebastian Abeck	Universität Karlsruhe
Berthold Butscher	GDM FOKUS/DeTeBerkom
Wolfgang Effelsberg	Universität Mannheim
Walter Gora	Corporate Systems Sulzbach
Heinz-Gerd Hegering	Universität München
Bernhard Hohlfeld	Daimler-Benz AG
Elmar Holler	Forschungszentrum Karlsruhe
Uwe Hübner	TU Chemnitz-Zwickau
Nina Kalt	SNI München
Udo Krieger	DBP Telekom Darmstadt
Paul J. Kühn	Universität Stuttgart
Horst Langendörfer	TU Braunschweig
Mathias Leclerc	Dresdner Bank
Lothar Mackert	IBM Sindelfingen
Peter Martini	Universität Bonn
Eckart Raubold	GMD Darmstadt
Kurt Rothermel	Universität Stuttgart
Alexander Schill	TU Dresden
Otto Spaniol	RWTH Aachen
Heiner Stüttgen	IBM Heidelberg
Joachim Swoboda	TU München
Martina Zitterbart	TU Braunschweig

Die Deutsche Bibliothek – CIP-Einheitsaufnahme

Kommunikation in verteilten Systemen : GI/ITG-Fachtagung ... – Berlin; Heidelberg; New York;
Barcelona; Budapest; Hongkong; London; Mailand; Paris; Santa Clara; Singapur; Tokio: Springer.
(Informatik aktuell)
Beitr. teilw. dt., teilw. engl. – Teilw. mit der Ausgabe: ITG/GI-Fachtagung
ISSN 0720-5503
NE: Gesellschaft für Informatik; Informationstechnische Gesellschaft 1997. Braunschweig,
19.–21. Februar 1997. – 1997
ISBN-13: 978-3-540-62565-0   e-ISBN-13: 978-3-642-60729-5
DOI: 10.1007/ 978-3-642-60729-5

CR Subject Classification (1997): A.0

ISBN-13: 978-3-540-62565-0 Springer-Verlag Berlin Heidelberg New York

© Springer-Verlag Berlin Heidelberg 1997

Satz: Reproduktionsfertige Vorlage vom Autor/Herausgeber

SPIN: 10547240   33/3142-543210 – Gedruckt auf säurefreiem Papier

Vorwort

Der vorliegende Tagungsband enthält Beiträge der 10. Fachtagung Kommunikation in Verteilten Systemen (KiVS), die im Februar 1997 in Braunschweig stattfand. Der adressierte Forschungsbereich ist nach wie vor außerordentlich vital und geprägt durch spannende Entwicklungen, beispielsweise die steigende Integration von Kommunikationssystemen im kommerziellen aber auch im privaten Bereich. WWW soll hier nur als ein prägnantes Schlagwort genannt werden. Electronic Commerce ist eine weitere hochinteressante Anwendung, der im Rahmen dieser Tagung Raum gewidmet ist.

Steigende und neuartige Anforderungen, etwa von seiten verteilter multimedialer Anwendungen (z.B. Videokonferenzing, CSCW), erfordern immer effizientere und flexiblere Kommunikationssysteme. Vor allem die immens wachsende Bedeutung von Mechanismen zur Gewährleistung von Sicherheit in Verteilten Systemen ist anzuführen. Darüber hinaus stellen Ansprüche an Dienstqualitäten in den sich etablierenden ATM-Netzen einen wichtigen Gesichtspunkt dar. Weiterhin stellt ein Paradigmenwechsel von der Individualkommunikation hin zur Gruppenkommunikation als grundlegendes Kommunikationsmuster eine außerordentlich wichtige Entwicklungsrichtung dar. All diesen Themen sind jeweils dedizierte Sitzungen mit hochinteressanten Beiträgen aus Industrie und Forschung gewidmet.

Nicht weniger interessant sind die Beiträge zu formalen Beschreibungstechniken, die sich hier mit richtungsweisenden Weiterentwicklungen befassen. Dasselbe gilt für die Sitzung zu den Themen Verteilte Systeme, Netzwerkmanagement und Middleware.

Eine weitere hochaktuelle Entwicklungsrichtung ist in der Mobilkommunikation zu sehen. Die Sitzung Mobilkommunikation sowie der eingeladene Vortrag zum Thema Mobility Management präsentieren hier richtungsweisende Trends.

Die KiVS ist eine Tagung mit langer Tradition, die sich direkt im Spannungsfeld zwischen Industrie und Forschung angesiedelt sieht. Dies reflektieren auch die teilweise sehr industrienahen Vorträge sowie besonders die Sitzung zur Thematik Multimedia-Anwendungen im industriellen Umfeld.

Von besonderem Interesse ist die Sitzung mit Vorträgen der Preisträger. Hier wird jungen Wissenschaftlerinnen und Wissenschaftlern die Möglichkeit geboten, ihre herausragenden Leistungen in ihrer Diplom- bzw. Doktorarbeit einem breiten Publikum zu präsentieren. Diese Arbeiten wurden von der GI-Fachgruppe Kommunikation und Verteilte Systeme jeweils als beste Arbeiten des Jahres 1995 bzw. 1996 ausgezeichnet.

Dank geht an alle, die bei der Organisation der Tagung beteiligt waren. Namentlich erwähnt seien hier Urs Thürmann und Ralph Wittmann, die sich um viele doch so wichtige "Kleinigkeiten" und Details gekümmert haben.

Braunschweig, im November 1996   Martina Zitterbart

Inhaltsverzeichnis

Session 1:

Multimedia-Anwendungen: Elektronische Märkte

Online Casinos

Rolf Oppliger and Jean-Luc Nottaris

University of Berne
Institute for Computer Science and Applied Mathematics (IAM)
Neubrückstrasse 10, CH-3012 Berne, Switzerland

Abstract. Online casinos allow arbitrary users to remotely participate in mental game playing, such as e.g. Mental Poker or Mental Black Jack. Two recent developments have brought the realization of online casinos closer to reality: On the one hand, cryptographic research has come up with practical solutions and corresponding protocols to the problems of how to play games mentally and how to spend money over open networks, and on the other hand, the Internet has become a globally accessible packet-switched (inter)networking infrastructure that provides support for multicast communications. This paper overviews the basic principles of mental games and digital payment schemes, and proposes a model that can be used to set up and run online casinos within a multicast environment, such as e.g. provided by the Internet Multicast Backbone (MBone). The paper also addresses a prototype implementation that has been done at the University of Berne.

1   Introduction

If one area exists where stand-alone computer systems have been far more successful than computer networks and distributed systems, that area is games. We have seen a wide proliferation of computer games during the last decade, and many companies make a good living from selling corresponding software packages. While some of these games are really good at incorporating multimedia streams, such as audio, video, and animations, only few of them also support multi-user and multi-player capabilities. The vast majority of these games are designed to be played by just one person at a time. By contrast, games on computer networks and distributed systems are designed for multi-player use, but in doing so they tend to sacrifice most multimedia features. What they gain, however, is the possibility of global, simultaneous game playing among large numbers of players, and this possibility is required for casinos to go online.

In this paper, the term online casino is used to refer to a casino that offers its service, which is game playing, over open networks, such as e.g. the Internet, to a potentially very wide audience. Thus, an online casino allows arbitrary users to remotely participate in mental game playing, such as e.g. Mental Poker or Mental Black Jack. The primary gaming technology on the Internet today are multi-user environments in which each player must log on a particular host and maintain a TCP/IP connection to this host accordingly. Thus, n connections are required for n participants to play simultaneously, and this may not scale for large n.

Two recent developments have brought the realization of online casinos closer to reality: On the one hand, cryptographic research has come up with practical solutions and corresponding protocols to the problems of how to play games mentally and how to use money over open networks, and on the other hand, the Internet has become a globally accessible packet-switched (inter)networking infrastructure that provides support for multicast communications. The term multicast refers to a technique which allows a single datagram to be passed to selected destinations. It can thus be considered as a generalization of the broadcast and unicast techniques. A datagram is unicast, if it is delivered from one source to one destination, and it is broadcast, if it is delivered to all hosts attached to a network. IP multicast is an extension of local area networking multicast to TCP/IP networks [5, 4]. It provides support for the transmission of an IP datagram to a host group which is a set of hosts identified by a single class D IP destination address [6]. A multicast datagram is delivered to all members of its destination host group with the same best efforts quality of service as regular unicast IP datagrams, i.e., the datagram is not guaranteed to arrive intact at all members of the host group or in the same order relative to other datagrams. The membership of a host group is dynamic, and hosts can join and leave groups at any time. There is no restriction on the location or number of members in a host group, and a host may be a member of more than just one host group at a time. Also, a host need not be a member of a group to send datagrams to it. A host group may be permanent or transient.

- A permanent host group has a well-known, administratively assigned class D IP address. Note that it is the address, not the membership of the host group, that is permanent. At any time a permanent host group may have any number of members, even zero.
- Those class D IP multicast addresses that are not reserved for permanent groups are available for dynamic assignment to transient host groups. These groups exist only as long as they have members.

Internet forwarding of IP multicast datagrams is handled by multicast routers (mrouters), which may be co-resident with, or separate from, normal Internet routers. A host transmits an IP multicast datagram as a local network multicast that reaches all immediately-neighboring members of the destination host group. If the datagram has an IP time-to-live (TTL) value that is greater than 1, the mrouter(s) attached to the local network take responsibility for forwarding it towards all other networks that have members of the destination group. On those other member networks that are reachable within the TTL, an attached mrouter completes delivery by transmitting the datagram as a local multicast. In order to participate in IP multicast, a host must be able to send and receive multicast datagrams. In IPv4, a host communicates its group membership by using the Internet Group Management Protcol (IGMP). In IPv6 (or IPng respectively), the IGMP is incorporated into the Internet Control Management Protcol (ICMP) [10, 11].

The Multicast Backbone (MBone) is an experimental network that is overlaid on the existing IPv4-based Internet to carry IP multicast datagrams [14, 7]. It originated from experiments during IETF meetings in which live audio and video were transmitted around the world. Application tools, such as `vat` (visual audio tool), `nevot` (network voice terminal), `nv` (network video), `ivs` (inria videoconferencing system), `vic` (video conferencing) and `wb` (whiteboard) are publicly available today. They can be used to hold multimedia conference sessions over the MBone. In addition to that, session directory tools, such as `sd` or `sdr`, can be used to announce MBone conference sessions in public, and to have MBone application tools start up according to the session parameters.

This paper overviews the basic principles of mental games and digital payment schemes, and proposes a model that can be used to set up and run online casinos within a multicast environment, such as e.g. the MBone. The paper also addresses a prototype implementation that has been done at the Institute for Computer Science and Applied Mathematics (IAM) of the University of Berne. The rest of the paper is organized as follows: The terminology that is used to subsequently describe the cryptographic protocols is summarized in section 2. The basic principles of mental games and digital payment schemes are overviewed in sections 3 and 4, and a model for online casinos is proposed in section 5. A prototype implementation is addressed in section 6, and conclusions are drawn in section 7.

2 Terminology

A protocol specifies the format and relative timing of messages exchanged between communicating entities. A cryptographic protocol is a protocol that uses cryptography, meaning that all or parts of the messages are encrypted on the sender' side and decrypted on the receiver' side [17]. The following notation is used to describe cryptographic protocols:

- The term K is used to refer to a secret key, which is a key taken from a secret key cryptosystem, whereas the term (k, k^{-1}) is used to refer to a public key pair, which is a key pair taken from a public key cryptosystem. In either case, key subscripts may be used to refer to particular entities.
- The term $\{m\}K$ is used to refer to a message m that is encrypted with the secret key K. The same key is used for decryption; thus, $\{\{m\}K\}K$ equals m.
- Similarly, the term $\{m\}k$ is used to refer to a message m that is encrypted with the public key k. The message can be decrypted only with the corresponding private key k^{-1}; thus, $\{\{m\}k\}k^{-1}$ equals m.
- In a digital signature scheme, a user's private key is used to digitally sign messages, and the corresponding public key is used to verify the signatures. Referring to the OSI terminology, the term $\{m\}k^{-1}$ is used to denote a digital signature giving message recovery, whereas the term $\langle m \rangle k^{-1}$ is used to denote a digital signature with appendix [12]. Note that in the second case, $\langle m \rangle k^{-1}$ in fact abbreviates $m, \{h(m)\}k^{-1}$, with h referring to a collision-resistant one-way hash function.

– In accordance to international standardization, the term $X \ll Y \gg$ is used to refer to a certificate that has been issued by X for Y's long-term public key k_Y. This certificate may conform to any standard in use today, such as e.g. ITU-T X.509 [13].

In addition to that, π_n is used to refer to a permutation of n numbers, L_n to a list of n random numbers, and square brackets $[]^+$ to an iteration of one or more times.

3   Mental Games

Mental game playing is an application that has attracted many cryptographers in the past. The rules for a mental game are just like its regular counterpart, except that players may communicate over a public and open network, such as e.g. the public switched telephone network (PSTN), the integrated services digital network (ISDN), or even the Internet. There are many games that can be played mentally. They range from rather simple games, such as e.g. coin flipping, to more sophisticated games, such as e.g. Mental Poker.

Playing Mental Poker is actually a very difficult problem for several reasons. The foremost reason is that it is impossible from an information-theoretic point of view. This result is due to Shamir, Rivest, and Adleman [18]. The same authors, however, have also proposed a protocol for playing mental poker that relies on the difficulty of inverting certain cryptographic transformations. The protocol was shown to be insecure by Lipton and Coppersmith. Lipton found a way to determine one bit about the messages using the fact that exponentiation modulo n preserves quadratic residuosity. This leakage of partial information was fixed by Goldwasser and Micali in the two-player case, using probabilistic encryption [9]. Unfortunately, their scheme does not extend to a larger number of players. Several protocols that have been proposed so far address the multi-player problem instance. Unfortunately, they all make special assumptions, such as the players' inability to establish secret communications [19] or the existence of a trusted third party [8]. In 1985, Crépeau came up with a protocol for playing Mental Poker that minimizes the effect of player coalitions [2], and one year later, he even presented an enhanced version of the protocol that does not require that players reveal their cards at the end of the game to show that they didn't cheat. This protocol allows players to keep secret their strategy, and to keep up a poker face accordingly [3]. In 1987, Goldreich, Micali, and Wigderson proposed a generalization of this protocol. In fact, they came up with a polynomial-time algorithm that, given as input the description of a mental game with incomplete information and any number of players, produces a protocol for playing the game that leaks no partial information, provided the majority of the players is honest.

This paper does not further elaborate on the theory of mental game playing. Instead, it focuses on Mental Black Jack (also known as "21") as an exemplary (and sufficiently simple) game that can be used to set up and run an online casino within a multicast environment. Black Jack is at present considered as one of the world's most popular games played with cards. The aim of Black Jack, which is played against a bank, is to acquire a total card value as near as possible to 21, without exceeding it. To determine his value, the player must remember that cards from two to nine take their pip or number value. Tens, Jacks, Queens, and Kings count ten each. Aces, at the player's option, count 1 or 11. At start, the banker deals two cards and the player may stand, refusing other cards, or hit, asking for one or more cards to improve his count. If he goes over 21, he busts and loses his bets. If he decides to stand, the banker gives himself one or more cards following the rules of the game. However, the banker must give himself a card if his count totals 16 or less, while he must stand if his count totals 17 or more. If a player's first two cards are a ten or a court card and an ace, he has a Black Jack. He has "21" when a count of 21 is obtained with three or more cards. When the banker has a Black Jack, all players lose their bets except the ones also having a Black Jack, as the bet is called off. In this case, no one loses or wins. The bet can be left for the next deal or can be withdrawn. A Black Jack is paid 3 to 2, except in the event of tie (same count) with the banker. If nobody has a Black Jack, the count which is nearest to 21 wins. If the count is lower than the banker's, bets are lost. If there is a tie, the bet is called off. If 21 is exceeded, the banker wins. If the banker busts, bets win.

There are some variations of the game making it possible to increase the initial bet and hence the winnings, when the initial cards have already been dealt. These variations refer to double-down, split Pair, and insurance. Note that the model proposed in section 5 is designed to handle Mental Black Jack as an exemplary game that can be played mentally within an online casino. The same model is (at least conceptually) able to handle any cryptographic protocol that one may think of and come up with. The variations mentioned above are therefore not further addressed in this paper.

4 Digital Payment Schemes

A digital payment scheme addresses the problem of how to securely spend money over a public and inherently open network, such as e.g. the Internet, and how to securely process financial transactions accordingly. The availability of digital payment schemes is a crucial prerequisite for online casinos to be used and widely deployed. There are many digital payment schemes available today. They can be divided into two major categories:

- Payment schemes that follow the credit card model, where a customer uses his credit card to buy and postpay goods and services. The most important example of this category is the Secure Electronic Transaction (SET) protocol as specified by the major credit card companies and software vendors, including Visa International, MasterCard, and Microsoft.
- Payment schemes that follow the debit card model, where a customer buys and prepays tickets that he can later use to obtain goods and services. In the simplest case, the tickets refer to digital cash. There are three parties

involved in a digital cash system: customers, merchants, and a bank. Every customer and every merchant is assumed to have an account with the bank. The customer withdraws digital cash from his account and spends it with a merchant. The merchant, in turn, deposits the cash he receives from the customer on his account. Digital cash protocols are protocols for the interactions between customers, merchants, and a bank. During the last decade, various digital cash protocols have been proposed to be used either in online or offline systems:

- Online systems require the merchant to communicate with the bank at every sale, whereas
- offline systems require no communication between the merchant and the bank until after the transaction between the merchant and the customer.

From a security point of view, online systems are advantageous. If there is a problem, the bank simply doesn't accept the cash and the customer cannot cheat. Offline systems can't prevent a customer from cheating, but instead detect cheating. Another way is to create a special smart card containing a tamperproof chip (which is often called an observer). The observer keeps a database of all the pieces of digital cash spent by the smart card. If a customer attempts to copy some digital cash and spend it twice, the observer detects the attempt and does not allow the transaction. Since the chip is tamperproof, the customer can't erase the database without permanently damaging the smart card. Digital cash protocols can also be divided along another line. Electronic coins have a fixed value; people using this system need several coins in different denominations. Electronic checks can be used for any amount up to a maximum value and then returned for a refund of the unspent portion. Another distinction is made whether a digital cash protocol preserves the customers' anonymity. The cryptographic techniques that can be used to provide anonymous digital cash are blind digital signatures [1].

Both categories provide suitable payment schemes for online casinos. Payment schemes that follow the debit card model are appropriate for games with small stakes, whereas payment schemes that follow the credit card model better fit the requirements of games with larger stakes. With special regard to online casinos, micropayment schemes provide a viable alternative. Micropayments schemes are a special kind of payment schemes for applications in which each payment is sufficiently small. To support micropayments, efficiency is required; otherwise, the cost of the mechanism will exceed the value of the payments. The area of micropayments has attracted considerable attention recently, and several researchers have proposed corresponding schemes.

It is assumed that there will be many digital payment schemes in the future, and that there must be a negotiation layer on top of the corresponding protocols. This negotiation layer and its protocols are being defined by the Joint Electronic Payment Initiative (JEPI) jointly announced by the CommerceNet and World Wide Web Consortium (W3C). The model proposed next does not require a particular payment scheme, but assumes different payment schemes to coexist simultaneously . Thus, it is up to the user to specify a particular payment scheme (that is supported by the online casino), and to buy and sell chips accordingly.

5 Model

Having introduced the basic principles of mental games and digital payment schemes, this section works towards a synthesis of both in a model for online casinos. The processes involved and the cryptographic protocols are overviewed in the following subsections.

5.1 Process Overview

It is assumed that online casino $\mathcal{C}$ is managed by a casino manager process C, and that C creates and stops table processes $T_i(i = 1, \ldots, n)$ according to user demand. Referring to the real world, C represents the casino manager, whereas each T_i represents the dealer running table i. T_i not only represents the dealer of table i, but the banker (or cashier) as well. In this model, every table has a banker of its own, and payments are considered locally, meaning that players buy and sell chips from the dealer of the table they play at. This approach has been chosen for simplicity, and there is no underlying reason, why a cashier would not be able to serve an entire casino.

In addition to that, it is assumed that C has a public key pair (k_C, k_C^{-1}) of which k_C is publicly available and generally trusted, and each T_i has a public key pair $(k_{T_i}, k_{T_i}^{-1})$ of which k_{T_i} is publicly available but not generally trusted. It is up to C to certify k_{T_i}, and to provide T_i with a corresponding certificate $C \ll T_i \gg$.

Each T_i has chips of size $s_{i1}, \ldots, s_{il_i}$. For every chip size $s_{ir}(r = 1, \ldots, l_i)$ he holds a public key pair $(k_{s_{ir}}, k_{s_{ir}}^{-1})$ of which $k_{s_{ir}}$ is publicly available, certified, and distributed by T_i, whereas $k_{s_{ir}}^{-1}$ is kept private and is used only to sell and buy chips. To keep the protocols sufficiently simple, it is assumed that each T_i has 4 decks of 13 cards each, resulting in a total number of $n = 52$ cards.

Figure 1 illustrates the model for an online casino. It shows the casino manager and table processes, the communication channels between them, as well as the corresponding message flows. With regard to the communication channels, it is assumed that C is assigned a permanent IP class D address, which is denoted as Adr_C, and each T_i is assigned a transient IP class D addresses from a pool. Consequently, there is a multicast channel assigned to C and each T_i. In addition to that, there are several unicast channels between players and table processes.

5.2 Cryptographic Protocols

In principle, a user can enter the casino, join a table, play games at that table, quit it, and leave the casino. The corresponding protocols are overviewed next.

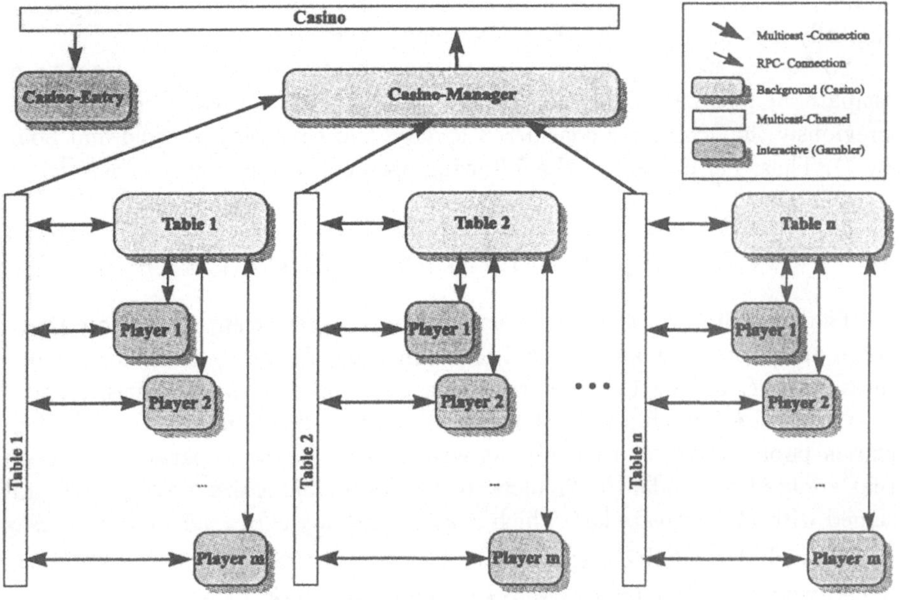

Fig. 1. Model for an online casino

Enter the Casino If user U wants to enter the casino, he has to grab the information that C periodically multicasts to Adr_C. This information includes a description of each table T_i $(i = 1, \ldots, n)$ that is up and running, and that U can join and play at. U (or his user agent respectively) can interpret the information locally and render a graphical representation accordingly.

Join a Table If user U wants to join table T_i, he has to randomly select a public key pair (k, k^{-1}) and run the following join table protocol:

$$1 : U \longrightarrow Adr_{T_i} : \text{JOIN\_TABLE\_REQUEST}(U, k)$$
$$2 : T_i \longrightarrow Adr_{T_i} : \text{JOIN\_TABLE\_CONFIRMATION}(\langle U, j, T_i \ll P_{ij} \gg \rangle k_{T_i}^{-1})$$

In step 1, U multicasts a join table request message to Adr_{T_i}. The message includes U and k. T_i grabs the message and decides whether he's going to serve U at table i. If he's going to serve U, he selects a track number $1 \leq j \leq m$ for U, and returns a corresponding join table confirmation message to Adr_{T_i} in step 2. In this case, the message includes U, j, and a certificate $T_i \ll P_{ij} \gg$ for U's public key k. The message is digitally signed by T_i with its private key $k_{T_i}^{-1}$. If T_i is not going to serve U at table i, he simply returns a value for j that is equal to zero.

If $j > 0$, U becomes a legitimate player on track $1 \leq j \leq m$ of table i. In this case, P_{ij} is used to refer to this user, and $(k_{P_{ij}}, k_{P_{ij}}^{-1})$ is used to refer to P_{ij}'s

10

public key pair (formerly denoted as (k, k^{-1})). P_{ij} uses this private key $k_{P_{ij}}^{-1}$ do digitally sign messages that he subsequently sends out.

So far, P_{ij} has only received permission to play at table i. In order to participate, he still has to buy some chips from T_i. It has already been mentioned previously that chips are considered locally, and that they are sold and bought by T_i. Thus, P_{ij} has to use the following protocol to buy a chip of size s_{ir}:

$$1 : P_{ij} \longrightarrow T_i \ : \text{BUY\_CHIP\_REQUEST}(\langle s_{ir}, k, params \rangle k_{P_{ij}}^{-1})$$
$$2 : T_i \longrightarrow P_{ij} : \text{BUY\_CHIPS\_CONFIRMATION}(\langle \{k\} k_{s_{ir}}^{-1} \rangle k_{T_i}^{-1})$$

The buy chip protocol can be used by any player at any time. Note that its communication flows are not multicast. Instead, P_{ij} sends a buy chip request message to T_i in step 1, and T_i returns a buy chip confirmation message to P_{ij} in step 2. The buy chip request message includes the chip size s_{ir}, a randomly chosen public key k for this chip, as well as some payment parameters $params$ that are used to handle the financial transaction. The entire message is digitally signed with P_{ij}'s private key, which is $k_{P_{ij}}^{-1}$. The buy chip confirmation message, in turn, includes k digitally signed with $k_{s_{ir}}^{-1}$. Again, the whole message is digitally signed with its originator's private key, which is now $k_{T_i}^{-1}$.

If P_{ij} wants to buy several chips, he (or his user agent respectively) has to iteratively initiate and rerun the buy chip protocol. It is also possible to modify the protocol to support buying several chips in a single protocol run. This possibility, however, does not extend the overall functionality and is therefore omitted in this paper.

Play Games Having joined T_i and bought some chips, $P_{ij}(i = 1, \ldots, n; j = 1, \ldots, m)$ can play multiple games at table i. For every single game g $(g = 1, \ldots)$, T_i has to shuffle the cards, have the players bet, deal the cards, play the game, and pay off. The corresponding protocols are overviewed next.

To shuffle the cards, T_i has to randomly select a permutation $\pi_n^{(g)}$ of n cards, and each player P_{ij} has to randomly select a list of n numbers $L_n^{(ijg)}$ that he has to keep secret. They all commit to their selection by multicasting a one-way hash value of $\pi_n^{(g)}$ and $L_n^{(ijg)}$ to Adr_{T_i}. Thus, T_i multicasts a shuffle card message to Adr_{T_i} that looks like

$$T_i \longrightarrow Adr_{T_i} : \text{SHUFFLE\_CARDS}(\langle T_i, g, h(\pi_n^{(g)}) \rangle k_{T_i}^{-1})$$

and each player P_{ij} multicasts a similar message to Adr_{T_i}

$$P_{ij} \longrightarrow Adr_{T_i} : \text{SHUFFLE\_CARDS}(\langle P_{ij}, g, h(L_n^{(ijg)}) \rangle k_{P_{ij}}^{-1})$$

Note that the messages are digitally signed by their originators. Before dealing the cards, each player must place his bets. In a real casino, this step refers to the step in which each player puts some chips on the table. In principle, each chip represents a bet. In an online casino, the corresponding protocol can be summarized as follows:

$$
\begin{aligned}
&1 : T_i \longrightarrow Adr_{T_i} : \text{BET\_START}(\langle T_i, g, start\rangle k_{T_i}^{-1}) \\
&2 : P_{ij} \longrightarrow Adr_{T_i} : \text{BET\_REQUEST}(\langle P_{ij}, T_i, g, s_{ir}, \{k\}k_{s_{ir}}^{-1}\rangle k_{P_{ij}}^{-1}) \\
&3 : T_i \longrightarrow P_{ij} : \text{BET\_CHALLENGE}(\langle T_i, g, c, N\rangle k_{T_i}^{-1}) \\
&4 : P_{ij} \longrightarrow T_i : \text{BET\_RESPONSE}(\langle T_i, g, c, N\rangle k^{-1}) \\
&5 : T_i \longrightarrow Adr_{T_i} : \text{BET\_STOP}(\langle T_i, g, stop\rangle k_{T_i}^{-1}) \\
&6 : T_i \longrightarrow Adr_{T_i} : \text{BET\_CONFIRMATION}(\langle T_i, g, [(P_{ir}, V_{ir})]^{+}\rangle k_{T_i}^{-1})
\end{aligned}
$$

In step 1, T_i initializes the protcol run by multicasting a bet start message to Adr_{T_i}. The message includes T_i and g. It is digitally signed with T_i's private key $k_{T_i}^{-1}$. It is now up to each P_{ij} to place his bets. If P_{ij} wants to place a bet, he multicasts a bet request message to Adr_{T_i} in step 2. The message includes P_{ij}, T_i, g, s_{ir}, and $\{k\}k_{s_{ir}}^{-1}$. Again, it is digitally signed with the originator's private key, which is now $k_{P_{ij}}^{-1}$. Note that $\{k\}k_{s_{ir}}^{-1}$ represents a chip of size s_{ir}. To prove legitimate ownership of the chip, P_{ij} has to run a challenge-response handshake with T_i. In step 3, T_i challenges P_{ij} with a bet challenge message that includes a bet counter c and a nonce N. The bet counter is incremented by one for every single bet of P_{ij} in game g, whereas the nonce is randomly chosen by T_i. In step 4, P_{ij} has to provide T_i with a correct response which corresponds to the same message digitally signed with the private key k^{-1} that belongs to the chip's public key k. Protocol steps 2 to 4 can be iterated an arbitrary number of times. After a certain amount of time, T_i multicasts a bet stop message in step 5 and a bet confirmation message in step 6. The first message indicates that bets are going to be accepted only for a certain amount of time, whereas the second message indicates the fact that time has run out and bets are no longer accepted. Both messages are digitally signed by T_i with his private key $k_{T_i}^{-1}$. The bet confirmation message also carries information about the players P_{ir} and their total bet values $V_{ir}(r = 1, \ldots, m)$. Again, the message is digitally signed by T_i.

To deal card d $(d = 1, \ldots, n)$ and provide P_{ij} with a card, T_i has to run the following protocol:

$$
\begin{aligned}
&1 : T_i \longrightarrow Adr_{T_i} : \text{DEAL\_CARD\_REQUEST}(\langle T_i, g, d\rangle k_{T_i}^{-1}) \\
&2 : P_{ir} \longrightarrow Adr_{T_i} : \text{DEAL\_CARD\_SHIFT}(\langle P_{ir}, g, d, L_n^{(irg)}[d]\rangle k_{P_{ir}}^{-1}) \\
&3 : T_i \longrightarrow Adr_{T_i} : \text{DEAL\_CARD\_SHOW}(\langle T_i, g, d, P_{ij}, \\
&\phantom{3 : T_i \longrightarrow Adr_{T_i} :} : \pi_n^{(g)}[\textstyle\sum_r L_n^{(irg)}[d](mod\ n - d)]\rangle k_{T_i}^{-1})
\end{aligned}
$$

In step 1, T_i multicasts a deal card request message to Adr_{T_i}. The message includes T_i, g, and d. It is digitally signed by T_i with $k_{T_i}^{-1}$. It is now up to each player $P_{ir}(r = 1, \ldots, m)$ to multicast a deal card shift message to Adr_{T_i}. This message includes P_{ir}, g, d, and $L_n^{(irg)}[d]$, with $L_n^{(irg)}[d]$ referring to element d in P_{ir}'s random number list $L_n^{(irg)}$. Again, the message is digitally signed with the originator's private key, which is $k_{P_{ir}}^{-1}$. After all players have sent out their messages in step 2, T_i multicasts a deal card show message to Adr_{T_i} in step 3. This message reveals card d to P_{ij}. It includes T_i, g, d, P_{ij}, and $\pi_n^{(g)}[\sum_r L_n^{(irg)}[d](mod\ n - d)]$. The whole message is digitally signed with $k_{T_i}^{-1}$. It is important that T_i drops card d from $\pi_n^{(g)}$ after the protocol run. Thus, the list becomes shorter. Multiple cards can be dealt by running the deal card protocol iteratively.

To play game k, T_i has to run a handshake protocol with each player P_{ij}. The protocol consists of two steps that can be summarized as follows:

$$1 : T_i \longrightarrow Adr_{T_i} : \text{PLAY\_REQUEST}(\langle T_i, g, j, N \rangle k_{T_i}^{-1})$$
$$2 : P_{ij} \longrightarrow Adr_{T_i} : \text{PLAY\_CONFIRMATION}(\langle P_{ij}, g, N, hit \mid stand \rangle k_{P_{ij}}^{-1})$$

In step 1, T_i multicasts a play request message to Adr_{T_i}. The message includes T_i, g, j, and a nonce N. It addresses player j and is digitally signed by T_i with $k_{T_i}^{-1}$. It is now up to P_{ij} to grab the message and return a play confirmation message to Adr_{T_i} in step 2. The message has to include P_{ij}, g, N, and either hit or $stand$. It is digitally signed by P_{ij} with $k_{P_{ij}}^{-1}$. If P_{ij} returns hit, the deal card protocol is relaunched. If the sum of the cards exceeds 21, P_{ij} loses and T_i addresses the next player. If P_{ij} returns $stand$, T_i automatically addresses the next player.

After the game, T_j has to pay off the players. The corresponding protocol is quite similar to the buy chip protocol and can be summarized as follows:

$$1 : T_i \longrightarrow Adr_{T_i} : \text{PAY\_OFF\_ANNOUNCE}(\langle T_i, g, [P_{ij}, W_{ij}]^+ \rangle k_{T_i}^{-1})$$
$$2 : P_{ij} \longrightarrow T_i \quad\ : \text{PAY\_OFF\_REQUEST}(\langle g, (k', k'', \ldots) \rangle k_{P_{ij}}^{-1})$$
$$3 : T_i \longrightarrow P_{ij} \quad\ : \text{PAY\_OFF\_CONFIRMATION}(\langle g, (\{k'\}k_{s_{ir}}^{-1}, \{k'\}k_{s_{ir}}^{-1}, \ldots) \rangle k_{T_i}^{-1})$$

In step 1, T_i multicasts a pay off announce message to Adr_{T_i}. The message includes T_i, g, and a list of pairs that contain both P_{ij} and P_{ij}'s wins W_{ij}. The message is digitally signed by T_i with $k_{T_i}^{-1}$. In step 2, it is up to each winning player P_{ij} to send a pay off request message to T_i. The message includes g and a set of public keys $(k', k'', \ldots)$. It is digitally signed by P_{ij} with $k_{P_{ij}}^{-1}$. Finally, T_i returns a pay off confirmation message to each winning player P_{ij} in step 3. Each message includes g and some public keys that are digitally signed by T_i with the private keys that belong to the appropriate chip sizes. Note that messages 2 and 3 are not multicast but addressed directly to T_i or P_{ij} respectively. Also note that at the end of the game, T_i has to publish his initial permutation $\pi_n^{(g)}$, and each player P_{ij} has to publish his list of random numbers $L_n^{(ijg)}$. If they all hash to the values previously announced, everybody has played honestly.

Quit a Table If P_{ij} wants to quit table i, he has to sell his remaining chips to T_i. Again, the corresponding sell chip protocol is similar to the buy chip and pay off protocols. It is thus omitted in this paper.

Leave the Casino Having sold all his chips to T_i, P_{ij} is free to leave the casino without doing any further action. He simply disconnects from the network and becomes user U again.

6 Prototype Implementation

With the proliferation of network and Internet applications, interpreted programming and scripting languages have become popular again. Examples are

Java and Tcl (Tool Command Language). While Java is a full-featured interpreted programming language that gives programmers access to low-level details, such as threaded processes, Tcl is a significantly simpler language that can act as a high-level scripting tool e.g. for linking Java applets. It is possible and very likely that Java will be the programming language of choice for Internet tool programmers, and that Tcl will be the high-level language that novice and sophisticated users alike will use to knit these tools together. Tcl complements Java, and many companies, including Sun Microsystems, actively support both Tcl/Tk and Java. Tcl usually comes with a user-interface toolkit, called Tk, that displays a consistent interface on any platform. This makes Tcl/Tk an ideal candidate for multiplatform development [16]. Tcl-DP is a distributed programming extension to Tcl/Tk that is freely available and well suited for writing client/server applications using sockets. Tcl-DP provides UDP and TCP/IP connection management, remote procedure call (RPC), and a simple distributed object system. As with Tcl, the goal of Tcl-DP is ease of programming for applications, not maximal performance. This makes Tcl/Tk and Tcl-DP an ideal prototyping environment for Internet and MBone applications.

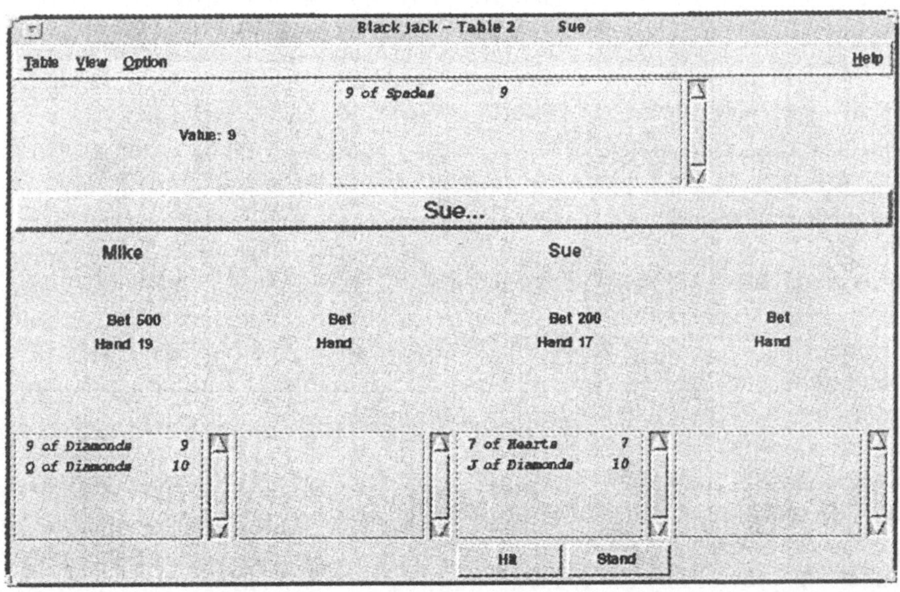

Fig. 2. Graphical user interface for an exemplary table

The model proposed in the previous section has been prototyped at the Institute for Computer Science and Applied Mathematics (IAM) of the University of Berne. Figure 2 shows the graphical user interface after having joined an exemplary table. In a first step, Tcl/Tk and Tcl-DP are used as development environments. In addition to that, SecuDE from GMD is used for cryptographic transformations. Most protocols are implemented in a multicast fashion. For example, the join table protocol consists of two messages that are both multicast. Some protocols, however, combine multicast messages with unicast. In this case, unicast messages are implemented with Tcl-DP's RPC facility. For example, the buy chip request protocol consist of a handshake that is implemented with RPC. In the current implementation of the deal cards protocol, both approaches are being combined, meaning that all messages are multicast, except for the handshake between the dealer T_i and each player P_{ij} which is unicast and implemented with an RPC.

In October 1996, the prototype implementation was released for public scrutiny [15]. The implementation consists of two software modules; one to set up and run a casino (which is the server module), and one to participate as a player (which is the client module). One thing that has not been implemented so far, however, is the use of a digital payment scheme in general, and the support of the outcome of JEPI in particular. Further information about online casinos in general, and the prototype implementation in particular can be found on the World Wide Web (WWW) by following the URL `http://iamwww.unibe.ch/~oppliger/Research/casinos.html`.

7   Conclusions

This paper has overviewed the basic principles of mental games and digital payment schemes, and has proposed a model that can be used to set up and run online casinos within a multicast environment, such as e.g. the Internet Multicast Backbone (MBone). The model can be used to incorporate other games, such as e.g. Mental Poker, American Roulette, Boule, Craps, or Punto Banco. The principles remain the same, although the corresponding protocols may gain in complexity. The paper has also addressed a prototype implementation that has been done at the University of Berne. Early experiments with the prototype implementation have shown that the MBone can serve as a communications infrastructure for online casinos. It is not clear, however, how the prototype behaves if players are widely distributed, and if the network becomes lossy and starts dropping IP packets. With regard to lossy networks, it is assumed that a more realistic approach would be to use a reliable multicast transport service, such as e.g. provided by the Reliable Multicast Protocol (RMP). RMP provides a reliable, ordered, and fault-tolerant transport service from multiple senders to multiple destinations that suits the requirements of online casinos. Another modification that seems to be appropriate and important for online casinos to become widely deployed is the provision of practical solutions to the problem of client module software distribution. It should not be necessary for a user to first download a software module that he can then use for participating in mental game playing. Instead, he should be able to simply click on a button and the system should be able to automatically download and install the module on his local machine. Java applets and Java-aware browsers, such as HotJava from Sun Microsystems or Netscape's Navigator, may provide the technology required to address these issues.

In addition to the technical issues discussed in this paper, there are also legal issues to address when it comes to a wide deployment of online casinos within the MBone. For example, there are states that allow gambling, and others that don't. Obviously, the states that allow gambling make a good living from the taxes they earn. The situation is even more obscure, as there are states that allow gambling only if the players are physically living a certain distance away from the casino they play at. Policies like that are difficult to maintain with regard to online casinos. What does it mean if an online casino is accessible from anywhere? Wouldn't this casino attract the attention of citizens that are coincidentally living in states that prohibit gambling? It is assumed that the proliferation of online casinos will also lead to a world wide harmonization of legislation for gambling.

Acknowledgements

The authors would like to thank Dieter Hogrefe and Hansjürg Mey for their encouragement and support.

References

1. CHAUM, D. Achieving Electronic Privacy. *Scientific American* (August 1992), 96 – 101.
2. CRÉPEAU, C. A Secure Poker Protocol that Minimizes the Effect of Player Coalitions. In *Advances in Cryptology — CRYPTO '85* (1986), H. Williams, Ed., Springer-Verlag, pp. 73 – 86.
3. CRÉPEAU, C. A zero-knowledge protocol that achieves confidentiality of the players' strategy or how to achieve an electronic poker face. In *Advances in Cryptology — CRYPTO '86* (1987), A. Odlyzko, Ed., Springer-Verlag, pp. 239 – 247.
4. DEERING, S. Host Extensions for IP Multicast. Request for Comments 1112, August 1989.
5. DEERING, S., AND CHERITON, D. Host Groups: A Multicast Extension to the Internet Protocol. Request for Comments 966, December 1985.
6. DEERING, S., AND CHERITON, D. Multicast Routing in Datagram Internetworks and Extended LANs. *ACM Transactions on Computer Systems 8*, 2 (1990), 85 – 110.
7. ERIKSSON, H. MBONE: The Multicast Backbone. *Communications of the ACM 37*, 8 (1994), 54 – 60.
8. FORTUNE, S., AND MERRITT, M. Poker Protocols. In *Advances in Cryptology — CRYPTO '84* (1985), G. Blakley and D. Chaum, Eds., Springer-Verlag, pp. 454 – 464.
9. GOLDWASSER, S., AND MICALI, S. Probabilistic Encryption and How to Play Mental Poker Keeping Secret All Partial Information. In *Proceedings of ACM Symposium on Theory of Computing* (New York, 1982), ACM Press, pp. 365 – 377.

10. HINDEN, R. IP Next Generation Overview. *Communications of the ACM 39*, 6 (1996), 61 – 71.

11. HUITEMA, C. *IPv6: The New Internet Protocol.* Prentice-Hall, New Jersey, 1996.

12. ISO/IEC. Information Processing Systems — Open Systems Interconnection Reference Model — Part 2: Security Architecture. ISO/IEC 7498-2, 1989.

13. ITU. The Directory — Authentication Framework. Recommendation X.509, Geneva, Switzerland, November 1987.

14. MACEDONIA, M., AND BRUTZMAN, D. MBone Provides Audio and Video Across the Internet. *IEEE Computer 27*, 4 (April 1994), 30 – 36.

15. NOTTARIS, J. Prototypimplementierung eines virtuellen Casinos in einer Multicast-Umgebung. Diplomarbeit, Universität Bern, 1996.

16. OUSTERHOUT, J. *Tcl and the Tk Toolkit.* Addison-Wesley Publishing Company, Inc., Reading, MA, 1994.

17. SCHNEIER, B. *Applied Cryptography: Protocols, Algorithms, and Source Code in C.* John Wiley & Sons, Inc., New York, NY, 1994.

18. SHAMIR, A., RIVEST, R., AND ADLEMAN, L. Mental poker. Technical Report MIT/LCS/TR-125, Massachusetts Institute of Technology (MIT), Cambridge, MA, 1979.

19. YUNG, M. Cryptoprotocols: Subscription to a Public Key, the Secret Blocking and the Multi-Player Mental Poker Game. In *Advances in Cryptology — CRYPTO '84* (1985), G. Blakley and D. Chaum, Eds., Springer-Verlag, pp. 439 – 453.

Einsatz von Tradingdiensten in WWW-basierten elektronischen Marktplätzen

Axel Küpper und Horst Herzog

RWTH Aachen, Informatik IV   GMD Fokus

Ahornstr. 55, 52056 Aachen   Hardernbergplatz 2, 10623 Berlin

kuepper@informatik.rwth-aachen.de   herzog@fokus.gmd.de

Zusammenfassung

Das World Wide Web (WWW) ist aufgrund seiner hohen Akzeptanz bei Nutzern und Anbietern gleichermaßen ein bedeutender strategischer Ausgangspunkt für die Entwicklung zukünftiger elektronischer Dienstmärkte. Neue Techniken, welche den Einsatz von verteilten CORBA-Anwendungen im WWW ermöglichen, beschleunigen diesen Trend. Die Akzeptanz elektronischer Marktplätze hängt jedoch entscheidend von den verfügbaren Werkzeugen zum Auffinden und zur Vermittlung der angebotenen Dienste statt. Die heutigen konventionellen Verzeichnis- und Suchdienste bieten lediglich stichwortbasierte Ansätze.

Dieser Beitrag beschreibt die Realisierung von Trading Communities im WWW, die bisher zur Vermittlung von Diensten in verteilten Systemen eingesetzt wurden. Zu diesem Zweck wurde mit der Internetprogrammiersprache Java und der Verteilungsplattform CORBA ein sogenannter Trading Agent verwirklicht, der eine Schnittstelle zwischen dem Trader und dem WWW-Anwender herstellt. Es wird ein dreistufiges Konzept präsentiert, welches die Spezifikation von Nutzeranforderungen für den Import sowie die Formulierung von Dienstangeboten für den Export von Diensten in elektronischen Marktplätzen unterstützt.*

1 Einführung

Der anhaltende Einzug von Computersystemen in Büros und Privathaushalte und der Zugang zu globalen Informationsnetzwerken hat die Entstehung eines elektronischen Dienstmarkts zur Folge. Ein solcher Dienstmarkt wird durch eine Vielzahl von Anbietern charakterisiert, welche ihre Produkte und Dienstleistungen den Kunden über das neue Medium offerieren. Hierbei kann es sich sowohl um konventionelle Güter des täglichen Gebrauchs als auch um völlig neue Dienstleistungen handeln, welche erst durch die Vernetzung von Computersystemen entstehen. Als Beispiele seien hier die Speicherung, die Übermittlung oder die Verarbeitung von Daten genannt. Ein bedeutendes Merkmal elektronischer Dienstmärkte ist der Wettbewerb, da Dienste und Güter gleicher Art von mehreren Anbietern zu verschiedenen Kon-

---

* Die beschriebene Entwicklung wurde vom Projekt TRACE in Auftrag gegeben und finanziert. TRACE (TRAding in a Co-operative Environment) ist ein Projekt im Rahmen des F&E-Programmes der DeTeBerkom GmbH, einem Tochterunternehmen der Deutschen Telekom.

ditionen verfügbar sind. Darüber hinaus sind elektronische Märkte durch eine hohe Dynamik gekennzeichnet. Ständig kommen sowohl neue Dienste als auch neue Dienstarten hinzu, andere verschwinden, weil sie unpopulär geworden sind oder nicht am Markt etabliert werden konnten.

Die Entwicklung von Systemen und Kommunikationsprotokollen zur Etablierung eines elektronischen Marktes und deren Zusammenschluß zu einer einheitlichen Architektur ist gegenwärtig Bestandteil vieler Forschungsarbeiten. [GG 95] präsentiert ein objektorientiertes Rahmenwerk für offene Dienstmärkte. Dienste werden als Objekt modelliert, deren Zustand und Implementierung voneinander entkoppelt sind. Hierdurch ist es möglich, daß die Erbringung eines Dienstes, die gewöhnlich von einer Sequenz von Methodenaufrufen ausgelöst wird, durch verschiedene Instanzen, sogenannte *Engines*, vollzogen wird. Ein anderer objektorientierter Ansatz wird von [KüPo 95] vorgestellt, der Anbieter, Angebote, Diensttypen und Dienste als Managed Objects im Sinne des OSI-Netzwerkmanagements beschreibt, zueinander in Beziehung setzt und somit einen Beitrag zum Konfigurationsmanagement leistet. [MML 96] beschreibt eine agentenbasierte Plattform für den *Common Open Service Market* (COSM), mit der die Beschaffung von Dienstbeschreibungen und Referenzen von Dienstanbietern unterstützt wird.

All diese Ansätze haben gemeinsam, daß sie sich auf Verteilungsplattformen stützen. Die Internationale Standard Organisation (ISO) arbeitet seit Beginn der neunziger Jahre im Rahmen des *Referenzmodells für Open Distributed Processing* (ODP) an Richtlinien zur Entwicklung von Anwendungen, die auf Verteilungsplattformen aufsetzen. Ein Gremium einer großen Anzahl von Firmen der verschiedensten Branchen ist die *Object Management Group* (OMG), die mit ihrer *Common Object Request Broker Architecture* (CORBA) [OMG 92] ebenfalls um die Etablierung eines Standards bemüht ist. Hier gibt es bereits eine Reihe von Produkten, beispielsweise Orbix der Firma Iona oder Neo von Sun. Es existieren Bemühungen zur Anpassung der beiden Standards.

Wichtig für die Akzeptanz eines elektronischen Marktplatzes ist jedoch die Verbreitung der zugrundeliegenden Plattform. Aus diesem Grund wird die Entwicklung auf diesem Gebiet am heutigen WWW nicht vorbeigehen. Neue Produkte, wie die Internetprogrammiersprache Java, und diverse Techniken für Sicherheits- und Zahlungsvorgänge im WWW deuten darauf hin.

Aufgrund des dynamischen Charakters und des hohen Wettbewerbs in elektronischen Dienstmärkten ist ein Kernstück für deren Erfolg und Akzeptanz die Existenz von Verfahren zur Lokalisierung und Vermittlung von Diensten. Im WWW gibt es für diese Zwecke lediglich rudimentäre Verzeichnis- und Suchdienste, wie beispielsweise Yahoo und AltaVista. Erstere gestatten das Auffinden von WWW-Dokumenten anhand einer Schlagworthierarchie, während letztere Dokumenttitel und -inhalte auf die vom Benutzer spezifizierten Schlagwörter hin durchsuchen.

Sowohl der ODP-Standard als auch Produkte des CORBA-Standards sehen für die Vermittlung von Diensten sogenannte Trader vor. Hierbei werden Nutzeranforderungen bei der Suche nach Diensten berücksichtigt. Des weiteren besteht die Möglichkeit, den Suchprozeß zu parametrisieren und mehrere Trader zu Föderationen zusammenzuschließen, um den Angebotsraum zu vergrößern. Dieses Paper beschreibt die Integration von Tradern in offene elektronische Dienstmärkte auf der Basis des WWW.

Das folgende Kapitel gibt einen Überblick über Dienste in verteilten Systemen und im WWW und schildert existierende Vermittlungs- und Lokalisierungstechniken. Des weiteren wird der kombinierte Ansatz dieser beiden Plattformen durch die Integration des CORBA-Standards ins WWW vorgestellt. Diese Kombination bildet die Grundlage für die neu entwickelte Architektur zum Einsatz von Tradern im WWW, die in Kapitel 3 präsentiert wird. Hier wird die Abstraktion von WWW-Diensten sowie die Funktionsweise von Trading Agents beschrieben, die durch Interaktionen mit einem Tradingsystem die Vermittlung von Diensten im WWW ermöglichen. Abschnitt 4 erläutert die Realisierung des Prototyps, welcher auf den zuvor beschriebenen Konzepten basiert. Die Schlußbemerkungen fassen schließlich die wichtigsten Ergebnisse zusammen und gegeben einen Überblick über zur Zeit laufende Arbeiten.

2 Dienste und ihre Vermittlung in elektronischen Märkten

Elektronische Dienstmärkte funktionieren nach dem Client/Server-Prinzip. Der Dienstnutzer (Client) nimmt die Ressourcen eines Dienstanbieters (Server) in Anspruch. Damit Client und Server interagieren können, wird eine gemeinsame Kommunikationsplattform benötigt. Diese Plattform stellt Protokolle und Mechanismen bereit, um diese Interaktionen bewerkstelligen zu können. Dabei werden je nach Plattform verschiedene Aspekte der Transparenz, Heterogenität und Sicherheit berücksichtigt. Die populärsten Plattformen, welche nach diesem Prinzip funktionieren, sind die verteilten Systeme nach dem ODP- oder CORBA-Standard und das WWW.

Beide Plattformen unterscheiden sich stark durch die technische Sichtweise der von ihnen angebotenen Dienste. Entsprechend unterschiedlich sind auch die Mechanismen zur Lokalisierung und Vermittlung. Im folgenden werden die spezifischen Merkmale diesbezüglich kurz erläutert und gegenübergestellt.

2.1 Dienste in verteilten Systemen

In verteilten Systemen werden Dienste explizit durch ihren zugehörigen *Diensttyp* klassifiziert. Ein Diensttyp legt verbindlich die Signatur und Semantik für alle Dienste fest, welche diesem Typ zugeordnet sind. Hierfür existiert eine *Schnittstellenbeschreibungssprache* (Interface Description Language, IDL), mit der die Signatur eines Diensttyps spezifiziert wird. Auf Basis dieser Schnittstellenspezifikation wird Applikationssoftware für den Client und den Server erstellt, die sich konform zu der vorgegebenen Semantik des Diensttyps verhalten muß. Die Dienste der verteilten Systeme sind also Dienste mit *typspezifischer Schnittstelle*, durch die eine explizite Klassifizierung der Dienste gegeben ist.

Darüber hinaus wird durch den Diensttyp eine Menge von *Diensteigenschaften* vorgegeben, mit denen sich Merkmale eines Dienstes beschreiben lassen, die nicht durch seine Schnittstelle festgelegt sind. Es ist vorgesehen, zwischen statischen, dynamischen und modifizierbaren

Diensteigenschaften zu unterscheiden. Der Diensttyp und seine Diensteigenschaften bilden die Grundlage für die Vermittlung von Diensten durch den Trader.

Zu jedem angebotenen Dienst ist ein assoziiertes *Dienstangebot* in einer Datenbank des Traders enthalten, welches den Diensttyp, die Diensteigenschaften und die Referenz des Dienstanbieters enthält [SPM 94]. Durch Angabe des gewünschten Diensttyps und sogenannter *Matching Constraints* können Anfragen an den Trader gerichtet werden. Dieser gibt als Ergebnis der Suche eine Liste geeigneter Referenzen zurück. Die Matching Constraints sind hierbei Anforderungen bezüglich der Diensteigenschaften.

Trader können durch entsprechende Links in ihrem Suchbaum zu Kooperationen zusammengeschlossen werden. Hierdurch können andere Trader in den Suchvorgang nach einem bestimmten Angebot involviert werden. Dieser Vorgang verläuft für den anfragenden Benutzer transparent. Ferner ist der Tradingprozeß durch die Spezifikation sogenannter Policies parametrisierbar.

Der Trader ist eng mit anderen Komponenten in einem verteilten System verknüpft. Hierzu gehören beispielsweise das *Type Repository* [ODP Ty] zur Verwaltung von Diensttypen oder der *Trader Administrator,* der Policies definiert und deren Einhaltung überwacht. Die so entstehende Ansammlung von kooperierenden Instanzen wird als *Trading Community* bezeichnet [ODP Tr].

2.2 Dienste im WWW

Während bei den verteilten Systemen Client- und Server-Software applikationsspezifisch sind, wird im WWW lediglich ein WWW-Browser und ein WWW-Server als gemeinsame Plattform benötigt. Dienste liegen als statische Dokumente in der *HyperText Markup Language* (HTML) vor, die mit dem *HyperText Transfer Protocol* (HTTP) zwischen Server und Browser übertragen werden [Sch 96]. Durch das *Common Gateway Interface* (CGI) auf der Seite des WWW-Servers können HTML-Dokumente dynamisch, beispielsweise in Abhängigkeit von Benutzereingaben, kreiert werden. Durch die Internetprogrammiersprache *Java* ergeben sich eine Reihe neuer Anwendungen für das WWW. Kleine Programme, sogenannte *Java-Applets*, können mittels HTTP geladen und von einer virtuellen Maschine innerhalb des WWW-Browsers auf dem Host des Benutzers automatisch initialisiert und gestartet werden. Die Dienste des WWW haben also eine *allgemeine Schnittstelle*, nach der, im Gegensatz zu den verteilten Systemen, keine Klassifizierung vorgenommen werden kann.

Trotz der großen Popularität des WWWs sind die verfügbaren Mechanismen zur Lokalisierung von Diensten sehr rudimentär. Es existieren für diese Zwecke lediglich konventionelle Verzeichnis- und Suchdienste wie beispielsweise Yahoo und AltaVista. Erstere gestatten das Auffinden von WWW-Dokumenten anhand einer Schlagworthierarchie während letztere Dokumenttitel und -inhalte auf vom Benutzer spezifizierte Schlagwörter durchsuchen [Be 96]. Wird das gesuchte Wort gefunden, so erhält der Benutzer eine Referenz des Dienstes.

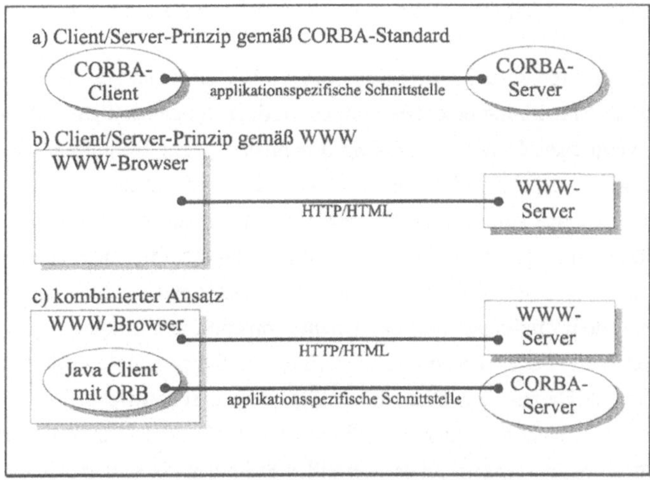

Abbildung 1: Offene und geschlossene Applikationen im WWW

2.3 Der kombinierte Ansatz: Verteilte Systeme im WWW

Sowohl verteilte Systeme als auch das WWW haben im Kontext der elektronischen Märkte Vor- und Nachteile, welche in [GGP+ 95] diskutiert werden. Die formale Beschreibung von Diensten bei den verteilten Systemen erlaubt zwar eine exakte Klassifizierung der Dienste, sie steht jedoch im Gegensatz zur Dynamik der Märkte, da die entsprechende Software standardisiert und beim Nutzer verfügbar sein muß. Hingegen ermöglicht das WWW zwar die geforderte Dynamik, da es jedoch lediglich eine Schnittstelle für den menschlichen Benutzer liefert, wird es den Ansprüchen vieler denkbarer Anwendungen nicht gerecht.

Den Ausweg aus dieser Misere verspricht die Entwicklung von CORBA-Applikationen in der Internetprogrammiersprache Java. Erste Produkte, welche die Abbildung der CORBA-Technologie auf Java ermöglichen, sind OrbixWeb von Iona oder BlackWidow von Sun. Hierdurch wird portable Clientsoftware per Java-Applet über das WWW zugänglich gemacht. Diese Applets sind dann in der Lage, sowohl auf bereits verfügbare als auch auf zukünftig entwickelte CORBA-Dienste zuzugreifen. Abbildung 1 verdeutlicht den Unterschied zwischen den verteilten Systemen, dem WWW und dem kombinierten Ansatz.

Durch diese Technik wird nun auch der Einsatz der ODP-basierten Dienstvermittlungstechniken im WWW möglich und sinnvoll. Die folgenden Abschnitte stellen ein System vor, welches in Zusammenarbeit zwischen der GMD Fokus und dem Lehrstuhl für Informatik IV der RWTH Aachen für die Vermittlung von Diensten im WWW entwickelt wurde.

3 Trading Communities im World Wide Web

Nach [ODP Tr] gehören einer *Trading Community* alle Objekte an, die am Prozeß der Dienstvermittlung unter Einwirkung einer bestimmten Trading Policy beteiligt sind. Hierzu gehören
neben dem eigentlichen Trader ein *Trading Administrator* zur Definition und Durchsetzung
der Policies, sowie *Importer* (Dienstnutzer) und *Exporter* (Dienstanbieter). Eine Trading
Community ist also eine autonom agierende Einheit, deren zugehörige Objekte einer gemeinsamen Verwaltung (durch den Trading Administrator) unterworfen sind. Dieser Abschnitt beschreibt eine Trading Community, welche im WWW eingesetzt werden kann. Sie besteht aus
einem Backend (dem Tradingsystem) und einem Frontend (dem Trading Agent). Die Verbindung zwischen den einzelnen Komponenten eines Tradingsystems und dem Trading Agent
zeigt Abbildung 2. Da zur Zeit Dienste mit allgemeiner Schnittstelle den WWW-basierten
elektronischen Marktplatz dominieren, muß ein Modell für deren Klassifizierung geschaffen
werden, welches mit dem Ansatz bei den verteilten Systemen koexistiert.

3.1 Klassifikation von Diensten im WWW

Eine Klassifizierung von HTML-Dokumenten kann lediglich durch ihre Zuordnung zu bestimmten Themenbereichen erfolgen, da eine typspezifische Schnittstelle nicht gegeben ist.
Solche Zuordnungen finden sich beispielsweise in den oben erwähnten Suchdiensten. Hierdurch werden Dienste aber nur sehr rudimentär abstrahiert.

Eine stärkere Abstraktion wird durch die Beschreibung mit Diensteigenschaften erzielt, ähnlich zu den Diensten mit typspezifischer Schnittstelle. Alle Dienste, die sich mit einer bestimmten Menge von Diensteigenschaften beschreiben lassen, gehören einem Diensttyp an.
Unter den Gesichtspunkten des Tradings ist eine solche Klassifizierung bereits ausreichend,
da eine typspezifische Schnittstelle nicht notwendig ist. Auf diese Weise wird ein Vergleich
von Diensten eines Typs unter gleichen Kriterien ermöglicht. Darüber hinaus können Dienste
mit typspezifischer und allgemeiner Schnittstelle gemeinsam durch ein Tradingsystem verwaltet werden, was für zukünftige elektronische Marktplätze von großer Bedeutung ist.

Zwischen den so gebildeten Diensttypen existieren vielerlei Beziehungen, welche durch einen
Type Manager verwaltet werden. Eine der bedeutensten Beziehungen ist die Vererbungsrela-
tion. Ein Diensttyp mit allgemeiner Schnittstelle ist ein Untertyp eines anderen Diensttyps,
wenn ihm mindestens alle Diensteigenschaften dieses Typs zugeordnet sind. Durch generische
Diensttypen, zu denen keinerlei Dienste existieren, sondern die lediglich ihre Diensteigenschaften anderen Typen vererben, kann die Existenz von Diensteigenschaften in allen Diensttypen oder in denen eines bestimmten Teilbaums der Vererbungshierarchie erreicht werden.
Aufgrund der immer größer werdenden Anzahl von HTML-Dialekten ist beispielsweise die
Erzwingung einer Diensteigenschaft `HTML_Type` in allen WWW-basierten Diensttypen sinnvoll.

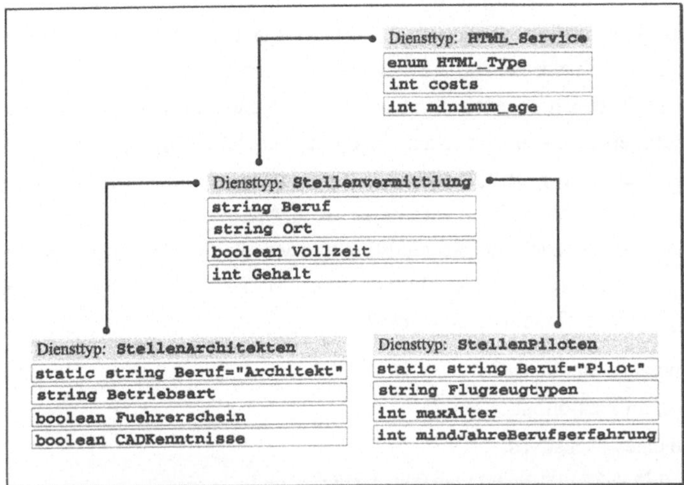

Abbildung 2: Vererbungsbeziehung zwischen HTML-Diensttypen

Abbildung 2 zeigt ein Beispiel für die Vererbungsbeziehung zwischen Diensttypen, welche eine gemeinsame Klasse von HTML-Dokumenten mit Eigenschaften beschreiben. Durch die Ansiedlung eines allgemeinen generischen Diensttyps `HTML_Service` an der Wurzel der Hierarchie wird die Angabe des HTML-Formats, der Kosten und des Mindestalters in allen Dienstangeboten erzwungen.

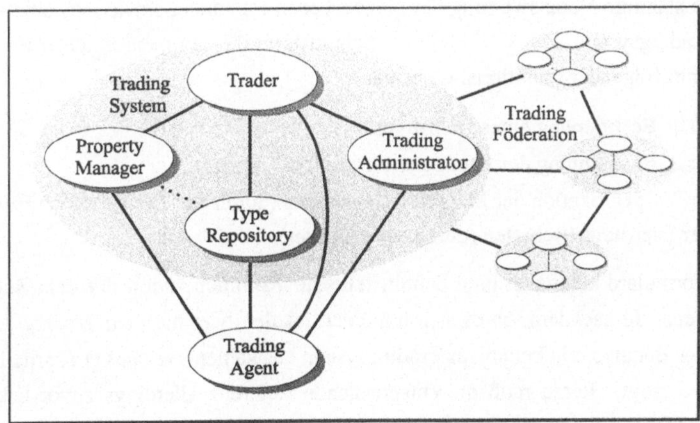

Abbildung 3: Trading System

3.2 Trading Agent

Ein sogenannter Trading Agent stellt die Verbindung zwischen dem Tradingsystem und dem menschlichen Anwender her. Der Trading Agent erlaubt sowohl den *Import*, also die Beschaffung von Dienstreferenzen, als auch den *Export*, also die Bereitstellung von Dienstangeboten durch den Dienstanbieter.

Im allgemeinen ist ein Agent ein weitestgehend autonom agierendes Softwareelement, welches im Auftrag einer (humanen) Instanz oder eines anderen Agenten handelt. Agenten werden für ein breites Spektrum von Anwendungen eingesetzt. Entsprechend vielfältig sind die Merkmale, nach denen Agenten und Agententechnologien klassifiziert werden können. [Ma95] präsentiert einen ausführlichen Überblick und stellt Anforderungen den zum Einsatz kommenden Techniken gegenüber. Gemäß der dort vorgenommenen Klassifizierung ist der Trading Agent ein persönlicher Assistent. Er ist in Abhängigkeit der zugrundeliegenden Implementierung (siehe nächster Abschnitt) entweder als lokaler oder als mobiler Agent verfügbar. Für die Erfordernisse elektronischer Marktplätze werden u.a. die folgenden Anforderungen an den Trading Agent gestellt:

- hohe Benutzerfreundlichkeit,
- hohes Maß an Flexibilität,
- Selektion eines Diensttyps,
- Spezifikation der benötigten Diensteigenschaften und
- Parametrisierung des Dienstauswahlprozesses.

Um diese Anforderungen zu erreichen, wird der Trading Agent durch Instanzen des Tradingsystems unterstützt. Die Interaktionen zwischen dem Frontend und dem Backend sind in Abbildung 4 dargestellt.

Der Trading Agent wird asynchron zu den Komponenten des Backends ausgeführt. Er stellt ein *Graphical User Interface* (GUI) bereit, mit dessen Hilfe die erforderlichen Parameter beim Import bzw. Export von Diensten eingegeben werden. Während des Spezifikationsprozesses erfolgt eine ständige Vorauswertung der eingegebenen Parameter sowie ggf. eine Interaktion mit dem Tradingsystem. Das GUI stellt als Schnittstelle für den menschlichen Benutzer drei Formulare mit folgender Funktionalität bereit:

- Formular 1: Bestimmung eines Diensttyps
- Formular 2: Bestimmung der Parameter für den Tradingprozeß
- Formular 3: Spezifikation der Matching Constraints (durch den Dienstnutzer) bzw. Spezifikation der Diensteigenschaften (durch den Anbieter).

Jedes der Formulare beinhaltet eine Schnittstelle zur Kommunikation mit dem Backend des Tradingsystems. Je nachdem, ob es sich um einen lokalen oder mobilen Trading Agent handelt, kann der Benutzer ein beliebiges Tradingsystem auswählen, welches er für die Dienstvermittlung bevorzugt. Hierzu muß die entsprechende Referenz allerdings zuvor bekannt sein und angegeben werden.

Wie Abbildung 4 zeigt, startet der Trading Agent bei Initialisierung einen Request zur Erlangung der Schlagworthierarchie und der Policy-Defaultwerte zur Parametrisierung des Tradingprozesses. Diese Strukturen werden bei jedem Aufruf des Trading Agents erneut geladen, da sie sich permanent ändern können.

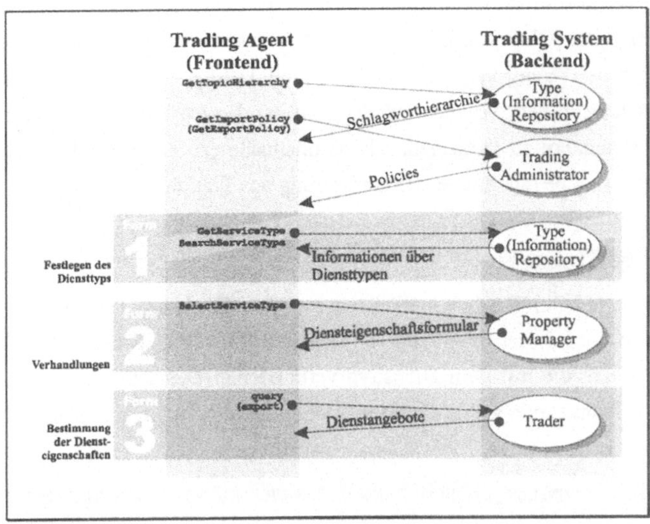

Abbildung 4: Interaktionen zwischen Frontend und Backend

3.3 Type Information Repository

Mit dem ersten Formular wird der Diensttyp festgelegt, auf den sich der nachfolgende Import- bzw. Exportvorgang bezieht. Die Selektion eines Diensttyps wird durch das *Type Information Repository* unterstützt, welches Bestandteil des Type Repositorys ist, in dem Diensttypen enthalten sind und verwaltet werden. Die in dem Information Repository enthaltenen Dokumente beschreiben einen Diensttyp sowohl formal als auch informell. Beispielsweise können die technische Schnittstelle oder die unterstützten Diensteigenschaften durch ein Textdokument für den Anwender zugänglich gemacht werden. Anhand von Grafiken und Animationen kann der Benutzer Demonstrationen und weitergehende Erläuterungen, wie beispielsweise Benutzermanuals, erhalten. Ein Diensttyp kann einem oder mehreren Schlagwörtern zugeordnet sein, mit deren Hilfe ein Anwender beim Auffinden eines für seine Zwecke geeigneten Diensttyps unterstützt wird. Die Schlagworthierarchie wird bei der Initialisierung des Trading Agents beim Type Information Repository angefordert. Mit Hilfe einer Search Engine kann darüber hinaus gezielt nach bestimmten Stichwörtern gesucht werden, die mit den Diensttypen verbunden sind.

3.4 Trading Administrator

Im zweiten Formular spezifiziert der Benutzer seine Präferenzen bezüglich des Tradingprozesses. Die unterstützen Policyparameter sowie durch den Trading Administrator vorgegebene Grenz- und Defaultwerte werden bei Initialisierung des Agents geladen und bestimmen somit den Inhalt des zweiten Formulars. Der Trading Agent überprüft die Präferenzen des Benutzers auf Verletzung der Trading Policies und fordert ggf. zur Korrektur der eingegebenen Werte auf.

Die Parametertypen sind abhängig davon, ob der Anwender des Trading Agents ein Anbieter oder eine Nutzer ist. [ODP Tr] definiert für den Import eine Reihe von Policies, welche ein standardkonformes Tradingsystem unterstützen muß. Denkbar wäre die Entwicklung eines erweiterten Ansatzes, in dem Policies von der Identität des Anwenders abhängig sind. Die Zuordnung von Benutzern zu Domänen, z.B. Großabnehmer, Stammkunden oder Endverbraucher, ermöglicht so eine qualitative Differenzierung des Tradingprozesses.

3.5 Property Manager

Das dritte Formular ist abhängig von dem ausgewählten Diensttyp. Mittels der Operation `SelectService` wird dieser dem Property Manager übergeben. Dieser übermittelt daraufhin dem Trading Agent die mit dem Diensttyp verbundenen Diensteigenschaften. Die IDL-Beschreibung der Schnittstelle von `SelectService` hat die folgende Form:

```
enum PropertyDataType{BOOLEAN, INTEGER, FLOAT, STRING, ENUMERATION};

typedef <String> EnumerationElement;

struct StatistBoolean {short PercentageOfFalse;
   short PercentageOfTrue; };

struct StatistInteger {
   short Min; short Max; short Average; };

struct StatistFloat {
   float Min; float Max; float Average; };

struct StatistString {string Min; string Max; };

struct StatistEnumeration {
   EnumerationElement el; short Percentage; };

sequence <StatistEnumeration> StatistEnumerationList;

union PropertyAttributes switch (PropertyDataType) {
   case BOOLEAN: StatistBoolean b;
   case INTEGER: StatistInteger i;
   case FLOAT:    StatistFloat f;
   case STRING:   StatistString s;
   case ENUMERATION:       StatistEnumerationList e; };

struct PropertyType {
   NameType PropertyTypeName; PropertyAttributes Attributes; };

sequence <PropertyType> PropertyTypeList;

void SelectType (in oid Identifier, out short NumberOfOffers,
         out PropertyTypeList props) raises (reject);
```

Hieraus wird deutlich, daß neben der Bezeichnung der Diensteigenschaften und deren Datentypen auch statistische Werte bezüglich aller Eigenschaften des jeweiligen Diensttyps bereitgestellt werden, um dem Anbieter einen Eindruck über den verfügbaren Wertebereich zu vermitteln. Abbildung 5 zeigt ein Dienstanforderungsformular eines Diensttyps `Stellenanzeige` des realisierten Prototyps.

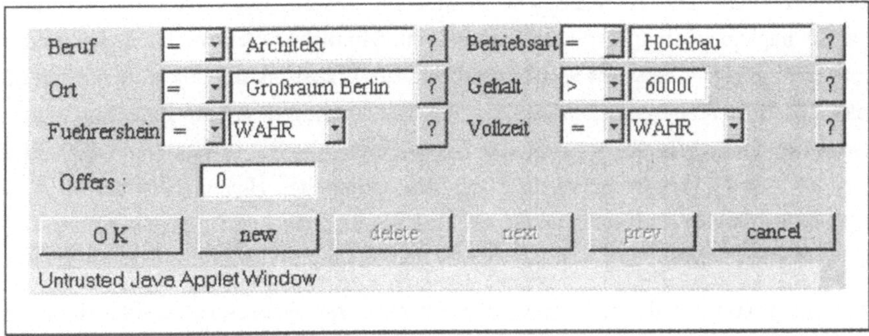

Abbildung 5: Dienstanforderungsformular eines Diensttyps `Stellenmarkt`

Die Statistiken werden durch den Property Manager erstellt und ständig aktualisiert. Zu diesem Zweck leitet der Trader jede Modifikation seiner Datenbank an den Property Manager weiter. Erreicht den Trader ein neues Dienstangebot, so fließt dieses in die Statistik des zugehörigen Diensttyps ein. Wird ein Dienstangebot entfernt, findet eine Korrektur der Statistik statt. Der Property Manager steht also ständig mit dem Trader und dem Trading Agent in Kontakt. Darüber hinaus kann eine Verbindung zum Type Repository nötig werden, wenn über den Datentyp einer Diensteigenschaft Unklarheit herrscht. Dies ist beispielsweise dann der Fall, wenn Diensteigenschaften dem Trader nicht in einer kanonischen Form, sondern in einer Zeichenkette übergeben werden. Ist dem Property Manager der zugehörige Diensttyp zudem unbekannt, ist es nicht möglich, eindeutig auf den Datentyp einer Diensteigenschaft zu schließen. Beispielsweise kann zwischen `string` und `enumeration` nicht unterschieden werden. In diesem Fall wird eine Anfrage an das zugehörige Type Repository notwendig.

3.6 Trader

Die in den Formularen ausgehandelten Parameter werden auf die Operationen `query` (beim Import) bzw. `export` abgebildet. Beim Import gibt der Trader eine Liste mit Referenzen der Dienste zurück, welche den Anforderungen des Clients entsprechen. Beim Export erhält der Anbieter eine Bestätigung, daß das Dienstangebot in die Datenbank des Traders eingefügt wurde.

Der in dem Tradingsystem zum Einsatz kommende Trader wurde von der GMD Fokus entwickelt[*].

4 Realisierung des Prototyps

Die Elemente des Tradingsystems und der Trading Agent sind - wie bereits erwähnt - miteinander interagierende Applikationen auf der Basis eines Object Request Brokers (ORB), wie

---

[*]   http://www.fokus.gmd.de/minos/trace/entry.html
      http://www.fokus.gmd.de/minos/toi/entry.html

Abbildung 6 zeigt. Das Tradingsystem ist unter dem Betriebssystem Solaris mit C++ und der CORBA-Implementierung Orbix 2.0 verwirklicht. Sämtliche Daten werden in der Datenbank Postgres 95 abgelegt. Postgres 95 ist eine relationale Datenbank mit objektorientierten Merkmalen und der Abfragesprache SQL [Post 95]. Für den Zugriff auf die Datenbank durch die Tradingkomponenten stellt Postgres eine C++-Klassenbibliothek bereit, welche die Anfragen über eine TCP/IP-Verbindung an die Datenbank weiterleitet. Hierdurch ist die Möglichkeit gegeben, für Zwecke der Lastverteilung das Tradingsystem und die Datenbank auf verschiedenen Hosts einzurichten.

Der Trading Agent ist als Java-Applet innerhalb eines WWW-Browsers ausführbar und kommuniziert über einen Java-ORB mit dem Tradingsystem. Der Java-ORB ist eine Klassenbibliothek, welche den Aufruf von Methoden des entfernten Backends ermöglicht. Grundlage hierfür bildet die Schnittstellenspezifikation der einzelnen Tradingkomponenten. Durch einen IDL-Compiler werden aus dieser Schnittstellenspezifikation Javaklassen zur Codierung und Dekodierung der mit den Methoden übergebenen Parameter generiert. Die codierten Daten werden dann über das Internet Inter-ORB Protocol (IIOP) an die ORBs der Trading Community übertragen. Das IIOP ermöglicht die Interoperabilität zwischen ORBs verschiedener Hersteller, z.B. zwischen BlackWidow und Orbix. Bei der Realisierung der Trading Agents werden zwei unterschiedliche Ansätze verfolgt. Beide Ansätze haben gemeinsam, daß sie als Java-Applets innerhalb eines WWW-Browsers ausführbar sind und über einen Java-ORB mit einem Tradingsystem kommunizieren.

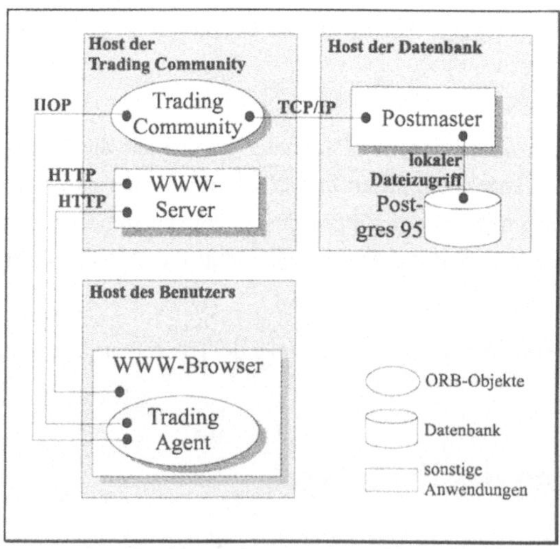

Abbildung 6: Realisierung der Trading Community

Die beiden unterschiedlichen Ansätze resultieren aus den strengen Sicherheitsrestriktionen gegen Java-Applets, wenn sie von einem WWW-Servers eines entfernten Hosts auf den Rechner des Benutzers geladen, automatisch initialisiert und ausgeführt werden [Fla 96]. Insbesondere ist es diesen Applets nicht gestattet, die folgenden Operationen auszuführen:

- Verbindungsaufbau zu einem Serverprozeß, der nicht auf dem Host des WWW-Servers läuft, von dem das Applet stammt,
- Schreib- und Lesezugriff auf das lokale Dateisystem und
- Auslesen und Weitergabe der Benutzerkennung.

In einem ersten, bereits realisierten Ansatz ist der Trading Agent als mobiler Agent verwirklicht. Durch Angabe des Uniform Resource Locators (URL) des dem Tradingsystem zugeordneten WWW-Servers wird die assoziierte Java-Klassenbibliothek geladen, gestartet und ausgeführt. Eine Kontaktaufnahme ist dann ausschließlich zu dem Tradingsystem möglich, von dem der Trading Agent stammt. Des weiteren ist es dem Benutzer nicht möglich, einmal vorgenommene Spezifikationen zu speichern, um sie für spätere Tradingsitzungen wiederzuverwenden.

Die zweite Version des Trading Agents gehört in die Kategorie der lokalen Agenten. Diese zeichnen sich im Vergleich zu den mobilen Agenten dadurch aus, daß sie auf einem Host fest angesiedelt sind und nicht migrieren können. Eine Möglichkeit zur Interaktion mit anderen Objekten im Netz ist jedoch gegeben. Bevor ein lokaler Trading Agent genutzt werden kann, muß er zunächst im lokalen Dateisystem installiert werden. Erst danach kann er innerhalb eines Browsers vom lokalen Dateisystem geladen und ausgeführt werden. Im Unterschied zu der mobilen Version ist der Benutzer nun in der Lage, durch Angabe einer IP-Adresse das Backend frei zu wählen und ohne Umwege über eine Föderation zu kontaktieren. Darüber hinaus können Benutzerprofile abgespeichert und verwaltet werden, was den Spezifikationsprozeß erheblich erleichtert. Abbildung 7 gibt einen Überblick über die beiden Versionen und ihre Vor- und Nachteile.

5 Schlußbemerkungen

Das Paper präsentiert einen Ansatz zur Vermittlung von Diensten in WWW-basierten elektronischen Marktplätzen, der in Zusammenarbeit zwischen der GMD Fokus und dem Lehrstuhl für Informatik IV der RWTH Aachen entstanden ist. Der Ansatz basiert auf einem Modell zur Klassifizierung von Diensten mit allgemeiner Schnittstelle, wie sie heutzutage im WWW in Form von HTML-Dokumenten verfügbar und für jedermann zugänglich sind. Durch die Verknüpfung inhaltlich gleicher bzw. ähnlicher Dienste mit einer Menge von Diensteigenschaften wird eine Typisierung vorgenommen, die sich von dem äquivalenten Ansatz bei den verteilten Systemen nur durch das Fehlen der typspezifischen Schnittstelle unterscheidet.

Auf diese Weise wird erreicht, daß im WWW eingesetzte Tradingsysteme die Dienste aus beiden Plattformen, den verteilten Systemen und dem WWW, parallel verwalten und vermitteln können. Dies ist um so wichtiger, da beide Plattformen durch die Verfügbarkeit neuer Techniken, wie etwa der Integration von ORBs in Java-Applets, zukünftig immer mehr verschmelzen werden und somit einen qualitativ hochwertigen und vielseitigen elektronischen Dienstmarkt bilden.

Agent	Merkmale	Vorteil	Nachteil
mobil	• als Java Applet • automatische Initalisierung und Ausführung nach dem Laden von einem WWW-Server	• nach dem Ladevorgang sofort ausführbar • Benutzer arbeitet automatisch immer mit der neuesten Version	• Verbindung nur zu dem Host des WWW-Servers möglich • Speicherung von Benutzerpräferenzen im lokalen Dateisystem des Benutzers nicht möglich
lokal	• als Java-Applikation • erfordert zunächst Installation im lokalen Dateisystem des Benutzers	• Verbindung zu beliebigen Trading Communities • Auswertung dynamischer Diensteigenschaften durch den Benutzer • Speicherung von Benutzerpräferenzen möglich • keine Wartezeiten beim Laden des Trading Agents	• Installationsprozeß • kein automatisches Softwareupdate

Abbildung 7: Gegenüberstellung mobiler und lokaler Trading Agents

Das verwirklichte Konzept des Trading Agents liefert eine Schnittstelle für den menschlichen Anwender, welches über ein hohes Maß an Benutzerfreundlichkeit verfügt und durch Interaktionen mit einem Tradingsystem wichtige Parameter des Dienstvermittlungsprozesses aushandelt. Eine wichtige Komponente ist hierbei der Property Manager, welcher im Kontext des gewählten Diensttyps entsprechende Formulare zur Spezifikation von Diensteigenschaften und Dienstanforderungen bereitstellt.

Zukünftige Arbeiten konzentrieren sich auf die Auswertung dynamischer Diensteigenschaften durch den Trading Agent selbst, um eine Entlastung des Traders zu erreichen [KPM 96]. Zudem ist die Entwicklung eines Ansatzes geplant, bei dem die Anbieter von Diensten autorisiert werden, neue Diensttypen durch Modifikation von Diensteigenschaften eigenständig zu kreieren. Hierbei muß allerdings eine explizite Differenzierung von Basistypen und erweiterten Typen vorgenommen werden, damit für den Tradingprozeß eine Vergleichsbasis für Dienste konkurrierender Anbieter garantiert wird.

Literatur

[Be 96]   Berghel, H.: *The Client Side of the Web*. In: Communications of the ACM. Januar 1996, Volume 39 No 1, pp 30-40

[Fla 96]   Flanagan, D.: *Java in a Nutshell*. O'Reilly & Associates, Inc., 1996

[GG 95]   Gründer, G.; Geihs, K.: *An Object-Oriented Framework for Open Service Markets*. In: Proceedings of 1st International Workshop on High Speed Networks and Open Distributed Platforms. St. Petersburg, 1995.

[GGP+ 95] Geihs, G.; Gründer, H.; Puder, A.; Lamersdorf, W.; Merz, M.; Müller, K.: *System-unterstützung für offene verteilte Dienstmärkte*. In: KiVS '95 - Kommunikation in verteilten Systemen, Chemnitz, 1995, Springer-Verlag

[KPM 96] Küpper, A.; Popien, C.; Meyer, B.: *Service Management using up-to-date quality properties*. In: Proceedings of the IFIP/IEEE International Conference on Distributed Platforms, Chapman & Hall, Dresden, Februar 1996

[KüPo 95] Küpper, A.; Popien, C.: *Ein Managementszenario für die Dienstvermittlung in Verteilten Systemen*. In: KiVS '95 - Kommunikation in verteilten Systemen, Chemnitz, 1995, Springer-Verlag

[Ma 95]   Magedanz, T.: *On the Impacts of Intelligent Agent Concepts on Future Telecommunication Environments*. In: Proceedings of 3rd International Conference on Intelligence in Broatband Service and Networks (IS&N '95), Springer-Verlag, 1995

[MML 96] Merz, M.; Müller-Jones, K.; Lamersdorf, W.: *Agents, services, and electronic markets: how do they integrate*. In: Proceedings of the IFIP/IEEE International Conference on Distributed Platforms, Chapman & Hall, Dresden, Februar 1996

[ODP Tr]   Draft Rec. X.950 I ISO/IEC DIS 13235 - *ODP Trading Function*, März 1996

[ODP Ty]   ISO/IEC JTC1/SC21/WG7. Open Distributed Processing Type Repository Function. International Standardisation Organisation, November 1995

[OMG 92] *Object Management Architecture Guide*. Revision 2.0, OMG Document 92-11-1, John Wiley & Sons, 1992

[Post 95]   Yu, A.; Chen, J.: The Postgres95 User Manual. Computer Science Div., Dept. Of EECS, University of California at Berkeley, 1995

[Sch 96]   Schulzrinne, H.: World Wide Web: Whence, Whiter, What Next? In: IEEE Network, März/April 1996, Vol. 10 No 2, pp 10-17

[SPM 94] Spaniol, O.; Popien, C.; Meyer, B.: *Dienste und Dienstvermittlung in Client/Server-Systemen*. Thomsons Aktuelle Tutorien, International Thomson Publishing, 1994

SPMP - ein Protokoll für einen Payment Management Service

Holger Reif, Jörg Deutschmann, Dietrich Reschke
TU Ilmenau
Fakultät für Informatik und Automatisierung
Institut Praktische Informatik und Medieninformatik
Fachgebiet Telematik
{Holger.Reif, Joerg.Deutschmann, Dieter.Reschke}@PrakInf.TU-Ilmenau.DE

Kurzfassung

Die sich abzeichnende Vielfalt von Zahlungssystemen im Internet erschwert die Festlegung eines geeigneten Systems. Die Arbeit beschreibt einen zu bestehenden Standards kompatiblen Dienst, der die Auswahl automatisiert. Ein Payment Manager übernimmt als eigenständiges Modul die erforderlichen Verhandlungen für den Nutzer. Der eigentliche Zahlungsvorgang ist davon unabhängig und wird mit bestehenden Systemen abgewickelt. Die Autoren schlagen eine Protokollspezifikation vor. Anhand einer Prototypimplementierung wird der Kaufablauf bei Nutzung dieses Protokolls vorgestellt.

1. Übersicht

Das Internet als offenes Netz hatte in den letzten Jahren ein exponentielles Wachstum zu verzeichnen. Dieser Trend wird sich auch in Zukunft fortsetzen. Insbesondere frei zugängliche Informationssysteme, allen voran das World Wide Web (WWW), tragen diesen Zuwachs. Heute ist praktisch jedem der Zugang über einen Internet Service Provider (ISP) zu diesem Netz möglich.

Allerdings steht dem überproportionalen Anstieg der Nutzerzahlen und der angebotenen Inhalte keinesfalls eine adäquate Zunahme der Netzkapazität gegenüber. Darüberhinaus fallen vermehrt staatliche Unterstützungen für Ausbau und Erhalt der Netzinfrastruktur weg, so daß zunehmend Privatinitiative gefordert wird und daraus folgend ein Zuwachs kommerzieller Inhalte zu verzeichnen ist. Um jedoch meßbare Einkünfte damit zu erzielen, muß das Angebot über reine Werbung und Selbstdarstellung hinausgehen und beispielsweise auch gebührenpflichtige Informationen, Dienstleistungen oder Waren umfassen.

Haupthindernis dafür ist bislang der Mangel an praktikablen und sicheren Zahlungsmöglichkeiten über das Internet. Obwohl bereits frühzeitig Arbeiten zu diesen

Themen veröffentlich wurden ([Chau82], [Duka92]), dominiert immer noch die Zahlung per Kreditkarte (gesicherte oder offene Übertragung der Kartennummer etc., [Reif96a]). Andere Syteme ([PaCo96], [ecas95], [SSBR95]) erreichen nur eine geringe Marktakzeptanz. Eine Änderung ist erst mit Verabschiedung des SET-Standards (Secure Electronic Transaction, [SET96]) oder des Electronic Check Projects des FSTC (Financial Service Technology Consortium, [Doug95]) zu erwarten. Aber auch dann werden mehrere Verfahren gleichberechtigt nebeneinander existieren, da sie für unterschiedliche Dienstleistungs- oder Warenarten verschieden gut geeignet sind. Beispielsweise akzeptiert nicht jeder Anbieter jede Kreditkarte. Außerdem ist eine Kreditkarte zum Bezahlen eines Betrages im Pfennigbreich (Online-Artikel, Telefonnummernrecherche etc.) denkbar schlecht geeignet. Dies entspricht auch der heute im täglichen Leben gewohnten Vielfalt von Zahlungsinstrumenten (z.B. Bargeld, Scheck, Kreditkarte).

Praktisch alle derzeitig realisierten Online-Einkaufsmöglichkeiten (sog. Malls) sind ähnlich einem Selbstbedienungsladen nach folgendem Schema organisiert: Der Händler führt einen Warenkorb für jeden in seinem System befindlichen Käufer, den dieser mit Waren füllt (*Auswahl von Waren*). Danach begibt er sich zum Checkpoint, an dem er die *Rechnung* präsentiert bekommt. Der Käufer bezahlt - meist indem er seine Kreditkartendaten ungesichert übermittelt - (*Bezahlung*) und erhält die gewünschten Waren (*Lieferung*). Völlig vernachlässigt wird heute gewöhnlich die *Auswahl des Zahlungsinstruments* bzw. Zahlungssystems (ZS).

Aus der Vielzahl der sich etablierenden Zahlungssysteme (jedes System verwendet i.a. ein eigenständiges Client-Modul) und des internationalen Charakters des Zahlungsvorgangs (verschiedene Währungen, Transferkosten) ergeben sich für den Nutzer Probleme in der Auswahl des für ihn günstigsten Zahlungsinstruments. Es wird zwar an Lösungen gearbeitet ([Waid96], [JEPI95]), diese sind jedoch mit der bestehenden Infrastruktur nicht kompatibel und werden einige Zeit benötigen, bevor sie breite Verwendung finden.

In dieser Arbeit wird ein Payment Management Service vorgestellt. Dieser Dienst ermittelt für den Nutzer in Kenntnis seiner Preferenzen und der zur Verfügung stehenden Zahlungsinstrumente das zweckmäßigste Zahlungsverfahren. Die Abwicklung des eigentlichen Zahlungsvorgangs selbst gehört nicht zu den Aufgaben dieses Dienstes sondern wird von einem auf das jeweilige Zahlungssystem spezialisierten Dienst übernommen.

Die weiteren Teile der Arbeit sind wie folgt strukturiert: Abschnitt 2 untersucht die Aufgaben eines Payment Management Services. Im Abschnitt 3 erfolgt die Auseinandersetzung mit einem Vorschlag, der ein ähnliches Ziel verfolgt. Anschließend wird im Abschnitt 4 der eigene Lösungsansatz vorgestellt und im Abschnitt 5 das Protokoll spezifiziert. Den Ablauf eines Kaufvorganges für eine Prototypimplementierung beschreibt Abschnitt 6. Abschließend wird die Arbeit im Abschnitt 7 zusammengefaßt und auf ungelöste Probleme hingewiesen.

2. Aufgaben und Anfoderungen

Der Payment Management Service besteht aus dem Payment Management Service Agent (nachfolgend *Payment Manager* bzw. PM genannt) und dem *Payment Management Server* (PMS). Unter *Nutzer* bzw. Käufer wird derjenige verstanden, der eine Zahlung zu leisten hat. Der Payment Manager agiert auf dessen Seite. *Anbieter* oder Händler ist der Empfänger einer Zahlung. Er betreibt den Payment Management Server.

Bei der Formulierung der Forderungen ist vor allem die Nutzerseite zu berücksichtigen. Demgegenüber sind die Bedürfnisse des Anbieters zweitrangig. Das oberste Ziel eines solch wichtigen Dienstes ist die Akzeptanz beim Käufer. Einem Händler, der ohnehin spezielle Dienste realisiert, kann dagegen ein höherer Aufwand zugemutet werden.

Der Payment Management Service soll folgendes leisten:

- Wahl des Zahlungssystems (z.B. kreditkartenbasiertes System)

- Wahl des Systemanbieters (z.B. kreditkartenausgebende Stelle)

- Wahl der Währungseinheit

- Festlegung des endgültigen Zahlungsbetrages inklusive aller systemspezifischen Zusatzkosten (z.B. Scheckgebühren)

Die Prüfung der Korrektheit des Zahlungsbetrags gehört nicht zu den Aufgaben des Payment Managers. Dafür werden umfangreichere Informationen benötigt, die sich nicht ohne weiteres gewinnen lassen. Beispielsweise ist dazu die Führung eines Schatten-Warenkorbes notwendig, um die Warenauswahl des Nutzers zu verfolgen. Da jedes Händlersystem diesen Warenauswahlprozeß verschieden handhabt, ist ein automatisches Nachvollziehen praktisch unmöglich. Eine Lösung dafür besteht in der Definition eines Standardformates für die Rechnung. Der Käufer prüft dann die Richtigkeit der einzelnen Positionen und der Payment Manager sichert die formale Korrektheit des Rechnungsbetrages.

Ursprünglich wurde neben der Auswahlfunktion auch noch eine Vorbereitung des Zahlungsvorgangs in Erwägung gezogen, da der PM aus der Kenntnis des verwendeten Zahlungssystems, der Währung und des Betrages eine Rechnung für den Zahlungssystem-Client erstellen kann. Davon wird abgegangen, da der Service Agent dafür die internen Formate jedes Zahlungssystems kennen muß. Diese sind z.T. nicht offengelegt oder können sich ändern. Damit wird auch die Integration neuer Verfahren verzögert. Ein weiterer Gesichtspunkt ist die Diversität der Zahlungssysteme. Einige verwenden keinen Service Agent im eigentlichen Sinne (Bei [SSBR95] trägt der Nutzer z.B. eine ID in ein Formular ein.), andere erfordern eine kryptografische Sicherung der Rechnung (siehe [Wayn96]). Die Berücksichtigung all dieser Umstände verkompliziert die Realisierung deutlich ohne einen adäquaten Nutzen zu erzielen.

Die Plazierung des Payment Management Services im Kaufablauf ist aus Abbildung 1 ersichtlich.

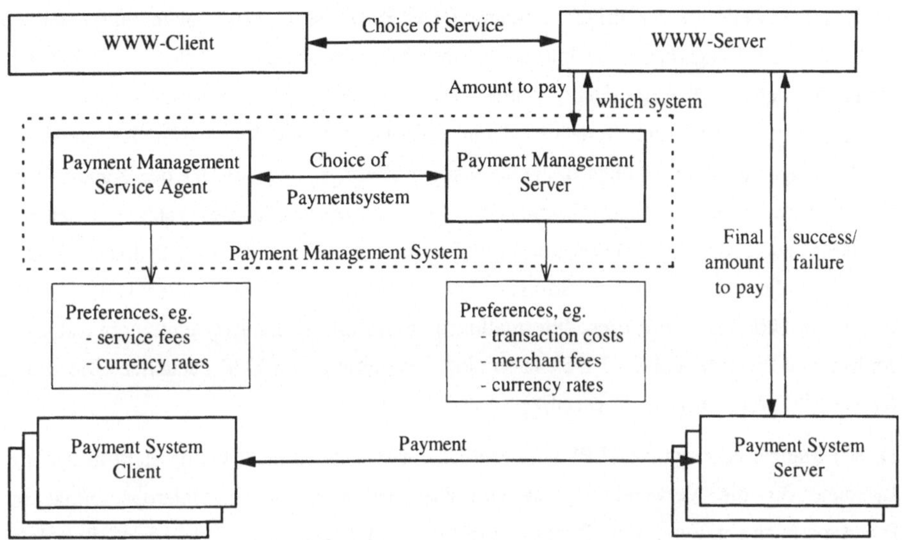

Abb. 1. Kaufablauf

3. Andere Arbeiten

Die Joint Electronic Payment Initiative (JEPI), ein im Dezember 1995 begonnenes gemeinsames Projekt von WWW-Konsortium und CommerceNet, an dem sich auch interessierte Technologieprovider und Händler beteiligen, verfolgt ähnliche Ziele wie diese Arbeit. Anliegen des Projekts ist es, Technologien zu untersuchen, die Verhandlungen über verschiedene Zahlungsinstrumente, Protokolle und Transportmedien ermöglichen. Eine nahtlose Integration wird angestrebt. In der kürzlich erschienenen Arbeit [EaKM96] wurde der gewählte Ansatz verdeutlicht. Das Konsortium verwendet die beiden Internet Drafts PEP (Protocol Extension Protocol) und UPP (Universal Payment Preamble).

PEP ([Khar96]) ist eine Erweiterung des WWW-Protokolls HTTP und soll Bestandteil der zukünftigen Spezifikation 1.2 werden. Es kann als Fortführung des allerdings wenig genutzten Content-Negotiation Mechanismus verstanden werden, der einem Browser die Angabe der von ihm akzeptierten und bevorzugten Dokumentenformate ermöglicht. Das Protocol Extension Protocol liefert den formalen Rahmen für die abwärtskompatible Integration von HTTP-Erweiterungen und Aushandlung ihrer Anwendung. Da PEP ein relativ neuer

Vorschlag ist, gibt es bislang kaum Anwendungen dafür. Neben dem JEPI-Konzept ist nur eine Verwendung innerhalb von PICS (Platform for Internet Content Rating, [MiRS96]) bekannt. Die Umsetzung von PEP, insbesondere die Integration in universelle WWW-Browser, ist noch unklar.

UPP, mittlerweile in der dritten Fassung ([East96a]), hatte ursprünglich zum Ziel, ein einheitliches Messageformat zur Initiierung eines Zahlungsvorgangs zu schaffen. Offenbar im Rahmen der JEPI-Aktivitäten wurde die Zielstellung verfeinert: Auswahl des Zahlungssystems und Einbettung des Zahlungsvorgangs in die Käufer-Händler-Interaktion. UPP schlägt die Verhandlungsparameter *amount* (Betrag), *account* (ID des Kunden beim Betreiber des Zahlungssystems), *transport* (URL, an welche die erste zahlungsspezifische Nachricht zu senden ist), *success* und *failure* (URL, mit der die Käufer-Händler-Interaktion nach dem Zahlungsvorgang im Erfolgs- bzw. Fehlerfall fortgeführt werden soll) vor. Der Autor von UPP bezeichnet diese Informationen als für alle Zahlungssysteme notwendig und fordert, daß die Protokolle aller Systeme eine Erweiterung von UPP darstellen. Die exakte Syntax der Parameter ist nicht spezifiziert.

Diesen Mangel beseitigt die JEPI-Veröffentlichung zwar auch nicht völlig, stellt aber einige Beispiele für die Verwendung von UPP-über-PEP vor, die die Interoperabilität der Prototypimplementierung der Projektteilnehmer sicherstellen soll. In diesen Beispielen werden jedoch (neben den für das jeweilige Zahlungssystem spezifischen) nur die Parameter amount und account benutzt. Dies deckt sich mit eigenen Untersuchungen, die zeigen, daß zum einen der Zahlungsvorgang meist gut in den Kaufablauf integriert ist und sowohl im Fehler- als auch Erfolgsfall sehr spezifische Dokumente angezeigt werden, die sich nicht in das Schema der success- und failure-Parameter einordnen lassen. Die Angabe des transport-Parameters erscheint ebenfalls nicht zweckmäßig, da der Zahlungsvorgang i.a. durch eine Rechnung des Anbieters initiiert wird, welche diese Angaben systemspezifisch enthält.

Die Verwendung des Protocol Extension Protocol bietet den Vorteil, daß der Händler bereits beim erstmaligen Kontakt mit dem Käufer (z.B. Anforderung der Einstiegsseite) Informationen liefern kann, welche Zahlungssysteme unterstützt werden. Der Kunde kann somit vorab prüfen, ob ihm eine Zahlung prinzipiell möglich ist. Das entspricht den üblichen Hinweiszeichen mit den akzeptierten Kreditkarten am Eingang eines Geschäfts. Auf der anderen Seite beherrscht keiner der heute verfügbaren WWW-Browser PEP und es ist auch nicht abzusehen, wann und wie eine solche Unterstützung, die ja dynamische Konfigurationsmöglichkeiten beinhaltet, implementiert wird.

4. Eigener Lösungsansatz

4.1 Integrationsmöglichkeiten

Für den Payment Management Service wird ein anderer Weg beschritten. Eine Untersuchung der Integrationsmöglichkeiten eines einzelnen Zahlungssystems in WWW-Komponenten ([Zimm96]) beschreibt fünf Ansätze: Client-API, Plug-ins, Java-Applets, Skriptsprachen und die Verwendung des MIME-Mechanismus (Multipurpose Internet Mail Extensions, [BoFr93]). Es zeigt sich, daß derzeit nur letzterer sinnvoll eingesetzt werden kann. Die API's und Scriptsprachen sind produktspezifisch und zum Teil als experimentell deklariert, was einen ständigen Aufwand für Weiterentwicklung und Portierung bedeutet. Das Plug-in-Konzept von Netscape wird sich zwar wahrscheinlich zu einem Quasistandard entwickeln, die frei zugängliche Dokumentation ist aber nicht ausreichend für eine abschließende Beurteilung. Java-Applets als portabler und nachladbarer Programmcode verfügen aufgrund ihres Sicherheitskonzepts nur über eng begrenzte Interaktionaktionsmöglichkeiten mit der Browserumgebung. Somit wurde dem MIME-Mechanismus der Vorzug gegeben.

MIME-fähige Applikationen erkennen aus bestimmten Headerzeilen den Typ eines Dokuments. Eine Anwendung, die diesen Typ nicht selbst bearbeiten kann (z.B. Darstellung auf dem Bildschirm, Abarbeitung als Skript), bedient sich einer sogenannten Helper-Applikation für den entsprechenden Dokumententyp. Die Verbindung zwischen Typ und Helper wird beispielsweise über eine Zuordnungsdatei hergestellt. Der ursprünglich für Mailanwendungen geschaffene MIME-Mechanismus wird von allen verbreiteten WWW-Browsern unterstützt.

Aus den oben angeführten Gründen und den Erfahrungen mit dem Prototyp aus [Zimm96] wurde für die Integration des Payment Management Services das MIME-Modell ausgewählt. Der Payment Manager auf Kundenseite stellt eine eigenständige Helper-Applikation dar. Er wird von der MIME-Applikation (WWW-Browser) gestartet. Der Payment Management Server beim Anbieter kann sowohl direkt durch den PM angesprochen oder ebenfalls über eine MIME-Applikation aufgerufen werden.

4.2 Verhandlungsparameter

Für die Auswahl der in die Verhandlung einzubeziehenden Parameter wird auf [East96a] und [Reif96b] zurückgegriffen. Um allgemeingültig zu bleiben, wird neben dem Zahlungssystem (*method*) nur noch ein Unterscheidungsmerkmal (*submethod*) vereinbart. Dieses kann beispielsweise den Betreiber des Systems bezeichnen (nicht globales System wie ecash, [ecas95]) oder eine andere wesentliche Eigenschaft (Einschränkung der akzeptierten Kreditkarten für SET) angeben. Eine weitere Unterteilung erscheint nicht sinnvoll, da diese dann stark systemabhängig ist. Mit einem Unterscheidungsmerkmal läßt sich für alle in [Reif96b] untersuchten Zahlungssysteme entscheiden, ob Kunde und Anbieter miteinander kompatibel sind, also einen Zahlungsvorgang durchführen können. Die Vereinbarung zusätzlicher systemspezifischer Parameter liegt im Aufgabenbereich des eigentlichen Zahlungssystems.

Weiterhin wird der Preis (*amount*) in die Verhandlung mit einbezogen. Darunter ist das Festlegen des Endpreises unter Berücksichtigung etwaiger systemspezifischer Gebühren, Werbeaktionen usw. durch den Händler zu verstehen. Der Payment Manager benötigt diese Information zur Entscheidung über das für den Käufer günstigste System (ebenfalls unter Berücksichtigung etwaiger fester oder volumenabhängiger Gebühren für den Kunden). Schließlich wird noch die Währung (*currency*) ausgehandelt. Dies ist für den globalen Einsatz unerläßlich. Zum einen kann die Menge der verwendbaren Währungen beschränkt sein, andererseits können die Umtauschkurse von Händler und Käufer differieren.

4.3 Verhandlungsablauf

Preise (für eine bestimmte Währung) dürfen nur vom PMS vorgeschlagen werden, der Payment Manager darf diese im Zusammenhang mit einem akzeptierten Angebot nur wiederholen. Da die Initiative vom Payment Management Server ausgeht, schlägt dieser die verwendbaren Zahlungssysteme vor. Der PM antwortet mit einem oder mehreren von ihm akzeptierten Systemen. Ein Unterscheidungsmerkmal ist beim Verhandlungsbeginn nicht erforderlich. Dieses kann entweder in der Antwort vom Payment Manager angeboten werden oder in der zweiten Nachricht des PMS für die übereinstimmenden Zahlungssysteme spezifiziert werden. Ebenso muß über eine Währung erst verhandelt werden, nachdem das Unterscheidungsmerkmal feststeht.

Der Payment Management Server ist dafür verantwortlich, die Verhandlung voranzutreiben. Der Payment Manager kann seinerseits Angebote unterbreiten, muß es aber nicht. Diese Festlegung dient dem Schutz der Privatsphäre des Kunden: er ist nicht gezwungen seine Möglichkeiten in vollem Umfang offenzulegen. Den Interessen des Händlers kommt die Festlegung entgegegen, daß der Endpreis erst genannt werden braucht, wenn die gemeinsam nutzbaren Zahlungssysteme nebst Unterscheidungsmerkmal und verfügbaren Währungen feststehen. Somit ist er nicht zu einer kompletten Offenlegung seiner Preispolitik in Abhängigkeit vom verwendeten Zahlungssystem gezwungen.

Es liegt im Ermessen des Payment Management Servers, wie detailliert er Angebote vorlegt. Neben der Berücksichtigung der Händlerinteressen ist auch eine Abwägung zwischen Menge der zu übertragenden Daten (=> Durchsatz) und Anzahl der Verhandlungsrunden (=> Umlaufzeit) vorzunehmen. Insbesondere wenn der Händler mehrere Zahlungsinstrumente in unterschiedlichen Währungen akzeptiert, erscheint ein detailliertes und entsprechend umfangreiches Angebot in der ersten Runde als nicht sinnvoll.

Eine Fallback-Strategie ist nicht vorgesehen. Wenn der Payment Manager ein unterstütztes, aber unvorteilhaftes Zahlungssystem (z.B. hohe Gebühren für Kunden) ablehnt, kann dieses nicht wieder in die Verhandlung eingebracht werden. Falls sich nach der nächsten Verhandlungsrunde herausstellt, daß für das vom PM akzeptierte Zahlungssystem keine gemeinsame Währung existiert, wird die Verhandlung als gescheitert betrachtet. Deshalb liegt es im Interesse beider Seiten, die Angebote so vollständig wie möglich und nur so restriktiv wie nötig vorzulegen.

Eine Verhandlung ist spätestens nach vier Runden abgeschlossen, da die Gebote immer spezieller werden und nur vier Parameter zu vereinbaren sind. Danach steht entweder der Endpreis und das Zahlungsinstrument oder das Scheitern der Verhandlungen fest. Sollte die Erfolglosigkeit durch ein zu restriktives Verhalten verursacht werden, muß durch den Payment Management Server eine neue Verhandlung begonnen werden. Allerdings ist unklar, wie dieser ein zu restriktives Verhalten des PM erkennt. Außerdem benötigt einer der beiden Partner eine Gedächtnisfunktion, um ein erneutes Scheitern in der nächsten Verhandlung zu verhindern.

5. Simple Payment Management Protokoll

5.1 Aufbau des Messageblocks

Ein Angebot besteht aus einem Messageblock, der durch eine Start- und eine Endezeile begrenzt wird.

Beide Zeilen beginnen mit mindestens fünf Minuszeichen ("-") und dem darauffolgenden Text `BEGIN SPMP MESSAGE` bzw. `END SPMP MESSAGE`. Die Zeile kann vor dem Zeilenwechsel weitere Minuszeichen enthalten. Leerzeichen sind außerhalb des Labels nicht zulässig.

Innerhalb des Messageblocks besteht jede Zeile aus einem SPMP-Primitiv gefolgt von einem Doppelpunkt (":") und einem oder mehreren, durch Komma getrennten Werten. Ein Wert wird als ASCII-Zeichenfolge dargestellt. Leerzeichen und Tabulatoren sind ohne Bedeutung. Es sind sechs Primitive definiert, von denen vier den zu verhandelnden Parametern entsprechen.

5.2 SPMP Primitve

`SPMP-method` legt das Zahlungssystem fest. Die Werte dieser Primitve sind nicht frei wählbar, sondern entstammen einer Menge vordefinierter Bezeichner. Die Definition bzw. der Registrierungsmechanismus für solche Bezeichner ist nicht Gegenstand des Protokolls. Falls mehrere Werte für das Primitv angegeben werden, darf kein Unterscheidungsmerkmal folgen.

SPMP-submethod spezifiziert das Unterscheidungsmerkmal. Es bezieht sich auf das letzte angegebene Zahlungssystem. Je Zahlungssystem sind mehrere Zeilen mit Angabe des Unterscheidungsmerkmals zulässig. Die Festlegungen für den Wertebereich des SPMP-method-Primitivs gelten analog.

SPMP-currency bezeichnet die Währung. Das Primitiv bezieht sich auf das letzte angegebene Unterscheidungsmerkmal. Je Unterscheidungsmerkmal sind mehrere Währungen zulässig. Als Wertebereich werden die dreibuchstabigen ISO-Currency-Codes vorgeschlagen. Ist die Währung darin nicht enthalten (also keine offizielle Landeswährung), gelten die Festlegungen unter SPMP-method sinngemäß.

SPMP-amount legt den Geldbetrag fest. Der Wert muß einer gültigen int- oder float-Konstante der Sprache C entsprechen.

SPMP-transaction-ID dient der Zuordnung des Messageblocks zu einer laufenden Verhandlung. Falls dieses Primitiv verwendet wird, muß es nach der Startzeile eines Messageblocks stehen und in der Antwort wiederholt werden. Sowohl PM als auch PMS können es einführen.

```
         ----------BEGIN SPMP MESSAGE----------
SPMP-transaction-ID: 0123456789abcdef
SPMP-contact: spmp://spmp-host.domain.de:1234/
SPMP-method: SET
   SPMP-submethod: VISA, EuroCard
      SPMP-currency: USD
        SPMP-amount: 100
      SPMP-currency: DEM
        SPMP-amount: 160
   SPMP-submethod: AmericanExpress
      SPMP-currency: USD
        SPMP-amount: 105
SPMP-method: CyberCash
   SPMP-submethod: VISA
      SPMP-currency: USD
SPMP-method: ecash
   SPMP-submethod: MarkTwain
      SPMP-currency: USD
   SPMP-submethod: DeutscheBank
      SPMP-currency: DEM
         ----------END SPMP MESSAGE----------
```

Abb. 2. Beispiel eines SPMP Messageblocks

Das Primitiv SPMP-contact wird vom Payment Management Server verwendet, um seine Adresse an den Payment Manager zu übermitteln. Es darf nur im ersten vom PMS gesendeten Messageblock benutzt werden und muß vor dem ersten SPMP-method-Primitiv stehen. Der Wert muß eine gültige URL bezeichnen. Abbildung 2 zeigt ein Beispiel für einen Messageblock. Die Einrückungen erfolgen zur besseren Übersicht und haben keine Bedeutung.

5.3 SPMP und URL

Um die Verwendung eines dedizierten Payment Management Servers innerhalb einer URL auszudrücken, wurde ein neues Zugriffsschema (spmp) definiert. Der zugehörige schemaspezifische Teil der URL folgt der "Common Internet Scheme Syntax" ([BLMM94]) und gibt den Hostnamen sowie den Port an. Die Verwendung von Nutzername, Paßwort oder Pfadangaben ist nicht vorgesehen. SPMP stellt einen transparenten, kryptografisch ungeschützten TCP-Kanal für die Übertragung der Messageblöcke zur Verfügung. Die Verbindung bleibt bis zum Abschluß der Verhandlungen bestehen und wird vom PMS abgebaut.

Das Simple Payment Management Protokoll kann in andere Protokolle gekapselt werden. Neben der Verwendung von SMTP (Simple Mail Transfer Protocol, [Post82]) mit dem Nachteil hoher Umlaufzeiten wird vor allem die Kapselung in HTTP vorgeschlagen. Dies ist insbesondere in firewall-geschützten Umgebungen sinnvoll, da dort ein Verbindungsaufbau zu einem dedizierten PMS mit hoher Wahrscheinlichkeit unterbunden wird. Der Mechanismus der Kapselung wird bei der prototypischen Realisierung genauer beschrieben.

6. Realisierung als Prototyp

6.1 Auswahl der Zahlungssysteme

Zum Test des Protokolls auf Verwendbarkeit wurde mit der Implementierung eines Prototyps begonnen. Bei den Arbeiten erwies sich das Finden geeigneter Zahlungssysteme für die Einbindung in den Prototyp als eines der größten Probleme. Zwar ist bereits eine Reihe von Systemen in Betrieb ([Reif96b]), eine Verwendung kommt aber nicht in Betracht, da bei diesen stets reales Geld involviert ist. Schließlich werden folgende Zahlungssysteme integriert: ecash, MagicMoney und ein selbstgeschaffenes System. Alle drei Systeme realisieren die Vorschläge aus Arbeiten von Chaum ([Chau82]) und beruhen auf digital signierten Bitstrings mit inhärentem Wert (eine Übersicht findet sich z.B. in [Reif95a]).

Ecash ([ecas95]) ist ein Produkt der Firma Digicash. Die frei erhältlichen Client-Programme können mehrere Währungen verwalten, entsprechende Server-Programme (Bank) stehen jedoch nicht zur Verfügung. Für den Prototyp wurde auf das CyberBuck-Experiment (internetweiter Betatest des Systems, [ecas94]) mit Geld ohne realen Wert zurückgegriffen, da Digicash den Server auch nach Testende weiter betreibt. MagicMoney ([Cyph94]) ist ein Softwarepaket des anonymen Autors Pr0duct Cypher, das sowohl Client- als auch Server-Programm enthält. Das Paket unterstützt mehrere Währungen. Das eigene Zahlungssystem ([Zimm96]) ist ähnlich, benutzt aber serverseitig eine Datenbank. Perspektivisch ist eine Integration des GlobeID-Systems ([PaCo96]), derzeit Pilotprojekt, und des Anfang September beginnenden CyberCoin-Projekts ([East96b]) vorgesehen.

6.2 Ablauf des Kaufvorgangs

Für den Prototyp wird kein separater SPMP-Server verwendet. Stattdessen werden die Messageblöcke in HTTP-Requests gekapselt. Der PMS ist dabei als CGI-Programm (Common Gateway Interface) realisiert. Den Ablauf eines kompletten Kaufvorgangs zeigt Abbildung 3.

Beim Aufruf einer kostenpflichtigen Seite (1) startet der HTTP-Server ein CGI-Programm (A), welches eine Antwort im *multipart*-MIME-Format sendet. Diese enthält zunächst eine (optionale) durch den Browser anzuzeigende Nachricht (2a) mit dem Hinweis auf die beginnenden Verhandlungen und den ersten Messageblock für den Payment Manager (2b). Letztere ist durch den selbstdefinierten MIME-Typ `application/x-spmp` gekennzeichnet. Die TCP-Verbindung wird aufrecht erhalten.

Der PM nimmt Verbindung zu der im Messageblock angegebenen URL mit dem Zugriffsschema `http` auf (3). Hinter dieser Adresse verbirgt sich wiederum ein CGI-Programm (B). Da die Zugriffsmethode innerhalb einer URL nicht kodiert werden kann, wird die Anwendung der `POST`-Methode für das Zugriffschema `http` explizit festgelegt. Die Verwendung der `Keep-Alive`-Option im Header des HTTP-Requests verhindert den Verbindungsabbau durch den HTTP-Server. Damit wird zum einen dem zustandsbehafteten Charakter der Verhandlung entsprochen und andererseits der Aufwand für den erneuten Start des PMS vermieden. Unterstützt der verwendete HTTP-Server kein Aufrechterhalten der Verbindung, muß der Payment Management Server den aktuellen Stand der Verhandlungen persistent ablegen und zu Beginn der nächsten Verhandlungsrunde (neuer Aufruf des PMS) mit Hilfe der Transaktionsnummer (`SPMP-transaction-ID`-Zeile des Messageblocks) laden. In der Abbildung ist aus Gründen der Übersicht nur eine Verhandlungsrunde dargestellt.

Nach Abschluß der Verhandlungen sendet der PMS einen Messageblock mit der Bestätigung der ausgewählten Parameter (4). Außerdem erfolgt eine Benachrichtigung des CGI-Programms (A) über das Ergebnis der Verhandlungen. Im Prototyp werden dazu UNIX-Pipes verwendet. Der Name der Pipe setzt sich aus einem konstanten Pfad und der Prozeß-ID von (A), welche Bestandteil der Transaktionsnummer ist, zusammen.

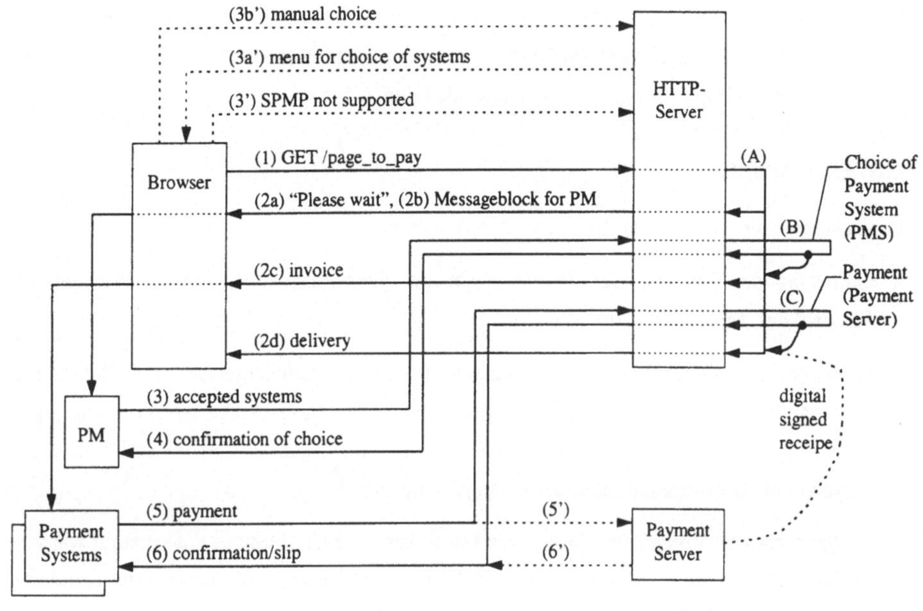

Abb. 3. Ablauf eines Kaufvorgangs

Als dritten Teil der Antwort auf die Anforderung der kostenpflichtigen Seite erhält der Browser nun eine Rechnung (2c). Aus der MIME-Kennzeichnung erkennt der Browser, welcher Zahlungssystem-Client zu starten ist. Die Bezahlung (5, 6) erfolgt beim Prototyp ähnlich wie die Verhandlung gekapselt in HTTP über den Aufruf eines CGI-Programmes (C). Alternativ ist die Verwendung eines separaten Zahlungsservers angedeutet (5', 6'). Allerdings gestaltet sich dann die Benachrichtigung von (A) schwieriger - insbesondere, wenn Zahlungsserver und HTTP-Server auf verschiedenen Hosts laufen. Dann ist die Verwendung einer digital signierten Quitting unerläßlich.

Nach erfolgter Bezahlung erhält der Browser die gewünschte Ware als vierten und letzten Teil der Antwort (2d). Das kann die Information selbst, ein Verweis auf eine temporäre URL oder auch nur eine verbale Bestätigung der Bezahlung im Falle der Bestellung physischer Waren sein. Die Anzeige des ersten Antwortteils (2a) im Browserfenster wird damit ersetzt.

Für den Fall, daß der Payment Manager vom Browser nicht aufgerufen werden kann (PM nicht installiert, Zuordnung des entsprechenden MIME-Typs nicht vorhanden), wird wie in Abbildung 3 gestrichelt angedeutet vorgegangen. Der erste Antwortteil beim Aufruf der kostenpflichtigen Seite (2a) enthält einen Hinweis auf diesen möglichen Fehler (MIME-Typ `application/x-spmp` unbekannt) und einen Verweis auf eine alternative Seite. Nach Aufruf dieser Ausweichseite (3') erhält der Nutzer eine Menüauswahl (3a'), aus der er das von ihm gewünschte Zahlungssystem selbst auswählen muß (3b').

6.3 Eigenschaften

Das beschriebene Szenario hat folgende Eigenschaften:

- *Entlastung* des Nutzers. Der Payment Manager übernimmt die immer wiederkehrende Auswahl des Zahlungssystem.

- *Kompatibilität* mit existierenden Lösungen. Damit wird sichergestellt, daß der Dienst sofort mit der installierten Softwarebasis zusammenarbeiten kann. Das ist um so wichtiger, da die Entwicklung mehr vom Angebot als von der Nachfrage (also auch der Bereitschaft, die gewohnte Software aufzugeben) vorangetrieben wird.

- Verwendung von *Standardmechanismen*. Damit kann die Einführungszeit verkürzt werden. Zum einen sind diese Mechanismen als hinreichend getestet anzusehen, zum anderen existieren für deren Bearbeitung bereits oft nachnutzbare Lösungen

- *Funktionsmodulare* Realisierung. Das vermeidet die Reimplementierung von bereits vorhandener Funktionalität und ermöglicht die Integration von neuen Zahlungssystemen ohne zusätzlichen Aufwand.

- Modellierung *vertrauter Abläufe* für den Nutzer. Nur so ist eine schnelle Akzeptanz ohne Eingewöhnungsphase zu erreichen.

7. Zusammenfassung und Ausblick

Der in dieser Arbeit beschriebene Dienst für die automatisierte Auswahl eines von Händler und Käufer unterstützten Zahlungssystems fügt sich durch die Verwendung des MIME-Mechanismus nahtlos in die bestehende Softwareinfrastruktur ein. Das spezifizierte Simple Payment Management Protocol stellt die Grundlage für eine prototypische Realisierung des Payment Management Service dar. Mit dieser wird zugleich die Kapselung von SPMP in HTTP demonstriert. Weiterhin zeigt sie eine mögliche nutzerfreundliche Reaktion auf eine fehlende SPMP-Unterstützung des Kunden.

Ein ungelöstes Problem ist der Umstand, daß das Verhandlungsergebnis nicht verallgemeinert, also auf andere kostenpflichtige Seiten ausgedehnt werden kann. Außerdem ist eine wünschenswerte Verhandlung vor Beginn der Warenauswahl derzeit nicht möglich.

Eine Schwierigkeit bereitet das nutzerfreundliche Erstellen der Preferences sowie deren kompakte Abspeicherung. Die Preferences beinhalten keine konkreten Fallentscheidungen sondern die gesamten Möglichkeiten des Nutzers, die er möglicherweise selbst nicht vollständig überblickt. Hier muß nach einem allgemeingültigen Modell für die vier Parameter gesucht werden.

Letztlich stellt sich die Frage, ob verallgemeinerte Anwendung des Verhandlungs-mechanismus' beim Kaufvorgang möglich ist. Denkbar wäre das Einfordern von Mengenrabatten oder die Aushandlung eines Hauspreises.

[BGHH95]   M. Bellare, J. Garay, R. Hauser, A. Herzberg u.a.: "*i*KP: - A Family of Secure Electronic Payment Protocols"; Zürich 1995.
<http://www.zurich.ibm.com/Technology/Security/ecommerce/>

[BLMM94]   T. Berners-Lee, L. Masinter, M. McCahill: "Uniform Resource Locators (URL)", RFC 1738; 1994. < ftp://ds.internic.net/rfc/rfc1738.txt>

[BoFr93]   N. Borenstein, N. Freed: "MIME (Multipurpose Internet Mail Extensions) Part One: Mechanisms for Specifying and Describing the Format of Internet Message Bodies", RFC 1521; 1993. <ftp://ds.internic.net/rfc/rfc1521.txt>

[Chau82]   D. Chaum: "Blind Signatures for Untraceable Payments"; In: Advances of Cryptology: Proceedings of Crypto '82, Plenum, (1983), 199-203.

[Cyph94]   Pr0duct Cypher: "Magic Money Digital Cash System"; 1994.
<http://www.c2.org/~mark/pgp/mm-readme.html>

[Dogg95]   J. Dogget: "FSTC Electronic Check Project"; Boston, 1995.
<http://www.fstc.org/echeck/>

[Duka92]   S. Dukach: "SNPP: A Simple Network Payment Protocol"; Cambridge, MA, 1992. <ftp://mercury.lcs.mit.edu/pub/snpp/snpp-paper.ps>

[EaKM96]   D. Eastlake, R. Khare, J. Miller: "Selecting Payment Mechanisms Over HTTP. Or, Seven Examples of UPP Over PEP (as used in JEPI)", Internet Draft (work in progress); August 1996.
<ftp://ds.internic.net/internet-drafts/draft-khare-jepi-uppflow-00.txt >

[East96a]   D. Eastlake: "Universal Payment Preamble", Internet Draft (work in progress); 1995, 1996.   <ftp://ds.internic.net/internet-drafts/draft-eastlake-universal-payment-02.txt>

[East96b]   D. Eastlake: "[Micropayments]"; Vortrag, August 1996.
<ftp://ftp.cybercash.com/pub/dee/micropayment21aug96.ppt>

[ecas94]   o.V.: "About the ecash trial"; Amsterdam 1994, 1995, 1996.
<http://www.digicash.com/ecash/trial.html>

[ecas95]   o.V.: "About ecash"; Amsterdam 1995, 1996.
<http://www.digicash.com/ecash/about.html>

[JEPI95]   o.V.: "Joint Electronic Payment Initiative"; Cambridge, MA, Dezember 1995.
<http://www.w3.org/pub/WWW/Payment/JEPI.html>

[Khar96]   R. Khare: "HTTP/1.2 Extension Protocol (PEP)", Internet Draft (work in progress); Mai 1996. <http: //www.w3.org/pub/WWW/TR/WD-http-pep.html>

[MiRS96] J. Miller, P. Resnick, D. Singer: "Rating Services and Rating Systems (and Their Machine Readable Descriptions)", Internet Draft (work in progress); 1996. <http://www.w3.org/pub/WWW/PICS/services.html>

[PaCo96] P.-A. Pays, F. de Comarmond: "An Intermediation and Payment System Technology", In: Proceedings 5. International WWW Conference, Paris, Mai 1996.

[Post82] J. Postel: "Simple Mail Transfer Protocol", RFC 821; 1982. <ftp://ds.internic.net/rfc/rfc821.txt>

[Reif95] H. Reif: "Elektronischer Handel: Zahlungsmöglichkeiten im Internet. Ein Überblick"; In: Proceedings Workshop Multimediale Kommunikations- und Informationssysteme, Ilmenau, 1995

[Reif96a] H. Reif: "Cyber-Dollars. Elektronisches Geld im Internet"; In: Magazin für Computertechnik (1996) 144-199.

[Reif96b] H. Reif: "Vergleichende Betrachtung von Zahlungssystemen mit Einsatzschwerpunkt Internet", unveröffentlichter Entwurf; Ilmenau, 1996.

[SSBR95] L. Stein, E. Stefferud, N. Borenstein, M. Rose: "The Green Commerce Model", Draft, San Diego, CA, 1995. <http://www.fv.com/pubdocs/green-model.txt>

[SET96] o.V.: "Secure Electronic Transactions (SET). Draft for testing"; Juli 1996. <http://www.mastercard.com/set/>

[Waid96] M. Waidner: "Secure Electronic Commerce: SEMPER"; Vortrag, 1. Deutscher Internetkongreß, Leipzig, 1996.

[Wayn96] P. Wayner: "Digital Cash. Commerce On the Net"; Academic Press, London 1995.

[Zimm96] S. Zimmermann: "Untersuchungen zur Integrierbarkeit von Paymentsystemen in die Konzepte des World Wide Web", Diplomarbeit im Fachgebiet Telematik der TU Ilmenau; Ilmenau, 1996.

Session 2:
Security

Host-orientiertes Netz-Audit
Ein neuer Ansatz zur Protokollierung von Netzaktivitäten

Birk Richter   *Michael Sobirey*   *Hartmut König*
Brandenburgische Technische Universität Cottbus
Lehrstuhl für Rechnernetze und Kommunikationssysteme
Postfach 10 13 44   D-03013 Cottbus
{richter, sobirey, koenig}@informatik.tu-cottbus.de

Zusammenfassung Sicherheitsaspekte spielen bei der Gestaltung
künftiger Kommunikationsnetze eine entscheidende Rolle. Die Aufzeichnung von Netzaktivitäten durch Auditing und die Auswertung dieser Daten mittels Intrusion Detection-Systemen sind dabei eine wesentliche Komponente. Die bisherigen Realisierungen im Bereich des
Netz-Audits werden den Anforderungen künftiger Kommunikationssysteme (verschlüsselter Netzverkehr, Switch-Technologien, wesentlich höhere Übertragungsraten) nicht mehr gerecht. In dem vorliegenden Beitrag
stellen wir mit dem Host-orientierten Netz-Audit einen neuen Ansatz
zur Protokollierung von Netzaktivitäten vor, mit dem die derzeitigen
technologischen Schwachstellen bisheriger Realisierungen innerhalb dieses Funktionsbereichs entscheidend kompensiert werden können.

1   Einleitung

Informationstechnische (IT-) Systeme sind aus unterschiedlichsten Gründen
inhärent unsicher. Ursachen hierfür liegen u.a. in konzeptionellen Schwachstellen, Implementations- und Konfigurationsfehlern. Selbst im Falle hypothetisch
technisch absolut sicherer IT-Systeme würden dem sicheren Betrieb dieser Systeme immer noch menschliche Schwächen entgegenstehen. Hat ein Angreifer erst
einmal die Authentifikation passiert, ist er für die Zugriffskontrolle zweifelsfrei
identifiziert. Sie ist von da ab nicht mehr in der Lage, ihn an der Inanspruchnahme der in unzulässiger Weise erlangten Zugriffsrechte zu hindern. Initiierte
Zugriffsanforderungen werden von der Zugriffskontrolle *einzeln* anhand der gesetzten Zugriffsrechte verifiziert. IT-Sicherheitsverletzungen sind jedoch in der
Mehrzahl der Fälle das Ergebnis mehrerer aufeinander abgestimmter und von
der Zugriffskontrolle akzeptierter Aktionen, die unter gezielter Ausnutzung si-
cherheitsrelevanter Schwachstellen erfolgen. Um IT-Sicherheitsverletzungen erkennen zu können, bedarf es folglich der Analyse von Aktionssequenzen.

Audit ist eine elementare Sicherheitsfunktion in IT-Systemen, deren Aufgabe in der Generierung, Aufzeichnung und Analyse von Daten über sicherheitsrelevante system- bzw. netzinterne Aktivitäten besteht. Die mittels Auditing
protokollierten Nachweise liefern detaillierte Informationen darüber, *wer, wann*
und *wo* auf *was wie* zugegriffen hat bzw. zuzugreifen versuchte. Aufgrund des
direkten Benutzerbezugs dieser Daten ist in Schadensfällen die Feststellung

der Verursacher möglich. Auditfunktionen sind integriert in Betriebssystemen [USL93, MC95] sowie in Applikationen, z.B. Datenbank-Managementsystemen [Bo88], einschließlich Kommunikationsprotokollen (z.B. TCP-Wrapper [Ve92]). In Anbetracht der beim Auditing anfallenden Datenmengen (bis zu mehreren MBytes je Nutzer pro Tag) und des komplexen Informationsgehalts erweist sich eine weitgehend manuelle, lediglich mit einfachen Tools unterstützte Analyse als recht anspruchsvoll und extrem zeitaufwendig. Erst der Einsatz leistungsstarker automatischer Analyseverfahren ermöglicht einen praktikablen Umgang mit den Auditdaten.

Intrusion Detection-Systeme realisieren eine derartige automatische Analyse von Auditdaten. Im einzelnen decken sie folgende Funktionsbereiche ab: Vorverarbeiten und Verwalten der zur Verfügung stehenden Auditdaten, automatisierte Analyse dieser Daten mittels Verfahren der Künstlichen Intelligenz bzw. statistischen Verfahren, Benachrichtigung des Sicherheitsadministrators sowie ggf. Einleitung von Gegenmaßnahmen zur Abwehr erkannter Angriffe. In den vergangenen Jahren wurde eine Vielzahl unterschiedlichster Intrusion Detection-Systeme entwickelt, mit denen sensitive Applikationen [Te89], einzelne Großrechner [Se$^+$88], die Kommunikation innerhalb lokaler Netze [He$^+$90] und mehrere Rechner in lokalen Netzen ohne bzw. mit Berücksichtigung der netzinternen Kommunikation ([Lu90] bzw. [Sna$^+$91]) überwacht werden können.

Im vorliegenden Beitrag konzentrieren wir uns auf Probleme der auditgestützten Netzüberwachung. Erforderlich sind hierfür detaillierte Informationen darüber, was *auf* und *zwischen* den jeweiligen Rechnern passiert. Vorgestellt wird ein neuer Ansatz zur Protokollierung von Netzaktivitäten, das Host-orientierte Netz-Audit. Dieser Ansatz ist unabhängig vom verwendeten Netzzugriffsverfahren und ermöglicht zudem die Aufzeichnung von Protokolldaten auch bei verschlüsseltem Netzverkehr, was besonders im Hinblick auf IPv6 von Bedeutung ist. Durch die gleichzeitige Aufzeichnung von Host- und netzbasierten Auditdaten wird eine umfassendere Überwachung von Netzaktivitäten in unterschiedlichen Schichten möglich.

Der Beitrag ist inhaltlich wie folgt gegliedert. In Kapitel 2 werden bisherige Ansätze zur Protokollierung von Netzaktivitäten und deren Realisierungen vorgestellt, klassifiziert und im Hinblick auf ihr derzeitiges und perspektivisches technologisches Leistungsvermögen bewertet. Darauf aufbauend wird in Kapitel 3 das Konzept des Host-orientierten Netz-Audits und in Kapitel 4 dessen Realisierung erläutert. Anschließend folgen eine Zusammenfassung sowie ein Ausblick.

2 Aufzeichnung von Netzaktivitäten

2.1 Auditrelevante Daten in Netzwerkschichten

Die bei der Erbringung von Netzdiensten in den jeweiligen Schichten ausgetauschten protokollspezifischen Daten weisen unterschiedliche Relevanz für eine auditgestützte Netzüberwachung auf. Wir beziehen uns nachfolgend auf den Internet-Protokollstack [Co88].

In der Anwendungsschicht sind dienstspezifische Daten, insbesondere Benutzer-Identifikatoren, Ressourcen-Namen sowie Dienstkommandos verfügbar. In dieser Schicht ist es möglich zu erkennen, ob bspw. ein *put-* oder *get-* Kommando innerhalb von *ftp* initiiert wurde. Daten zu Dienstzugangspunkten, z.B. TCP- oder UDP-Ports, sowie die beim Verbindungsaufbau erforderlichen Parameter werden in der Transportschicht ausgetauscht und verarbeitet. Desweiteren sind für das Netz-Audit die in der Netzwerkschicht verfügbaren (globalen) Quell- und Zieladressen einer Aktivität von Bedeutung, z.B. die IP-Adressen der miteinander kommunizierenden Hosts. Die im Subnetz verfügbaren Informationen, insbesondere MAC-Adressen, sind lediglich lokal relevant [Ri+96]. Die Aufzeichnung derartiger Daten erfolgt mittels Betriebssystem-Audit sowie durch Netzmonitore.

2.2 Betriebssystem-Audit

Das *Betriebssystem-Audit* protokolliert an Systemrufe bzw. spezielle Applikationen gebundene Aktionen, die *auf* dem jeweiligen überwachten Rechner von Nutzern oder deren Prozessen initiiert wurden. Die Generierung der Auditdaten erfolgt dabei im Betriebssystemkern. Das Auftreten dieser Aktionen wird durch Auditereignisse (audit events) dokumentiert, die wiederum bestimmten Auditklassen (z.B. für Filezugriffe, Prozeßmanagement, Systemadministration, Netzwerkzugriffe) zugeordnet werden. Die Möglichkeiten und Einschränkungen des Betriebssystem-Audits bei der Protokollierung von Netzaktivitäten sollen exemplarisch am Beispiel von Solaris 2.x aufgezeigt werden.

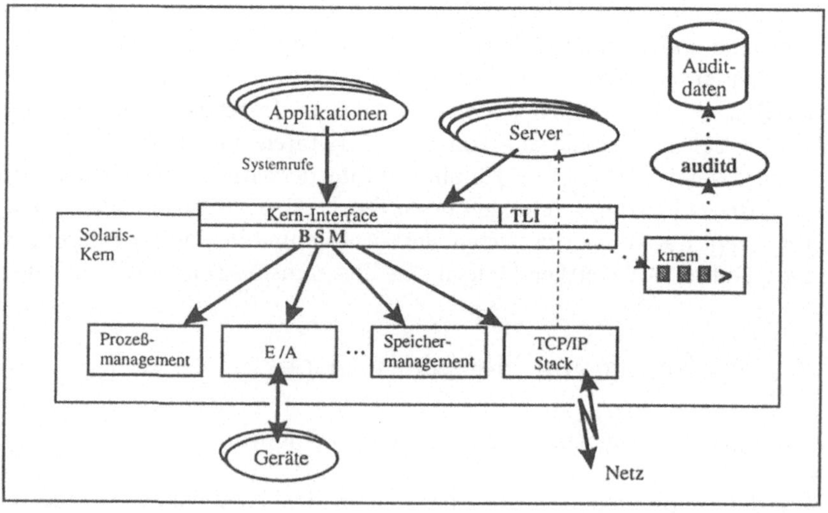

Abbildung1. Funktionsprinzip des Betriebssystem-Audits in Solaris 2.x

In Solaris generiert das Basic Security Modul (BSM) Auditdaten und puffert sie im kerninternen Arbeitsspeicher. Dort werden sie vom Audit-Daemon *(auditd)* entnommen und in ein Datenfile geschrieben (siehe Abb. 1). Insgesamt werden 278, mit Systemrufen und high level-Aktionen (z.B. login, logout) korrespondierende Auditereignisse definiert, die wiederum 17 Audit-Ereignisklassen zugeordnet werden.

Lediglich die Klasse *network* definiert Auditereignisse, die netzwerkspezifischen Aktionen zugeordnet sind. Diese Aktionen bilden das Transportschicht-Interface, eine vom darunterliegenden Protokoll-Stack und Netzwerkschichten unabhängige Programmierschnittstelle (unter BSD-Unix die *socket*-Schnittstelle [Le+89], unter Unix System V das *Transport Layer Interface* [Sun93]). Die Auditereignisse lassen sich in Aktionen zum *Senden* und *Empfangen* von Daten sowie zum *Management* von Netzzugriffen unterteilen. Für die Erkennung von Netzangriffen interessieren bei der Protokollierung von Netzaktivitäten insbesondere die Aktionen zum Empfangen von Daten. Nur diese enthalten relevante Informationen zu Netzaktivitäten, die auf *anderen* Rechnern initiiert wurden und den überwachten Rechner zum Ziel haben.

Damit ergeben sich folgende Randbedingungen für die Aufzeichnung von eingehenden Netzaktivitäten (Abb. 2 a) durch das Betriebssystem-Audit:

1. Eingehende Daten müssen auf dem überwachten Rechner von einem, in der Anwendungsschicht befindlichen Prozeß empfangen werden. Für gewöhnlich erfolgt dies durch Server-Prozesse, mit denen die durch die Netzaktivitäten angesprochenen Dienstzugangspunkte kontrolliert werden.

2. Dieser Prozeß muß für den Empfang der Daten das Transportschicht-Interface benutzen.

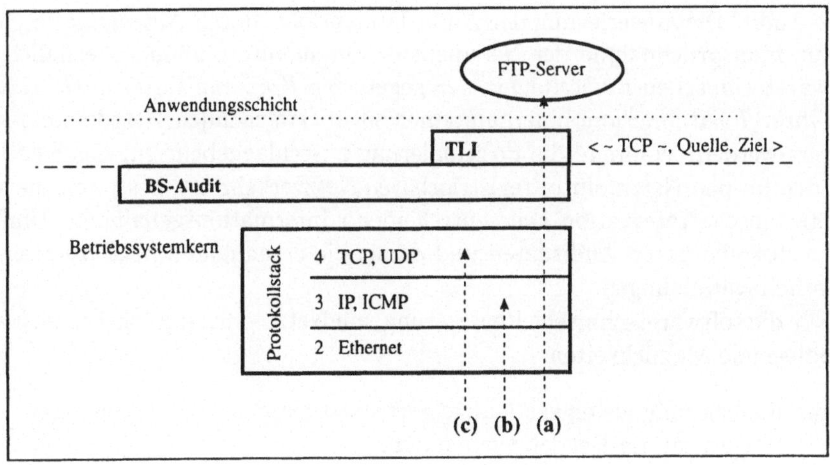

Abbildung2. Sichtbarkeit von Netzaktivitäten für das Betriebssystem-Audit

Bei Einhaltung der oben genannten Bedingungen können durch das Betriebssystem-Audit relevante Daten des verwendeten Transportprotokolls, sowie die Quell- und Zieladressen protokolliert werden (siehe Abb. 2). Dadurch sind allerdings folgende Netzaktivitäten für das Betriebssystem-Audit *nicht* registrierbar: Netzaktivitäten, die nur Protokolle benutzen, die *innerhalb* des Betriebssystemkerns abgearbeitet werden (z.B. ICMP in Schicht 3, Abb. 2 b) sowie für die auf dem angesprochenen Rechner kein empfangender Prozeß existiert (z.B. port probing, Abb. 2 c). Dienstspezifische Daten der Anwendungsschicht sind, sofern sie nicht von den jeweiligen Servern zur Verfügung gestellt werden, durch das Betriebssystem-Audit ebenfalls nicht protokollierbar.

Unsere Untersuchungen des Audits von SunOS und Solaris offenbarten weitere entscheidende Einschränkungen bei der Protokollierung von Netzaktivitäten. Vom SunOS-Audit werden *keine* Aktionen aufgezeichnet, die den Empfang von Netzdaten erlauben. Es erfolgt lediglich die Protokollierung des Verbindungsaufbaus *(connect, accept)*, womit z.B. über UDP erfolgende Netzaktivitäten nicht sichtbar sind. Außerdem werden Aktionen zum Management von Netzzugriffen *(bind, setsockopt)* protokolliert. Das Solaris-Audit wiederum zeichnet *keine* Aktivitäten der Transportschicht-Schnittstelle auf. Hier erfolgt die Protokollierung von Aktivitäten des Transport Service Interfaces (TSI), einem zusätzlichen Interface zwischen der Transportschicht-Schnittstelle und den Transportprotokollen [Go94]. Eine Zuordnung der protokollierten Aktionen zu den Aktionen der Transportschicht-Schnittstelle ist wegen der Komplexität des TSI (Nutzung von Streams) und dem Fehlen relevanter Netzdaten nicht möglich.

2.3 Netzmonitore

Netzdienste sind im allgemeinen entsprechend dem Client-Server-Prinzip realisiert. Die zur Erbringung des angeforderten Dienstes zwischen Client und Server ausgetauschten protokollspezifischen Daten bilden die Grundlage für das Netz-Audit. Die Generierung der Auditdaten erfolgt durch *Netzmonitore* parallel zur Inanspruchnahme der Netzdienste. Netzmonitore können bezüglich der softwaretechnischen *Einbettung in den* gegebenen *Kommunikationsarchitekturen* und ihrer *Positionierung* innerhalb einer zu überwachenden Netzdomäne klassifiziert werden. Während die Positionierung ausschlaggebend für das Sichtfeld, d.h. den für den Netzmonitor registrierbaren Netzverkehr, ist, bestimmt die softwaretechnische Integration ganz entscheidend Informationsgehalt und Umfang der protokollierbaren Auditdaten und damit die erkennbaren netzbasierten IT-Sicherheitsverletzungen.

Für die softwaretechnische Realisierung von Netzmonitoren ergeben sich zwei grundlegende Möglichkeiten:

– die Realisierung als eigenständige *vertrauenswürdige Applikation* oder
– die Integration im Betriebssystemkern.

Im folgenden werden einige wesentliche Entwicklungen von Netzmonitoren vorgestellt (siehe Abb. 3), wobei die Art und Weise der Generierung von Netz-

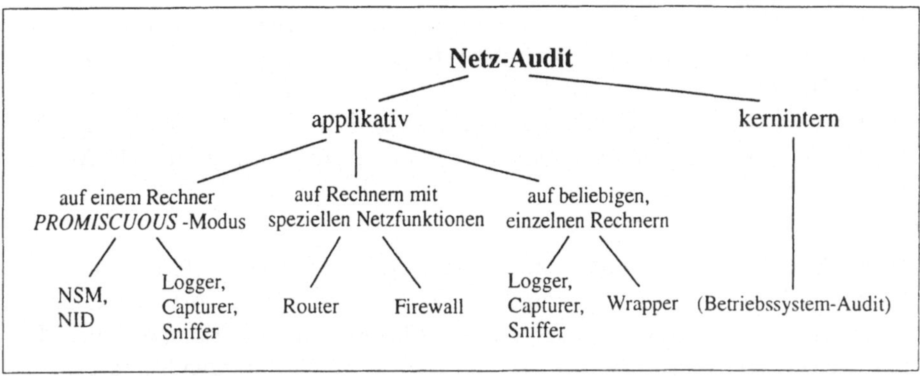

Abbildung3. Bisherige Realisierungen des Netz-Audits im Überblick

Auditdaten im Vordergrund steht. Sämtliche bisherigen Netzmonitore sind applikativ realisiert.

NSM und NID Der an der University of California in Davis entwickelte *NSM (Network Security Monitor)*, u.a. eingesetzt im Intrusion Detection-System DIDS (Distributed Intrusion Detection System) [Sna+91], sowie weiterentwickelt am Lawrence Livermore National Laboratory zum NID (siehe http://ciac.llnl.gov/CSPCSaroyanAbs.html) sind Beispiele für Realisierungen als eigenständige vertrauenswürdige Applikation. Diese Netzmonitore laufen auf einem separaten Rechner, dessen Netzschnittstelle im *Promiscuous*-Modus betrieben wird [He+90]. Auf diese Weise ist die Aufzeichnung und Analyse sämtlicher, innerhalb der überwachten Domäne transferierter Datenpakete möglich. Dies setzt jedoch voraus, daß die MAC-Ebene jedes, innerhalb der Domäne transferierte Paket, jedem Rechner (z.B. mittels Broadcast) zur Verfügung stellt. Die vom NSM, unabhängig vom Betriebssystem-Audit innerhalb der überwachten Domäne, generierten Netz-Auditdaten enthalten Quell- und Zieladresse, den Dienst der Netzaktivität sowie eine Verbindungsreferenz.

Logger, Sniffer und Capturer Für die Aufzeichnung von Protokolldaten der Schichten 2 - 4 mittels Applikationen existieren mit Loggern, Sniffern und Capturern effiziente Realisierungen. Diese Tools interagieren direkt mit dem Protokollstack des Betriebssystems. Aufgrund ihrer Filterfunktionen sind die Tools in der Lage, Pakete eines vorgegebenen Protokolls aus dem Netzverkehr herauszufiltern und entsprechende auditrelevante protokollspezifische Daten aufzuzeichnen. Sie ermöglichen weitgehend die Überwachung des gesamten Adreßraums der Dienstzugangspunkte eines Rechners, ohne dabei jedoch speziell die Protokolldaten zu dem jeweiligen Dienst selbst filtern zu können, da sie dessen Protokoll nicht kennen. Ungeachtet dessen können sie zumindest Beginn und Ende von Sitzungen erkennen sowie den bloßen, nicht interpretierbaren Inhalt der Pakete aufzeichnen.

Diese primär für das Netzmanagement entwickelten Netzmonitore gehören zum Lieferumfang heutiger Betriebssysteme (z.B. *etherfind* für SunOS 4.1.x, *snoop* für Solaris 2.x) bzw. sind als public domain Software frei verfügbar (z.B. *tcpdump* der Lawrence Berkeley Laboratories). Mit *Argus* wurde an der Carnegie Mellon University ein Netzmonitor entwickelt, der speziell für Netz-Auditing vorgesehen ist [BuDiF95].

Netz-Audit von Firewalls und Routern Die meisten heute im Einsatz befindlichen Firewalls bieten optional das Aufzeichnen von Protokolldaten des von ihnen bearbeiteten Netzverkehrs an. Je nach Firewall-Typ (Proxies, Paketfilter) unterscheiden sich die protokollierbaren Daten erheblich in Menge und Qualität. Bei einfachen Paketfilter-Mechanismen erfolgt, wie bei Routern, nur die Aufzeichnung von Aktivitäten bis zur Schicht 4. Der Einsatz von Proxy-Servern[1] erlaubt zusätzlich die Aufzeichnung von Aktivitäten der Service-Schicht.

Beispiele für Router mit Netz-Audit - Funktionen sind die Router der Firma NSC. Sie sind in der Lage, Auditereignisse zu *ARP (Address Resolution Protocol)* und *FDDI* in Schicht 2, zu *ICMP* in Schicht 3, zu *TCP* und *UDP* in Schicht 4 sowie zu diversen, von der Konsole aus initiierten Ereignissen zu generieren [HLI94a].

Dienstspezifisches Netz-Audit von Wrappern *Wrapper* sind Mechanismen, die Zugriffsanforderungen auf die von ihnen überwachten Netzdienste auf der Grundlage der in der Vermittlungs- und Transportschicht ausgetauschten Protokolldaten anhand eigener Autorisierungsdaten überprüfen und protokollieren. Der nachfolgende Audit-Record soll den Informationsgehalt von Auditdaten, die von Wrappern generiert wurden, veranschaulichen.

```
Apr 13 15:15:31 bear in.telnetd[2454]:connect from duck.cs.tu- ...
< Datum, Zeit, Ziel (Rechnername), Netzdienst, Quelle >
```

Wrapper können entweder im Diensterbringer (Server) oder in einem Super-Server, wie z.B. im *inet*-Dämon unter UNIX [Ve92]) integriert werden. Bei der Verwendung eines Super-Servers sind nur die ihm (durch Konfigurationsdateien) bekannten Zugangspunkte überprüfbar. Nach der Erteilung der Zugriffserlaubnis durch den Wrapper erfolgt die weitere Kommunikation (*ohne* Protokollierung) direkt zwischen Anforderer und Erbringer. Wrapper wurden auch für RPC-basierte Dienste implementiert.

2.4 Anstehende Entwicklungen

Die sich für die nächsten Jahre abzeichnenden Entwicklungen in der Netzwerktechnik haben zum Teil gravierende Auswirkungen auf die bislang benutzten Verfahren zur Protokollierung von Netzaktivitäten:

---

[1] Proxy-Server erfüllen die Funktionalität von "Trusted Application Gateways" [El94].

1. Die Verschlüsselung des Netzverkehrs, wie sie z.B. in IPv6 bzw. IP Next Generation [At95] vorgesehen ist, macht den Einsatz der Netzmonitore NSM und NID sowie von Loggern *wirkungslos*. Die für eine Protokollierung notwendige Entschlüsselung der Protokolldaten kann nur von den jeweiligen Quell- und Zielrechnern vorgenommen werden. Somit sind diese Netzmonitore nicht in der Lage, die im Netz transferierten, für andere Rechner bestimmten Dateneinheiten, zu interpretieren.

2. Für sämtliche Realisierungen, die im Promiscuous-Modus betriebene Netzwerkschnittstellen verwenden, zeichnen sich durch den Einsatz von Switch-Technologien (Ethernet-, IP-Switches, Frame Relay, ATM) mit der damit verbundenen Einschränkung des Broadcast-Mechanismus gravierende Einsatzprobleme ab. Die angestrebte Protokollierung *aller* Netzaktivitäten einer Domäne ist potentiell *nicht* mehr möglich.

3. Der Einsatz von leistungsfähigeren Übertragungsverfahren und -medien kann zu Performance-Problemen beim Einsatz solcher Netzmonitore, wie dem NSM sowie von Loggern und Sniffern führen. Momentan ist der Datendurchsatz der benutzten Netzwerke (z.B. Ethernet mit theoretisch 10 MBit/s) weit geringer als der angeschlossener Rechner (z.B. SPARCstation 20 mit theoretisch ca. 100 MByte/s). Dem angestrebten Ziel, prinzipiell alle Netzaktivitäten innerhalb einer Domäne protokollieren zu können, stehen die bedeutend höheren Übertragungsraten (z.B. ATM mit 622 MBit/s ... 2,48 GBit/s) entgegen.

Für die Realisierung eines detaillierten und umfassenden Netz-Auditings in derzeitigen und künftigen Kommunikationsnetzen sind deshalb neue Herangehensweisen erforderlich. Ein entsprechender Ansatz wird im folgenden Abschnitt vorgestellt.

3 Host-orientiertes Netz-Audit

Dem Konzept des Host-orientierten Netz-Audits wird die folgende Prämisse zugrundegelegt:
Netzangriffe sind gegen bestimmte Rechner (bzw. netzspezifische Geräte) gerichtet. Infolge dessen sollten netzbasierte Auditdaten, die ein Nachvollziehen dieser Angriffe ermöglichen, **auf den betroffenen Rechnern** *generiert werden.*
Vorgesehen hierfür ist die Ergänzung des Betriebssystem-Audits überwachungsrelevanter Rechner um Netzmonitore. Diese Netzmonitore überwachen im Protokollstack erfolgende sowie applikationsspezifische Netzaktivitäten der jeweiligen Diensterbringer.
Das Betriebssystem-Audit umfaßt Funktionseinheiten zur Generierung und Aufzeichnung der Auditdaten sowie zum eigenen Management. Außerdem stellt es eine Programmierschnittstelle für die Generierung benutzerspezifischer Auditdaten zur Verfügung. Davon ausgehend ist eine Erweiterung des bisherigen Betriebssystem-Audits zur Aufzeichnung von Netzaktivitäten (siehe Kapitel 2.2) realisierbar. Aufgabe der dafür vorgesehenen Netzmonitore ist es, ausschließlich Netzaktivitäten aufzuzeichnen, die auf anderen Rechnern initiiert wurden

und den zu überwachenden Rechner zum Ziel haben. Auf diese Weise ist ein im Promiscuous-Modus betriebenes Netzwerkinterface *nicht* erforderlich. Zur Gewährleistung einer einheitlichen Audit-Trail, die sowohl Host- *als auch* netzbasierte Auditdaten enthält, werden die vom Betriebssystem-Audit bereitgestellten Funktionen zur Generierung und Aufzeichnung von Auditdaten genutzt.

Diese Netzmonitore können entweder *kernintegriert* oder *applikativ* realisiert werden. Durch den Protokollstack werden die Protokolle der Schichten 2 bis 4 innerhalb des Betriebssystemkerns realisiert. Ein Großteil der von einem Netzmonitor zu erbringenden Funktionen (Filtern und Analysieren von Paket-Headern) wird vom Protokollstack abgedeckt. Die Aufzeichnung von Netz-Auditdaten bedarf weniger Änderungen, erfordert jedoch die Verfügbarkeit des Quellcodes und würde zudem eine spezielle, nur für diesen Protokollstack geltende Lösung darstellen[2]. Die Nutzung von allgemeinen Programmierschnittstellen für den Zugang zum Netzwerk ist hier die bessere und auch flexiblere Lösung. Eine Kernintegration des Netzmonitors bringt neben Leistungs- (das Kopieren von Daten aus bzw. in den Kernspeicher entfällt) auch Sicherheitsvorteile. Der Netzmonitor läuft innerhalb des Kerns und ist somit nicht ohne weiteres für andere Prozesse (Nutzer) erreichbar.

Wird von dem benutzten Betriebssystem eine Kernintegration des Netzmonitors nicht unterstützt, muß dessen Implementierung als eigenständige Applikation erfolgen. Aus den oben genannten Gründen favorisieren wir für die Generierung von Netz-Auditdaten bzgl. der Schichten 2 bis 4 kernintegrierte Netzmonitore. Für beide alternative Realisierungen (siehe Abb. 4, a bzw. b) ist zu beachten, daß der Zugang zum Protokollstack so erfolgt, daß auch Rechner, die über mehr als eine Netzschnittstelle verfügen, z.B. Router und Gateways, unterstützt werden.

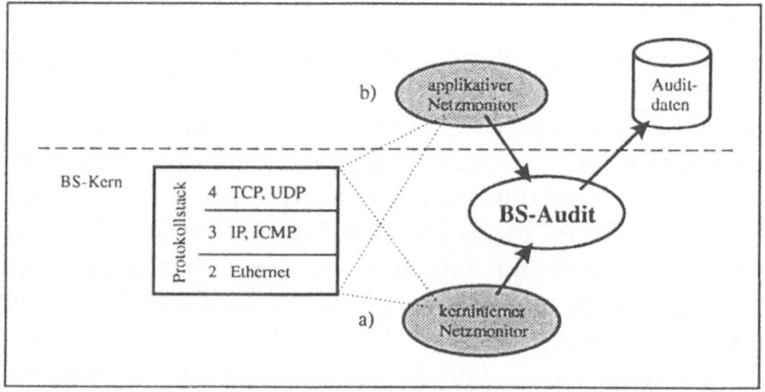

Abbildung4. Alternative Realisierungen der Netzmonitore

---

[2] Die einfachste Lösung für den Linux-Kern besteht z.B. in dem Einbringen eines zusätzlichen *kprintf* in die Routine zur Bearbeitung von eingehenden IP-Paketen.

Für das Netz-Auditing der Anwendungsschicht ergeben sich zwei prinzipielle Möglichkeiten. Kerninterne Netzmonitore könnten um entsprechende Funktionalität ergänzt werden. Problematisch ist hierbei allerdings die Vielzahl der in der Anwendungsschicht befindlichen Dienste, was zu einer hohen Komplexität des Netzmonitors führen würde. Vorteilhafter ist die Erweiterung der jeweiligen Diensterbringer (Server) um applikationsspezifisches Netz-Audit (siehe Abb. 5). Dabei können allgemeine Programmierschnittstellen (z.B. Audit-API von Haystack [HLI94b]) genutzt werden.

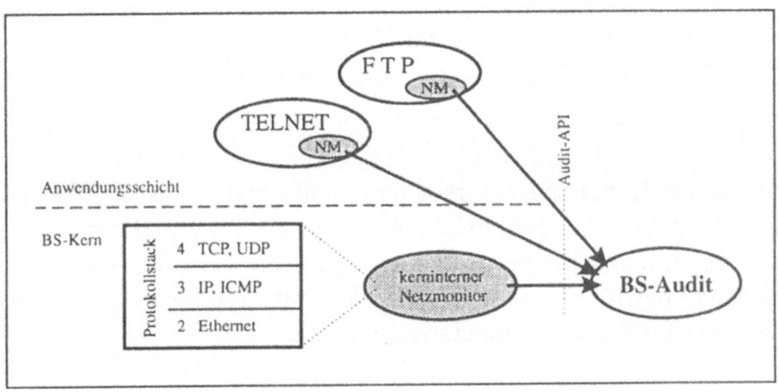

Abbildung 5. Gesamtkonzept des Host-orientierten Netz-Audits

Die in den vorhergehenden Kapiteln aufgezeigten technologischen Nachteile der bisherigen Ansätze für Netz-Audit sowie die informationellen Defizite des Betriebssystem-Audits können mit dem vorgestellten Konzept entscheidend kompensiert werden. Im einzelnen ergeben sich folgende Vorteile:

- Eine Aufzeichnung von Netz-Auditdaten ist auch bei verschlüsseltem Netzverkehr möglich, da der Protokollstack die für ihn bestimmten Datenpakete entschlüsseln muß, um sie überhaupt interpretieren und verarbeiten zu können.
- Das Host-orientierte Netz-Audit ist unabhängig vom verwendeten Netzzugriffsverfahren als auch vom Datendurchsatz im Subnetz.
- Der Ansatz ermöglicht eine gute Skalierbarkeit des "Blickwinkels" der Monitore auf die Netzaktivitäten in der zu überwachenden Netzdomäne. Ausfälle einzelner Netzmonitore haben nur lokale Auswirkungen.

Die als Nachteil zu nennende Mehrbelastung der Rechner hält sich in Grenzen. Zum Leistungsvergleich wurden Tests mit Loggern durchgeführt (Netzwerk-Interface nicht im Promiscuous-Modus). Diese Tests zeigten keine wesentlichen Einschränkungen im Rechnerbetrieb.

4 Realisierung der kerninternen Netzmonitore

Entsprechend den funktionalen Schichten von Netzmonitoren (Paketentnahme, Protokollanalyse/Filtern, Datenaufzeichnung, Report) ist folgendes bei der Realisierung der Netzmonitore für das Host-orientierte Netz-Audit zu beachten:

1. Wie erfolgt der Zugriff zum Protokollstack?
2. In welchen Netzwerkschichten müssen welche Protokolldaten aufgezeichnet werden?
3. Welche für die Auditanalyse relevanten Informationen sollen bereitgestellt werden? Wie "intelligent" soll der Netzmonitor sein?
4. Wie erfolgt die Interaktion der Netzmonitore mit dem Betriebssystem-Audit?

Dabei ist im Rahmen einer möglichst einfachen Anpassung des Konzepts an verschiedene Systemumgebungen von allgemeinen Programmierschnittstellen Gebrauch zu machen bzw. sind solche zu definieren. Abbildung 6 zeigt das Zusammenspiel der für den zu realisierenden Netzmonitor notwendigen Module sowie die benötigten Programmierschnittstellen.

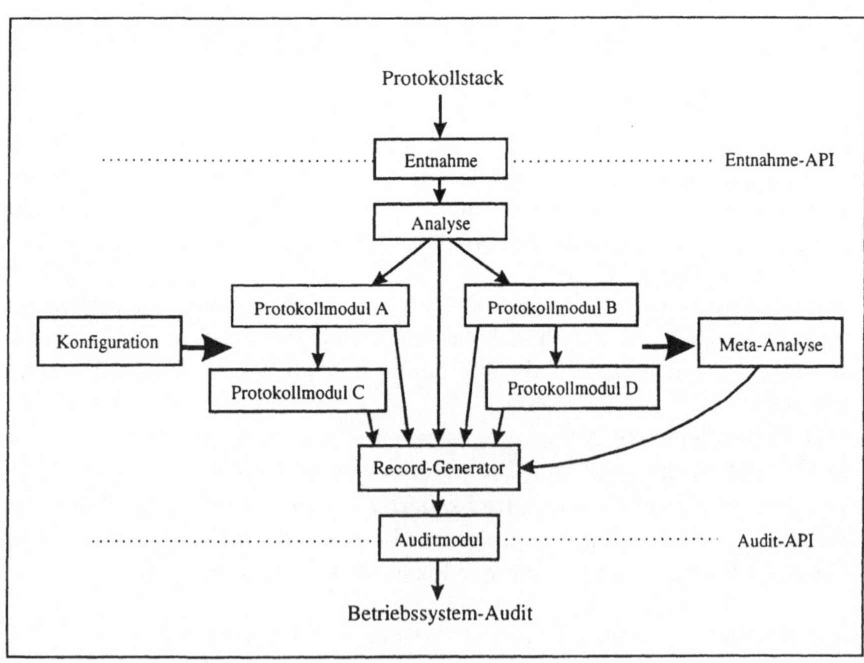

Abbildung 6. Funktionsmodule des Netzmonitors

Das *Entnahme-Modul* realisiert den Zugang des Netzmonitors zu den notwendigen Netzwerkschichten. Dabei werden die vom Protokollstack bereitgestellten Funktionen genutzt. Um das Entnahme-Modul von den Spezifiken der jeweils zugrunde liegenden Protokollstacks unabhängig zu machen, erfolgt die Nutzung einer allgemeinen Programmierschnittstelle (Application Programming Interface, API). Durch dieses Entnahme-API wird auch der transparente Zugriff auf den Protokollstack bei einer applikativen bzw. Kernimplementierung gewährleistet.

Das *Analysemodul* stellt Filter[3]- und Analysemechanismen für die unterste durch den Netzmonitor überwachte Netzwerkschicht bereit. Über das Entnahme-Modul greift das Analysemodul auf den Protokollstack zu. Durch die weiteren *Protokollmodule* werden die Filter- und Analysemechanismen für die darüberliegenden zu überwachenden Protokolle bereitgestellt. Der Aufruf der Protokollmodule bei der Bearbeitung von Paketen erfolgt in der Reihenfolge der beteiligten Netzwerkschichten (z.B. Ethernet - IP - TCP - FTP). Zur Generierung der Audit-Records werden von dem Analysemodul und den Protokollmodulen die benötigten Protokolldaten an den *Recordgenerator* weitergegeben. Der Recordgenerator legt den Informationsgehalt der Audit-Records fest. Entsprechend dem vom Recordgenerator vorgegebenen Format können Daten zu allen beteiligten Protokollen oder nur zu bestimmten Protokollen in den Audit-Datensätzen aufgezeichnet werden (siehe Abb. 7).

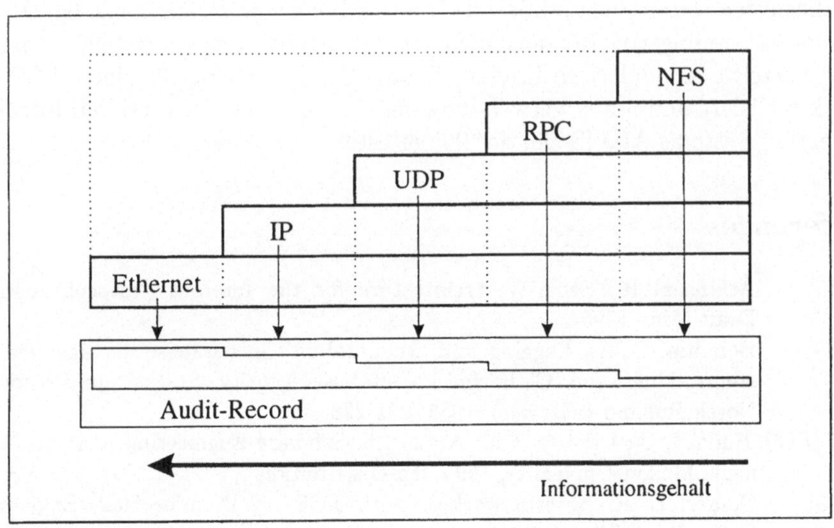

Abbildung7. Informationsgehalt eines NFS-Audit-Records

---

[3] zum Beispiel nach Quelladressen

Das *Auditmodul* gewährleistet über eine allgemeine Programmierschnittstelle die Interaktion mit dem Betriebssystem-Audit, so daß der generierte Audit-Record in die einheitliche Auditdatei eingefügt werden kann. Über das *Konfigurationsmodul* werden Funktionen zum Management des Netzmonitors bereitgestellt, so z.B. die Aktivierung von Protokollmodulen und Filtern und die Initiierung von Statusabfragen. Durch die *Meta-Analyse* werden die zur Erfüllung des dritten Entwurfskriteriums notwendigen Funktionen bereitgestellt. Unter Meta-Analyse soll hier die Fähigkeit verstanden werden, Sessions zu erkennen. Damit erhält ein Netzmonitor die Möglichkeit, Daten zu bestehenden Sessions zu sammeln, so daß "summierende" Audit-Records generiert werden können.

5   Zusammenfassung und Ausblick

In diesem Beitrag wurde ein neues Konzept zur auditgestützten Überwachung von Netzaktivitäten vorgestellt. Der Ansatz favorisiert kernintegrierte Netzmonitore für die Generierung von Netz-Auditdaten der Schichten 2 bis 4 sowie die Erweiterung der Diensterbringer um applikationsspezifisches Netz-Audit. Dies ermöglicht eine vom jeweiligen Netzzugangsverfahren sowie vom Datendurchsatz im Subnetz unabhängige Aufzeichnung von Netz-Auditdaten auch bei verschlüsseltem Netzverkehr. Der Ansatz bietet zudem eine gute Skalierbarkeit hinsichtlich des Blickwinkels auf die zu überwachenden Netzdomänen. Durch die Interaktion des Host-orientierten Netz-Audits mit dem Betriebssystem-Audit der überwachten Rechner ist durch die gleichzeitige Protokollierung von Host- und netzbasierten Daten eine umfassende Überwachung von Netzwerken möglich, was für die Erkennung von Netzangriffen erforderlich ist. Das vorgestellte Konzept wird derzeitig exemplarisch in einer Solaris 2.x Umgebung für einen TCP/IP-Stack realisiert und unter Verwendung des am Lehrstuhl entwickelten Intrusion Detection-Systems AID [So96, So+96] getestet.

References

[At95]   Atkinson, R.: Security Architecture for the Internet Protocol, Internet Draft, May 1995

[Bo88]   Bonyum, D. A.: Logging and accountability in database management systems, Landwehr, C. E. (ed.): Database security: Status and Prospects, North Holland (Elsevier), 1988, 223-228

[BuDiF95] Bullard, C.; DiFatta, Ch.: Argus 1.5, Software Engineering Institute, Carnegie Mellon University, 1995, ftp-Distribution

[Co88]   Comer, D. E.: Internetworking with TCP/IP, Prentice Hall, Englewood Cliffs, NJ., 1988

[El94]   Ellermann, U.: Firewalls-Isolations- und Audittechniken zum Schutz von lokalen Computer-Netzen, DFN-Bericht Nr. 76, Sept. 1994

[Go94]   Goodheart, B.; Cox, J.: The Magic Garden Explained, The internals of UNIX System V Release 4, An operating system design, Prentice-Hall, 1994

[HLI94a]   Haystack Laboratories, Inc.: Applying audit analysis to firewalls, Final Report, Nov. 14, 1994

[HLI94b] Haystack Laboratories, Inc.: Haystack's implementation of the POSIX 1003.1 interface for reading and writing of audit trails, 1994, online verfügbar über automatischen e-mail responder

[He+90] Heberlein, L. T.; Levitt, K. N.; Mukherjee, B.: A method to detect intrusive activity in a networked environment, Proc. of the 14th National Computer Security Conference, Washington D. C., Oct. 1991, 362-371

[Le+89] Leffler, S. J.; McKusick, M. K.; Karels, M. J.; Quarterman, J. S.: The Design and Implementation of the 4.3BSD Unix Operating System, Addison-Wesley, 1989

[Lu90] Lunt, T. F.: IDES: An intelligent system for detecting intruders, Proc. of the Symposium Computer Security, Threat and Countermeasures, Rom, Nov. 1990

[MC95] Microsoft Corp.: Microsoft Windows NT Guidelines for Security, Audit and Control, Microsoft Press, Redmont, Washington, 1995

[Ri+96] Richter, B.; Sobirey, M.; König, H.: Auditbasierte Netzüberwachung, Praxis der Informationsverarbeitung und Kommunikation (PIK) 1/96, 24-32

[Se+88] Sebring, M. M.; Sellhouse, E.; Hanna, M. E.; Whitehurst, R. A.: Expert system in intrusion detection: A case study, Proc. of the 11th National Computer Security Conference, Baltimore, MD, Oct. 1988, 74-81

[Sna+91] Snapp, S. R. et. al.: DIDS - Motivation, architecture, and an early prototype, Proc. of the 14th NCSC, Washington, D. C., Oct. 1991, 167-176

[So96] Sobirey, M.: Auditgestützte Einbruchserkennung in Netzen, Ergebnisse aus dem Projekt AID, in: Kubicek, H.; Müller, G.; Neumann, K.-H.; Raubold, E.; Roßnagel, A. (Hrsg.): Jahrbuch Telekommunikation und Gesellschaft, Bd. 4, 1996, Öffnung der Telekommunikation, Heidelberg, R. v. Decker's Verlag, 284-286

[So+96] Sobirey, M.; Richter, B.; König, H.: The Intrusion Detection System AID. Architecture, and experiences in automated audit analysis, in Horster, P. (ed.): Communications and Multimedia Security II, Proc. of the IFIP TC6/TC11 International Conference on Communications and Multimedia Security, Essen, Germany, Sept. 1996, Chapman & Hall, London, 278-290

[Sun93] Sun Microsystems, Inc.: SunOS 5.3 Network Interfaces Programmer's Guide, 1993

[Te89] Tener, W. T.: Discovery: An expert system in the commercial data security environment, Proc. of the 4th IFIP TC11 International Conference on Security, IFIP Sec'86, Monte Carlo, North Holland, Amsterdam, 1989, 261-266

[USL93] Unix System Laboratories: Audit Trail Administration, Prentice Hall, Englewood Cliffs, NJ, 1993

[Ve92] Venema, W.: TCP-Wrapper. Network monitoring, access control, and booby traps, Proc. of the 3th USENIX Unix Security Symposium, Baltimore, MD, Sept. 1992, 85-92

Authentikation als Grundlage der Skalierung von Sicherheit in der Kommunikationstechnik[1]

Reiner Sailer
sailer@ind.uni-stuttgart.de

Institut für Nachrichtenvermittlung und Datenverarbeitung, Universität Stuttgart
Prof. Dr.-Ing. Dr. h.c. P.J. Kühn

Kurzfassung

Moderne Kommunikationsnetze ermöglichen zunehmend flexible, nutzerkonfigurierbare Dienste. Durch die Anwendung der Kommunikationstechnik zur Verarbeitung sensitiver Daten sind die Anforderungen an die Sicherheit gestiegen, welche oftmals bei der Einführung neuer Systeme und Dienste noch nicht konkretisiert sind und deshalb nur unzureichend Berücksichtigung finden. Die zunehmende Auswertung personenbezogener Daten, die zur Realisierung von Diensten im Kommunikationsnetz verarbeitet werden, macht auch diese Daten schützenswert. Die Qualität eines Dienstes wird deshalb in Zukunft auch an seiner Möglichkeit gemessen werden, individuelle Sicherheitsanforderungen effizient zu realisieren oder mindestens zu unterstützen. Die vorliegende Arbeit stellt ein Konzept vor, welches durch Betrachtung verschiedener Kriterien eine wirtschaftliche und effiziente Sicherung von Kommunikationssystemen ermöglicht. Die Verfahren zur sicheren Identifikation von Kommunikationspartnern (Authentikation) und die Verteilung von geheimen Schlüsseln zur Sicherung der übermittelten Daten werden aufgrund ihrer Bedeutung detailliert behandelt. Eine Integration vorgeschlagener Sicherungsmechanismen auf Protokollebene wird am Beispiel der Dienstanforderung im Schmalband-ISDN skizziert.

1 Einführung

Moderne öffentliche Kommunikationsnetze bieten dem Nutzer eine Fülle von Diensten an, mit deren Hilfe Informationen über beliebige Entfernungen übertragen werden können. Telekommunikationsdienste werden zunehmend flexibel und lassen sich auf Wunsch nutzerspezifisch konfigurieren. Beispiele sind das Einrichten zeit- und ursprungsabhängiger Rufumleitungen beim Telefondienst. Aspekte der Datensicherheit und des Datenschutzes standen jedoch bei der Definition der Qualitätsparameter nicht im Vordergrund und sind im Augenblick nicht genügend berücksichtigt.

Gemeinsam genutzte öffentliche Netze sind sehr effizient bezüglich der Ausnutzung ihrer Ressourcen (Economy of Scale, Bündelungsgewinn). Die gemeinsame Nutzung von Netzressourcen impliziert jedoch, daß die Daten verschiedener Nutzer, die sich gegenseitig nicht vertrauen, gemeinsam verarbeitet werden. Kommt es bei dieser Verarbeitung zu Fehlern, so ist nicht mehr gewährleistet, daß die übermittelten Informationen nur für den erwarteten Empfänger zugänglich sind. Dabei spielt es keine Rolle, ob der Fehler beim Nutzer liegt oder Fehler in der hochkomplexen Netzfunktionalität vorliegen.

Durch die absehbare Entwicklung, immer mehr und flexiblere Dienste innerhalb eines Netzes zu realisieren (z.B. im Intelligenten Netz [1]), wird ohne entsprechende Sicherungsmöglichkeiten den Nutzern auf lange Sicht zunehmend die Kontrolle über die durch das Kommunikationsnetz vermittelten bzw. im Kommunikationsnetz verarbeiteten Daten entzogen.

Durch die zunehmende Menge persönlicher Informationen, mit denen diese flexiblen Dienste nutzerspezifisch konfiguriert werden können, entstehen auch datenschutzrechtliche Probleme,

---

[1]Besonderer Dank gilt der Gottlieb Daimler- und Karl Benz-Stiftung in Ladenburg und deren Mitarbeitern und Förderern für ihre freundliche Unterstützung und die finanzielle Förderung dieser Arbeit.

die nicht einfach zu lösen sein werden, die Akzeptanz der Dienste aber wesentlich beeinflussen können. Illustriert wird die Entwicklung des Bewußtseins der Kunden auch am Beispiel des vieldiskutierten Video-On-Demand. Da hier für jeden Film getrennt abgerechnet wird, können aus den Abrechnungsdaten Interessendaten der Kunden abgeleitet werden. Deshalb werden dort mit Nachdruck anonyme Zahlungsmöglichkeiten (z.B. Debitkarten) verlangt, die eine Erfassung abgerufener Filme (zu Abrechnungszwecken) umgehen.

Besonders augenscheinlich wird das Sammeln von Kommunikationsdaten und das Extrahieren von Interessendaten von Teilnehmern im Zusammenhang mit neuen Marktstrategien, die im Internet zunehmend Verbreitung finden. Diese Strategien zielen auf die Sammlung möglichst vieler Daten über Teilnehmer ab (Kreditwürdigkeit anhand der Kreditkartenart, Interessen, Wohngebiet, Telefonnummern, Anschriften) und verwenden sie für Marktstudien und Werbeaktionen.

Im Bereich der öffentlichen Kommunikationsnetze sind kommerziell erhältliche CD-ROMs zu nennen, deren Erzeuger finanziellen Gewinn daraus ziehen, daß sie persönliche Daten von Millionen von Teilnehmern der Bundesrepublik elektronisch verarbeitbar mit entsprechenden Anwendungsprogrammen zur Verfügung stellen. Vorstellbar für die Zukunft sind auch das Einbeziehen der Kommunikationshäufigkeit, der Nutzung von Mehrwertdiensten und der Ableitung von Interessen der einzelnen Teilnehmer der Bundesrepublik bzw. deren berufliche Orientierung, um diese gezielt mit - gegebenenfalls von diesen Personen unerwünschtem - Werbematerial zu überhäufen. Eine Verknüpfung mit Informationen aus dem Internet und anderen Informationsquellen kann die Problematik zusätzlich verschärfen. Auch die Integrität der zugänglichen Informationen kann nicht geprüft werden. So kann das Unterschieben falscher Information zur Benachteiligung von Personen führen.

Weiterhin wird die Kommunikationstechnik in immer stärkerem Maße in sensitiven Bereichen (z.B. im Gesundheitswesen) eingesetzt, in denen ein Kontrollverlust über Informationen bei der Nutzung öffentlicher Netze verhindert werden muß.

Dies alles zeigt, daß ehemals bedenkenlos bereitgestellte persönliche Angaben aufgrund ihrer zunehmenden Verfügbarkeit in digitalisierter Form (z.B. durch Nutzung von Kommunikationsdiensten) und der resultierenden einfachen Verarbeitbarkeit zu einem Kontrollverlust für die betroffenen Personen führen können. Elektronisch erfaßte Daten wurden beispielsweise in den USA zur Kontrolle des Einkommens von Sozialleistungsempfängern verwendet [2].

Der zunehmende Kontrollverlust über sensitive Informationen zusammen mit der zunehmenden Abhängigkeit der (Informations-) Gesellschaft von den Telekommunikationsdiensten und der daraus resultierenden Verletzlichkeit durch Fehlfunktion der Netze [3] macht die „Nachrüstung" der Telekommunikationsnetze mit Mechanismen erforderlich, die die steigenden Sicherheitsanforderungen der Nutzer und auch der Netzbetreiber bzw. Dienstanbieter garantieren können.

1.1 Möglichkeiten der Kompensation des Kontrollverlustes

Sicherheit beschreibt die Erfüllung der an ein System gestellten Sicherheitsanforderungen. Wir unterscheiden zwischen den Anforderungen:

- *Vertraulichkeit* von Informationsträgern (Schutz gegen unautorisierte Kenntnisnahme),
- *Integrität* von Daten (Schutz gegen unautorisierte, unerkannte Veränderung) und
- *Verfügbarkeit* von Daten und Diensten.

Diese Sicherheitsanforderungen werden im allgemeinen mit schützenswerten Objekten verknüpft. Eine solche Verknüpfung wird im folgenden *Schutzziel* genannt.

Eine Möglichkeit, den Zugriff auf schützenswerte Informationen auch in nicht kontrollierbaren Bereichen zu sichern, stellt die Verschlüsselung dar. Eine Verschlüsselung bildet die interpretierbaren Daten mit Hilfe einer umkehrbaren Abbildung auf nicht interpretierbare Daten ab. Diese Abbildung kann nur unter Kenntnis eines „Geheimnisses" umgekehrt werden.

Zwar ist der Zugriff auf die nichtinterpretierbaren Daten weiterhin nicht kontrollierbar, doch können Angreifer „lediglich" die Verfügbarkeit der übertragenen Daten stören. Sie können nicht mehr unautorisiert Informationen erlangen (Störung der Vertraulichkeit) oder die zu übermittelnde Information durch Manipulation der Informationsträger unbemerkt verändern (Störung der Integrität).

Wesentliche Bedeutung für die Effizienz von Sicherheitsfunktionen - d.h. die wirtschaftliche Erfüllung aller Sicherheitsanforderungen - hat die *Allokation* dieser Funktionen. Die Allokation bestimmt die Stellen innerhalb eines Kommunikationssystems, an denen Sicherheitsfunktionen realisiert werden. Für die Lokalisierung von Sicherheitsfunktionen bieten sich aus Teilnehmersicht drei Möglichkeiten:

- innerhalb des teilnehmerkontrollierten Bereiches
- innerhalb des Netzes (kontrolliert durch den Netzbetreiber bzw. Dienstanbieter)
- ausgelagert in vertrauenswürdige Organisationen (unabhängig kontrolliert, zertifiziert)

Sicherheitsmechanismen können nur in vertrauenswürdigen, d.h. als sicher angenommenen Umgebungen realisiert werden, da sonst die Implementierung der Mechanismen nicht manipulationssicher wäre. Deshalb ist es wichtig, inwieweit ein solches Vertrauen bezüglich der Garantie verschiedener Schutzziele gegeben ist bzw. gewonnen werden kann.

Ähnlich wie beim Postdienst, der in Zusammenarbeit mit den Kunden Inhalte durch Briefumschläge schützt, ist auch in Kommunikationsnetzen ein sogenannter Grundschutz vorstellbar, der für alle Kommunikationsvorgänge automatisch Anwendung findet. Im Postdienst steigt dadurch der Aufwand potentieller Angreifer, Briefe mit interessantem Inhalt zu identifizieren. Ähnlich kann eine allgemein angewendete, jedoch nur bis zu einem bestimmten Maße vertrauenswürdige Grundsicherheit innerhalb des Netzes erheblich zum Vertrauensgewinn beitragen, indem an kritischen Stellen der Aufwand für Angriffe erhöht wird.

Das Maß an Vertrauen in den Netzbetreiber bzw. Dienstanbieter und die Sicherheitsanforderungen an einen Kommunikationsdienst bestimmen, ob zusätzlich individuelle Sicherheitsmaßnahmen ergriffen werden müssen. Solche Sicherungsmaßnahmen können eine Verschlüsselung in den Endgeräten oder die beglaubigte Aufzeichnung der in Anspruch genommenen abrechnungspflichtigen Leistungen des Netzbetreibers bzw. Dienstanbieters darstellen.

Die ungenügende Beachtung der Aspekte des Datenschutzes und der Datensicherheit bei der Planung und Entwicklung vieler heute im Betrieb befindlicher Kommunikationssysteme schafft harte Randbedingungen für eine sicherheitstechnische Nachrüstung der Kommunikationsinfrastruktur im Teilnehmer- und Netzbereich. Die durch diese Nachrüstung zu erwartenden hohen Kosten erzwingen eine effiziente Realisierung von Schutzzielen. Es ist genau zu überlegen, welche Sicherheitsmechanismen notwendig sind und wo diese effizient lokalisiert werden können.

Der vorliegende Beitrag beschäftigt sich mit Sicherheitsaspekten bei der Inanspruchnahme von Telekommunikations-Dienstleistungen an der Schnittstelle zwischen Teilnehmerbereich und Netzbereich. Es werden Ausprägungen und Integrationsmöglichkeiten von Sicherheitsfunktionen zur Realisierung zukünftig erwarteter Sicherheitsanforderungen an einem konkreten Beispiel besprochen.

1.2 Szenario der zukünftigen Dienstnutzung und Sicherheitsanforderungen

Die Anforderungen an die Unterstützung der Mobilität von Teilnehmern werden zukünftig auch im Festnetzbereich steigen (Universal Personal Telecommunications [4]). Mobile Teilnehmer werden private oder öffentliche Endgeräte an öffentlichen oder gemeinsam genutzten Anschlüssen bargeldlos nutzen. Dazu müssen bei der Dienstanforderung die in Anspruch genommenen Leistungen sicher dem jeweiligen Nutzer zugeordnet werden können. Außerdem muß der Zugriff auf mehrwertige Dienste auf der Basis von Teilnehmeridentitäten kontrollierbar sein. Nutzer- und nutzungsspezifische Tarife setzen dabei eine eindeutige Identifikation der Dienstnehmer beispielsweise als Grundlage einer flexiblen und korrekten Zuordnung der Gebühren (Accounting) voraus.

Bei der Realisierung von Diensten und entsprechender Infrastruktur zur Unterstützung der Teilnehmermobilität müssen Aspekte des Datenschutzes und der Datensicherheit in ausreichendem Maße mitberücksichtigt werden.

Im weiteren Verlauf der Arbeit werden vor allem Möglichkeiten zur gegenseitigen Identifikation von Dienstnutzer und Dienstanbieter und zum Schutz von übermittelten Anwendungs- bzw. Kommunikationsdaten untersucht. Dabei spielt die Integrationsfähigkeit von Mechanismen an der Schnittstelle von Teilnehmer- und Netzbereich zur Realisierung individueller Sicherheitsanforderungen in bestehenden Kommunikationsnetzen eine wichtige Rolle.

Bild 1 zeigt die zugrundeliegende Konfiguration. Das Sicherheitsmodul (SM) vertritt den Teilnehmer gegenüber dem Endgerät und dem Kommunikationsnetz bei der Realisierung und Anwendung von Sicherheitsfunktionen.

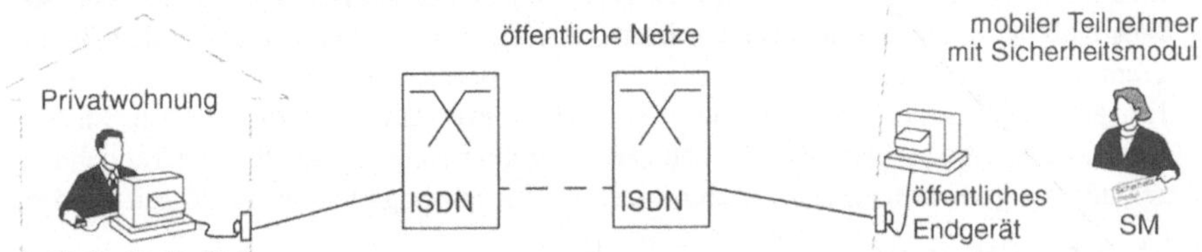

Bild 1: *Aufgliederung des Telekommunikationsnetzes in Bereiche*

Abschnitt 2 führt zunächst in allgemeine Konzepte zur Realisierung verschiedener Sicherheitsanforderungen ein. Abschnitt 3 bespricht Mechanismen zur Authentikation, welche als Grundlage dienen für das in Abschnitt 4 dargestellte Protokoll zur Sicherung der Teilnehmer-Netz-Schnittstelle im ISDN.

2 Bildung von Bereichen zur Integration von Sicherheitsfunktionen

Zur effizienten Sicherung von Kommunikationsnetzen werden diese zunächst in Bereiche aufgegliedert, die separat gesichert werden können. Für eine effiziente Sicherung bietet sich die Aufteilung des Netzes nach folgenden Kriterien an [5]:

- Zuständigkeit und Verantwortlichkeit für Management, Administration und Organisation,
- technische und organisatorische Gegebenheiten und
- geltende Sicherheitsanforderungen bzw. vorgegebene Schutzziele.

Durch die Abbildung der Systemkonfiguration auf hinsichtlich der genannten Kriterien unterscheidbare Bereiche können die einzubringenden Sicherheitsmechanismen an die jeweiligen *Gegebenheiten* und resultierende *Angriffsmöglichkeiten* angepaßt werden.

Sicherheitsmechanismen können wirkungsvoll nur in Bereichen realisiert werden, deren Verantwortlichen Vertrauen entgegengebracht wird, da Sicherheitsmechanismen auch verwaltet, aktuelle Software-Versionen installiert, Zugriffsrechte gesetzt, Schlüssel installiert und aktualisiert und Überwachungsergebnisse (z. B. Protokoll-Dateien, siehe [6]) interpretiert werden müssen.

Die verschiedenen Bereiche müssen gegeneinander abgegrenzt und Bereichsübergänge müssen abgesichert werden. Die Zugriffskontrolle für Dienste und Daten sowie die Anpassung der Sicherheitsanforderungen zwischen Teilnehmerbereich und Netzbereich stellen Beispiele für Funktionen an Bereichsgrenzen dar.

Die dargestellte Konfiguration aus Bild 1 unterscheidet bezüglich der Verantwortlichkeiten und der Vertrauenswürdigkeit lokalisierter Sicherheitsmechanismen die Bereiche Privatwohnung, öffentliche Netze, öffentliches Endgerät und mobiler Teilnehmer bzw. SM.

Zwei wichtige Mechanismen, die dem Bereichskonzept zugrundeliegen, sind die *Separation* und die *Mediation* [7].

- *Separation* zielt auf die gegenseitige Abgrenzung von Informationsträgern (Nutzdaten und Steuerdaten) ab, die verschiedenen Sicherheitsanforderungen unterliegen. In Bild 1 kann innerhalb des Kommunikationsnetzes zwischen der Teilnehmeranschlußleitung und dem Zwischenamtsbereich unterschieden werden. Unter der Annahme, daß Angriffe an der zugänglichen Teilnehmeranschlußleitung eher erwartet werden, können die Informationsträger in diesem Teilbereich durch kryptographische Verschlüsselung zusätzlich gesichert werden. Durch diese Aufteilung entsteht eine *Skalierbarkeit* der zusätzlich notwendigen Sicherheitsmechanismen abhängig von zugrundeliegenden Schutzzielen und Annahmen über Bedrohungen, welche in den jeweiligen Teilbereichen relevant sind.

- *Mediation* realisiert die Vermittlung zwischen verschiedenen Bereichen und sichert so die innerhalb der aneinandergrenzenden Bereiche vorgegebenen Schutzziele an den Bereichsgrenzen ab. Alle Informationsträger, welche einen Bereich verlassen oder in einen Bereich Eingang finden sollen, müssen durch das Mediationsverfahren geprüft werden. Im obigen Beispiel sorgt die Mediation dafür, daß Daten vor ihrer Übertragung über die Teilnehmeranschlußleitung im Teilnehmerbereich bzw. in der Vermittlungsstelle verschlüsselt werden.

2.1 Separationskonzept

Die Separation kann verschiedene Ausprägungen erfahren. Prinzipiell sind die physikalische, temporäre, logische und kryptographische Separation unterscheidbar.

Durch Separation können sowohl Informationsträger (Nutz- und Steuerdaten) als auch Funktionen (Telekommunikationsdienste, kryptographische Funktionen) geschützt werden. Die verschiedenen Ausprägungen der Separation werden nachfolgend anhand des Szenarios aus Bild 1 an Beispielen veranschaulicht.

Physikalische Separation: Eine physikalische Separation kann zur Sicherung von besonders schützenswerten Daten genutzt werden. Sie wird dadurch realisiert, daß z.B. geheime kryptographische Schlüssel auf separate Sicherheitsmodule verteilt werden und dort ausforschungssicher nur für die zugehörigen Teilnehmer nutzbar sind. Sicherheitsmodule realisieren meist auch die durch diese geheimen Schlüssel parametrisierten Funktionen (z.B. Signaturdienst), da die geheimen Schlüssel den vertrauenswürdigen Bereich nicht verlassen sollen [8].

An der Schnittstelle des Sicherheitsmoduls zum Menschen ist eine Identitätsprüfung bzw. Zugriffskontrolle aufbauend auf biometrischen Verfahren in naher Zukunft denkbar. Der Schutz des Menschen vor der Nutzung gefälschter Module kann durch Echtheitsmerkmale realisiert werden. Eine physikalische Separation der Module selbst durch ihren Besitzer kann zusätzlich vor Diebstahl oder Unterschieben gefälschter Sicherheitsmodule schützen.

Temporäre Separation: Die temporäre Separation kann durch die Personalisierung des Endgerätes mit Hilfe eines Sicherheitsmoduls durch den jeweiligen Nutzer erfolgen. Damit diese Separation vertrauenswürdig ist, können die Endgeräte unabhängig kontrolliert werden und ein gültiges Zertifikat gegenüber dem Teilnehmer (z.B. durch eine Plakette) oder gegenüber dessen SM (in Form elektronisch signierter Nachweise) nachweisen. Sie müssen nach der Nutzung in einen definierten Grundzustand übergehen (z.B. durch Löschen des Wahlwiederholspeichers bei Telefonen), so daß keine Information über vorherige Nutzer durch nachfolgende Nutzer ableitbar ist.

Logische Separation: Zugriffskontrollverfahren für Informationen und Dienste realisieren eine logische Separation. Aufbauend auf der Identität einer Instanz wird der Zugriffsschutz auf Informationsträger oder Dienste mit Hilfe sogenannter Zugriffskontroll-Listen (Access Control List) realisiert [9]. Diese Zugriffskontroll-Listen können in Form von Tabellen realisiert werden, die für Gruppen oder Einzelne die zugelassenen Zugriffsarten auf Ressourcen (z.B. durch Dienst-Profile, Schreib- bzw. Lese-Rechte für Daten) beschreiben. Jeder Zugriff auf logisch separierte Ressourcen muß durch einen Monitor überwacht werden. Dieser Monitor entscheidet auf der Grundlage der Zugriffskontroll-Listen, ob ein Zugriff zugelassen oder abgewiesen wird.

Kryptographische Separation: Die kryptographische Separation realisiert eine Separation der Verständlichkeitsmenge der Informationsträger von autorisierten Zugreifern bezüglich der Verständlichkeitsmenge unautorisierter Zugreifer dadurch, daß sie die Interpretierbarkeit von Daten bzw. die Nutzung von Diensten an die Kenntnis eines nur autorisierten Zugreifern bekannten Geheimnisses knüpft. Die kryptographische Separation der Informationsträger wird hier auf die (physikalische) Separation der geheimen kryptographischen Schlüssel bzw. die (logische oder physikalische) Separation der diese Schlüssel schützenden SM abgebildet.

In Kommunikationsnetzen können folgende Separations-Mechanismen zur Abgrenzung von Daten verschiedener Verbindungen unterschieden werden:

- *Physikalische Separation* durch räumlich begrenzte Ausdehnung des Übertragungsmediums (Funkzelle, Übertragungsleitung) und physikalischen Zugangsschutz der Vermittlungsstellen.

- *Logische Separation* durch Modulationsverfahren (Frequenzmultiplex, Zeitmultiplex, Wellenlängenmultiplex) oder logische Kanalnummern und Adressen auf den Übertragungsstrecken bzw. getrennte Speicherbereiche bei der parallelen Verarbeitung verschiedener Verbindungen innerhalb einer Vermittlungsstelle.

- *Temporäre Separation* durch getrennte Übermittlung der Daten zeitlich nicht überlappend aktiver Verbindungen.

Die temporäre und die logische Separation sind nur innerhalb vertrauenswürdiger Bereiche realisierbar, da ihre Wirksamkeit auf der Implementierung des jeweiligen Zugriffverfahrens beruht. Die physikalische Separation der durch Kommunikationsdienste übertragenen oder verarbeiteten Informationsträger einzelner Verbindungen widerspricht den Zielen der gemeinsamen Nutzung von Netzressourcen (Bündelungsgewinn). Für den Schutz von Informationen in nicht kontrollierbaren Kommunikationsnetzen wird deshalb die kryptographische Separation vorgeschlagen. Durch *kryptographische Separation* kann zusätzlich realisiert werden:

- die Abgrenzung von Daten verschiedener Verbindungen (Anwendungsdaten etc.) während der gemeinsamen Verarbeitung in der Vermittlungsstelle – z.B. zum Schutz gegen Fehlfunktion des Netzes oder falsche Zieladressen – und

- der Schutz von Daten gegen Angreifer an nicht kontrollierbaren Übertragungsstrecken bzw. innerhalb von Netzknoten.

Bei kryptographisch separierten Verbindungen kann ein Fehlrouten die Vertraulichkeit und Integrität der zugehörigen Daten nicht stören, da das „neue" Ziel die falsch gerouteten Daten nicht interpretieren oder unbemerkt ändern und wiedereinspielen kann. Eine entsprechende kryptographische Separation kann beispielsweise in den Endgeräten oder in Zusatzgeräten im Teilnehmerbereich [10] realisiert werden. In [11] werden anschaulich negative Auswirkungen beschrieben, welche durch das Verwählen bei der Nutzung eines Telefax-Dienstes entstehen können.

2.2 Mediationskonzept

Die Mediation hat die Aufgabe, Sicherheitsanforderungen verschiedener Bereiche an den Übergängen dieser Bereiche zu sichern. Ein Mediator sichert also den Übergang von einem Bereich in einen angrenzenden Bereich. Die Vermittlung zwischen Mediatoren muß deshalb in einer Umgebung realisiert werden, die für alle Bereiche vertrauenswürdig ist, deren Sicherheitsanforderungen an den Bereichsgrenzen umgesetzt werden müssen. Falls diese Bereiche keinen gemeinsamen Vertrauensbereich besitzen, dann muß die vermittelnde Funktionalität in einen neu zu schaffenden gemeinsamen Vertrauensbereich ausgelagert werden.

Ein Vertrauensbereich stellt einen abgeschlossenen Bereich dar, der bezüglich der geltenden Sicherheitsanforderungen als vertrauenswürdig angenommen wird. Es werden in diesem Bereich keine Angreifer oder Angriffsmöglichkeiten angenommen. Durch welche technischen, rechtlichen oder organisatorischen Maßnahmen diese Vertrauenswürdigkeit einer Instanz – bzw. eines durch sie verantworteten Bereiches – gegenüber anderen Instanzen gewonnen werden kann und welche Voraussetzungen dafür gegeben sein müssen, wird in [12] näher betrachtet.

Eine Instanz, die einen solchen ausgelagerten gemeinsamen Vertrauensbereich realisiert, wird im folgenden Vertraute Instanz (VI) genannt.

Das Prinzip der VI als Vermittler zwischen Mediatoren verschiedener Bereiche wird am Beispiel der sicheren Zuordenbarkeit der Inanspruchnahme von Dienstleistungen im Umfeld der Telekommunikation erläutert (Accounting, Rechteprüfung). Es dient als Grundlage für das in Abschnitt 4 vorgestellte Protokoll zur Sicherung dieser Schnittstelle.

Bei den verantwortlichen Instanzen handelt es sich um den Teilnehmer, der einen Dienst anfordert und um den Netzbetreiber der den Dienst abrechnet bzw. um den Dienstanbieter, der die Berechtigung prüft (siehe Bild 2). Der Teilnehmer fordert, daß nur jene Dienste abgerechnet werden, die auch vom ihm in Anspruch genommen werden. Der Dienstanbieter und der Netzbetreiber fordern, daß alle genutzten Dienste abgerechnet und den Teilnehmern korrekt zugeordnet werden. Zur Befriedigung dieser Anforderungen müssen alle genutzten Dienste eindeutig dem richtigen Teilnehmer zugeordnet werden können.

Durch die Mobilität von Teilnehmern kann die Zuordnung von Dienstanforderungen nicht an ortsfeste Netzanschlüsse gebunden werden und somit nicht vom Netzbetreiber zweifelsfrei anhand der Anschlußlage einer Teilnehmeranschlußleitung bestimmt werden. Ein entsprechender Mediator für den Netzbereich (M^N) schützt Netzbetreiber und Dienstanbieter vor unautorisierter Dienstnutzung von außerhalb des Netzbereiches und muß die Zuordenbarkeit der anfallenden Gebühren nachweisbar gestalten.

Durch die absehbare Vielfalt an Dienstanbietern und entsprechend unterschiedlichen Tarifen muß der Teilnehmer die Möglichkeit besitzen, den Dienstanbieter bzw. den in Anspruch genommenen Dienst eindeutig – und eventuell auch nachweisbar – zu identifizieren. Ein Mediator für den Teilnehmerbereich (M^T) muß dazu die Identität des Dienstanbieter bzw. des genutzten Dienstes vor der Dienstnutzung prüfen.

Abschnitt 3 führt in ein international standardisiertes kryptographisches Verfahren ein, welches von den Mediatoren zur Identitätsprüfung genutzt werden kann. Das vorgestellte Verfahren hat den Vorteil, daß eine Instanz ihre Identität nachweisen kann, ohne daß der Prüfer die dabei erhaltenen Informationen nutzen könnte, um diese geprüfte Instanz gegenüber anderen Instanzen zu imitieren. Dies ist in unserem Beispiel notwendig, da der prüfenden Instanz nicht uneingeschränkt vertraut werden soll. Die prüfende Instanz muß über den Inhaber der zu prüfenden Identität keinerlei weitere Kenntnis besitzen. Damit ist das Verfahren auch für die Nutzung von Fremdnetzen über Zugangsnetze anwendbar. Dieses spielt gerade bei mobilen Teilnehmern und bei der Diversität von Netzbetreibern eine wichtige Rolle.

Die Mediatoren M^T und M^N (siehe Bild 2) fordern bei Bedarf die zur Prüfung einer Identität notwendige Prüfinformation bei einer VI an. Die entsprechende Funktionalität zur Verwaltung dieser Prüfinformation kann deshalb durch eine von Teilnehmer und Netzbetreiber bzw. Dienstanbieter unabhängige, vertrauenswürdige Instanz realisiert werden. Diese VI muß bei jeder Dienstanforderung den Mediatoren zugänglich sein. Eine effiziente Realisierungsmöglichkeit bietet deshalb ihre Einbeziehung in die Signalisierung zur Dienstanforderung. Diese Möglichkeit wird in Abschnitt 4 näher untersucht.

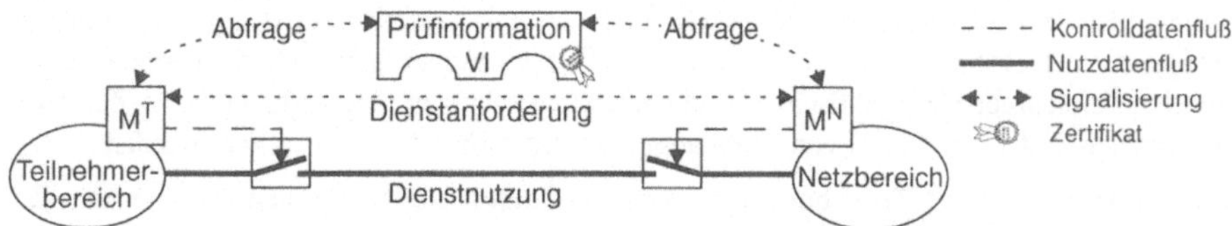

Bild 2: *Vertraute Instanzen als Vermittler zwischen Bereichen*

Weitere Aufgaben einer VI können auch im Schutz von Daten liegen, die gegenwärtig im Kommunikationsnetz verarbeitet werden und deren Verbleib für den Teilnehmer dadurch nicht kontrollierbar ist. Damit verschiedene Kommunikationsereignisse nicht aufgrund der Identität eines Teilnehmers miteinander in Beziehung gesetzt werden können – woraus zusätzliche Informationen über Teilnehmer ableitbar wären –, ist es denkbar, daß für jede Dienstnutzung temporäre Identitäten (Pseudonyme) vergeben werden. Die Auflösung der Pseudonyme muß durch die VI zur Weitergabe der Gebühren an den Teilnehmer und zur Bestimmung von Berechtigungen möglich sein. Das Netz würde bei entsprechender Realisierung die Gebühren der VI zuordnen, welche diese Gebühren nach Auflösung der Pseudonyme an die entsprechenden Verursacher weitergibt. Die Bekanntgabe der Berechtigungen der jeweiligen Teilnehmer durch die VI genügt im Netz für die Prüfung der Dienstanforderung. Auf diese erweiterten Möglichkeiten zur Vermeidung persönlicher Daten im Netz durch die Einbeziehung von Vertrauten Instanzen wird im weiteren nicht näher eingegangen.

3 Authentikation im Anwendungsfeld Telekommunikation

Authentikation beschreibt den Vorgang der „sicheren" Identifikation von Objekten oder Instanzen. In der Kommunikationstechnik dient die Authentikation vor allem im Vorfeld einer Zugriffskontrolle (Access Control) zur Klärung der Identität der zugriffsfordernden Instanz.

Die Bindung einer Identität an eine Instanz kann prinzipiell durch ein eindeutiges biometrisches Merkmal (z.B. einen bestimmten Fingerabdruck), durch Besitz eines Sicherheitsmoduls, durch Wissen um ein Geheimnis oder eine Kombination von Wissen und Besitz realisiert werden. Innerhalb von Kommunikationssystemen bietet sich der Identitätsnachweis durch Besitz oder Wissen an. An der Schnittstelle des Menschen zur Technik sind biometrische Verfahren eher geeignet. Bild 3 zeigt, wie die Authentikation zweier Teilnehmer A und B als Dienst nach dem Vorbild des OSI-Referenzmodelles dargestellt und realisiert werden kann.

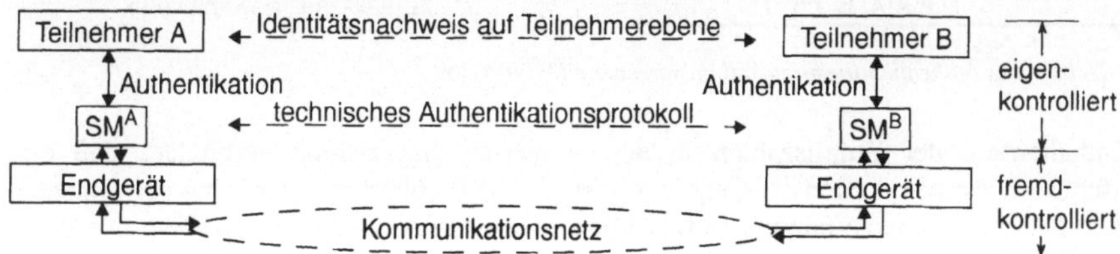

Bild 3: *Kommunikationsmodell der Authentikation zwischen zwei Teilnehmern*

Zunächst authentisiert sich der Teilnehmer gegenüber seinem Sicherheitsmodul. Dadurch wird das Sicherheitsmodul bei Verlust gegen unbefugte Nutzung gesichert. Für diese Authentikation sind biometrische Verfahren besonders geeignet [13], da bei Paßwörtern etc. menschliche Gedächtnisschwächen und die Anwendung der Verfahren in öffentlichen Gebäuden zu Sicherheitslücken – z.B. durch „Schultergucker" – führen können.

Bei zugriffskontrollierten Endgeräten muß vor der Nutzung des Endgerätes zur Bestimmung der Identität des Teilnehmers eine Authentikation des diesen Teilnehmer vertretenden Sicherheitsmoduls gegenüber dem Endgerät stattfinden. In diesem Bereich existieren verschiedene Authentikationsprotokolle, von denen einige in [14] dargestellt sind. Umgekehrt muß das Endgerät einen Beweis seiner Vertrauenswürdigkeit gegenüber dem Sicherheitsmodul liefern, um den Teilnehmer vor „gefälschten Endgeräten" zu schützen. Dieses kann durch Zertifikate (begrenzter Gültigkeitsdauer) von unabhängigen Kontrollinstanzen unterstützt werden.

Die Authentikation auf Teilnehmerebene kann nun durch die technischen Vertreter der Teilnehmer (hier: SM^A, SM^B) auf eine Authentikation auf technischer Ebene abgebildet werden.

Da nicht alle während der späteren Kommunikation schützenswerten Daten zur Sicherung durch das Sicherheitsmodul geleitet werden können, wird einem zertifizierten Endgerät aus Aufwandsgründen meist vertraut werden müssen. Ein während des Authentikationsvorganges zwischen den Sicherheitsmodulen ausgehandelter Kommunikationsschlüssel wird an das Endgerät weitergegeben, welches die Sicherung der übertragenen Daten und damit deren Authentisierung übernimmt. Da zwischen der Informationsquelle (Teilnehmer) und der Sicherheitsfunktion (Verschlüsselungsmodul im Endgerät) ein unkontrollierter Bereich liegt, sind die übertragenen Daten höchstens so sicher wie dieser Bereich.

Als Beispiel für den Protokollablauf einer Authentikation wird im folgenden ein Basisverfahren vorgestellt, welches den Identitätsnachweis auf der Grundlage des Wissens eines geheimen Schlüssels realisiert. Anschließend wird die Sicherheit des vorgestellten Authentikationsverfahrens in Bezug auf seine Robustheit gegen vorstellbare Angriffsversuche untersucht.

3.1 Basis-Protokoll für eine kryptographische Authentikation

Das vorgestellte Protokoll basiert auf der X.509-Empfehlung der ITU-T [15],[16] und damit auf einem asymmetrischen Signatursystem [17], bei dem jeder Identität ein geheimer (privater Schlüssel) zur Unterschrift und ein öffentlich bekannter Schlüssel zur Prüfung der Echtheit dieser Unterschrift durch jedermann zugeordnet ist.

Die die Authentikation initiierende Instanz A schickt eine signierte Nachricht N1 zur Partnerinstanz B (Bild 4). Instanz B beweist ihre Identität durch das Signieren der in N1 enthaltenen Zufallszahl r^A in N2 mit ihrem geheimen Schlüssel. Zusätzlich fordert sie von A, die in N2 enthaltene Zufallszahl r^B zu signieren. Instanz A beweist ihre Identität gegenüber B dadurch, daß sie diese Zufallszahl in N3 mit dem nur ihr bekannten geheimen Signaturschlüssel signiert und an B übermittelt.

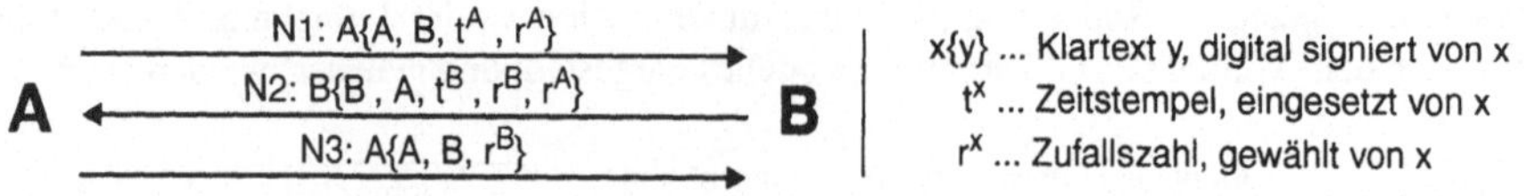

A   N1: A{A, B, t^A , r^A} →   B   x{y} ... Klartext y, digital signiert von x

      ← N2: B{B , A, t^B , r^B, r^A} t^x ... Zeitstempel, eingesetzt von x

      N3: A{A, B, r^B} → r^x ... Zufallszahl, gewählt von x

Bild 4: *Technisches Authentikationsprotokoll basierend auf ITU-T X.509*

Das Enthaltensein der Zufallszahlen in den signierten Nachrichten verhindert, daß ein Angreifer einen Authentikationsvorgang zwischen A und B abhört und die dabei gewonnenen signierten Nachrichten dazu nutzt, sich fälschlicherweise für A oder B auszugeben. Die Zeitstempel t^x beschränken die Gültigkeitsdauer von Nachrichten und ermöglichen so, daß sich die verwendeten Zufallszahlen verschiedener signierter Nachrichten – im Bezug auf die Sicherheit des Verfahrens gegen das Wiedereinspielen abgehörter Nachrichten – nur innerhalb des Gültigkeitszeitraumes unterscheiden müssen. Dieses Verfahren vereinfacht die Wahl einer „neuen" Zufallszahl aus Sicht des Senders, da innerhalb verschiedener Gültigkeitszeiträume gleiche Zufallszahlen nicht zu wiederverwendbaren Nachrichten führen.

Zur Realisierung des Verfahrens wird ein (asymmetrisches) Signatursystem benötigt. Die an der Authentikation teilnehmenden Instanzen müssen zur Prüfung der Signaturen über den öffentlichen Schlüssel der zu authentisierenden Partnerinstanz verfügen.

Dieser öffentliche Schlüssel muß authentisch sein, d.h. tatsächlich zu der Identität gehören, deren Signatur mit dem öffentlichen Schlüssel geprüft wird. Die Verwaltung dieser öffentlichen Schlüssel kann von sogenannten Verzeichnisdiensten übernommen werden. Diese liefern auf Anfrage den zu einer Identität gehörigen gültigen öffentlichen Schlüssel. Diese Verzeichnisdienste können auch die Sperrung von Schlüsseln realisieren, deren zugehörige geheime Schlüssel bekannt geworden sind (kompromittierte Schlüssel). Die Vertrauenswürdigkeit der Authentikation hängt direkt von der Authentizität der öffentlichen Schlüssel ab und damit von der Vertrauenswürdigkeit des Verzeichnisdienstes, der i.a. über das Kommunikationsnetz angesprochen wird. Interessante Ansätze und Gestaltungsalternativen für vertrauenswürdige Verzeichnisdienste werden in [18] besprochen. Die VI in Bild 2 kann beispielsweise einen solchen Verzeichnisdienst realisieren.

Prinzipiell könnte der Identitätsnachweis auch mit Hilfe symmetrischer Verschlüsselungsverfahren realisiert werden. Die mit symmetrischen Verschlüsselungssystemen erzeugten Signaturen werden auch Message Authentication Codes (MAC) genannt. Zur Bildung des MAC können geheime Schlüssel – welche ausschließlich den zu authentisierenden Instanzen bekannt sind – in die Berechnung eines Hash-Wertes über die zu signierende Nachricht einbezogen werden [19]. Dieses Verfahren erscheint in offenen Systemen insbesondere bei der spontanen Kommunikation mit vorher nicht bekannten Kommunikationspartnern unpraktikabel beziehungsweise setzt zur Installation gemeinsamer geheimer Schlüssel seinerseits ein asymmetrisches Verschlüsselungssystem voraus. Die Urheberschaft von Nachrichten kann mit symmetrischen Verfahren nicht nachgewiesen werden. Außerdem darf der geheime Schlüssel nicht außerhalb des Vertrauensbereiches der zu authentisierenden Instanzen vorliegen. Deshalb können sich Instanzen, die sich nicht gegenseitig vertrauen, mit diesen Verfahren nur über den Umweg einer Authentikation gegenüber einer gemeinsamen VI indirekt authentisieren.

3.2 „Angriffsmodell" für die Authentikation

Gelingt einem Angreifer ein erfolgreicher Angriff auf das Authentikationsverfahren, so kann er sich fälschlicherweise als Inhaber einer Identität ausgeben und erbt die zu dieser Identität gehörigen Rechte.

Die Sicherheit des vorgestellten Authentikationsverfahrens ist abhängig von der Korrektheit der Implementierung des verwendeten Verfahrens [20] und der Sicherungsmechanismen des zugrundeliegenden Protokolles. Das Signatursystem muß u.a. robust sein gegen die allgemein bekannten Angriffsversuche zur Erlangung des geheimen Schlüssels [21], der dem Verschlüsselungssystem zugrundeliegt. Durch die Wahl geeigneter Schlüssel und eine sorgfältige Implementierung in sicherer Umgebung können viele dieser Angriffe so erschwert werden, daß sie i.a. als nicht mehr relevant einzustufen sind. Gegenwärtig empfehlenswerte minimale Schlüssellängen werden in [22] und [23] diskutiert.

Das Protokoll zur Authentikation muß u.a. resistent sein gegen das Wiedereinspielen abgehörter signierter Nachrichten aus parallel ablaufenden oder zeitlich zurückliegenden Authentikationsvorgängen. Außerdem müssen die zum Zwecke der Authentikation zwischen den Partnern ausgetauschten Nachrichten (N1 bis N3 in Bild 4) während der Übertragung vor Veränderung geschützt werden. Die Authentizität des zur Prüfung der signierten Nachrichten benutzten öffentlichen Schlüssels muß gewährleistet sein, um eine sogenannte Maskerade (Vorspiegeln einer falschen Identität) durch Einführen falscher Schlüssel zur Signaturprüfung zu verhindern.

Bei geeigneter Implementierung des Signatursystems – Implementierung der Funktionen, Schlüsselwahl und -aufbewahrung – verbleiben folgende relevante Angriffsmöglichkeiten, welche durch Mechanismen des Authentikationsprotokolles kompensiert werden müssen:

(a) Impersonation durch Angabe einer falschen Identität,

(b) Einführen falscher öffentlicher Schlüssel,

(c) Stehlen geheimer Schlüssel,

(d) Ändern des Chiffrats,

(e) Ändern des Klartextes und

(f) Wiedereinspielen abgehörter Nachrichten.

Den Angriffen (a), (d), (e) und (f) kann durch die Verwendung sicherer Signatursysteme, durch Zeitstempel von synchronisierten Uhren, Zufallszahlen, Prüfsummen oder einfache Redundanz entgegengewirkt werden [24],[25],[26].

Die Angriffe (b) und (c) können nur durch eine entsprechende Sicherungsinfrastruktur [18] kompensiert werden. Dabei kann sich u.U. das häufige Wechseln von Schlüsseln zur Kompensation von Angriff (c) bei ungenügender Realisierung der Sicherungsinfrastruktur negativ auf die Robustheit gegen Angriff (b) auswirken, da die Konsistenz des Schlüsselverzeichnisses aufwendiger und damit fehleranfälliger werden kann. Der sogenannte „Man-in-the-Middle" Angriff, bei dem sich der Angreifer in die Kommunikation der zu authentisierenden Kommunikationspartner einschleust und den jeweils anderen Partner „spielt", ist durch vertrauenswürdige Zertifikate und gute Signatursysteme ebenfalls ausgeschlossen.

Die Verfügbarkeit zertifizierter öffentlicher Schlüssel und ihre authentische Verteilung sowie die sichere Aufbewahrung und korrekte Anwendung der geheimen Schlüssel sind deshalb Voraussetzung für ein sicheres Authentikationsverfahren.

4 Unterstützung von Separation und Mediation durch Authentikation in offenen Telekommunikationssystemen

Dieser Abschnitt zeigt die Anwendung der bisherigen Ergebnisse anhand von Protokollen, die an der Schnittstelle zwischen Teilnehmer- und Netzbereich zur Realisierung der folgenden Sicherheitsanforderungen integriert werden können:

(A) Authentikation zwischen Teilnehmer und Dienst (Berechtigungsprüfung, etc.)

(B) Sicherung der übermittelten Nutzdaten auf der Teilnehmeranschlußleitung

(C) Authentikation der Kommunikationspartner (indirekt unter Mitwirkung des Netzes)

Abschnitt 4.1 bespricht ein Protokoll zur Realisierung dieser Forderungen unter der Voraussetzung, daß die Kommunikations- und Nutzdaten innerhalb der Netze sicher sind, d.h. daß dem Netzbetreiber und Dienstanbieter bezüglich der Sicherheit der übermittelten Daten innerhalb des Netzes vertraut wird. Der Schwerpunkt der Betrachtungen liegt auf dem Aufbau und Inhalt der Nachrichten, welche zur Realisierung der Forderungen zwischen Teilnehmer und Netz ausgetauscht werden müssen. Abschnitt 4.2 skizziert die Integration dieser Nachrichten in die Teilnehmersignalisierung im Schmalband-ISDN (N-ISDN).

4.1 Integration von Sicherheit unter Mitwirkung des Netzbetreibers

Dieser Abschnitt stellt ein Protokoll vor, mit dem die Anforderungen (A) bis (C) unter Mitwirkung des Netzbetreibers realisiert werden können. Das Protokoll basiert auf dem Authentikationsprotokoll aus Bild 4.

Bild 5 zeigt ein Protokoll, das die genannten Anforderungen unterstützt. Die Nachrichtenteile S^{ix} enthalten die für die Authentikation notwendigen Parameter der *Nachricht i* aus Bild 4 zur

Authentikation von *Teilnehmer x* und *Vermittlungsstelle V^x*. Zusätzlich beinhalten die signierten Nachrichten weitere Parameter zur Realisierung der Forderungen (B) und (C), welche durch ihre Bindung an die Authentikation ebenfalls authentisch sind.

In die Authentikationsvorgänge zwischen Teilnehmer und Teilnehmervermittlungsstellen wird zur Installation eines gemeinsamen geheimen Schlüssels (Sitzungsschlüssel, SKey) das sogenannte Diffie-Hellman-Verfahren eingebettet [27]. Mit diesem Sitzungsschlüssel kann anschließend die Kommunikation zwischen Endgerät und Vermittlungsstelle verschlüsselt werden (Forderung B). Jeder Kommunikationspartner wählt bei diesem Verfahren einen Schlüsselteil Skey^x. Die Berechnung des Sitzungsschlüssels aus den Schlüsselteilen ist nur den Kommunikationspartnern möglich, die einen der Schlüsselteile erzeugt haben. Deshalb müssen die Schlüsselteile während der Übertragung nicht geheim gehalten werden. Schwächen des Diffi-Hellman-Verfahrens [28] werden durch die zugrundeliegende Authentikation kompensiert.

Das in Bild 5 dargestellte Authentikationsprotokoll realisiert auch für mobile Teilnehmer weitgehende Sicherheit unter Einbeziehung des Netzbetreibers. Dieser kann aufgrund der bekannten Identität des rufenden Teilnehmers die Zuordnung der Gebühren selbst vornehmen. Die Vertraute Instanz dient lediglich als Verzeichnisdienst für öffentliche Schlüssel (Protokollnachrichten 2 und 3) und muß bei entsprechenden Caching-Verfahren innerhalb der Vermittlungsstelle nicht bei jeder Dienstanforderung zwischengeschaltet werden (siehe auch Bild 2).

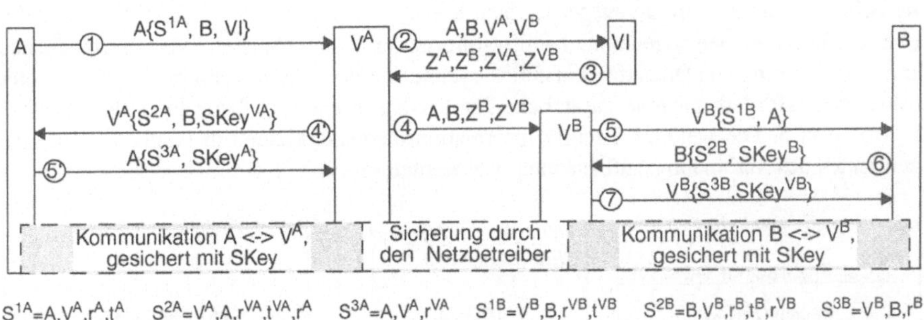

Bild 5: *Sicherung der Teilnehmer-Netz-Schnittstelle unter Einbeziehung des Netzes*

Die Caching-Strategie muß natürlich ausgleichen zwischen möglichst geringer zusätzlicher Netzlast durch Abfragen bei der Vertrauten Instanz und der Aktualität der Zertifikate. Das Sperren ungültiger öffentlicher Schlüssel kann bei der Nutzung zwischengespeicherter Zertifikate nicht berücksichtigt werden. Die Zertifikate Z^B und Z^{VB} für die gerufene Seite werden von der Vermittlungsstelle V^A des rufenden Teilnehmers zur Zielvermittlungsstelle V^B übertragen, um weitere Abfragen einzusparen. Ebenso werden die Identitäten A und B der Teilnehmer übermittelt. Falls das Netz die Verbindung nur dann durchschaltet, wenn die Authentikation der Teilnehmer A und B erfolgreich verläuft, dann ist auch Forderung (C) erfüllt.

4.2 Integration des Protokolles in die ISDN-Teilnehmersignalisierung

Die Implementierung der Protokolle im ISDN-Teilnehmerbereich erfordert zunächst die Kodierung der Nachrichten (1) bis (7) aus Bild 5. Die Anwendung, welche die Nachrichten generiert bzw. prüft, soll an dieser Stelle nicht näher beschrieben werden. Die in Tabelle 1 angegebenen Längen von Nachrichtenelementen sind als Richtwerte gedacht und sollen als Ausgangspunkt für die Bewertung der Integrationsfähigkeit des Protokolles in bestehende Signalisierprotokolle im Teilnehmerbereich dienen.

Aus dieser Kodierung folgt, daß die Nachrichtenlängen kleiner als 1536 Bits (= 192 Oktetts) sind. Die Signatur kann also bei Verschlüsselung mit 1536 Bit-Schlüsseln[1] mit einem asymmetrischen Verschlüsselungssystem in einem Block erfolgen. Die Signaturprüfung kann dadurch erfolgen, daß die Nachrichten mit dem öffentlichen Schlüssel des angeblichen Senders entschlüsselt werden und in der entschlüsselten Nachricht die enthaltene Identität des Senders mit der zum öffentlichen Schlüssel gehörigen Identität verglichen wird. Die Redundanz zur Bestimmung der Authentizität einer Nachricht besteht hier aus der Nachrichtenstruktur und dem Inhalt bestimmter Felder, welche bei der Prüfung mit dem falschen öffentlichen Schlüssel mit größter Wahrscheinlichkeit nicht mit den erwarteten Werten übereinstimmen werden.

Identitäten (A,B,V^A,V^B,VI)	8 Oktetts (16 Ziffern, 2^{64} Identitäten)
Zeitstempel (t^A,t^B,t^{VA},t^{VB})	8 Oktetts (Y,M,D,H,M,S,Timezone)
Zufallszahlen (r^A,r^B,r^{VA},r^{VB})	4 Oktetts
Schlüsselhälften nach Diffie-Hellman (SKey^X)	128 Oktetts (Modulo 1024bit)

Tabelle 1: Mögliche Längenkodierung der Nachrichtenelemente des Protokolles

Bei den in die bestehende Teilnehmersignalisierung im ISDN zu integrierenden Nachrichten kann eine Länge von 1536 Bits angenommen werden. Zur effizienten Entschlüsselung beim Empfänger ist es sinnvoll, die Identität des Signaturerzeugers unverschlüsselt voranzustellen.

Bild 6 zeigt die Signalisierung eines erfolgreichen Verbindungsaufbaus im ISDN [29],[30]. Die beim Verbindungsaufbau ausgetauschten Signale werden um die Nachrichten aus Bild 5 erweitert. Dazu werden sogenannte Facility-Informationselemente (FAC) verwendet, die auch für die Aktivierung von Dienstmerkmalen verwendet werden. Die Integration des Nachrichtenaustausches erfordert nur eine zusätzliche Facility-Nachricht zur Übertragung der Nachricht (5') aus Bild 5. Die weiteren Facility-Informationselemente können in reguläre Signalisiernachrichten des Verbindungsaufbaus integriert werden.

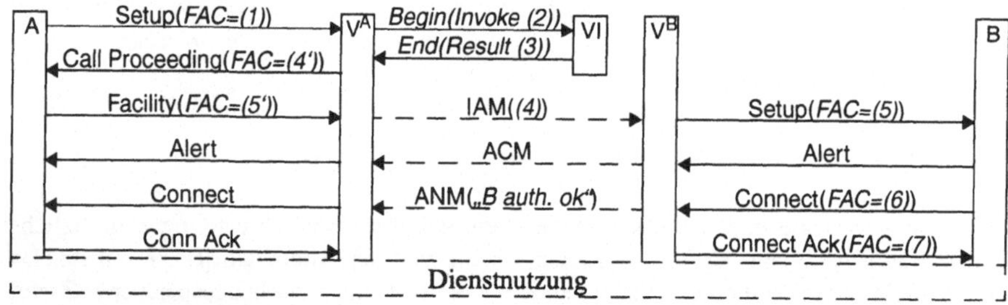

Bild 6: Integration der Nachrichten in die Verbindungssignalisierung im (N-) ISDN

Zur Abfrage gültiger Zertifikate der öffentlichen Schlüssel wird das Transaction Capability Application Service Element verwendet, welches im Zwischenamtsbereich für die verbindungsunabhängige Signalisierung zur Verfügung steht. Da die Signalisierung eine gesicherte Übertragung bietet (bezüglich Verlust von Nachrichten und Übertragungsfehlern) und die Zertifikate sowieso signiert sind, wird diese Abfrage der VI nicht speziell gesichert. Die Teilnehmer können die Zertifikate der Vermittlungsstellen bei Bedarf z.B. über ein Dienstmerkmal anfordern.

---

[1] Das öffentliche Signatursystem ist universell verwendbar und sollte größtmögliche Sicherheit bieten. Das Diffie-Hellman-Verfahren braucht nicht sicherer zu sein, als die anschließende Verschlüsselung bzw. die vom Netz im Zwischenamtsbereich gebotene Sicherheit. Die Schlüssellängen sind aus [23], S. 162, Tab. 7.6 abgeleitet.

Die maximale Nachrichtenlänge der dargestellten Signalisiernachrichten innerhalb der Teilnehmersignalisierung beträgt im (N-) ISDN 260 Oktetts. Die Länge der zur Zeit verwendeten Nachrichten beim normalen Verbindungsaufbau liegt meist deutlich unter 50 Oktetts, so daß die zusätzlichen Daten integrierbar sind, ohne eine Segmentierung erforderlich zu machen.

Falls eine Authentikation erfolglos verläuft, sollte dies dem A-Teilnehmer angezeigt und die Dienstanforderung abgebrochen werden. Da die Identität des rufenden Teilnehmers mit der Durchschaltung des Rufes zum gerufenen Teilnehmer feststeht, kann dem B-Teilnehmer – falls vom A-Teilnehmer gewünscht – die geprüfte Identität von A angezeigt werden (Forderung C).

Bewertung des Verfahrens:

Die Teilnehmer sind vor dem Durchschalten einer Verbindung authentisiert, da deren Authentikation mit der Weiterleitung der Connect-Nachricht abgeschlossen ist. Die Authentikation des rufenden Teilnehmers ist schon vor der Einleitung des Verbindungsaufbaus abgeschlossen. Der gerufene Teilnehmer wird bei gemeinsam genutzten Endgeräten sein Sicherheitsmodul erst nach der Dienstanzeige (Klingelsignal beim Telefon) in das Endgerät einführen, so daß Nachricht 6 in Bild 6 frühestens mit der Connect-Nachricht übertragen werden kann.

Zur Sicherung der Datenaustauschphase wird während des Verbindungsaufbaus ein gemeinsamer Schlüssel zwischen Endgerät und Vermittlungsstelle installiert, während innerhalb der Netze die Sicherung der Daten dem Netzbetreiber übertragen wird. Deshalb muß dieser für beide Teilnehmer vertrauenswürdig sein. Aufgrund bekannter rechtlicher Anforderungen an den Netzbetreiber sind die übertragenen Informationen mit diesem Verfahren nicht gegen Zugriffe in- und ausländischer staatlicher Dienste geschützt.

5 Zusammenfassung und Ausblick

Das vorgestellte Konzept zur Bereichsbildung zeigt einen Weg zur wirtschaftlichen Integration von Sicherheitsmechanismen auf. Es bezieht gegebene Sicherheitsanforderungen, Verantwortlichkeiten und technische Randbedingungen ein und ermöglicht dadurch effiziente Sicherheitsmechanismen. Separation und Mediation bilden die Basis für die Einordnung von Sicherheitsmechanismen und fördern das Verständnis für deren Wirkung. Die Bedeutung gemeinsamer Vertrauter Instanzen und Möglichkeiten für deren Einbindung in die Dienstanforderung im ISDN wurden an einem Beispiel erläutert.

Vertrauenswürdige Verzeichnisdienste spielen im Umfeld der spontanen, sicheren Kommunikation in offenen Systemen eine zentrale Rolle. Deshalb wird für die Nutzung von Kommunikationsdiensten in privaten und öffentlichen Bereichen wegweisend sein, wie die Vertrauenswürdigkeit verschiedener Interessengruppen gewonnen werden kann. Aus technischer Sicht sind hier vor allem die Zertifikation zu nennen [31], der im Rahmen der Zuverlässigkeit und der unabhängigen Kontrolle als Basis für die Vertrauenswürdigkeit von Technik eine zentrale Rolle zukommt. Die Implementierung von Verzeichnisdiensten kann im Intelligenten Netz durch zertifizierte Dienste unabhängiger Netzbetreiber realisiert werden.

Das vorgestellte Protokoll zur Sicherung der Teilnehmer-Netz-Schnittstelle wurde bezüglich der Länge von Nachrichten auf seine Integrationsfähigkeit in die Teilnehmersignalisierung im Schmalband-ISDN geprüft. Untersuchungen von Zeitverzögerungen, die durch die Generierung und Prüfung der zusätzlichen Nachrichtenteile (Signaturerzeugung, Signaturprüfung) innerhalb des Protokollablaufs entstehen, müssen im Rahmen einer Simulation durchgeführt werden. Die Vorteile einer Auslagerung der gesamten Authentikation und damit zusammenhängender Netzfunktionen in Vertraute Instanzen muß in Zusammenhang mit den neuen Möglichkeiten, welche das Intelligente Netz bieten wird, untersucht werden.

Literatur

[1] *T. Magedanz, R. Popescu-Zeletin:* „Intelligent Networks - Basic Technology, Standards and Evolution", International Thomson Computer Press, 1996

[2] *J. Shattuck:* „Computer Matching Is A Serious Threat to Individual Rights", Comm. ACM, Vol. 27, No. 6, June, 1984, pp. 538-541

[3] *A. Roßnagel, P. Wedde, V. Hammer, U. Pordesch:* „Die Verletzlichkeit der Informationsgesellschaft", 2. Auflage, Westdeutscher Verlag GmbH, Opladen, 1990

[4] *G. Arndt, R. Lueder:* „Bewegungsfreiheit in allen Netzen", Siemens telcom report *16*, 2/1993, pp. 67-69

[5] *R. Sailer, P. J. Kühn:* „Ein Domain-Konzept zur systematischen und wirtschaftlichen Integration von Sicherheit in Kommunikationsnetze", it+ti Informationstechnik und Technische Informatik, Heft 4, 1996

[6] *B. Richter, M. Sobirey, H. König:* „Auditbasierte Netzüberwachung", *PIK*, 19, 1996, Heft 1, pp. 24-32

[7] *J. Rushby, B. Randell:* „A Distributed Secure System", IEEE Computer, July, 1983, pp. 55-67

[8] *A. Pfitzmann, B. Pfitzmann, M. Schunter, M. Waidner:* „Vertrauenswürdiger Entwurf portabler Benutzerendgeräte und Sicherheitsmodule", Proc. Verläßliche Informationssysteme (VIS‘ 95), Vieweg, 1995

[9] *R. Sandhu, P. Samarati:* „Access Control: Principles and Practice", IEEE Comm. Magazine, 9/1994, pp. 40ff

[10] *N. Pohlmann:* „Schutz von LANs und LAN-Kopplung über öffentliche Netze", *DATACOM*, 6, 1995, pp. 50ff

[11] *M. Warwick:* „Feeling Insecure?", Communications International, January 1996, pp. 37

[12] *W. Langenheder, U. Pordesch:* „Sicherheit und Vertrauen in der Kommunikationstechnik - Soziologische Ansätze und Methoden", it+ti Informationstechnik und Technische Informatik, Schwerpunktheft 4, 1996

[13] *B. Miller:* „Vital signs of identity", IEEE Spectrum, February 1994, pp. 22-30

[14] *H.-P. Königs:* „Cryptographic Identification Methods for Smart Cards in the Process of Standardization", IEEE Communications Magazine, June 1991, pp. 42-48

[15] „Data Networks And Open System Communications, Directory, Information Technology - Open Systems Interconnection - The Directory: Authentication Framework", ITU-T Recommendation X.509, 1993

[16] *C. I'Anson, C. Mitchell:* „Security Defects in CCITT Recommendation X.509 - The Directory Authentication Framework", ACM Computer Communication Review, Vol. 20, No. 2, April, 1990, pp. 30-34

[17] *R. L. Rivest, A. Shamir, L. Adleman:* „A Method for Obtaining Digital Signatures and Public-Key Cryptosystems", Comm. ACM, Volume 21, No. 2, February 1978, pp. 120-126

[18] *V. Hammer (Hrsg.), M. J. Schneider, A. Roßnagel, J. Bizer, C. Kumbruck, U. Pordesch:* „Sicherheitsinfrastrukturen - Gestaltungsvorschläge für Technik, Organisation und Recht", Springer Verlag, 1995

[19] *G. Tsudik:* „Message Authentication with One-Way Hash Functions", *ACM Computer Communication Review,* Vol. 22, No. 5, October, 1992, pp. 29-38

[20] *J. H. Moore:* „Protocol Failures in Cryptosystems", *Proc. IEEE,* Vol. 76, No. 5, May, 1988, pp. 594-602

[21] *A. Beutelspacher, J. Schwenk, K. - D. Wolfenstetter:* „Moderne Verfahren der Kryptographie", Vieweg, 1995

[22] *M. Blaze, W. Diffie, R. L. Rivest, B. Schneier, T. Shimomura, E. Thomson, M. Wiener:* „Minimal Key Lengths For Symmetric Ciphers To Provide Adequate Commercial Security", ftp://ftp.research.att.com/dist/mab/keylength.ps, January, 1996

[23] *B. Schneier:* „Applied Cryptography", 2nd ed., John Wiley & Sons, Inc., 1996

[24] *M. Abadi, R. Needham:* „Prudent Engineering Practice for Cryptographic Protocols", Digital, Systems Research Center, Research Report No. 125, Palo Alto, California, June 1994

[25] *B. C. Neuman, S. G. Stubblebine:* „A Note on the Use of Timestamps as Nonces", ACM Operating Systems Review, Vol. 27, No. 2, April, 1993, pp. 10-14

[26] *T. Y. C. Woo, S. S. Lam:* „A Lesson on Authentication Protocol Design", ACM Operating Systems Review, Vol. 28, No. 3, July 1994, pp. 24-37

[27] *W. Diffie, M. E. Hellman:* „New Directions in Cryptography", IEEE Transactions On Information Theory, Volume 22, No. 6, November 1976, pp. 644-654

[28] *R. L. Rivest, A. Shamir:* „How to Expose an Eavesdropper", *Comm. ACM*, Vol. 27, No. 4, 1984, pp. 393-395

[29] *G. Bandow, H. Gottschalk, D. Gehrmann, W. Hlavac, H. Koch, W. Müller, D. Schwetje:* „Zeichengabesysteme - Eine neue Generation für ISDN und intelligente Netze", L.T.U. - Vertriebsgesellschaft mbH, Bremen, 2. Auflage, 1995

[30] „Digital Subscriber Signalling System No. 1 (DSS1), Network Layer, User-Network Management", ITU-T Recommendations Q.930-Q.940, Geneva, 1989

[31] *K. Rannenberg:* „Evaluationskriterien zur IT-Sicherheit - Entwicklungen und Perspektiven in der Normung und außerhalb", Verläßliche IT-Systeme, GI-Fachtagung, Vieweg, April 1995

Ein Vertraulichkeit gewährendes Erreichbarkeitsverfahren[*]

Schutz des Aufenthaltsortes in künftigen Mobilkommunikationssystemen

Hannes Federrath, Elke Franz, Anja Jerichow, Jan Müller, Andreas Pfitzmann

Technische Universität Dresden, Institut für Theoretische Informatik, 01062 Dresden
{federrath, ef1, jerichow, jm4, pfitza}@inf.tu-dresden.de

Zusammenfassung

Es wird ein Verfahren zur Verwaltung von Aufenthaltsinformationen in Mobilkommunikationssystemen vorgestellt. Dabei wird von dem in existierenden Netzen verwendeten Konzept der mehrstufigen Speicherung von Aufenthaltsinformationen ausgegangen. Das Verfahren erfüllt die Datenschutzforderung nach Vertraulichkeit des Aufenthaltsorts von Mobilkommunikationsteilnehmern. Es ermöglicht die Speicherung unterschiedlich granularer, geographischer Aufenthaltsinformationen unter Pseudonymen (statt der wahren Identität der Teilnehmer). Die Pseudonyme werden über Register unterschiedlicher Netzbetreiber miteinander verkettet. Somit ist die Erstellung von Bewegungsprofilen von mobilen Teilnehmern nicht möglich.

1   Motivation

Vertraulichkeit, Integrität und Verfügbarkeit sind grundsätzliche Forderungen an ein datenschutzgerechtes Kommunikationssystem. Dem Schutz des Aufenthaltsorts von Mobilkommunikationsteilnehmern als Teil von Vertraulichkeit wird in bestehenden Mobilkommunikationssystemen kaum Bedeutung beigemessen. Die Teilnehmer sind beobachtbar, da ihre Erreichbarkeit meist durch Speicherung der Aufenthaltsinformation gewährleistet wird. Zumindest dem Netzbetreiber ist so stets der aktuelle Aufenthaltsort jedes erreichbaren Teilnehmers bekannt.

1.1   Bestehende zellulare Funknetze

In einem zellularen Funknetz ist das Versorgungsgebiet gewöhnlich in Location Areas (LA) eingeteilt. Um einen mobilen Teilnehmer bei einem ankommenden Verbindungswunsch stets effizient erreichen zu können, muß dem Netz die aktuelle Location Area Identification (LAI) des Teilnehmers zur Signalisierung bekannt sein. Bewegt sich ein mobiler Teilnehmer von einem LA in ein anderes, löst seine Mobilstation (MS) *automatisch* ein Location Update (LUP) aus und meldet dem Netz so, vom Teilnehmer unbeeinflußt, seinen neuen Aufenthaltsort. Damit ist auch ein *passiver* Teilnehmer mit angemeldeter MS vom Netz stets verfolgbar, d.h. der Netzbetreiber kann *Bewegungsprofile* seiner Teilnehmer erstellen.

Im GSM (Global System for Mobile Communication) [GSM_93], einem zellularen Funknetz, werden die Aufenthaltsinformationen der Mobilteilnehmer aus Performancegründen *mehrstufig* im Home Location Register (HLR) und Visitor Location Register (VLR) gespeichert. So wird im VLR die LAI des Teilnehmers hinterlegt, während im HLR die aktuelle VLR-Adresse ge-

---

[*] Wir danken der Deutschen Forschungsgemeinschaft (DFG) und der Gottlieb Daimler- und Karl Benz- Stiftung Ladenburg für die finanzielle Unterstützung. Für Anregungen, Diskussionen und Kritik geht unser Dank an Dagmar Schönfeld und Dogan Kesdogan.

speichert wird. Bild 1 veranschaulicht die Mehrstufigkeit der Speicherung in voller Allgemeinheit.

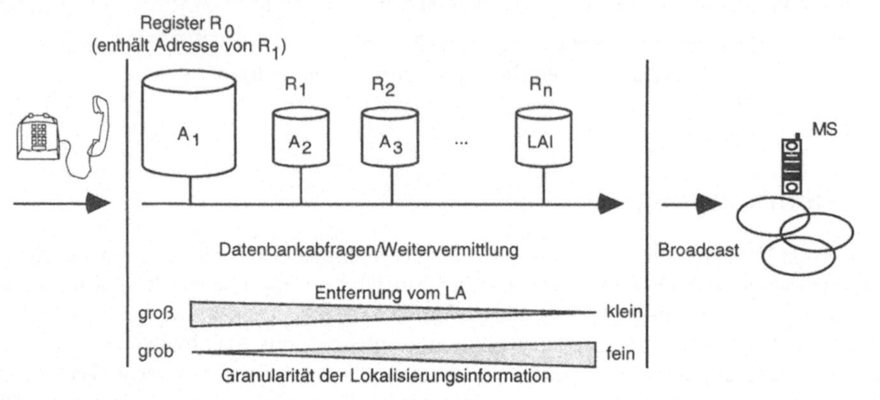

Bild 1: Mehrstufige Speicherung von Lokalisierungsinformation

Durch die Mehrstufigkeit sind in den einzelnen Ebenen des Netzes unterschiedlich genaue Lokalisierungsinformationen verfügbar. Das bringt beim LUP den Vorteil, daß stets nur die Register aktualisiert werden müssen, bei denen sich die Lokalisierungsinformation des Teilnehmers geändert hat. Dadurch erfolgt die LUP-Signalisierung meist nur über kurze Entfernungen im VLR-Bereich. Eine Signalisierung über große Entfernungen zum HLR ist nur selten erforderlich. Die Verteilung von Lokalisierungsinformationen führt dagegen zu einem aufwendigeren Verbindungsaufbau, da im Gegensatz zur zentralen Verwaltung zusätzliche Datenbankabfragen notwendig sind. Jedoch wird dieser Nachteil durch Einsparung an Bandbreite beim weitaus häufiger notwendigen LUP kompensiert.

Für den Datenschutz bedeutet diese Verteilung von Lokalisierungsinformation jedoch keine automatische Verbesserung. Zum einen hat ein Netzbetreiber in einem Mobilfunksystem wie GSM stets die globale Sicht auf alle Daten. Er kann also die verteilten Lokalisierungsinformationen verketten und Bewegungsprofile erstellen. Zum anderen wurden bisher noch keine Aussagen gemacht, unter welcher Identität die Datenbanken Lokalisierungsinformationen abspeichern. Im GSM-Netz erfolgt die Speicherung im HLR und VLR unter der Identität des Teilnehmers (der MSISDN, Mobile Subscriber ISDN Number bzw. der IMSI, International Mobile Subscriber Identity).

1.2 Künftige zellulare Funknetze

Ein künftiges System könnte verschiedene zellulare Funknetze integrieren. Das ist eine realistische Annahme. Z.B. ist bei UMTS (Universal Mobile Telecommunication System) [Mitt_94], einem in der Standardisierung befindlichen allgemeinen Mobilfunknetz, die Integration verschiedener Systeme geplant.

Das Eingliedern verschiedener Netze in ein Gesamtsystem erlaubt es, Daten unterschiedlich großer Versorgungsgebiete bei unterschiedlichen Betreibern zu speichern. Wir bezeichnen dies ebenfalls als mehrstufige Speicherung. Die Zellbereiche können sich dabei hierarchisch überlagern (siehe auch [FJKP_95]).

Im Bild 2 werden durch die verschiedenen Zellgrößen vier sich überlagernde Netze dargestellt, wobei das grau gezeichnete Netz einerseits ein separates, die anderen überlagerndes Netz darstellt. Andererseits übernimmt es auch Aufgaben als Gesamtsystem. Die drei schwarz dargestellten Netze versorgen Teilgebiete des alles überlagernden grauen Netzes. Jedem der Netze sind in den verschiedenen Ebenen Register R_i (i=0...3) zur Speicherung der Aufenthaltsinformationen zugeordnet. R_0 übernimmt ähnlich dem HLR in GSM eine zentrale Verwaltungsfunktion. In dem dargestellten Beispiel versorgt jeweils ein einzelnes Netz einen Bereich des Gesamtgebietes. Es ist jedoch wünschenswert, daß den Nutzern in jedem Bereich mehrere Netze bzw. Register verschiedener Betreiber zur Verfügung stehen, aus denen sie wählen können. Beispielsweise könnten neben R_2 noch die Register R_4 und R_5 existieren.

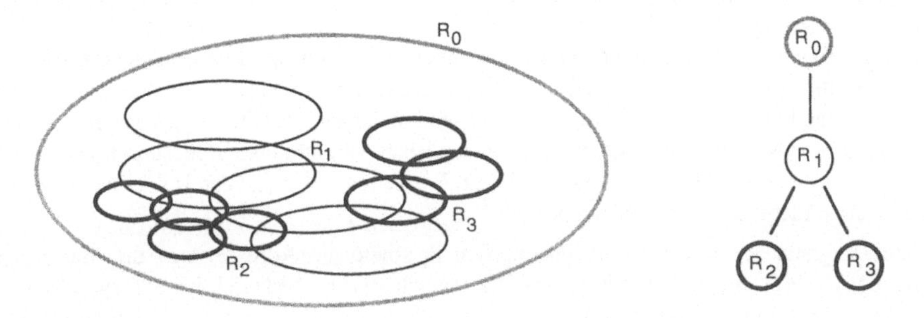

Bild 2: Integration verschiedener Netze

1.3 Mobilkommunikationssysteme der Zukunft

Ein in Zukunft vorstellbares System soll die Datenschutzforderung nach Anonymität, hier Erreichbarkeit ohne Verfolgbarkeit, gewährleisten und die Vorteile existierender Systeme nutzen. Eine Mobilstation muß häufiger ihren Aufenthaltsort zur Gewährleistung des Location Management signalisieren, als tatsächlich Verbindungen benötigt werden. Erreichbarkeit ohne Verfolgbarkeit bedeutet somit Schutz des Aufenthaltsortes während der Signalisierungsphase.

Folgendes ist von einem allgemeinen Mobilkommunikationssystem zu fordern.

- Mehrstufige Speicherung: Aufenthaltsdaten sollen verteilt in verschiedenen Registern R_i mit i=0...n gespeichert werden, wobei die Register *nicht* heimlich zusammenarbeiten. Das ist realistisch, wenn die Register mit Blick auf künftige Netze verschiedenen Betreibern unterstehen.

- Einsatz von Pseudonymen: Die Einträge der Teilnehmer in den Registern erfolgen unter Pseudonymen. Betreiber können die Identität eines Teilnehmers nicht mit seinem Pseudonym verketten. Ein Teilnehmer muß in der Lage sein, dem Netz seinen aktuellen Aufenthaltsort unter einem Pseudonym zu signalisieren.

In der Literatur [Hets_93, MüSt_95, Pfit_93, Walk_94] finden sich eine Reihe von Lösungen des Problems, die von einer vertrauenswürdigen Feststation ausgehen.

Im folgenden wird ein die Erreichbarkeit gewährleistendes Verfahren vorgestellt, das zum einen beim LUP effizient durch die mehrstufige Speicherung der Lokalisierungsinformation und zum anderen die Anonymität der mobilen Teilnehmer während der Signalisierungsphase gewährleistet. Die Verwendung von Kryptographie ist notwendig. Wir schlagen ein hybrides System vor, d.h. mittels asymmetrischer Verschlüsselung wird der Signalisierungspfad sehr aufwendig aufgebaut. Im Anschluß daran kann die Verbindung weniger aufwendig mittels symmetrischer Kryptographie mehrfach genutzt werden, ohne den Schutz der Kommunikationsbeziehung aufzugeben.

2 Mehrstufige Speicherung mit Pseudonymen

Es wird die in [KeFo_95], [KFJP_96] und [FeJP_96] formulierte Idee aufgegriffen, Aufenthaltsinformationen mehrstufig und pseudonym zu speichern. Neue Ansätze bezüglich des Generierens der Pseudonyme werden vorgestellt.

2.1 Das allgemeine Prinzip

Gegeben sei ein Vermittlungsnetz. Die Knoten, hier Register genannt, speichern und verwalten die Lokalisierungsinformationen für die sich in bestimmten geographischen Bereichen befindlichen Teilnehmer. Teilnehmer am Kommunikationsverkehr sind unter einem definierten Namen, ihrer MSISDN, erreichbar. Ein Teilnehmer generiert mehrere Pseudonyme für seine Identität und hinterlegt in jedem Register ein Pseudonympaar. Nur das Register ist in der Lage, ein eingehendes Pseudonym mit einem ausgehenden zu verknüpfen. Diese Zuordnung wird im Text durch einen Pfeil $P_i \rightarrow P_{i+1}$ dargestellt. Im Wurzelregister R_0 ist der Teilnehmer unter seiner wahren Identität, der MSISDN, bekannt.

Jedes Register R_i muß also ein Pseudonym P_i sowie die Adresse A_{i+1} und das Folgepseudonym P_{i+1} des nächsten Registers R_{i+1} speichern. Das bedeutet, jeweils zwei Register teilen ein Geheimnis. Wenn man in der Lage ist, alle in den Registern gespeicherten Informationen zusammenzusetzen, so entsteht eine über Pseudonyme verkettete Liste, welche die Lokalisierungsinformation für die MS beschreibt.

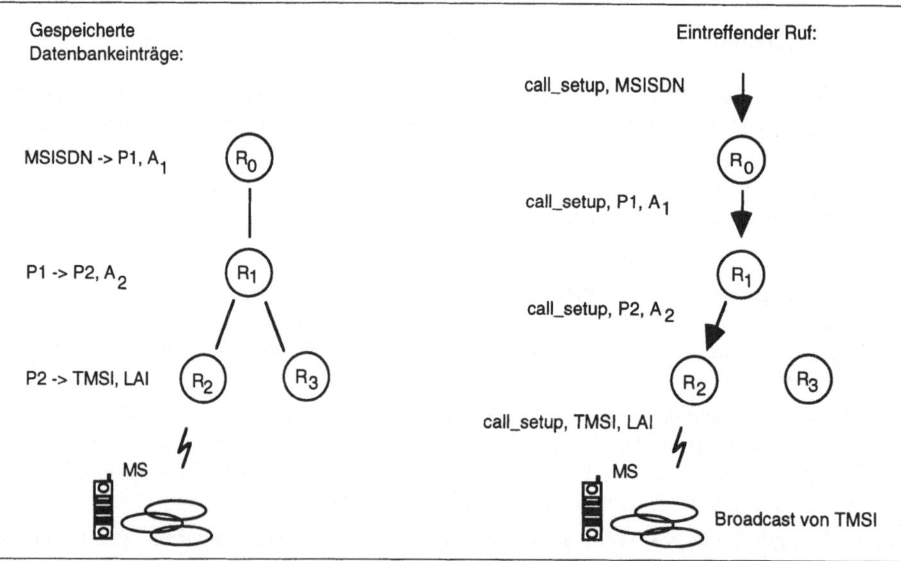

Bild 3: a) Beispiel für mehrstufige Verwaltung   b) Erreichen einer MS

Bei einem ankommenden Ruf für MSISDN wird die Nachricht "call_setup" durch das Netz geschickt. Eine bei R_i ankommende Nachricht wird anhand des eingehenden Pseudonyms dem gespeicherten Folgepseudonym zugeordnet und an die Adresse von R_{i+1} weitergeleitet. Das letzte Register der Kette speichert für sein Pseudonym die LAI und eine vom Teilnehmer generierte implizite Adresse TMSI (Temporary Mobile Subscriber Identity) für die Paging-Nachricht auf der Funkschnittstelle. Im Bild 3 kennt R_2 die Zuordnung $P2 \rightarrow TMSI, LAI$.

Einem Register ist nur das gespeicherte Pseudonympaar P_i und P_{i+1} bekannt. In unserem Beispiel weiß der Betreiber des Registers R_1 nur, daß jemand mit dem Pseudonym P1 sich in dem durch A_2 beschriebenen geographischen Bereich aufhalten muß, an welchen es die Nachricht mit dem Pseudonym P2 weiterleitet. Selbst wenn ein Register korrumpiert ist, erhält es keine Information über die wahre Identität des Teilnehmers.

2.2 Angreifermodell

Wie in 1.2 und 1.3 beschrieben, ermöglicht die Eingliederung verschiedener unabhängiger Kommunikationssysteme in ein Gesamtsystem die Annahme, daß die Register der einzelnen Systeme zur Datenverwaltung nicht heimlich miteinander kooperieren. Aus dieser Annahme kann ein Angreifermodell abgeleitet werden. Ein Angreifermodell definiert die Stärke möglicher Angreifer. Ein System sollte möglichst starken Angriffen widerstehen können. Folgende Annahmen werden getroffen:

- Jegliche Kommunikation im Netz ist beobachtbar.

- In den Registern kann nicht gelesen werden, d.h. eingehende und ausgehende Pseudonyme sind nicht verkettbar.

- Die Register kooperieren nicht heimlich miteinander.

- Zwei benachbarte Register teilen ein Geheimnis, ein Pseudonym.

Um diese Forderungen zu erfüllen, sind an Register und Pseudonyme spezielle Anforderungen zu stellen. Kapitel 3 beschäftigt sich mit der Generierung der Pseudonyme.

Die Register empfangen und senden Nachrichten im Batch (auch Schub genannt), d.h. es werden entsprechend der Batchgröße Nachrichten erst gesammelt und dann *zu einem Zeittakt zusammen* weitergeleitet. Sonst wäre eine zeitliche Verkettung der Nachrichten möglich. Auch das Aussehen der Nachrichten muß sich ändern. Hierzu wird das den MIXen zugrundeliegende Konzept [Chau_81, PfPW_88, PfPW_91] genutzt: Ein MIX-Netz besteht aus mehreren MIXen und dient dem Schutz der Kommunikationsbeziehung zwischen Sender und Empfänger. Die Nachrichten werden im Batch von einem MIX zum anderen geschickt. In den MIXen erfolgt ein Umkodieren und Umsortieren der Nachrichten, so daß keine Rückschlüsse von den ein- auf die ausgehenden Nachrichten möglich sind. Aus diesem Grund wird auch die Länge der Nachrichten im gesamten Netz beibehalten, was als längentreue Umkodierung bezeichnet wird.

2.3 Verwaltung der Aufenthaltsinformation

Verwalten von Aufenthaltsinformationen (location management) bei der Signalisierung heißt Registrieren eines Teilnehmers, Aktualisieren seiner Aufenthaltsinformationen in den Registern und Abmelden.

2.3.1 Aufenthaltsregistrierung

Die Aufenthaltsregistrierung besteht darin, den Knoten R_i (i = 0...n) mitzuteilen, welchen Eintrag sie vorzunehmen haben. So kann später die Mobilstation effizient und mit geringem Signalisierungsaufwand erreicht werden.

Hierzu muß die Mobilstation jedoch wissen, welche R_i (i=0...n) für eine Registrierung in Frage kommen. Es ist außerdem wichtig, daß die MS zwischen vielen R_i unterschiedlicher Betreiber in jeder Ebene wählen kann (siehe 1.2). Dadurch wird die Vertrauenswürdigkeit verbessert. Die verfügbaren Register der verschiedenen Aufenthaltsgebiete können gebroadcastet oder durch die Teilnehmer aus einer Datenbasis abgefragt werden. Das Lesen aus dieser Datenbank muß natürlich so geschehen, daß nicht erkannt werden kann, welche Einträge für welche LAs gelesen wurden. Eine mögliche Lösung dieses Problems ist das in [CoBi_95] vorgestellte "Blinde Lesen". Bei diesem Verfahren wird gewährleistet, daß die Interessensdaten der Lesenden nicht offenbar werden.

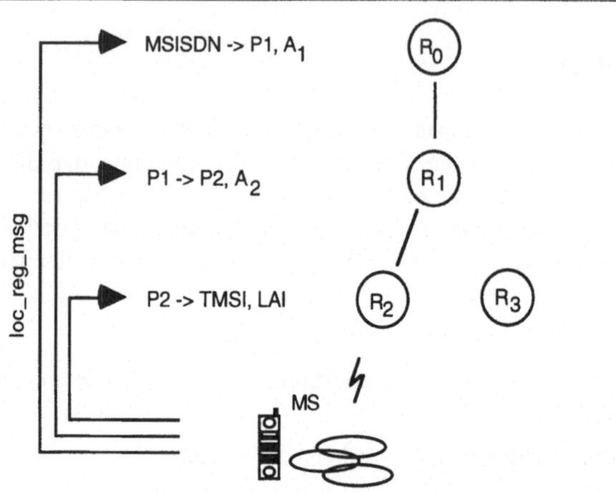

Bild 4: Location Registration

2.3.2 Aktualisieren der Register

Beim LUP erfragt die MS die für das Aufenthaltsgebiet verfügbaren Register (siehe 2.3.1), aus denen sie nach bestimmten Kriterien, wie z.B. Lastsituation im Netz oder Vertrauenswürdigkeit des Betreibers, auswählt. Daraus ermittelt sie, in welchen Registern Einträge vorzunehmen bzw. zu erneuern sind und berechnet die zu signalisierenden Nachrichten.

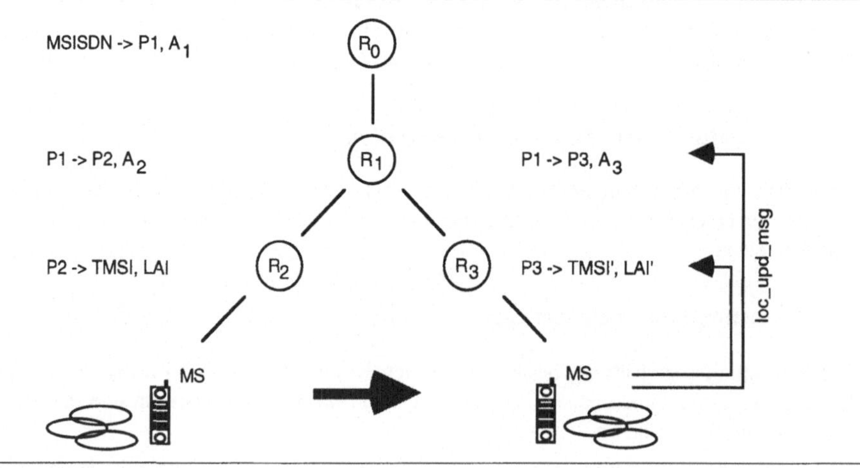

Bild 5: Location Update

Befinden sich die R_i mit wachsendem i näher beim LA, wird Signalisierungsaufwand im Fernbereich gespart, da nur die sich ändernden Lokalisierungsinformationen zu aktualisieren sind. Im Bild 5 bleibt z.B. der Eintrag von R_0 unverändert.

2.3.3 Abmelden

Die Daten der nicht mehr benutzten Register könnten nach einer bestimmten Zeit verfallen, oder es wird mittels einer Nachricht "Löschen" dies den entsprechenden Registern mitgeteilt.

Letzteres erscheint sinnvoll, da die Verbindung sonst auch dann aufgelöst werden könnte, wenn der Pfad längere Zeit nicht genutzt und die Zeitgrenze überschritten wird.

3   Pseudonymverwaltung

Einmal in den Registern hinterlegt, bilden die Pseudonyme einen *Signalisierungspfad*. Ziel der Verwendung der Pseudonyme als Kennzeichen ist es, einen einmal aufgebauten Pfad für die folgende Signalisierung (call setup, location update) effizient nutzen zu können. Ein Pfad wird mehrfach genutzt, ohne erneut den Registrierungsprozeß zu durchlaufen.

3.1   Forderungen an die Pseudonyme

- Das Hinterlegen der Pseudonyme in den verschiedenen Registern muß so erfolgen, daß nicht zugeordnet werden kann, welche MS die Nachricht gesendet hat. Sie müssen anonym hinterlegt werden.

- Um replay-Angriffe zu verhindern, darf ein Pseudonym nur einmal verwendet werden.

- Der Teilnehmer muß die Datensätze in den Registern aktualisieren können, da ein LUP immer von ihm initiiert wird.

- Die Gültigkeit der Pseudonyme ist zeitlich begrenzt.

Die Forderungen können durch die Verwendung eines "Zählers" (oder einer Zeitbasis) erfüllt werden, indem nach jeder Pseudonymverwendung (bzw. einer abgelaufenen Zeit) ein neues Pseudonym über einen Pseudozufallszahlengenerator generiert wird. Es wäre auch möglich, über eine global einheitliche Zeitbasis T die Pseudonyme synchron weiterzuschalten. Die Weiterschaltung wäre dann unabhängig von den zu übermittelnden Nachrichten. Wenn das Schalten über eine global bekannte Funktion f erfolgt, muß die Mobilstation beim Einbuchen bzw. LUP einen Initialwert[1] $P_{i,init}$ senden, über den die Pseudonyme nach der Vorschrift $P_i' := f(T,P_{i,init})$ gebildet werden. Das Hinterlegen der Pseudonyme könnte durch MIXe erfolgen. Das bedeutet, jedes Register ist Empfänger einer Nachricht $[P_i \rightarrow P_{i+1}, A_{i+1}]$. Diese wird unter Wahrung der Anonymität der MS von ihr über das MIX-Netz an die Registerknoten übermittelt.

Statt jedes Pseudonym separat zu hinterlegen, könnten die Register zusätzliche Funktionen übernehmen. Ähnlich zu den MIXen sammeln die Register bereits die ankommenden Verbindungswünsche und schicken sie im Batch weiter. Die MS könnte denselben Weg nutzen, um von ihr generierte Pseudonyme in den entsprechenden Registern zu hinterlegen.

Im Gegensatz zu den MIXen sind die Register an geographische Bereiche gebunden. Durch Batchbetrieb und längentreue Umkodierung der Nachrichten kann jedoch keine Zuordnung erfolgen, vorausgesetzt die Anzahl der übermittelten Nachrichten ist groß genug. Gegebenenfalls

---

[1]   z.B. eine Zufallszahl, entspricht dem beim Einbuchen hinterlegten Pseudonym

müssen in den Registern bedeutungslose Nachrichten generiert werden, um diese Bedingung zu gewährleisten. Die Register kennen nur die Adresse des jeweils nächsten Registers. Eine Verkettung der Lokalisierungsinformation ist nur dann möglich, wenn die Register verdeckt zusammenarbeiten. Dies widerspricht aber dem Angreifermodell.

3.2 Generieren der Pseudonyme

3.2.1 Aufenthaltsregistrierung

Die Pseudonyme werden von der MS generiert und bei der Aufenthaltsregistrierung hinterlegt. In den Registern soll jeweils ein Datensatz $[k_i,P_i{\rightarrow}P_{i+1},A_{i+1}]$ gespeichert werden. Hierzu wird an ein Register R_i jeweils eine Nachricht $m_i := c_i(A_{i-1},k_i,P_i{\rightarrow}P_{i+1},A_{i+1},m_{i-1})$ geschickt. A_{i-1} ist die Adresse des Registers, an welches "loc_reg_msg,m_{i-1}" weitergeleitet wird. k_i ist der zum späteren Umkodieren der Nachrichten notwendige symmetrische Schlüssel. P_i und P_{i+1} sind die in den Registern gespeicherten Pseudonyme. A_{i+1} ist die für die Signalisierung eines Verbindungswunsches (call_setup) notwendige nächste Zieladresse.

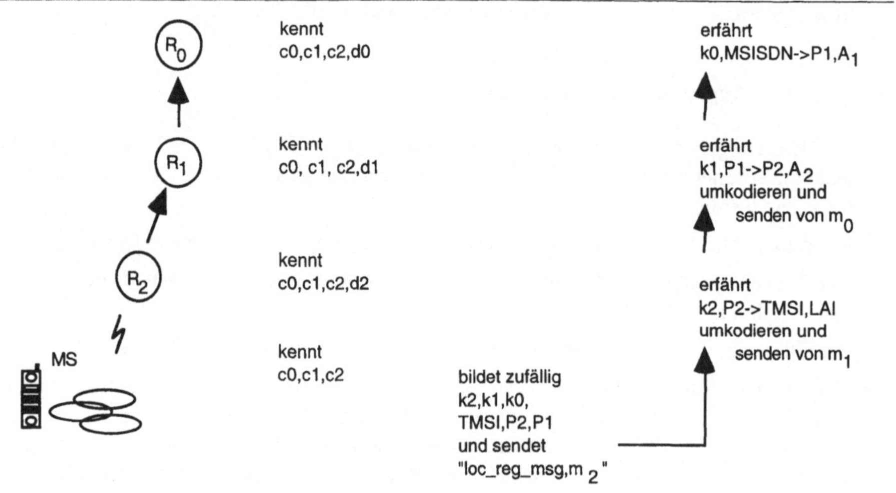

Bild 6: Veranschaulichung des Einbuchens

Der Teilnehmer benötigt ein Kennzeichen, um die Datensätze im Register zur Pseudonymberechnung bzw. -hinterlegung nach einer Signalisierung ansprechen zu können. Solche Registerkennzeichen müssen deshalb vom Teilnehmer generiert werden bzw. dem Teilnehmer bekannt sein. Es bietet sich an, den symmetrischen Schlüssel, der im Datensatz enthalten ist, hierfür zu nutzen (siehe auch 3.3).

Will eine MS einbuchen, wird nach Auswahl der zu durchlaufenden R_i mit i=0...n sowie dem Generieren der Pseudonyme für die R_i eine Nachricht m_n folgendermaßen gebildet.

$$m_0 := c_0(k_0,MSISDN{\rightarrow}P_1,A_1)$$

$$m_i := c_i(A_{i-1},k_i,P_i{\rightarrow}P_{i+1},A_{i+1},m_{i-1}) \qquad \text{für i=1...n}$$

MS schickt die Nachricht $N := $ "loc_reg_msg,m_n" an das erste, ihr zugängliche Register R_n, wobei A_{n+1} der eigenen Ortsinformation, der LAI, und P_{n+1} der TMSI entspricht.

Kommt also m_i bei R_i an, so wird m_i mit dem privaten Schlüssel d_i (passend zu c_i) des Registers entschlüsselt. Die in m_i mitgeschickten Pseudonyme P_i und P_{i+1} werden gemeinsam mit k_i und A_{i+1} als Datensatz in R_i gespeichert. A_{i+1} ist die Adresse, an die später ein bei R_i anliegender Verbindungswunsch weitergeleitet werden soll. Der Rest der Nachricht wird an die beim Entschlüsseln gefundene Folgeadresse A_{i-1} mit dem Vermerk "loc_reg_msg" weitergeschickt.

R_0 erkennt sich als Empfänger, da keine Adresse angegeben ist, an die die angekommene Nachricht weiterzuleiten ist. In R_0 werden die MSISDN, die Abbildung auf das erste Pseudonym P_1 und die beim "call_setup" notwendige erste Zieladresse A_1 gespeichert.

3.2.2 Aufenthaltsaktualisierung

Die MS bewegt sich von einem LA in ein anderes. Um am neuen Aufenthaltsort erreichbar zu sein, muß der Signalisierungspfad aktualisiert, also teilweise neu aufgebaut werden. Die MS generiert für die neuen Register die relevanten Daten. Entsprechend dem Einbuchen werden diese Informationen in der Nachricht "loc_update,m_m" kodiert, die an das Register R'_m im neuen LA geschickt wird[2].

Ein Vorteil der mehrstufigen Speicherung ist, daß nicht mehr der gesamte Pfad neu aufgebaut werden muß. In den neuen Registern erfolgt im Prinzip eine Aufenthaltsregistrierung, wirklich aktualisiert wird nur das tiefste, für alten und neuen Signalisierungspfad gleichgebliebene Register R_k. In R_k wird ein neuer Datensatz (z.B. in Bild 7 [k1,P1$\rightarrow$P3,A3]) eingetragen.

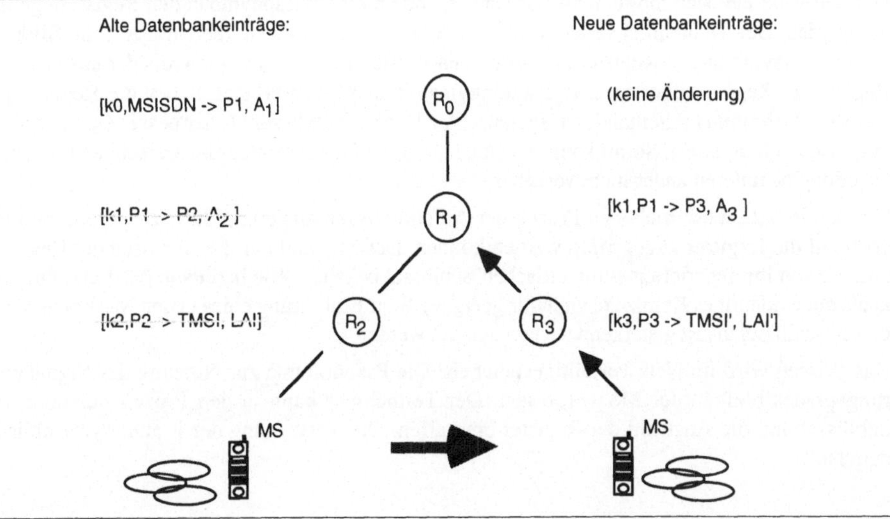

Bild 7: Beispiel für konkretisiertes Location Update

Der Pfad wird umgelenkt. Am mitgesendeten Vermerk "loc_update" erkennt das Register im Umlenkpunkt die ankommende Nachricht. Um die symmetrisch verschlüsselte Nachricht entschlüsseln zu können, muß es alle gespeicherten Schlüssel durchprobieren. Am gleichbleibenden k_k bzw. P_k wird beim Signalisieren eines Verbindungswunsches der neue Signalisierungspfad zu R'_{k+1} mit A'_{k+1} erkannt. In R_k wird die Nachricht mit der neuen Folgeadresse A'_{k+1}

---

[2] Als Index wird hier "m" verwendet, da die Anzahl der Register im neuen Signalisierungspfad nicht zwingend gleich der Anzahl "n" im alten Pfad ist. Es kann auch m>n oder m<n gelten.

und dem zugehörigen neuen Initialwert P'_{k+1} für das nächste Register eingetragen. Die Nachricht m_m wird wie folgt gebildet:

$$m_k \quad := \quad k'_k(P_k{\rightarrow}P'_{k+1},A'_{k+1})$$

$$m_i \quad := \quad c'_i(A'_{i-1},k'_i,P'_i{\rightarrow}P'_{i+1},A'_{i+1},m_{i-1}) \qquad \text{für } i=k+1...m$$

wobei P'_{m+1} der neuen TMSI' und A'_{m+1} der neuen LAI' entspricht. Die Datensätze der Register des alten, nicht mehr benötigten Teils des Signalisierungspfades, also der Register R_i (mit $i=k+1...n$), können wiederum durch eine Löschmeldung freigegeben werden, bzw. sie verfallen nach einer bestimmten Zeit.

Da die Pseudonyme nur einmal verwendet werden, entsteht für die MS zusätzlicher Aufwand. Sie muß die an die Register geschickten Pseudonyme speichern und bei jeder Neuberechnung der Pseudonyme den gespeicherten Stand aktualisieren. Es bietet sich also die oben beschriebene Variante der global einheitlichen Zeitbasis an. Dann braucht erst bei einer Aufenthaltsaktualisierung die in 3.1 erwähnte Vorschrift zur Berechnung von P_i angewendet zu werden. Eine andere Möglichkeit wird im folgenden Abschnitt beschrieben.

3.3   Effizientes Generieren der Pseudonyme

Wenn der Teilnehmer alle Pseudonyme generieren muß, so entsteht beträchtlicher Übertragungsaufwand, da bei der Aufenthaltsregistrierung asymmetrisch verschlüsselt werden und die Längentreue gewährleistet sein muß.

Der Aufwand läßt sich möglicherweise senken, indem die Pseudonyme in den Registern gebildet werden. Der Teilnehmer generiert nur den Startwert für das erste Register. Auf die Bildung der Pseudonyme in den Registern hat er keinen Einfluß mehr. Damit ein Outsider aus den von Register zu Register übertragenen Pseudonymen kein Wissen erlangt, haben die Register jeweils ein Geheimnis miteinander ausgetauscht, z.B. eine Zufallszahl (oder besser einen kryptographischen Schlüssel). Somit kann ein Outsider keine Folgepseudonyme berechnen und auch Pseudonyme untereinander nicht verketten.

Um den in 3.2.2 beschriebenen Prozeß der Aufenthaltsaktualisierung durchzuführen, muß jedoch auf die Register zugegriffen werden können. Der MS sind nur die Adressen der Register und die von ihr generierten symmetrischen Schlüssel bekannt. Wie bereits in 3.2.1 erwähnt, ist k_i als ein eindeutiges Kennzeichen dafür geeignet. Statt Einführung eines neuen Merkmals kann dieser Schlüssel als Registerkennzeichen genutzt werden.

Das Wissen wird im Netz verteilt gespeichert. Die Pseudonyme zur Nutzung des Signalisierungspfades bleiben der MS verborgen. Der Teilnehmer kann in den Prozeß nur über die Schlüssel und die Auswahl der Register eingreifen. Die Verwaltung der Pseudonyme obliegt dem Netz.

3.3.1   Aufenthaltsregistrierung

Will sich eine MS im Netz einbuchen, werden die zu durchlaufenden Register R_i ($i=0...n$) ausgewählt. Die MS schickt die Nachricht "loc_reg_msg,m_n,T_{init}" an das erste Register R_n. T_{init} ist der Initialwert für die Pseudonymbildung.

$$m_0 \quad := \quad c_0(k_0,\text{MSISDN},A_1)$$

$$m_i \quad := \quad c_i(A_{i-1},k_i,A_{i+1},m_{i-1}) \qquad\qquad\qquad \text{für } i=1...n$$

wobei A_{n+1} der LAI entspricht. Aus T_{init} wird das erste Pseudonym für R_n gebildet und als Pseudonympaar $P_n{\rightarrow}T_{init}$ gespeichert.

Vom Register R_i wird m_i sowie ein in R_{i+1} gebildetes Pseudonym P_{i+1} empfangen. Als erstes wird mittels privatem Schlüssel d_i die Nachricht entschlüsselt. Die Entschlüsselung $d_i(c_i(A_{i-1},k_i,A_{i+1},m_{i-1})$ ergibt die nächste Registeradresse A_{i-1}, den symmetrischen Schlüssel bzw. das Registerkennzeichen k_i, die Rückadresse A_{i+1} für das call_setup und die Restnachricht m_{i-1}.

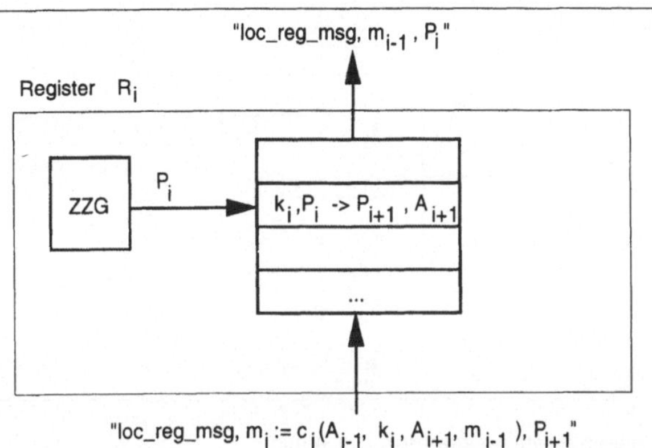

Bild 8: Allgemeines Schema zur Generierung der Startwerte bei der Registrierung

Durch "loc_reg_msg" initiiert, generiert das Register R_i unabhängig vom empfangenen P_{i+1} ein Pseudonym P_i mittels eines Zufallszahlengenerators (ZZG). Der Teilnehmer hat also keinen Einfluß auf die Pseudonymbildung. Nur R_i kann P_i und P_{i+1} miteinander verketten, beide Pseudonyme sowie Schlüssel und Rückadresse werden als Datensatz gespeichert. Die Restnachricht m_{i-1}, der Vermerk "loc_reg_msg" und das im Register gebildete P_i werden an das nächste Register übermittelt.

3.3.2 Aufenthaltsaktualisierung

Der Teilnehmer kennt die von ihm in den Registern hinterlegten k_i. Bei Änderung des Signalisierungspfades wird über die neuen Register R'_i mit i=m...k+1 bis zum k-ten Register R_k eine Aktualisierungsnachricht übermittelt.

An R'_m wird dabei die folgende Nachricht N := loc_update,m_m,T'_{init} geschickt, mit

$$m_k \quad := \quad c_k(k_k,A_k)$$
$$m_i \quad := \quad c'_i(A'_{i-1},k'_i,A'_{i+1},m_{i-1}) \qquad \text{für } i=k+1...m$$

Das Bilden der Pseudonyme erfolgt entsprechend dem Einbuchen.

3.3.3 Signalisieren eines Verbindungswunsches

Bei der Nutzung des Pfades zum Signalisieren (call_setup) werden eventuell nicht öffentliche Signalisierungsdaten (z.B. die Nummer eines ihn rufenden Teilnehmers oder spezielle Gebühreninformationen) übertragen. Diese werden mittels der in den Registern enthaltenen Schlüssel k_i von jedem Register verschlüsselt. Nur der Teilnehmer selbst, der alle k_i kennt, kann wieder entschlüsseln und somit die Daten lesen.

Nach einmaliger Nutzung des Pfades müssen wiederum neue Pseudonyme generiert werden. Das bedeutet, der Datensatz ist zu aktualisieren. Wie bereits erwähnt, darf der Algorithmus zum Generieren der Pseudonyme nur den jeweils beteiligten Registern bekannt sein. Wird wie im

Bild 9 hierfür ein Pseudozufallszahlengenerator (PZZG) verwendet, so besteht das Geheimnis zwischen den Registern R_{i-1} und R_i im Zufallszahlenanteil zz1, und zwischen R_i und R_{i+1} ist es entsprechend zz2.

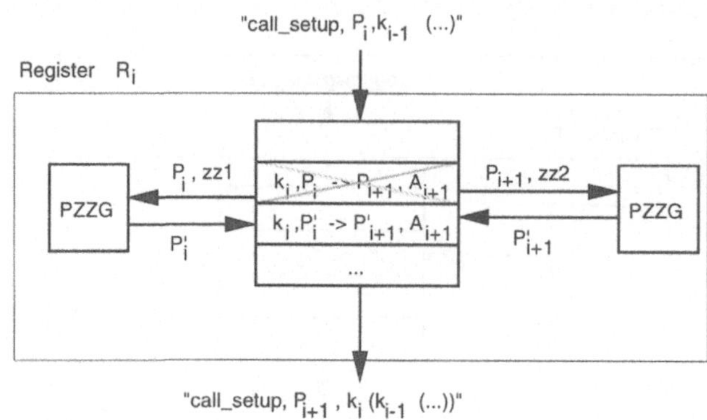

Bild 9: Bilden der neuen Pseudonyme beim call_setup

Das Problem von Replay-Angriffen wurde bereits erwähnt. Ein Angreifer könnte eine Verbindungswunschnachricht abfangen und erneut senden. Würden die Pseudonyme nach einmaligem Zugriff nicht wechseln, könnte ein Angreifer eine Nachricht mehrmals schicken und würde aufgrund derselben Ausgabenachricht Kenntnisse über den Signalisierungspfad und somit auch über den Aufenthaltsort der MS erlangen.

3.3.4   Einsparen von Übertragungsaufwand

Beim Übertragen von Daten wird Bandbreite benötigt. Dem Register ist das Vorgängerregister sowie das nachfolgende Register bekannt, da alle Kommunikation im Netz abhörbar ist. Deshalb ist das Mitschicken der Rückadressen nicht zwingend erforderlich. Ein Register R_i kann anhand des Senders R_{i+1} selbständig die Adresse A_{i+1} des späteren Empfängers speichern.

Eine weitere Einsparung kann darin bestehen, daß der Teilnehmer statt der Schlüssel und Pseudonyme nur jeweils eine kurze Zufallsbitfolge schickt, aus der dann die relevanten Daten von den Registern selbst generiert werden. Natürlich muß hier ein solcher Algorithmus verfügbar sein, der keinem Outsider bzw. anderen Registern das Nachvollziehen der Berechnungen ermöglicht.

4   Diskussion des Angreifermodells

4.1   Bisheriges Angreifermodell

Bisher wurde bei der Diskussion der Sicherheit des vorgeschlagenen Verfahrens das in Kapitel 2.2 aufgestellte Angreifermodell benutzt. Die grundlegende Annahme in diesem Modell lautet, daß die Register R_i nicht kooperieren. Damit ist der stärkste Angreifer ein Register, denn es kann, wie jeder außenstehende Angreifer, den Netzverkehr beobachten und besitzt zusätzlich noch Informationen für die Pseudonymverkettung im eigenen Register. Der dadurch entstehende Informationsgewinn ist gering. Das Register R_0 kann als Angreifer ermitteln, in welchem Register der Ebene 1 der Teilnehmer angemeldet ist. Ein anderes Register R_i kann 2

Pseudonyme verketten, aber keiner Identität zuordnen. Das Verfahren ist demzufolge unter den getroffenen Festlegungen sicher. In diesem Kapitel wird ein schärferes Angreifermodell betrachtet und diskutiert, inwieweit das vorgestellte Verfahren diesem standhält.

4.2 Ein schärferes Angreifermodell

4.2.1 Angreifermodell

Das in 4.1 beschriebene Angreifermodell setzt ein wenig korrumpiertes System voraus. Durch das Angreifermodell des MIX-Netzes angeregt, wird dem Kommunikationsnetz im folgenden ein schärferes Angreifermodell zugrundegelegt.

- Jegliche Kommunikation im Netz ist beobachtbar.
- Von n Registern kooperieren maximal n-1 Register.

Die folgenden Überlegungen werden zeigen, daß unter diesen schärferen Annahmen das vorgeschlagene Verfahren gebrochen werden kann. Es existieren jedoch Möglichkeiten, den Angriff zu erschweren!

4.2.2 Ein Angriff

Unter dem Angreifermodell aus 4.2.1 ist folgender Angriff denkbar und erfolgreich: Ein Register, z.B. R_k soll überbrückt werden. Man nehme an, R_k sei das einzige vertrauenswürdige Register auf dem Signalisierungspfad des Teilnehmers. Der Angreifer kennt durch seine Mächtigkeit bereits alle Pseudonymumsetzungen außerhalb von R_k und natürlich das zwischen R_{k-1} und R_k bzw. R_k und R_{k+1} ausgetauschte Geheimnis.

Wird dem angegriffenen Teilnehmer signalisiert, so kann der Angreifer den Ausgabebatch B1 von R_k beobachten und speichern. Er kann aber die in R_k gespeicherten P_k und P_{k+1} nicht verketten. Nach dem Weiterleiten der Nachricht generiert R_k neue Pseudonyme P'_k und P'_{k+1} (entsprechend 3.3.3). Wird dem angegriffenen Teilnehmer *erneut* signalisiert, speichert der Angreifer wiederum den Ausgabebatch B2. Da R_{k+1} aufgrund des mit R_k ausgetauschten Geheimnisses die Pseudonyme P_{k+1} und P'_{k+1} ebenfalls verketten kann, kann jetzt das Register R_{k+1} prüfen, wie oft P_{k+1} in B1 und P'_{k+1} in B2 enthalten ist. Ist diese Zuordnung nur für ein Paar erfolgreich, so hat der Angreifer damit die Pseudonyme P_k und P_{k+1} verkettet und somit R_k überbrückt.

Der gesamte Signalisierungspfad läßt sich vom ersten bis zum letzten Register nachvollziehen. Mit diesem Angriff ist ein Teilnehmer somit lokalisierbar und verfolgbar, wenn nur ihm in zwei Batchen B1 und B2 signalisiert wird.

Dieser Angriff ist derart verallgemeinerbar, daß bereits die Kooperation zweier beliebig weit auseinanderliegender Register genügt, um den Aufenthaltsort eines Teilnehmers bei erneuter Signalisierung offenzulegen.

4.2.3 Erschweren des Angriffs

Man kann den oben beschriebenen Angriff erschweren, wenn man die Register im Pool- statt Batchbetrieb verwendet. Beim Poolbetrieb werden im Register Nachrichten gesammelt, bis eine vorher definierte Poolgröße erreicht worden ist. Danach wird für jede eingehende Nachricht eine zufällig gewählte freigegeben. Der Angreifer kann dadurch den Ausgabezeitpunkt der Nachrichten nicht berechnen. Sein Aufwand steigt. Außerdem ist es möglich, daß die zweite Signalisierungsnachricht vor der ersten ausgegeben wird. Die Wahrscheinlichkeit steigt, daß während des Angriffs noch mindestens einem anderen Teilnehmer zweimal signalisiert wird.

Der Nachteil des Poolbetriebs liegt in der Dienstqualität, da keine maximale Durchlaufverzögerung der Signalisierung garantiert werden kann.

Betrachtet man die in den Registern gespeicherten Teilnehmer als Anonymitätsgruppe, läßt sich der in 4.2.2 beschriebene Angriff bereits im Batchbetrieb erschweren, wenn für jeden Teilnehmer der Gruppe eine Signalisierungsnachricht in jedem Batch enthalten ist. Dies wird beispielsweise beim Verfahren der ISDN-MIXe [PfPW_91] angewendet. Unter Anonymitätsgruppe versteht man eine Gruppe, deren Zusammensetzung sich während des bestehenden Signalisierungspfades nicht ändert. Durch diese Forderungen ist der Einsatz in einem Mobilkommunikationsnetz mit Terminal Mobility jedoch nicht mehr effektiv möglich. In Situationen mit geringer Teilnehmermobilität ist ein statischer Signalisierpfad vorteilhaft, da er dann potentiell mehrfach genutzt wird. Solche Mobilitätsmuster findet man z.B. im Bereich Personal Mobility, wenn sich ein Teilnehmer (etwa an seinem Arbeitsplatz) für längere Zeit an einem Ort aufhält. Da hier die Abstände zwischen zwei Aufenthaltsaktualisierungen meist größer sind, bleiben auch die Anonymitätsgruppen über einen längeren Zeitraum bestehen.

5   Schlußbemerkungen

Ein Mobilkommunikationssystem wurde beschrieben, das bei der Verwaltung von Aufenthaltsinformationen die Anonymität der Teilnehmer in der Signalisierungsphase gewährleistet, jedoch die Erreichbarkeit nicht einschränkt.

Eine Abschätzung der Leistung des Verfahrens zeigt folgendes:

Durch die Pseudonymverwaltung erhöht sich der Speicheraufwand gegenüber existierenden Systemen. Die Datenschutzforderung nach Vertraulichkeit des Aufenthaltsortes wird erfüllt, natürlich ist damit höherer Realisierungsaufwand des Kommunikationssystems verbunden.

Der Managementaufwand für die Mobilstation soll möglichst gering gehalten werden. Unter 3.3 wird eine Möglichkeit dazu durch effizientes Generieren der Pseudonyme vorgestellt.

Es wird angestrebt, daß auf jeder Ebene zu jeder Zeit immer genügend Register unterschiedlicher Betreiber zur Auswahl stehen. Erst dadurch wird die Vertrauenswürdigkeit gewährleistet. Durch diese Auswahlmöglichkeit kann außerdem auf unterschiedliche Lastsituationen im Netz reagiert werden.

Die Aufenthaltsinformationen werden pseudonym und mehrstufig verwaltet. Sind die Teilnehmer mobil, so erfolgt aufgrund der mehrstufigen Speicherung die Aufenthaltsaktualisierung in der Regel nur innerhalb eines Teilnetzes. Dann muß nicht im gesamten Netz signalisiert werden.

Die Verwendung hybrider kryptographischer Systeme ermöglicht nach einmaligem Aufbau eines Signalisierungspfades dessen mehrmalige effiziente Nutzung. Im ersten Schritt werden symmetrische Schlüssel in den Vermittlungsknoten (Registern) mittels eines asymmetrischen Verfahrens hinterlegt. In den folgenden Schritten können dann die symmetrischen Schlüssel genutzt werden. Beim Location Update kann Aufwand gespart werden, da nur ein Teil des Signalisierungspfades erneuert werden muß. Im Umlenkpunkt kann sogar symmetrisch gearbeitet werden. Durch hybride Systeme werden die Vorteile von asymmetrischer und symmetrischer Kryptographie miteinander verknüpft. Die Verwendung kryptographischer Funktionen erhöht jedoch den Signalisierungsaufwand.

Die Diskussion eines schärferen Angreifermodells zeigt, daß Modifikationen ursprünglicher Annahmen auch Veränderungen im Verfahren nach sich ziehen. Je mehr Stärke den Angreifern zugestanden wird, desto mehr Forderungen werden an das Verfahren gestellt. Bei nicht miteinander kooperierenden Registern werden keine besonderen Annahmen über die Teilnehmer getroffen. Wird das Angreifermodell jedoch modifiziert (siehe Kapitel 4), hält das Verfahren

Angriffen nur stand, wenn die Teilnehmer Anonymitätsgruppen zugeordnet werden. Eine andere Variante wird in [FeJP_96] aufgezeigt, wo die Unverkettbarkeit der Registerinformationen durch zwischengeschaltete Mixe gewährleistet wird. Aufgrund verschiedener Einsatzmöglichkeiten ist die Betrachtung verschiedener Szenarien wichtig.

6 Literatur

Chau_81   David Chaum: Untraceable Electronic Mail, Return Addresses, and Digital Pseudonyms; Communications of the ACM 24/2 (1981) 84-88.

CoBi_95   David A. Cooper, Kenneth P. Birman: Preserving Privacy in a Network of Mobile Computers; 1995 IEEE Symposium on Research in Security and Privacy, IEEE Computer Society Press, Los Alamitos 1995, 26-38.

FeJP_96   Hannes Federrath, Anja Jerichow, Andreas Pfitzmann: Mixes in mobile communication systems: location management with privacy, Proc. of the Workshop on Information Hiding, Cambridge (UK), Univ.of Cambridge, Isaac Newton Institute, 30.5.-1.6.96.

FJKP_95   Hannes Federrath, Anja Jerichow, Dogan Kesdogan, Andreas Pfitzmann: Security in Public Mobile Communication Networks; Proc. of the IFIP TC 6 International Workshop on Personal Wireless Communications, Verlag der Augustinus Buchhandlung Aachen, 1995, 105-116.

GSM_93   ETSI: GSM Recommendations: GSM 01.02 - 12.21; February 1993, Release 92.

Hets_93   Thomas Hetschold: Aufbewahrbarkeit von Erreichbarkeits- und Schlüsselinformation im Gewahrsam des Endbenutzers unter Erhaltung der GSM-Funktionalität eines Funknetzes; GMD-Studien no. 222, Oktober 1993.

KeFo_95   Dogan Kesdogan, Xavier Fouletier: Secure Location Information Management in Cellular Radio Systems; IEEE Wireless Communication System Symposium 95, Proceedings, Long Island (1995) 35-46.

KFJP_96   Dogan Kesdogan, Hannes Federrath, Anja Jerichow, Andreas Pfitzmann: Location management strategies increasing privacy in mobile communication; 12th IFIP International Conference on Information Security (IFIP/Sec '96), Chapman & Hall, London 1996, 37-38.

Mitt_94   H. Mitts: Universal Mobile Telecommunication Systems - Mobile access to Broadband ISDN; in Broadland Islands '94: Connecting with the End-User, W. Bauerfeld, O. Spaniol, F. Williams (Editors) 1994, 203-209.

MüSt_95   Günter Müller, Frank Stoll: Der Freiburger Kommunikationsassistent - Sicherheit in multimedialen Kommunikationsnetzen durch nutzerbezogene Dezentralisation. Dokumentation zum Symposium "Multimedia und Datenschutz" des Berliner Datenschutzbeauftragen, Internationale Funkausstellung Berlin, August 1995, 1-16.

Pfit_93   Andreas Pfitzmann: Technischer Datenschutz in öffentlichen Funknetzen; Datenschutz und Datensicherung DuD 17/8 (1993) 451-463.

PfPW_88   Andreas Pfitzmann, Birgit Pfitzmann, Michael Waidner: Datenschutz garantierende offene Kommunikationsnetze; Informatik-Spektrum 11/3 (1988) 118-142.

PfPW_91   Andreas Pfitzmann, Birgit Pfitzmann, Michael Waidner: ISDN-MIXes – Untraceable Communication with Very Small Bandwidth Overhead; Proc. Kommunikation in verteilten Systemen, IFB 267, Springer-Verlag, Heidelberg 1991, 451-463.

Walk_94   Bernhard Walke: Technik-Akzeptanz und -Verträglichkeit von mobilen Kommunikationsnetzen; ITG-Fachtagung "Herausforderung Informationstechnik", VDE-Verlag, München, 18.-20.Oktober 1994.

Session 3:
ATM und Quality of Service

Multimediale Anwendungen in globalen ATM-Netzen

Reinhold Eberhardt, Christian Rueß, Rolf Sigle
Daimler-Benz AG
Forschung und Technik
Postfach 2360
89013 Ulm
{eberhardt, ruess, sigle}@dbag.ulm.DaimlerBenz.COM

Zusammenfassung

Die Daimler-Benz Forschung und das International Computer Science Institute (ICSI) nehmen am ersten interkontinentalen „Asynchroner Transfer Mode" (ATM) Feldtest teil. Dieser Tagungsbericht gibt erste Erfahrungen mit multimedialen Anwendungen in globalen ATM-Netzen wieder. Insbesondere werden verschiedene Anwendungsszenarien und Ergebnisse von Performancemessungen diskutiert.

1   Einleitung

Auf den weltweiten Wettbewerb reagieren Unternehmen heute mit weltweitem Vertrieb, Produktion, Forschung und Entwicklung. Das damit institutionalisierte weltweit vernetzte Arbeiten erfordert neue Formen der Zusammenarbeit. Die Daimler-Benz Forschung erarbeitet hierfür einen ganzheitlichen Lösungsansatz mit den Elementen Computer Supported Cooperative Work, Concurrent Engineering und High Performance Communications. Dieser ganzheitliche Lösungsansatz benötigt i.a. eine flexiblere Netzinfrastruktur und höhere Bandbreite als in heutigen Corporate Networks üblich. Deshalb beteiligt sich Daimler-Benz am ersten interkontinentalen ATM-Feldtest. Die hierfür notwendige Infrastruktur wird durch das Projekt „Multimedia Applications on Intercontinental Highways" (MAY) bereitgestellt. Das Projekt MAY wurde von DeTeBerkom, einer Gesellschaft für Forschung und Entwicklung von Anwendungen, Diensten und Endsystemen für die Telekommunikation und Tochterfirma der Deutschen Telekom, initiiert. Als Netzbetreiber nehmen die Deutsche Telekom, Sprint, GlobalOne und Teleglobe an diesem Pilotprojekt teil. Die durch die Netzbetreiber bereitgestellte Verbindung wird durch Firmen und Forschungseinrichtungen für Tests von Anwendungen und Kommunikationsprotokollen genutzt. Bei Daimler-Benz werden in Zusammenarbeit mit dem ICSI prototypisch Entwicklungsabläufe für weltweite Zusammenarbeit untersucht.

In diesem Tagungsbeitrag werden die im ersten Projektabschnitt gemachten Erfahrungen diskutiert. Aus Anwendersicht waren zunächst die drei Schwerpunkte „ATM-Infrastruktur im internationalen Weitverkehrsbereich",

„transparente Nutzung bestehender Applikationen" und eine grobe Abschätzung der „Leistungsfähigkeit eines transatlantischen ATM-Netzes" von Bedeutung. Deshalb ist dieser Beitrag folgendermaßen unterteilt: Abschnitt 2 gibt einen Überblick über die MAY-Netzinfrastruktur, in Abschnitt 3 werden die Anwendungsszenarien und -erfahrungen beschrieben. Die Ergebnisse und Bewertung von Performancemessungen sind in Abschnitt 4 dargestellt, Abschnitt 5 gibt einen Ausblick über zukünftige Arbeiten.

2 MAY-Netzinfrastruktur

Die neuartige Netztechnologie ATM ermöglicht erstmalig durchgängige Hochgeschwindigkeitskommunikation in lokalen und in Weitverkehrsnetzen. Im Gegensatz zur heutigen Situation, in der unterschiedliche Dienste und unterschiedliche Netzstrukturen eingesetzt werden, bildet ATM für alle Arten von Anwendungen ein ideales Trägermedium. Dies gilt sowohl für den privaten, als auch für den öffentlichen Sektor genauso wie für Sprach- und Datenübertragung. Diese Universalität von ATM bildet eine ideale Ausgangsbasis für multimediale Anwendungen.

Das interkontinentale ATM-Netzwerk für das MAY-Projekt wird von der Deutschen Telekom, Sprint, GlobalOne und Teleglobe zur Verfügung gestellt. Die Verbindung zwischen dem ICSI in Berkeley und Daimler-Benz in Ulm setzt sich aus vielen einzelnen Verbindungen der unterschiedlichen Diensteanbieter zusammen (Abbildung 1).

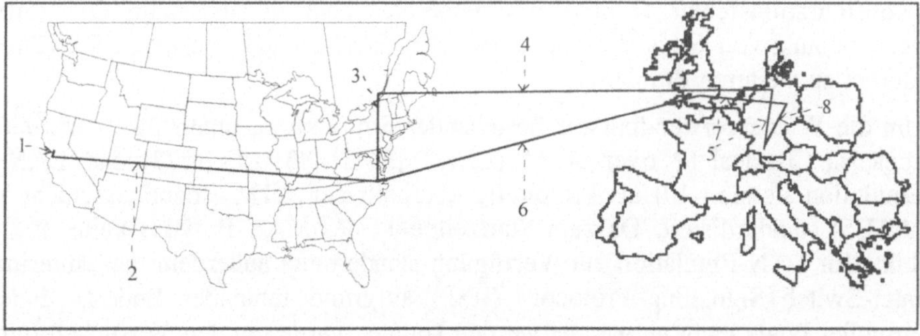

Abbildung 1: ATM-Verbindung zwischen ICSI (Berkeley/USA) und Ulm

Die Teilverbindungen mit den zugehörenden Diensteanbietern und maximaler Bandbreite sind in Tabelle 1 dargestellt.

Verbindungs-nummer	von	nach	Diensteanbieter	max. Bandbreite [Mbit/s]
1	ICSI (Berkeley)	Burlingame	Pacific Bell	155 (Sonet OC3)
2	Burlingame	Reston	Sprint	45 (DS3)
3	Reston	Montreal	GlobalOne	45 (DS3)
4	Montreal	Hamburg	Teleglobe	155 (Sonet OC3)
5	Hamburg	Ulm	Deutsche Telekom	155 (SDH STM1)
6	Reston	London	GlobalOne	2 (E1)
7	London	Berlin	Deutsche Telekom	2 (E1)
8	Berlin	Ulm	Deutsche Telekom	155 (SDH STM1)

Tabelle 1: ATM Verbindungen zwischen Berkeley und Ulm

Da in ATM-Weitverkehrsnetzen bisher noch keine Signalisierung eingeführt wurde, stehen für Versuche lediglich permanente virtuelle Verbindungen (PVC) zur Verfügung. Die Workstations bei Daimler-Benz in Ulm sowie am ICSI sind über lokale ATM-Vermittlungsknoten direkt an diese interkontinentalen Verbindungen angeschlossen.

Für den Aufbau einer Ende-zu-Ende ATM-Verbindung zwischen Daimler-Benz Ulm und dem ICSI in Berkeley sind zwischen Berkeley und Hamburg bzw. Berlin eine begrenzte Anzahl von PVCs dauerhaft geschaltet. Für die Verbindung zwischen Hamburg bzw. Berlin und Ulm müssen für Tests PVCs beim Netzmanagementzentrum der Deutschen Telekom in Köln beantragt werden. Da bei diesem Szenario neben den lokalen Systemadministratoren noch weitere fünf Netzbetreiber beteiligt sind, ist die Lokalisierung von Fehlern (Konfigurationsfehler, Hardwareprobleme etc.) sehr zeitaufwendig. Die Zeitverschiebung von 6 bis 9 Stunden zwischen Deutschland und den USA führt hierbei zu weiteren Problemen.

Um die Wiederverwendbarkeit bestehender Software zu unterstützen wurden zunächst Classical IP over ATM (CLIP) [RFC1483, RFC1577] und LAN-Emulation Version 1.0 als Protokolle oberhalb der ATM Adaptionsschicht 5 (AAL5) standardisiert. Da zum Startzeitpunkt des MAY-Projekts keine Produkte für LAN-Emulation zur Verfügung standen und außerdem das „Interim Inter-Switch Signalling Protocol" (IISP) aufgrund fehlender Ende-zu-Ende virtueller Pfade nicht verwendet werden konnte, wurden in den Versuchen nur CLIP PVCs verwendet.

Aus Sicht des Endanwenders sind noch zusätzliche Leistungsmerkmale wünschenswert:

- Möglichkeiten zur Überwachung von Verbindungen und Verbindungsreservierungen.
- Ende zu Ende virtuelle Pfade - Voraussetzung für die Nutzung von IISP (PNNI Phase 0).

- Unterstützung von Verkehrsströme mit variabler Bitrate.

- Signalisierung in Weitverkehrsnetzen, d.h. Ende-zu-Ende SVCs (switched virtual circuits).

Die Kosten für den Aufbau einer lokalen ATM-Netzinfrastruktur, der Anschluß an ein ATM-Weitverkehrsnetz und die laufenden fixen und variablen monatlichen Kosten sind sehr hoch.

3 Anwendungen

Für eine interkontinentale Zusammenarbeit von Gruppen müssen verschiedenste Werkzeuge bereitgestellt werden. Diese Werkzeuge haben abhängig von der Aufgabe unterschiedliches Gewicht. Beispielsweise ist bei der Konstruktion von Fahrzeugteilen eine Audioverbindung mit hoher Qualität wesentlich wichtiger als eine hochqualitative Videoverbindung. Werkzeuge wie Videokonferenzsysteme und Werkzeuge, welche die gemeinsame Benutzung von Anwendungen (application sharing) ermöglichen, werden in allen Aufgabenbereichen benötigt. Da das primäre Anwendungsumfeld die weltweite Konstruktion und das Design von Fahrzeugen ist, werden nur Workstation-basierte Lösungen untersucht. Insbesondere generieren diese Anwendungen Daten, die über die bestehende Kommunikationsinfrastruktur wegen zu geringer Bandbreite und fehlender Dienstgüte nicht übertragen werden können. Da in den Versuchen eine ATM-Infrastruktur mit den in Abschnitt 2 beschriebenen Beschränkungen verwendet wird, wurden lediglich IP-basierte Produkte betrachtet. Die in der ATM-Technologie vorhandene Garantie von Dienstgüteparametern kann aufgrund der verwendeten Protokolle bisher nicht ausgenutzt werden.

3.1 Videokonferenz

Videokonferenzen werden in den unterschiedlichsten Anwendungsszenarien benötigt. Diese reichen von Rücksprachen zwischen Monteur und Konstrukteur, über fachliche Diskussionen zwischen zwei an dem selben Projekt arbeitenden Entwicklern hin zu Besprechungen mehrerer Manager. Neben Audio und Video kommen sogenannte „Whiteboard"-Werkzeuge zum Einsatz, die als gemeinsam benutzbare Notizzettel dienen und teilweise über Importmöglichkeiten (z.B. Postscriptdokumente) verfügen. Die Anforderungen an die Qualität der Audio- und Videoverbindung ist hoch, da bei diesen Szenarien die Telekommunikation als Ersatz für Besprechungen dient.

Die Vielfalt von Werkzeugen für diese Anwendungen ist sehr groß. Aufgrund fehlender Standardisierung sind diese jedoch untereinander und mit ISDN-basierten Produkten noch nicht interoperabel. Als kostengünstige Möglichkeit können die für den Multicast-Backbone des Internets (MBone [kumar]) entwikkelten Werkzeuge [MBoneApps] verwendet werden. Es stehen mehrere „Public

Domain" Audio-, Video- und Whiteboard-Werkzeuge für unterschiedliche Rechner- und Betriebssystemplattformen zur Verfügung. Bei unseren Tests zeichneten sich insbesondere die am Lawrence Berkeley National Laboratory (LBNL) entwickelten Werkzeuge vat [vat], vic [vic] und wb [wb] durch problemlose Installation und große Verfügbarkeit auf vielen Plattformen aus. Diese Werkzeuge verfügen über einen großen Funktionsumfang, haben jedoch alle unterschiedliche Bedienschnittstellen. Dadurch sind sie für den Einsatz in den meisten betrachteten Szenarien nur bedingt geeignet. Durch das an der Universität Hannover entwickelte Konferenzsteuerungswerkzeug „Confman" [conf] wird das Starten einer Konferenz erheblich vereinfacht.

Im Gegensatz zu den MBone-Werkzeugen stehen kaufbare Produkte unterschiedlicher Hersteller. Dabei handelt es sich um integrierte Werkzeuge mit einheitlicher Bedienschnittstelle. Die meisten dieser Werkzeuge sind jedoch nur für einzelne Hardwareplattformen und Betriebssysteme verfügbar.

3.2 Gemeinsame Dokumentenbearbeitung

Speziell in den technischen Bereichen ist zusätzlich zur Sprach- und Bildübertragung das gemeinsame Betrachten und Bearbeiten von Dokumenten von besonderer Bedeutung. Im Vergleich zur Videokonferenz sinken bei dieser Anwendung die Anforderungen an das Video. Beobachtungen von Anwendern haben gezeigt, daß in den meisten Fällen Video nur während der Begrüßungsphase wichtig ist. Sobald die Diskussion über das weitere Vorgehen abgeschlossen ist, kann im allgemeinen auf Video im weiteren Verlauf der Konferenz verzichtet werden. Im Gegensatz dazu ist die Qualität der Audioverbindung weiterhin besonders wichtig.

Für die verteilte Betrachtung und Bearbeitung von Dokumenten werden von verschiedenen Herstellern integrierte Produkte angeboten, die u.a. über eine Komponente zum gemeinsamen Bearbeiten beliebiger X-Protokoll-basierter Anwendungen verfügen. Dabei spielt ein spezieller Prozeß (X-Multiplexer) für die Anwendung die Rolle des X-Servers und gleichzeitig kann er zu mehreren X-Servern als X-Client Kontakt aufnehmen, d.h. die Anwendung läuft lediglich auf der Workstation des Initiators und es wird für jeden Teilnehmer der Konferenz die graphische Bedienschnittstelle generiert. Der X-Multiplexer repliziert und filtert X-Protokoll-Primitive, die zwischen X-Servern und der Anwendung ausgetauscht werden. In diesen Produkten ist außerdem ein Token-basiertes Protokoll zur Weitergabe des Bearbeitungsrechts für das gemeinsam bearbeitete Dokument implementiert. Durch die Möglichkeit, Bemerkungen auf eine unsichtbare Folie, die über dem bearbeiteten Dokument liegt, zu schreiben und die Anzeige des Mauszeigers auf entfernten Rechnern (Telepointer) wird die Diskussion des Dokuments weiter unterstützt.

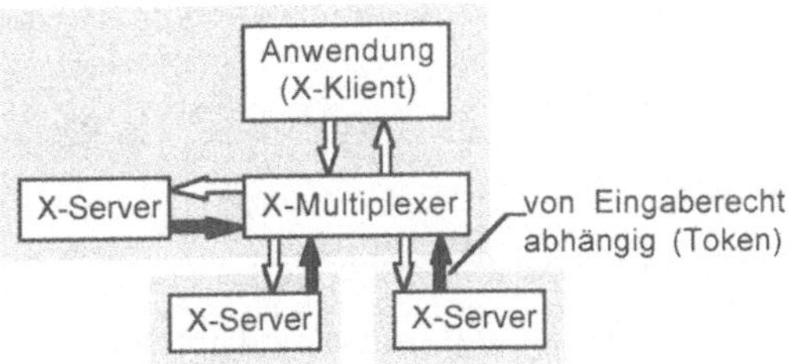

Abbildung 2: X-Multiplexer

Diese Applikationen haben den großen Vorteil, daß die zur Dokumentenbearbeitung verwendete Anwendung nur auf dem Rechner des Initiators benötigt wird, da alle anderen Konferenzteilnehmer lediglich eine Kopie der Bedienschnittstelle bekommen. Einzelne Produkte bieten auch eine Version für Microsoft Windows an, wodurch auch PC-Benutzer in einer Konferenz an der Bearbeitung eines Dokuments mit einer UNIX-basierten Applikation teilnehmen können.

Zu Problemen kann es kommen, wenn die Applikationen Erweiterungen des X-Protokolls verwenden, die entweder vom X-Multiplexer oder einem der X-Server der Konferenzteilnehmer nicht unterstützt werden. In diesem Fall kommt es meistens zum Absturz der Anwendung. Das X-Protokoll wurde ursprünglich für die Kommunikation zwischen X-Server und X-Client im lokalen Bereich entwickelt und beinhaltet den Austausch vieler kleiner Nachrichten. Deshalb ist die Performance der gemeinsamen Dokumentenbetrachtung bei großen Entfernungen (große Laufzeit zwischen X-Server und X-Client) nicht sehr gut.

3.3 Verteilte Konstruktion und verteiltes Design

Bei der Konstruktion und beim Design von Fahrzeugen werden in der Regel hochperformante Workstations mit speziellen CAD-Anwendungen eingesetzt. Zunehmend werden auch „Virtual Reality"-Techniken verwendet. Diese Anwendungen ermöglichen noch keine gemeinsame und gleichzeitige Bearbeitung von Konstruktionsmodellen an verschiedenen Standorten. Diese Applikationen verwenden meist spezielle Grafikerweiterungen des X-Servers. Deshalb können die in Abschnitt 3.2 beschriebenen Werkzeuge zur gemeinsamen Dokumentenbearbeitung nicht verwendet werden. Aus diesem Grund werden für dieses Umfeld spezielle Lösungen entwickelt. An sie werden unter anderem folgende Anforderungen gestellt:

- Verteilte Betrachtung von CAD-Modellen.

- Annotationen.

- Dokumentationsunterstützung.

- Unterstützung der Bearbeitung in verschiedenen Zeitzonen (work around the clock).

- Auslagerung von rechenintensiven Aufgaben auf Hochleistungsrechner.

- Integrierte Sicherheit.

- Hohe Audioqualität im Konstruktionsbereich.

- Höchste Audio- und Videoqualität im Designbereich.

4 Performancemessungen

Mit Hilfe von Performancemessungen wurde die Leistung von ATM-Netzen sowohl im lokalen, als auch auf der transatlantischen Verbindung näher untersucht. Dabei soll insbesondere die Leistungsfähigkeit bzw. die Schwächen von Standardprotokollen und Anwendungen offengelegt werden. Insbesondere wurden Protokolle der TCP/IP-Familie sowie die Performance von Videoübertragung betrachtet.

4.1 Netzwerkkonfiguration

Für die Durchführung der Tests standen mehrere SUN Workstations zur Verfügung, welche mit ATM-Adaptern von Fore ausgestattet sind. Abbildung 3 zeigt die Topologie der Workstations.

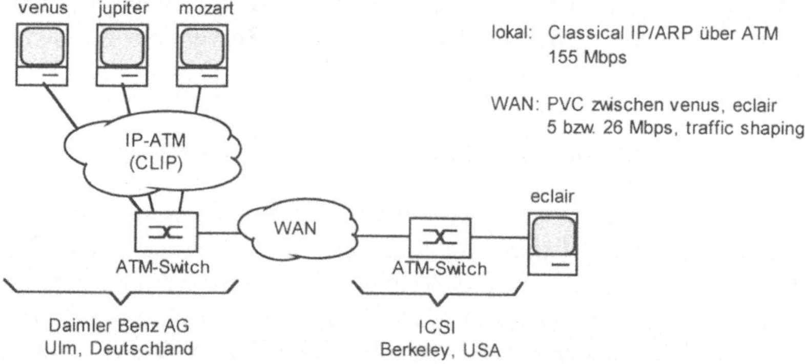

Abbildung 3: Topologie der ATM Testumgebung

Die Workstations benutzen „Classical IP over ATM" (CLIP) [RFC1483, RFC1577]. Im Weitverkehrsbereich wird manuell eine permanente virtuelle Verbindung (PVC) zwischen „venus" und „eclair" eingerichtet. Für diese Verbindung wurden Bandbreiten von 5 bzw. 26 Mbit/s bereitgestellt. Beim jeweiligen Sender wurde die Senderate auf diesen Wert beschränkt, um Zellverluste in den dazwischenliegenden Vermittlungsknoten zu vermeiden.

Folgende Tabelle gibt einen Überblick über die verwendete Hardware:

	Typ	ATM-Adapter
venus	SUN SPARCstation 20, Solaris 2.5	Fore SBA-200
jupiter	SUN SPARCstation 10, Solaris 2.5	Fore SBA-200
mozart	SUN SPARCstation 5, Solaris 2.4	Fore SBA-200
eclair	SUN SPARCstation 5, Solaris 2.5	Fore SBA-200

4.2 Benchmark-Programme

Um die Leistungsfähigkeit von ATM und die Verwendbarkeit vorhandener Standardprotokolle im Hochgeschwindigkeitsbereich zu testen, wurden sowohl im lokalen Bereich als auch im Weitverkehrsbereich Performancemessungen durchgeführt.

Das Werkzeug „netperf" ([np]) von Hewlett-Packard ist frei verfügbar. Es ermöglicht viele verschiedene Performancemessungen. Insbesondere ist es möglich, aufbauend auf TCP oder UDP die sogenannte „bulk data transfer performance" zu messen. Des weiteren bietet netperf die Möglichkeit, die „Request/Response"-Zeit und somit die Zeitverzögerung einer Netzverbindung zu bestimmen. Dies ist auch mit dem Hilfsprogramm „ping" mit der Option „-s" möglich, wobei in diesem Fall ICMP als Protokoll verwendet wird.

Als Alternative zu netperf kann für die Messung der Übertragungsgeschwindigkeit das Werkzeug „TTCP" verwendet werden. Es bietet jedoch lediglich einen Teil der Optionen von netperf.

Bei den Messungen der Übertragungsraten können als Parameter die Socketgrößen, sowie die Nachrichtengrößen auf Sende und Empfangsseite variiert werden. Bei ungesicherten Übertragungsmethoden (z.B. UDP) ist die Verlustrate von besonderer Bedeutung.

4.3 Messungen im lokalen Bereich

Zwischen den Rechnern jupiter und venus wurden TCP-Transferraten in Abhängigkeit der Nachrichtengröße gemessen (siehe Abbildung 4). Die Puffergrößen der beiden Sockets wurden dabei auf den Maximalwert von 64 kByte gesetzt.

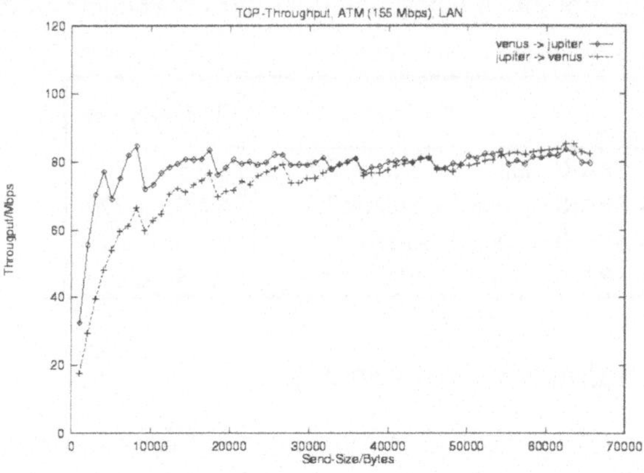

Abbildung 4: ATM-Messung im LAN

Die Nachrichtengröße wurde in Schritten von 1024 Bytes erhöht. Die Rechner sowie das ATM-Netz waren während der Messung ansonsten unbenutzt.

An den gemessenen Maximalwerten läßt sich erkennen, daß die Rechenleistung der Endsysteme nicht ausreicht, um die zur Verfügung stehende Bandbreite zu nutzen. Betrachtet man den Overhead der einzelnen Protokollebenen (SONET-OC3, ATM, AAL5), so steht oberhalb von AAL5 eine Bandbreite von 135.6 Mbit/s zur Verfügung (siehe [atmarp], [krivda]). CLIP- und TCP-Overhead können diesen Wert durch SNAP Header, AAL5 Trailer und Padding wiederum auf 135.1 Mbit/s (9180 Byte MTU) bzw. 125.2 Mbit/s (576 Byte MTU) reduzieren.

Zu beachten ist, daß die verwendeten ATM-Adapter die Verarbeitung der ATM-Zellen in Hardware durchführen und somit keine zusätzliche Rechenlast beim Endsystem entsteht. Die Adapterkarten stellen eine AAL5-Schnittstelle bereit.

Bei den Messungen sind in regelmäßigen Abständen von ca. 8 kByte Einbrüche in der Transferrate zu erkennen. Dies ist auf die MTU-Größe bei CLIP zurückzuführen, welche 9180 Bytes beträgt. Wird ein TCP-Paket gesendet, dessen Größe die MTU übersteigt, so muß es für die Übertragung fragmentiert und beim Empfänger reassembliert werden. Diese Operation belastet den Prozessor des Endsystems, wodurch auch die Gesamtperformance abnimmt. Bei ungünstiger Fragmentierung (z.B. bei 9216 oder 18432 Bytes) steigt zusätzlich der Protokolloverhead (siehe auch [mol]).

Bei den UDP-Messungen konnte ebenfalls festgestellt werden, daß die erreichbare Übertragungsrate durch die Rechenleistung der Endsysteme beschränkt wird. Durch das Fehlen einer Flußkontrolle kann es jedoch dazu kommen, daß ein langsames Empfangssystem durch einen schnellen Sender überlastet wird.

Sender	Empfänger	Max. Senderate	Empfangsrate
SUN SPARCstation 10 (jupiter)	SUN SPARCstation 20 (venus)	62 Mbit/s	62 Mbit/s
SUN SPARCstation 20 (venus)	SUN SPARCstation 10 (jupiter)	102 Mbit/s	<0.1 Mbit/s

Im vorliegenden Test konnten von einer SUN SPARCstation 10 (jupiter) zu einer SUN SPARCstation 20 (venus) bis zu 62 Mbit/s nahezu verlustfrei übertragen werden. In der umgekehrten Richtung konnte die SUN SPARCstation 20 bis zu 102 Mbit/s senden, wobei vom Empfänger nahezu keine Daten angenommen werden konnten (unter 0.1 Mbit/s).

4.4 Messungen auf der transatlantischen Verbindung

Für die Messung im Weitverkehrsbereich wurde ein PVC zwischen zwei Rechnern eingerichtet (siehe Abbildung 3). Für die Messungen standen Bandbreiten von 5 Mbit/s und 26 Mbit/s zur Verfügung.

Die Roundtrip-Zeit wurde bei unbelastetem Netz sowohl mit netperf, als auch mit ping gemessen und erreichte 200 ms.

Um Zellverluste in den zwischen den Endsystemen liegenden Vermittlungsknoten zu vermeiden, wurde auf der Senderseite die Datenrate beschränkt (siehe [atmarp]). Die folgende Tabelle gibt einen Überblick über die erhaltenen Meßergebnisse.

Bandbreite	TCP	UDP-Send	UDP-Recv
5 Mbit/s	0.5-2.13 Mbit/s	4-4.5 Mbit/s	ohne Verluste
26 Mbit/s	1.14-2.27 Mbit/s	19.6-22.3 Mbit/s	siehe unten

Für die TCP-Messungen wurde wiederum die Nachrichtengröße variiert und die Socketgrößen auf die Maximalwerte gesetzt. Sowohl für die 5 Mbit/s-, als auch für die 26 Mbit/s-Verbindung konnte lediglich ein Bruchteil der zur Verfügung stehenden Bandbreite genutzt werden (ca. 2.2 Mbit/s). Eine Erhöhung der Bandbreite von 5 auf 26 Mbit/s führte kaum zu einer meßbaren Verbesserung.

Die verwendete Standardimplementierung des TCP-Protokolls ist für schnelle Netzverbindungen mit einer großen Verzögerungszeit (hohe Pfadkapazität - Produkt aus Bandbreite und der durch die Signallaufzeit bedingten Verzögerung) ungeeignet. Bei TCP kann der Sender nur in begrenztem Umfang weitersenden, bis er eine Bestätigung für die gesendeten Daten vom Empfänger erhält (Sliding Window Prinzip, siehe [comer, brzi96]). Angenommen, der Sender wartet nach dem Senden von 64 kByte (maximale Fenstergröße) auf das Eintreffen einer Bestätigung, so bedeutet dies, daß sich im besten Fall 64 kByte „auf der Leitung" befinden können. Bei einer Roundtrip-Zeit von 200 ms beschränkt dies die von TCP nutzbare Bandbreite auf 64 kByte/200ms=2.6 Mbit/s.

Für TCP wurden Erweiterungen vorgeschlagen, welche diese Problematik betreffen (siehe [RFC1323]), allerdings sind diese TCP-Optionen in heutigen Implementierungen meistens nicht verfügbar. Angesichts der rasch fortschreitenden Entwicklung im Bereich der Hochgeschwindigkeitsnetze und insbesondere deren Einsatz im Weitverkehrsbereich sollte sich in naher Zukunft eine neue Version oder Alternative zu TCP durchsetzen.

Bei den Messungen mit dem UDP-Protokoll kann man obiger Tabelle entnehmen, daß bei den gegebenen Bandbreiten die Rechenleistung der Endsysteme keinen entscheidenden Einfluß auf die Senderate nimmt. Bei der Verbindung mit 5 Mbit/s konnte in über 40 Messungen keine Paketverluste festgestellt werden, was auf die zuverlässige ATM-Verbindung und die ausreichende Rechenleistung der Endsysteme zurückzuführen ist.

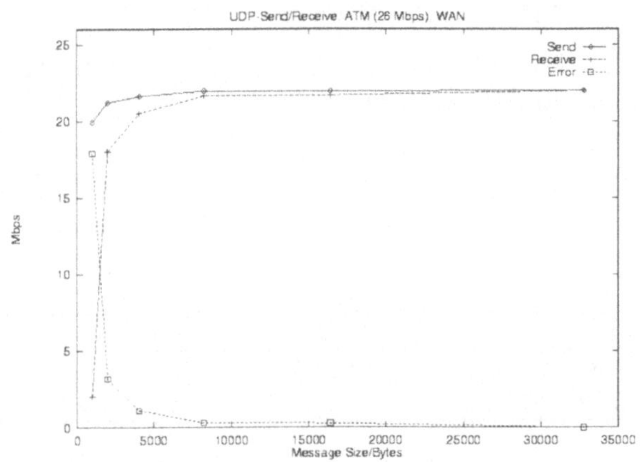

Abbildung 5: UDP-Meßergebnisse

Die Messungen bei 26 Mbit/s wurden von einer SUN SPARCstation 20 zu einer SUN SPARCstation 5 ausgeführt. Wie in der Abbildung 5 zu erkennen ist, konnte der sendende Rechner nahezu mit der vollen Bandbreite senden. Bei kleinen Paketgrößen kommt es allerdings zu hohen Fehlerraten. Durch Monitoring der ATM-Verbindung konnte sichergestellt werden, daß diese Fehler nicht auf Probleme in der ATM-Verbindung (Zellverluste) zurückzuführen sind.

Vielmehr liegt es nahe, daß bei dieser Netzgeschwindigkeit der Empfangsrechner an die Grenze seiner Empfangskapazität stößt. Bei kleinen Paketgrößen wird der Empfänger wesentlich stärker mit der Verarbeitung der UDP/IP-Header belastet; zusätzlich wird beim Empfang jedes Paketes ein Interrupt beim empfangenden Rechner ausgelöst.

4.5 Messungen auf der Anwendungsebene

Zusätzlich zu den bisher vorgestellten Messungen auf der Transportschichtebene haben wir den Einfluß von begrenzten Workstation- und Netzwerkressourcen auf multimediale Werkzeuge näher untersucht. In unsere Test sendeten wir lediglich ein Medium (Video) in eine Richtung. Dadurch kann der Einfluß der CPU-Belastung durch die Dekodierung beim Empfänger isoliert untersucht werden.

Als sendende Workstation verwendeten wir eine SUN SPARCstation 20, die mit einem Parallax Videoboard ausgerüstet ist. Dieses Videoboard unterstützt M-JPEG Videokompression in Hardware. Dadurch kann die Sende-Bildwiederholrate in einem großen Bereich variiert werden, ohne daß die CPU dieser Workstation stark belastet wird. Als Empfänger wurde eine SUN SPARCstation 5 verwendet, welche mit einem SUN-Videoboard ausgerüstet ist. Dieses Videoboard unterstützt nicht die gleiche Hardwarekompression wie das Parallax-Board, deshalb muß das Dekodieren des Videorahmens beim Empfänger in Software durchgeführt werden. Diese Aufgabe belastet die CPU des Empfängers in starkem Maße.

Die beiden Workstations waren bei diesem Test über das MAY-Netzwerk verbunden, wobei die Bandbreite auf 1.5 Mbit/s begrenzt war. Zur Übertragung des Videos wurde das MBone Werkzeug vic verwendet. Bei unterschiedlichen Sende-Bildwiederholraten wurde die empfangene Bildwiederholrate, die Belastung der Empfänger-CPU und der ATM-Durchsatz gemessen. Die Meßwerte für die Bildwiederholraten werden durch das Videowerkzeug selbst bereitgestellt. Die Belastung der CPU wurde mit Hilfe des UNIX-top-Kommandos ermittelt und der Durchsatz auf ATM-Ebene wurde mit proprietären Werkzeugen für den verwendeten Synoptics ATM-Vermittlungsknoten gemessen.

Die Ergebnisse der Messungen sind in Abbildung 6 dargestellt. Bei Steigerung der Sende-Bildwiederholrate folgt die beim Empfänger dargestellte Bildwiederholrate zunächst der Senderate. Ab einer Sende-Bildwiederholrate von 16 Bilder/Sekunde ist die CPU des Empfängers überlastet, d.h. nicht alle gesendeten Rahmen werden beim Empfänger dargestellt. Bei einer weiteren Steigerung der Sende-Bildwiederholrate auf über 19 Bilder/Sekunde kommt es zur Überlastung der ATM-Verbindung, wodurch im Netz ATM-Zellen zufällig verworfen werden. Deshalb bricht die Bildwiederholrate beim Empfänger drastisch ein.

Die Messungen haben gezeigt, daß bei Sättigung von Netzwerk- oder Host-Ressourcen eine weitere Erhöhung der Bildwiederholrate des Senders zur Verschwendung von Ressourcen und zu einer Abnahme der Videoqualität beim Empfänger führt. Parallel laufende Anwendungen (z. B. eine zweite Videoverbindung, Application Sharing, ...) beeinflussen die Videoübertragung zusätzlich negativ. Zur Vermeidung dieser Effekte wird in [AlSi96] eine Architektur für multimediale Anwendungen vorgestellt, bei dem die zur Verfügung stehenden Ressourcen ständig überwacht werden. Diese Informationen werden dazu benutzt, um die Parameter für die einzelnen Medien entsprechend den Wünschen der Benutzer einzustellen und somit die bestmögliche Ressourcenausnutzung und Befriedigung der Benutzerbedürfnisse zu garantieren.

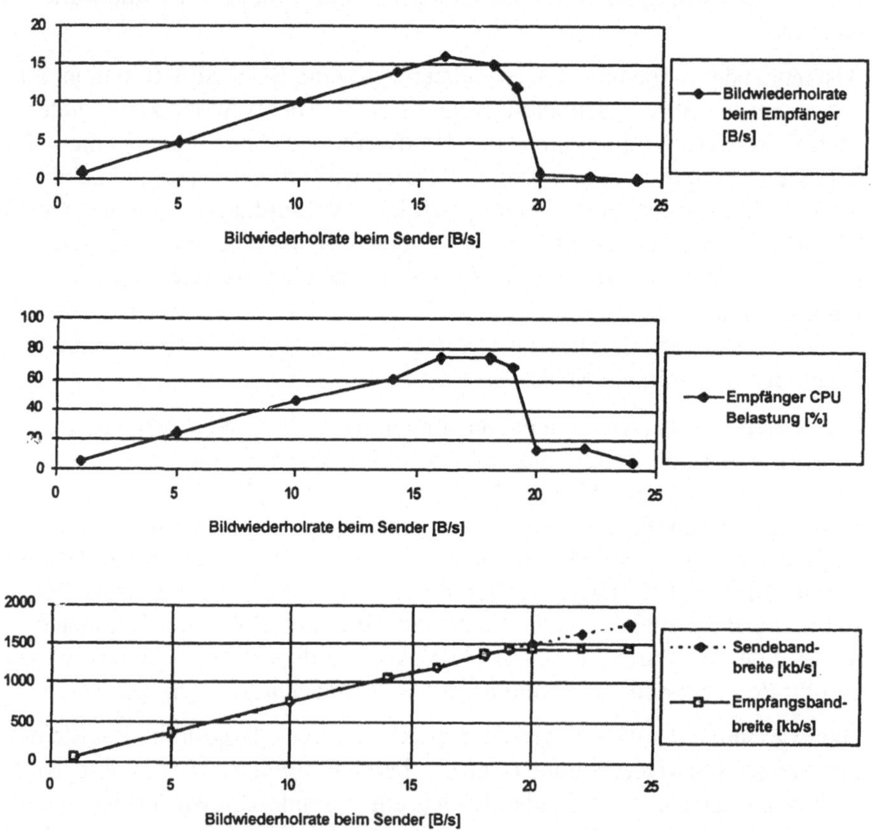

Abbildung 6: Messung bei unidirektionaler Videoübertragung

4.6 Bewertung

Wie die oben dargestellten Ergebnisse zeigen, sind die momentan verfügbaren Protokolle der TCP/IP-Familie nur eingeschränkt für zukünftige Netzinfrastrukturen geeignet. Hohe Bandbreiten erfordern leichtgewichtige Protokolle, durch welche ein Endsystem die hohe Netzgeschwindigkeit effizient nutzen kann. Die Prozessorleistung des Endsystems sollte in erster Linie der eigentlichen Anwendung zur Verfügung stehen und nicht für die Kommunikation verloren gehen.

Hohe Bandbreite in Verbindung mit einer hohen Verzögerungszeit auf dem Kommunikationspfad stellen weitere Anforderungen an ein effizientes Übertragungsprotokoll. Das bisher von TCP verwendete Verfahren kann bei hoher Pfadkapazität (Produkt aus Bandbreite und der durch die Signallaufzeit bedingten Verzögerung) lediglich einen Bruchteil der Bandbreite nutzen.

Um Workstation- und Netzwerkressourcen optimal auszunutzen, werden bei multimedialen Anwendungen Mechanismen benötigt, damit bei Sättigung einer Workstation-CPU nicht unnötig Netzbandbreite verschwendet wird, bzw. bei auftretenden Problemen im Netz die Sendeparameter an die gegebenen Verhältnisse angepaßt werden.

5 Ausblick

Die ersten Erfahrungen mit ATM im Weitverkehrsbereich haben gezeigt, daß das Potential von ATM bisher nur bedingt ausgenutzt werden kann. Damit alle Möglichkeiten ausgeschöpft werden können, sind Erweiterungen beim Diensteangebot der Netzbetreiber (z.B. Signalisierung im Weitverkehrsbereich, VBR-Dienste usw.) notwendig. Darüber hinaus besteht der Bedarf an neuen verbesserten Transportprotokollen basierend auf ATM. Die Daimler-Benz Forschung wird deshalb weitere Untersuchungen im Bereich der Transportprotokolle durchführen. Im weiteren werden insbesondere die Anwendungsszenarien von verteilter Konstruktion und verteiltem Design betrachtet. Außerdem wird als neuer Anwendungsbereich das „Teleteaching" untersucht.

Literatur

[AlSi96]   Alfano M.., Sigle R., *Controlling Resources in a Collaborative Multimedia Environment*, Proceedings 5th IEEE International Symposium on High-Performance Distributed Computing (HPDC-5), Syracruse, USA, 1996

[atmarp]   Manual Page zu atmarp, Fore Systems, 2/1996

[brzi96]   Braun T., Zitterbart M., *Hochleistungskommunikation, Band 2: Transportdienste und -protokolle*, Oldenbourg 1996, ISBN 3-486-23088-3

[comer]   Comer, Douglas E.: *Internetworking with TCP/IP*, Volume I, Second Edition, Prentice Hall 1991, ISBN 0-13-468505-9

[conf]   Universität Hannover, Rechnernetze und Verteilte Systeme, *Confman Distribution*, http://www.rvs.uni-hannover.de/products/confman/

[krivda]   Krivda, Cheryl D.: *Analyzing ATM Adapter Performance, The Real World Meaning of Benchmarks*, Efficient Networks Inc., 1996, http://www.efficient.com/doc/EM.html

[kumar]   Kumar V.: *MBone: Interactive Multimedia On The Internet*, Macmillan Publishing, Simon & Schuster 1995

[MBoneApps]   Kumar V.: *Mbone Desktop Applications*, http://www.best.com/~prince/techinfo/mc-soft.html

[mol]   Moldeklev, Kjersti u.a.: *The effect of end system hardware and software on TCP/IP throughput performance over a local ATM network*, Telektronikk, Band 91, S. 155-167, 2/3 - 1995

[np]   Netperf, www, http://www.cup.hp.com/netperf/NetperfPage.html

[RFC1323]   Jacobson V., Braden B., Borman D.: *TCP Extensions for high-performance*, Request for Comments 1323, Mai 1992

[RFC1483]   Heinanen J.: *Multiprotocol Encapsulation over ATM Adaptation Layer 5*, Request for Comment 1483, Juli 1993

[RFC1577]   Laubach, M.: *Classical IP and ARP over ATM*, Request for Comments 1577, Januar 1993

[vat]   LBNL: *The Audio Conferencing Tool vat*, http://www-nrg.ee.lbl.gov/vat

[vic]   LBNL: *The Video Conferencing Tool vic*, http://www-nrg.ee.lbl.gov/vic

[wb]   LBNL: *The Shared Whiteboard wb*, http://www-nrg.ee.lbl.gov/wb

Quality-of-Service Support for IP Flows over ATM

Torsten Braun and Stefano Giorcelli
IBM European Networking Center
Vangerowstr. 18
D-69115 Heidelberg
Phone: +49 6221 59-4352
Fax: +49 6221 59-3300
Email: braun@heidelbg.ibm.com

Abstract. This paper describes an extension of a classical IP over ATM implementation which allows to support quality-of-service for IP flows. While standard classical IP over ATM implementations use shared VCs for several IP flows between two end systems, the classical IP over ATM implementation extensions allow to establish separate VCs with individual quality-of-service parameters for single IP flows. The paper describes the modifications of an AIX 4.2 kernel implementation. Mbone video applications using RSVP for resource reservation have been implemented on top of the classical IP over ATM implementation.

1 Introduction

An IP flow is a sequence of packets exchanged between two end points identified by the pair of IP address and port number. A flow is identified by the so-called flow identifier. In IPv4, this is the combination of the two end point identifiers, while in IPv6 the flow identifier may consist of the flow label and the source IP address.

ATM connection establishment following the classical IP over ATM concept [15] means that a single, shared best-effort virtual connection (VC) is established for several flows between any pair of ATM attached IP systems. The single VC is established with quality-of-service (QoS) parameters supporting best-effort service according to [17]. In some situations it is desirable to establish and use a dedicated VC for a flow, in particular for data flows with high quality-of-service requirements. Another application of using dedicated VCs for IP flows is a RSVP based environment. The Resource ReSerVation Protocol (RSVP) [7] is being used in the Internet world to reserve resources in order to provide quality-of-service. ATM VCs can be considered as a very important resource for quality-of-service guarantees. Signalling parameters for ATM VC establishment can be derived from quality-of-service parameters of IP flows exchanged between RSVP systems.

The paper describes an implementation architecture to provide ATM QoS support for IP flows. The architecture is based on a classical IP over ATM implementation, which has been extended to support QoS on application level. System calls have been implemented, which allow to specify traffic descriptor parameters to be used in SETUP messages for VC establishment. If a dedicated VC exists for a flow, the packets of the flow are sent over this VC, otherwise a best-effort VC is used, which must be shared with other flows. The advantage of this approach is that applications need only slightly to be modified to take advantage of the QoS extensions of the classical IP over ATM implementation. Internet addresses can still be used, only additional function calls specifying the desired quality-of-service are required. On transport level, TCP and UDP are currently supported. The architecture is open to other protocols over IP.

After an overview about IP over ATM in Section 2, the implementation architecture of the QoS extensions of the classical IP over ATM implementation is illustrated in Section 3. Section 4 describes applications which can use the QoS extensions. Section 5 gives an outlook to future work.

2 IP over ATM

2.1 Classical IP over ATM

The original Internet architecture (classical IP model) assumes an interconnection of networks. Each network can be divided into many subnetworks (IP subnets). According to the classical IP model, hosts within the same subnet can communicate directly, while hosts on different subnets must exchange packets via routers. When a host wishes to communicate with another host, the destination address is analyzed whether the destination is local (host on the same subnet) or remote (host on a different subnet). In the first case, the packet can be sent directly to the destination, while in the second case it has to be sent to a router, which is has to forward it to the next hop.

These concepts are applied with slight modifications also in the case of ATM subnets. In particular, the notion of Logical IP Subnet (LIS) has been introduced. A LIS consists of a group of hosts and routers which are connected to the same ATM network and belong to the same IP subnet. Only hosts connected to the same LIS communicate directly with each other, while routers are used to reach destinations outside the LIS. Two protocols are used to map IP addresses to ATM addresses within a LIS. The ATM Address Resolution Protocol (ATM ARP) resolves IP addresses to ATM addresses. The Inverse ATM Address Resolution Protocol resolves ATM addresses to IP addresses.

The ATM ARP is based on a centralized approach. Each LIS has an ATM ARP server, which maintains a table of IP and ATM address pairs. The ATM ARP server address has to be statically configured in each host within the LIS. When a host first connects to a LIS, it establishes a connection to the ATM ARP server using the configured address. In response to this connection establishment, the ATM ARP server sends an Inverse ARP request to the host, in order to determine its IP address. The host replies with an Inverse ARP reply, and the resulting address binding is then stored in the server's ATM ARP table.

If a host A wants to send a packet to a host B, it first checks whether the destination IP address is local or not. IF host B resides on the same LIS, a connection can be directly established to it. Host A looks for the IP address of host B in its local ATM ARP table, which stores mappings between IP and ATM addresses. If it is the first packet for host B, no entry can be found in the local ATM ARP table. Therefore, host A must request the ATM address of host B from the ATM ARP server. Host A sends an ATMARP_request to the ATM ARP server and receives from it an ATMARP_reply message containing the ATM address of host B (Figure 1). Host A stores the address mapping in its cache and establishes an ATM VC to host B by an SETUP message. The SETUP message contains quality-of-service parameters for a best-effort service according to [17]. The establishment of the VC requires the reception of a CONNECT message in response to the SETUP message. The following packets from host A to host B are sent via the best-effort VC as soon as it is established.

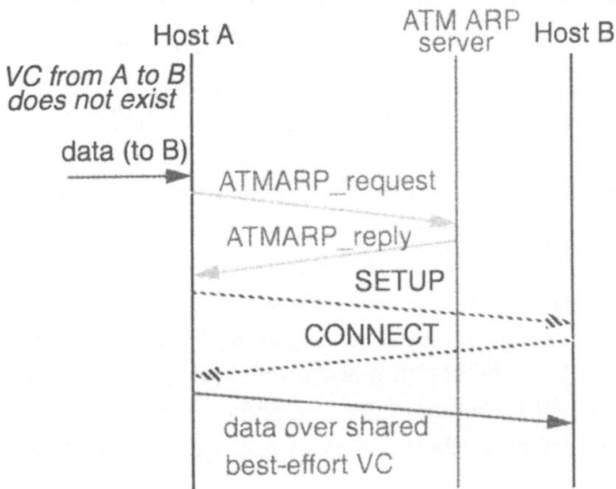

Figure 1: Classical IP over ATM and ATM ARP

The classical IP over ATM model suffers from several limitations. One limitation is that direct VCs between hosts are only established between hosts of a common logical IP subnet. If two hosts do not belong to a common IP subnet, IP traffic must be forwarded via routers although the ATM network infrastructure would allow a direct ATM VC between the two hosts. This short-cut is not allowed by the classical model, so that resulting routes are not optimal, and routers may become performance bottlenecks. The short-cut functionality is enabled by the Next Hop Resolution Protocol (NHRP) [14], developed by the IETF routing over large clouds working group. NHRP allows hosts or routers to find the ATM address of the next hop, given the IP address of the destination. It minimizes the number of hops and allows hosts residing on the same ATM network to establish a direct VC although the hosts are not members of a common IP subnetwork.

2.2 Quality-of-Service support

Another problem of the classical IP over ATM approach is that it does not support quality-of-service on application or IP flow level. This problem is addressed by the Application REquested IP over ATM (AREQUIPA) proposal [1]. It allows ATM attached hosts to set up single ATM connections with QoS requested for dedicated IP flows. Applications can directly benefit from ATM ability to guarantee quality of service. The approach introduces three new API functions in the TCP/IP protocol suite `Arequipa_expect`, `Arequipa_preset` and `Arequipa_close`.

If host A wants to establish a connection to host B, the hosts first exchange their ATM addresses and the port numbers. Host B then invokes `Arequipa_expect` to accept an incoming ATM connection from host A. This function requires as parameters the socket descriptor, the IP address of host A, the port number and the ATM address. Host A invokes

`Arequipa_preset` to open an ATM VC to host B. This function requires a socket descriptor, host B's IP address, port number, ATM address, and QoS parameters. AREQUIPA functions cannot be performed on a router because they do not include complete information about the flow identifier of transmitted data. Only the remote address is passed to the functions, while a router would have to set also the source addresses. The AREQUIPA approach only works in contexts where ATM connectivity is provided end-to-end.

A different approach are interfaces providing the application direct access to ATM (so-called native ATM interfaces). Applications are running directly over AAL5 but not over TCP/IP protocols. Several solutions use existing socket function calls [12][13], where ATM addresses instead of the Internet addresses are used. The socket calls have to be modified and applications have to get and set desired quality-of-service parameters of the ATM connection to be established. Native ATM interfaces are limited to a homogeneous ATM network, and the application also needs to know the ATM address of the receiver host. This can be avoided by adding ATM addresses into the domain name system data base. Another advantage of native ATM sockets is reduced processing overhead due to missing IP and UDP/TCP processing compared to UDP/TCP sockets. However, in [20] it is shown that there are only minor performance differences between a UDP/IP protocol stack and native ATM sockets. A drawback of native ATM interfaces is the lack of reliable services such as required for WWW applications.

To allow applications to specify their QoS requirements the resource reservation protocol (RSVP) has been developed by the IETF [7]. It exchanges QoS requests between end systems and routers. RSVP runs on top of IP or UDP. Similar to ICMP, IGMP or routing protocols, it does not carry user data. RSVP has been designed for simplex data flows. Resources are reserved in only one direction. RSVP is no routing protocol, it obtains routes from a routing protocol and uses this information to forward QoS requests along paths. Within routers, incoming packets are classified by a packet classifier, which looks for the routes and the QoS class for each packet. The packet scheduler of the outgoing interface passes the packets to the underlying link layer providing the appropriate QoS. RSVP allows dynamic QoS reservations. Receivers may request or change resource reservations at any time. The architecture described hereafter can be used to run RSVP over ATM [5]. ATM resources can be reserved for IP flows based on RSVP message exchange. This results in the establishment of QoS-based ATM VCs.

3 Implementation of IP over ATM with quality-of-service-support

3.1 Implementation architecture

The architecture of the classical IP over ATM implementation with QoS support is shown in Figure 2. A1, A2 and A3 are three applications having access to a shared, best-effort VC established by the classical IP over ATM implementation. At a given time, the applications might require a QoS-based ATM VC, either through a RSVP reservation, or directly through an I/O control (ioctl) call to the kernel. After the private QoS-based VC has been established, it is exclusively used for the requesting application. The best-effort VC is kept up for other IP flows after the dedicated VCs are established. The extensions of the classical IP over ATM implementation extension can be divided into four parts:

- the administration of an additional ATM ARP table together with the definition of new data structures to store QoS and flow identifier information (ATM ARP QoS table),

- the introduction of new ioctl commands to set, get, and delete entries from this ATM ARP QoS table,

- the modification of the sender part of the classical IP over ATM implementation taking into account the possible presence of a dedicated VC, and

- the modification of the receiver part of the classical IP over ATM implementation to avoid sending Inverse ARP requests for unidirectional VCs.

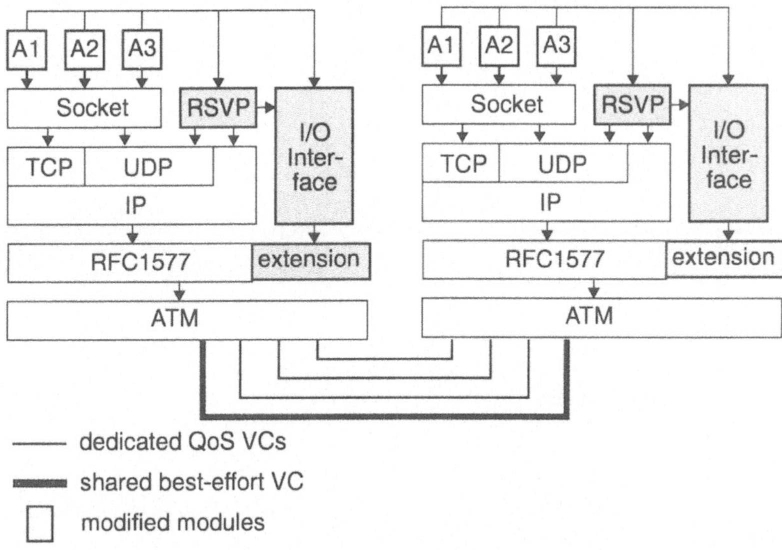

Figure 2: QoS extensions of classical IP over implementation

3.1.1 ATM ARP QoS table

The normal classical IP over ATM implementation builds an ATM ARP table to store the ATM addresses of end systems, together with their IP address and a VC identifier identifying the VC to be used for sending IP datagrams to the specified destination. Several internal functions of the classical IP over ATM implementation access and modify the contents of this table. In order to allow applications or reservation protocols such as RSVP to request a special quality-of-service to be used for a certain IP flow, a second ATM ARP table has been added in addition to the standard ATM ARP table. This ATM ARP QoS table stores information such as the flow identifiers and the corresponding QoS parameters. The functions to access and modify this table and the actions resulting from the modifications are described in the next subsection.

The standard ATM ARP table consists of an array of pointers to double-linked lists indexed through a hash function. To allow the same handling procedures on the ATM ARP QoS entries, the additional ATM ARP QoS table has been designed with a similar format as the standard one (see Figure 3). The two different tables are necessary because the default, best-effort VCs need to be kept up even after the establishment of private QoS connections to allow other flows and best-effort messages to be exchanged.

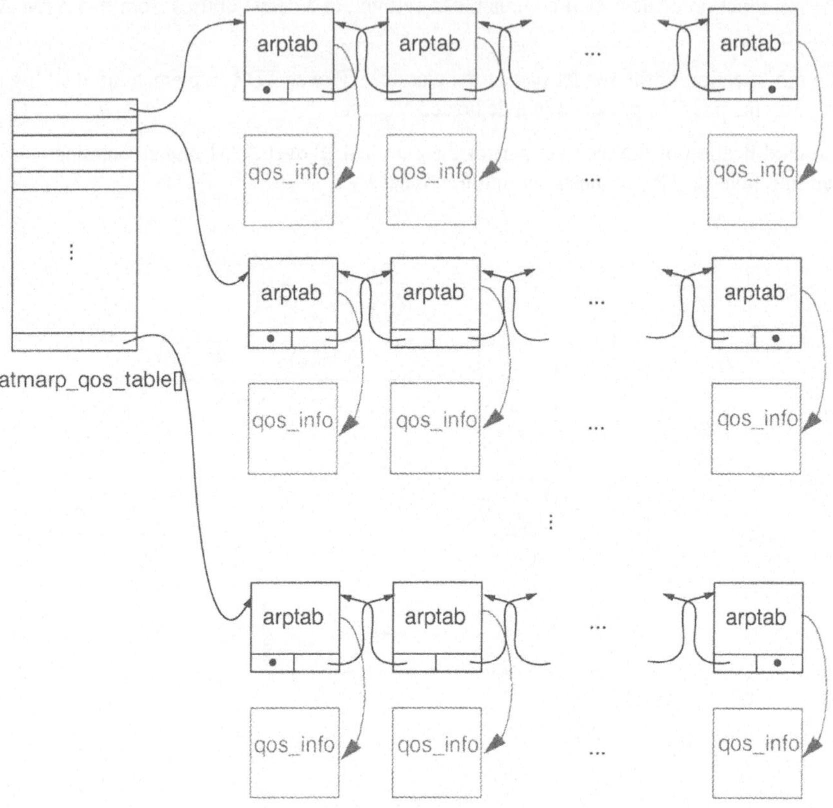

Figure 3: QoS-ATMARP table

To store the information regarding the flow identifier and QoS parameters in each of these ARP table entries, a subfield within this structure is used as a pointer to a new structure, called qos_info. The definition of this structure is given below:

```
struct qos_info {
  flowid_t flowid;
  c_par_t conn_par;
  cause_t cause;
};

typedef struct flowid {
  struct in_addr srcaddr;
  int srcport;
  struct in_addr dstaddr;
  int dstport;
} flowid_t;
```

```
typedef struct conn_par {
  int fwd_peakrate_hp;
  int fwd_peakrate_lp;
  int fwd_sus_rate_hp;
  int fwd_sus_rate_lp;
  int fwd_bur_size_hp;
  int fwd_bur_size_lp;
  int best_effort;
} c_par_t;
```

The `c_par_t` type includes a subset of the standard ATM QoS parameters to set up a certain ATM connection with the QoS parameters requested by the application. It could easily be enhanced by additional parameters. The `flow_id_t` type has been defined for the use in IPv4 and contains the IP address and the port number for the source and the destination. The `cause_t` type of the `qos_info` structure contains in the case of a connection setup failure information about the reason for which it was not possible to establish the connection.

3.2 Application programming interface

New I/O control commands allow to create, modify, read, and delete entries in the additional ATM ARP QoS table maintained in the kernel. The user interface to access the table consists of additional commands for the ioctl function.

```
int ioctl (FileDescriptor, Command, ifr)
int FileDescriptor, Command;
struct ifreq *ifr;
```

An application should set an entry for the requesting IP flow in this ATM ARP QoS table through an `ioctl` call to the kernel using the **ATM_SQOS** command. A RSVP implementation sets this entry after receiving the flow specification parameters from the next hop by a reservation message. An entry with the same flow identifier must not be already present in the table. However, an entry with the same destination address is required in the normal ATM ARP table. In a RSVP scenario this assumption is always true. When the RSVP reservation message is received, RSVP path messages have been sent by the source over the best-effort VC before and the destination ATM address is already stored in the ATM ARP table. This entry can be used in order to complete the ATM ARP QoS table entry with the destination ATM address. The **ATM_SQOS** command requires the parameters next hop address, flow identifier and ATM connection parameters.

The **ATM_GQOS** command gets (reads) an entry from the ATM ARP QoS table corresponding to a specific flow identifier given as a parameter. For example, when RSVP reservation messages arrive at a sending RSVP node, one has to check using the **ATM_GQOS** command, whether there is already an ATM ARP QoS table entry for the flow specified in the RSVP reservation message.

The **ATM_DQOS** command deletes an entry from the ATM ARP QoS table. Deleting the entry for a certain IP flow in the ATM ARP QoS table results in the termination of the corresponding VC. Packets of the deleted flow will again be sent over the best-effort VC. The **ATM_GQOS** and the **ATM_DQOS** commands need the next hop address and the flow identifier as parameters.

The `ATM_DUMPQOS` command dumps the contents of the ATM ARP QoS table. It is mainly used for debugging and monitoring purposes.

3.3 Sender modifications

When a data packet for a certain flow has to be sent, the extended classical IP over ATM implementation looks if there is an entry for the flow in the ATM ARP QoS table. If an entry is found and a VC does not exist, it tries to establish the VC by sending a `SETUP` message. In the meantime it sends the packets of the flow for which the connection is being established over the best-effort VC to the destination. As soon as the dedicated VC is established, packets belonging to the flow will be sent over the dedicated VC. For a packet to be sent, the following operations are performed (Figure 5):

- If no ATM ARP QoS table entry is found for the destination address, the normal ATM ARP operations are performed.

- If at least one entry is found, the complete flow identifier is extracted from the packet headers. The source and destination addresses are extracted from the IP header, the source and destination ports from the TCP/UDP header. Only TCP and UDP protocols are currently supported. Another lookup is performed on the ATM ARP QoS table for the complete flow identifier.

  - If no ATM ARP QoS table entry is found, the packet is sent over the best-effort VC.

  - If the ATM ARP QoS table entry is found, there are three cases:

    - If the VC is `UP` the packet is sent over the dedicated QoS VC.

    - If the VC is `CONNECTING` the packet is sent over the best-effort VC.

    - If the VC is `DOWN` a function call is performed in order to get the VC connected, and the packet is sent over the best-effort VC.

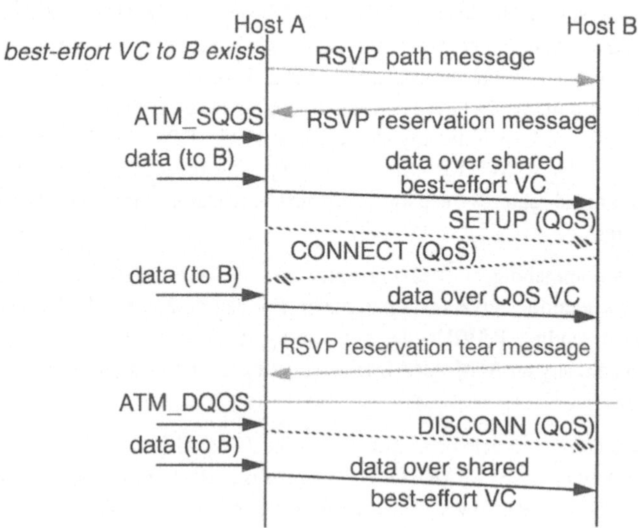

Figure 4: VC setup for IP flows with QoS requirements

The number of additional operations of the sending routine have been kept very low compared to the original classical IP over ATM implementation in order to minimize the performance overhead.

Figure 4 shows the behavior of the sender part of the classical IP over ATM implementation. Data are sent over the QoS VC as soon as it is established. VC establishment is triggered by an `ATM_SQOS` command, e.g. after an RSVP message exchange. VCs are deleted by the `ATM_-DQOS` command, e.g. after tearing the RSVP reservation. After deleting the VC data are sent over the best-effort VC again. The QoS parameters of the ATM ARP QoS entries, which have been configured by an `ATM_SQOS` command, are used for ATM connection setup. The connection parameters, which are included in the `qos_info` structure, are copied into the corresponding fields of the SETUP message.

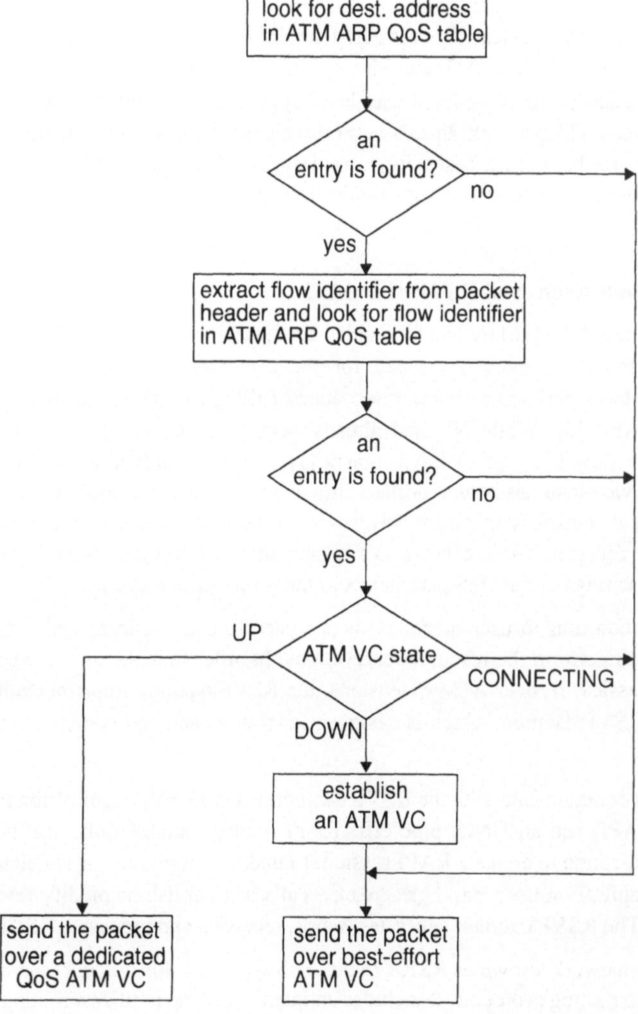

Figure 5: QoS extensions of the sender part of the classical IP over ATM implementation

3.4 Receiver modifications

Handling of incoming calls has also been modified, i.e. the classical IP over ATM implementation had to be adapted. In a normal classical IP over ATM implementation an Inverse ARP message is sent back to the calling system in order to find out its IP address when a connection establishment request is received. Since the additional VCs with QoS support are unidirectional (as RSVP reservations are unidirectional), this Inverse ARP message will not be sent for QoS VCs. QoS VCs are identified by having the broadband Bearer Capability class set to C (for best-effort VCs the used class is X), and the backward sustainable cell rate set to 0 (unidirectional VC).

4 Applications

The extensions to the classical IP over ATM implementation allow user-level programs to establish dedicated VCs for IP flows with specific QoS. Thus, it becomes possible for a resource reservation protocol or for a user-level application to benefit from QoS guarantees across an IP over ATM network. In this section we describe how to use the classical IP over ATM extensions for both of the cases. First, we describe Mbone applications using RSVP over ATM. Second, we explain how to design applications in order to use directly the quality-of-service interface.

4.1 Mbone Applications and RSVP over ATM

The network video (NV) [10] tool and the video conferencing tool (vic) [16] are one of numerous video conferencing tools developed for the use over the IETF multicast backbone (Mbone). Both tools perform resource reservations calling the RSVP daemon [21] using the RSVP API (RAPI) [8]. While NV had already been prepared for the use over RSVP, we adapted vic for its use in an RSVP environment [9]. Currently, only unicast communication is supported. The vic menu has been modified allowing the receiver to specify the desired bandwidth. The actual transmission rate is advertised in the path message according to [18] and displayed at the receiver. The receiving user is then able to select the reserved bandwidth that determines the settings of the QoS parameters in the reservation messages.

The RSVP daemon runs in user space and is designed to communicate with a traffic control kernel in order to perform the resource reservations. In order to make use of the features provided by the classical IP over ATM extensions, the RSVP daemon implementation had to be modified. The RSVP daemon, which is designed for routers and end systems, has three major interfaces:

- Applications communicate with the RSVP daemon via the RSVP Application Programming Interface (RAPI) and an UNIX pipe. The RAPI library routines linked to the application allow an application to create a RAPI session, to make reservations, or to delete them. E.g., a receiver application uses `rapi_reserve` calls to establish or modify reservations for the session. The RSVP daemon generates, sends, receives, and processes RSVP messages.

- A general framework known as RSRR (Routing Support for Resource Reservation) is used as interface to routing protocols. It includes an interface to the multicast routing code and an unicast routing interface to the kernel routing table.

- The RSVP daemon communicates with a traffic control kernel through a traffic control (TC) adaptation module which is a part of the RSVP daemon. The RSVP daemon can be used to establish reservation states in hosts and routers. The daemon may pass this state to the traffic control kernel via the kernel-specific TC adaptation module. The packet classifier, packet scheduler and the admission control module can be considered as parts of a traffic control kernel.

The original release contained a TC adaptation module for the MIT ISPS kernel. In order to perform the additionally defined ioctl calls of the kernel extensions and to reserve ATM resources, a new TC adaptation module for ATM has been implemented. The RSVP daemon cooperates with the TC adaptation module through several function calls. Their interfaces have been nearly kept unchanged compared to the original release.

Within the resulting implementation the Mbone application calls the RSVP daemon by RAPI calls. The RSVP daemon in turn performs function calls to the TC adaptation module. The TC adaptation module then establishes dedicated QoS ATM VCs through the classical IP over ATM implementation extensions. This scenario is shown in Figure 6. The TC adaptation module is the interface between the RSVP daemon and the classical IP over ATM QoS extensions. The TC adaptation module provides several interface functions.

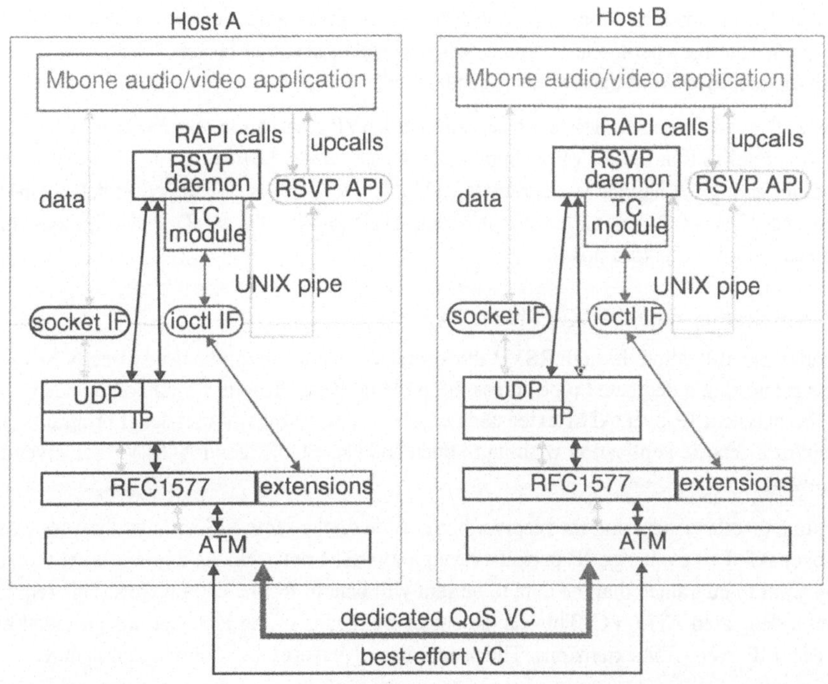

Figure 6: Mbone multimedia application over RSVP and ATM

A RAPI call at the receiver (host B) to `rapi_reserve` triggers the sending of a reservation message to the sender (host A). After receiving a reservation message the RSVP daemon at host A calls the traffic control function `TC_AddFlowspec` using the parameters desired flow specification and sender traffic specification. The function translates the QoS parameters into ATM connection parameters, and returns a pointer to the created structure as a handle to the RSVP daemon. QoS mapping between IETF service classes and ATM connection parameters is described in [6].

The RSVP daemon then calls the `TC_SetFilter` function within the TC module, in order to associate the entry created by `TC_AddFlowspec` to a specific IP flow, and to add the complete entry to the ATM ARP QoS table. The `TC_SetFilter` function performs an `ATM_GQOS` ioctl call, in order to check whether a private VC already exists for this flow. If no entry is found, an `ATM_SQOS` can be performed, and the VC is prepared to be established. As soon as a data packet has to be sent by host A, the setup procedure for the private VC is triggered, while the packet is sent over the best-effort VC. When the VC is fully established, packets belonging to this specific flow are sent over the dedicated QoS VC.

If host B now changes its reservation (e.g., asking for a higher bandwidth), a new RSVP reservation message is sent to host A. At host A, the `TC_ModFlowspec` function is called by the RSVP daemon, with the handle and the modified flow specification as parameters. This function first checks the existence of the entry passed as a parameter within the ATM ARP QoS table (through a `ATM_GQOS` call). If the entry is found, it deletes it through an `ATM_DQOS` call, thus tearing down the private VC. It then translates the new QoS parameters into ATM connection parameters. Finally, it calls `ATM_SQOS` to set a new entry in the ATM ARP QoS table with the new parameters. Again, when a packet needs to be sent by host A, a new VC with the modified ATM parameters is established.

If host B finally wants to delete a reservation, a RSVP reservation tear message is sent to host A. This implies that the RSVP daemon calls the `TC_DelFlowspec` function within the TC module, giving the handle as a parameter. The `TC_DelFlowspec` function deletes the entry from the ATM ARP QoS table through an ioctl call to `ATM_DQOS`. This also implies that the corresponding VC is torn down.

4.2 Application-requested QoS-based VCs

Besides the utilization through RSVP, the kernel extensions might be used directly by applications requesting a dedicated pipe across the ATM network. The new ioctl commands provided by the classical IP over ATM extensions can be accessed by any user-level program. Guidelines for a generic application wishing to open and use a QoS-based ATM VC are given in the following.

Assume that the sender and the receiver both reside on the same LIS and that they use classical IP over ATM to exchange IP packets through an ATM network. At a given time, the sender may want to guarantee that the data to be sent will benefit from a certain QoS. This requires to open a dedicated ATM VC. This can be set up by means of the ioctl options provided by the classical IP over ATM extensions. The sender has to perform the following procedure.

- First, a socket must be opened to allow the ioctl function to be called.

- A data structure containing several parameters for the `ATM_GQOS` call must be filled with the destination IP address, the complete flow identifier (source and destination IP addresses and port numbers), and the QoS parameters for the ATM connection such as peak rate, sustainable rate, and maximum burst size.

- An `ATM_GQOS` ioctl call must be performed in order to make sure that no other dedicated VC already exists for the specified flow.

- An `ATM_SQOS` ioctl must be performed to set an entry in the ATM ARP QoS table and to prepare the kernel to establish the private VC.

- When the first data packet for the specified flow has to be sent, the kernel extensions will try to set up the VC, while sending the first packet over the best-effort VC. Once the connection is established, packets will start to flow over the private VC established with dedicated QoS parameters.

- If the sender wants to close the private VC, it must call a `ATM_DQOS` ioctl command. The ATM connection is released and the corresponding entry is removed from the ATM ARP QoS table.

No modifications of the procedure to send data are required. The socket interface is still being used with no additional parameters. The ioctl calls can be performed at any time during a socket connection, and they influence only packets sent after an `ATM_SQOS` call. No modifications are required to the application on the receiver side. It will keep on receiving data through the same socket without any modification.

5 Future work

The classical IP over ATM implementation does currently not support IP multicast. IP multicast over ATM is still a matter of specification [2]. The implementation architecture is prepared to support multicast and only minor modifications are needed to adapt it. In particular, the ATM ARP QoS table entries should be modified in order to store a list of ATM addresses, instead of a single one to be able to establish point-to-multipoint VCs. The shared explicit reservation style is not implemented in the used RSVP implementation. The kernel extensions do not support it as well. In order to support this style, slight modifications would be needed in the data structures, i.e. the table entry should include a list of senders, instead of a single sender [11].

An important issue which is currently under study at the IETF is the QoS parameters mapping between IETF service classes and ATM service classes [6]. The implementation does not focus specifically on this topic, which is left for future improvements. However, functions calls to translate the QoS are provided within the TC adaptation module of the RSVP daemon, such that only the body of these functions must be modified to change the QoS mapping. The QoS mapping is done in the user space. This simplifies to evaluate different schemes to map IETF integrated services classes and parameters [4][19][22] to ATM parameters [3].

The architecture presented in this paper is a good basis for experiments. Several functional extensions are under discussion. It may be desirable to establish a VC immediately after calling an `ATM_SQOS` command and not together with the first data packet. This allows that data of the supported flow can be exchanged earlier over the QoS VC. However, if there are no data to exchange directly after the `ATM_SQOS` command, the early VC setup would waste ATM resources. Another option would be a command to modify the QoS parameters of a flow. In that case, the old VC is torn down after an additional VC with the modified QoS parameters has been established. This avoids that data are exchanged over the best-effort VC between releasing the old VC and the availability of the new VC. However, the probability that the new VC can not be set up because of missing resources increases. Given that a switch can support X Mbps of a single port, modifying the QoS requirements from Y Mbps to Z Mbps is not possible using a modify command as proposed above, if $Y + Z > X$.

6 Conclusions

The implemented classical IP over ATM implementation extensions allow any application to establish and use dedicated VCs across an ATM network through a well-defined interface, while the standard TCP-UDP/IP socket calls remain unchanged. The QoS VC establishment can be made at any time during the data transmission, and the existing sockets need not to be closed and re-opened. Implementation in routers is possible, and heterogeneous IP over ATM networks are supported through utilization of RSVP. The QoS-based VC management is based on well-defined interfaces, such as new ioctl commands or the RSVP API. The only obvious disadvantage compared to native ATM interfaces consists in the lack of direct VCs between end systems on different LISs. Integrating NHRP into the protocol architecture would eliminate this drawback. Several advantages over native ATM interfaces make the proposed approach attractive to allow QoS support for existing Internet applications over ATM.

7 References

[1]   W. Almesberger, J.Y. LeBoudec, P. Oechslin: Application REQuested IP over ATM (AREQUIPA), Internet Draft, June 1996

[2]   G. Armitage: Support for Multicast over UNI 3.0/3.1 based ATM Networks, February 1996

[3]   ATM Forum Technical Committee: User-Network Interface Specification Version 3.1, ATM Forum, September 1994

[4]   F. Baker, R. Guerin, D. Kandlur: Specification of Committed Rate Quality-of-Service, Internet Draft, June 1996

[5]   S. Berson: IP Integrated Services Support in ATM, Internet Draft, September 1996

[6]   M. Borden: Interoperation of Controlled-Load and Guaranteed Service with ATM, Internet Draft, September 1996

[7]   R. Braden, L. Zhang, S. Berson, S. Herzog, S. Jamin: Resource ReSerVation Protocol (RSVP) - Version 1 Functional Specification, Internet Draft, May 1996

[8]   R. Braden, D. Hoffman: RSVP Application Programming Interface (RAPI) for SunOS/ BSD, Internet Draft, August 1995

[9]   S. Bretz: Integration of a RSVP Resource Reservation Module into a MBone Multimedia Application, Diploma Thesis, BA Mannheim, September 1996

[10]   R. Frederick: Experiences with real-time software video compression, ftp:// parcftp.xerox.com/pub/net-research/nv-paper.ps, 1994

[11]   S. Giorcelli: RSVP over Implementation over ATM, Professional Thesis, Eurecom Sophia-Antipolis, July 1996

[12] W. J. Hymas, H. Stüttgen, S. Sharma, S. Wise: Socket Extensions for Native ATM, IEEE ATM '96 Workshop, San Francisco, August 26-28, 1996

[13] D. Kandlur, D. Saha, M. Willebeek-LeMair: Protocol Architecture for Multimedia Applications over ATM Networks, ACM Computer Communication Review, Vol. 25, No. 3, July 1995, pp. 33-43

[14] D. Katz, D. Piscitello, J. Luciani: NBMA Next Hop Resolution Protocol (NHRP), Internet Draft, September 1996

[15] M. Laubach: Classical IP and ARP over ATM, RFC 1577, January 1994

[16] S. McCanne, V. Jacobson: vic: A Flexible Framework Framework for Packet Video, ACM Multimedia '95

[17] M. Perez, F. Liaw, A. Mankin, E. Hoffman, D. Grossman, A. Malis: ATM Signaling Support for IP over ATM, RFC 1755, February 1995

[18] S. Shenker, L. Breslau: Two Issues in Reservation Establishment, ACM SIGCOMM '95, pp. 14-26

[19] S. Shenker, C. Partridge, R. Guerin: Specification of Guaranteed Quality of Service, Internet Draft, August 1996

[20] R.K. Singh, S.G. Tell, and S.J. Bharat: Comparison of Raw and Internet Protocols in a HIPPI/ATM/SONET Based Gigabit Network, ACM Computer Communication Review, Vol. 26, No. 1, January 1996, pp. 18-28

[21] URL: ftp://ftp.isi.edu/rsvp/release

[22] J. Wroclawski: Specification of the Controlled-Load Network Element Service, Internet Draft, June 1996

Hochleistungsfähige Implementierung von Protokollen mit zellenbasierten Fehlerkontrollmechanismen für ATM-Netze

Georg Carle, Institut für Telematik, Universität Karlsruhe
Jochen Schiller, Institutionen för Datorteknik, Uppsala Universitet, Schweden
E-Mail: [g.carle, j.schiller]@ieee.org

Kurzfassung

Der Asynchrone Transfermodus (ATM) beginnt sich mehr und mehr als wichtige Netzwerktechnologie sowohl in privaten als auch öffentlichen Netzen durchzusetzen. Es besteht aber immer noch ein großer Mangel an Erfahrung mit Implementierungen leistungsfähiger, an das ATM-Umfeld angepaßter Protokolle auf unterschiedlichen Implementierungsplattformen. Wichtig ist hierbei, daß der Nutzen neuartiger Protokolle durch reale Implementierungen oder praxisnahe Simulationen nachgewiesen werden kann. Der vorliegende Artikel beschreibt anhand eines Protokolls mit zellenbasierten Vorwärtsfehlerkorrekturmechanismen [CaEG95a, CaEG95b] in der ATM-Adaptionsschicht sowie eines Protokolls mit ATM-spezifischen Übertragungswiederholungsmechanismen [CaZi95] unser Vorgehen bei der Gewinnung von Leistungsaussagen. Zur Untersuchung der Protokollimplementierungen werden preiswerte, PC-basierte Systeme, die Emulation von ATM-Netzwerken auf Arbeitsplatzrechnern und schließlich die Implementierung auf hochleistungsfähiger Hardware aufgeführt. Als ein Resultat der Arbeiten kann der Nutzen des gewählten Protokolls und der Implementierungen anhand konkreter Leistungskenndaten aufgezeigt werden.

1 Einleitung

Die Einführung von ATM-Netzen stellt in mehrerer Hinsicht ein Paradigmenwechsel dar. So wird mit ATM in Zukunft ein System zur Verfügung stehen, das mit einem einheitlichen Übertragungsverfahren, dem Asynchronen Transfermodus, eine Vielfalt unterschiedlicher Endsysteme miteinander verbinden wird. Zusätzlich bietet ATM die Möglichkeit, vielerlei unterschiedlicher Dienste, wie Audio, Video und Massendatentransfer mit garantierter Dienstgüte unter Zuhilfenahme von sogenannten Adaptionsschichten anzubieten. Für herkömmliche Netze entwickelte Kommunikationsprotokolle höherer Schichten sind nun aufgrund dieser Veränderungen oft nicht mehr adäquat für den Einsatz oberhalb der ATM-Schicht. Zusätzlich sind neue Dienste wie die Gruppenkommunikation gefordert, die von gängigen Protokollen nicht oder nur unzureichend unterstützt werden. Aus diesen Gründen ist eine Neuentwicklung angepaßter Protokolle unabdingbar für die vollständige Ausnutzung der Leistungsfähigkeit von ATM.
Ein wichtiger Schritt im Rahmen der Protokollentwicklung ist der Praxistest. Ein Protokoll sollte nicht nur in der Theorie fehlerfrei funktionieren, sondern vor allem im realen Einsatz seine Leistungsfähigkeit und Funktionalität unter Beweis stellen. Eine weitere wesentliche Eigenschaft eines Protokolls ist die Möglichkeit der einfachen Integration in verschiedene Implementierungsarchitekturen. Beispiele für solche Architekturen sind preiswerte Standard-PCs als Endgeräte, leistungsfähige Arbeitsplatzrechner für den technisch-wissenschaftlichen Einsatzbereich sowie dedizierte, hochleistungsfähige Zwischensysteme.

Im folgenden Abschnitt erfolgt eine Einführung in das als Protokollbeispiel gewählte Verfahren zur Vorwärtsfehlerkorrektur. Im 3. Abschnitt wird dann die Integration dieses Protokolls in die ATM-Adaptionsschicht aufgezeigt. Anschließend wird im 4. Abschnitt anhand einer Protokolltestumgebung auf Arbeitsplatzrechnern aufgezeigt, wie sich das Verhalten des Protokolls unter verschiedenen Umgebungsbedingungen wirklichkeitsgetreu überprüfen läßt. Als leistungsfähigste Implementierung des Protokolls wird im 5. Abschnitt eine dedizierte Hardware-Einheit zur Unterstützung der Protokollabarbeitung vorgestellt. Anschließend erfolgt eine Übersicht über die im Rahmen dieser Arbeiten gewonnenen Ergebnisse.

2 Fehlerkontrollmechanismen in ATM-Netzwerken

ATM-Netze erlauben es, bei Diensten mit variabler Bitrate die Bandbreite dynamisch zwischen mehreren Verbindungen aufzuteilen, wodurch sich ein statistischer Multiplexgewinn erzielen läßt. Bei der Überlagerung stoßartiger Datenströme kann es dabei zum Verlust von Zellen durch Pufferüberläufe kommen. In Breitbandnetzen mit optischer Übertragung, die sehr kleine Bitfehlerwahrscheinlichkeiten besitzen, sind Zellverluste durch Pufferüberläufe weitaus häufiger als Zellverluste durch Übertragungsfehler. Pufferüberläufe sind keine unabhängigen Ereignisse, sondern zeigen ein stark korreliertes Verhalten [OhKi91]. Die Wahrscheinlichkeit für Zellverluste kann für verschiedene Dienste über einen großen Bereich variieren [StGr94]. Für Quellen mit stark stoßartigem Sendeverhalten kann eine akzeptable Netzauslastung häufig nur erreicht werden, wenn höhere Zellverlustwahrscheinlichkeit in Kauf genommen werden [WoFD93]. Für den Sender einer Multicastverbindung steigt mit wachsender Anzahl von Empfängern auch die Wahrscheinlichkeit für das Auftreten von Fehlern.
Zellverluste können entweder durch Übertragungswiederholungen (Automatic Repeat Request, ARQ) oder durch Vorwärtsfehlerkorrektur (Forward Error Correction, FEC) behoben werden. ARQ-Verfahren besitzen schlechte Skalierungseigenschaften für große Pfadkapazitäten sowie für Gruppenkommunikation mit vielen Empfängern. Die Leistungsfähigkeit von FEC-Verfahren ist unabhängig von Entfernung und Pfadkapazität. FEC-Verfahren besitzen außerdem für Multicastverbindungen sehr gute Skalierungseigenschaften, weil ihre Leistungsfähigkeit unabhängig von der Gruppengröße ist. Als Nachteil ist der permanent erforderliche Mehraufwand für die Redundanzdaten zu sehen.

2.1 Motivation für die Entwicklung leistungsfähiger Adaptionsschichtprotokolle

Die Schwächen der für heterogene Netze entwickelten Kommunikationsprotokolle beim Einsatz in einem homogenen ATM-Netz sind darauf zurückzuführen, daß ATM-Netze gegenüber den bisherigen Netzen in mehrerer Hinsicht einen Paradigmenwechsel darstellen. Die für heterogene Netze entwickelten Kommunikationsprotokolle für zuverlässige Gruppenkommunikation haben in der neuen Umgebung funktionale und leistungsbezogene Defizite.
Durch die hohe vermittelbare Bandbreite in ATM-Netzen wurde die Protokollverarbeitung, die zur Sicherstellung eines zuverlässigen Ende-zu-Ende-Dienstes erforderlich ist, zum potentiellen Leistungsengpaß.
Neben unzureichender Verarbeitungsleistung kann ein Leistungsengpaß auch darauf zurückzuführen sein, daß Protokollmechanismen unzureichend an die Eigenschaften des darunterliegenden Netzwerks angepaßt sind. Während die konventionellen Internetzwerke in der Regel von einer verbindungslosen Netzwerkschicht geprägt sind, ist ATM ein verbindungsorientiertes

Protokoll. Aus diesem Grund eignen sich die für eine verbindungslose Netzwerkschicht entwickelten Transportprotokolle nur bedingt für ATM-Netze.

In bestehenden paketvermittelten Netzwerken treten Pakete variabler Länge auf, die häufig mehrere Kilobyte groß sind. Im Überlastfall treten in den Netzknoten Pufferüberläufe auf, bei denen Pakete verworfen werden. In den Netzknoten bieten diese Pakete variabler Länge die Basiseinheit des Multiplexens zur Zuteilung von Netzressourcen. Im Gegensatz dazu bilden in ATM-Netzen kurze Zellen mit einer Länge von 53 byte die Basiseinheit des Multiplexens. Überlastete ATM-Knoten verwerfen einzelne Zellen. Bei Verwendung der Adaptionstypen AAL3/4 und AAL5 hat schon ein einzelner Zellverlust zur Folge, daß ein aus bis zu mehreren hundert Zellen bestehendes Paket komplett verloren geht [StGr94]. Daher ist eine Fehlerbehebung in der Transportschicht, wo immer der Verlust ganzer Pakete behoben werden muß, nicht geeignet, Fehler durch beschädigte oder verlorene ATM-Zellen effizient zu beheben. Bei einer Behebung von Zellverlusten in der Transportschicht führt häufig schon eine verhältnismäßig geringe Zellverlustwahrscheinlichkeit zu einem dramatischen Einbruch der Dienstqualität [Roma93].

Um zuverlässige Gruppenkommunikationsdienste in ATM-Netzen auf effizientere Weise als mit den bisher vorhandenen Protokollen erbringen zu können, ist die Entwicklung neuer Protokolle erforderlich, die an die spezifischen Randbedingungen in ATM-Netzen besser angepaßt sind. Dabei ist es wichtig, Fehlerkontrollmechanismen zur Verfügung zu haben, die beim Auftreten von Zellverlusten eine große Leistungsfähigkeit besitzen. Da bei der Gruppenkommunikation eine Vielzahl unterschiedlicher Randbedingungen möglich sind, ist es auch wichtig, Fehlerkontrollmechanismen einsetzen zu können, die an die charakteristischen Eigenschaften eines Kommunikationsszenarios angepaßt sind. Gleichzeitig müssen diese Mechanismen mit geringem Implementierungsaufwand realisierbar sein, um Leistungsengpässe durch die Protokollverarbeitung zu vermeiden.

2.2 FEC-SSCS: Dienstspezifische Konvergenzteilschicht mit FEC für AAL5

Ein Schwerpunkt unserer Untersuchungen bildete ein Adaptionsschichtprotokoll mit Vorwärtsfehlerkorrektur, dessen Schichtmodell in Abbildung 1 gezeigt ist. Bei dem innerhalb des ATM-Forums diskutierten Protokolls FEC-SSCS (FEC Service Specific Convergence Sublayer, [CaEG95a, CaEG95b]) handelt es sich um eine dienstspezifische Konvergenzteilschicht für AAL5, die zellenbasierte Vorwärtsfehlerkorrektur mit einer vom Sender dynamisch anpaßbaren Anzahl von Redundanzzellen ermöglicht. FEC-SSCS verwendet pro 46 byte großem Datensegment einen Protokollkopf von 2 byte Länge, der eine Zellsequenznummer sowie die Prüfsumme CRC-10 enthält. Damit können Bitfehler und Zellverluste erkannt werden. Zur Fehlerkorrektur werden innerhalb der AAL5-Nutzlast zusätzliche 46 byte große Redundanzsegmente hinzugefügt, die zusammen mit dem Protokollkopf die sogenannten Redundanzzellen bilden. Die Protokollverarbeitung beim Empfänger ist im verlustlosen Fall sehr gering, da lediglich die ursprüngliche Nutzdaten reassembliert werden müssen und die Redundanzzellen einfach verworfen werden können. Während die ursprüngliche Spezifikation von FEC-SSCS [CaEG95b] ausschließlich Reed-Solomon-Codes zur Generierung der Redundanzzellen einsetzt, untersuchten wir zusätzlich eine Generierung von Redundanzzellen mit einem Matrixbasierten XOR-Verfahren.

Wie in [EsCa95] gezeigt, läßt sich FEC-SSCS auch sehr vorteilhaft in Verbindung mit dem Protokoll SSCOP [Q2110] als höhere Schicht einsetzen. Unsere Implementierung von FEC-SSCS erlaubt, wie in Abschnitt 6 gezeigt, den Einsatz von SSCOP über FEC-SSCS.

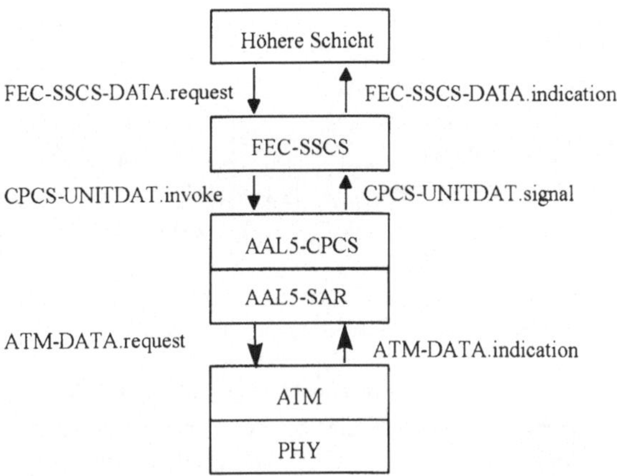

Abbildung 1: Dienstspezifische Konvergenzteilschicht mit FEC für AAL5

2.3 RMC-SSCS: Dienstspezifische Konvergenzteilschicht mit zellenbasierter Vorwärtsfehlerkorrektur und Übertragungswiederholung für AAL5

Das RMC-AAL-Protokoll (Reliable Multicast ATM Adaptation Layer, [CaZi95]) wurde für die Dienstspezifische Konvergenzteilschicht (SSCS) von AAL5 entwickelt und daher auch als RMC-SSCS bezeichnet. Es verfügt neben zellenbasierter FEC über die Möglichkeit, rahmenbasierte oder zellenbasierte Übertragungswiederholungen durchzuführen. RMC-SSCS kann sowohl in Endsystemen als auch in speziellen Zwischensystemen, sogenannten Gruppenkommunikationsservern, eingesetzt werden, siehe Abbildung 3 [CaZi95].

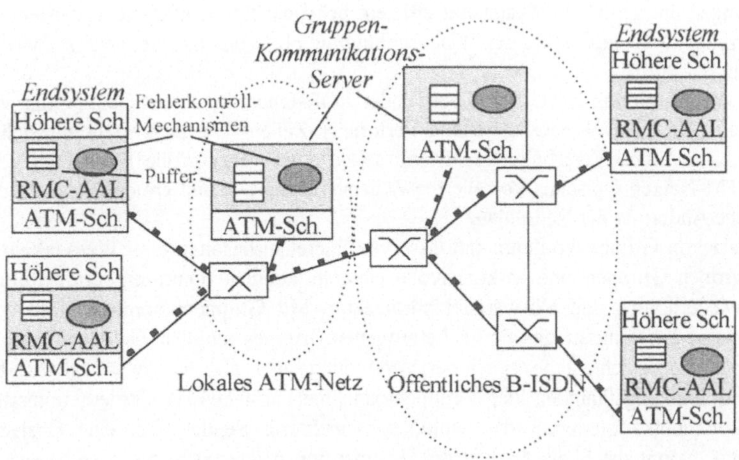

Abbildung 2: Adaptionsschichtprotokoll RMC-AAL mit Mechanismen zur Unterstützung zuverlässiger Multicastkommunikation

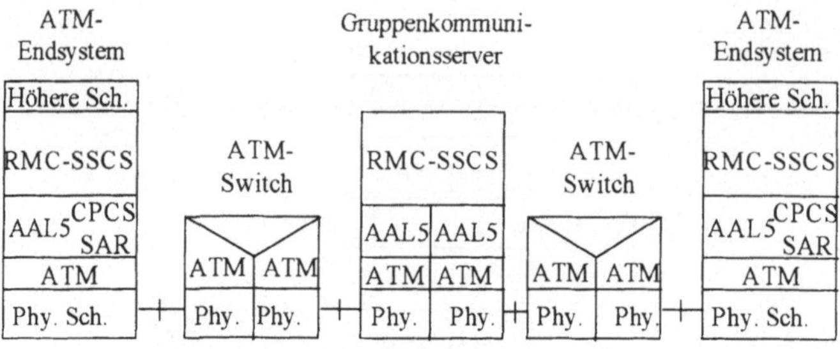

Abbildung 3: Schichtmodell für RMC-AAL

RMC-SSCS verwendet einen Rahmenkopf von 10 byte und kann dadurch zuverlässige Dienste mit einer höheren Effizienz erbringen, als dies bei der Verwendung eines Transportprotokolls wie TCP oder XTP möglich wäre, die einen deutlich größeren Paketkopf verwenden. Durch ein spezielles Quittungsformat mit Binärfeldern stellt die Quittungsverarbeitung von RMC-SSCS auch für eine große Empfängerzahl nur geringe Anforderungen an die Verarbeitungsleistung, wodurch sich das Problem einer Quittungsimplosion abschwächen läßt.

Für höhere Zellverlustwahrscheinlichkeiten sowie für Anwendungen, die besonders niedrige Verzögerungszeiten fordern, verfügt RMC-SSCS über einen Fehlerkontrollmechanismus mit zellenbasierter Übertragungswiederholung. Durch die Unterstützung des Strommodus kann mit RMC-SSCS im Vergleich zu konventionellen Protokollen eine besonders niedrige Verzögerung erzielt werden, da beim Sender auch von unvollständig vorliegende Rahmen schon einzelne Zellen gesendet werden können, und beim Empfänger Fehler auch schon bei unvollständig empfangenen Rahmen erkannt werden können.

RMC-SSCS verwendet hierarchische Sequenznummern, bestehend aus einer Rahmensequenznummer von 24 bit Länge und einer Zellsequenznummer von 6 bit Länge. Gegenüber existierenden Vorschlägen für eine zellenbasierte Fehlerkontrolle [BoLa93] konnte der zusätzliche Bandbreitenbedarf deutlich gesenkt werden. Durch die Einführung von sogenannten Rahmenfragmenten für die zellenbasierte Übertragungswiederholung lassen sich Zellverluste auch für Verbindungen mit großer Pfadkapazität effizient beheben. Rahmenfragmente bestehen aus einer Kopfzelle zur Identifikation der Wiederholung, gefolgt von einer Sequenz zu wiederholender Zellen.

Das FEC-Verfahren von RMC-SSCS verwendet XOR-Operationen zur Generierung von Redundanzzellen und zur Wiederherstellung verlorener Zellen. Dieses Verfahren zeichnet sich durch einen geringen Verarbeitungsaufwand sowie durch einer große Robustheit gegenüber den in ATM-Netzen typischen korrelierten Zellenverlusten aus und ermöglicht außerdem eine dynamische Änderung der Redundanz.

Der Einsatz von Gruppenkommunikationsservern bietet insbesondere im Weitverkehrsbereich und bei großen Gruppen eine wirkungsvolle Unterstützung für Quittungsverarbeitung, Übertragungswiederholung und Vorwärtsfehlerkorrektur. Mit Gruppenkommunikationsservern ist außerdem eine Leistungssteigerung bei heterogenen Gruppen möglich, bei denen innerhalb der Gruppe große Unterschiede bezüglich der Verbindungseigenschaften sowie bezüglich Funktionalität und Leistungsfähigkeit der Gruppenteilnehmer bestehen. Außerdem unterstützt ein Gruppenkommunikationsserver das Multiplexen mehrerer Sender über eine einzige ATM-Verbindung, womit die Skalierbarkeit bei Gruppen mit mehreren Sendern verbessert werden kann.

3 Implementierung von Protokollmechanismen in die ATM-Adaptionsschicht

Die vollständig funktionsfähige Implementierung der Fehlerkorrekturmechanismen wurde auf PCs unter dem Betriebssystem Linux [Linux] ausgestattet mit 155 Mbps ATM-Adaptern [ENI96] durchgeführt. Abbildung 4 zeigt dabei die Lage des FEC-Moduls innerhalb des Schichtenmodells an. Das FEC-Modul befindet sich auf der Hardware-unabhängigen Seite, so daß es prinzipiell für beliebige ATM-Adapterkarten einsetzbar ist. Das Modul ATM-sockets stellt die Treiberschnittstelle für Anwendungsprogramme dar. Hierüber können außer den üblichen Befehlen zur Datenübertragung alle FEC-Parameter beinflußt werden. Ein Beispiel hierfür ist der folgende Befehl, der die FEC-Parameter auf 2 Redundanzzellen pro AAL-Rahmen, Reed-Solomon-Algorithmus und aktivierte Bitkorrektur setzt.

```
ioctl(socket, FEC_SETMODE, FEC_MODE(2, FEC_REEDSOLOMON,
      FEC_BITCORRECTION));
```

Die aktuell gültigen FEC-Parameter können mittels

```
result = ioctl(socket, FEC_GETMODE, 0);
```

abgefragt werden. Die Anwenderschnittstelle wurde also in die bereits vorhandene Schnittstelle zur Steuerung der Gerätetreiberoptionen (ioctl, input/ouput control) eingebunden. Der Vorteil dieser Schnittstelle liegt in der einfachen Handhabung und Aufrufbarkeit. Für die FEC-Parameter selbst wurde ein bisher ungenutztes Feld innerhalb der socket-Struktur verwendet. Ein weiterer Vorteil dieser Lösung liegt darin, daß bereits existierende Anwendungen, die kein Gebrauch der FEC-Erweiterung machen, weiterhin problemlos betrieben werden können, da für sie kein Unterschied in der Anwenderschnittstelle sichtbar ist.

Das Modul ATM-Koordination ist für die gesamte Steuerung des Hardware-unabhängigen Teils des Treibers zuständig, darunter auch für Senden und Empfang der Daten. Die Steuerung des Zugriffs auf die Hardware der Adapterkarte führt das Modul PHY-Treiber durch, die Segmentierung und Reassemblierung der Daten übernimmt das Modul SAR-Treiber.

Das implementierte FEC-Modul (siehe Abbildung 4) erhält von der ATM-Koordination die zu sendende Nutzdateneinheit. Nun wird die für die zugehörige Verbindung gültige FEC-Einstellung verwendet, um entweder im Reed-Solomon- oder im XOR-Kodierer Redundanzsymbole für die Nutzdateneinheit zu berechnen. Die Einstellungen für die Verbindungen sind dabei jeweils unabhängig voneinander. Die Nutzdateneinheit wird nun um einen SSCS-PDU-Kopf erweitert und zusammen mit den Redundanzdaten in Segmente von 46 byte Länge zerlegt, von denen jedes mit einem Erkennungskopf versehen wird. Diese Datensegmente werden dem SAR-Treiber zum Versand übergeben. Ist der Bitfehler-Erkennungsmodus aktiviert, so wird jedem Erkennungskopf eines Datensegments noch eine CRC-10-Prüfsumme hinzugefügt.

Beim Empfang von Daten werden diese vom SAR-Treiber an das FEC-Modul weitergeleitet. Anhand des SSCS-PDU-Kopfes wird die ursprüngliche Größe des Datenblocks und die verwendeten FEC-Parameter ermittelt. Verlorengegangene Zellen können leicht mittels des Erkennungskopfes ermittelt werden. Bei aktivierter Bitfehlererkennung werden zusätzlich noch die Prüfsummen der einzelnen Zellen überprüft. Bei einem Prüfsummenfehler wird eine Zelle als verloren markiert. Sind keine Übertragungsfehler aufgetreten, so werden die Nutzdaten extrahiert und an die ATM-Koordination weitergeleitet. Sind jedoch Fehler aufgetreten, so wird die beschädigte SSCS-PDU mit einer Liste der verlorenen Zellen je nach FEC-Parameter an die Reed-Solomon- bzw. XOR-Einheit weitergeleitet. Hier wird mit Hilfe der Redundanz versucht, die ursprünglichen Daten wieder herzustellen. Ist dies möglich, so wird das Paket wie im fehlerfreien Fall weitergeleitet ansonsten verworfen.

Die Implementierung des FEC-Moduls geschah vollständig im Kern des Betriebssystems Linux, da hier ATM-Gerätetreiber und das Betriebssystem als Quellcode vorhanden sind.

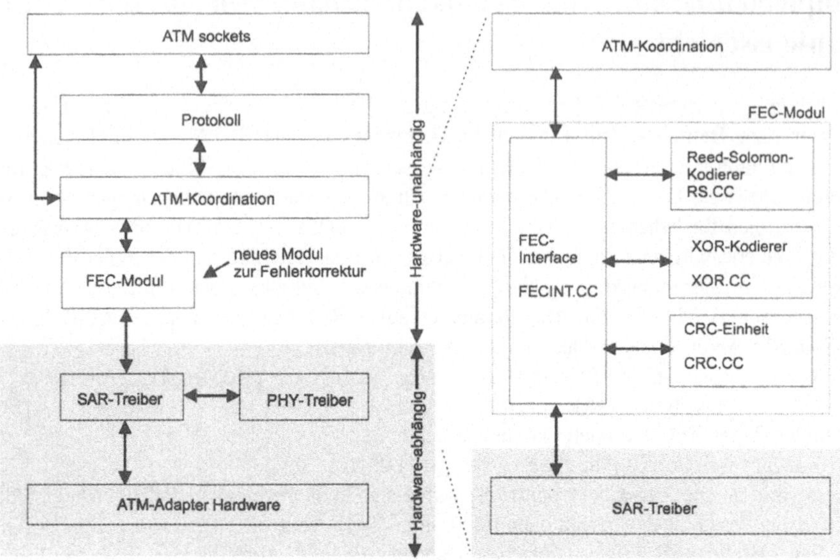

Abbildung 4: Modularer Aufbau des FEC-Moduls

4 Protokolltestumgebung

Mehr noch als bei konventionellen Protokollen gilt es bei Protokollen für die Gruppenkommunikation das Verhalten für eine große Anzahl an Teilnehmern unter realistischen Bedingungen zu testen. Für das hier gewählte Beispiel bedeutet dies unter anderem, daß die Leistungsfähigkeit der Fehlerkorrektur für verschiedene Fehlerwahrscheinlichkeiten nachgewiesen werden muß. Basierend auf realer ATM-Hardware lassen sich solche Untersuchungen nur sehr schwer durchführen, da sich beispielsweise Parameter wie Zellverlustrate oder Puffergröße innerhalb eines ATM-switches im allgemeinen nicht beeinflussen lassen. Aus diesem Grund wurde im Rahmen dieser Arbeiten auf das ATM-Softwarepaket VINCE (Vendor Independent Network Control Entity, [MaHP94]) zurückgegriffen, das eine Emulation von ATM-Netzwerken und ATM-Vermittlungseinrichtungen basierend auf konventionellen Netzen (mit TCP/IP) und Rechnern gestattet. Zwar liegt die absolute Leistungsfähigkeit dieser Software-Emulation um eine Größenordnung unter der realer ATM-Hardware, doch können nun relativ einfach alle benötigten Parameter beeinflußt werden.

Abbildung 5 gibt den Aufbau des Protokollstapels von VINCE mit der Erweiterung zur Fehlererzeugung und -behebung basierend auf TCP/IP an.

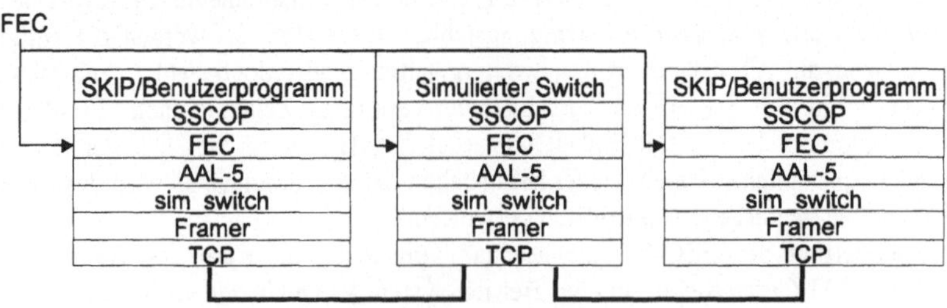

Abbildung 5: Schichtenaufbau der Protokolltestumgebung

Die Nachbildung der ATM-Hardware geschieht in den Schichten sim_switch und Framer. Darunter wird über eine Socket-Schnittstelle auf TCP/IP und die reale Hardware zugegriffen. Die Fehlererzeugung für die Testumgebung wurde in die Schicht sim_switch integriert, da sie Fehler im ATM-Netz nachbilden soll, d.h. die Möglichkeit zum Manipulieren bzw. Verwerfen von ATM-Zellen besitzen muß. Oberhalb von AAL5 folgen die Schicht zur Fehlerbehebung (FEC), darüber SSCOP (Service Specific Convergence Protocol) und schließlich die Benutzerprogramme/SKIP zur Steuerung von VINCE. Hier können nun zum Programmstart oder während der Laufzeit Funktionen innerhalb von VINCE (z.B. Erzeugen eines Switches, Verbindungsverwaltung) ausgeführt werden.

Als Anwendung wurde ein Programm zum Darstellen von MPEG-codierten Videosequenzen gewählt. Auf diese Weise ist es für einen Betrachter sehr einfach möglich, die Auswirkungen von Fehlern und die Fähigkeiten der Fehlerkorrektur zu bewerten. Abbildung 6 zeigt die Oberfläche des Programms XVINCE zur Eingabe der benötigten Parameter für die Fehlererzeugung und -behebung. Neben der Eingabe von Netzadressen und Befehlen können im oberen Teil des Fensters verschiedene Makros ausgeführt werden (Verbindungsaufbau etc.). Im mittleren Teil können für beliebige emulierte ATM-Switches Parameter wie Zellverlustrate, Bitfehlerwahrscheinlichkeit oder Anzahl der FEC-Redundanzzellen eingestellt werden. Sobald mit Hilfe dieser Software Verbindungen aufgebaut wurden, können beliebige Daten übertragen werden. Während der Übertragung können nun die Parameter geändert werden, um so direkt die Auswirkungen zu beobachten.

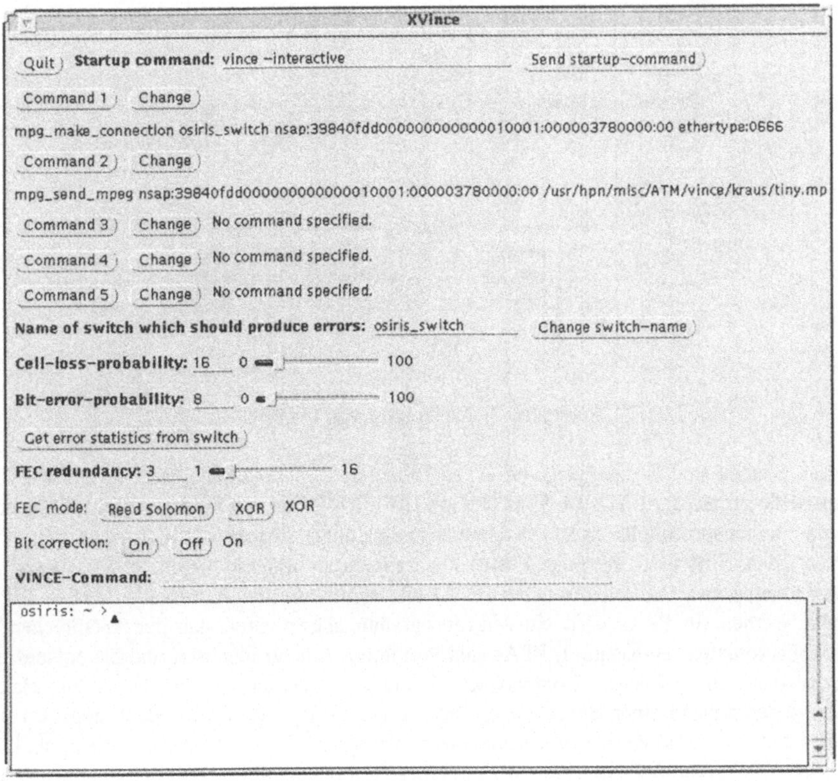

Abbildung 6: Oberfläche von XVINCE zur Steuerung der Parameter eines Software-switches

5 GAPPU: Generic ATM Protocol Processing Unit

Die in den vorigen Abschnitten vorgestellten Mechanismen zur Fehlerkorrektur können eine relativ große Rechenleistung erfordern. Dies gilt insbesondere beim Einsatz dieser Mechanismen in Zwischensystemen, die eine sehr große Gruppe von Empfängern zu bedienen haben. Hinzu kommt, daß es wesentlich wirtschaftlicher ist, in einigen wenigen Zwischensystemen eine sehr hohe Rechenleistung zur Verfügung zu stellen, um dann im Gegenzug Endsysteme relativ einfach gestalten zu können. So sollten beispielsweise Zwischensysteme mit adäquaten Fehlerkorrekturmechnismen für mobile, leistungsschwächere Endsysteme und hochleistungsfähige Arbeitsplatzrechner ausgestattet sein.

Um die für diese Heterogenität erforderliche Rechenleistung erbringen zu können, wurde das Konzept der Protokollverarbeitungseinheit GAPPU (Generic ATM Protocol Processing Unit) entwickelt. GAPPU stellt ein Rahmenwerk dar, das mehrere RISC-Prozessoren, dedizierte Hardware und Speicher umfaßt. Wesentlich ist hierbei, daß alle Komponenten durch eine hochgradig parallele Kopplungseinheit (Kreuzschienenverteiler) verbunden werden, die zusätzlich für einen vorhersagbaren und steuerbaren Datenaustausch zwischen den Komponenten sorgt. Dies bedeutet, daß im Rahmen der Datenübertragung innerhalb der Architektur im Gegensatz zu gängigen Systemen eine vorher festgelegte Dienstgüte garantiert werden kann. Abbildung 7 zeigt die Architektur von GAPPU, die vom Konzept her vergleichbar mit dem Multimedia-Prozessor TMS320C80 [Texa95] ist.

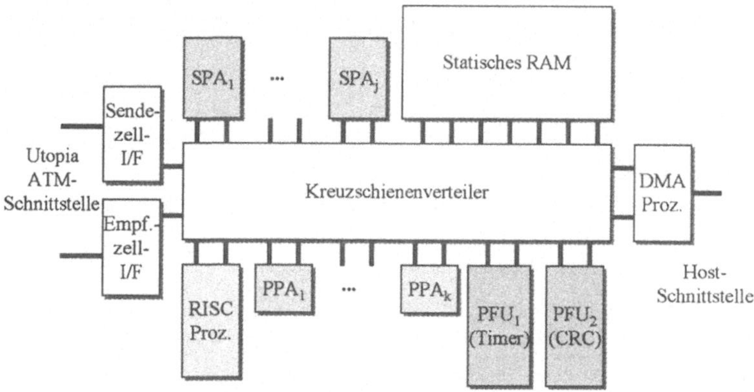

Abbildung 7: Architektur von GAPPU

Für das Senden und Empfangen von ATM-Zellen verfügt GAPPU über eine ATM-PHY-Schnittstelle gemäß der UTOPIA-Spezifikation [AFUT94]. Für leistungsunkritische Teile eines Kommunikationsprotokolls (z.B. Verbindungsverwaltung) können RISC-Prozessoren integriert werden. Sind leistungsfähige Protokollautomaten zu implementieren, so kann zwischen programmierbaren Protokollautomaten (PPA) und synthetisierten Protokollautomaten (SPA) gewählt werden. In PPAs wird ein Mikroprogramm abgearbeitet, das den entsprechenden Protokollautomaten repräsentiert. PPAs sind von ihrem Aufbau identisch und bieten spezielle Mechanismen zum schnellen Kontextwechsel und zur Verwaltung von Verbindungsdaten. SPAs werden anhand einer Beschreibung eines Protokollautomaten individuell generiert und stellen somit eine exakt an den jeweiligen Automaten angepaßte Hardware dar. Weiterhin können spezielle Funktionen zur Unterstützung eines Kommunikationsprotokolls in sogenannten Protocol Function Units (PFU) implementiert werden. Diese Einheiten werden von Hand entworfen, da hier eine außerordentlich hohe Leistungsfähigkeit erforderlich ist. Beispiele hierfür sind CRC- und Zeitgebereinheiten [Schi96]. Allen Komponenten steht außer lokalem Speicher auf der Komponenten selbst noch ein gemeinsames statisches RAM zur Verfügung. Die Anbindung an zusätzliches dynamisches RAM geschieht über eine DMA-Einheit. Alle Komponenten innerhalb GAPPU besitzen identische Schnittstellen zur Ankopplung an den Kreuzschienenverteiler und können via Nachrichtenaustausch oder gemeinsamen Speicher miteinander kommunizieren.

In Abhängigkeit von der zu implementierenden Funktionalität und der gewünschten Leistungsfähigkeit können nun unterschiedliche Komponenten integriert werden. Die Architektur zielt auf eine Implementierung als leistungsfähiger ASIC (Application Specific Integrated Circuit) ab. Dafür wurden die Rahmenarchitektur und wesentliche Komponenten mit Hilfe der Hardware-Beschreibungssprache VHDL [IEEE87, LeWS94] beschrieben, simuliert und auf verschiedene Zieltechnologien synthetisiert. Anhand der Simulationsergebnisse läßt sich die Funktionalität des Entwurfs überprüfen. Die Synthese dient sowohl der Leistungsabschätzung als auch der Ermittlung des Flächenbedarfs als Chip.

Als Vielzweckprozessor zur Abarbeitung von Protokollautomaten wird im Rahmen von GAPPU auf den RISC-Prozessor DLX [HePa94, SaKa96, FeRe94] zurückgegriffen, der eine gemeinsame Untermenge der wesentlichen Eigenschaften gängiger RISC-Prozessoren umfaßt und sowohl als Simulationsmodell als auch in einer vollständig synthetisierbaren Version vorliegt. Wie in [Gumm95] gezeigt, läßt sich ein DLX-Prozessor mit lediglich 60.000 Transistoren realisieren. Als dedizierte Komponenten zur Unterstützung der Protokollabarbeitung (PFU) wurden seither eine Einheit zur Verwaltung dynamischer Datenstrukturen, eine Zeitgeberverwaltung sowie Komponenten zur Berechnung von Redundanzdaten für die Vorwärtsfehlerkorrektur entworfen, simuliert und auf programmierbare Bausteine (FPGAs [Virt95, Xili94]) und 0,7 μm CMOS-ASICs synthetisiert [Euro94, Syno94, Cade94]. Bei den entworfenen Einheiten handelt es sich jeweils um Komponenten, welche die RISC-Prozessoren von besonders zeitintensiven Rechenoperationen entlasten. Dieses Konzept ist vergleichbar mit dem Einsatz von speziellen Gleitkommaarithmetikeinheiten in gängigen PCs [Schi95]. Bei Gruppenkommunikation mit hohen Datenraten würde die Abarbeitung dieser Funktionen in Software aufgrund der großen Anzahl von zu unterstützenden Verbindungen und Empfängern zu Leistungsengpässen und zu einer Verschlechterung der Dienstgüte führen. Geforderte Garantien für die Dienstgüte könnten bei der angestrebten Leistungsfähigkeit somit nicht mehr eingehalten werden.

Im Rahmen des Entwurfs eines Kommunikationssystems ist es ebenfalls von großer Wichtigkeit, daß Kommunikationsprotokolle ohne Abänderung der Protokolle selbst auf den bisher vorgestellten unterschiedlichen Plattformen realisiert werden können. Besonders wichtig ist die effiziente und einfache Implementierung auf einer Hardware-Realisierung wie es das System GAPPU darstellt. Ausgangspunkt unserer Protokollimplementierung stellt die Spezifikation des Kommunikationssystems in der standardisierten und im Telekommunikationsbereich weit verbreiteten Sprache SDL [CCIT89] dar. Basierend auf dieser Spezifikation kann nun C-Code für eine Software-Implementierung [Veri95] oder VHDL-Code für eine Hardware-Implementierung als SPA automatisch generiert werden [Schi96]. Falls flexible Protokollautomaten höchster Leistungsfähigkeit benötigt werden, so müssen PPAs eingesetzt werden. Hier wird ebenfalls mit Compiler-Unterstützung ein für den Menschen einfach lesbarer Assemblercode direkt in Microcode für den Protokollautomaten abgebildet.

Besonders elegant ist hierbei die Möglichkeit der Übersetzung eines C-Programms in den Maschinencode für den DLX-RISC-Prozessor mit Hilfe eines GNU-C-Compilers. Dies bedeutet, daß C-Code für reine Software-Implementierungen übernommen und nun auf den RISC-Prozessoren innerhalb der GAPPU abgearbeitet werden kann. Eine natürliche Aufteilung des Programmes auf die verschiedenen Prozessoren ergibt sich im allgemeinen aus der Tatsache, daß RMC-SSCS wie auch zahlreiche andere Kommunikationsprotokolle aus einer Menge miteinander kommunizierender Automaten besteht. So können nun, in Abhängigkeit von der benötigten Leistungsfähigkeit ein/mehrere Protokollautomat(en) auf eine RISC-CPU abgebildet werden.

Die Automatisierung der Abbildung einer Protokollspezifikation auf leistungsfähige Implementierungen stellt eine wesentliche Erhöhung der Korrektheit der Systeme dar, da viele Fehler der Handimplementierung ausgeschlossen werden können.

6 Ergebnisse

Für die Leistungsmessungen der Implementierung der FEC-Mechanismen unter Linux wurde ein 90 MHz Pentium-PC mit 16 Mbyte RAM und 155 Mbps ATM-Adapter eingesetzt. Das Testprogramm übertrug pro Kombination der FEC-Parameter fünf Mal eine 3 Mbyte große Datei und ermittelte dabei den mittleren Datendurchsatz und die mittlere Kodierzeit. Hierbei wurden die Zellverluste so eingestellt, daß für das FEC-Modul jeweils der maximale Dekodieraufwand entstand. In Abbildung 8 macht sich, wie zu erwarten, der Geschwindigkeitsgewinn des einfacheren XOR-Verfahrens deutlich bemerkbar.

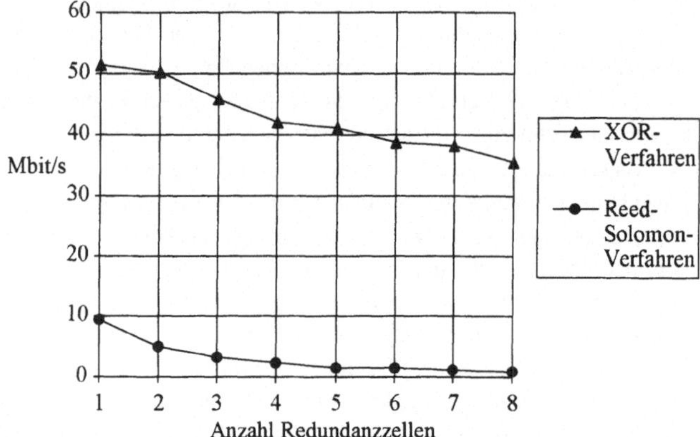

Abbildung 8: Leistungsvergleich der FEC-Verfahren bei Software-Implementierung (Intel)

Anhand der Ergebnisse läßt sich feststellen, daß das Reed-Solomon-Verfahren für eine reine Software-Implementierung zu rechenintensiv ist. Mit dem XOR-Verfahren lassen sich deutlich höhere Übertragungsraten erzielen, jedoch muß auch hierbei beachtet werden, daß bei den in Abbildung 8 angegebenen Datenraten die CPU des Rechners vollständig mit der Kodierung/Dekodierung ausgelastet ist und keine weiteren Kapazitäten für Anwendungen verfügbar sind. Hinzu kommt, daß das XOR-Verfahren außerordentlich einfach in Hardware zu implementieren ist, auch für das RS-Verfahren existieren Hardware-Ansätze. Insgesamt wäre also eine Unterstützung dieser Funktionalität in Hardware auf dem ATM-Adapter wünschenswert.

Da noch nicht alle benötigten Komponenten vollständig simuliert und synthetisiert wurden, mußten sich bisherige Leistungsmessungen der GAPPU auf Teilkomponenten beschränken. Die dabei erzielten Ergebnisse zeigen, daß gegenüber einer Software-Lösung eine deutliche Leistungssteigerung erreicht werden kann, so daß der Ansatz insgesamt als sehr vielversprechend bezeichnet werden kann. Zusammengefaßt konnten seither folgende Kenngrößen ermittelt werden. Bei der Analyse der Verarbeitungszeit in Abbildung 9 wurde von einer Verarbeitung des RMC-SSCS-Protokolls auf einer GAPPU mit 6 RISC-Prozessoren sowie weiteren

135

dedizierten Hardware-Komponenten ausgegangen. Hierbei wurden 32-bit RISC-Prozessoren mit einer mittleren Verarbeitungsleistung von 100 MIPS vorausgesetzt, was beim heutigen Stand der Technik eine konservative Annahme darstellt. Als PFUs wurden Hardware-Komponenten für Segmentierung und Reassemblierung, für die Berechnung der CRC-Prüfsummen und für die Vorwärtsfehlerkorrektur vorausgesetzt. Die Verarbeitung von Nutzzellen des RMC-SSCS-Protokolls erfolgt in den Komponenten Empfangsprozessor, Frame Manager Receive, Frame Manager Send, Send Manager und Sendprozessor. Abbildung 9 zeigt die Verarbeitungszeiten der einzelnen Komponenten für die unterschiedlichen Fehlerkontrollverfahren des RMC-SSCS-Protokolls. Hierbei wird die Verarbeitungszeit der Komponente Frame Manager Receive in drei Funktionsbereiche unterteilt: ARQ rahmenbasiert, ARQ zellenbasiert, und FEC. Für das rahmenbasierte ARQ-Verfahren von RMC-SSCS muß lediglich der Funktionsbereich ARQ rahmenbasiert verarbeitet werden, wobei sich die geringste Verarbeitungszeit ergibt. Für das zellenbasierte ARQ-Verfahren müssen die Funktionsbereiche ARQ rahmenbasiert und ARQ zellenbasiert verarbeitet werden. Für rahmenbasiertes ARQ mit FEC müssen die Funktionsbereiche ARQ rahmenbasiert und FEC verarbeitet werden, während für zellbasiertes ARQ mit FEC alle drei Funktionsbereiche verarbeitet werden müssen. Da im untersuchten Fall von einer dedizierten PFU für FEC ausgegangen wird, fallen für den Funktionsbereich FEC pro verarbeiteter Zelle lediglich 0,11 µs zur Kommunikation mit der FEC-Komponente an.

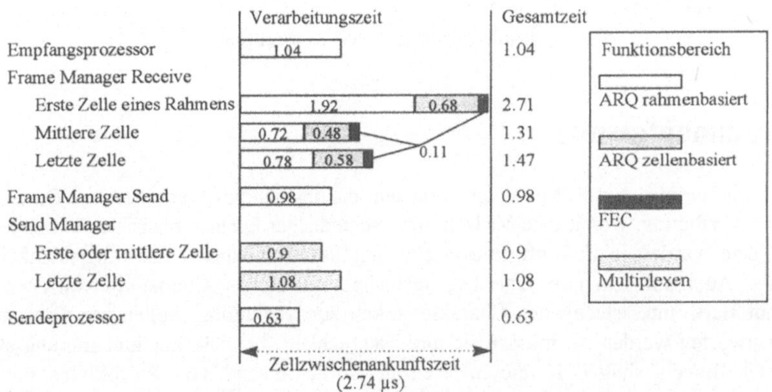

Abbildung 9: Verarbeitungszeit für Nutzzellen in den einzelnen Prozessoren

Eine Integration von 6 DLX-RISC-Prozessoren, dedizierten Komponenten für die Verwaltung dynamischer Datenstrukturen und Zeitgebern, plus ein 16 bit breiter Kreuzschienenverteiler für 14 Sender-/Empfänger resultiert in einem Flächenbedarf von unter 200000 Gattern. Dabei nehmen die RISC-Prozessoren 60%, der Kreuzschienenverteiler 18%, die dedizierten Hardware-Einheiten zur Unterstützung der Prozessoren 11% und schließlich die restliche Logik (Schnittstellen, Treiber, Testpfad etc.) ebenfalls 11% der Chipfläche ein. Hinzu kommt der Flächenbedarf für lokalen Speicher. Im Vergleich dazu besitzt der Prozessor TMS320C80 ca. 4 Millionen Transistoren, was in etwa 1 Million Gatter entspricht. Diese Ergebnisse sprechen also für die Realisierbarkeit des Entwurfs. Als maximale Taktfrequenz des bisherigen Entwurfs wurde unter konservativen Annahmen 50 MHz ermittelt. Diese im Vergleich zu RISC-Prozessoren niedrige Frequenz liegt darin begründet, daß pro Takt innerhalb der GAPPU eine wesentlich höhere Funktionalität abgearbeitet wird. Als Beispiel hierfür dient die Listenverwaltung, deren Leistung in Abbildung 10 mit einem gängigen RISC-Prozessor verglichen wird.

Dazu wurde die mittlere Verarbeitungszeit für das Einfügen eines neuen Eintrags in eine listenbasierte Zeitgeberverwaltung untersucht. Hier zeigt sich deutlich, wie trotz einer niedrigeren Taktfrequenz von 20 MHz bei der FPGA-Lösung eine höhere Leistungsfähigkeit als bei der Verwendung eines Alpha-AXP-Prozessors mit einer Taktfrequenz von 175 MHz erreicht werden kann. Bei der Software-Implementierung auf dem RISC-Prozessor wurden einmal die Meßwerte ohne die gleichzeitige Überprüfung auf einen Alarm (AXP21064, ohne) und einmal mit dieser Überprüfung ermittelt. Ein positiver Effekt der niedrigen Frequenz der FPGA-Lösung ist eine wesentliche Vereinfachung des Systementwurfs und die Möglichkeit, billigere Teilkomponenten (z.B. Speicher) zu verwenden.

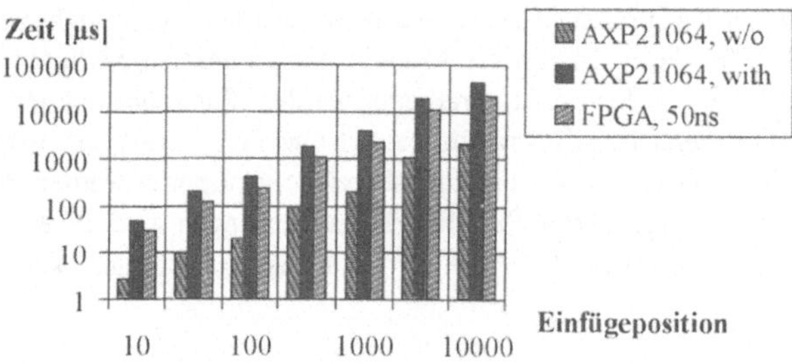

Abbildung 10: Leistungsvergleich zwischen Software- und Hardware-Implementierung von Zeitgebern

7 Zusammenfassung

Mit der Einführung von ATM-Netzen steht ein leistungsfähiges Verfahren zur Datenübertragung zur Verfügung, womit eine Vielzahl unterschiedlicher Dienste realisiert werden kann. An diese Netze werden in Zukunft Endsysteme mit unterschiedlicher Leistungsfähigkeit angeschlossen. Auch auf Seiten der Übertragungstechnologie stehen Alternativen von Glasfaser bis Funk mit stark unterschiedlichen Charakteristiken zur Verfügung. Sollen nun Protokolle für ATM entworfen werden, so müssen sie ihre Tauglichkeit für viele Implementierungsalternativen unter Beweis stellen. In diesem Beitrag wurde anhand von Protokollen mit ATM-spezifischen Fehlerkontrollmechanismen für FEC und ARQ aufgezeigt, wie Implementierungsalternativen realisiert und getestet werden können. Die betrachteten Protokolle eigenen sich nicht nur für den Einsatz in Endsystemen, sondern auch für spezielle Gruppenkommunikationsserver. Wie in einer ausführlichen Motivation dargestellt, ist diese Art von Protokollen von besonderem Interesse, sollen in Zukunft beispielsweise Konferenzsysteme mit einer Vielzahl von Teilnehmern oder andere verteilte Anwendungen kostengünstig und dennoch leistungsfähig aufgebaut werden. Traditionelle Protokolle sind nur schlecht mit der Teilnehmerzahl skalierbar und schwer an die ATM-Technologie anpaßbar. Insbesondere für mobile Anwendungen stellt die Verlagerung der Fehlerkorrektur in Zwischensysteme den einzig sinnvollen Weg dar, da hier höhere Fehlerwahrscheinlichkeiten zwischen Feststation und Mobilteilnehmer auftreten, und ohne eine Fehlerkontrolle in den Zwischensystemen die Dienstqualität aller Empfänger einer Gruppe in Mitleidenschaft gezogen würde.

Die FEC-Mechanismen wurden in Software und Hardware implementiert und vermessen. Hierbei konnte mit Hilfe einer ATM-Emulation das Verhalten der Mechanismen unter verschiedenen Fehlerwahrscheinlichkeiten überprüft werden. Mit gängigen PCs reicht dabei die Leistungsfähigkeit aus, um die Auswirkungen anhand eines MPEG-Videodatenstroms optisch nachzuvollziehen. Um jedoch das Konzept der Vorwärtsfehlerkorrektur sinnvoll für große Gruppen einsetzen zu können, ist eine Hardware-Komponente wie die entworfene GAPPU unabdingbar. GAPPU stellt eine hochleistungsfähige Architektur für Zwischensysteme dar, die eine Vielzahl von Protokollfunktionen übernehmen kann. Es wurde anhand von Leistungsmessungen gezeigt, daß diese Hardware leistungsfähig genug ist, um selbst komplexe Operationen innerhalb von Zwischenankunftszeiten von ATM-Zellen durchzuführen.

Aktuelle Arbeiten umfassen vor allem die Erweiterung der Funktionseinheiten für GAPPU und deren vollständige Synthese als ASIC. Hierzu wurden bereits detaillierte Beschreibungen in VHDL vorgenommen. Zum Test der einzelnen Funktionen werden diese zusätzlich auf ein in einen Arbeitsplatzrechner integriertes FPGA-Board abgebildet.

8 Literatur

[AFUT94] ATM Forum: UTOPIA, An ATM-PHY Interface Specification, Level 1, Version 2, März 1994

[BoLa93] Bondi, A.; Lai, W.-S.: The influence of cell loss patterns and overheads on retransmission choices in broadband ISDN, Computer Networks and ISDN Systems 26, S. 585-598, 1994

[Cade94] Cadence Design Systems, Inc.: Dokumentation zur Entwurfsumgebung DFW II, Cadence Design Systems, Inc., San Jose, U.S.A., 1994

[CaSc95] Carle, G.; Schiller, J.: Enabling High Bandwidth Applications by High-Performance Multicast Transfer Protocol Processing, 6th IFIP Conference on Performance of Computer Networks, PCN95, Istanbul, Türkei, Oktober 1995

[CaEG95a] Carle, G.; Esaki, H.; Guha, A.; Tsunoda, K.; Kanai, K.: Necessity of an FEC Scheme for ATM Networks, Contribution ATMF/95-0325; ATM Forum Technical Committee 'Service Aspects and Applications SA&A', Denver, Colorado, U.S.A., April 1995

[CaEG95b] Carle, G.; Esaki, H.; Guha, A.; Tsunoda, K.; Kanai, K.: Proposal for Specification of FEC-SSCS for AAL Type 5, Contribution ATMF/95-0326; ATM Forum Technical Committee 'Service Aspects and Applications SA&A', Denver, Colorado, U.S.A., April 1995

[CaZi95] Carle, G.; Zitterbart, M.: ATM Adaptation Layer and Group Communication Servers for High-Performance Multipoint Services, 7th IEEE Workshop on Local and Metropolitan Area Networks, Marathon, Florida, März 1995

[CCIT89] CCITT: Functional Specification and Description Language (SDL), Recommendations Z.100-Z.104, Blue Book, Oktober 1989

[EsCa95] Esaki, H.; Carle, G.: Combination of SSCOP and an AAL-Level FEC Scheme, Contribution ATMF/95-1560; ATM Forum Plenary, London, U.K., Dezember 1995

[ENI96] Efficient Networks, Inc.: ATM Adapter ENI 155p for PCI Bus Product Information, Hardware Installation Guide, Hardware Device Interface User's Guide, 1996

[Euro94] European Silicon Structures: Dokumentation zur 0,7 µm-Bibliothek, European Silicon Structures, Rousset, Frankreich, 1994

[Gumm95] Gumm, M.: VHDL-Modelling and Synthesis of the DLXS-RISC-Prozessor; VLSI Design Course, Institut für Parallele und Verteilte Höchstleistungsrechner (IPVR), Universität Stuttgart, 1995

[FeRe94] Feldman, J.M.; Retter, C.T.: Computer architecture: a designer's text based on a generic RISC, McGraw-Hill, 1994

[HePa94] Hennessy, J.L.; Patterson, D.A.: Rechnerarchitektur: Analyse, Entwurf, Implementierung und Bewertung, Vieweg Verlag, Braunschweig, 1994

[IEEE87] IEEE Std 1076-1987, VHDL: VHSIC Hardware Description Language

[KrKS93] Krishnakumar, A.S.; Kneuer, J.G.; Shaw, A.J.: HIPOD: An Architecture for High-Speed Protocol Implementations, in: Danthine, A.; Spaniol, O. (Eds.): High Performance Networking, IV, IFIP, North-Holland, 1993, S. 383-396

[KiFa95] Kim, H.; Farber, D.: The Failure of Conservative Congestion Control in High-Speed Networks, Proceedings of Second Gigabit Networking Workshop (GBN'95), Boston, MA, U.S.A., April 1995

[LeWS94] Lehmann, Wunder, Selz: Schaltungsdesign mit VHDL, Franzis-Verlag, 1994

[Linux] Linux Homepage, http://www.linux.org/

[MaHP94] Mankin, A.; Hoffman, E.; Perez, M.: Vendor Independent (and Architecture Flexible) Network Control Entity, Proceedings of INET'94, Internet Society, Prag, Juni 1994

[OhKi91] Ohta, H., Kitami, T.: A Cell Loss Recovery Method Using FEC in ATM Networks, IEEE Journal on Selected Areas in Communications, Vol. 9, No. 9, Dezember 1991, S.1471-1483

[Q2110] ITU-T Draft Recommendation Q.2110: B-ISDN Adaptation Layer - Service Specific Connection Oriented Protocol (SSCOP), International Telecommunication Union, Genf, 1994

[Roma93] Romanov, A.: Some Results on the Performance of TCP over ATM, Second IEEE Workshop on the Architecture and Implementation of High Performance Communication Subsystems HPCS'93, Williamsburg, Virginia, U.S.A., September 1993

[SaKa96] Sailer, P.M.; Kaeli, D.R.: The DLX Instruction Set Architecture Handbook, Morgan Kaufmann Publishers Inc., San Francisco, USA, 1996

[Schi95] Schiller, J.: A Flexible Co-Processor for High-Performance Communication Support, IEEE Globecom'95, Singapore, November 1995

[Schi96] Schiller, J.: Teilautomatisierter Entwurf modularer Prozessorsysteme für die Hochleistungskommunikation, Fortschrittsberichte VDI, Reihe 10, Nr. 426, VDI-Verlag Düsseldorf, 1996

[ScZi95] Schiller, J.; Zitterbart, M.: Modular VLSI Implementation Architecture for High-Performance Communication Support, 7th IEEE Workshop on Local and Metropolitan Area Networks, Marathon, Florida, März 1995

[StGr94] Stock, T; Grünenfelder, R.: Frame Loss vs. Cell Loss in ATM Concentrators and Policing Units, Proceedings of 12th Annual Conference on European Fibre Optic Communications an Networks, Heidelberg, Juni 1994

[Stee94] Steenkiste, Peter A.: A Systematic Approach to Host Interface Design for High-Speed Networks, IEEE Computer, März 1994, S. 47-57

[Syno94] Synopsys Inc.: Dokumentation zu Simulator, Design Compiler, Design Analyzer, Version 3.0b, Synopsys Inc., Mountain View, USA, 1994

[Texa95] Texas Instruments Inc.: TMS320C80 Multimedia Video Processor: Technical Reference, Texas Instruments Inc., http://www.ti.com/

[Veri95] Verilog SA: Dokumentation zu Geode, Verilog SA, Toulouse, Frankreich

[Virt95] Virtual Computer Corporation: EVC1s technical reference, Virtual Computer Corporation, Reseda, U.S.A., 1995

[WoFD93] Worster, T.; Fischer, W.; Davis, S.P.: Resource Allocation for Packet Data Traffic on ATM: Problems and Solutions, in Gerner, N.; Hegering, H.-G.; Swoboda, J. (Hrsg.): Proceedings of „Kommunikation in Verteilten Systemen"; München, März 1993, Springer-Verlag, S. 100-113

[Xili94] Xilinx: The programmable logic data handbook, Xilinx, San Jose, U.S.A., 1994

Session 4:

Formale Beschreibungstechniken

Conformance Testing of Objects in Distributed Processing Systems

Brigitte Bär and Kurt Geihs
Computer Science Department
Johann Wolfgang Goethe-Universität Frankfurt
PO Box 11 19 32, D-60054 Frankfurt, Germany
Phone/Fax: +49 69 798-28196 / -22643
E-mail: *[baer,geihs]@informatik.uni-frankfurt.de*

Abstract

The object model is a very popular paradigm for building distributed applications. Several standardisation efforts are underway that define architectures for distributed computing based on the object model. With object-based service specifications the need for conformance testing of object implementations arises to ensure that objects act as intended. The issue of conformance testing is of particular importance in distributed systems where objects from different sources and manufacturers have to interwork. We discuss the requirements of object conformance testing and the relationship to established protocol conformance testing methodology. For OMG CORBA objects, we propose a test architecture and explain the development of test cases using the standardised test notation TTCN.

1. Introduction

The object model has proven to be a powerful programming model for building reusable and re-configurable software components. The logical distribution that is inherent in an object-oriented software design makes the object model an ideal candidate for distributed system structures. The Object Management Group (OMG) has recognised the potential of object orientation for distributed systems and has developed specifications for an infrastructure that provides for interoperability in heterogeneous distributed environments. The infrastructure is called the OMG Common Object Request Broker Architecture (CORBA) [OMG91, OMG95]. The pivotal component of the architecture is a so called Object Request Broker (ORB) which enables objects to interoperate across a network. The CORBA is widely accepted by users and software manufacturers as one of the major middleware foundations for client/server-computing. Other OMG standards, such as standards for object services, are built on the CORBA standard [OMG93].

Distributed processing also has been a subject of official standardisation committees for some time. The International Organisation for Standardisation (ISO), the International Telecommunication Union (ITU), and their member organisations have been working on a Reference Model for Open Distributed Processing (RM-ODP) [ISO10746]. The major parts provide a descriptive framework for distributed processing systems in general as well as prescriptive specifications for open distributed processing systems. ISO and others have also finished an ODP Trader standard [ISO13235]. The trader is a matchmaker for service providers and service requesters. Such a component was identified by ISO in its ODP work as an important infrastructure service for distributed systems.

The basic technical goals of ODP and OMG are very similar. Both provide a foundation for interoperability in heterogeneous distributed computing systems. Although the ISO RM-ODP necessarily is more abstract in nature than the OMG specifications, the two organisations have established an official liaison in order to keep their activities aligned and to benefit from each other. For example, the ISO is using the CORBA Interface Definition Language (IDL) to specify computational ODP interfaces, while OMG has launched a request for technology for a trader component.

The two standardisation activities underline the need for standards in a heterogeneous world of computing in order to build truly open systems. Just like the OMG, ISO has chosen the object model as the basic modelling paradigm for its reference model. One issue that has not been addressed sufficiently so far is the conformance of object implementations to their specifications. In distributed systems where object implementations from different origins have to interwork, conformance testing is essential in order to increase the level of confidence that object implementations behave as defined in their specifications.

The issue of conformance testing has been studied in great detail for standardised protocols in the context of the ISO Reference Model for Open Systems Interconnection (OSI). Conformance of a protocol implementation to the corresponding protocol standard is one of the key activities to ensure interworking within open systems. ISO has published a framework [ISO9646] in order to harmonise the process of testing and certification. However, conformance testing is not only of importance for protocol implementations but also for every implementation that claims to implement a standard. In particular, this holds true for object implementations offering (standardised) services that are integrated into applications.

Some work on object conformance testing has been done in the area of network and systems management [Bär96, CTS92, EWOS92, ISO93]. Network and system resources are modelled as managed objects [Sta93]. The conformance testing activities for managed objects have shown that the OSI protocol conformance testing methodology can be adapted. In this paper, we investigate the conformance testing for general objects in distributed object systems based on the experiences gained with the testing of managed objects and well established OSI conformance testing principles. Our results are applied to the testing of CORBA objects.

Both, OMG and ISO ODP have recognised the need for conformance testing. Conformance of CORBA based implementations will be tested by the X/Open organisation [OMG95b]. The testing process has not been established and details have not been published yet. For the ISO RM-ODP, some preliminary statements on conformance points are contained in the RM documents and some additional research has been done [PROST93]. However, there is a common agreement that much more discussion is needed on the ODP conformance issues. This is future work for ISO ODP.

In this paper, we do not address the theory of conformance testing (as discussed, for example, in [Bri88, Pha92, Tre92]). Our emphasis is on a practical methodology and on tools to support the software engineering for distributed object systems. In Section 2, we briefly present the basic concepts of the OSI methodology for testing the conformance of communication protocols. In Section 3, we discuss the requirements for conformance testing of objects and the applicability of the OSI testing methodology for CORBA objects. A test architecture is presented and it is shown that an already existing test notation of ISO can be carried over for object testing. Using this test notation, test cases can be specified and executed following the guidelines of the OSI testing methodology. In Section 4 an example for the development of test cases is presented. In our conclusions at the end of the paper, we summarise the pros and cons of our approach and point to open research questions.

2. Conformance Testing Concepts

In the *Conformance Testing Methodology and Framework* [ISO9646], conformance testing is defined to be the assessment process for determining whether the externally visible behaviour of an OSI implementation conforms to the behaviour defined in the relevant specification. A real system is said to exhibit conformance in its communication with other real systems if it complies with the conformance requirements, e.g. certain capabilities or allowable behaviours defined in the corresponding OSI standard. Since exhaustive testing is impossible, conformance and interworking cannot be guaranteed. However, the purpose of conformance testing is to increase the probability that different (OSI protocol) implementations are able to interwork.

In order to harmonise the process of testing and certification for OSI implementations, the framework provides a methodology for specifying conformance test suites and defines procedures to be followed by implementation providers and test houses. A test suite consists of a collection of individual test cases each of which addresses one or more conformance requirements derived from a certain protocol specification. A test case specifies a sequence of interactions (test events) at the interfaces between a test system and the *Implementation Under Test* (IUT).

In the world of OSI communication protocols, testing is realised through the exchange of *Abstract Service Primitives* (ASPs) and/or *Protocol Data Units* (PDUs) between the test system and the IUT at so called *Points of Control and Observation* (PCOs). In each test case, a positive test verdict is only given if the response received from the IUT as a result of a sent event initiated by the test system complies with the expected response as defined in the test case. The conceptual test architecture is shown in Figure 1.

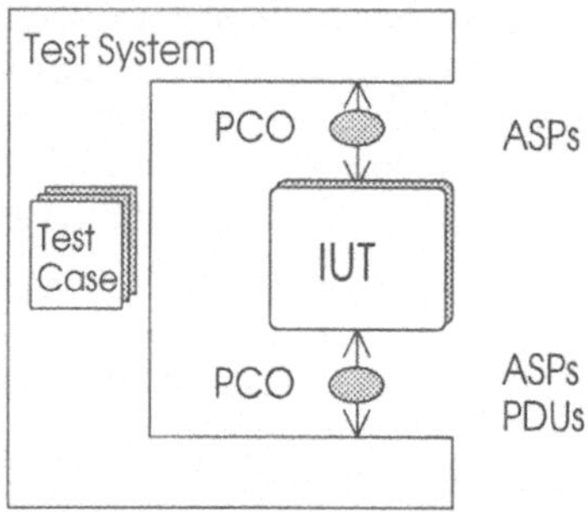

Fig. 1: Protocol test architecture

Conformance of a protocol implementation is determined by executing the test cases of a test suite defined for the corresponding protocol standard according to the guidelines given in [ISO9646]. The results are analysed and summarised in a test report. The use of standardised test suites and common procedures for testing the conformance of OSI implementations leads to comparability and acceptance of test results.

ISO has defined a test specification language called *Tree and Tabular Combined Notation* (TTCN) for the development of abstract test suites. TTCN aims at providing a common language in which test cases can be expressed on an abstract level. The development of a test suite involves defining the (abstract) data types of test events, i.e. the information exchanged between test system and IUT, in a declaration part. For example, the declaration part includes definitions for ASP and PDU types. In TTCN the Abstract Syntax Notation One (ASN.1

[ISO8824]) is used for that purpose. The behaviour part of a test suite contains the test cases which specify the test event sequences (ASPs and/or PDUs) needed to test a certain conformance requirement. For readability reasons, the data values to be transmitted in a *send event* and expected in a *receive event* are located in a separate part of a test suite, the constraints part. For further details of TTCN test suites the reader is referred to the standards [ISO9646].

3. Testing CORBA Objects

We investigate the conformance testing of objects that sit on top of a CORBA platform and interact via the object broker, e.g. an implementation of a particular CORBA Object Service [OMG93]. Note that we are not addressing the conformance of CORBA implementations themselves, i.e. we are not looking at the behaviour of an ORB or the interoperability of different ORB implementations as specified in the CORBA 2.0 specifications [OMG95].

Applying the OSI conformance testing definitions, an object is said to exhibit conformance if it complies with the conformance requirements of its corresponding service specification. A test method is needed that allows for the observation and manipulation of objects. In addition, test cases have to be developed that are suitable for testing the conformance requirements identified for a certain service specification. Before addressing conformance of CORBA objects in more detail, we give a brief overview of the CORBA and its Interface Definition Language (IDL).

3.1. CORBA and CORBA IDL

Figure 2 shows the basic architecture with the ORB as the central component. Application objects invoke operations on other objects via the broker. According to the object model, objects are encapsulated and all access to an object's state is performed via the object's interface. In CORBA, object interfaces are specified using the CORBA Interface Definition Language (IDL) [OMG91].

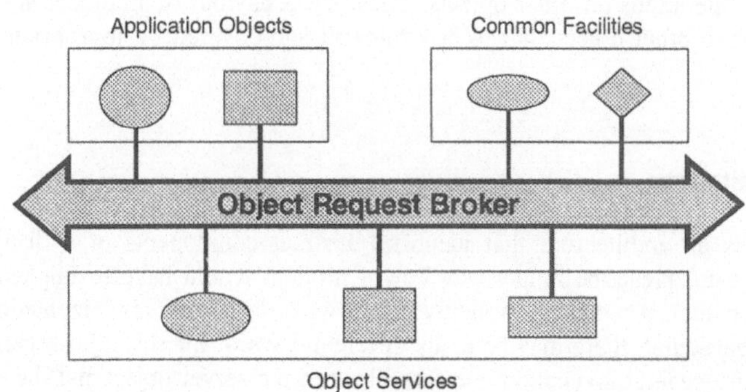

Fig. 2: Common Object Request Broker Architecture [OMG91]

The IDL is a purely declarative language whose design was influenced heavily by the programming language C++ with some additions for distribution. An IDL specification consists of type definitions for modules, interfaces, exceptions, etc. Modules mainly serve structuring purposes, i.e. a module defines a name space for internal type names. An interface defines the object's operations and attributes accessible by the clients of the object. An interface specification may inherit properties (operations and attributes) from other interface specifications. Exceptions are used in the definition of operations in order to specify error messages that have to be returned under certain error conditions. So called *scoped names* are used to uniquely identify a type name of an IDL specification. In the following, we assume that the reader is somewhat familiar with the CORBA IDL.

3.2. Object Conformance Requirements

Plain IDL interface descriptions are not sufficient for the derivation of conformance requirements for a certain service, since they remain purely syntactic. In addition to the syntactic interface definition, conformance testing requires a semantic specification of the expected object behaviour as well as clearly stated conformance requirements. (Obviously, accepted software engineering principles demand service and conformance specifications for all software modules; unfortunately the practice of software development often looks quite different.)

Access to CORBA objects is restricted to invoking operations at the interfaces. As a result, testing an object for conformance is based on the observation of the object's externally visible behaviour through the effects of operation invocations only. The object operations to be tested include attribute oriented operations and all inherited operations, if applicable. The effects of an operation are not only visible in the values of output parameters, in the return value, or in error messages. Attribute value changes as a result of an operation invocation have to be considered as well.

Two levels of object testing must be distinguished. On the one hand, an object has to be tested in isolation as a single, encapsulated unit by looking at the responses from the object. On the other hand, in practice an object never acts independently, but generally is part of an interrelated and interacting set of objects. There are many possible forms and representations of object relationships. For example, object relationships may be explicitly expressed via the CORBA relationship service [OMG94], or they may be represented by means of object references and operations on other objects. Thus, the behaviour of an object in the context of its relationships to other objects has to be evaluated and covered by appropriate test cases as well.

3.3. Test Architecture

The CORBA is an architecture that identifies abstract components of a distributed object system. It does not prescribe in any way how a product would have to implement the ORB functionality. In fact, it is stated explicitly that a wide variety of implementations should be permitted. In particular, there may be many different ways of interfacing a server to its ORB. Thus, there is no general invocation interface between the server object and the ORB which is accessible from the outside world. Furthermore, the client is not aware of the mechanisms used to communicate with server objects. The only general way of accessing a server object is from a client object that resides on the same (or an interconnected) ORB.

Consequently, our test architecture as shown in Figure 3 has a test system object as a client object. The test system is responsible for executing the test cases defined for an object specification. It invokes the operations of the server objects under test via the ORB and compares the results with the expected results defined in the underlying service specifications. As emphasised before, CORBA objects rarely are completely independent units. Therefore, the effect of operations that induce state changes in related CORBA objects have to be evaluated as well. Consequently, several CORBA objects have to be observed in conjunction as shown in the test architecture.

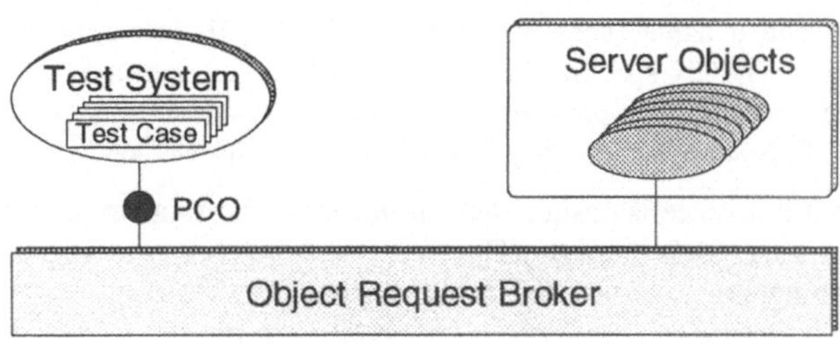

Fig. 3: Test architecture for CORBA objects

In order to test an object's behaviour it is irrelevant whether the operations were invoked via the static or the dynamic ORB interface. The CORBA specification states explicitly that a server object would not notice any difference between the two types of invocation interfaces. The test PCO (Point of Control and Observation, see Section 2) can either be the static or the dynamic interface.

3.4. Mapping of TTCN to IDL

The basis for testing the conformance of CORBA objects is the object's service specification including a (syntactic) interface specification and a (semantic) behaviour specification. For comparability and acceptance of test results, standardised test cases are required. We want to specify abstract test cases for CORBA objects by utilising established OSI testing methodology.

According to the OSI conformance testing methodology, abstract test cases are defined in TTCN. In order to be able to use TTCN for the development of abstract test cases for IDL interface specifications, we have defined an IDL to TTCN language mapping [Bär96]. This provides a transformation of IDL elements (type definitions and invocations of operations including parameters) to TTCN and ASN.1. Based on the mapping we can specify test cases for CORBA objects in TTCN and thus use much of the conformance testing methodology and tools that have been developed for OSI testing previously.

Let us explain our IDL to TTCN mapping approach by using the following example IDL specification:

```
module ObjectIdentity {
    typedef unsigned long OID;
    interface identifiableObject{
        readonly attribute OID constant_random_id;
        boolean is_identical{in IdentifiableObject
                                    other_object};
    };
};
```

It shows excerpts from a CORBA object service specification [OMG94]. According to the semantics of the service specification, the operation `is_identical` determines whether two given objects are identical. Let us look at some of the peculiarities of mapping CORBA IDL constructs to TTCN.

Scoped Names, Modules, Interfaces, and Object References

The concept of scoped names does not exist in TTCN. IDL identifiers have to be made globally unique in a TTCN specification. This is done by an appropriate concatenation of module, interface, and/or other type names. The concepts of module and interface are not used explicitly in the TTCN specification; they appear only in the chosen identifiers.

A CORBA Object Reference is opaque, but can be converted to a string by calling a special ORB operation via the ORB interface. Therefore, we have chosen to map object references onto an ASN.1 string, i.e.

```
Object ::= IA5String
```

Operations

Operations defined in an IDL interface can be mapped to the concept of ASPs. Because invocations result in the synchronous execution of an operation, and because conceptually TTCN requires an asynchronous communication, an operation is split into a request and a return primitive. For every primitive, a globally unique identifier has to be assigned. For example, the operation `is_identical` is split into an

```
ObjectIdentity_identifiableObject_is_identical_Request
```
and an

```
ObjectIdentity_identifiableObject_is_identical_Result
```
primitive.

Invoking an operation requires the specification of the object to be invoked and the parameters to be supplied. Object references identifying CORBA objects are represented in terms of the ASN.1 type `Object`. Therefore, the first parameter of each primitive which is defined in terms of a struct-like ASN.1 type has to provide for a value of type `Object`. 'Input' parameters as well as 'inout' parameters are assigned to the request primitive. An optional parameter for context specific information is also needed in the request primitive. All 'output' parameters (including 'inout' parameters) and a parameter for the return value are part of the result primitive. The complete mapping of the operation `is_identical` is shown below:

```
ObjectIdentity_identifiableObject_is_identical_Request :=
SEQUENCE {
    object  Object,
    other_object    Object,
    context IA5String OPTIONAL
    }


ObjectIdentity_identifiableObject_is_identical_Result :=
SEQUENCE {
    object  Object OPTIONAL,
    result  BOOLEAN OPTIONAL,
    error   StandardException OPTIONAL
    }
```

In order to take exceptions into account, a parameter for error messages is part of every result primitive. If defined for an operation, this parameter will have the type of a user defined exception. Otherwise, the type of the error parameter has the type of a standard exception. Because there can be either a result or an error message, both parameters are defined as optional. For further details on the mapping of operations the reader is referred to [Bär96].

Attributes, IDL Data Types, and Exceptions

Attributes in IDL specifications are logically equivalent to two operations that read and write the attribute. For 'readonly' attributes only the read operation is available. The mapping of attributes is treated in nearly the same way as operations, e.g. the attribute `constant_random_id` is converted to:

```
ObjectIdentity_constant_random_id_get_Request := SEQUENCE {
    object  Object
    }


ObjectIdentity_constant_random_id_get_Result := SEQUENCE {
    object  Object OPTIONAL,
    result  OID OPTIONAL,
    error   StandardException OPTIONAL
    }
```

We have also defined mappings for all simple and structured data types. The expressive power of ASN.1 makes it quite easy to find appropriate representations.

IDL exceptions are converted to the structured ASN.1 type SEQUENCE. In addition, a structured ASN.1 type supporting all standard exceptions is provided in every TTCN specification.

Inheritance

The concept of inheritance has a minor impact on the testing procedures. Each operation and attribute defined for an object has to be tested regardless whether it is inherited or defined locally. When specifying a test suite, declarations of inherited operations and attributes can be reused for derived interfaces assuming they are not overloaded locally.

4. Test Case Development

Test objectives for abstract test cases are aligned with the conformance requirements of a certain specification. Each conformance requirement identified has to be addressed in one or more test cases where each test case is based on the observation and manipulation of CORBA objects by making use of operation invocations only. Let us look at an example test case defined in TTCN.

Test Case Dynamic Behavior	
Test Case Name :	ObjectIdentity_identifiableObject_is_identical_1
Group :	ObjectIdentity_identifiableObject
Purpose :	verify that the operation is_identical returns true if the objects are identical
Default :	
Comments :	example test case for operation is_identical

Nr	Label	Behavior Description	Constraints Ref	Verdict
1		!ObjectIdentity_identifiableObject_is_identical_Request START Timer	is_identical_request	
2		?ObjectIdentity_identifiableObject_is_identical_Request CANCEL Timer	is_identical_result	(PASS)
3		?OTHERWISE CANCEL Timer		(FAIL)
4		?TIMEOUT CANCEL Timer		(INCONC)

This test case focuses on the requirement that the operation `is_identical` has to return the value 'True' if the object invoked and the other object (given by a parameter of the invocation) are identical.

The TTCN test case consists of a header containing overview information like a test case name, the test purpose etc., and a body for the test case behaviour. The body is partitioned into different columns. In the *Behavior Description* column, test events to be sent to the objects under test and its possible responses are defined. Send events are indicated by a '!'. A '?' is used to denote receive events. An entry in the *Constraints Ref* column refers to a specification of the data values (parameters) to be transmitted in a send event or expected as part of a received event. In the *Verdict* column, a verdict for the received test event is given.

In the example, an `ObjectIdentity_identifiableObject_is_identical_Request` is sent to an object which is responsible for executing the corresponding operation. The object to be invoked and the reference of the other object are specified in the constraint `is_identical_request` (see behaviour line 1). In this example, we assume that the object references of both objects (as defined in the corresponding constraint) are identical. Different receive events have to be distinguished as a result of the sent event. If an `ObjectIdentity_identifiableObject_is_identical_Result` event occurs and the data received complies with the data specified in the constraint `is_identical_result`, the test case verdict 'PASS' is assigned. In this example, the return value 'True' is expected stating that the references of the objects are identical. In the case that a result primitive with invalid data values or any other event is received (see behaviour line 3), the test case verdict is 'FAIL'. Considering that no response may be received, a timer is started whenever a new test event is sent (see behaviour line 1). A 'TIMEOUT' event is generated by the test system indicating that no events have been received within the specified interval. In [ISO9646], time-out events cause a test case verdict 'INCONCLUSIVE' (see behaviour line 4).

The example test case represents a typical test case for objects. A complete test suite for a service specification is comprised of all test cases needed to test the identified conformance requirements. Because of object relationships, several objects may be addressed in one test case. For the execution of the test cases, the conformance assessment process defined in the OSI testing methodology can be applied.

5. Conclusions

It is obvious that in a world of inter-networking and highly diverse, decentralised autonomous computing components there is a need for interoperability standards and for standardised services. Since the object model has been chosen as the basic modelling paradigm for distributed system standards, the conformance of object implementations will be an important issue in future open distributed systems.

In this paper, we have shown how conformance testing for distributed object systems can be built on established OSI protocol conformance testing methodology. We have applied our findings to the testing of CORBA objects. A test architecture needed for the observation and manipulation of CORBA objects has been presented. Due to the lack of a standardised test notation for object systems, we have pointed out how TTCN can be used for the definition of abstract test cases for CORBA service specifications. The applicability of the TTCN test notation enables the reuse of existing test technology. In [BäMa94], it was demonstrated that the approach works in a similar way when applied to the conformance testing of managed objects in standardised network and system management solutions. It should also be applicable to other object-based approaches such as ODP, since it does not rely on any particular CORBA-specific features.

Although we were quite satisfied with the results, the TTCN notation has some limitations when applied to object systems. For example, time dependent test criteria cannot be specified in TTCN. Likewise, it is not suited for the specification of tests that check the persistence property of objects, and clearly it is not adapted to special application requirements, i.e. multimedia applications. We are currently investigating a test notation that can do better in this respect. Furthermore, we need powerful tools to support the steps of the test procedure. There is ample room for improvement here.

Acknowledgements

The work of B. Bär was supported by a grant from IBM European Networking Centre, Germany.

References

[BäMa94]   B. Bär, A. Mann, *A Methodology for Conformance Testing of Managed Objects,* 14th Int. IFIP Symposium on Protocol Specification, Testing and Verification, Vancouver/Canada (1994)

[Bär96]   B. Bär, *Konformitätstesten von Managementobjekten im Netz- und Systemmanagement,* Shaker Verlag, Aachen (1996) *(in German)*

[Bri88]   E. Brinksma, *A Theory for the Derivation of Tests,* Proceedings of 8th International Conference on Protocol Specification, Testing and Verification, Elsevier Science Publishers, Amsterdam (1988)

[CTS92]   CTS3-NM Project, *Methodology Report on Object Testing,* Deliverable 3, European Community Directorate Generale XIII-E4, Brussels (1992)

[EWOS92]   EWOS PT-16, *Framework for Conformance and Testing of Network ManagementProfiles,* Report 1, EWOS/EG NM/PT-16 (1992)

[ISO10746]   ISO, *Information Technology - Basic Reference Model of Open Distributed Processing, Parts 1-4,* IS 10746

[ISO13235]   ISO, *Information Technology - Open Distributed Processing - ODP Trading Function,* DIS 13235

[ISO8824]   ISO, *Specification of Abstract Syntax Notation One (ASN.1),* IS 8824

[ISO93]   ISO, *Draft Answer to Q1/63.2 on Testability of Managed Objects,* ISO/IEC JTC 1/SC 21/N 8009 (1993)

[ISO9646]   ISO, *Information Processing Systems - Open Systems Interconnection - Conformance Testing Methodology and Framework*, IS 9646

[OMG91]   Object Management Group and X/Open: *The Common Object Request Broker: Architecture and Specification*, OMG Document 91-12-1 (1991)

[OMG93]   Object Management Group: *Joint Object Services Submission: Submission Overview*, OMG Document 93-7-1 (1993)

[OMG94]   Object Management Group: *Joint Object Services Submission: Relationship Service Specification*, OMG Document 94-5-5 (1994)

[OMG95]   Object Management Group: *The Common Object Request Broker: Architecture and Specification*, Version 2.0 (1995)

[OMG95b]   Private communication with R. Soley, OMG Vice President

[PROST93]   PROST-ODP, *Report of the Study on Testing for Open Distributed Processing*, Programme of Research on Open Systems Testing (1993)

[Pha92]   M. Phalippou, *The Limited Power of Testing*, Proceedings of 5th International Workshop on Protocol Test Systems, Pau (1993)

[Sta93]   W. Stallings, *SNMP, SNMPv2, and CMIP: The Practical Guide to Network Management Standards*, Addison-Wesley (1993)

[Tre92]   J. Tretmans, *A Formal Approach to Conformance Testing*, Ph.D. Thesis, Twente University (1992)

A description model to support test suite derivation for concurrent systems

ANDREAS ULRICH
Fakultät für Informatik, Otto-von-Guericke-Universität,
PF 4120, 39016 Magdeburg, Germany,
e-mail: ulrich@cs.uni-magdeburg.de

The paper presents a concurrency model, called *behavior machine*, to describe concurrent systems in a finite representation of recursive behavior and free of interleaving. Thus, the new model alleviates the state explosion problem. After introducing the notion of a behavior machine, the paper shows how a behavior machine can be constructed from a set of communicating finite state machines using the theory of Petri net unfoldings. The concurrency model is finally applied to support test suite derivation for concurrent systems.

1 Introduction

Due to the limited power of verification, testing has always been an important method in practice to validate the correctness of software systems. Big efforts have been spent to provide methods for test suite derivation of communication protocols described by a sequential finite state machine (FSM). Results of the research on this issue are test suite derivation algorithms, like the transition tour method, UIO-method, or W-method [BoUy91].

Although these methods generate test suites of high test coverage, they fail if they are applied to concurrent systems described by a set of communicating FSMs. In this case, communicating FSMs are merged in order to obtain again a single FSM using interleaving semantics rules. This operation is particularly aggravated by state explosion in the constructed FSM resulting in a huge description model that cannot be used efficiently for test suite derivation.

This paper continues work on the use of partial order semantics for test suite derivation of concurrent systems. It improves the previous work done in [UlCh95] and also other known work on this subject (e.g. [YaCh92] [KCV93] [KCK+96]) by providing a sound concurrency model that can be constructed automatically from a set of communicating FSMs. The new concurrency model, called *behavior machine* (BM), is an interleaved-free and finite description of concurrent and recursive behavior. For many applications, a behavior machine can be computed in reasonable time and memory space.

After having introduced the new concurrency model in this paper, its construction algorithm is presented. The algorithm starts from a system description given as a set of communicating FSMs. First, the FSMs are mapped into a single Petri net representing the system. This Petri net is further used to construct its *unfolding*, another Petri net with a simpler structure, using an algorithm from [ERV96]. It is then shown how a behavior machine is constructed from the finite prefix of a Petri net unfolding.

In a further section of the paper, the behavior machine serves as model for the purpose of test suite derivation. An algorithm to construct a *concurrent transition tour*, an adaptation of the transition tour for a single FSM to the concurrent world, is presented.

The paper is organized as follows. Section 2 introduces the model assumptions on a concurrent system and a specification language. Section 3 sets up the new concurrency model. Section 4 explains some Petri net notions needed for an easy understanding of the construction algorithm. Section 5 presents the algorithm to compute a behavior machine. Section 6 shows the application of the concurrency model to test suite derivation for concurrent systems. Finally, Section 7 concludes the paper.

2 A model for distributed concurrent systems

2.1 Assumptions on the model

Generally, a distributed concurrent software system consists of a number of software modules running on different host machines connected through a computer network. Each module is implemented as a sequential unit realizing a certain function of the system. Due to the fact that different modules run on different machines, true concurrency between the modules and the lack of a global clock are elementary features of a distributed concurrent system.

Modules solely communicate via interaction points with each other. The communication pattern used is either synchronous or asynchronous. Taking into account the high complexity in testing distributed systems, we simplify the communication pattern by allowing synchronous communication between modules only. This is, however, not a serious restriction since programming languages for distributed systems, like Ada, and function calls in high-level network programming, like remote procedure calls, which are also used in CORBA-based systems, rely on the rendezvous principle as communication pattern.

2.2 Specification language for distributed concurrent systems

Starting point of our investigations is a formal specification that defines completely the desired behavior of the distributed system. Sequential behavior of a module in a distributed system is modelled as a *finite state machine* (FSM). The model of a FSM is an abstraction that focuses on interactions of a module with other modules in the system and/or with the environment of the system. It is a state transition diagram containing all the states the module can reach and all the transitions it can perform (see Figure 1 for simple examples of FSMs).

Definition (1): (FSM)
A *finite state machine* (FSM) is defined by the quadruple $(S, A, \rightarrow, s_0)$, where
- S is a finite set of states;
- A is a finite set of actions (the alphabet);
- $\rightarrow \subseteq S \times A \times S$ is a transition relation; and
- $s_0 \in S$ is the initial state.

The distributed concurrent system $\mathcal{S}$ is composed from a set of communicating FSMs by means of a composition operator $\parallel$ similar to that used in CSP. $P \parallel Q$ is the parallel composition of modules P and Q with synchronization of the actions common to both of their alphabets and interleaving of the others:

$$\mathfrak{S} = FSM_1 \parallel FSM_2 \parallel \ldots \parallel FSM_n.$$

The parallel composition $P \parallel Q$ of two FSMs $P = (S_1, A_1, \rightarrow_1, s_1)$ and $Q = (S_2, A_2, \rightarrow_2, s_2)$ is defined as $(S, A, \rightarrow, s)$, where $S = S_1 \times S_2$, $A = A_1 \cup A_2$, $s = (s_1, s_2)$, and $\rightarrow$ is given by the three transition rules:

- **If $P -a\rightarrow_1 P'$ then $(P \parallel Q) -a\rightarrow (P' \parallel Q)$ if $a \notin A_2$.**
- **If $Q -a\rightarrow_2 Q'$ then $(P \parallel Q) -a\rightarrow (P \parallel Q')$ if $a \notin A_1$.**
- **If $P -a\rightarrow_1 P'$ and $Q -a\rightarrow_2 Q'$ then $(P \parallel Q) -a\rightarrow (P' \parallel Q')$ if $a \in A_1 \cap A_2$.**

The third rule defines synchronization between modules. The application of the rules for the parallel operator is based on the interleaving framework. We realize that with an increasing number of modules in the parallel composition, the state space increases exponentially (see Figure 1 for a parallel composition of two simple FSMs).

3 A concurrency model

The representation of behavior in a global FSM is accomplished by a tedious repetition of concurrent actions in order to construct all possible total orders due to the interleaving framework. However, concurrent actions are independent to a certain extent from their occurrence in a total order. Instead of interpreting causality information in an interleaved-based model, we apply the notion of a *labeled partially ordered set* and its extension to a *partially ordered multiset* which are interleaved-free representations of concurrent behavior [Pra86].

Definition (2): (Lposets)
A *lposet* (*labeled partially ordered set*) is defined by the quadruple $(E, A, \leq, l)$, where
- E is a set of event names;
- A is a set of action names;
- $\leq$ is a partial order expressing the causality information between events, i.e. $e \leq f$ if event e precedes event f in time $(e, f \in E)$;
- $l: E \rightarrow A$ is a labeling function assigning action names to events. Each labeled event represents an occurrence of the action labelling it, with the same action possibly having multiple occurrences.

A *pomset* (*partially ordered multiset*) is then the isomorphism class of an *lposet*, denoted $[E, A, \leq, l]$.

A *process* describing the behavior of concurrent system $\mathfrak{S}$ is a set of pomsets where each pomset describes a possible execution sequence of concurrent actions. Since the behavior of a system is frequently infinite due to recursive parts in the system description, the pomsets of a process are infinite, too. If branching occurs in a process, the set of pomsets forms an infinite pomtree where an arc in the pomtree is a lposet, and a vertex is a branching point of the process (see Figure 3 as an example).

In order to construct a finite model of global behavior of a concurrent system, one could apply the construction rules of the interleaving framework to obtain a global FSM (see Section 2.2).

However, the construction of the global FSM from a set of communicating FSMs is not feasible in many cases due to state explosion.

It follows that we need a new model that combines the advantages of both concepts: true concurrency between actions (as preserved in a lposet) and finiteness of the description (as preserved in a FSM). This model is a *behavior machine* (BM). A behavior machine is a similar model to the one introduced in [PLL+91]. However, the main advantage of a behavior machine is that it can be constructed automatically from a set of communicating FSMs, as it will be shown in the paper.

Definition (3): (Behavior machine)
The *behavior machine* of a concurrent system $\mathfrak{S}$ is a quadruple $BM_{\mathfrak{S}} = (G, LPO, T, g_0)$ consisting of
- a finite set of global states G, where each element of G is an n-tuple of local states of all FSMs of $\mathfrak{S}$, i.e. $G \subseteq S_1 \times \ldots \times S_n$;
- a set of finite lposets LPO, where each lposet $lpo \in LPO$ is derived from system $\mathfrak{S}$;
- a concurrent transition relation $T \subseteq G \times LPO \times G$ that maps a start state to a end state by performing the actions of the given lposet;
- and an initial global state $g_0 = (s_1, \ldots, s_n) \in G$.

The definition of a behavior machine is similar in structural terms to the definition of a FSM. The main difference lies in the use of lposets in the behavior machine instead of actions in the FSM. A global state of behavior machine $BM_{\mathfrak{S}}$, excluding its initial state, expresses always a branching point or a recurrence point within concurrent system $\mathfrak{S}$. A branching point is a global state where further behavior of the system diverges. A recurrence point is a global state where the behavior of the system repeatedly continues. Since global states are present in a behavior machine only if they possess at least one of these two properties, the set of global states represented explicitly in a behavior machine is usually a very small subset of the set of reachable global states in the system.

As a matter of fact, a pomtree is obtained from the behavior machine if its concurrent transitions are unrolled. In this case, branching points in the behavior machine correspond to branching points in the pomtree, whereas recurrence points are not represented in the pomtree. Thus, unrolling a behavior machine is similar to the construction of a spanning tree from a directed graph.

Consider the following simple system $\mathfrak{S} = A \parallel B$ whose FSMs are given in Figure 1 as an example. Under the assumption that the actions a and c in each FSM synchronize, removal of parallel operator $\parallel$ by applying the interleaved-based semantics rules yields the global FSM $\mathfrak{S}$.

Figure 2 shows the behavior machine of the same system $\mathfrak{S} = A \parallel B$. It contains three global states (S_0, S_1, S_2) and four concurrent transitions (t_1–t_4) and describes the same behavior of system $\mathfrak{S}$ as given in Figure 1. Each concurrent transition is described by a lposet that exhibits concurrency among actions (see transition t_4). If the behavior machine is unrolled, the pomtree of Figure 3 is obtained. The process of unrolling makes the concurrency between events visible. For instance, if transitions t_2 and t_4 are concatenated, we realize that event b is concurrent to event e.

Although the behavior machine in Figure 2 is not the smallest representation of concurrent behavior due to the construction algorithm discussed below, it is still a very compact representation of concurrent behavior. Furthermore, it is able to distinguish concurrency from branching. This knowledge is lost in the description based on interleaving in Figure 1.

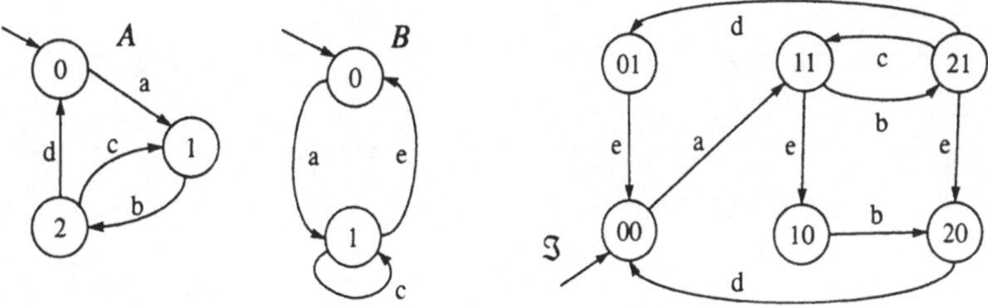

FIGURE 1. FSM A and B and the combined FSM $\Im = A \parallel B$.

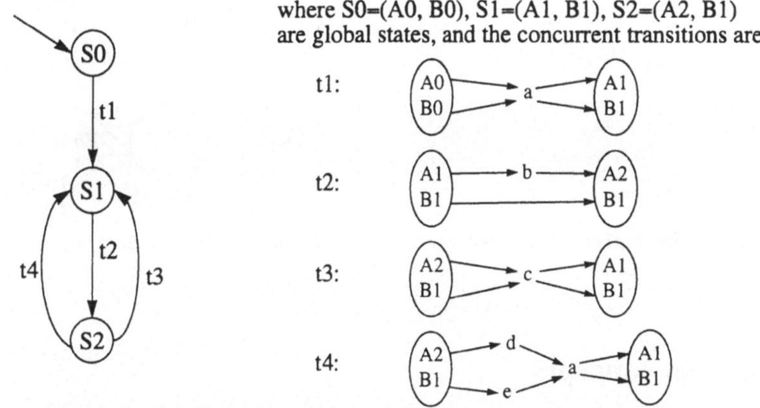

where S0=(A0, B0), S1=(A1, B1), S2=(A2, B1) are global states, and the concurrent transitions are

FIGURE 2. The behavior machine of system $\Im$.

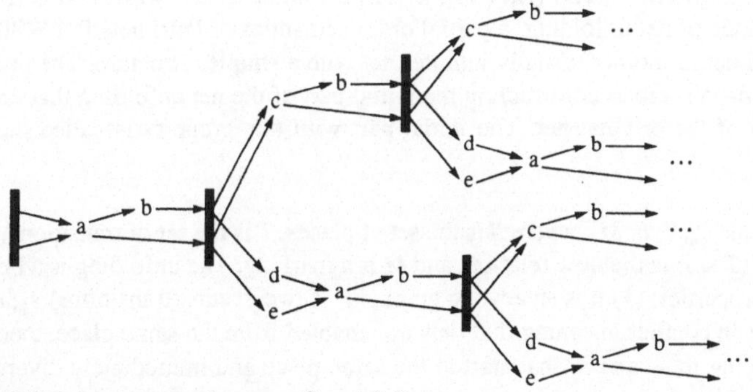

FIGURE 3. A pomtree of system $\Im = A \parallel B$.

In the sequel of this paper, we show how a behavior machine is constructed from a set of communicating FSMs using a Petri net and its unfolding as intermediate model. However before we can start, we need to introduce further notions.

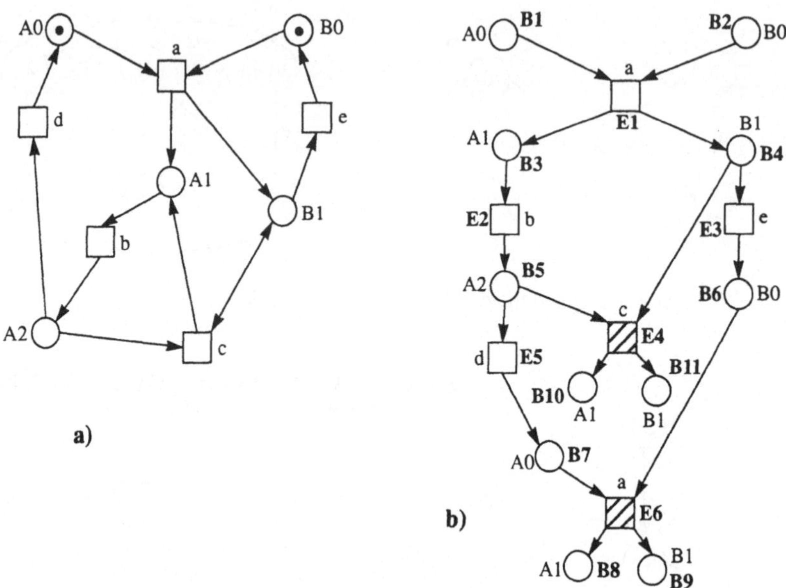

FIGURE 4. The marked Petri net of system $\mathfrak{S} = A \parallel B$ (a) and its unfolding (b).

4 Petri net concepts

The construction algorithm of a behavior machine is based on a Petri net description of the concurrent system. In [McM95] and [ERV96], a verification approach was described that is based on the technique of net unfolding, a partial order semantics of Petri nets [NPW80]. The unfolding of a Petri net is another (usually infinite) net with a simpler structure. The proposed algorithms in both papers aim at constructing the initial part of the net unfolding that contains all reachable states of the original net. The initial part with this property is called the *finite complete prefix*.

A Petri net is a 4-tuple (S, T, F, M), where S is the set of places, T is the set of transitions, $S \cap T = \varnothing$, $F \subseteq (S \times T) \cup (T \times S)$ is the flow relation, and M is a marking. The unfolding is a Petri net (B, E, F) with the properties: (1) it is an acyclic graph, (2) if two events (transitions) $e_1, e_2 \in E$ of the unfolding are in conflict, meaning that they are enabled from the same place, then there exist two paths leading to e_1 and e_2 that start at the same place and immediately diverge, (3) the nodes in the unfolding have a finite number of predecessors, and (4) no event is in self-conflict.

Figure 4 depicts the Petri net description of system $\mathfrak{S}$ and the initial part of its unfolding. Note that the unfolding is not finite. For instance, if event **E4** is performed, the unfolding continues by substituting place **B10** with **B3** and **B11** with **B4**, respectively. This applies similarly to event **E6**. Events **E4** and **E6** are also in conflict. The branching point where the paths leading to the events diverge is the marking {**B5**, **B4**}.

A *local configuration* [e] of event e in the unfolding describes a possible partially ordered run of the system which executes event e as its last event. It is a set of events satisfying the following two conditions: (1) if any event is in the local configuration, then so are all of its predecessors, and (2) a local configuration is conflict-free. The local configuration captures the precedence relation between events. Any total order on these events that is consistent with the partial order is an allowed totally ordered run of the system. Throughout the paper, we use the notions *local configuration* and *configuration* interchangeable.

To compute the finite complete prefix of a Petri net, it is necessary to define a break-off condition to stop the construction of the unfolding. This is done by introducing *cut-off events*. An event e is a cut-off event if the local configuration $[e]$ belonging to event e reaches a marking $Mark([e])$ in the unfolding that was reached before by a smaller local configuration of a different event.

Consider the unfolding in Figure 4b. The configuration of event **E6** is the set of events $[E6] = \{E1, E2, E3, E5, E6\}$. The reachable marking of this configuration is $Mark([E6]) = \{A1, B1\}$. This marking was reached before, however, by configuration $[E1] = \{E1\}$. We say, event **E6** corresponds to event **E1**. Since the configuration of **E1** has fewer elements than the configuration of **E6**, it follows that **E6** is a cut-off event. The second cut-off event in this example is **E4**.

In Section 5 that presents the construction algorithm of a behavior machine, we exploit the property of a Petri net unfolding that the complete state space of a specific system can be constructed if all cut-off events and their corresponding events existing in the unfolding are known. Those events are contained in the finite complete prefix.

Let (B, E, F) the unfolding of a 1-save Petri net[1]. The finite set of tuples of cut-off and corresponding events from E is given as

$$\{ (e_{\text{cutoff}_1}, e_{\text{corresp}_1}), (e_{\text{cutoff}_2}, e_{\text{corresp}_2}), ..., (e_{\text{cutoff}_n}, e_{\text{corresp}_n}) \}$$

where the two configurations of events in a tuple reach the same marking, i.e.

$$Mark([e_{\text{cutoff}_i}]) = Mark([e_{\text{corresp}_i}])$$

The theory of unfoldings and construction of finite complete prefixes and their application in the verification process of concurrent systems are discussed in depth in [McM95] and [ERV96]. In our paper, we use the unfolding to construct a behavior machine and apply the behavior machine as input for test suite derivation. This approach is motivated by the fact that the prefix of an unfolding constructed by the algorithms in [ERV96] is complete, i.e., it covers all reachable states and all allowed paths through the system, but it also preserves true concurrency in the system description.

---

1 A *1-safe net* is a net which places contain at most one token each at a certain time. A 1-safe net is obtained if the net is constructed from a set of FSMs communicating synchronously as discussed in this paper.

5 Construction algorithm of a behavior machine

5.1 Preparation

The first step in constructing a behavior machine from a set of communicating FSMs is a transformation of the FSMs into a Petri net. After the transformation, the unfolding algorithm is applied to construct the finite complete prefix of the net. Finally, the behavior machine is constructed from the prefix.

The construction of a Petri net from a set of communicating FSMs is simple. The following algorithm is applied: first, each single FSM is transformed into a Petri net; then, all Petri nets are merged according to the synchronization constraints in order to obtain a single net. This transformation was already presented in [GaSi90] and is used in the *Cæsar/Aldebaran* toolset that supports verification of specifications given in the formal description language LOTOS.

In the first step, each state in a FSM is transformed into a place in the Petri net; each FSM transition is transformed into a Petri net transition between two places. To obtain a single net, pairs of Petri net transitions with the same action name are merged. The following figure demonstrates the second transformation step:

Figure 4a shows the Petri net constructed from the two FSMs in Figure 1. The next step is the construction of the finite complete prefix. This is done by applying the algorithm presented in [ERV96]. Figure 4b depicts the prefix of the example system. The last step, the construction of the behavior machine, is described in the next sub-section.

5.2 Construction algorithm

We assume that the finite complete prefix of a Petri net unfolding, including the set of cut-off and corresponding events is given. Algorithm (1) returns the local configuration of an event e in the unfolding (B, E, F).

The local configuration of an event describes an execution path through the behavior machine from the initial state to this particular event. The marking reached by the configuration of an event is also of interest since it defines a global state in the behavior of a concurrent system. The reachable marking of a local configuration $Mark([e])$ is found by means of Algorithm (2).

The reachable marking of a configuration can be identified with places in the unfolding that are reached if all events in the configuration are executed. Since the construction of a Petri net is done from a set of communicating FSMs, the number of tokens in a reachable marking is equal to the number of FSMs in the system.

1	• let *e* be an event of the unfolding;
2	*local_configuration* = {*e*}; *event_set* = {*e*}; *place_set* = ∅;
3	**while** (*event_set* is not empty) **do**
4	**forall** events *e* ∈ *event_set* **do**
5	*place_set* = *place_set* ∪ predecessors(*e*);
6	**end**
7	*event_set* = ∅;
8	**forall** places *p* ∈ *place_set* **do**
9	*event_set* = *event_set* ∪ predecessors(*p*);
10	**end**
11	*local_configuration* = *local_configuration* ∪ *event_set*;
12	*place_set* = ∅;
13	**end**
14	**return** *local_configuration*;

ALGORITHM 1. Construction of a local configuration from an event.

1	• let *configuration* be a configuration from an event in the unfolding;
2	*reachable_marks* = ∅;
3	**forall** events *e* ∈ *configuration* **do**
4	*place_set* = successors(*e*);
5	**forall** places *p* ∈ *place_set* **do**
6	**if** (successors(*p*) are not contained in *configuration*) **then**
7	*reachable_marks* = *reachable_marks* ∪ {*p*};
8	**end**
9	**end**
10	**return** *reachable_marks*;

ALGORITHM 2. Construction of the reachable marking of a configuration.

If the behavior machine is constructed, it is not necessary to compute the reachable marking for each configuration in the unfolding. Instead, only those reachable markings have to be known that are recurrence or branching points. The cut-off events and events corresponding to them define recurrence points of the behavior machine. Yet, branching points have to be computed.

To identify the branching points, we do the following considerations. Given the finite complete prefix of an unfolding, each local configuration of a cut-off event or a corresponding event starts in the initial state of the system, i.e. the initial marking, and ends in a marking reached by the configurations of those events. Since the finite complete prefix covers all reachable states of the system, branching points can exist only somewhere inside the configurations of cut-off and corresponding events.

If we analyze any two configurations from the same unfolding $[e_1]$ and $[e_2]$ with $e_1 \neq e_2$, we realize that the configurations start with a same subset of events and diverge after a certain event e_{branch} occurred in both configurations. Now, a branching point can be defined exactly by the reachable marking of the configuration formed by this event e_{branch} assuming that $e_{\text{branch}} \in [e_i]$; and $[e_{\text{branch}}]$ is the maximum configuration that holds the condition $[e_{\text{branch}}] \subset [e_i]$, with $i = \{1, 2\}$.

```
1      • let E be the set of cut-off events and corresponding events in a finite
           complete prefix;
2      • let 𝓔 initially be the set of configurations from all events in E, i.e.
           𝓔 = {[e₁], [e₂], ... };
3      forall configurations [e] ∈ 𝓔 do
4          forall events d ∈ [e] with d ≠ e do
5              if (([d] ∉ 𝓔) AND (successors(d) are branching places)) then
6                  • mark d as branching event;
7                  𝓔 = 𝓔 ∪ [d];
8              end
9          end
10     end
11     forall configurations [e] ∈ 𝓔 do
12         forall configurations [d] ∈ 𝓔 do
13             if ((|[e]| < |[d]|) AND ([e] ⊂ [d])) then
14                 • mark [e] if it is the maximum configuration contained in [d];
15             end
16         end
17     forall configurations [e] ∈ 𝓔 do
18         if ((e is a branching event) AND
           ([e] is marked as maximum configuration less than twice)) then
19             𝓔 = 𝓔 \ {[e]};
20         end
21     return 𝓔;
```

ALGORITHM 3. Generation of configurations relevant in the behavior machine.

This observation leads to the construction algorithm of a behavior machine. It takes as input the set of cut-off events and corresponding events that are contained in the finite complete prefix of an unfolding. The idea of this algorithm is to construct the configurations of the given cut-off and corresponding events first. Then, the events in the configurations are analyzed in order to identify the branching points.

As discussed above, a branching point is defined by the reachable marking of a configuration of maximum size contained within two or more other configurations. To identify these points, we analyze the successor places of an event e. If at least one of the successor places has more than one successor event, the reachable marking of the configuration $[e]$ might be a branching point in the behavior machine. Since this result is obtained from a local analysis of a single event rather than from an analysis of the global system, not all events found refer really to a branching point. The following Algorithm (3) takes into account this aspect and returns only those events and their configurations that will be finally considered in the construction of a behavior machine.

The initial set of configurations $\mathcal{E}$ is obtained from the configurations of cut-off and corresponding events contained in the prefix of the unfolding (line 2 in Algorithm (3)). In the next step, further configurations of events are added to $\mathcal{E}$ if these events possess successor places that cause branching (lines 3–10). The third step (lines 11–16) determines whether a configuration is contained in another one and marks the maximum configuration that fulfills this property. The final step (lines 17–20) deletes configurations of events added before to $\mathcal{E}$ if they are not marked as maximum configuration or if they are marked only once in another configuration. That means, configurations that do not determine a branch in the behavior are omitted in the construction of the behavior machine.

1	• let $\mathcal{E}$ be the set of configurations computed in Algorithm (3);
2	*global_states* = ∅;
3	**forall** configurations $[d] \in \mathcal{E}$ **do**
4	• compute the reachable marking *reachable_marks* of $[d]$;
5	*global_states* = *global_states* ∪ {*reachable_marks*};
6	**end**
7	*conc_trans* = ∅;
8	**forall** configurations $[d] \in \mathcal{E}$ **do**
9	• let $[e]$ be the maximum configuration of $[d]$;
10	*conc_trans* = *conc_trans* ∪ {$[d] \setminus [e]$};
11	**end**
12	**return** *global_states*, *conc_trans*;

ALGORITHM 4. Construction of global states and concurrent transitions in a BM.

Algorithm (3) returns the set of configurations $\mathcal{E}$ relevant in the construction of the behavior machine, i.e., the configurations have the property that they reach a marking of a recurrence point or a branching point. In the next Algorithm (4), this knowledge is used to construct the global states and the concurrent transitions of the behavior machine corresponding to the unfolding of a concurrent system.

In line 4 of Algorithm (4), the reachable marking is computed according to Algorithm (2). Note that the reachable markings are the same for the configuration of a cut-off event and the configuration of its corresponding event, thus the second computation is redundant. A concurrent transition in a behavior machine is computed in line 10. It is simply the difference of configuration $[d]$ and the maximum configuration $[e]$ contained in $[d]$. This computation is correct since the configuration $[e]$ is a subset of $[d]$, and all events in $[e]$ occur in the behavior machine in one or more other concurrent transitions.

The behavior machine is now nearly complete. The missing initial global state of the behavior machine is computed from the reachable marking of the empty configuration, i.e., it is the initial set of tokens in the Petri net.

5.3 Complexity analysis

The construction algorithm of a behavior machine exploits the advantages of the theory of net unfoldings. It was shown in [McM95] and [ERV96] that the size of the finite complete prefix of an unfolding depends on the degree of branching in the system. The size is bounded on $\mathcal{O}\left(\binom{n}{k}\right) = \mathcal{O}(n^k)$, where n is the number of places in the unfolding, and k is the largest number of successor places of any transition. In [ERV96], the upper bound of the running time of the unfolding algorithm was given as $\mathcal{O}\left(\left(\frac{n}{k}\right)^k\right)$.

The construction of a behavior machine is based on cut-off events and corresponding events in the finite complete prefix and the configurations belonging to them. Constructing configurations and their reachable markings is linear in time since it can be implemented as a sequential search over the unfolding. The highest complexity of the construction algorithm is contained in Algorithm (3), lines 11–16. The complexity of these few lines is bound on $\mathcal{O}(n^2 \cdot (\log_k n)^2)$, where n is the number of places in the finite complete prefix, and k is the largest number of successor places of any transition. All other parts of the construction algorithm are less complex.

To demonstrate the feasibility of the construction algorithm, we compute the behavior machines for a variable number of processes of the classic Dining Philosophers example. The results are given in the table below.

# philosophers	# reachable states	# concurrent transitions	# global states	mem. usage (kByte)	computation time (sec)[a]
5	392	35	16	36	0.11
7	4,247	77	36	61	0.73
9	46,763	135	64	98	2.96
11	510,116	209	100	151	9.12
13	5,564,522	299	144	222	22.76
15	—[b]	405	196	314	48.83

TABLE 1. Results of the Dining Philosophers example.

a. computed on a SPARC Station 5.

b. value not computed.

The second column of the table shows the number of reachable states computed in a traditional reachability analysis. This number of states grows clearly exponentially with the number of philosophers. The following two columns reveal the numbers of concurrent transitions and global states of the constructed behavior machines. We realize that the number of global states increases slightly worse than quadratic. Even though the computation time increases fast and seems to be bounded on $O(n^{5.5})$, where n is the number of philosophers, the time is still reasonable small. This is also particularly true for the memory space used. The computation time of the finite complete prefix that is used as input for our construction algorithm was always less or around few seconds.

5.4 Properties of behavior machines

The behavior machine is constructed from the finite complete prefix of an unfolding. Due to the construction algorithm of the prefix, the resulting behavior machine may not be the minimal representation of concurrent behavior. Figure 2 shows a behavior machine that is obviously not the smallest representation of the system $\mathfrak{S} = A \parallel B$ in Figure 1. In this specific example, the action a is redundantly represented within the concurrent transitions t_1 and t_4 what can be avoided in the minimal description. However, the behavior machine found is still a smaller description of concurrent behavior compared to its interleaved-based counterpart.

The behavior machine constructed from the given algorithm is minimal in another sense: it introduces a global state only if it is a branching point or recurrence point. Thus, it is able to distinguish concurrency from branching. Unlike a finite state machine, the global states of a behavior machine do not represent all reachable global states. That means, there exist other global states that are not explicitly given. Nevertheless, all reachable global states of a system are omnipresent in the behavior machine. They can be constructed by exploiting the recurrence structure of the concurrent system, i.e., by generating the pomtree of the system [Esp94].

Since a behavior machine represents only reachable global states, its graph structure yields a connected graph. Further graph properties cannot be assumed. For instance, the behavior machine of a system does not necessary need to be strongly connected even if all of its sequential FSMs have this property.

6 Test suite generation based on partial orders

6.1 Test architecture and concurrent transition tour

Talking about test suite generation, we first need to introduce a suitable test architecture to test a concurrent system. In this paper, we assume that a test architecture is described by a parallel composition of a tester and an implementation under test (IUT), which represents the implementation of the concurrent system to be tested: *Tester* || *IUT.*

The tester shall be a single module described in the same way as the modules of the concurrent system, i.e. a single FSM. Furthermore, the tester shall have access to all interactions of the modules in the system (grey-box test method). Regardless these simplifying assumptions, the introduced test architecture is sufficient to demonstrate the use of partial orders in testing concurrent systems. A more elaborated approach to a distributed test architecture can be found in [UlCh95].

To derive test suites for concurrent systems, we extend the notion of a *transition tour* [SiLe89] and apply it as a test case for distributed systems. A transition tour is defined for a single FSM as the shortest path that covers all transitions in the FSM at least once. In the context of distributed systems, the transition tour is extended to a *concurrent transition tour* (CTT) in such a way that all transitions in all modules of the system are visited at least once on the shortest possible path through the system [UlCh95].

Definition (4): (CTT)
A *concurrent transition tour* through a concurrent system $\Im = FSM_1 \, \| \, ... \, \| \, FSM_n$ is a minimal pomset $CTT = [E_{CTT}, A_{CTT}, \leq, l]$ such that all actions of $\Im$ are covered at least once in the pomset, i.e. if $a \in A_1 \cup A_2 \cup ... \cup A_n$, then $a \in A_{CTT}$, and E_{CTT} is minimal.

In the case of a single FSM, Definition (4) is analogous to the definition of a transition tour. The given definition of a CTT relates to the "all edges between concurrency states" selection criterion given in [TLK92] that covers all edges that exist between the global states. To reduce testing costs, it is essential that the CTT has a minimal length, i.e., the system should be traversed completely with the shortest path.

6.2 Derivation algorithm of a CTT

Derivation of a CTT from a behavior machine of a concurrent system is straightforward. Since the description of concurrent behavior is reduced to a finite directed graph, simple graph algorithms can be applied. To construct a CTT, an algorithm that solves the Chinese postman problem is appropriate. A *Chinese postman tour* is a tour through a graph that contains all edges in the graph at least once and, thus, it fulfills the properties of a CTT over a behavior machine. It can be constructed in polynomial time for directed, strongly-connected graphs as shown in [ADL+91].

Since a constructed behavior machine does not need to be strongly-connected, a modified test derivation approach is used. First, all strongly-connected components of maximum size contained in a behavior machine are computed using, e.g., an algorithm from [CLR90]. After that, a CTT is derived for each strongly-connected component. This approach assures full coverage of all transitions in the behavior machine. The complete algorithm is given in Algorithm (5).

1	Find all strongly-connected subgraphs of maximum size $bm^s_1, ..., bm^s_n$ in behavior machine *bm*.
2	For each bm^s_i find the shortest path p_i from the initial state of *bm* to a state in bm^s_i.
3	For each bm^s_i find the Chinese postman tour pt_i through this subgraph.
4	A CTT for a subgraph of *bm* is found by concatenation of p_i and pt_i: $CTT_i = p_i \oplus pt_i$.
5	The test suite is the set of all CTTs found: $TS = \{CTT_1, ..., CTT_n\}$.

ALGORITHM 5. Test suite derivation.

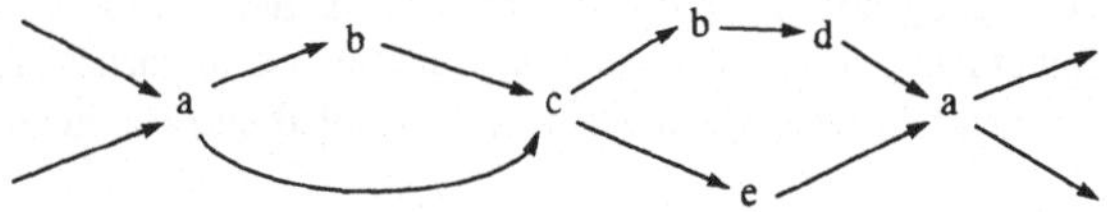

FIGURE 5. A concurrent transition tour of system $\mathfrak{I} = A \parallel B$.

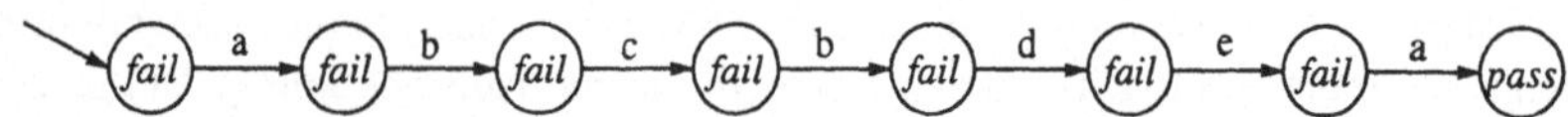

FIGURE 6. The specification of a tester as a single FSM to test system $\mathfrak{I} = A \parallel B$.

The operation $t_1 \oplus t_2$ expresses concatenation of two concurrent transitions in a behavior machine. Concatenation is carried out in the way that the local states of the end state in t_1 are connected with the same local states of the start state in t_2. Since the definition of a CTT does not represent states, they are finally dropped to obtain the resulting CTT.

Consider the behavior machine of system $\mathfrak{I} = A \parallel B$ in Figure 2. It contains one strongly-connected component consisting of the states S_1 and S_2. The initial path to reach this component is given by concurrent transition t_1. The Chinese postman tour through the component is the sequence of concurrent transitions $t_2 \oplus t_3 \oplus t_2 \oplus t_4$. Thus, the final test suite of system $\mathfrak{I}$ contains only a single CTT and can be given as $TS_{\mathfrak{I}} = \{CTT\} = \{t_1 \oplus t_2 \oplus t_3 \oplus t_2 \oplus t_4\}$ (see Figure 5). This test suite describes the shortest path through the concurrent system fulfilling the requirements of a CTT, i.e., it contains all transitions of the single FSMs A and B at least once.

6.3 Test execution

If we use the derived CTT, we are able to construct the tester in the following way. Assuming that the tester shall be implemented as a single FSM running in parallel with the IUT, concurrent actions in the CTT need to be serialized according to the causality relations among them, i.e., we construct a totally ordered run from the CTT. Any interleaving sequence of actions that can be obtained from a CTT is sufficient in this case.

The CTT in Figure 5 represents three allowed interleaving sequences. We choose the sequence *abcbdea* to be implemented in the tester. The other two sequences are *abcbeda* and *abcebda*. The tester is now constructed as a FSM as shown in Figure 6.

The tester contains 8 states where 7 states are labeled with the test verdict *fail*, and the final state is labeled *pass*. Since the tester communicates with the IUT synchronously, test execution stops in a certain state of the tester if the IUT is not able to participate in an action that is required by the tester. Only if the IUT participates in all actions of the implemented test sequence, the tester reaches the *pass*-state indicating a successful test run through the system.

7 Conclusions

The model of a behavior machine is used in this paper to support test suite derivation for concurrent systems. The model has its merits as a finite description of concurrent systems that still exhibits true concurrency among actions. The main contribution in our paper is the presentation of an algorithm that constructs a behavior machine from the finite complete prefix of a Petri net unfolding. The algorithm requires that the concurrent system is specified as Petri net or is mapped into an adequate net first. Such mapping algorithm from a set of communicating FSMs to a Petri net is also presented.

The main advantage of a behavior machine as concurrency model is its suitability to cover completely the behavior of a concurrent system in a finite description. Furthermore, a behavior machine makes the recurrent and branching structure of the concurrent system visible. Vertices in the behavior machine refer to a small subset of the set of reachable global states in the system. Only the minimum number of global states is represented in a behavior machine that is necessary to identify recurrence and branching points.

In a further part of the paper, the application of a behavior machine in the area of test suite derivation is shown. An adaptation of the transition tour to concurrent systems, the concurrent transition tour, is given. Its derivation from a behavior machine is discussed. Test suite derivation methods, like an adapted W- or UIO-method, could be applied for a behavior machine, too. However, these methods require mostly some further graph properties that may be not readily fulfilled by a behavior machine in advance. Properties of behavior machines have to be subject of further studies to apply also these methods.

Since the construction of a behavior machine is based on a Petri net, other synchronization models of concurrent systems can be used as long as the resulting Petri net is a 1-safe net. For instance, to support non-blocking asynchronous communication among the FSMs in the system, only the algorithm that constructs the Petri net must be changed.

The proposed approach to test suite derivation is implemented as a prototype tool and is integrated in the LOTOS tool environment *Caesar/Aldebaran* [GaSi90] in connection with the Petri net toolset PEP [GrBe96]. Since the LOTOS static analyzer *Cæsar* supports symbolic evaluation of LOTOS data types, full data flow dependencies are considered in the derived test suite, too.

8 References

[ADL+91]   A. V. Aho, A. T. Dahbura, D. Lee, M. Ü. Uyar: *An optimization technique for protocol conformance test generation based on UIO sequences and rural Chinese postman tours*; IEEE Transactions on Communications, vol. 39, no. 11 (Nov. 1991); pp. 1604–1615.

[BoUy91]   B. S. Bosik, M. Ü. Uyar: *Finite state machine based formal methods in protocol conformance testing: from theory to implementation*; Computer Networks and ISDN Systems 22 (1); 1991; pp. 7–33.

[CLR90]   Th. H. Cormen, Ch. E. Leiserson, R. L. Rivest: *Introduction to algorithms*; The MIT Press; McGraw-Hill, New York; 1990; ISBN 0-07-013143-0.

[ERV96]   J. Esparza, S. Römer, W. Vogler: *An improvement of McMillan's unfolding algorithm*; 2nd International Workshop on Tools and Algorithms for the Construction and Analysis of Systems (TACAS'96); Passau, Germany; 1996.

[Esp95]   J. Esparza: *Model checking using net unfoldings*; Science of Computer Programming, vol. 23 (1994); pp. 151–195.

[GaSi90]   H. Garavel, J. Sifakis: *Compilation and verification of Lotos specifications*; 10th International Symposium on Protocol Specification, Testing and Verification (PSTV'90); Ottawa, Canada; 1990; pp. 379–394.

[GrBe96]   B. Grahlmann, E. Best: *PEP – More than a Petri net tool*; 2nd International Workshop on Tools and Algorithms for the Construction and Analysis of Systems (TACAS'96); Passau, Germany; 1996.

[KCV93]   M. C. Kim, S. T. Chanson, S. T. Vuong: *Concurrency model and its application to formal protocol specifications*; IEEE INFOCOM, vol. 2; San Francisco, USA; 1993; pp. 766–773.

[KCK+96]   M. C. Kim, S. T. Chanson, S. W. Kang, J. W. Shin: *An approach for testing asynchronous communicating systems*; 9th International Workshop on Testing of Communicating Systems (IWTCS'96); Darmstadt, Germany; Sep. 1996.

[McM95]   K. L. McMillan: *A technique of state space search based on unfolding*; Formal Methods in System Design, vol. 6, no. 1 (Jan. 1995); pp. 45–65.

[NPW80]   M. Nielsen, G. Plotkin, G. Winskel: *Petri nets, event structures and domains*; Theoretical Computer Science, vol. 13, no. 1 (1980); pp. 85–108.

[Pra86]   V. Pratt: Modelling *Concurrency with partial orders*; International Journal of Parallel Programming, vol. 15, no. 1 (Feb. 1986); pp. 33–71.

[PLL+91]   D. K. Probst, H. F. Li, K. G. Larsen, A. Skou: *Partial-order model checking: a guide for the perplexed*; 3nd International Conference on Computer-aided Verification (CAV'91); Aalborg, Denmark; 1991.

[SiLe89]   D. P. Sidhu, T. K. Leung: *Formal methods for protocol testing: a detailed study*; IEEE Transactions on Software Engineering, vol. 15, no. 4 (Apr. 1989); pp. 413–426.

[TLK92]   R. N. Taylor, D. L. Levine, Ch. D. Kelly: *Structural testing of concurrent programs*; IEEE Transactions on Software Engineering, vol. 18, no. 3 (March 1992); pp. 206–215.

[UlCh95]   A. Ulrich, S. T. Chanson: *An approach to testing distributed software systems;* 15th International Symposium on Protocol Specification, Testing and Verification (PSTV'95); Warsaw, Poland; pp. 107–122; 1995.

[YaCh92]   R. D. Yang, C. G. Chung: *Path analysis testing of concurrent programs*; Information and Software Technology; vol. 34, no. 1 (Jan. 1992); pp. 43–56.

Erkennung von Wechselwirkungen
zwischen Dienstmerkmalen im Intelligenten Netz
mit Hilfe formaler Techniken

Dirk O. Keck

Universität Stuttgart
Institut für Nachrichtenvermittlung und Datenverarbeitung[1]
Prof. Dr.-Ing. Dr. h. c. Paul J. Kühn
Seidenstr. 36, D-70174 Stuttgart
Telefon (0711) 121 2484, Fax (0711) 121 2477
E-mail: keck@ind.uni-stuttgart.de

Kurzfassung. Das Intelligente Netz (IN) ist ein Architekturkonzept, das die schnelle und kostengünstige Einführung neuer Kommunikationsdienste unterstützt und erleichtert. Wechselwirkungen
zwischen Diensten im IN stellen ein ernstzunehmendes Problem dar, da sie den sicheren und benut-
zerfreundlichen Betrieb eines Telekommunikationsnetzes gefährden können. In dieser Arbeit wird
ein Verfahren zur Erkennung solcher Wechselwirkungen vorgestellt, das in einer frühen Phase der
Dienstentwicklung ansetzt. Dabei wird gezeigt, daß die Ursache für solche Wechselwirkungen
darin liegt, daß mehrere Dienste gemeinsame Einflußbereiche besitzen und über Auswirkungen auf
diese Bereiche miteinander in Wechselwirkung treten können. Mit Hilfe einer formalen Beschreibung der Rufbehandlung und Dienstbearbeitung im IN können unter Verwendung formaler Techniken wie der Erreichbarkeitsanalyse solche Wechselwirkungen erkannt werden.

1 Einführung

1.1 Das Intelligente Netz (IN)

Benutzer des Telefonnetzes stellen immer höhere Erwartungen an dessen Funktionalität. Entwicklung und Aufbau des diensteintegrierenden digitalen Fernsprechnetzes ISDN trug diesen
Anforderungen Rechnung, indem eine Anzahl von Erweiterungen des Basisdienstes, die sogenannten zusätzlichen Dienstmerkmale (engl. Supplementary Services) hinzugefügt wurden.
Jedes dieser Dienstmerkmale erfordert einen Eingriff in die Software jeder Vermittlungsstelle.
Diese Methode für die Realisierung zusätzlicher Dienste ist teuer und inflexibel, da stets der
gesamte Entwicklungszyklus für eine neue Version der Vermittlungssoftware durchlaufen und
diese neue Software dann in allen Vermittlungsstellen im Netz installiert werden muß.

Der Bedarf an einer Erleichterung der Erstellung neuer Dienste und Dienstmerkmale führte
zur Entwicklung des Intelligenten Netzes (IN) als neuartigem Architekturkonzept. Es handelt
sich entgegen seiner Bezeichnung nicht um ein weiteres Telekommunikationsnetz, sondern um
ein allgemeingültiges Konzept zur Realisierung neuer Dienste und Dienstmerkmale. Die
wesentliche Eigenschaft dieses Konzepts liegt in der Trennung von Vermittlung und Dienstbearbeitung. Für die Vermittlung und Rufbehandlung sind die Vermittlungsstellen des Netzes
verantwortlich, wie auch in herkömmlichen Netzen. Die Bearbeitung von zusätzlichen Diensten bzw. Dienstmerkmalen erfolgt nicht mehr in den Vermittlungssystemen, sondern in davon
getrennten Dienststeuerknoten, sogenannten Service Control Points (SCPs). Dies sind in der
Regel leistungsfähige Universalrechner, die über ein Anwendungsprotokoll, das INAP (Intelli-

1 Diese Arbeit wird in Zusammenarbeit mit der Alcatel SEL AG, Stuttgart, durchgeführt und durch das Software
Labor der Universität Stuttgart, Breitwiesenstr. 20-22, D-70565 Stuttgart unterstützt.

gent Network Application Protocol) mit den Vermittlungsstellen kommunizieren und auf die Rufbehandlung Einfluß nehmen können.

Das IN-Konzept beinhaltet vier Sichtweisen (Ebenen) mit unterschiedlichem Abstraktionsgrad, denen allen das zentrale Element des Dienstes bzw. Dienstmerkmales gemeinsam ist [8]. Auf der obersten Betrachtungsebene, der sogenannten Service Plane (SP), wird ein Dienst nur durch eine Beschreibung ohne Berücksichtigung von Realisierungsaspekten charakterisiert. Eine Ebene darunter, auf der Global Functional Plane (GFP), wird der Dienst als eine Aneinanderreihung von standardisierten Bausteinen, den sogenannten Service Independent Building Blocks (SIBs) betrachtet. Mit Hilfe dieser Beschreibungsform kann der Dienstablauf vollständig charakterisiert werden. Sie enthält genügend Informationen, um daraus die Implementierung des Dienstes mit Hilfe von geeigneten Programmwerkzeugen generieren zu können. Die nächste Ebene, die Distributed Functional Plane (DFP), bietet eine Sicht auf die funktionalen Einheiten und deren logische Beziehungen im Netz, die in Zusammenarbeit die auf den höheren Ebenen charakterisierten Dienste erbringen können. Die unterste Ebene schließlich, als Physical Plane (PP) bezeichnet, beschreibt die Zuordnung dieser logischen funktionalen Einheiten zu realen Einrichtungen im Netz und geht auch auf die erforderlichen Protokollarchitekturen näher ein. Für ausführlichere Informationen über die Architektur des IN sei der Leser auf die einführenden Arbeiten [5, 7, 13, 14] verwiesen.

1.2 Dienstentwicklung im Intelligenten Netz

Dienste für das IN erweitern die Grundfunktionen der Rufbehandlung um zusätzliche Merkmale. Da das IN als Architektur zur Unterstützung einer schnellen und kostengünstigen Realisierung neuer Dienste entwickelt wurde, ist die Dienstentwicklung (engl. Service Creation) von vorne herein integraler Bestandteil des Konzepts. Die Entwicklung neuer Dienste beginnt in der Regel mit der Erstellung einer informellen Spezifikation des Dienstes. Diese Spezifikation dient als Ausgangpunkt für eine Beschreibung des Dienstablaufes mit Hilfe von vorgegebenen Bausteinen (SIBs) in einer formalisierten graphischen Notation, die einem Flußdiagramm ähnelt. Ausgehend von dieser Beschreibung eines neuen Dienstes kann mit Hilfe von Programmwerkzeugen ein ausführbarer Dienst generiert werden. Dieser Dienst wird im weiteren unter Zuhilfenahme von Management-Funktionen, die ebenfalls Bestandteil des IN-Konzepts sind, in einen in das IN integrierten Dienststeuerknoten (SCP) eingebracht.

Die Aufgabe, in einer frühen Phase während des Lebenszyklus eines neuen Dienstes dessen korrekte Funktion unter allen Umständen sicherzustellen, liegt im vitalen Interesse aller beteiligten Parteien. Formale Beschreibungs- und Verifikationstechniken können hier einen wertvollen Beitrag leisten und demonstrieren, wie sie für reale Probleme gewinnbringend eingesetzt werden können.

1.3 Wechselwirkungen zwischen Diensten im Intelligenten Netz

1.3.1 Das Problem

Während der Spezifikation und Entwicklung neuer Dienste bzw. Dienstmerkmale werden diese in der Regel einzeln betrachtet. Diese Sicht wird durch die standardisierten Schnittstellen zwischen Basisdienst und neuen Diensten im IN und durch die Behandlung der Dienste als unabhängige und voneinander getrennte Einheiten unterstützt. Das reale Umfeld eines neu entwickelten Dienstes im Netz unterscheidet sich von der Situation während der Spezifikation und Entwicklung eines neuen Dienstes grundlegend. Neben dem neu entwickelten Dienst bzw. Dienstmerkmal koexistieren gleichzeitig eine Vielzahl weiterer IN-Dienste im Netz; außerdem besitzen moderne digitale Vermittlungssysteme zusätzlich noch eine Reihe weiterer Dienstmerkmale, die nicht in Form von IN-Diensten, sondern als konventionelle Dienste ausgeführt sind, die die Funktion der Vermittlungsstelle erweitern.

Die Tatsache, daß all diese Dienste unabhängig voneinander Möglichkeiten besitzen, auf die Rufbehandlung zu wirken, hat zur Folge, daß ein neu entwickelter Dienst mit bestehenden Diensten oder anderen, zur gleichen Zeit neu entwickelten Diensten in Wechselwirkung treten kann. Obwohl dieses Verhalten nicht zwangsläufig zu Schwierigkeiten führen muß, liegt ein Einsatzkontext für einen Dienst vor, für den dieser nicht spezifiziert ist und in vielen Fällen auch nicht spezifiziert werden kann, da der Dienstentwickler ein nur unvollständiges Wissen über andere Dienste im Netz besitzt.

Die Folgen solcher Wechselwirkungen können erheblich sein. Teilnehmer können verwirrt und verärgert werden, da sie aufgrund ihrer beschränkten Sicht auf die Vorgänge im Netz nicht mehr verstehen können, was gerade geschieht – eine Problematik, die besonders im IN durch die in der Regel recht beschränkte Benutzerschnittstelle in Form gewöhnlicher Telefonapparate ohne Anzeigemöglichkeiten noch gefördert wird. Wesentlich kritischer sind Gefahren zu betrachten, die zu fehlerhafter Vergebührung und damit zu erheblichen finanziellen Verlusten bei Kunden, Diensteanbietern und Netzbetreibern führen können, oder die letztlich sogar die Stabilität und Verfügbarkeit des Netzes gefährden.

Diese Wechselwirkungs-Probleme, im Englischen auch *Feature Interaction Problems* genannt, sind ein wesentliches Hindernis auf dem Weg zur schnellen Erstellung neuer Dienste im Rahmen der IN-Architektur [1]. Die Erkennung solcher Wechselwirkungen zu einem möglichst frühen Zeitpunkt während des Entwicklungszyklus' eines neuen Dienstes ist ein wichtiger und notwendiger Schritt auf dem Wege zur Lösung dieses Problems und Gegenstand des vorliegenden Beitrags.

1.3.2 *Einteilung von Lösungsansätzen für das Problem der Wechselwirkungen*

In einer grundlegenden Übersicht haben Cameron und Velthuijsen [3] die Möglichkeiten zur Lösung dieses Problems in drei Klassen eingeteilt:

- *Vermeidung (engl. „avoidance").* Durch die verwendete Entwicklungsmethode oder die zugrunde liegende Architektur des Netzes wird das Auftreten unerwünschter Wechselwirkungen prinzipiell unterdrückt.

- *Erkennung (engl. „detection").* Eine vorgegebene Menge von Diensten bzw. Dienstmerkmalen wird daraufhin untersucht, ob (unerwünschte) Wechselwirkungen zwischen diesen Diensten existieren. Diese Untersuchung wird im Idealfall von einem Entwicklungswerkzeug unterstützt bzw. automatisch durchgeführt.

- *Auflösung (engl. „resolution").* Darunter versteht man Mechanismen, die beim Auftreten einer (unerwünschten) Wechselwirkung selbsttätig dazu führen, daß trotzdem ein möglichst für alle beteiligten Parteien akzeptables Ergebnis gefunden wird.

Unter diesen Klassen nimmt die Erkennung von Wechselwirkungen eine Schlüsselposition ein. Ohne sie ist weder die Vermeidung noch die Auflösung von Wechselwirkungen denkbar, da für beide Einsicht in die Mechanismen der Entstehung von Wechselwirkungen vorhanden sein muß und deshalb zunächst auch das Problem der Erkennung gelöst werden muß.

1.3.3 *Definitionen des Begriffs der Wechselwirkung zwischen Diensten*

Zum Verständnis des Problems der Wechselwirkungen zwischen Diensten muß zunächst der *Begriff der Wechselwirkung* scharf umrissen werden. Eine Wechselwirkung zwischen Dienstmerkmalen tritt dann auf, wenn das Verhalten eines Dienstmerkmals beim gleichzeitigem Vorhandensein eines anderen (aktiven) Dienstmerkmals von dem Verhalten ohne dieses andere Dienstmerkmal abweicht. Geht man weiter und spricht von unerwünschten Wechselwirkungen, verschärft sich das Problem: es muß nun bekannt sein, welches Verhalten im konkreten Falle erwünscht ist, was im allgemeinen nicht aus der (funktionalen oder deskriptiven) Dienstspezifikation des Einzeldienstes zu entnehmen ist, sondern für den konkreten Fall oder als gesondertes Regelwerk spezifiziert werden muß.

Eine üblicherweise verwendete Definition für Wechselwirkungen zwischen Diensten lautet: *Für eine Anzahl von n Dienstmerkmalen F_1, ... , F_n existiert eine Wechselwirkung genau dann, wenn für jedes i ($1 \leq i \leq n$) das Dienstmerkmal F_i in Kombination mit dem zugrunde liegenden Basisdienst N die Anforderung P_i erfüllt, eine Kombination der Dienstmerkmale jedoch die Kombination der Anforderungen nicht erfüllt* [6].

Es gibt zahlreiche Ansätze, das Problem der Wechselwirkungen unter Zuhilfenahme formaler Methoden zu lösen. Sie beruhen auf einer Beschreibung des Systems und seiner Eigenschaften gemäß dieser Definition. Wechselwirkungen manifestieren sich dann dadurch, daß durch Hinzufügen eines zweiten Dienstmerkmals bestimmte Eigenschaften nicht mehr erfüllt werden können. Velthuijsen [15] liefert einen kurzen Überblick über Arbeiten, in denen mit Hilfe formaler Methoden Wechselwirkungen zwischen Diensten erkannt werden und geht auf die Schwierigkeiten ein, die sich bei diesen Vorgehensweisen bieten:

- Die Funktionalität des Telefondienstes wird durch die Hinzunahme von zusätzlichen Dienstmerkmalen erweitert und damit auch verändert. Dadurch wird es sehr schwierig, wenn nicht gar unmöglich, Eigenschaften zu formulieren, die immer erfüllt sein müssen – also auch dann, wenn vollkommen beliebige, noch nicht vorhandenen Dienste im Netz existieren und mit dem betrachteten Dienst zusammen eingesetzt werden können.

- Es gibt sehr viele Bedingungen in einem System, die für die Beschreibung eines bestimmten Dienstmerkmals zunächst nicht relevant scheinen, jedoch dann Bedeutung bekommen, wenn andere Dienstmerkmale hinzukommen.

Aufgrund der genannten Schwierigkeiten baut der hier vorgestellte Ansatz an einer in [11] gegebenen Definition auf, nach der man zwei grundlegende Arten von Wechselwirkungen unterscheiden muß, nämlich solche, die durch nicht lösbare Konflikte in den Anforderungen an zwei Dienste zustande kommen und solche, die dadurch entstehen, daß dasselbe Objekt durch mehrere Dienste benutzt werden soll. Dieser Ansatz orientiert sich an letzterer Sichtweise. Formale Methoden werden eingesetzt, um solche Objekt-Konflikte zu erkennen. Es kann dabei nicht zwischen erwünschten und unerwünschten Wechselwirkungen unterschieden werden. Das stellt jedoch keinen großen Verlust dar, da diese Unterscheidung in zahlreichen Fällen schwierig ist und z. T. willkürlich erfolgt. Beispiele hierfür finden sich u. a. in [2].

1.3.4 *Ursachen für Wechselwirkungen zwischen Diensten*

Dienste im Intelligenten Netz besitzen gemeinsame Einflußbereiche, d. h. Objekte im Netz, die von mehr als einem Dienst beeinflußt werden können bzw. die mehr als einen Dienst beeinflussen können. Es handelt sich dabei um

(a)   private (dienstinterne) Daten, die von anderen Diensten in keiner Situation gelesen oder verändert werden können,

(b)   Daten des bearbeiteten Rufes, wie z. B. Nummern des rufenden und gerufenen Teilnehmers, die sowohl von der Rufbehandlung als auch von mehreren Diensten gelesen oder verändert werden,

(c)   den Ablauf eines Rufes, der im Rahmen eines IN-Rufes von mehreren Diensten beeinflußt werden kann und

(d)   die Reservierung von bestimmten, von mehreren Diensten erreichbaren Ressourcen im Netz.

Wechselwirkungen zwischen zwei Diensten entstehen dann, wenn diese sich über die gemeinsamen Einflußbereiche (b, c, d) gegenseitig beeinflussen können (Bild 1). Anhand der Untersuchung von Zugriffen auf diese Bereiche lassen sich Wechselwirkungen erkennen. Dies kann durch Verwendung formaler Techniken erfolgen, was zunächst ein geeignetes formales Systemmodell erforderlich macht, das in einem folgenden Abschnitt näher beschrieben wird.

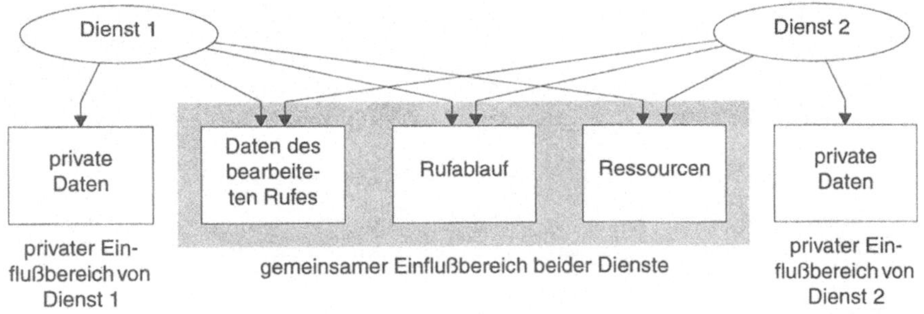

Bild 1: Einflußbereiche von zwei IN-Diensten

1.3.5 Erkennung von Wechselwirkungen

Die Vorgehensweise zur Erkennung von Wechselwirkungen unter Verwendung formaler Techniken, auf die in den folgenden Abschnitten genauer eingegangen wird, läßt sich folgendermaßen skizzieren:

- Erstellung einer formalen Beschreibung der Rufbehandlung, der Dienstbearbeitung und der interessierenden Daten und Ressourcen in der formalen Spezifikationssprache LOTOS (Language Of Temporal Ordering Specifications) [12]. Dies wird in Abschnitt 2 beschrieben.

- Auswahl von Dienstmerkmalen, die auf Wechselwirkungen untersucht werden sollen und Erzeugung von Rufszenarien mit diesen Dienstmerkmalen. Dies ist Gegenstand von Abschnitt 3. Es werden hier nur Paare von Dienstmerkmalen untersucht. Prinzipiell ist das Verfahren auch für mehr als zwei Dienstmerkmale anwendbar.

- Durchführung einer Erreichbarkeitsanalyse und Auswertung derselben. Mit Hilfe einfacher Techniken können Wechselwirkungen anhand der gemeinsamen Einflußbereiche mehrerer Dienste erkannt werden, was in Abschnitt 4 näher ausgeführt wird.

Diese Vorgehensweise ermöglicht es, Dienste bzw. Dienstmerkmale für das IN weitgehend automatisierbar anhand deren gemeinsamer Einflußbereiche auf mögliche Wechselwirkungen hin zu untersuchen.

2 Modellierung von IN-Rufen mit LOTOS

2.1 Modellierung auf der Ebene verteilter Funktionen

Die Modellierung von IN-Rufen erfolgt auf der Ebene verteilter Funktionen (Distributed Functional Plane, DFP) im IN-Architekturmodell. Die Betrachtung auf dieser Ebene bietet genügend Abstraktion von physikalischen Gegebenheiten im Netz, gleichzeitig sind auf dieser Ebene Abläufe sowohl im Bereich der Rufbehandlung als auch bei der Dienstbearbeitung detailliert zu erkennen. Zur formalen Beschreibung der gewonnenen Modelle kommt die standardisierte Spezifikationssprache LOTOS zum Einsatz. Ziel der Modellierung ist die Bereitstellung einer Modellplattform für die Ausführung von IN-Rufszenarien mit Diensten zum Zweck der Erkennung von Wechselwirkungen, die durch Überlappung der Einflußbereiche von Diensten zustande kommen. Aus diesem Grund ist die Modellierung im Vergleich zum vollständigen IN-Systemmodell vereinfacht; durch die reduzierte Komplexität wird gleichzeitig der Einsatz formaler Techniken wie der Erreichbarkeitsanalyse erleichtert. Bild 2 gibt einen

Überblick über die Struktur der Spezifikation für die Ausführung von IN-Rufszenarien und zeigt einen Ausschnitt aus der Verhaltensbeschreibung. Diese wird in den folgenden Unterabschnitten näher erläutert.

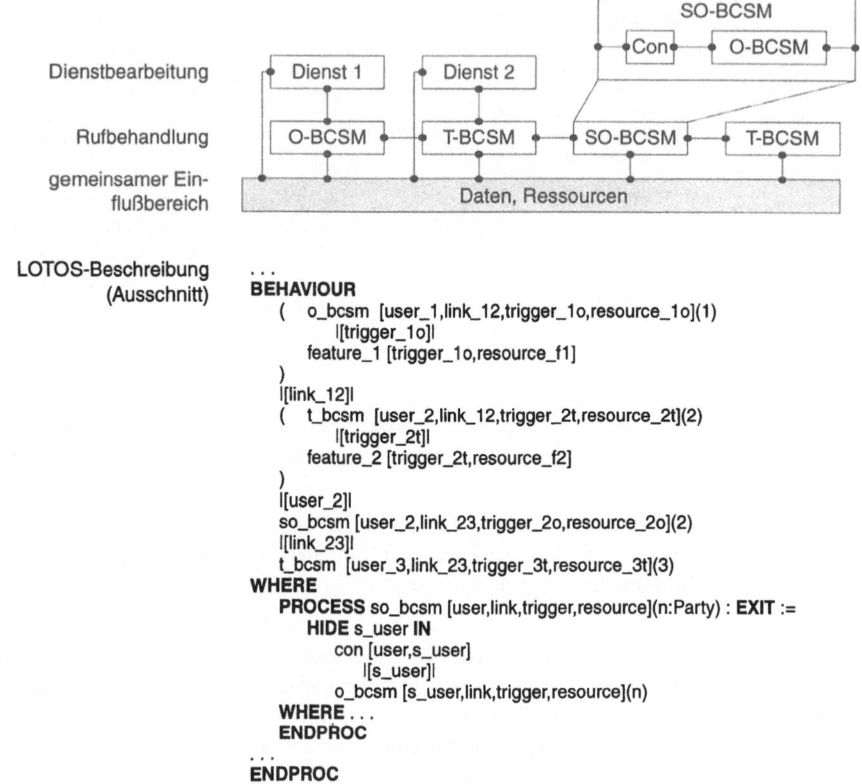


```
BEHAVIOUR
    (   o_bcsm [user_1,link_12,trigger_1o,resource_1o](1)
            |[trigger_1o]|
        feature_1 [trigger_1o,resource_f1]
    )
    |[link_12]|
    (   t_bcsm [user_2,link_12,trigger_2t,resource_2t](2)
            |[trigger_2t]|
        feature_2 [trigger_2t,resource_f2]
    )
    |[user_2]|
    so_bcsm [user_2,link_23,trigger_2o,resource_2o](2)
    |[link_23]|
    t_bcsm [user_3,link_23,trigger_3t,resource_3t](3)
WHERE
    PROCESS so_bcsm [user,link,trigger,resource](n:Party) : EXIT :=
        HIDE s_user IN
            con [user,s_user]
                |[s_user]|
            o_bcsm [s_user,link,trigger,resource](n)
    WHERE ...
    ENDPROC
    ...
ENDPROC
```

Bild 2: Struktur der LOTOS-Verhaltensbeschreibung des Systemmodells

2.2 Rufmodellierung

Als Spezifikationsstil für die Rufbehandlung wurde ein zustandsorientierter Stil ausgewählt, wie er in [16] beschrieben ist. Dieser Stil ermöglicht sehr gut die Wiedergabe der Rufmodelle (Basic Call State Models, BCSMs) aus Q.1214 [9], deren Darstellung auf kommunizierenden endlichen Zustandsautomaten basiert. Das IN-Rufmodell teilt sich in Hälften für den rufenden und den gerufenen Teilnehmer auf, in das sogenannte Originating bzw. Terminating Basic Call State Model (O- bzw. T-BCSM). Diese beiden Modelle können untereinander kommunizieren. Im Netz wird diese Kommunikation mit Hilfe von ISUP-Meldungen (ISDN User Part) oder durch vermittlungsstelleninterne Protokolle durchgeführt. Außerdem ist in den Ortsvermittlungsstellen Informationsaustausch mit dem Teilnehmer erforderlich, was im ISDN mit D-Kanal-Protokollen erreicht wird.

Es ist möglich, Rufmodelle so miteinander zu verketten, daß lineare Strukturen entstehen, wie sie z. B. für eine Anrufweiterschaltung erforderlich sind. Dazu ist ein Verbindungsglied zwischen der gerufenen Modellhälfte und der nachfolgenden rufenden Modellhälfte erforderlich. Es sind auch Verzweigungen möglich, wie sie z. B. bei einer Rückfrage auftreten, bei der ein Teilnehmer in eine Wartestellung kommt, während gleichzeitig ein zweites Gespräch zur Rückfrage bei einem anderen Teilnehmer geführt wird.

Die Elemente der LOTOS-Beschreibungen für die Rufbehandlung sind in Bild 2 enthalten. Sie beinhalten Prozesse für die rufende und gerufene Seite *(O-BCSM* und *T-BCSM)* und für das Verbindungsglied zwischen gerufener und nachfolgender rufender Modellhälfte *(Con)*, das zusammen mit dem Prozeß für eine rufende Modellhälfte kombiniert wird *(SO-BCSM*, subsequent O-BCSM). Diese wird z. B. für die Anrufweiterschaltung benötigt. Ein Verzweigungselement für die Umschaltung zwischen zwei Ruf-Hälften des gleichen Typs (z. B. für Rückfragen) ist nicht dargestellt. Auf diese Weise können die Funktionen der Rufbehandlung auf der Ebene der verteilten Funktionen des IN-Architekturmodells als Grundlage für die Realisierung von IN-Diensten nachgebildet werden.

2.3 Auslösung von Diensten

Aufgrund der Trennung zwischen Ruf- und Dienstbearbeitung im IN ist eine klar definierte Eingriffsmöglichkeit von Diensten in die Rufbehandlung erforderlich. Diese Möglichkeit wird durch Ergänzung der aus Zuständen (Point in Call) und Zustandsübergängen bestehenden Rufmodelle um sogenannte Detection Points (DPs) erreicht.

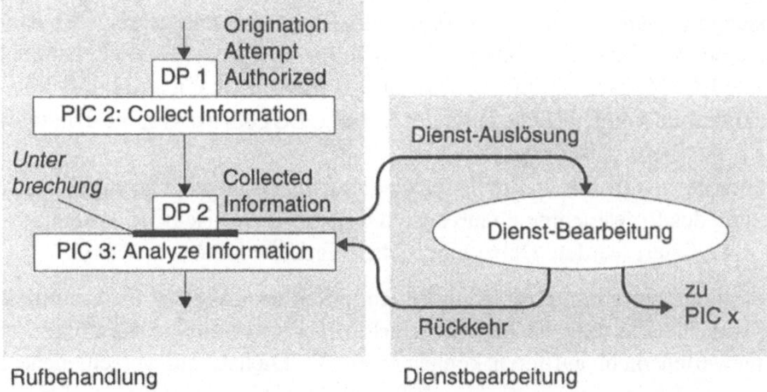

Bild 3: Points in Call (PIC), Detection Points (DP) und Dienstbearbeitung

Diese Detection Points ermöglichen es, die Rufbehandlung an genau definierten Stellen zu unterbrechen und eine Dienstlogik aufzurufen. Da für die Dienstlogik in der Regel nur wenige Detection Points relevant sind, können diese aktiviert bzw. deaktiviert werden. Dies kann sowohl statisch durch eine übergeordneten Instanz (Netz- bzw. Dienst-Management) als auch dynamisch durch eine ablaufende Dienstlogik erfolgen. Bild 3 illustriert den Ablauf einer Dienstlogikausführung mit Hilfe dieses Mechanismus. Dargestellt ist ein Ausschnitt aus dem Rufmodell eines rufenden Teilnehmers. Nach Abheben des Hörers wird der inaktive Detection Point *DP 1* übergangen und der Zustand *PIC 2* erreicht. Nachdem dort die Wählinformation vom Benutzer eingegeben worden ist, wird der aktive Detection Point *DP 2* erreicht. Hier wird die Rufbehandlung unterbrochen, was im Bild durch einen schwarzen Balken symbolisiert ist, und ein Dienst ausgelöst, der nicht näher bestimmt ist. Diese Dienstlogik besitzt zwei mögliche Ausgänge, den Sprung zu einem anderen, hier nicht näher charakterisierten Zustand *PIC x* und die Wiederaufnahme der Rufbehandlung bei *PIC 3*.

In Bild 3 nicht eingezeichnet ist die Möglichkeit, einen Detection Point nur dazu zu verwenden, eine Mitteilung an die Dienstlogik zu übermitteln, ohne die Rufbehandlung dafür zu unterbrechen (sog. Notification).

In der LOTOS-Modellierung wird der Mechanismus der Detection Points mit Hilfe von Interaktionspunkten realisiert, die für die unterschiedlichen Alternativen der Fortsetzung geeignete Ereignisse anbieten. Der Aktivierungsmechanismus wird mit Hilfe von abstrakten Datentypen und Guarded Commands realisiert.

2.4 Dienstmodellierung

Im IN-Architekturmodell werden Dienste als abgeschlossene Einheiten betrachtet, die einen definierten Eingang (sog. Point of Initiation) und mindestens einen Ausgang (sog. Point of Return) besitzen. Die Auswahl des Ausganges entscheidet dabei über die Art der Fortsetzung des Rufes. Wird in einem der Rufmodelle ein Detection Point erreicht, der als Auslöser für einen IN-Dienst aktiviert wurde, so wird an dieser Stelle die Rufbehandlung unterbrochen und mittels einer Trigger-Meldung die Bearbeitung der Dienstlogik (Service Logic) am genau definierten Eingang der Dienstlogik angestoßen. Die Dienstlogik wird dann durchlaufen. Für die durchgeführten Untersuchungen zur Erkennung von Wechselwirkungen ist es nicht erforderlich, diese Dienstlogik in ihrer inneren Funktionsweise vollständig zu erfassen, da alle Aspekte, die nur private, dienstinterne Daten betreffen, für Wechselwirkungen nicht relevant sind. Lediglich die Aktionen, durch die eine Dienstlogik mit ihrer Umgebung im Rahmen des gemeinsamen Einflußbereiches in Verbindung tritt, müssen erfaßt werden. Nach ihrer Abarbeitung kehrt die Dienstlogik mit entsprechenden Anweisungen zur Rufbehandlung zurück. Solche Anweisungen können z. B. der Abbruch des Rufes, die Fortsetzung des Rufes oder die Herstellung einer Verbindung zu einem anderen Teilnehmer sein. Die Rufbehandlung, d. h. das entsprechende BCSM, kann auf diese Anweisungen geeignet reagieren. In [4] wird ein Verfahren zur Spezifikation von IN-Diensten in der Sprache LOTOS vorgestellt. Die in dieser Arbeit verwendete Modellierung ist daran angelehnt.

Da die Dienste mittels der an die Rufbehandlung zurückgegebenen Ergebnisse Einfluß auf die Fortsetzung des Rufes nehmen, muß auch die Vorgehensweise beim Vorhandensein mehrerer Dienste spezifiziert werden. Dabei gibt es die folgenden Fälle:

- Die Dienste werden in unterschiedlichen Rufmodellen ausgelöst. Eine explizite Vorschrift für die Dienstausführung ist hier nicht erforderlich, da direkte Konflikte zwischen den Rückgabewerten nicht auftreten können, weil die Dienste auf verschiedene Rufmodelle wirken.

- Die Dienste werden im selben Rufmodell, aber von unterschiedlichen Detection Points ausgelöst. Da die Kontrolle nach dem Ablauf eines Dienstes wieder an die Rufbehandlung zurückgeht, können hier ebenfalls keine direkten Konflikte zwischen den Rückgabewerten der Dienste auftreten.[2]

- Die Dienste werden im selben Rufmodell von demselben Detection Point aktiviert. Hier können Konflikte auftreten, die geklärt werden müssen, indem Ablaufreihenfolge der Dienste und Reaktionen auf Ergebnisse der Dienstausführung z. B. in Form einer Priorisierung explizit angegeben werden, da zu jedem Zeitpunkt immer nur ein Dienst die Kontrolle über ein Rufmodell haben darf.

3 Ermittlung von Rufszenarien mit Diensten

Ein *Rufszenario* beschreibt die Struktur einer IN-Rufbeziehung unter Berücksichtigung von Diensten und allen beteiligten Teilnehmern sowie deren zugeordneten Rufmodellen (BCSMs). Ein solches Rufszenario wird durch eine LOTOS-Verhaltensbeschreibung nachgebildet (siehe Bild 2) und bietet damit die Grundlage für die Durchführung weiterer Analysen. Auf die Erstellung solcher Rufszenarien unter Verwendung vorgegebener Dienste wird nun näher eingegangen.

---

2 Die Vorgehensweise für Dienste, die eine Kontrollbeziehung (Control Relationship [9]) über längere Zeit aufrecht erhalten, wurde bisher noch nicht näher untersucht, da der Standard in einer solchen Situation die Möglichkeit zum Aufruf eines zweiten Dienstes nicht vorsieht.

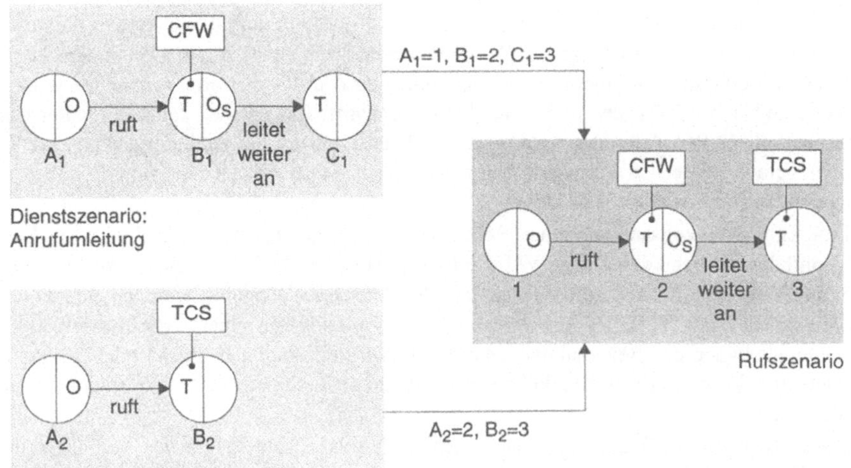

Bild 4: Erzeugung eines Rufszenarios aus zwei Dienstszenarien

Jeder einzelne Dienst im IN besitzt einen Standard-Anwendungsfall, der sich in Form eines sogenannten *Dienstszenarios* darstellen läßt. Ein solches Dienstszenario besteht aus den Teilnehmern, die zum Ablauf eines Dienstes gehören, beispielsweise bei einer Anrufumleitung der rufende Teilnehmer, der weiterleitende Teilnehmer, der Empfänger des weitergeleiteten Rufes, sowie aus den Rufmodellen (BCSMs), die bei diesen Teilnehmern im Rahmen des IN-Dienstes beteiligt sind. Besonders hervorzuheben ist in diesem Zusammenhang das Rufmodell, durch das der Dienst ausgelöst wird, das ist im Beispiel der Anrufweiterschaltung das gerufene Modell beim weiterleitenden Teilnehmer. In Bild 4 sind in der linken Bildhälfte solche Szenarien beispielhaft für die Dienste „Anrufumleitung" (CFW, Call Forwarding) und „Abweisen unerwünschter Anrufer" (TCS, Terminating Call Screening) dargestellt. Die Pfeile in den Szenarien markieren die zusammengehörigen Rufmodellhälften, die Auslösung eines Dienstes wird symbolisiert durch einen Punkt in dem Rufmodell, das den Detection Point für den Dienst enthält.

Ein Rufszenario kann mit Hilfe solcher Dienstszenarien dadurch erzeugt werden, daß den Teilnehmern in den Dienstszenarien reale Teilnehmer zugeordnet werden. Dieser Vorgang ist in Bild 4 in der rechten Bildhälfte dargestellt. Auf diese Weise kann aus zwei Dienstszenarien eine Anzahl topologisch unterschiedlicher Rufszenarien gewonnen werden. In [10] werden Bedingungen vorgestellt, mit deren Hilfe aus dieser Menge von Rufszenarien diejenigen extrahiert werden können, die aufgrund bestimmter Eigenschaften potentielle Quellen für Wechselwirkungen sind. Es wurde gezeigt, daß es genügt, solche Rufszenarien zu betrachten, in denen mindestens ein Zweig, bestehend aus einander zugeordneten rufenden und gerufenen Rufmodellen, existiert, der sowohl in beiden beteiligten Dienstszenarien vorhanden ist als auch den Dienst-Auslöser für mindestens einen der Dienste im Rufszenario enthält.

4 Techniken zur Ermittlung von Wechselwirkungen

4.1 Erreichbarkeitsanalyse

Mit Hilfe der Erreichbarkeitsanalyse ist es möglich, zu erkennen, daß ein Dienst den Rufablauf so beeinflußt, daß ein anderer Dienst auf diese Weise nie zum Einsatz kommen kann oder der gleiche Dienst erneut ausgelöst wird, was einen Hinweis auf (Endlos-)Schleifen liefern kann. Ein Beispiel für das Nichterreichen eines Dienst-Auslösers soll diesen Sachverhalt illustrieren:

„Anrufbeantworter im Belegtfall" (VMB, Voicemail on Busy) ist ein Dienst, bei dem ein Anrufer im Belegtfall mit einem im Netz befindlichen Anrufbeantworter verbunden wird, auf dem er eine Nachricht für den nicht erreichten Teilnehmer hinterlassen kann. „Erneuter Anruf im Belegtfall" (ARC, Automatic Recall) ist ein Dienst, der im Fall, daß der gewünschte Teilnehmer gerade belegt ist, automatisch einen zweiten Anrufversuch unternimmt, sobald der belegte Teilnehmer wieder frei ist.

Eine Erreichbarkeitsanalyse eines Szenarios, in dem der rufende Teilnehmer den Dienst ARC und der gerufene den Dienst VMB aktiviert haben, ergibt für die Dienst-Auslöser in der rufenden Modellhälfte das Ergebnis, daß der ARC-Dienst nie ausgelöst werden kann, da durch die Aktivierung des VMB-Dienstes wegen der Verbindung mit einem Anrufbeantworter im Netz die Rückgabe des Belegtsignals unterdrückt wird und damit beim rufenden Teilnehmer der Detection Point für den Belegtfall nie erreicht und dadurch der ARC-Dienst nicht ausgelöst werden kann.

Dieses Szenario wirft die Frage nach dem erwünschten bzw. erwarteten Verhalten dieser beiden Dienste im Zusammenspiel auf, und zwar auf der Ebene der prinzipiellen Erfüllbarkeit der Anforderungen beider Dienste [11], was jedoch nicht Gegenstand dieses Beitrags ist. Auf der rein funktionalen Ebene wird die Wechselwirkung durch die Erreichbarkeitsanalyse klar aufgedeckt.

4.2 Datenflußanalyse

Die Datenflußanalyse erlaubt es, den Weg und die Einflüsse eines bestimmten Datums während einer Rufbeziehung zu verfolgen. Mit ihrer Hilfe läßt sich eine ganze Klasse von Wechselwirkungen erkennen, die über die Veränderung und Benutzung von Informationen wie der gewählten Rufnummer, der gerufenen Nummer und der Nummer des rufenden Teilnehmers zustande kommen. Diese Informationen ändern sich in der Regel während des Fortschreitens eines IN-Rufes dadurch, daß Rufbehandlung und Dienste diese Daten verändern. Gleichzeitig ist jedoch auch ein Lesen bzw. Auswerten dieser Informationen durch eine Dienstlogik und durch die Rufbehandlung möglich, was dazu führt, daß die Auswertung derselben Datenstruktur zu verschiedenen Zeitpunkten zu unterschiedlichen Ergebnissen führen kann – ganz offensichtlich eine Quelle für Wechselwirkungen.

Als erstes erläuterndes Beispiel dient das bereits in Bild 4 dargestellte Rufszenario. Der IN-Dienst „Abweisen unerwünschter Anrufer" (TCS) entscheidet aufgrund einer schwarzen Liste, ob der Anruf eines bestimmten Teilnehmers entgegengenommen werden soll. „Anrufumleitung" (CFW) leitet einen Anruf von einem Teilnehmer an einen anderen Teilnehmer weiter. Die Wechselwirkung in diesem Szenario besteht in der Möglichkeit, daß ein Teilnehmer von einem Teilnehmer, der eigentlich abgeblockt werden sollte, erreicht wird, wenn eine Anrufweiterschaltung dazwischen steht und damit der weiterleitende Teilnehmer und nicht mehr der ursprüngliche als Anrufer gilt.

Das in diesem Beispiel betrachtete Datum ist die Telefonnummer des rufenden Teilnehmers. Aus einer Erreichbarkeitsanalyse für dieses Szenario wurden die möglichen Manipulationen für die Nummer des rufenden Teilnehmers extrahiert (Bild 5). Es sind folgende Vorgänge erkennbar (Die mit i bezeichneten Übergänge sind „leere" Übergänge und dehalb ohne Bedeutung für die hier durchgeführten Untersuchungen):

(a) Die Rufbehandlung für das erste Segment zwischen Teilnehmer 1 und 2 initialisiert die Nummer des gerufenen Teilnehmers nach dem Abheben, vor Aufbau eines neuen Rufes, im Graphen durch W^1 markiert.

(b) Die Weiterleitung beeinflußt dieses Datum dadurch, daß die Rufbehandlung für das weitergeleitete Segment zwischen Teilnehmer 2 und 3 den Wert neu setzt (W^2).

(c) Das „Abblocken unerwünschter Anrufer" liest den aktuellen Wert (R^{TCS}) und entscheidet, ob der Ruf entgegengenommen werden darf, oder ob er abgebrochen wird.

Die Nummer des rufenden Teilnehmers wird gesetzt und anschließend geändert, bevor der Dienst „Abweisen unerwünschter Anrufer" die Entscheidung über die Fortsetzung des Rufes fällt. Der erste Wert ist durch helle Unterlegung, der zweite durch dunklere Unterlegung in Bild 5 markiert. Die Wechselwirkung manifestiert sich durch die für diesen Dienst fehlende Sicht bis an den Anfang des Rufes.

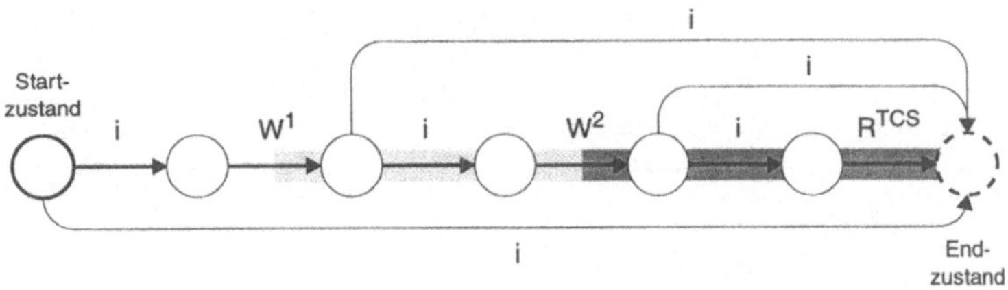

Bild 5: Nummer des rufenden Teilnehmers im Erreichbarkeitsgraph für die Dienste „Abweisen unerwünschter Anrufer" (TCS) und „Anrufumleitung" (CFW)

Als zweites Beispiel dient ein ähnliches Szenario, in Bild 6 a dargestellt. „Schwarze Liste" (OCS, Originating Call Screening) ist ein Dienstmerkmal, das anhand der Nummer des gerufenen Teilnehmers und einer sogenannten „schwarzen Liste" von Rufnummern, die als Rufziel nicht erwünscht sind, entscheidet, ob ein Ruf zugelassen oder nicht zugelassen, also abgebrochen wird. Dieser Dienst wird mit einer Anrufumleitung kombiniert.

Hier besteht die Schwierigkeit darin, daß nicht eindeutig gesagt werden kann, welche der beiden denkbaren Verhaltensweisen die erwünschte bzw. durch die Benutzer erwartete ist. Die erste Variante, den Ruf an einen Teilnehmer weiterzuleiten, obwohl dieser auf der schwarzen Liste steht, resultiert in einem Anruf bei einem Teilnehmer, der eigentlich nicht erreichbar sein sollte. Für diese Vorgehensweise spricht jedoch die Tatsache, daß das Ziel der Weiterleitung Sache des Weiterleitenden ist, da dieser in der Regel auch für den weitergeleiteten Zweig des Rufes bezahlt. Die zweite Variante, den Ruf abzubrechen, wenn das Ziel der Weiterleitung auf der schwarzen Liste steht, könnte den Rufer erheblich verwirren, da es ihm unter Umständen einmal gelingt und einmal mißlingt, bei ein und derselben Rufnummer anzurufen, je nach dem, ob bzw. wie dieser gerufene Teilnehmer eine Umleitung aktiviert hat. Dieses Beispiel illustriert auch die Probleme der Entscheidung zwischen erwünschten und unerwünschten Wechselwirkungen, die auch daher rührt, daß die Umleitung mit ganz unterschiedlichen Intentionen aktiviert werden kann [17].

Durch Betrachtung der gerufenen Nummer in einem Erreichbarkeitsgraphen[3] (Bild 6 b) läßt sich das Problem auf dem etwas dicker gezeichneten Weg klar erkennen. Zunächst wird der Wert nach der Eingabe der Rufnummer durch die Rufbehandlung initialisiert (W^1). Der Dienst OCS wertet daraufhin diese Rufnummer, durch helle Unterlegung gekennzeichnet, aus und entscheidet, ob der Ruf abgebrochen wird oder nicht (R^{OCS}). Diese Entscheidung hat Auswirkungen auf die gesamte Rufbeziehung. Zur Herstellung einer Verbindung zum ursprünglich gerufenen Teilnehmer wird die Rufnummer durch die Rufbehandlung ausgewertet (R^1). Beim diesem Teilnehmer, der weiterleitet, setzt die CFW-Dienstlogik die Rufnummer um auf die des Empfängers der Weiterleitung (W^2), was durch dunkle Unterlegung gekennzeichnet wird, und verändert damit die Voraussetzung, anhand derer der OCS-Dienst die Entscheidung für die gesamte Rufbeziehung getroffen hat. Die neue Rufnummer wird durch die Rufbehandlung dar-

---

3 Erstellt mit Hilfe der LOTOS-Werkzeuge Caesar und Aldébaran.

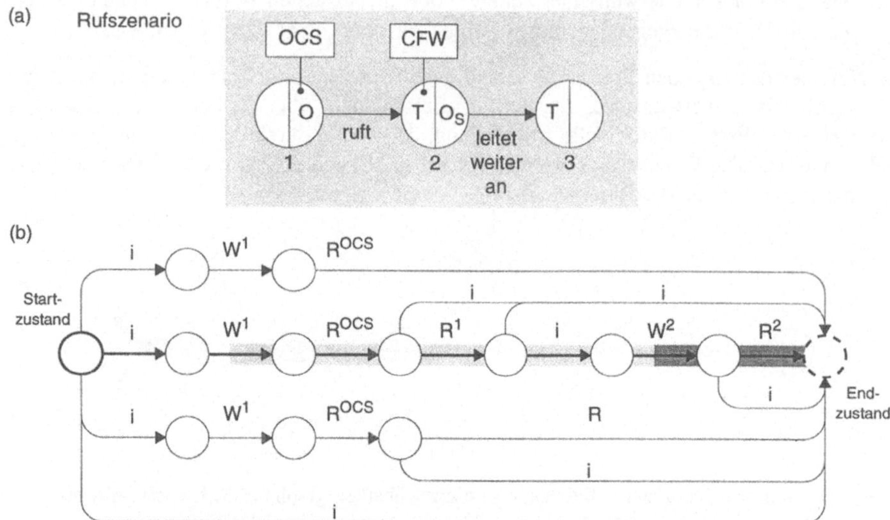

Bild 6: Nummer des gerufenen Teilnehmers im Erreichbarkeitsgraph für die
Dienste „Schwarze Liste" (OCS) und Anrufweiterschaltung (CFW)

aufhin noch ausgewertet (R^2), um die Verbindung herzustellen. Die Wechselwirkung äußert sich darin, daß der durch die „schware Liste" zur Entscheidung für die gesamte Rufbeziehung herangezogene Wert im späteren Verlauf verändert und erneut ausgewertet wird.

Durch die Realisierung der Dienste im IN steht das Verhalten dieses Dienstszenarios faktisch fest, da es hier prinzipiell nicht möglich ist, zum Zeitpunkt des OCS-Aufrufs das Ziel der späteren Weiterleitung festzustellen. Dennoch handelt es sich um eine Wechselwirkung, bei der das Verhalten eines Dienstes durch den anderen beeinflußt wird.

4.3 Überwachung von Ressourcen

Durch Überwachung von Ressourcen im Netz läßt sich aus dem Erreichbarkeitsgraphen erkennen, ob Konflikte vorliegen, die auf Wechselwirkungen hinweisen. Dabei ist zu betonen, daß diese Wechselwirkungen nicht zwangsläufig unerwünscht sein müssen.

Das in [2] angeführte Beispiel für die Wechselwirkung zwischen Kreditkartenruf und Anrufbeantworterdienst fällt in die Kategorie, die mit diesem Verfahren aufgedeckt werden können. Beim dort beschriebenen Kreditkartenruf dient die Betätigung der #-Taste dazu, ein Gespräch zu beenden, um die Möglichkeit zu bekommen, ohne erneute Eingabe der Kartennummer ein neues Gespräch zu führen. Beim Anrufbeantworterdienst besitzt die #-Taste ebenfalls eine bestimmte Funktion. Wird der Kreditkartenruf genutzt, um den Anrufbeantworter zu bedienen, so ist die Reaktion auf die #-Taste unklar, weil diese in beiden Dienste (unterschiedliche) Bedeutungen besitzt.

Diese Wechselwirkung läßt sich erkennen, indem ein Modell #-Taste als Ressource mit den Zuständen „verfügbar" und „reserviert" bereitgestellt wird (s. LOTOS-Fragment in Bild 7) und durch die die Prozesse der Systemspezifikation eine Reservierung bzw. Freigabe dieser Ressource durchführen läßt. Der in diesem Fall zweite Dienst, der Anrufbeantworter, trifft auf eine bereits reservierte #-Taste, was in Form einer Verklemmung bei der Erreichbarkeitsanalyse auf die Wechselwirkung hinweist.

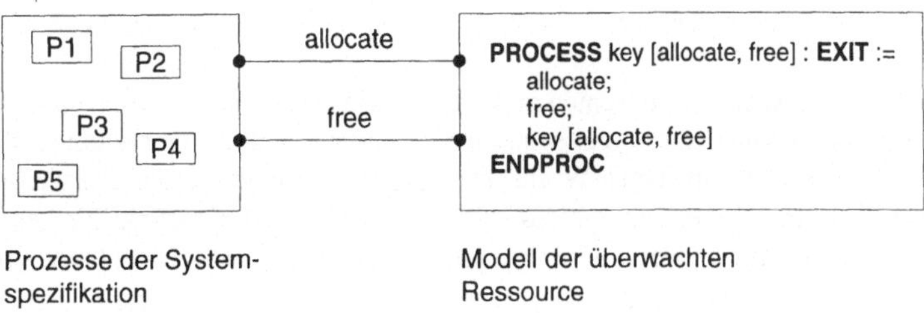

Bild 7: LOTOS-Beschreibung einer einfachen Ressource

5 Integration der Verfahren

Nachdem zuvor die einzelnen Schritte zur Erkennung von Wechselwirkungen erläutert worden sind, werden diese nun zu einem durchgängigen Verfahren kombiniert. Ausgangssituation ist eine Sammlung von IN-Diensten, zu denen ein neuer Dienst hinzugefügt werden soll. Dieser soll auf Wechselwirkungen mit den bestehenden Diensten untersucht werden. Der erste Schritt besteht in einer Spezifikation dieses neuen Dienstes in der Sprache LOTOS, die alle Informationen über die nicht-privaten Einflußbereiche des Dienstes, d. h. gemeinsame Daten und Ressourcen sowie die Auswirkungen auf den Rufablauf in Form von Rückgabewerten enthält und die mit den Rufmodellen, deren LOTOS-Beschreibung ebenfalls vorliegt, zusammenarbeiten kann. Dabei wird vorausgesetzt, daß für die anderen Dienste ebenfalls die Beschreibungen in dieser Form bereits vorliegen. Erfolgte die Erstellung des Dienstes mittels eines Service Creation Environments (SCE), dann kann die Dienst-Spezifikation in LOTOS bei Vorliegen einer Schnittstelle für Dienstbeschreibungen auch automatisch aus den Informationen über die einzelnen Dienst-Bausteine (SIBs) generiert werden.

Weiterhin ist für den neuen Dienst ein Dienstszenario erforderlich, das die im Standardfall beteiligten Teilnehmer enthält. Aus diesem werden zusammen mit den Dienstszenarien der bereits vorhandenen Dienste Rufszenarien erzeugt, die als Ausgangspunkte für die weiteren Untersuchungen dienen. Diese Rufszenarien werden in LOTOS-Verhaltensbeschreibungen umgesetzt, was nichts anderes als ein Zusammensetzen der bereits vorhandenen LOTOS-Dienstbeschreibungen mit den Prozessen der Rufbehandlung bedeutet.

Die nun für die einzelnen Rufszenarien vorliegenden, in sich abgeschlossenen LOTOS-Beschreibungen werden den oben beschriebenen Techniken zur Erkennung von Wechselwirkungen unterzogen, d. h. Erreichbarkeitsanalyse, Datenflußanalyse und Untersuchung von Ressourcen-Konflikten. Die dabei unter Umständen erkannten Wechselwirkungen treten mit einiger Wahrscheinlichkeit in mehreren unterschiedlichen Rufszenarien auf, obwohl sie auf dieselbe Ursache zurückzuführen sind. Die Reduktion der Ergebnisse auf die prinzipiell unterschiedlichen Wechselwirkungen ist deshalb eine wichtige Aufgabe und wesentlicher Bestandteil der Ergebnisnachbearbeitung. Hierbei können u. a. auch Minimierungsverfahren zum Einsatz kommen.

6 Einschränkungen

Die vorgestellte Arbeit beruht auf der Durchführung von Erreichbarkeitsanalysen auf einem in der formalen Sprache LOTOS erstellten Modell der Rufbehandlung und Dienstebearbeitung im IN. Dieses Modell vereinfacht und abstrahiert von der Realität, indem weggelassen wird, was für die Funktionen der Rufbehandlung und Dienstbearbeitung nicht relevant ist, um den Zustandsraum des Systems so klein wie möglich zu halten und dem Problem der Zustandsraumexplosion zu entgehen. Wechselwirkungen werden über die Einflüsse von Diensten auf bestimmte Objekte erkannt. Die vollständige Erkennung und richtige Modellierung der relevanten Einflußbereiche ist deshalb Schlüssel zu einer umfassenden Erkennung von Wechselwirkungen.

Es wird nicht zwischen erwünschten und unerwünschten Wechselwirkungen unterschieden. Bisher liegen noch keine Erfahrungen vor, wie groß das Verhältnis von erkannten Wechselwirkungen zu wirklich unerwünschten Wechselwirkungen ist. Da jedoch auch erwünschte Wechselwirkungen, die mit dieser Methode identifiziert werden, auf Konflikte hinweisen können, liefern auch diese möglicherweise wichtige Anhaltspunkte für später auftretende Probleme.

Die Erkennung von Wechselwirkungen zwischen Diensten und deren Ursachen ist ein wichtiger Schritt auf dem Weg zur Beherrschung dieses Problems. Zur Vermeidung und Auflösung von Wechselwirkungen kann trägt die hier vorgestellte Methode die Einsicht bei, daß Dienste in Wechselwirkung treten, wenn sie überlappende Einflußbereiche besitzen, und daß umgekehrt Wechselwirkungen dadurch vermieden werden könnten, daß man für disjunkte Einflußbereiche sorgt – eine Eigenschaft, die jedoch wegen der in der IN-Architektur von mehreren Diensten beeinflußbaren Rufbehandlung praktisch nicht erfüllbar ist.

7 Zusammenfassung

Dieser Beitrag stellt ein Verfahren zur Erkennung von Wechselwirkungen zwischen Diensten für das Intelligente Netz vor. Dieses Verfahren trifft keine Entscheidungen bezüglich der Erwünschtheit oder Unerwünschtheit einer Wechselwirkung, sondern identifiziert Wechselwirkungen anhand der Beobachtung der gemeinsamen Einflußbereiche der untersuchten Dienste und der Rufbehandlung. Es beruht auf einer Modellierung der Rufbehandlung und der Dienstbearbeitung im Intelligenten Netz auf der Ebene verteilter Funktionen in der formalen Spezifikationssprache LOTOS. Aus den Standardszenarien für einzelne Dienste werden auf Wechselwirkungen hin zu untersuchende Rufszenarien erzeugt, die in der formalen Sprache beschrieben werden. Diese Beschreibung wird mit Hilfe formaler Techniken untersucht. Aus dem Erreichbarkeitsgraphen können Informationen über die Erreichbarkeit bestimmter Detection Points ermittelt werden. Die Datenflußanalyse liefert Wechselwirkungen, die über den Zugriff auf gemeinsame Daten entstehen, und durch die Modellierung gemeinsamer Ressourcen können Konflikte bei der Benutzung derselben im Laufe eines Rufs ermittelt werden.

Die in diesem Beitrag berichteten Ergebnisse entstammen einem laufenden Forschungsvorhaben. Weitere Bemühungen werden der Verbesserung der Modellierung von Rufbehandlung und Dienstbearbeitung sowie einer Verfeinerung und Automatisierung der Analysemethoden für die mit Hilfe formaler Techniken wie der Erreichbarkeitsanalyse gewonnenen Ergebnisse gelten. Ferner ist Unterstützung der automatischen Generierung von formalen Dienst-Beschreibungen aus den Dienstbeschreibungen der Dienstentwicklungsumgebung (SCE) Gegenstand weiterer Untersuchungen.

Literatur

[1] T. F. Bowen, F. S. Dworack, C. H. Chow, N. Griffeth, G. E. Herman, Y.-J. Lin, "The Feature Interaction Problem in Telecommunications Systems," *Proceedings of the 7th International Conference on Software Engineering for Telecommunications Switching Systems,* Bournemouth, U.K., Juli 1989, pp. 59-62.

[2] E. J. Cameron, N. D. Griffeth, Y.-J. Lin, M. E. Nilson, W. K. Schnure, "A Feature Interaction Benchmark for IN and Beyond," in *Feature Interactions in Telecommunications Systems,* L. G. Bouma, H. Velthuijsen (Eds.), IOS Press, 1994, pp. 1-23.

[3] E. J. Cameron, H. Velthuijsen, "Feature Interactions in Telecommunications Systems," in *IEEE Communications Magazine,* Vol. 31, No 8, August 1993, pp. 18-23.

[4] K. E. Cheng, "Towards a Formal Model for Incremental Service Specification and Interaction Management Support," in *Feature Interactions in Telecommunications Systems,* L. G. Bouma, H. Velthuijsen (Eds.), IOS Press, 1994, pp. 152-166.

[5] J. J. GARRAHAN, P. A. RUSSO, K. KITAMI, R. KUNG, "Intelligent Network Overview," IEEE Communications Magazine, Vol. 31, No. 3, March 1993, pp. 30-36.

[6] J. C. GODSKESEN, "A Formal Framework for Feature Interaction with Emphasis on Testing," in *Feature Interactions in Telecommunications Systems III*, K. E. Cheng, T. Ohta (Eds.), IOS Press, 1995, pp. 21-30.

[7] J. HARJU, T. KARTTUNEN, O. MARTIKAINEN, "Introduction to Intelligent Networks," in *Intelligent Networks (Proceedings of the IFIP workshop on intelligent networks 1994)*, J. Harju, T. Karttunen, O. Martikainen (Eds.), Chapman & Hall, 1995, pp. 1-33.

[8] ITU-T Recommendation Q.1201 "Principles of Intelligent Network Architecture," Geneva, October 1992.

[9] ITU-T Recommendation Q.1214 "Distributed Functional Plane for Intelligent Network CS-1," Geneva, March 1993.

[10] D. O. KECK, "Identification of Call Scenarios with Potential Feature Interactions," in *International Workshop on Advanced Intelligent Networks (AIN '96)*, T. Margaria (Ed.), Lehrstuhl für Informatik, Universität Passau MIP-9604, Passau, März 1996, pp. 42-55.

[11] K. KIMBLER, H. VELTHUIJSEN, "Feature Interaction Benchmark," vorgetragen auf dem *Feature Interaction Workshop 1995*, Kyoto (Japan), October 1995.

[12] L. LOGRIPPO, M. FACI, M. HAJ-HUSSEIN, "An introduction to LOTOS: learning by examples," in *Computer Networks and ISDN Systems*, 23 (1992), pp. 325-342.

[13] T. MAGEDANZ, R. POPESCU-ZELETIN, *Intelligent Networks – Basic Technology, Standards and Evolution*, International Thomson Computer Press, London, Boston, 1996.

[14] J. THÖRNER, *Intelligent Networks*, Artech House, Boston, London, 1994.

[15] H. VELTHUIJSEN, "Issues of Non-Monotonicity in Feature-Interaction Detection," in *Feature Interactions in Telecommunications Systems III*, K. E. Cheng, T. Ohta (Eds.), IOS Press, 1995, pp. 31-42.

[16] C. A. VISSERS, "Architecture and Specification Style in Formal Descriptions of Distributed Systems," in *Protocol Specification, Testing, and Verification VIII*, S. Aggarwal, K. Sabnani (Eds.), Elsevier Science Publishers B. V. (North-Holland), 1988, pp. 189-204.

[17] P. ZAVE, "Secrets of call forwarding: A specification case study," in *Formal Description Techniques VIII*, G. v. Bochmann, R. Dssouli, O. Rafiq (Eds.), Chapman & Hall, 1996, pp. 169-184.

A Proposal for a Real-Time Extension of TTCN

Thomas Walter[1] and Jens Grabowski[2]

[1] Eidgenössische Technische Hochschule Zürich, Institut für Technische Informatik
(TIK), 8092 Zürich, Schweiz, e-mail: walter@tik.ee.ethz.ch
[2] Medizinische Universität zu Lübeck, Institut für Telematik, Ratzeburger Allee 160,
23538 Lübeck, Deutschland, e-mail: jens@itm.mu-luebeck.de

Abstract. In this paper we propose an extension of TTCN (Tree and
Tabular Combined Notation) to *real-time TTCN*. The extension is defined on a syntactical and semantical level. Syntactically, we provide
facilities to annotate TTCN statements with two time values, namely an
earliest execution time (EET) and a latest execution time (LET). The
informal interpretation of these time values is that a TTCN statement
may be executed if it has been continuously enabled for at least EET
units and it must be executed if it has been continuously enabled for LET
units. The operational semantics of real-time TTCN is defined by means
of timed transition systems. In timed transition systems an execution of
a system is modelled by a timed state sequence which counts for time
(progress of time) and state (execution of TTCN statements) activities.
We define a mapping of real-time TTCN to timed transition systems and
give examples in order to show the applicability of our approach.

1 Introduction

TTCN (Tree and Tabular Combined Notation) [10] is a notation for the definition
of conformance test suites for OSI (Open Systems Interconnection) protocol
specifications. Test suites are used for ensuring that different implementations
of the same protocol specification are checked for the same set of requirements
[8, 9]. Test suites are collections of test cases where each test case is defined
with a specific test purpose in mind. Test cases are specified as sequences of test
events. Essentially, test events are input and output events of abstract service
primitives (ASP) or protocol data units (PDU). A test case describes how a
tester should drive an implementation under test (IUT) through a sequence of
test events in order to reach the test purpose. The relative ordering of test events
is defined in a *behaviour description*. A behaviour description may also include
tester specific events, e.g., initialisation of variables or start of timers.

Although TTCN provides a timer mechanism which allows to set timers
and to check their status, the absolute and relative timing of events cannot
be specified. The TTCN timer mechanism might be sufficient for functional
tests of traditional OSI protocols, but it is insufficient for testing *non-functional*
requirements of multimedia and real-time communication protocols.

Due to the increasing dissemination of multimedia applications, testing of
the corresponding protocol implementations will become an issue. We propose a

real-time extension of TTCN so that TTCN can be used in testing multimedia and real-time communication protocols.

Our extension of TTCN to *real-time TTCN* is on a syntactical and a semantical level. In particular, the syntactical difference is that for real-time TTCN we allow an annotation of test events with an earliest execution time (*EET*) and a latest execution time (*LET*). Informally, a test event may be executed if it has been continuously enabled for at least *EET* time units and it must be executed if it has been continuously enabled for *LET* time units. Test events are executed instantaneously. For the definition of an operational semantics of real-time TTCN we adopted timed transition systems [7].

A number of techniques for the specification of real-time constraints have been proposed: time Petri Nets [2, 15], LOTOS [1, 6, 12, 17], SDL [6, 13] and ESTELLE [4]. As in the cited literature, our approach allows the timing of actions relative to the occurrence of previous actions. The difference of the cited approaches and ours is that the former are used for the specification of functional and real-time requirements of systems whereas our emphasise is put on testing real-time requirements. Real-time TTCN is used for the specification of properties of a test system and requirements on the IUT.

In this paper we focus on mechanisms for the specification of real time requirements in test cases. Other important issues like test suite validation, test realization and tool support are for further study.

The paper is structured as follows: Section 2 gives a brief introduction to TTCN. Section 3 explains real-time TTCN. The feasibility of our approach is shown in Section 4. Section 5 concludes the paper with an assessment of our approach and the identification of open issues.

2 TTCN - Tree and Tabular Combined Notation

TTCN is a notation for the description of test cases to be used in conformance testing. TTCN provides two syntactical forms, TTCN/MP as a machine processable (i.e., pure textual) form, and TTCN/GR as a graphical representation. For the purpose of this paper we mainly restrict our attention to TTCN/GR and TTCN concepts related to the description of the dynamic test case behaviour. Further details on TTCN can be found in [10, 14, 16, 18].

2.1 Abstract Testing Methods and TTCN

A test case specifies which outputs from an implementation under test (IUT) can be observed and which inputs to an IUT can be controlled. Inputs and outputs are either *abstract service primitives* (ASPs) or *protocol data units* (PDUs). An example of an *abstract test method* is the *Multi-Party Testing Context* [9]. Abstract testing functions, such as *lower tester* (LT), *upper tester* (UT) and *lower tester control function* (LTCF), are the active components. LTs and UTs control and observe the IUT at *points of control and observation* (PCOs) which are interfaces above and below the IUT. The LTCF is responsible for the creation and coordination of LTs and UTs. LTs, UTs and LTCF are referred to as test components (TCs). They run in parallel. TCs are interconnected by *coordination points* (CPs) through which they exchange *coordination messages* (CMs). LT and IUT logically communicate by exchanging PDUs which are embedded in ASPs exchanged at PCOs. Since in most cases the lower boundary of an IUT does not provide adequate PCO interfaces, LTs and IUT communicate by using services of an underlying service provider. PCOs and CPs are based on the same abstract model: a pair of unbounded FIFO queues (one for each direction of communication) which allow an asynchronous exchange of ASPs and CMs.

2.2 Test Case Dynamic Behaviour Descriptions

The behaviour description of a TC consists of *statements* and *verdict assignments*. A verdict assignment is a statement concerning the conformance of an IUT with respect to the sequence of events that have been performed. A PASS verdict is assigned if the IUT passes the test, FAIL is given if the IUT contradicts the specification, and INCONCLUSIVE is assigned if neither a PASS nor a FAIL verdict can be assigned. TTCN statements are *test events, constructs* and *pseudo events*.

Test events are SEND, IMPLICIT SEND, RECEIVE, OTHERWISE, TIMEOUT and DONE. SEND and IMPLICIT SEND specify the sending of ASPs, PDUs and CMs. RECEIVE and OTHERWISE denote the processing of received ASPs, PDUs and CMs. TIMEOUT events check for the expiration of a timer. DONE is used to check whether TCs have terminated. Test events may be qualified and/or followed by assignments and timer operations.

Constructs are CREATE, ATTACH, ACTIVATE, RETURN, GOTO and REPEAT. CREATE specifies the creation of a TC. The created TC executes in parallel with all other running TCs. ATTACH is a construct which allows to transmit control to a sub-behaviour description, called *test step*. The mechanism is comparable to the procedure concept in programming languages. ACTIVATE and RETURN deal with *default behaviour descriptions*. Usually, a default behaviour description handles all incoming events which are not treated in the main behaviour description. ACTIVATE allows to change the default behaviour during the test run and RETURN allows to return from a default behaviour back to the main description. GOTO transfers control to a specified statement. REPEAT is used for the specification of loops.

Pseudo-events are qualifiers (i.e. Boolean expressions), timer operations and assignments.

Statements can be grouped into *statement sequences* and *sets of alternatives*. In TTCN/GR, sequences of statements are represented one after the other on separate lines and being *indented* from left to right. The statements on lines 1 - 6 in Fig. 1 are a statement sequence. Statements on the same level of indentation and with the same predecessor are a set of alternatives. In Fig. 2 the statements on lines 4 and 6 form a set of alternatives. They are on the same level of indentation and have the statement on line 3 as their common predecessor.

<table>
<tr><td colspan="6" align="center">Test Case Dynamic Behaviour</td></tr>
<tr><td>Nr</td><td>Label</td><td>Behaviour Description</td><td>Constraints Ref</td><td>Verdict</td><td>Comments</td></tr>
<tr><td>1</td><td></td><td>CP ? CM</td><td>connected</td><td></td><td>RECEIVE</td></tr>
<tr><td>2</td><td></td><td>(NumOfSends := 0)</td><td></td><td></td><td>Assignment</td></tr>
<tr><td>3</td><td></td><td>REPEAT SendData</td><td></td><td></td><td>Construct</td></tr>
<tr><td></td><td></td><td>UNTIL [NumOfSends > MAX]</td><td></td><td></td><td></td></tr>
<tr><td>4</td><td></td><td>START Timer</td><td></td><td></td><td>Timer Operation</td></tr>
<tr><td>5</td><td></td><td>?TIMEOUT timer</td><td></td><td></td><td>TIMEOUT</td></tr>
<tr><td>6</td><td></td><td>L ! N-DATA request</td><td>data</td><td></td><td>SEND</td></tr>
</table>

Fig. 1. TTCN Behaviour Description - Sequence of Statements

<table>
<tr><td colspan="6" align="center">Test Case Dynamic Behaviour</td></tr>
<tr><td>Nr</td><td>Label</td><td>Behaviour Description</td><td>Constraints Ref</td><td>Verdict</td><td>Comments</td></tr>
<tr><td>1</td><td></td><td>[TRUE]</td><td></td><td></td><td>Qualifier</td></tr>
<tr><td>2</td><td>L1</td><td>(NumOfSends := NumOfSends + 1)</td><td></td><td></td><td></td></tr>
<tr><td>3</td><td></td><td>+SendData</td><td></td><td></td><td>ATTACH</td></tr>
<tr><td>4</td><td></td><td>[NOT NumOfSends > MAX]</td><td></td><td></td><td>Alternative 1</td></tr>
<tr><td>5</td><td></td><td>-> L1</td><td></td><td></td><td>GOTO</td></tr>
<tr><td>6</td><td></td><td>[NumOfSends > MAX]</td><td></td><td></td><td>Alternative 2</td></tr>
</table>

Fig. 2. TTCN Behaviour Description - Set of Alternatives

2.3 Test Case Execution and Test Component Execution

Test case execution starts with only the main test component running. The main test component which fulfils the role of the LTCF, creates all other TCs. Immediately after creation the TC starts executing its behaviour description.

The execution of a behaviour description starts with the first *level of indentation* (line 1 in Fig. 1), and proceeds towards the last level of indentation (line 6 in Fig. 1). If on a level of indentation a set of alternatives is found, only one alternative is executed and test case execution proceeds with the next level of indentation relative to the executed alternative. For example, in Fig. 2 the statements on line 4 and line 6 are alternatives. If the statement on line 4 is executed, processing continues with the statement on line 5. Each TC maintains its own set of local variables and may make use of a number of implicitly defined variables. Execution of a behaviour description stops if the last level of indentation is visited, a test verdict is assigned or a test case error occurs.

Before a set of alternatives is evaluated, a *snapshot* is taken [10], i.e., the state of the TC and the state of all PCOs, CPs and timers related to the TC are updated and frozen until the set of alternatives is evaluated. This guarantees that evaluation of a set of alternatives is an *atomic* and *deterministic action*.

Alternatives are evaluated in sequence and the first alternative which is *evaluated successfully* (i.e., all conditions of that alternative are fulfilled [10]) is executed. Then execution proceeds with the set of alternatives on the next level of indentation. If no alternative can be evaluated successfully, a new snapshot is taken and evaluation of the set of alternatives is started again.

2.4   TTCN and Real-Time Constraints

In TTCN no explicit time model is assumed in the sense that no predictions of the execution time of TTCN statements or the transmission times of ASPs, PDUs and CMs can be made. Only timers and the corresponding TIMEOUT event are a means for specifying real-time behaviour in TTCN. However, as stated in [10], a test case should be defined such that the relative speed of the systems executing the test case does not have an impact on the test result.

Timers can be started (with a timeout value from picoseconds to minutes), can be stopped and timer values can be read. The status of a timer can be checked in a set of alternatives using the TIMEOUT event. But, whenever a timer expires this has no immediate influence on the execution of a test component. If a timer expires while evaluation of a set of alternatives is in progress, expiration of that timer is not visible until the next snapshot is taken. An immediate reaction on the timeout event is not possible. Depending on the ordering of alternatives an expired timer may get undetected at all.

3   Real-Time TTCN

The extension of TTCN to real-time TTCN includes syntactical changes and the definition of an operational semantics. For the latter we define a mapping of real-time TTCN to timed transition systems [7]. Our choice of timed transition systems has been inspired by our work on the definition of an operational semantics for TTCN [20, 21].

3.1   Timed Transition Systems

As stated in the literature [2, 7, 15], real-time behaviour of systems can be expressed by assuming that execution of events is restricted by a finite interval of earliest and latest execution times and which assume that execution of events is instantaneous. In our approach we use timed transition systems for modelling real-time behaviour. In this section we quote the main definitions of [7].

A *transition system* [11] consists of a set V of variables, a set Σ of states, a subset $\Theta \subseteq \Sigma$ of initial states and a finite set $\mathcal{T}$ of transitions which also includes the idle transition t_I. Every transition $t \in \mathcal{T}$ is binary relations over states; i.e., it defines for every state $s \in \Sigma$ a possibly empty set $t(s) \subseteq \Sigma$ of so-called t-successors. A transition t is said to be *enabled* on state s if and only if $t(s) \neq \emptyset$. For the idle transition t_I we have that $t_I = \{(s, s) \mid s \in \Sigma\}$.

An infinite sequence $\sigma = s_0 s_1 \ldots$ is a *computation* of the underlying transition system if $s_0 \in \Theta$ is an initial state, and for all $i \geq 0$ there exists a $t \in \mathcal{T}$ such that $s_{i+1} \in t(s_i)$, denoted $s_i \stackrel{t}{\longrightarrow} s_{i+1}$, i.e., transition t is *taken* at position i of computation σ.

The extension of transition systems to timed transition systems is that we assume the existence of a real-valued global clock and that a system performs actions which either advance time or change a state [7]. Actions are executed instantaneously, i.e., they have no duration.

A *timed transition system* consists of an underlying transition system and, for each transition $t \in \mathcal{T}$, an earliest execution time $EET_t \in \mathbb{N}$ (with $\mathbb{N}$ the natural numbers including zero) and a latest execution time $LET_t \in \mathbb{N} \cup \{\infty\}$ is defined. We assume that $EET_t \leq LET_t$ and, by default, EET_t is zero and LET_t is ∞. For a transition t which is enabled on an initial state we have $LET_t = \infty$ and so for the idle transition t_I: $LET_{t_I} = \infty$. EET_t and LET_t define timing constraints which ensure that transitions cannot be performed neither to early (EET_t) nor too late (LET_t).

A *timed state sequence* $\rho = (\sigma, T)$ consists of an infinite sequence σ of states and an infinite sequence T of times $T_i \in \mathbb{R}$ (with $\mathbb{R}$ the real numbers) and T satisfies the following two conditions:

- *Monotonicity:* $\forall i \geq 0$ either $T_{i+1} = T_i$ or $T_{i+1} > T_i \wedge s_{i+1} = s_i$.
- *Progress:* $\forall t \in \mathbb{R} \, \exists \, i \geq 0$ such that $T_i \geq t$.

Monotonicity implies that time never decreases but possibly increases by any amount between two neighbouring states which are identical. If time increases this is called a *time step*. The transition being performed in a time step is the idle transition which is always enabled (see above). The progress condition states that time never converges, i.e., since $\mathbb{R}$ has no maximal element every timed state sequence has infinitely many time steps. Summarising, in timed state sequences state activities are interleaved with time activities. Throughout state activities time does not change, and throughout time steps the state does not change.

A timed state sequence $\rho = (\sigma, T)$ is a *computation* of a timed transition system if and only if state sequence σ is a computation of the underlying transition system and for every transition $t \in \mathcal{T}$ the following requirements are satisfied:

- for every transition $t \in \mathcal{T}$ and position $j \geq 0$ if t is taken at j then there exists a position i, $i \leq j$ such that $T_i + EET_t \leq T_j$ and t is enabled on $s_i, s_{i+1}, \ldots, s_{j-1}$ and is not taken at any of the positions $i, i+1, \ldots, j-1$, i.e., a transition must be continuously enabled for at least EET_t time units before the transition can be taken.
- for every transition $t \in \mathcal{T}$ and position $i \geq 0$, if t is enabled at position i, there exists a position j, $i \leq j$, such that $T_i + LET_t \geq T_j$ and either t is not enabled at j or t is taken at j, i.e., a transition must be taken if the transition has been continuously enabled for LET_t time units.

A finite timed state sequence is made infinite by adding idle transitions, so that we have an infinite sequence of time activities.

3.2 Syntax of Real-Time TTCN

For our real time extension of TTCN we add time information in the declarations and the dynamic part of a TTCN test suite. In the declarations part we specify time names and units to be used in TTCN behaviour descriptions. In the dynamic part we add time values to behaviour lines of behaviour descriptions.

Execution Time Declarations			
Time Name	Value	Unit	Comments
EET	1	s	EET value
LET	1	min	LET value
WFN	5	ms	Wait For Nothing
NoDur		min	No specified value

Fig. 3. Execution Time Declarations Table

Extensions of the Declarations Part. For the specification of EET and LET values and time units we introduce an Execution Time Declarations table (Fig. 3) and the keywords EET and LET.[3] The Time Name column can be used to declare names for EET and LET values. The names can be used instead of concrete values within behaviour description tables. Value and Unit columns are used to associate a time value and a time unit to a time name. As time units we allow the time units already used in TTCN (picoseconds (ps) to minutes (min)). Time values are converted to the default time unit whenever necessary, e.g., before time values are evaluated in a behaviour description.

EET and LET are predefined variables with 0 and ∞ as initial values. These initial values can be overwritten as shown in Fig. 3. Apart from column headings the table looks much like the TTCN Timer Declarations table.

For the time name NoDur (Figure 3) only the time unit min is given but no value. In this case, a value has to be provided during test case execution by means of an assignment. If a name is evaluated and no value is assigned, the test case will end with a dynamic test case error.

Due to practical reasons it is not appropriate to require that for each TTCN statement EET and LET values are specified. In this case the default values for EET $(= 0)$ and LET $(= \infty)$ are used. Additionally, we allow to overwrite these default values within an Execution Time Declarations table. For changing the default time values the keywords EET and LET are used. In Fig. 3, the default values for EET and LET are changed to 1 second and 1 minute, respectively.

Besides the static declarations of time values, a change of these values is also allowed within a behaviour description. During a test run time values can be changed by means of assignments. We only require that concrete EET and LET values can be determined when the corresponding TTCN statement is evaluated successfully and that the condition $0 \leq EET \leq LET$ holds. In all other cases the test case will end with a dynamic test case error.

Examples for the dynamic change of time values within a behaviour description can be found in Fig. 4. On line 2 the value 3 is assigned to the time name NoDur and on line 4 the default LET value is changed. This change becomes effective on the next level of indentation, i.e., for the TTCN statements on lines 5 and 6. As shown on line 6 it is also allowed to refer to default time values explicitly by using the keyword LET.

[3] We use different fonts for distinguishing between syntax, i.e., EET and LET, and semantics, i.e., EET and LET.

Test Case Dynamic Behaviour						
Nr	Label	Time	Behaviour Description	Constraints Ref	Verdict	Comments
1		2, 4	A ? DATA request			
2			(NoDur := 3)			Time assignment
3		2, NoDur	A ! DATA ack			
4			(LET := 50)			LET update (ms)
5			A ? Data request			
6		WFN, LET	B ? Alarm			

Fig. 4. Adding EET and LET values to behaviour lines

Extensions of the Dynamic Part. The changes in the dynamic part of a
TTCN test suite are related to behaviour lines in Test Case Dynamic Behaviour,
Default Dynamic Behaviour and Test Step Dynamic Behaviour tables. The structure of the behaviour lines is the same in all these tables. Therefore, we discuss
the syntactical changes by using a Test Case Dynamic Behaviour table only.

As indicated in Fig. 4 we add a Time column. An entry in the Time column
specifies EET and LET values for the corresponding behaviour line. Entries
may be variables or constants, e.g., the entry in Fig. 4 line 1 sets $EET = 2$ and
$LET = 4$ with default time unit ms. Within the Time column EET and LET
may also be specified by means of name references which have to be looked up
within the declarations part of the test suite. For instance, on line 3 of Fig. 4
the time name NoDur is used. NoDur has been declared in table Fig. 3 and has
been assigned a value on line 2 of Fig. 4.

3.3 Operational Semantics of Real-Time TTCN

The operational semantics of real-time TTCN is defined in two steps: Firstly, we
define the semantics of a TC in terms of a timed transition system which has
the real numbers $\mathbb{R}$ as *abstract* time domain (in contrast to the *concrete* time
domain in the syntactical extension of TTCN described in the previous section).
Secondly, we extend this definition so that the behaviour of several concurrent
TCs is modelled.

Operational Semantics of a Real-Time Test Component. With a given
definition of a TC we associate the following timed transition system: A state
$s \in \Sigma$ of a TC is given by a mapping of *variables* to *values*. The set of variables
V includes all variables defined for the TC in the test suite and, additionally,
a variable for each timer. Furthermore, we introduce a *control variable* π which
indicates the location of control in the behaviour description of the TC. π is
updated when a new level of indentation is visited. We even let PCOs and
CPs be pairs of variables so that each holds a queue of ASPs, PDUs or CMs
sent and received, respectively. PCO and CP variables and timer variables are
shared variables which can also be accessed from the environment of a TC.
For instance, received ASPs are put on the corresponding PCO variable by the
environment. Similarly, when a timer expires the value of the corresponding
timer variable is updated by the environment. The environment performs its
activities concurrently to the execution of the TC.

The initial state of a TC is the state with all variables having assigned their initial values (if specified) or being undefined. All PCO and CP variables have assigned an empty queue and all timer variables have assigned the value stop. The control variable π is initialised to the first level of indentation. If the TC is not running, i.e., the TC has not been created yet, then all variables are undefined.

The set $\mathcal{T}$ of transitions contains a transition for every TTCN statement in the TC behaviour description and the idle transition t_I. Furthermore, we have a transition t_E which models activities of the environment, i.e., reception of an ASP or expiration of a timer. t_E is not performed by the TC but may change the state of the TC, because a shared PCO, CP or timer variable is updated.

In the following we assume that the currently visited level of indentation has been expanded as defined in Annex B of [10] and has the following general form: $A_1[EET_1, LET_1], \ldots, A_n[EET_n, LET_n]$, where A_i denotes an alternative and EET_i, LET_i denote the earliest and latest execution times of alternative A_i.

We say that $A_i[EET_i, LET_i]$ is *potentially enabled* if $A_i[EET_i, LET_i]$ is in the set of alternatives. $A_i[EET_i, LET_i]$ is *enabled* if $A_i[EET_i, LET_i]$ is evaluated successfully (Sect. 2.3), $A_i[EET_i, LET_i]$ is *executable* if $A_i[EET_i, LET_i]$ is enabled and $A_i[EET_i, LET_i]$ has been potentially enabled for at least EET_i.

The mapping described above defines the set of possible computations of a TC as a set of timed state sequences with *potentially enabled* substituted for *enabled* in the definitions of Sect. 3.1. If an alternative cannot be successfully evaluated within LET time units then test case execution stops with an error indication. To make the evaluation of a real-time TTCN behaviour description more explicit we introduce the following refined snapshot semantics (Sect. 2.3). For the rest of this section we let $T, T', T'' \in \mathbb{R}$ with $T \leq T' \leq T''$.

1. The TC is put into its initial state.
2. If the level of indentation is visited for the first time then all alternatives are marked *potentially enabled* and the global time T is saved. The state of PCO and CP variables and expired timer variables is locked, so that they cannot be updated by the environment.
   If for an $A_i[EET_i, LET_i]$ in $A_1[EET_i, LET_i], \ldots, A_n[EET_i, LET_i]$, $LET_i < T' - T$, where T' the current global time and T the time when the alternative has been marked potentially enabled, then test case execution stops.
3. All alternatives which can be evaluated successfully are marked *enabled*. If no alternative in the set of alternatives can be evaluated successfully then PCO, CP and timer variables are unlocked (and the environment may again update these variables). Processing continues with Step 2.
4. An enabled alternative $A_i[EET_i, LET_i]$ is marked *executable* provided that $EET_i \leq T' - T \leq LET_i$ and if there is another enabled alternative $A_j[EET_j, LET_j]$ with $EET_j \leq T' - T \leq LET_j$ then $i < j$, i.e., the i-th alternative comes before the j-th alternative in the set of alternatives.
   If no alternative can be marked executable then PCO, CP and timer variables are unlocked. Processing continues with Step 2.

Test Case Dynamic Behaviour						
Nr	Label	Time	Behaviour Description	Constraints Ref	Verdict	Comments
1		2, 4	PCO1 ? N-DATA indication	info		
2			...			next level
3		2, 4	PCO2 ? N-ABORT indication	abort		
4			...			next level

Fig. 5. Partial Real-Time TTCN Behaviour Description

5. The alternative $A_i[EET_i, LET_i]$ marked executable in Step 4 is executed and control variable π is updated to the next level of indentation. PCO, CP and timer variables are unlocked. A test case terminates if the last level of indentation is reached, otherwise evaluation continues with Step 2.

Remarks: If a new level of indentation is visited for the first time (Step 2) then all alternatives become *potentially enabled* and time starts running although some alternatives may wait for some further conditions to become fulfilled. If a potentially enabled alternative cannot be evaluated successfully before the specified latest execution time then a specified real-time constraint has not been met and test case execution stops. If no alternative can be evaluated successfully (Step 3) then a next iteration of Steps 2 - 5 must be performed. But before, PCO, CP and timer variables are unlocked. In Step 4, the selection of alternatives for execution from the set of executable alternatives follows the same rules as in TTCN [10]. If a TC stops (Step 5) then the finite timed state sequence is extended to an infinite sequence by adding an infinite sequence of idle transitions. Every iteration of Steps 2 - 5 is *atomic*. This complies with the snapshot semantics of TTCN [10].

Example 1. We consider the partial behaviour description in real-time TTCN given in Fig. 5. Assume that the level of indentation with the two alternatives on lines 1 and 3 has been visited for the first time at T. The first alternative may be executed in the interval $EET_1 = 2$ and $LET_1 = 4$ provided that a N-DATA indication with data info has been received at PCO PCO1. Furthermore, let us assume that at T' an N-DATA indication is received. Then, the first alternative may be executed at T'' with $EET_1 \leq (T'' - T) \leq LET_1$, because this alternative is enabled (Step 3) and is executable (Step 4) and no other alternative is executable (no N-ABORT indication has been received yet). A corresponding computation might be:

$$\ldots \longrightarrow (s, T) \xrightarrow{t_I} (s, T') \xrightarrow{t_E} (s', T') \xrightarrow{t_I} (s', T'') \xrightarrow{t_1} (s'', T'') \longrightarrow \ldots$$

The reception of an N-DATA indication at time T' is a state activity, $(s, T') \xrightarrow{t_E} (s', T')$, because a PCO variable is updated by the environment performing transition t_E.

Suppose that an N-DATA indication and an N-ABORT indication have been received from the environment at some $T''' \leq T''$. Then, although both alternatives are executable, the first alternative is executed according to Step 4 because of the ordering of alternatives in the set of alternatives.

If no N-DATA indication and no N-ABORT indication have been received before LET_1 or LET_2 time units after the alternatives have been potentially enabled, test case execution stops (Step 2).

Operational Semantics of a Real-Time Test System. In general, more than one TC participates in the execution of a test case and, because of the multiplicity of executable alternatives, several TTCN statements may be executed in parallel. In timed transition systems the parallel behaviour of TCs is modelled as finite sequences of state activities which are not interleaved with time activities. Each state activity is performed by another test component.

Example 2. We assume a test system of n active or running TCs $TC_1, \ldots, TC_n$. Each TC has its own processor. Given these assumptions we associate the following timed transition system with the test system:

$V = V_1 \cup \ldots \cup V_n$ where $V_i \cap V_j = \emptyset$ for $0 \leq i, j \leq n$ and $i \neq j$, i.e., the set of variables is the union of the set of variables of all TCs. Σ contains all interpretations of V, i.e., the mapping from variables to values. The initial state $(\in \Theta)$ of the test system is the one where only the MTC is initialised. The set $\mathcal{T}$ of transitions consists of the idle transition t_I and the environment transition t_E plus the sets of transitions of all TCs labelled with the corresponding time values EET and LET of TTCN statements.

Assuming that during a test run every TC has an executable alternative ready at time T then execution of all executable alternatives may yield the following computation:

$$\ldots (s_0, T) \xrightarrow{t_1} (s_1, T) \xrightarrow{t_2} \ldots \xrightarrow{t_{n-1}} (s_{n-1}, T) \xrightarrow{t_n} (s_n, T) \ldots$$

i.e., a sequence of n state activities. Note that, scheduling the executable alternatives in a different order would have yielded another computation.

The model described above, which assumes that a processor is available for every TC, is termed *multiprocessing model* in [7]. In a *multiprogramming model*, a single processor is shared among a number of TCs. All TCs which are running on the same processor and which have an executable transition have to be scheduled for execution. Fortunately, as shown in [7], the semantics of the multiprogramming model can also be defined in terms of timed transition systems. The only additional constructs necessary are a special processor control variable μ which holds the identifier of the currently executing TC, and a scheduling transition t_S that changes the status of TCs by resuming a temporarily suspended TC. Executing the scheduling transition is a state activity that changes the processor control variable μ. In the initial state of a test system, the variable μ is assigned with the identifier of the MTC. In a computation of a test system scheduling transitions are interleaved with state activities and time steps. Unlike as in [7], scheduling another TC does not pre-empt any potentially enabled, enabled or executable transition of any other TC. A test system satisfying the defined real-time constraints must be sufficiently fast and scheduling of TCs must be done properly.

3.4 Discussion of the Proposal

If we assume that no time values are defined (in this case EET and LET are set to zero and ∞, respectively), execution of a test case results in the same sequence of state-transitions as in TTCN. In this sense our definition of real-time TTCN is downwards compatible.

Execution of a statement is modelled as an instantaneous change of state. However, it is common knowledge that execution of a statement has a finite duration. The point we would like to emphasise is that during execution of a statement a state becomes "transient" in the sense that the result of executing a statement is not available (or observable) immediately. If execution of a statement has come to an end, the result becomes permanent (or observable). In the approach employed, time instance when processing of a statement has terminated is recorded.

Real-time TTCN combines property and requirement oriented specification styles. Time labels for TTCN statements, in general, define real-time constraints for the test system. The test system is assumed to be sufficiently fast, so that a correctly behaving test system complies with the properties defined in the real-time TTCN behaviour description. Time labels for RECEIVE and OTHERWISE events, which imply a communication with the IUT, define requirements on the IUT and the underlying service provider. As well as the test system, the underlying service provider is assumed to be sufficiently reliable, particularly with respect to the timing of activities. Therefore, if a timing constraint of a RECEIVE or OTHERWISE event is violated, this clearly is an indication that the IUT is faulty and the test run should end with a FAIL verdict assignment.

4 An Application of Real-Time TTCN

Figure 6 is an example of a (partial) behaviour description for defining two real-time constraints. Firstly, every two time units the test system should generate an N-DATA request (lines 1 and 2). Secondly, the test system should receive every two to three time units a T-DATA indication (lines 3 and 4). Assuming a constant delay for the transmission of PDUs from an LT to the IUT the second constraint implies the requirement on the IUT that the IUT is capable of generating a T-DATA indication every two to three time units.

A TTCN behaviour description almost equivalent to the real-time TTCN behaviour description for the second constraint is shown in Fig. 7. The first timer is used for the lower execution time and the second timer is used to control the latest execution time. If the second TIMEOUT event can be observed, this is an indication for a erroneous behaviour of the IUT. This TTCN behaviour description, however, only is correct under the assumption that the test system is *infinitely* fast, so that no extra delay is introduced due to the execution of TTCN statements. In real-time TTCN all assumptions which are to be fulfilled by a test system are made explicit. Besides its conciseness (compare Figs. 6 and 7) this is a further advantage.

Test Case Dynamic Behaviour						
Nr	Label	Time	Behaviour Description	Constraints Ref	Verdict	Comments
1	L1	2, 2	PCO ! N-DATA request	req		
2			-> L1			GOTO
3	L2	2, 3	PCO ? T-DATA indication	ind		
4			-> L2			GOTO

Fig. 6. Continuous Sending and Receiving in Real-Time TTCN

Test Case Dynamic Behaviour					
Nr	Label	Behaviour Description	Constraints Ref	Verdict	Comments
1	L2	START timer(2)			
2		?TIMEOUT timer			
3		START timer(1)			
4		PCO ? T-DATA indication	ind		
5		STOP timer			
6		-> L2			
7		?TIMEOUT timer		FAIL	

Fig. 7. Time constraints in TTCN for Continuous Receiving

Test Case Dynamic Behaviour						
Nr	Label	Time	Behaviour Description	Constraints Ref	Verdict	Comments
1			(NumOfSends := 0)			Assignment
2			REPEAT SendData (L) UNTIL [NumOfSends > MAX]			
3		10, 12	L ! N-DATA request	req		
4			SendData (PCO)			
5		2, 2	PCO ! N-DATA request	req		

Fig. 8. Real-Time TTCN Test Case for QoS Testing

A more concrete example is an application of real-time TTCN to quality-of-service (QoS) testing [5, 19, 22]. Suppose that for a transport connection a specific *throughput*[4] QoS parameter value has been negotiated. A possible test purpose is that the IUT should abort the connection if the actual monitored throughput is less than the negotiated throughput.

Let the IUT be the receiving transport protocol implementation. The corresponding real-time TTCN test case is shown in Fig. 8. The behaviour description for the UT receiving transport data is similar to the one shown in Fig. 6 lines 3 and 4. From the negotiated throughput QoS parameter value we can compute the time interval between successive T-DATA indication ASPs that satisfies the negotiated throughput. The LT transmits transport data with N-DATA request at the computed rate. Delaying an N-DATA request (line 3 in Fig. 8) should cause the connection to be aborted (not shown in Fig. 8).

---

[4] Throughput is the ratio of the size of the last received transport service data unit to the time elapsed between the corresponding last and next T-DATA indications (and similar for the sending site) [3].

5 Conclusions and Outlook

In this paper we have discussed a proposal for a real-time extension of TTCN. The motivation for our work has been given by the demand for a test language that can express real-time constraints. This demand mainly comes from the use of multimedia applications which are quite restrictive with respect to the fulfilment of real-time requirements. Since TTCN cannot express real-time constraints, we have made a proposal for a syntactical and semantical extension of TTCN. On a syntactical level TTCN statements can be annotated by time labels which specify earliest and latest execution times. The operational semantics of our TTCN extension is based on timed transition systems [7]. In the paper we have described how real-time TTCN test cases are interpreted in timed transition systems.

In our approach a TTCN statement is annotated by time labels. The advantages of this approach are twofold: Firstly, only a few syntactical changes are necessary. Secondly, the extension of TTCN to real-time TTCN is downwards compatible: If we assume that zero and ∞ are earliest and latest execution times, a computation of a real-time TTCN test case is the same as in standard TTCN. A possible extension of our approach is to allow the annotation of test events, assignments and timer operations that are combined on a single statement line with time labels. A mapping of TTCN to transition systems at that level of detail has been investigated in [20, 21]. This mapping may be further extended and evaluated.

Based on the real-time extension of TTCN as proposed in this paper techniques for the analysis of the real-time behaviour of testers against specified test cases are to be defined. For this it seems necessary that the discussion of an operational semantics of real-time TTCN as discussed in Sect. 3.3 is being extended. Particularly, the different processing models (multiprocessing and multiprogramming models) have to be refined and, in a second step, the modelling of communication channels (PCOs, CPs and service provider) have to be integrated. Our future work will focus on these aspects.

Acknowledgements. The authors are indebted to Stefan Heymer for proofreading and for his detailed comments on earlier drafts of this paper. We are also grateful to the anonymous reviewers providing detailed comments and valuable suggestions which have improved contents and presentation of this paper.

References

1. H. Bowman, L. Blair, G. Blair, A. Chetwynd. *A Formal Description Technique Supporting Expression of Quality of Service and Media Synchronization*. Multimedia Transport and Teleservices. LNCS 882, 1994.
2. B. Berthomieu, M. Diaz. *Modeling and Verification of Time Dependent Systems Using Time Petri Nets*. IEEE Transactions on Software Engineering, Vol. 17, No. 3, March 1991.
3. A. Danthine, Y. Baguette, G. Leduc, Léonard. *The OSI 95 Connection-Mode Transport Service - The Enhanced QoS*. High Performance Networking, IFIP, 1992.

4. S. Fischer. *Spezifikation von Multimediasystemen mit Real-Time Estelle.* 6.tes GI/ITG Fachgespräch 'Formale Beschreibungstechniken für verteilte Systeme', Erlangen, June, 1996.

5. J. Grabowski, T. Walter. *Testing Quality-of-Service Aspects in Multimedia Applications.* Proceedings of the Second Workshop on Protocols for Multi-media Systems (PROMS), Salzburg, Austria, October 1995.

6. D. Hogrefe, S. Leue. *Specifying Real-Time Requirements for Communication Protocols.* Technical Report IAM 92-015, University of Berne, 1992.

7. T. Henzinger, Z. Manna, A. Pnueli. *Timed Transition Systems.* Real-Time: Theory in Practice. LNCS 600, 1991.

8. ISO/IEC. *Information Technology - OSI - Conformance Testing Methodology and Framework - Part 1: General Concepts.* ISO/IEC IS 9646-1, 1994.

9. ISO/IEC. *Information Technology - OSI - Conformance Testing Methodology and Framework - Part 2: Abstract Test Suite Specification.* ISO/IEC IS 9646-2, 1994.

10. ISO/IEC. *Information Technology - OSI - Conformance Testing Methodology and Framework - Part 3: The Tree and Tabular Combined Notation (TTCN).* ISO/IEC IS 9646-3, 1996.

11. R. Keller. *Formal Verification of Parallel Programs.* Communications of the ACM, Vol. 19, No. 7, 1976.

12. L. Léonard, G. Leduc. *An Enhanced Version of Timed LOTOS and its Application to a Case Study.* Formal Description Techniques VI, North-Holland, 1994.

13. S. Leue. *Specifying Real-Time Requirements for SDL Specifications - A Temporal Logic Based Approach.* Protocol Specification, Testing and Verification XV, 1995.

14. R. Linn. *Conformance Evaluation Methodology and Protocol Testing.* IEEE Journal on Selected Areas in Communications, Vol. 7, No. 7, 1989.

15. P. Merlin, D. Faber. *Recoverability of Communication Protocols.* IEEE Transactions on Communication, Vol. 24, No. 9, September 1976.

16. R. Probert, O. Monkewich. *TTCN: The International Notation for Specifying Tests of Communications Systems.* Computer Networks and ISDN Systems, Vol. 23, 1992.

17. J. Quemada, A. Fernandez. *Introduction of Quantitative Relative Time into LOTOS.* Protocol Specification, Testing and Verification VII, North-Holland, 1987.

18. B. Sarikaya. *Conformance Testing: Architectures and Test Sequences.* Computer Networks and ISDN Systems, Vol. 17, 1989.

19. J. Montiel, E. Rudolph, J. Burmeister (editors). *Methods for QoS Verification and Protocol Conformance Testing in IBC - Application Guidelines.* RACE Ref. 2088, 1993.

20. T. Walter, J. Ellsberger, F. Kristoffersen, P.v.d. Merkhof. *A Common Semantics Representation for SDL and TTCN.* Protocol Specification, Testing and Verification XII, North-Holland, 1992.

21. T. Walter, B. Plattner. *An Operational Semantics for Concurrent TTCN.* Proceedings Protocol Test Systems V, North-Holland, 1992.

22. T. Walter, J. Grabowski. *Towards the new Test Specification and Implementation Language 'TelCom TSL'.* 5.tes GI/ITG Fachgespräch 'Formale Beschreibungstechniken für verteilte Systeme', Kaiserslautern, June, 1995.

Session 5:
Verteilte Systeme

A Software Architecture for Control and Management of Distributed ATM Switching

M. Duque-Antón*, R. Günther*, R. Karabek**, T. Meuser*

*PHILIPS Research Laboratories,
Weisshausstr. 2, 52064 Aachen

**Technical University of Aachen, Dept. of Computer Science (Informatik IV)
Ahornstr. 55, 52074 Aachen

Abstract

Distributed switching will become a key feature for flexible and inexpensive workgroup switches as well as for dedicated high performance networking solutions. The Philips Research Laboratories in Aachen have demonstrated the feasibility of distributed ATM switching by developing a ring-based ATM switch. After solving the hardware related problems we are now focusing our efforts on the design of a distributed software platform for switch control and management purposes.

In this paper we present a distributed software architecture based on object oriented design that takes advantage of the inherent communication, processing and storage capabilities of the ATM hardware. The proposed architecture provides a framework for a location-transparent implementation, operation and maintenance of ATM switch applications like switch control, management and signalling as well as more specialized functions like location control for wireless ATM networks. The distributed, and consequently parallel execution of switch software on the proposed platform increases the overall flexibility and performance of the system.

1 The Need for Distributed ATM Switching

ATM has been adopted as the universal transfer mode for the future Broadband ISDN in public networks [1]. Most of the interest in ATM originates from its promise of vastly increased bandwidth and greater flexibility and manageability. Driven by the ATM Forum this technology has recently found its way into Local and Home Area Networks (LANs and HANs), yielding ATM-LANs and Residential Broadband Networks [2]. Thus ATM has become a 'total area' network technology providing a platform for data, control, entertainment, voice, and a variety of multimedia services.

Current ATMLAN concepts are mainly based on a *centralized switch* to which hosts are connected by dedicated trunks [3]. This is a convenient way to quickly deliver ATMLAN products, as centralized ATM switches are well-known from public networks. But if the specific traffic characteristics, system requirements and cost constraints of the in-house communications are to be better taken into account, it is necessary to develop a more dedicated switch architecture.

In our opinion, the infrastructure for private communications should be built up on a low initial investment basis and in a flexible way. Traditionally, the cost of a LAN is growing gradually with increasing user demands, and the network offers the freedom to change its configuration at any time and to any size. If a centralized switch, designed according to the concepts for public switching, is used for ATMLANs, this very attractive feature will, unfortunately, be lost. The centralized architecture restricts the flexibility of the network topology and will force the operator to make assumptions about the future extent of the network from the early beginning.

The use of ATM in private networks also requires additional user-friendliness: In LANs where transmission costs are low, a high link utilization is not of greatest concern. Instead, easy configuration and management, simplicity of use and system reliability are important.

Some future usage environments for ATM will even make mandatory the installation of *distributed switching*. A wireless ATMLAN without a dedicated base station (*ad hoc network scenario*) requires that the switching functionality is distributed over all connected terminals [4]. Networked multimedia in private HANs employing all entertainment equipment (TV, PC, telephone, settop boxes, etc.) leads to the integration of communication aspects into the application devices, requiring cost-effective network interfaces. The private user will not be willing to pay for a separate switch nor for additional management and control devices.

As a last example let us consider dedicated system applications like surveillance networks interconnecting ATM cameras along a highway around a metropolis like Paris. Taking centralized switches, one has to install a meshed network with an expensive cabling structure and a centralized control. Integrating ATM switch functions directly into the cameras enables us to build a network installation which follows the geography of the highway in a natural way.

2 The Distributed Switch Concept

At the Philips Research Laboratories in Aachen a distributed switch concept for ATM has been developed that has the potential to meet these new requirements [5]. The idea behind the concept is to identify the basic functionality of a switching network and to realize all necessary functions in a generic module. Such modules -- which we call *ATM transceivers* -- are interconnected as autonomous intelligent switching units to form a distributed switch. Each module contains all the hardware and software functionalities required to build up a switch of any size and in any topology by combining a sufficient number of modules.

The ability to physically separate a distributed switch into autonomous ATM transceivers allows flexible cabling topologies, see Figure 1. If the transceivers are distributed to different locations, a ring topology is obtained. If the transceivers are concentrated in a central place, a star topology results. Even combinations of both topologies are possible. All topologies provide scalability in terms of number of terminal ports, throughput, and geographical distance.

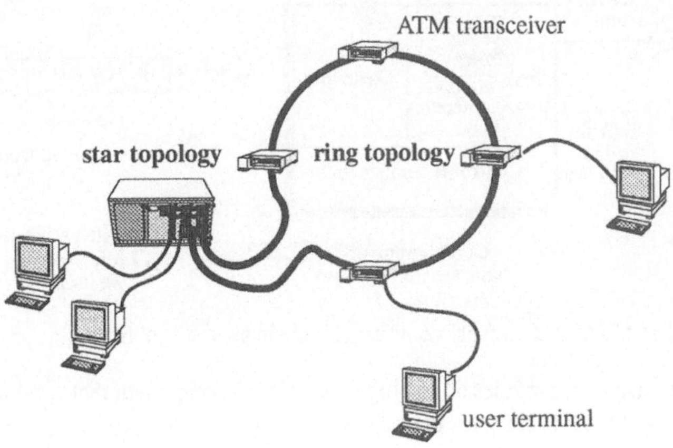

Figure 1: The distributed ATM switch supports both 'star' and 'ring' wiring

The main task of ATM networks is to transfer cells from one terminal port to one or more destinations, possibly over several interconnected switches. Analysing a general switching network shows three main functions which have to be performed by each transceiver (see Figure 2):

1. Terminal access and switch interconnection via ports

Each ATM transceiver has two bidirectional ports for transceiver interconnection plus one for the terminal access. The terminal port provides a standardized interface in accordance with ATM Forum specifications [6]. The necessary signalling and traffic management functions are supported by an embedded CPU. The VPI/VCIs in the headers of the incoming and outgoing cells are modified by a translator according to pre-defined routing values. For the physical interconnection each transceiver offers open interfaces that allow the use of different physical interfaces for electrical, optical and wireless media at different data rates.

2. Switching

The switching element routes the cells to either the terminal port, the two interconnection ports or an embedded control unit. It allows also a copying of cells for multicast and broadcast applications. To avoid congestion and to have a low cell loss probability, the arrived cells may be stored in a buffer of the switching element.

3. Control and Management

The control unit, realized by the embedded CPU, is connected to the switching element by an internal ATM interface over which it can receive and transmit cells. The control unit supports different tasks in the transceiver like controlling the terminal access, the signalling among terminal and switch module, and resource and traffic management. Furthermore, it supports the intercommunication between neighbouring transceivers. The distributed switch concept does not need a central server for operation. All functions - done by commonly used architectures in a central switch server - are supported here by the decentralized distributed control units. This has the advantage that the total CPU power grows proportionally to the number of installed switch modules and fits also directly to the required processing power of a switch.

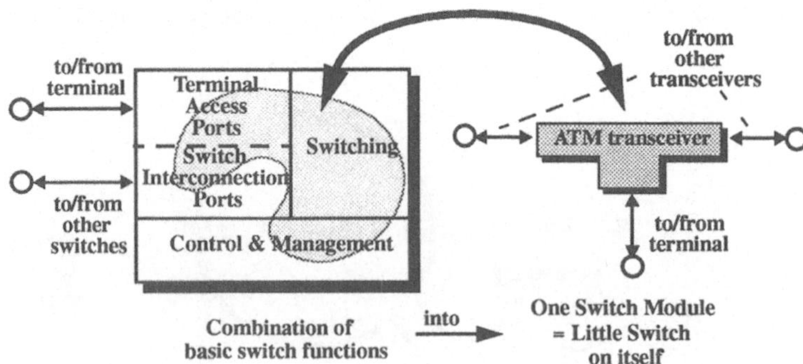

Figure 2: The 'ATM transceiver' combines all basic switch functions into one generic module

The ATM transceiver provides an intelligent switching component that combines the dedicated high-speed ATM hardware with the power and flexibility of a general-purpose MIPS microprocessor. Thus the distributed switch built by several transceivers provides distributed processing and storage capacity as a basis for the proposed software architecture.

3 A Layered Software Structure

The software layering should deliver structuring principles independent of the underlying physical transmission medium, e.g. wired or wireless. The basic idea is that the contents of the architectural components (e.g. algorithms) may vary but the interfaces between them remain unchanged. The architecture helps to identify the components that remain unchanged and supports re-use.

On top of the distributed hardware platform described above, the software is structured according to its main functionality. The resulting layering is shown in Figure 3.

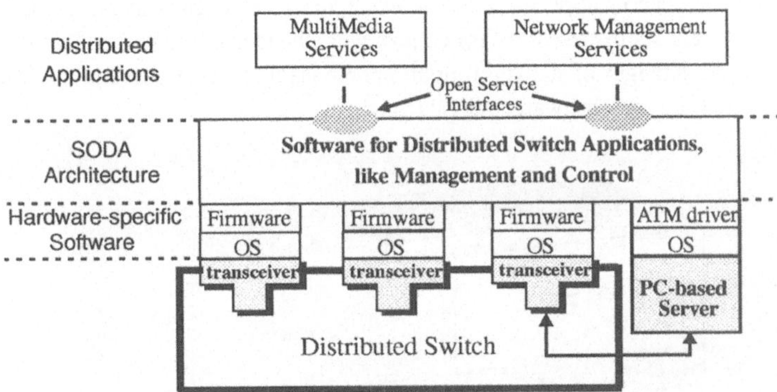

Figure 3: Software Layers on top of the distributed ATM Switch

On each transceiver, hardware-specific software, the *firmware*, provides facilities to send/receive AAL packets via ATM connections and change hardware-specific features, like routing tables. To make the distributed system work logically like a centralized ATM switch, the operations of the individual transceivers have to be coordinated by a fast management and control software. Such higher-layer software should be independent of the hardware-specific platform, the operating system (OS) and the firmware.

Therefore the *SODA architecture* (SOftware for Distributed Atm switching) has been designed that provides a separation including well-defined interfaces for hardware access. It also defines the framework for the implementation of distributed switch applications like management and control. We employ object-orientation as a well-known analysis and design methodology. Switch applications are realized by one or more software objects which can be flexibly arranged on the transceivers and optionally on a dedicated PC-based switch software server. The integration of PCs provides extended storage and processing capabilities.

Communication means have been provided for a location-transparent delivery of messages between the software objects in the system [7]. This allows the application components to communicate with each other without knowledge of their locations. The SODA architecture provides open interfaces to the application programmer for the design of all kinds of services as distributed applications.

Up to now control and management have been designed as switch applications. Setting up and removing communication channels are responsibilities of control. The management part carries out maintenance purposes in the system. Switch status information is presented to the outside world and modification requests are handled here. In addition, management applications configure the distributed switch, optimize its performance and allow integration into a global network management system. It should be noted that the SODA architecture does not exclude any other switch applications. For example in the wireless case, a location control performs locating of mobile terminals and deals with unsteady transmission qualities of radio links.

4 The SODA architecture

Keeping in mind the capacity of the underlying hardware and the requirements on the software, the SODA architecture has been designed as shown in Figure 4. Switch applications, e.g. *Control* and *Management*, use a common information storage component, the *Information Repository*. Data needed from both applications are stored here so that it can be accessed via a common interface. The system status necessary for control and management is mirrored in the information repository. All changes of status information here leads to corresponding modifications in the system's hardware and firmware and vice versa.

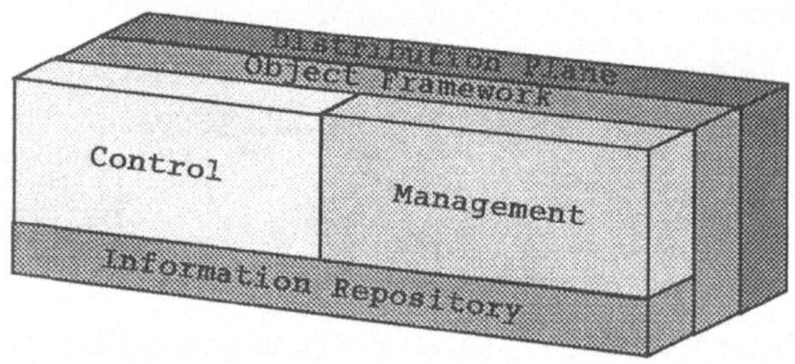

Figure 4: The SODA Architecture Reference Model

Control, management and the information repository consist of several software objects communicating without knowledge of the communication partner's location. This is achieved by a *Distribution Plane* offering its functionality to all software layers of the architecture. Since the distribution plane is extended over all system devices, it is possible to arrange the objects in any part of the system like a transceiver or a connected PC or workstation. The communication facility is offered in a common way independent of which system part (transceiver, PC or workstation) the objects are arranged on.

The *Object Framework* provides an object's living environment. It supports the dynamic creation and deletion of objects. A set of special functions allow the object registration and the inter-object communication. The object framework provides a common object representation for all kinds of system parts.

Now we discuss the features of these architectural components in more details. After that, switch applications which make use of the offered functionality are described in section 5.

4.1 The Object Framework

Objects used in the SODA architecture have the following functionality in common:

- Registration

  At the beginning of an object's lifetime the object has to announce its presence and its public methods to the distribution plane making them accessible to other objects.

- Object references

  After an object and its methods are registered it can communicate with any other object of the distributed system. Object references are a common way to access other objects. The object framework makes the necessary references available to the object. For the first call, it requests a reference from the distribution plane. After the initialization, the reference is stored and used for following method invocations of the same object.

- Communication

  The method invocation in other objects is done by sending a message. This message is built up in a common way indicating the remote object, the called method and the call parameters. The object framework supports two different ways of communication, *asynchronous* and *synchronous* calls. In each case the caller is responsible for putting the method's parameters in the right order. Type-checking is only done in the method's invocation step during runtime.

We call objects of that kind *embedded objects* and take them as building blocks for our architecture. The object framework provides the necessary environment to make an embedded one out of any object. Embedded objects are active, i.e. there are one or more threads of control per object to handle method invocation requests from other objects. Objects normally starts processing when a message from another object arrives. If there is a need for recurrent actions to be executed by objects, the object framework provides the functionality to invoke periodically specific methods of objects.

4.2 The Distribution Plane

Object framework and distribution plane are strongly related components as shown in Figure 5. The object framework supports the realization of software components as embedded objects. The distribution plane provides a communication facility for embedded objects.

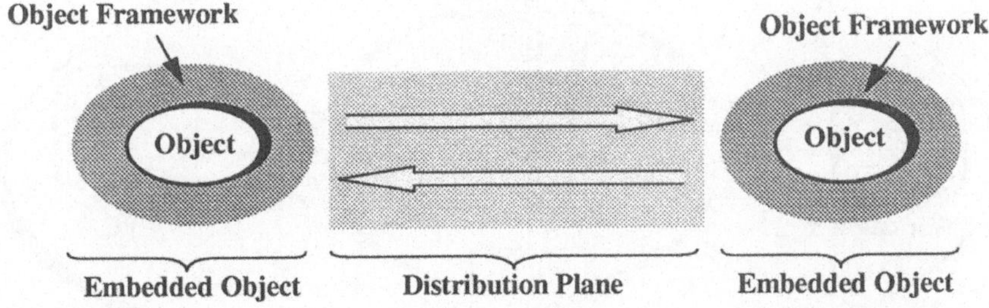

Figure 5: Relationship between Distribution Plane and Object Framework

The distribution plane is the software 'glue' connecting the parts of our distributed ATM switch. It is the architectural component dealing with distribution issues and comprising knowledge on the different software objects and their location. Software redundancy issues are also addressed here. The distribution plane consists of three main functional components (see Figure 6):

- The **distributor** is responsible for forwarding arriving messages from the firmware and from objects. Arriving messages are either diverted to embedded objects residing on the local system part or passed on to the firmware.

- The **name server** comprises the knowledge of all active objects in the whole system. The objects' locations are stored in a local object table. The mapping of an object's service to a corresponding object address is carried out by the name server. This mapping functionality gives the distribution plane the capability to change the destination object to which messages are routed transparently for the application. In addition to that, a description of the object classes, their methods and their signatures are available. They are mainly used for the representation of object interactions by a graphical user interface.

- The **replication control** deals with software redundancy. It comprises the knowledge of all replicated objects in the system. We favour a solution in which replicated services appear as if the service is provided by one object. A suitable replication scheme is for further study.

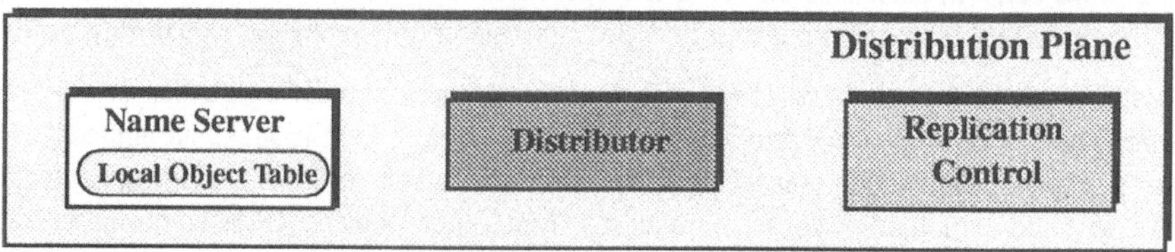

Figure 6: Structure of the Distribution Plane

4.2.1 Configuration of the Distribution Plane

The functionality of the distribution plane is realized by the interaction of autonomous distribution plane entities (DPEs) arranged on every system part (see Figure 7). Each DPE includes a *Name Server*, a *Distributor* and a *Replication Control*, as described above.

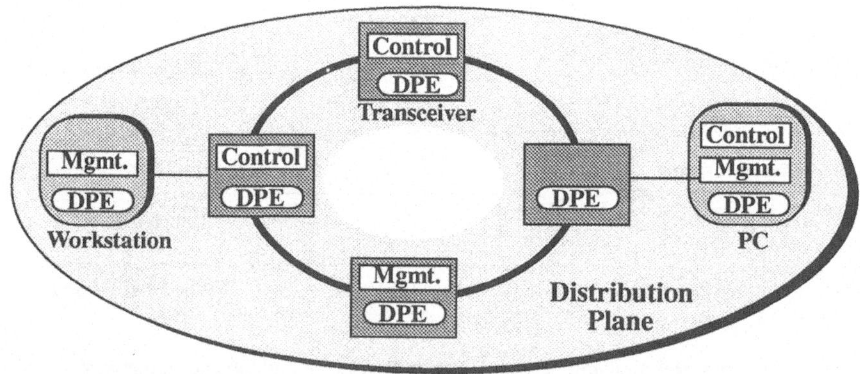

Figure 7: Building the Distribution Plane by autonomous DPEs

Architectural components like control, management and the information repository are split into several embedded objects. The distribution plane as the architectural backbone, however, does not consist of embedded objects for the following reasons. As mentioned above, different message streams have to be handled. Generally one task per stream seems to be an appropriate design solution. Consequently the distribution plane is built up of several tasks communicating efficiently via shared memory. The embedded object concept is not adequate here. Nevertheless, from the outside the distribution plane looks and behaves like a normal architectural component.

Embedded objects can be distributed over the distribution plane, i.e. over any system parts, in any way. Information on the objects is shared among the distribution plane's entities. It is a question of policy in which way the information is stored and forwarded between these entities and therefore not in the scope of this paper. Here it should just be emphasized that the architectural approach with distribution plane entities does not lead to any restriction on the policy algorithm.

The distributed switch must tolerate the removal of system parts and has to deal with the integration of new system parts. The distribution plane as the architectural backbone handles those situations with autonomous entities, each of them providing all distribution plane functionalities.

4.2.2 Internal and external interfaces

The distribution plane has external interfaces to the *firmware*, *object framework*, and *configuration management*. Besides that, an *internal interface* between the autonomous distribution plane entities is necessary.

- The **firmware** offers a message-based interface to the distribution plane. The distribution component uses it to send and receive information packets via ATM. Virtual channel identifiers on which the distribution plane's messages are forwarded are not part of the firmware interface. So most ATM-specific parameters are left for implementation on firmware side.

- An **object framework** communicates directly only with the DPE that resides on the same system part. The registration of an object encompasses the initialization and introduction of new objects and their methods. In addition, the replacement of running objects is also covered. This allows the framework architecture to support objects' movement and duplication.

  During an object's initialization, the object framework informs the distribution plane of the presence of an embedded object. The distribution plane, especially the name server, is the architectural component in charge of handling distribution aspects in the system.
  To address a method request, the calling object asks for the reference to the destination object. The distribution plane as the component with knowledge of the embedded object distribution has to provide these references using its local object table or asking other DPEs.
  For the message transfer itself the distribution plane offers primitives to be used by the object framework for sending and receiving method calls and pertinent replays from and to the network. If the called object resides on a remote system part, two distribution plane entities are involved and the message is sent via ATM to a remote distributor component. It is completely transparent for the calling object if the communication between objects residing on the same system part is being handled by the local distributor of its own.

- The **configuration management** and distribution plane both play an important role when the switch configuration changes due to the integration or removal of system parts. The distribution plane's responsibility is to inform the configuration management of the presence of new or loss of old switch elements. Therefore it checks the entities' presence frequently in short intervals by exchanging 'Alive'-messages between distribution plane entities. This is part of the intra-distribution plane functionality, which is described in the following.

- For the cooperation of the autonomous DPEs, which are arranged on each system part, the **internal interface** between the DPEs need to have the following functions:
  The distributed switch must tolerate that some of its system parts are not accessible during short time intervals or that they disappear completely. In such a situation communicating objects should get a direct response that their communication partner is not accessible anymore. Therefore the distribution plane has to know which DPEs are accessible at the moment.

During registration of an embedded object, the local name server entity has to ask all remote name server entities whether the new embedded object leads to any inconsistencies. For efficiency reasons, the name server's local object table comprises information on not just all local embedded objects, but also on some remote embedded objects. It is a policy and implementation question which remote embedded object entries are kept and when information on new embedded objects is diverted to name server entities. Anyhow, one DPE must inform all other DPEs of an object's registration and de-registration as well as on whether an object is replaced by another object.

During a replacement in which replacing and replaced objects are not on the same system part, the replacing name server entity has to ask the replaced name server entity. If the given capability is valid, then the state of the embedded object is transferred to the replacing name server entity. After that the replaced embedded object is removed by the remote name server. As mentioned above, the object framework requests references of objects from which a method should be invoked. On the distribution plane, first the name server's local object table is searched through. If the necessary information is not local then all remote name server entities are questioned for an appropriate object reference.

4.3 Information Repository

The task of the *Information Repository* is to facilitate access to shared information of the management objects and control objects as well as to coordinate access to low level firmware data and functions. Since most of the information, especially the low-level firmware data within the switch are generated at different locations, the information repository itself will be realised in a distributed fashion.

All aspects of distribution, concurrent access, and consistency are to be taken into account when designing the information repository. Furthermore to realise transparent access to all shared information, these aspects are to be shielded from the other software components. In addition to storing information, the information repository has several active functions:

- Uniform and location-transparent access to information shared by switch applications.

- Preparation of information that is available only as raw data or in a different format.

- In addition to directly retrieving the data, an object can specify a certain condition relating to an information entity under which it wishes to be notified. Such an event-based notification mechanism avoids frequent polling of an object which wants to perform a specific task, if the value of an information entity reaches a certain threshold.

- Control of firmware/hardware (HW/FW) changes initiated by software components as well as storage and maintenance of the related information are the responsibility of the information repository. Therefore it holds proxy objects representing exactly to one counterpart in the real HW/FW. After having received a notification from its counterpart, a proxy object adapts its state according to the change. In the other direction, the proxy objects offer the interface for control and management to access the HW/FW. For each modification access the proxy object initiates an action on the HW/FW and notes the modification in its data base.

Especially this last point makes it clear that certain aspects of the information repository have characteristics of a layer, since the information repository is the only entity in the system that may initiate hardware/firmware-related actions. This allows hardware independence for all software layers above the information repository.

5 Design of switch applications

Switch applications are intended to run automatically as part of each distributed switch. User interaction is necessary only for their configuration and management. The most essential switch applications are control and management. In order to cope with networks consisting of more than one distributed switch, *network applications* have to be installed. Examples for network applications are network-wide signalling, network management and mobility management.

At this point we should emphasize the differences between switch applications and network applications. In general, a network application will control several switch applications. Switch applications provide information and perform subtasks under control of network applications. Network applications communicate with the switch applications using ATM standard interfaces (UNI and NNI), meta-signalling protocols, and SNMP via the switch's AAL interface. Network applications are out of scope of this paper since they are not a part of the switch software, but they are using it. In the beginning, we are going to install the following switch applications as part of the SODA architecture:

5.1 Switch Control

Switch control software enables the user to set-up and tear down ATM connections either via UNI signalling [6], [8] or network management tools. For that, at call request time virtual channels are established as switched virtual channels (SVC's), or permanent virtual channels (PVC's) are pre-configured before operation. In both cases resources are allocated to connections using *call admission control* schemes and *resource control* mechanisms. Besides that, control has to perform *congestion control* and parts of the *traffic control*.

The design of the switch control supports *external call control* by applications that is suited to facilitate the introduction and operation of services from areas such as multimedia conferencing or virtual networking. Following the concept of *Open Switching* [9], a specific call and event control could be integrated as switch application in the distributed software architecture.

5.2 Switch Management

Following the principle that the distributed switch is logically considered as a single entity, the *switch management* has to perform all tasks to manage the distributed system like a central element and it should offer standardized management interfaces to the external world [10]. Thus the switch management could be a proprietary switch application, but the structure of information and protocols should comply with those of the global network management system.

As discussed in the introduction, the distributed switch realizes a communication system with embedded processing power and is intended for specific usage environments in the wireless and consumer markets. Therefore switch management has to be extended beyond a basic element manager that usually provides functions like switch configuration, fault detection, and provision of elementary management information. In addition to this internal management tasks, management applications which usually run on an external management platform should be performed by the switch management also. Thus switch management becomes responsible to carry out common management tasks such as *Fault Management, Topology Management, Configuration Management, Performance Management, Accounting Management,* and *Security Management.* The objective of integrating all management tasks as switch applications into the switch is the installation of a (semi-) automatic management system.

5.3 Location Control

This component is responsible for the *intra-switch* handover in the case of a wireless system where each ATM transceiver operates as a base station. The location control gets information of the actual signal quality and signal strengths of the radio channels measured by the mobile terminals. Based on this information, it initiates the handover of a mobile terminal to another base station, i.e. another transceiver. In particular, we can assume an interrupt-free handover, as time constraints allows for maintaining two connections simultaneously. The old one is released only after the new one was successfully established.

Location control allows for network-wide roaming. The mobile information concerning one distributed switch is kept within its local instance of location control. In order to allow for inter-switch handover (the mobile terminal is rooming to another switch) a mobility management, responsible network-wide roaming, uses the information of location control. Thus location control may receive a *Handover_Indication* from the mobile terminal (if an intra-switch handover has to be performed) as well as from mobility management (for inter-switch handover).

5.4 Switch Load Control

Switch load control offers access to the routing tables in order to allow for a network-wide load management application. When performing call admission for inter-switch calls, network load control is intended to interact with the local switch load controls to find the best route through the composed network. Using a meta-signalling protocol and the switch's AAL interface, such an application can initiate the setting and modification of the switch's routing table. On the other hand, network load management receives information on resource usage from the individual switches. Based on this information it optimizes the network-wide routing and forwards the routing tables to the switches. This way, global CAC and load balancing are supported.

6 First Prototypes and Other Related Work

As a first prototype outside our laboratory, a network using distributed ATM switching was installed at the campus of the University of Technology in Aachen. In this pilot network two physically centralized department switches and a physically distributed optical backbone were installed providing a broadband interconnection of all connected terminals and allowing the interworking with third party ATM equipment as well as the access to the Regional ATM Test-Bed (RTB-NRW) interconnecting several universities via public leased lines. The main objective for this installation is to evaluate the basic architecture in a realistic usage environment. Thereby the prototype is installed as cross-connect and provides only a simple user interface for control and management.

First experiences with the proposed software architecture were gained from a testbed implemented within the scope of the RACE 2101 project IMMUNE [11]. In order to provide a fast restoration system for the distributed switch, automatic self-healing mechanisms have been realized as switch application. Information on the configuration, resources, and the performance of the ATM transceiver ring is controlled by a distributed switch management. The call admission control and the IMMUNE objects make use of this decentralized information base to speed up processing. On the other hand, these objects also contribute to the update of the information base by reporting each detected failure to the management. After a fast automatic restoration, the management may initiate a post optimization by re-configuring the system.

Taking into account these first experiences we started to design the new SODA architecture described in this paper. It is the main objective to design and implement an efficient distributed software system for real-time communication environments. This should become independent of the underlying physical configuration and is open for all future broadband services for ATM networks such as external call control for multimedia applications and mobility control for wireless ATM networks.

When scanning the literature we can see several approaches defining distributed software architecture for system control and management. In the following the relationship between the SODA architecture and the main current standardization activities is briefly summarized.

The Telecommunications Information Networking Architecture (TINA) [12] defines a software architecture that can be used to define a modular structure for the control of switching nodes. Its main purpose, however, is to enable telecom networks to support the rapid and flexible introduction of new services and the ability to manage services and the network infrastructure in an integrated way. The TINA architecture covers several technical areas:

- The Computing Architecture defines a software sub-layer to support for distributed execution of software components, i.e. how they interact and how they communicate.

- The Service Architecture provides a set of concepts for specifying, designing, and operating service-related telecommunications software components.

- The Network Architecture describes a set generic components that provide high-level abstractions of network resources used by several service applications.

- The Management Architecture aims to provide a set of generic management principles for the management of Service, Network, and Computing Architecture.

The scope of TINA is much wider than the purpose of the SODA architecture. We do not aim at a service, network or management architecture, but only at a computing architecture which defines a 'software bus' for the interaction of software objects realizing any application.TINA, however, does not specify the software bus itself. It only requires the use of CORBA's IDL (Interface Definition Language) for interface specification.

The Object Management Group (OMG) has standardized a software bus, known as CORBA (Common Object Request Broker Architecture) [13]. CORBA's aim is to support distributed applications and to provide a standard for the interoperability of distributed objects in heterogeneous environments. This includes to address objects, to set up communication links to them and to finally invoke operations on objects.

CORBA and SODA have similar functionality and both are operating according to the same principles. Our target usage environment, however, which aims to distributed real-time control application requires for a dedicated solution. Thus we decided not to use a CORBA-compliant ORB but a more real-time, light-weight ORB. Some extensions concerning real-time objects become necessary. SODA supports multi-tasking, asynchronous remote procedure calls (RPC's) and multi-priority queuing. It allows for a direct use of ATM real-time communication facilities and addressing information. We restrict our platform only to those services required in our specific usage environment. Services for naming, persistence, concurrency control, and software exchange are installed as a inherent part of the ORB instead of being Object Services in the sense of CORBA.

The Distributed Component Object Model (DCOM) [14] were introduced by Microsoft Corporation as an extension to Windows operating systems. It describes the object model used for the communication between OLE (Object Linking and Embedding) applications providing means for application integration. In DCOM a method call of an application is transparently propagated to the actual object instance, being located inside the same process, inside another process on the same machine, or - in theory - on a remote machine. The underlying paradigm is the RPC.

While OLE / DCOM is now a common technology in the area of PC desktop application integration, its usage as distribution platform is still not possible because of the lack of remote communication and other distribution mechanisms. Rumours say that Microsoft will adopt an DCE implementation for remote communication, security and other services. Maybe DCE IDL will be the interface definition language for such an enhanced COM environment.

The intentions of SODA and DCOM are quite different. SODA is employed by communication devices and provides means for object interaction while leaving as much freedom as possible to the implementors of the application objects. On the other hand DCOM describes the integration of application objects themselves running on a PC. The required means for object interaction are not specified and have to be provided by services of distribution platforms like CORBA.

7 Literature

[1]   M. de Prycker: *Asynchronous Transfer Mode, Solution for Broadband ISDN*, 2. Edt., Ellis Horwood Limited, 1993.

[2]   P. Newman: *ATM Local Area Networks*, IEEE Communications Magazine, vol. 32, no. 3, March 1994, pp. 79 - 89.

[3]   E.W. Zegura: *Architectures for ATM Switching Systems*, IEEE Communications Magazine, vol. 31, no. 2, February 1993, pp. 28 - 37.

[4]   Y. Du: *System Architectures of a Home Wireless ATM Network*, Proc. of IEEE ICUPC - International Conference on Universal Personal Communications, September 1996.

[5]   Y. Du, R. Kraemer: *ATM local area networks using distributed switch architecture*, Proceedings of IEEE GLOBECOM'94, November 1994, pp. 1832 - 1838.

[6]   ATM Forum/94-1018R7: *User-Network Interface, Signalling, Version 4.0*, October 1995.

[7]   G. Booch: *The Booch Method: Distributed Systems*, Report on Object-Oriented Analysis, September 1995.

[8]   M. Duque-Anton, R. Günther, R. Karabek, T. Meuser: *A Switch Control Software Architecture for Future ATM Broadband Services*, submitted to the Seventh IFIP Conference on High Performance Networking, New York, April 1997.

[9]   M. Elixmann et al.: *Open Switching - Extending Control Architectures to Facilitate Applications*, Proc. of ISS'95, vol. 2, April 1995, pp. 239 - 243.

[10]   H. J. Fowler: *TMN-Based Broadband Network Management*, IEEE Communications Magazine, vol. 33, no. 3, March 1995, pp. 74 - 79.

[11]   K. P. May et al.: *A Fast Restoration System for ATM-Ring-Based LANs*, IEEE Communications Magazine, vol. 33, no. 9, September 1995, pp. 90 - 98.

[12]   H. Berndt, L.A. de la Fuente, P. Graubmann: *Service and Management Architecture in TINA-C*, Proc. TINA '95, Melbourne, Australia, February 1995.

[13]   Object Management Group OMG: *The Common Object Request Broker: Architecture and Specification* Revision 2.0, July 1995.

[14]   Microsoft Corp.: *The Component Object Model Specification*, Version 0.9, October 1995.

CoDO – Eine Entwurfsumgebung für verteilte objektorientierte CAE-Werkzeuge

Peter E. H. Hofmann, Utz G. Baitinger, Universität Stuttgart
Institut für Parallele und Verteilte Höchstleistungsrechner (IPVR)

1 Einleitung

Der Entwurf von höchstintegrierten Schaltungen wie beispielsweise Mikroprozessoren, Signal-prozessoren oder andere komplexe Schaltkreise kann nur mit Hilfe von speziellen Software-werkzeugen (CAE-Tools) durchgeführt werden.

Bei der Entwicklung von Entwurfswerkzeugen standen vor allem pragmatische Überlegungen im Vordergrund. Es ging im wesentlichen darum, schnell anwendbare Programme für den Einsatz in der täglichen Praxis zu schreiben. Auf eine einfache Bedienung oder auf einheitliche Schnittstellen für den Datenaustausch wurde ebensowenig Wert gelegt, wie auf eine modulare und leicht wartbare Struktur der Programme. Diese pragmatisch ausgerichtete Entwicklung führte sehr schnell zu Problemen: Beispielsweise erschwerten die unterschiedlichen Benutzer-oberflächen die Anwendung verschiedener Werkzeuge erheblich, da jedes Werkzeug individu-ell bedient werden mußte. Gleichzeitig verhinderten die nicht einheitlichen und undokumentierten Datenschnittstellen den Austausch von Entwurfsdaten zwischen den ver-schiedenen Werkzeugen.

Um den sich ständig verändernden technologischen Anforderungen nachkommen zu können, sind für zukünftige Generationen von Entwurfswerkzeugen vor allem die Aspekte Modularität, Stabilität, Wartbarkeit und Wiederverwendbarkeit von elementarer Bedeutung. Da objektorien-tierte Softwaresysteme über genau diese Eigenschaften verfügen, sollen diese Techniken ver-stärkt zur Implementierung neuer CAE-Werkzeuge eingesetzt werden. Eine weitere Anforderung von CAE-Werkzeugen ergibt sich aus der Tatsache, daß viele der eingesetzten Al-gorithmen zu der Klasse der NP-vollständigen Probleme gehören und somit als sehr rechenzeit-intensiv einzustufen sind.

Diese Beschleunigung dieser Algorithmen kann nur durch den Einsatz paralleler und verteilter Programmiertechniken erreicht werden. Das Problem dieser Techniken ist, daß sie nur mit Hilfe spezieller Hardwaresysteme und darauf abgestimmter Programmierumgebungen eingesetzt werden können. Hinzu kommt, daß es sehr schwierig ist, parallele Programme zu entwerfen und vor allem die Einhaltung moderner Softwareengineering Eigenschaften zu gewährleisten. Was fehlt ist demnach ein Konzept, welches die Vorteile des objektorientierten Ansatzes bei der Strukturierung großer Softwaresysteme mit den Vorteilen der nebenläufigen und verteilten Pro-grammierung bei der Beschleunigung rechenintensiver Verfahren verbindet.

Aus diesem Grund wurde im Rahmen des Projektes CoDO (*Concurrent Distributed Objects for sophisticated CAE Tools*) am Institut für Parallele und Verteilte Höchstleistungsrechner (IPVR) der Universität Stuttgart eine Entwurfsumgebung entwickelt, die diese Verbindung von objekt-orientierter und verteilter Programmierung unterstützt.

Die entwickelte Entwurfsumgebung CoDO, die im folgenden ausführlich vorgestellt wird, wur-de der Sprache Eiffel unter Solaris 2.4 entwickelt und prototypisch implementiert. Basierend auf dieser Entwicklungsumgebung wurden konkrete CAD-Algorithmen implementiert und ei-ner Laufzeitanalyse unterzogen, um dadurch Erfahrungen über die Stärken und Schwächen des Ansatzes zu gewinnen.

2 Eigenschaften von CAE-Werkzeugen

CAE-Werkzeuge sind große und sehr komplexe Softwaresysteme deren Erstellung einen sehr hohen Aufwand an Personal und Kosten erfordert. Zu den wichtigsten Aufgaben bei der Implementierung von CAE-Werkzeugen zählen die Modellierung der Datenstrukturen und die Optimierung der Verfahren, die auf sie angewendet werden.

Da die Aufgaben die von CAE-Werkzeugen Bearbeitet werden sehr vielschichtig sind, soll hier stellvertretend ein konkretes Anwendungsgebiet vorgestellt werden. Mit den heute verfügbaren Schaltkreistechnologien lassen sich integrierte Schaltungen mit mehreren Millionen Transistoren herstellen. Geht man von der vereinfachten Abschätzung aus, daß zur Realisierung eines Transistors, wie er in Abbildung 1 als Teil eines Inverters dargestellt ist, mit allen relevanten Verbindungsstrukturen durchschnittlich fünf Polygone benötigt werden, so kommt man bei einer Schaltung mit 20 Millionen Transistoren leicht auf 100 Millionen Polygone. Geht man weiter davon aus, daß jedes Polygon aus durchschnittlich fünf Kanten aufgebaut ist, so erhält man insgesamt etwa 500 Millionen elementare geometrische Strukturen, die in entsprechenden Datenstrukturen modelliert und verarbeitet werden müssen. Um derartig umfangreiche Datenmengen mit vertretbarer Rechenzeit und akzeptablem Speicherplatzbedarf bearbeiten zu können, müssen entsprechende Mechanismen entwickelt werden.

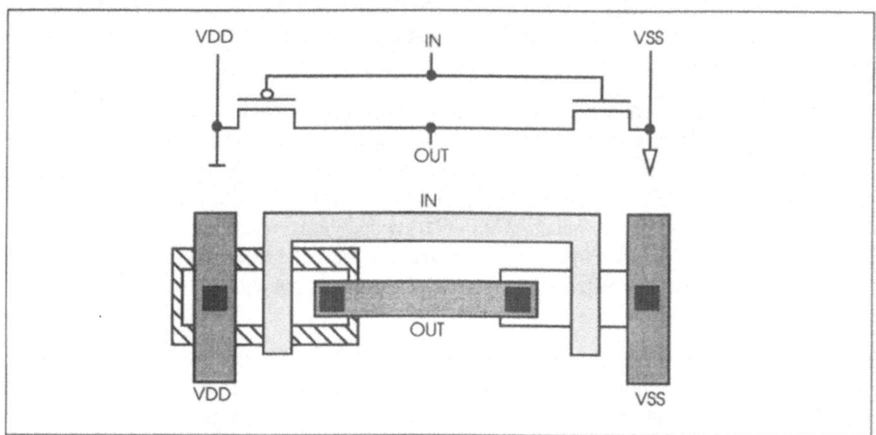

Abbildung 1: Schaltbild und Layout eines CMOS-Inverters

Übergang....

3 Die Entwurfsumgebung CoDO

Die Entwurfsumgebung CoDO („*Concurrent Distributed Objects for Sophisticated CAE Tools*") wurde mit dem Ziel entwickelt, die Implementierung von leistungsfähigen CAE-Werkzeugen auf der Basis des objektorientierten und nebenläufigen Paradigmas zu unterstützen. Die Entwurfsumgebung hat eine modulare Struktur, die es erlaubt, existierende Komponenten jederzeit auszutauschen oder das System um zusätzliche Eigenschaften zu erweitern. Die zentrale Komponente der Entwurfsumgebung CoDO ist das CAPO-System (Concurrent **AP**plication

Organisator), das die grundlegenden Mechanismen für die Verteilung von Objekten in einem Workstationcluster bereitstellt. Das CAPO-System basiert in der aktuellen Ausbaustufe auf einer objektorientierten Programmiersprache, die um nebenläufige Mechanismen auf der Basis eines Bibliotheksansatzes erweitert wurde, und auf einem UNIX-Betriebssystem, welches im wesentlichen die Interprozesskommunikationsmechanismen (IPC) liefert.

Neben dem CAPO-System wird für die Entwicklung nebenläufiger, objektorientierter CAE-Anwendungen auch eine leistungsfähige, objektorienierte Programmiersprache benötigt, die über Klassenbibliotheken mit elementaren Datenstrukturen verfügen muß.

Ein weiterer Bestandteil der Entwurfsumgebung ist eine Bibliothek mit Softwarebausteinen. Dabei handelt es sich um spezielle, auf der Basis des CoDO-Systems entwickelte Programmteile und Algorithmen, die für eine spätere Wiederverwendung gespeichert werden.

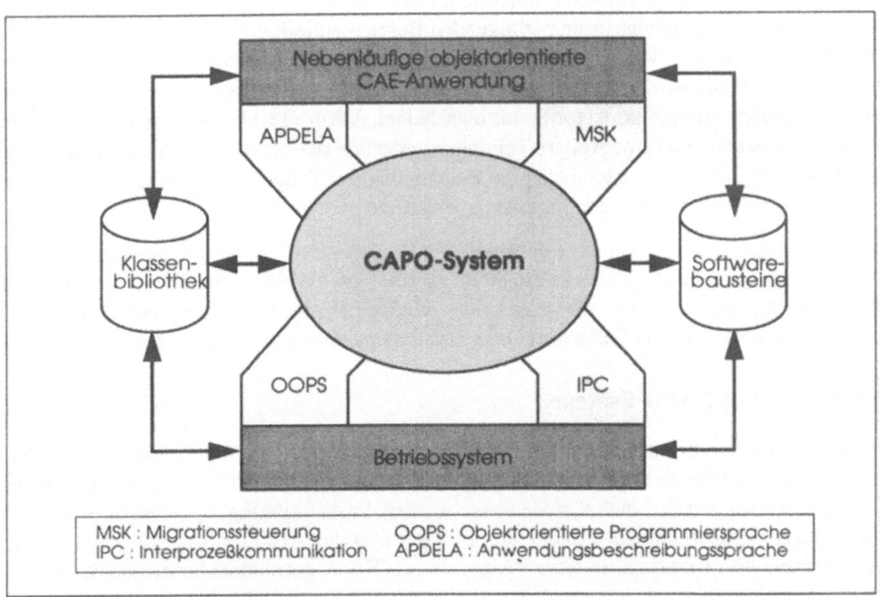

Abbildung 2: Aufbau der Entwurfsumgebung CoDO

Das CAPO-System (Concurrent APplication Organisator) stellt die zentrale Komponente der Entwurfsumgebung dar. Die Aufgabe dieser Komponente besteht im wesentlichen in der Verteilung und Ausführung eines entkoppelbaren Problems auf mehreren durch ein Netzwerk verbundenen Rechnern. Sie basiert auf einer objektorientierten Programmiersprache, deren Leistungsmerkmale um Mechanismen zur nebenläufigen Programmierung erweitert wurden. In der hier vorgestellten Entwurfsumgebung CoDO wurde die Sprache ISE-Eiffel 3 mit Hilfe einer entsprechenden Bibliothek um die erforderlichen Mechanismen erweitert. Es ist aber prinzipiell möglich, jede andere objektorientierte Programmiersprache zu verwenden. Einzige Voraussetzung ist deren Eignung zur Entwicklung großer und komplexer Softwaresysteme.

Da die vom CAPO-System bereitgestellten Mechanismen sehr systemnah realisiert wurden, sind zur Implementierung von CAE-Werkzeugen spezifische Kenntnisse der objektorientierten Sprache und der entwickelten Mechanismen erforderlich. Um die Entwicklung auch weniger geübten Anwendungsentwicklern zu ermöglichen, stellt die Entwicklungsumgebung die high-level-Sprache APDELA zur Verfügung. Mit Hilfe dieser Sprache werden keine spezifischen

Kenntnisse über das zugrundeliegende CAPO-System mehr benötigt. Der Anwender hat lediglich die Aufgabe, die einzelnen Objekte und ihre Methoden zu spezifizieren. Alles übrige wird dann vom Compiler übernommen.

Die Migrationssteuerungskomponente (MSK) hat die Aufgabe, die Verlagerung (Migration) von Objekten innerhalb des Workstationclusters zu steuern und zu überwachen. Objektmigration bedeutet die dynamische Lokationsänderung einzelner Objekte während der Laufzeit. Dadurch können Überlastungen einzelner Rechnerknoten durch die Verlagerung rechenintensiver Objekte auf weniger ausgelastete Rechner behoben werden.

3.1 Das CAPO-System

Die Lösung eines entkoppelbaren Problems läßt sich im wesentlichen in einen problemzergliedernden und einen ergebniszusammenfügenden Bereich aufteilen. Im ersten Bereich wird das Problem mittels des entwickelten Algorithmus in unabhängige Teilprobleme zerlegt. Auf jedes dieser Teilprobleme wird unabhängig voneinander derselbe Algorithmus solange angewendet, bis ein Abbruchkriterium im Algorithmus entscheidet, daß die Teilprobleme nun eine Granularität erreicht haben, wo keine weitere Teilung erforderlich ist und direkt gelöst werden können. Durch die Möglichkeit, eine unabhängige Berechnung der Teilprobleme vorzunehmen, bieten sich derartige Problemstellungen für eine nebenläufige und verteilte Bearbeitung an.

Jedes Teilproblem wird an einen eigenständigen Prozeß vergeben, der die entsprechende Lösung berechnet und das Ergebnis an die Stelle zurück gibt, die seine Berechnung veranlaßt hat. Die so berechneten Teilergebnisse werden dann durch einen „Result-Assembling"-Algorithmus Schritt für Schritt zu einem Gesamtergebnis zusammengefaßt und schließlich ausgegeben.

Der Aufbau des CAPO-Systems

Das CAPO-System besteht aus zwei zentralen Komponenten: der Algorithmenausführungskomponente (ALEX) und der Kommunikationsbasiskomponente (CUBA). Die Algorithmenausführungskomponente beinhaltet den eigentlichen Problemlösungsalgorithmus sowie den Algorithmus, der sich um das Zusammensetzen der einzelnen Teillösungen kümmert und aus diesem Grund als *„Result-Assembling"*-Algorithmus (RA-Algorithmus) bezeichnet wird.

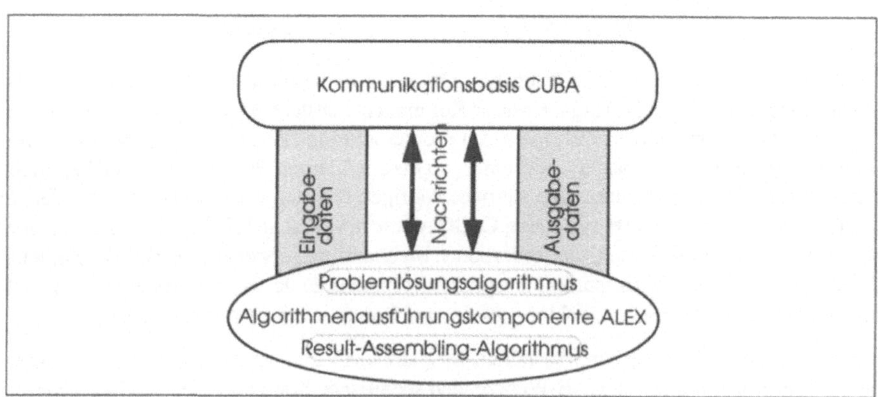

Abbildung 3: Modell des CAPO-Systems

Sämtliche Algorithmenausführungskomponenten werden von den lokalen Kommunikationsbasen verwaltet. Ihnen obliegt die Erzeugung, Initialisierung und Terminierung von jeder ALEX-Komponente, die sich auf dem Rechnerknoten befindet. Dabei ist es von zentraler Bedeutung, daß eine Kommunikationsbasis mehrere ALEX-Komponenten erzeugen und verwalten kann. Jede ALEX-Komponente ist aber nur in der Lage, mit ihrer lokalen Kommunikationsbasis zu kommunizieren.

Die Kommunikationsbasis CUBA übernimmt neben der Erzeugung und Initialisierung der Algorithmenausführungskomponenten auch die Kommunikation zwischen diesen Komponenten, sowohl lokal als auch über Rechnergrenzen hinweg. Darüberhinaus gehört auch die Verteilung von Aufträgen, die momentan aus Kapazitätsgründen nicht bearbeitet werden können, zu ihren Aufgaben. Diese Verteilung erfolgt nach folgendem Algorithmus: Jedes von einer ALEX-Komponente berechnete Teilproblem wird an die lokale CUBA zurückgegeben. Sie entscheidet dann, welche der Teilergebnisse lokal weiterbearbeitet werden können und welche an weniger stark ausgelastete Rechner im Workstationcluster weitergeleitet werden sollen.

Da es für eine deterministische Bearbeitung der Aufgabenstellung wichtig ist, die Teilergebnisse der vergebenen Aufträge kontrolliert an die Auftraggeber zurück zu senden, gehört die Verwaltung der Ergebnisrückgabe ebenfalls zu den Aufgaben einer Kommunikationsbasis.

3.2 Der Aufbau der Kommunikationsbasis CUBA

Um den komplexen Anforderungen, speziell nach einem möglichst hohen Nachrichtendurchsatz, nachkommen zu können, ist eine modulare Architektur entwickelt worden, die aus folgenden Komponenten besteht: Eingangspuffer (*Input-Buffer*), Auftragsbearbeiter (*Dealer*) und dem Verteiler (*Broker*), der wiederum aus dem Auftragspuffer (*Broker-Buffer*) und dem Auftragsverteiler (*Broker-Distributor*) aufgebaut ist.

Der Eingangspuffer dient zur Entkopplung der kommunizierenden Komponenten. Dadurch wird die asynchrone Bearbeitung der synchron eingehenden Nachrichten ermöglicht. Diese Nachrichten werden von der sogenannten *Dealer*-Komponente aus dem Puffer angefordert. Die so gelieferte Nachricht wird hinsichtlich ihrer Art (Auftrag, Systemnachricht oder Ergebnis) analysiert und eine entsprechende Aktion veranlaßt. Mögliche Aktionen, die von der Dealer-Komponente veranlaßt werden können, sind:

- die Erzeugung einer Algorithmenausführungskomponente,

- die Weiterleitung der Nachricht an den lokalen ALEX oder an eine entfernte Kommunikationskomponente.

Diese Weiterleitung der Nachrichten wird von einer weiteren Komponente, dem *Broker*, übernommen. Dieser wiederum besteht ebenfalls aus zwei unabhängigen Komponenten: dem *Broker-Puffer* und dem *Broker-Verteiler*. Der Broker-Puffer (*Broker-Buffer*) bekommt die Nachricht direkt vom Dealer, speichert sie zwischen und reicht sie auf Verlangen an den Broker-Verteiler (*Broker-Distributor*) weiter. Dieser besitzt eine Verbindung zum Empfänger oder baut eine zu diesem auf und entfernt die Nachricht entgültig aus der Kommunikationsbasis.

Jede dieser Komponenten stellt, um eine parallele Ausführung zu erreichen, einen eigenständigen Prozeß dar. Dadurch ist es möglich, sämtliche Komponenten zeitgleich auf einem Rechnerknoten ablaufen zu lassen. Dadurch werden die einzelnen Aufgaben nicht nur entkoppelt, sondern darüberhinaus optimiert. Die folgende Abbildung 8 stellt den Aufbau einer Kommunikationsbasis schematisch dar. Sie zeigt exemplarisch, wie unterschiedliche Nachrichten über das Netzwerk zur Kommunikationsbasis gesendet werden und wie für Aufträge entsprechende ALEX-Objekte erzeugt werden.

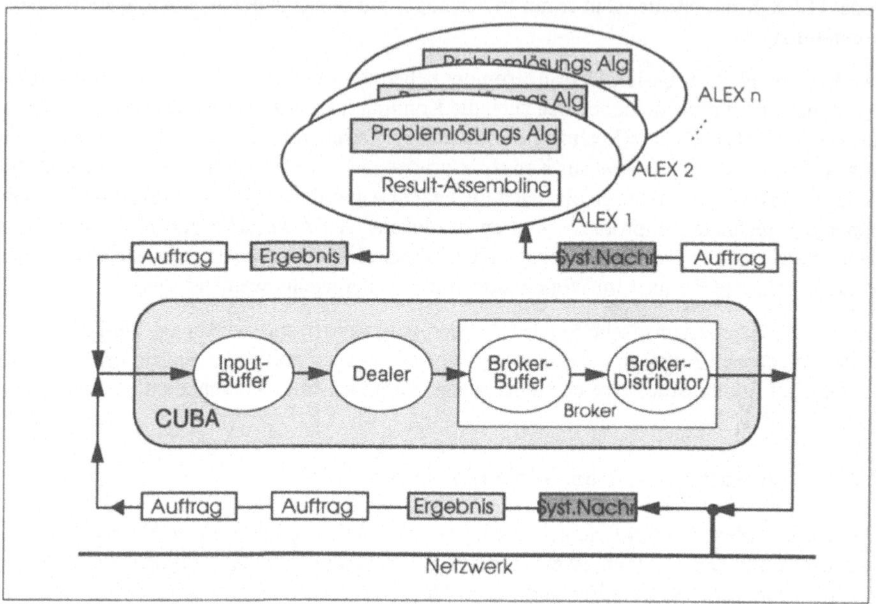

Abbildung 4: Modell der Kommunikationsbasis CUBA

3.3 Implementierung

Die gesamte Implementierung basiert auf der rein objektorientierten Sprache Eiffel [Meye 92], die mit Hilfe von speziell entwickelten Bibliotheken um nebenläufige und verteilte Mechanismen erweitert wurde. Als Entwicklungsumgebung wurde die Eiffel-3 Entwicklungsumgebung von der Firma Interactive Software Engineering Inc. (ISE) verwendet, die neben den grundlegenden Compiler- und Debugger-Werkzeugen auch umfangreiche Klassenbibliotheken bereitstellt.

Da die Entwicklungsumgebung der Firma ISE sowohl auf unterschiedlichen UNIX-Systemen als auch auf Personal Computern zur Verfügung steht, und gleichzeitig eine sehr leistungsfähige Programmiersprache bereitstellt, fiel die Entscheidung zugunsten der Sprache ISE-Eiffel-3 aus. Es ist jedoch darauf geachtet worden, die Konzepte weitgehend sprachunabhängig zu entwerfen, so daß eine einfache Portierung in andere Sprachen (speziell in C++) sehr leicht möglich ist. Für die Implementierung des CAPO-Systems und der Beispielanwendungen wurden folgende Bibliotheken verwendet: EiffelBase, EiffelVision und EiffelNet EiffelBase stellt elementare Klassen für alle gängigen Datenstrukturen und den Zugriff auf Betriebssystemfunktionen zur Verfügung. EiffelVision stellt Klassen für die Erstellung von graphischen Benutzeroberflächen bereit. EiffelNet stellt Klassen für die Erstellung von Client/Server-Anwendungen bereit.

Um Objekte mit ihren unterschiedlichen Beziehungen und Abhängigkeiten über Sockets übertragen zu können, müssen sie in eine lineare Struktur transformiert werden. Dazu wird die in der Eiffel-Bibliothek bereitgestellte Klasse STORABLE verwendet, die Objekte in eine externe

Datei vom Typ UNIX_FILE schreibt. Da Sockets vom UNIX-Betriebssystem genau wie Dateien behandelt werden, kann durch den technischen Trick, Sockets als Unterklassen von UNIX_FILE zu implementieren, erreicht werden, daß die Methoden (*features*) der Klasse STORABLE die Daten nicht in eine Datei sondern direkt an die jeweiligen Sockets übertragen.

Um das Laufzeitverhalten des CAPO-Systems verstehen zu können, wird die Arbeitsweise der spezifizierten Komponenten des CAPO-Systems anhand eines fiktiven Beispiels aufgezeigt. Anschließend wird dann das Laufzeitverhalten des entwickelten Systems anhand konkreter Beispiele analysiert und eine Bewertung der Ergebnisse durchgeführt.

3.3.1 Das Nachrichtenaufkommen im CAPO-System

Um die komplexen Abläufe und vor allem den Nachrichtenverkehr zwischen den einzelnen Komponenten erläutern zu können, soll die Bearbeitung eines Problems *P* betrachtet werden, das in zwei Teilprobleme *P1* und *P2* aufgeteilt werden kann. Die entstandenen Teilprobleme lassen sich unmittelbar lösen, so daß keine weitere Zerlegung mehr erforderlich ist und direkt mit der Ergebniszusammenführung begonnen werden kann.

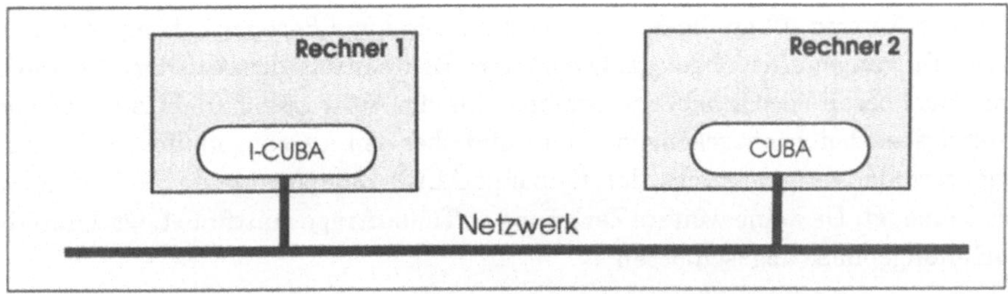

Abbildung 5: Startkonfiguration des CAPO-Systems

Abbildung 7-8 zeigt die zur Lösung des fiktiven Problems eingesetzte Rechnerkonfiguration bestehend aus zwei Arbeitsplatzrechnern. Auf *Rechner 1* ist die initiale Kommunikationsbasis (I-CUBA) installiert, die für die Bearbeitung des Ausgangsproblems (*P*) vorbereitet wurde und für die Initiierung der gesamten weiteren Bearbeitung verantwortlich ist. Auf *Rechner 2* ist ebenfalls eine Kommunikationsbasis installiert. Die Rechner sind über ein Netzwerk verbunden, so daß die Kommunikationsbasen in der Lage sind, Nachrichten auszutauschen.

Um die Vorgänge bei der Bearbeitung eines Problems graphisch zu veranschaulichen, wurde ein Ablauf-Zeit-Diagramm erstellt, welches in Abbildung 6 dargestellt ist. In dieser Abbildung sind die Komponenten der beiden Kommunikationsbasen und die zu erzeugenden ALEX-Komponenten in Form von Linien dargestellt. Jede Linie symbolisiert einen eigenständigen Prozeß, der mit den anderen Prozessen Nachrichten austauschen kann. Das dargestellte Ablauf-Zeit-Diagramm macht deutlich, daß die Hauptaktivität der Kommunikationsbasen beim Auftragsbearbeiter und beim Auftragsverteiler liegt, während die Eingangs- und Ausgangspuffer ein weitgehend passives Verhalten zeigen. Auftragsbearbeiter und

Auftragsverteiler prüfen in regelmäßigen Zeitabständen, ob im Eingangs- bzw. Ausgangspuffer Nachrichten eingegangen sind. Ist dies der Fall, werden die Nachrichten gelesen, analysiert und weiterverarbeitet.

Die Bearbeitung des Beispielproblems beginnt im Auftragsverteiler der initialen Kommunikationsbasis *I-CUBA*. Dieser Prozeß erzeugt eine erste ALEX-Komponente *ALEX 1*, die für die Bearbeitung des Gesamtproblems P zuständig ist. Im Verlauf der Bearbeitung wird das Gesamtproblem P zunächst in zwei Teilprobleme *P1* und *P2* zerlegt. Um die Bearbeitung dieser Teilprobleme zu veranlassen, werden zwei Auftragsnachrichten *A1* und *A2* erzeugt, und an den Eingangspuffer der initialen Kommunikationsbasis gesendet.

In der nächsten Aktivitätsphase des Auftragsbearbeiters wird die Auftragsnachricht *A1* gelesen und über den Ausgangspuffer an den Auftragsverteiler weitergeleitet. Da es sich um den ersten Auftrag handelt, erzeugt der Auftragsverteiler die lokale ALEX-Komponente *ALEX 2*. In der darauffolgenden Aktivitätsphase des Auftragsbearbeiters wird die Auftragsnachricht *A2* entgegengenommen und ebenfalls über den Ausgangspuffer an den Auftragsverteiler weitergeleitet. Da dieser zweite Auftrag nicht ebenfalls auf dem lokalen Rechner bearbeitet werden soll, wird der Auftrag *A2* an die Kommunikationsbasis von *Rechner 2* delegiert und in deren Eingangspuffer abgelegt. Die weitere Bearbeitung des Auftrags *A2* erfolgt nach dem bereits beschriebenen Schema, d.h. die Auftragsnachricht *A2* wird vom Auftragsbearbeiter entgegengenommen und über den Ausgangspuffer an den Auftragsverteiler weitergereicht, der dann eine ALEX-Komponente *ALEX 3* auf *Rechner 2* erzeugt. Da keine weitere Zerlegung in Teilaufträge stattfindet, ist damit die Verteilungsphase abgeschlossen.

Die beiden erzeugten ALEX-Komponenten *ALEX 2* und *ALEX 3* berechnen nun die Lösung der ihnen zugeordneten Teilprobleme. Nachdem die Komponente *ALEX 2* ihr Ergebnis *E1* berechnet hat, sendet sie dieses in Form einer Ergebnisnachricht an den Eingangspuffer der initialen Kommunikationsbasis. Danach terminiert diese ALEX-Komponente. Die Ergebnisnachricht wird vom Auftragsbearbeiter entgegengenommen, als Teilergebnis erkannt und über den Ausgangspuffer und den Auftragsverteiler an die übergeordnete ALEX-Komponente *ALEX 1* zur Ergebniszusammenführung weitergeleitet.

Auch die Komponente *ALEX 3* beendet ihre Berechnung mit der Erzeugung einer Ergebnisnachricht. Diese Nachricht *E2* wird jedoch nicht direkt an die initiale Kommunikationsbasis gesendet, sondern zunächst im Eingangspuffer der lokalen Kommunikationsbasis von *Rechner 2* abgelegt. Sie wird dann vom Auftragsbearbeiter entgegengenommen, als Ergebnisnachricht erkannt und danach über den Ausgangspuffer an den Auftragsverteiler weitergegeben. Dieser leitet die Nachricht dann an die initiale Kommunikationsbasis weiter. Die initiale Kommunikationsbasis bearbeitet diese Ergebnisnachricht analog zur Ergebnisnachricht *E1*.

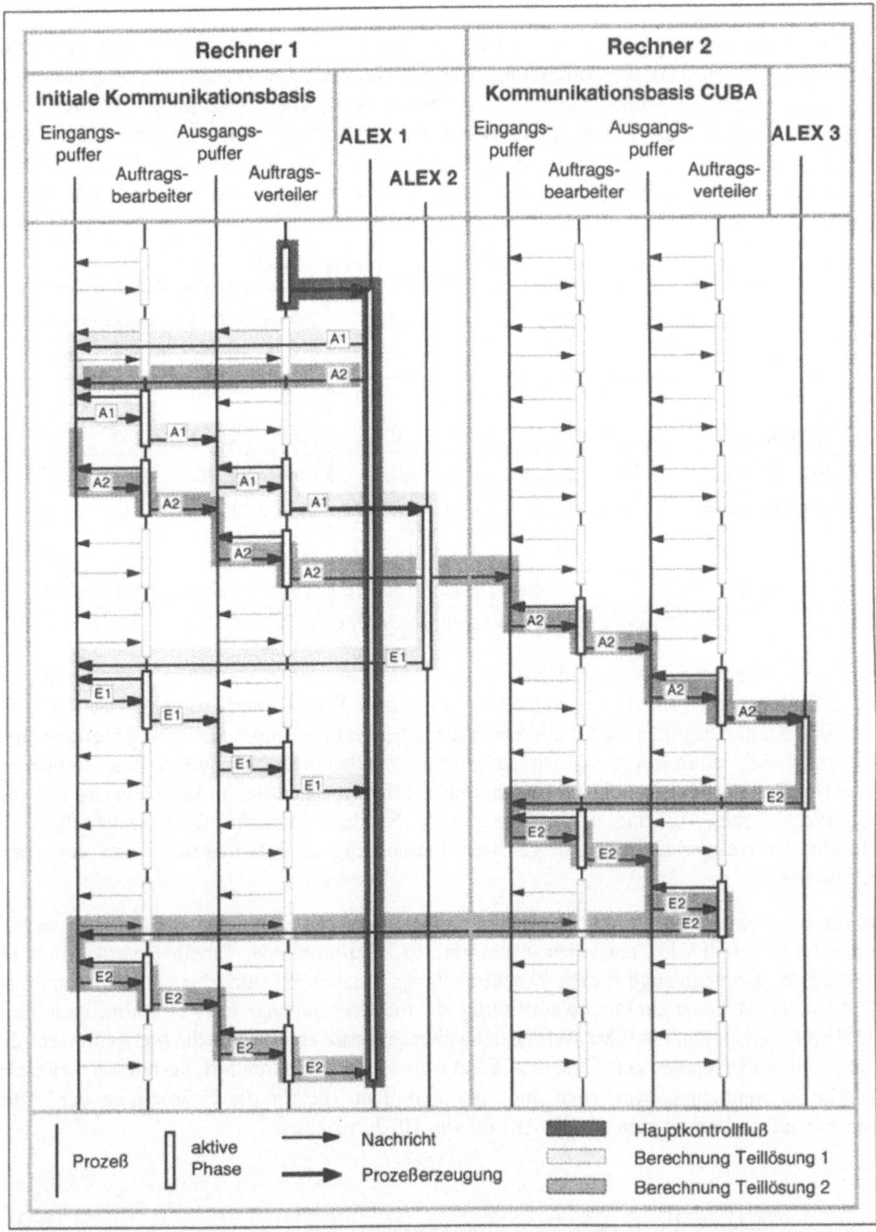

Abbildung 6: Nachrichtenaufkommen im CAPO-System

Sobald auch das zweite ausstehende Teilergebnis bei der für das Gesamtproblem zuständigen Komponente *ALEX 1* eingegangen ist, werden die beiden Teilergebnisse zu einem Gesamtergebnis verknüpft. Damit ist die gesamte Berechnung abgeschlossen und die Komponente *ALEX 1* terminiert.

4 Laufzeitanalyse

Neben der Bestimmung von einzelnen Laufzeitfaktoren – auf die hier aus Platzgründen nicht näher eingegangen wird, wurden Messungen an konkreten CAE-Verfahren vorgenommen. Im folgenden werden die Meßergebnisse für das bereits besprochene Floorplan-Verfahren vorgestellt. Das Verfahren wurde sowohl prozedural als auch objektorientiert auf einem SUN-Workstationcluster implementiert, um so die notwendigen vergleichswerte für die verteilte Implementierung zu besitzen. Die nachfolgende Tabelle faßt die ermittelten Ergebnisse zusammen:

| MinCut-Verfahren | Sequentielle Implementierung | | | | Nebenläufige Implementierung | | | |
| Programmiersprache | C (s) | | Eiffel (s) | | Eiffel und CAPO-System (s) (SLC) | | | |
Hardware	SLC	SS 10	SLC	SS 10	2 WS	4 WS	6 WS	8 WS
① 10 Knoten	0,005	0,001	0,006	0,001	0,101	0,388	0,581	0,772
② 100 Knoten	0,17	0,02	0,19	0,028	0,292	0,483	0,675	0,867
③ 1000 Knoten	1,6	0,38	1,66	0,42	1,699	1,882	2,071	2,256
④ 10.000 Knoten	28,5	4,32	28,3	4,29	16,24	12,73	17,98	31,88
⑤ 100.000 Knoten	255,2	87,41	259,8	83,42	191,6	169,56	221,34	260,21
⑥ 1000.000 Knoten	3011,1	648,2	3138,7	762,65	1234,1	1190,7	1475,9	3244,9

Tabelle 1: Laufzeitmessungen des MinCut-Verfahrens

Aus Laufzeitwerten geht hervor, daß die Kurven der Probleme ①, ② und ③ aufgrund ihrer geringen Problemgröße einen negativen *Speedup* besitzen. Erst ab einer Problemgröße von ungefähr 1000 Knoten beginnen sich die Vorteile der nebenläufigen Implementierung abzuzeichnen. Der erreichte Speedup von etwa 2,5 ist für ein entkoppelbares Problem, wie das hier implementierte MinCut-Verfahren, nicht sehr hoch und rechtfertigt eigentlich in keiner Weise den programmtechnischen Aufwand, der betrieben wurde. Für das Verständnis der Ursachen für dieses schlechte Laufzeitverhalten ist eine genauere Betrachtung der Arbeitsweise dieses Verfahrens erforderlich.

Für die Bearbeitung einer Knotenmenge mit beispielsweise 1024 Knoten, die schlimmstenfalls immer binär geteilt wird, entstehen insgesamt 1023 Teilprobleme. Tabelle 2 verdeutlicht am Beispiel der Knotenmenge diesen Zusammenhang. Ausgehend von einer Knotenmenge mit 1024 Knoten ist zuerst ein Prozeß notwendig, der die Knotenmenge in zwei Teilmengen mit je 512 Knoten aufspaltet. Für diese werden dann zwei Prozesse erzeugt, die die Menge in vier Teilmenge mit je 256 Knoten aufteilen, usw. Setzt man dieses Verfahren fort, bis nur noch zweielementige Knotenmengen vorliegen und summiert dann die für die Bearbeitung benötigten Prozesse auf, so kommt man auf die Anzahl von 1023 Prozessen.

Knotenmenge	1024	512	256	128	64	32	16	8	4	2	
Teilprobleme	1	2	4	8	16	32	64	128	256	512	Σ 1023

Tabelle 2: Anzahl der Teilprobleme bei binärer Spaltung

Für die Bearbeitung dieser Teilprobleme (*TP*) sind neben den Kosten für die Partionierung der Graphen auch die Kosten für die Initialisierung der Prozesse und die Übertragung der benötigten Daten zu berücksichtigen.

Anzahl der Teilprobleme:

$$TP = \sum_{i=1}^{n} 2^i = 2^{n+1} - 1 \qquad \text{wobei n = Anzahl der Knoten}$$

Kosten für Partionierung:

$$MC(k) = (k\log k) \times c \qquad \text{wobei } (\textit{klog k}) \text{ die Komplexität des Verwendeten Verfahrens ist}$$

Kosten   für   Prozesserzeu-

$$T_{Init}(k) = EP + D(k) \qquad \text{EP= Kosten für die Erzeugung eines Betriebssystemprozesses}$$

$$D(k) = \text{Kosten für das Kopieren des}$$

Kosten für sequentielles Floorplanning:

$$FP_{Seq}(n) = \sum_{i=0}^{ldn} 2^i MC\left(\frac{n}{2^i}\right) \qquad \left(\frac{n}{2^i}\right) \text{ Anzahl der verbleibenden zu partitionierenden Elemente der Knoten-}$$

Kosten für nebenläufiges Floorplanning:

$$FP_{Neben}(n) = \frac{\sum_{i=0}^{ldn} 2^i \left[MC\left(\frac{n}{2^i}\right) + T_{Init}\left(\frac{n}{2^i}\right) \right]}{|Prozessoren|}$$

Das Laufzeitverhalten der nebenläufigen Lösung wird stark beeinflußt durch die Kosten für die Prozesserzeugung. Selbst unter der Voraussetzung, daß für jede Teiberechnung ein eigener Prozessor zur Verfügung steht, ergibt sich aus den oben angegebenen Gleichungen, daß sich eine nebenläufige Berechnung genau dann lohnt, wenn die Prozeßerzeugungskosten deutlich geringer sind als die Kosten für eine sequentielle Berechnung. Dieser Zusammenhang läßt sich näherungsweise über folgende Gleichungen beschreiben:

$$MC\left(\frac{n}{2^i}\right) + T_{Init}\left(\frac{n}{2^i}\right) \ll 2^i \cdot MC\left(\frac{n}{2^i}\right)$$

$$T_{Init}\left(\frac{n}{2^i}\right) \ll 2^i - 1\, MC\left(\frac{n}{2^i}\right)$$

Daraus ergibt sich, daß sich der Einsatz eines nebenläufigen Verfahrens nur lohnt, wenn die Knotenmenge ausreichend groß ist. Für die Implementierung nebenläufiger Verfahren bedeutet dies, daß es nur sinnvoll ist, bis zu einer bestimmten Schranke *S* nebenläufig zu rechnen. Sobald sich die Problemgröße unter diese Schranke bewegt, ist eine sequentielle Bearbeitung wesentlich günstiger. Diese Schranke ist von unterschiedlichen Faktoren wie beispielsweise von der Art des zu lösenden Problems, der Geschwindigkeit der verwendeten Hardware oder der Implementierungssprache abhängig. Damit muß diese Schranke für jedes Verfahren individuell über die oben spezifizierten mathematischen Beziehungen bestimmt werden. Bei dem hier untersuchten MinCut-Verfahren liegt dieses Schranke bei etwa 1000 Knoten.

Aufgrund dieser Erkenntnis wurde das MinCut-Verfahren entsprechend modifiziert, so daß ab 1000 Knoten die entstehenden Teilprobleme nicht mehr nebenläufig, sondern sequentiell bearbeitet werden. Die dabei gemessenen Laufzeitverbesserungen sind in Abbildung 11 dargestellt.

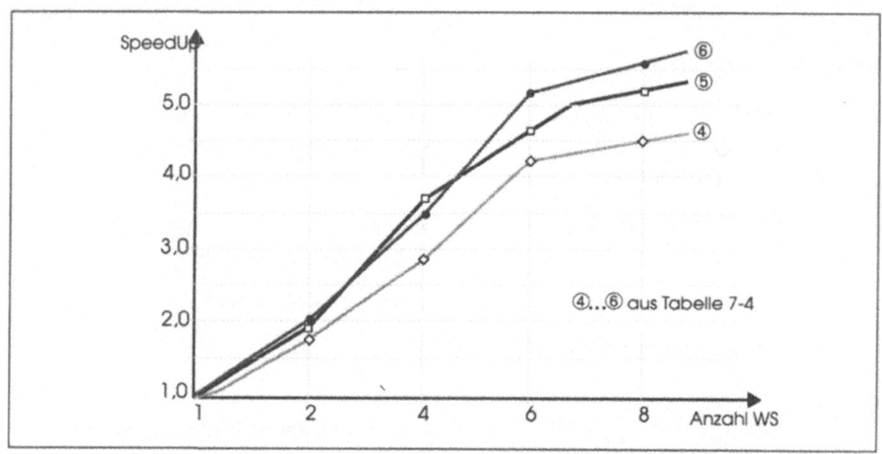

Abbildung 7: Laufzeitdiagramm des modifizierten MinCut-Verfahrens

Man erkennt hier ein deutlich verbessertes Laufzeitverhalten aller Meßreihen, die eine Problemgröße über 1000 Knoten besitzen. Im Gegensatz zu der nicht modifizierten Meßreihe, bricht hier der Speedup nicht so schnell zusammen, sondern beginnt ab etwa 6 Prozessoren langsam abzuflachen. Die so erreichte Optimierung könnte durch die Verwendung von leichtgewichtigen Prozessen bei der Implementierung der einzelnen Mechanismen noch weiter verbessert werden.

5   Zusammenfassung

Die vorgestellte Entwurfsumgebung ermöglicht die Entwicklung nebenläufiger und verteilter CAE-Anwendungen auf der Basis eines Workstationclusters. Als Implementierungssprache wurde Eiffel 3.2 verwendet. Eiffel bietet sich aufgrund der Tatsache an, daß es sich um eine rein objektorientierte Sprache handelt, die sehr mächtige Konstrukte zur Unterstützung von Softwareengineeringtechniken bereitstellt. Leider war es bisher nicht möglich, die vorgestellten Mechanismen auf der Basis leichtgewichtiger Prozesse zu implementieren. An einer derartigen Erweiterung wird derzeit intensiv gearbeitet. Die Erfahrungen mit Eiffel waren sehr gut. Studenten die keinerlei Erfahrungen in OOP hatten, konnten in ca. 2 Wochen erste eigene Programme entwickeln und nach ca. 6 Wochen beherrschten sie die Sprache soweit, um auch komplexere Problemstellungen lösen zu können. Die Integration verschiedener Programmteile, die bei einem größeren Projekt zwangsläufig auftreten konnten mit sehr geringem Aufwand realisiert werden. Was die Laufzeit der implementierten Anwendungen angeht, besteht allerdings noch ein Optimierungsbedarf.

Die vorgestellte Entwicklungsumgebung wird derzeit hinsichtlich zusätzlicher Mechanismen (z.B. Migrationssteuerung) erweitert und zur Implementierung nebenläufiger objektorientierter CAE-Werkzeuge eingesetzt. Mit Hilfe dieser Implementierungen sollen ausführlichere Laufzeituntersuchungen durchgeführt werden, die Aufschluß über die möglichen Optimierungspotentiale geben sollen. Desweiteren wird daran gearbeitet, die vorhandenen Mechanismen auch auf gekoppelte Problemstellunge anzuwenden, um dadurch die nebenläufige Zusammenarbeit verschiedener Dienste zu ermöglichen.

6   Literatur

[Agha 90]   G. Agha: *Concurrent Object-Oriented Programming*; Communications of the ACM September 1990

[BuLu 92]   R. Butler, E. Lusk: *User´s Guide to the P4 Parallel Programming System*; Argonne National Laboratory 1992

[Caro 93]   D. Caromel: *Toward a Methodic Approach of Object-Oriented Programming*; Communications of the ACM, Sept. 1993, S.90-99

[CBHS 93]   V. Cahill, S. Baker, C. Horn, G. Starovic: *Amadeus Project – Generic Runtime Support for Distributed Persistent Programming*; OOPSLA´93 Conference Proceedings 1993, S.144-161

[GHK 95]   H. Gall, M. Hauswirth, R. Klösch: *Objektorientierte Konzepte in Smalltalk, C++, Objective-C, Eiffel und Modula-3*; Informatik Spektrum 18, S. 195-202, Springer Verlag 1995

[KaLe 89]   D. Kafura, K. Lee: *Inheritance in Actor Based Concurrent Object-Oriented Programming Languages*; Proceedings ECOOP 1989, Cambridge University Press 1989

[KaBr 93]   M. Karaorman, J. Bruno: *Introducing Concurrency to a Sequential Language*; Communications of the ACM, Sept. 1993, S. 103-116

[Leng 90]   T. Lengauer: *Combinatorial Algorithms for Integrated Circuit Layout*; Teubner Verlag 1990

[Lewi 94]   T. Lewis: *Foundations of Parallel Programming – A Machine-Independent Approach*; IEEE Computer Press 1994

[Meye 90]   B. Meyer: *Objektorientierte Softwareentwicklung*; Hanser Verlag 1990

[MGH 93]   M. Mühlhäuser, W. Gerteis, L. Heuser: *DOCASE: A Methodic Approach to Distributed Programming*; Communication of the ACM, September 1993 Vol. 36, S. 127-138

[MüSch 92]   M. Mühlhäuser, A. Schill: *Software Engineering für verteilte Anwendungen*; Springer 1992

[NTMS 91]   O. Nierstrasz, D. Tsichritzis, V. Mey, M. Stadelmann: *Object + Scripts = Applications*; Proceedings, Esprit Conference, Kluwer Academic Publishers 1991

[Schi 91]   A. Schill: *Verteilte objektorientierte Systeme – Grundlagen und Erweiterungen*; Informatik Forschung und Entwicklung Ausgabe 6/1991, S. 14-27

[StScGi 95]   G. Stellner, M. Schumann, M. Gringhuber: *Vergleich von Programmbibliotheken mit der Analyseumgebung SPY*; Informationstechnik & Technische Informatik 37, Oldenbourg Verlag 1995

[SUN 85]   SUN Microsystems: *Remote Procedure Call Spezification*; SUN Microsystems Inc. 1985

[TrAk 88]   A. Tripathi, M. Aksit: *Communication, Scheduling and Resource Mangement in SINA*; Journal of Object-Oriented Programming, Nov./Dez. 1988 S. 24-36

[Veit 52]   E. Veitch: *A Chart Method for Simplifying Boolean Functions*; Proceedings of the ACM, S. 127-133, Vol. 5, Mai 1952

[YBS 86]   A. Yonezawa, J. Briot, E. Shibayama: *Object-Oriented Concurrent Programming in ABCL/1*; ACM OOPSLA 1986 , Orlando Florida S. 406-415

Evaluation of Multicast Methods to Maintain a Global Name Space for Transparent Process Migration in Workstation Clusters

Stefan Petri, Bettina Schnor, Matthias Becker, Bernd Hinrichs, Titus Tscharntke, Horst Langendörfer

Institut für Betriebssysteme und Rechnerverbund, TU Braunschweig,
Bültenweg 74/75, D-38106 Braunschweig, Germany
`petri@ibr.cs.tu-bs.de`

Abstract. In this paper we examine the performance and fault tolerance of different multicast based methods for maintaining the consistence of distributed data, depending on the network topology and packet loss probability. We present a system model and analytical results. This work is motivated by experiences with our process migration system ᴨBEAM. There we use a global virtual name space to achieve location transparency for process migration and checkpointing / rollback for distributed applications on clusters of Unix workstations. First measurements have shown that the maintenance of this global name space is critical for the performance of the entire system.

1   Introduction and Motivation

Clusters of Workstations are widely in use to provide interactive working facilities for the users. They have also become popular for parallel computing because of their price / performance ratio, and because typical installations exhibit low average CPU utilization and many idle times [4, 10].

However, compared to "real" parallel computers, workstation cluster computing has to consider additional problems. The machines are heterogeneous, users are running their applications independently, interactive users must not be obstructed, and the failure rate of nodes and networks is higher.

While there exist a number of tools to implement parallel applications on workstation clusters, load balancing and failure transparency still are challenging problems and an area of many current research activities.

All previously known work in this area puts strict limitations on the supported applications. Our ᴨBEAM system overcomes some important of these limitations.

We use process migration and checkpointing to achieve transparent load balancing and fault tolerance for distributed applications on clusters of Unix workstations. By migration, the process is moved in space, whereas by rollback it is (also) moved in time.

We are currently developing the ᴨBEAM system that

- offers high transparency, not only for file operations but also for IPC, signals and timers (so that distributed applications can be supported),

- runs in user space on off-the-shelf Unix systems, without kernel modifications,
- is portable to a wide range of platforms,
- supports consistent global checkpoints,
- and offers good performance.

We have implemented two methods to synchronize the distributed parts of the ϕBEAM system, to practically test their stability and performance in case of faulty networks, and we now examine some more, because this component has shown to be important for the performance of the entire ϕBEAM.

In the next sections we first give an overview of the system, in which we also briefly discuss related work, and present some measured performance figures. After that, we describe the alternative multicast methods for distributed name space synchronization that we are considering. We define a model for the network topology and failure rate, and present analytical results. We conclude with a description of our current and future work.

2 Overview of the ϕBEAM System

For both migration and checkpointing/rollback, we need to save the state of an application process, transfer the saved state information, and to create a new process from it. The application must not get aware of the moving in space (by migration) or in time (by rollback).

The previously known work in this area can be divided into kernel level systems (e.g. [8, 2, 12, 13]), user space systems (e.g. [10, 5, 20, 18], and application level systems (coded into each application individually). We have discussed the advantages and disadvantages of these three categories before [16, 17].

We have decided to built our migration system in user space, independent of the applications. In contrast to other systems, we can handle not only single processes without communication (e.g. Condor [11], `libckpt` [18]), and we do not require the applications to be based on a special message passing library (e.g. CoCheck [20], MPVM [5]).

We distinguish between the *internal* state of an application process (address space, registers), and the *external state*, its relation to the outside world (open files, parent and child processes, communication end points (sockets)). A process manipulates its external state through system services that are invoked with system calls. Most cited systems achieve location transparency by forwarding the system call parameters to the original (home) node of a process, where the system service is executed, and sending back the results. To avoid this dependency on the home node, and also to be able to handle global consistent checkpoints for groups of communicating processes, we use a different approach.

We have built a system wide virtual name space for process IDs (a global process table), transport addresses and file names [16]. We interpose the application's system calls and translate the parameters from the virtual into the underlying real Unix name spaces before really invoking the kernel services. Similarly, the return values are translated back into the virtual name space. This method does not only work for operations on regular files, but also for inter process communication (IPC). This interposition also enables us to trace the external state, so that we are able to reconstruct it at restart time, after migration or rollback.

The global process table contains the mapping between virtual process identifiers and the corresponding current real process location and identifier. Similarly, the global address table provides the information, which transport addresses are in use, by which process, and what are the currently corresponding real addresses. We have already described this global name space in more detail [16, 17].

Mobile IP (e.g. [15]) can provide location transparency for migrating an entire machine, but it does not work for migration of processes between machines.

Our +PBEAM system consists of (figure 1):

- a freeze/restart mechanism for single processes,
- a modified system library for the system call interposition,
- a **process-** and **port-number** information service (PPNIS) that maintains the virtual name space,
- a Resource Monitor and a Load Manager that collect information about resource usage and processor load of the participating processes and hosts, and make them available for the scheduler,
- a scheduler that evaluates the resource statistics, and takes the decisions about checkpointing and migration,
- and a dispatcher that executes the decisions that the scheduler has made.

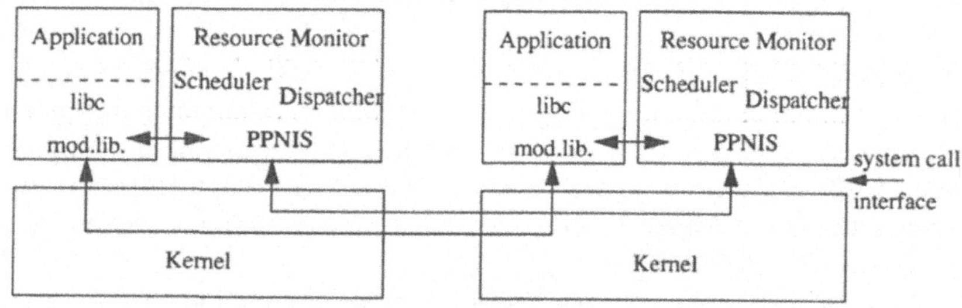

Fig. 1. +PBEAM System Components

2.1 Name Space Maintenance

One problem in maintaining the replicated global name space is to synchronize changes on all existing copies. We have implemented two versions of the name space. The first uses a simple master-slave method. Since we expect the master to become a performance and fault tolerance bottleneck in large system configurations, we also implemented a fully distributed version, using a majority consensus algorithm [9, 21].

In the master-slave version, the slaves only store information about the processes that are currently assigned to them, while the master maintains the global process and address tables. The master also is responsible to make decisions like generate unique process ids for new processes.

In the majority consensus version, the global process and address tables are stored on each node. The global tables contain only the information, which node this process or virtual address is currently assigned to. Generating new table entries requires a voting for write access. Lookup requests are forwarded to the host who is given as current "owner" of the process or address in the global table. If the supposed owner does not have that information, the host that generated the request obviously has an old version of the global tables, and voting for read access is done to get the most up-to-date versions [22].

3   First Results: Measured Performance Figures

In this section we show measured performance data for only one simple benchmark program that exercises the maintenance of the virtual transport address tables. We have presented some more performance data for other components of +PBEAM before [16, 17].

The measurements for all following figures were done at night time on an idle but not dedicated cluster of 35 SUN workstations, connected by a 10 MB/sec Ethernet. All figures show the average from five runs. Unless noted otherwise, the deviations in all cases were below 10 percent.

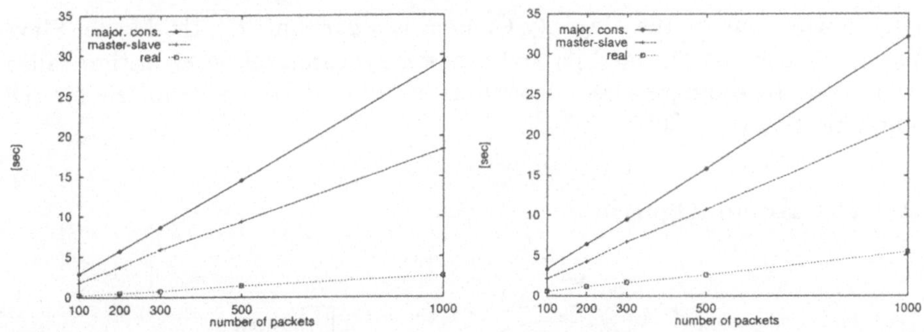

Fig. 2. Times for exchanging messages of 50 bytes (left) and 1000 bytes (right) with the master-slave and the majority consensus implementations of +PBEAM.

Figures 2 shows the execution times of a Pingpong-Benchmark which sends a number of messages forth and back between two hosts. This is not the expected typical distributed application, but a good example program to test the overhead for interposing the communication. The messages are sent by UDP between two SUN IPCs over a 10 MB Ethernet. The execution times are shown for small packets of 50 bytes (left) and larger ones of 1000 bytes (right). The results with the two synchronization methods ("maj. cons." and "master-slave") are compared with the runtime in the Unix name space ("real").

The figure shows that the majority consensus approach buys the added fault tolerance with a notably increased overhead.

During the measurements we also noted that a slow or overloaded node for the master server slows down the entire system. On the other hand, the majority consensus algorithm also is significantly harder to implement and debug.

The comparison of the left and right side of figure 2 shows that the dependency of the HBEAM-imposed overhead on the message size is neglectable.

Experiences with more realistic applications

The above figures might give the impression that we do not meet our stated goal of good performance. However, this pingpong program does not by far resemble the behavior of real world applications. We have used the NAS parallel benchmarks [1, 23] to test the overall behavior of the HBEAM system [17]. For these applications, we have measured the run time overhead imposed by HBEAM to be 10-20%. While doing the NAS benchmark runs, we have also found several approaches to further accelerate our current implementations, but the name space synchronization still remains a performance-critical component. Thus we started to investigate, which synchronization method is suited for which system configurations.

4 Comparison and evaluation of algorithms for synchronous and reliable delivery of multicasts

Now we will compare the Majority Consensus algorithm [21], the Master-Slave approach, Token on Demand [6] and a newer synchronization algorithm called Totem [14]. To compare these algorithms, we have developed a metric for the communication costs [3].

4.1 The Totem Algorithm

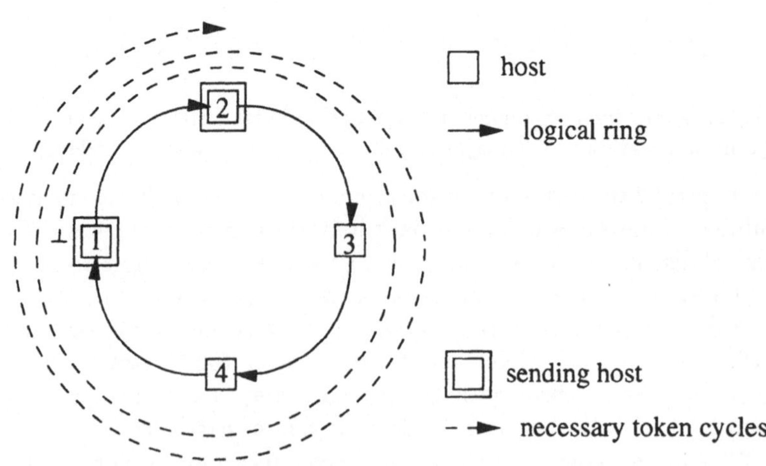

Fig. 3. The Totem Ring

In contrast to the other algorithms, Totem does not use explicit replies to acknowledge a message. All hosts involved in the Totem machine are organized in a virtual ring. A single token circulates along this ring. Only the host that "owns" the token is allowed to send a multicast and increase the message-id in the token. When a host receives the token, it can check if all of the messages were received. If not, the host puts its name into a list of hosts which have not received a certain message. The sender of the message can now repeat it when the token passes it the next time. Assuming the best case, the token needs to circle around only once to acknowledge the message for all involved hosts.

4.2   Network Model and Communication Costs

There are two main aspects of communication costs when comparing those algorithms. One is that synchronization and reliable delivery cause a certain network traffic and the second is that this needs a certain amount of time. These costs are not necessarily equivalent because in a network topology with different subnets it is possible to send two or more messages in the same period of time. For practical reasons, the time needed for reliable and ordered delivery of a multicast is more relevant than the network traffic.

To compare the algorithms we make some assumptions concerning the topologies on which the system works. First, there is the LAN, where the hosts are linked by e.g. Ethernet. We define the cost for a message between two hosts to be 1. Multicasts are supposed to be sent using either the IP multicast [7] or the built-in broadcast mechanism and also cost 1. Due to transmission errors, a multicast will not reach all of the potential receivers. The percentage of hosts who are not assumed to receive the multicast is expressed by the variable e. The same percentage of replies sent will not reach the sender. The sender of the multicast uses single messages to re-send the data to the hosts who have not yet received the multicast. There will be no error when doing this. The costs in time units are proportional to the costs in network traffic because there are no parallel messages possible in a single LAN.

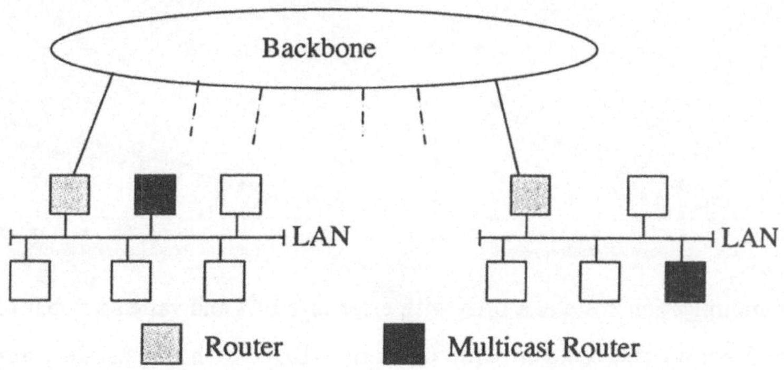

Fig. 4. A Multi-LAN: Backbone with subnets.

When using a Multi-LAN-topology (e.g. a backbone with attached subnets) we have to decide whether a message is sent from one host to another in the same or a different subnet. We distinguish between *external* and *internal* messages. To a different subnet, the message has to be routed through the router of the sending subnet over a backbone passing the router to the destination subnet and finally reaches the destination host. So the message does three hops to its destination. The multicast may need even more hops, we assumed five. The algorithms using explicit replies use a kind of hierarchical reply mechanism. We assume a reply-server in each subnet that collects the replies from all hosts in the subnet and send one reply back to the sender. If one host did not get the multicast, the reply-server is responsible to recover this.

The resulting equations are quite complex, so we give a simple example how we calculate the time costs in a LAN using the Totem algorithm (see equation 1). There are n hosts involved and s concurrent senders. U_i represents the costs of an internal message, and M the costs of a multicast. Passing the token to the next host causes costs of two internal messages $2U_i$. Assuming that the multicast is not perfect, the token has to circle around two times from each sender's point of view before the multicast is reliably delivered to all hosts. The token has to pass $2n + (s - 1)$ hosts. There will be $\frac{e}{100}(n - 1)$ hosts that will not receive the multicast.

$$c_{Totem}(n, s, e) = 2U_i\Big(2n + (s - 1)\Big) + s\Big(M + U_i\frac{e}{100}(n - 1)\Big) \qquad (1)$$

4.3 Analytical Results

The figures below show the communication costs in units of time. The costs in hops are different from these, but the relations between the two kinds of costs is almost constant. The left side of each plot shows the case that all hosts want to send a message at the same time, the right side shows the same scenario but with only one sending host.

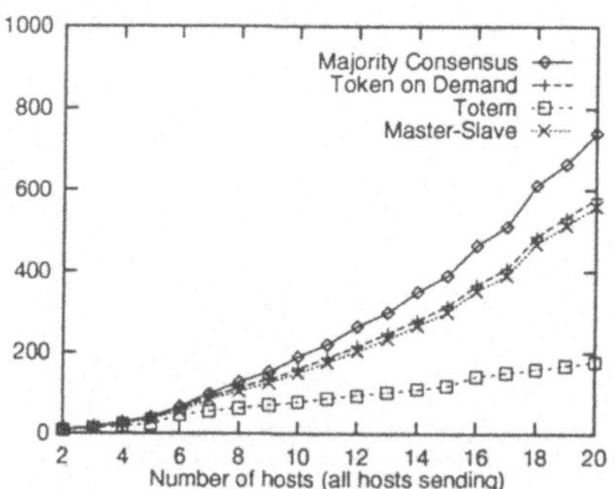

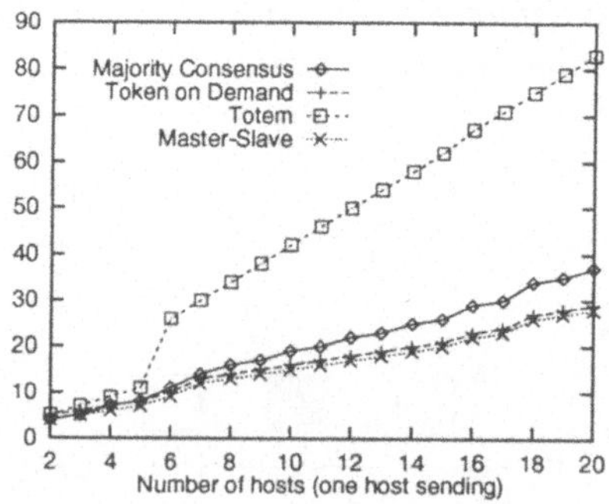

Fig. 5. Communication costs in a LAN with error rate 10% and varied number of hosts.

Figure 5 shows the costs in time units in a LAN with one sender, and with the number of senders equal to the number of hosts in the LAN. The classical algorithms keep the same relation in both cases, in contrast to Totem which causes low costs when there are many senders (in relation to the other algorithms) and high cost when there are few senders and many hosts. The reason is the virtual ring of Totem. The token has to circle around twice if at least one host did not get the multicast. This becomes clear when looking at the right plot: We calculated with rounded errors, so that with an error rate of 10% and five hosts exactly 0.5 (rounded up to 1.0) hosts do not receive the multicast. In this case the token needs a second turn and the costs increase.

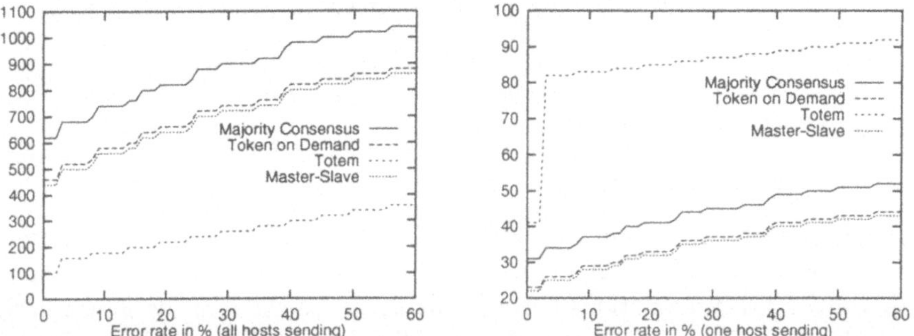

Fig. 6. Communication costs in a LAN with 20 hosts and varied error rate.

The advantage of Totem becomes clear in figure 6, where we see almost the same configuration as in figure 5. We assumed 20 hosts in the LAN. With increasing error rates, the algorithms cause more costs but Totem's costs increase only linear. With only one sender in a LAN (right side) Totem needs much more time than the other algorithms. The reason is the overhead caused by the token that needs up to two cycles to guarantee reliable delivery.

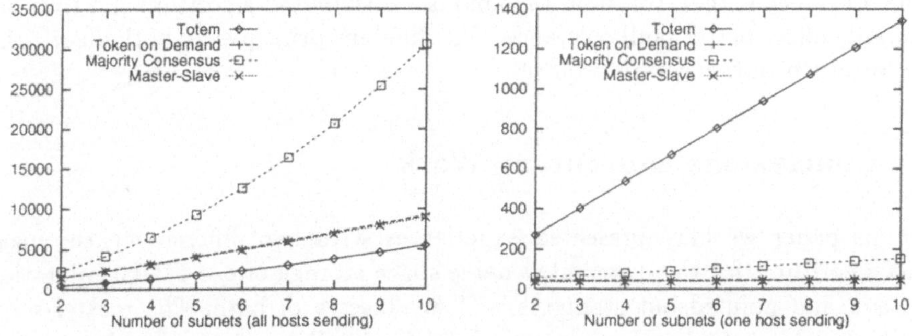

Fig. 7. Communication costs in a Multi-LAN with error rate 10% and varied number of subnets.

In figure 7 we see the costs in units of time in a Multi-LAN with 20 hosts in each subnet, and one sender in the left plot, and with each host sending in the right plot. The relations between the curves are nearly the same as in figure 5.

The right plot in figure 8 shows the costs in time units assuming six subnets in the Multi-LAN, with 20 hosts in each subnet. For the left side plot, each of these 120 hosts wishes to send a multicast. Totem causes less costs than the other algorithms if the error rate is below 35%. Above this limit, the algorithms using hierarchical reply mechanisms cause less costs than Totem because of the fact that we assumed the reply-servers are responsible for reliable message delivery

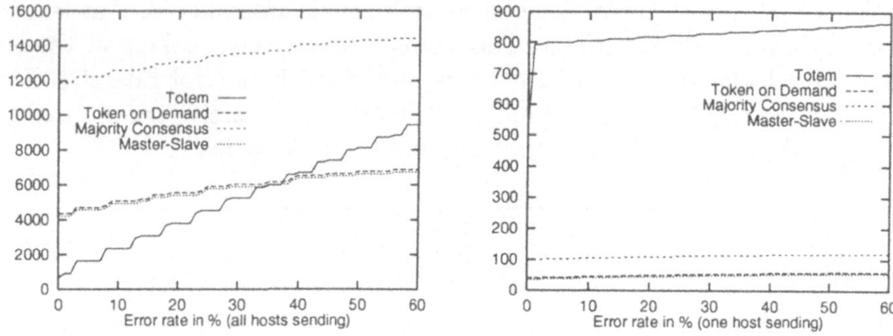

Fig. 8. Communication costs in a Multi-LAN with 6 subnets.

in their subnets. In Totem, the sender of a multicast is responsible for reliable delivery to all other hosts in the whole Multi-LAN. Assuming only one sender in the Multi-LAN, the relations between the costs are the same as shown in figure 6, with the difference that the costs for Token on Demand, Master-Slave and Majority Consensus are nearly constant because of hierarchical replies.

In conclusion we can state that when assuming a normally operating network with error rates below 30%, Totem has advantages when there are many hosts sending multicasts. The reason is that Totem does not use explicit replies. On the other hand, the virtual ring of hosts has to be cycled by the token even if there is only one sender. This causes an overhead that is bigger than the costs caused by explicit replies.

In all cases, Master-Slave causes nearly the same costs as Token on Demand. The difference is that Token on Demand is a distributed algorithm and thus potentially offers better fault tolerance. The different principles in both algorithms are regarded in this comparison.

5   Conclusions and Future Work

In this paper we have presented experiences with two different synchronization algorithms for the distributed name space storage of our +Beam migration system, and pointed out strengths and weaknesses of both. The master-slave method yields better performance, at least for smaller systems, and has proved to be much simpler to implement and easier to debug than the fully distributed algorithms.

For further investigation of the synchronization efficiency, we have defined a cost metric and a network model for distributed synchronization using multicasts, and have analytically compared the costs of several multicast algorithms under various number of hosts and various error rates. The comparison shows the performance advantages of the Totem algorithm depending on the operating conditions.

We are currently implementing the mentioned multicast algorithms to do practical tests with up to 200 workstations on the network of our university and verify our analytical results. One important point of interest is to find out, at which system size the master in the centralized approach really becomes the bottleneck.

We use ⊬PBEAM as experimentation platform to extend our ongoing research activities about scheduling in "configurational heterogeneous" workstation environments [19].

References

Our WWW page `http://www.cs.tu-bs.de/ibr/projects/load/` contains links to online available documents, and more information about our research activities.

1. D. Bailey, E. Barszcz, J. Barton, D. Browning, R. Carter, L. Dagum, R. Fatoohi, S. Fineberg, P. Frederickson, T. Lasinski, R. Schreiber, H. Simon, V. Venkatakrishnan, and S. Weeratunga. The NAS Parallel Benchmarks. Report RNR-94-007, Department of Mathematics and Computer Science, Emory University, March 1994.
2. Amnon Barak, Shai Guday, and Richard G. Wheeler. *The MOSIX Distributed Operating System*, volume 672 of *LNCS*. Springer Verlag, 1993.
3. Matthias Becker. Leistungsbewertung von Multicast Synchronisationsverfahren. Master's thesis, TU Braunschweig, 1996. In preparation.
4. Clemens H. Cap. Workstation Cluster Computing aus der Sicht des Anwenders. *PIK – Praxis der Informationsverarbeitung und Kommunikation*, 17(4):230–237, October 1994.
5. Jeremy Casas, Dan L. Clark, Ravi Konuru, Steve W. Otto, Robert M. Prouty, and Jonathan Walpole. MPVM: A migration transparent version of PVM. *Computing Systems*, 8(2):171–216, 1995.
6. K. Mani Chandy. A mutual exclusion algorithm for distributed systems. Technical report, University of Texas, 1982.
7. S. Deering. Host Extensions for IP Multicasting. RFC 1112, Stanford University, August 1989.
8. Fred Douglis and John Ousterhout. Transparent Process Migration: Design Alternatives and the Sprite Implementation. *Software – Practice and Experience*, 21(8):757–785, August 1991.
9. H. Langendörfer and B. Schnor. *Verteilte Systeme*. Hanser Verlag, München, 1994.
10. Michael J. Litzkow, Miron Livny, and Matt W. Mutka. Condor – A Hunter of Idle Workstations. In *Proceedings of the 8th International Conference on Distributed Computer Systems*, pages 104–111. IEEE, June 1988.
11. Michael J. Litzkow and Marvin Solomon. Supporting Checkpointing and Process Migration Outside the UNIX Kernel. In *Usenix Conference Proceedings*, pages 283–290, San Francisco, CA, January 1992.
12. Thomas Ludwig. *Automatische Lastverteilung für Parallelrechner*. Reihe Informatik. BI-Wissenschaftsverlag, 1993.
13. Dejan S. Milojičić. *Load Distribution – Implementation for the Mach Microkernel*. Vieweg Verlag, Braunschweig, 1994.
14. L.E. Moser, P.M. Melliar-Smith, D.A. Agarwal, R.K. Budhia, and C.A. Lingley-Papadopoulos. Totem: A fault-tolerant multicast group communication system. *Communications of the ACM*, 39(4):54–63, April 1996.

15. C. Perkins. IP Encapsulation within IP. Internet draft (work in progress), Mobile IP Working Group of the Internet Engineering Task Force (IETF) / IBM, May 1996. draft-ietf-mobileip-ip4inip4-03.txt.

16. S. Petri and H. Langendörfer. Load Balancing and Fault Tolerance in Workstation Clusters – Migrating Groups of Communicating Processes. *Operating Systems Review*, 29(4):25–36, October 1995.

17. S. Petri, B. Schnor, H. Langendörfer, and J. Steinborn. Consistent Global Checkpoints for Distributed Applications on Clusters of Unix Workstations. In H.G. Matthies and J. Schüle, editors, *Paralleles und verteiltes Rechnen – Beiträge zum 4. Workshop über wissenschaftliches Rechnen*, pages 77–86, Aachen, October 1996. TU Braunschweig, Shaker.

18. James S. Plank, Micah Beck, Gerry Kingsley, and Kai Li. Libckpt: Transparent Checkpointing under Unix. In *Usenix Conference Proceedings*. USENIX, January 1995.

19. B. Schnor, S. Petri, R. Oleyniczak, and H. Langendörfer. Scheduling of Parallel Applications on Heterogeneous Workstation Clusters. Will appear in proceedings of *PDCS'96 – Ninth International Conference on Parallel and Distributed Computing Systems*, September 1996.

20. Georg Stellner. Resource Management and Checkpointing for PVM. In *Proceedings of the Second European PVM User Group Meeting*, Lyon, 1995.

21. R.H. Thomas. A Majority Consensus Approach to Concurrency Control for Multiple Copy Databases. *ACM Transactions on Database Systems*, 4(2):180–209, 1979.

22. Bernd Hinrichs und Titus Tscharntke. Aufbau eines echt verteilten Namensraumservices für die transparente Prozeßmigration zwischen Workstations. Studienarbeit, August 1996.

23. S. White, A. Ålund, and V.S. Sunderam. Performance of the NAS Parallel Benchmarks on PVM Based Networks. Report RNR-94-008, Department of Mathematics and Computer Science, Emory University, May 1994.

Session 6:

Middleware: CORBA

Einbeziehung von Nutzerinteressen bei der QoS-basierten Dienstvermittlung unter CORBA

Peter Reichl, Claudia Linnhoff-Popien, Dirk Thißen

Lehrstuhl für Informatik IV, RWTH Aachen
Ahornstraße 55, 52056 Aachen
Tel.: ++49 241 8021411; Fax: ++49 241 8888220
Email: {reichl | popien}@i4.informatik.rwth-aachen.de
thissen@zeus.informatik.rwth-aachen.de

Abstract

Der wachsende Einsatz objektorientierter Technologien in immer komplexer werdenden Informationssystemen führte dazu, innerhalb der CORBA-Architektur einen Basisdienst zur Vermittlung von Diensten zu integrieren. Dieser sogenannte Trading Service ist durch Arbeiten im Bereich des Open Distributed Processing vorbereitet und bereits in verschiedenen Formen implementiert worden. Der vorliegende Artikel erweitert das Konzept des Standards, einen Dienst genau dann einem Nutzer anzubieten, wenn dessen Spezifikation exakt mit einem Dienstangebot übereinstimmt. Die Einbeziehung von Gewichtungen, mit denen ein Nutzer QoS-Attribute präferieren kann, erlaubt eine neue Qualität der Dienstvermittlung. Das Konzept der QoS- und QoSP-Funktionen wird vorgestellt und seine Implementierung erläutert. Der erweiterte Trader ist etwas langsamer als seine klassische Vorgängerversion, verfügt jedoch über eine für den Anwender ausgesprochen nützliche zusätzliche Funktionalität, die den zeitlichen Mehraufwand vertretbar erscheinen läßt.

Keywords: Verteilte Systeme, CORBA, Orbix, Trading Service, QoS, Entscheidungstheorie

1   Einführung

Dem zunehmenden Aufwand für die Entwicklung immer komplexer werdender verteilter Informationssysteme läßt sich am ehesten durch die Wiederverwendung bereits existierender Komponenten begegnen. Objektorientierte Technologien haben sich in diesem Zusammenhang als gut geeignet erwiesen und kommen daher mehr und mehr zum Einsatz. Insbesondere die Verwendung von Middleware erlaubt dabei, die Heterogenität von bestehenden Rechnern unterschiedlicher Hersteller zu überbrücken und sie in ein gemeinsames Rechnernetz zu integrieren.. Ein solcher Ansatz besitzt verschiedene Vorteile. Zum einen brauchen die Anwender ihre gewohnte und bereits installierte Umgebung nicht aufzugeben, zum anderen wird durch den Zugriff auf die neu involvierten Komponenten eine Vielzahl neuer Dienste angeboten.

Dem Problem der Entwicklung von Objekttechnologien widmet sich in besonderer Weise die 1989 gegründete Object Management Group (OMG). Sie versucht, innerhalb ihrer laufenden Standardisierungsarbeiten Aspekte wie die Wiederverwendung von Softwarekomponenten, Interoperabilität und Portabilität sowie die Integration bereits kommerziell verfügbarer Hard- und Software zu ermöglichen. Zu diesem Zweck werden seitens der OMG einheitliche abstrakte

Schnittstellen und Protokolle entwickelt. Dieses Konzept der Erstellung und Veröffentlichung copyrightfreier objektorientierter Standards stieß weltweit auf eine solche Akzeptanz, daß die OMG im Mai 1996 bereits 640 Mitglieder zählte.

Der Object Request Broker (ORB) bildet das Kernstück der Common Object Request Broker Architecture (CORBA) [CORBA, PSW96]. Er steht mit drei Klassen von Diensten in Verbindung. Zunächst gibt es Basisdienste, die sogenannten CORBAservices, welche unabhängig von bestimmten Anwendungen im CORBA-Standard spezifiziert sind und jedem Entwickler zur Verfügung stehen. Die Common Facilities sind anwendungsorientiert zum Beispiel auf bestimmte wirtschaftliche Gebiete wie etwa das Finanzwesen zugeschnitten, jedoch nicht unbedingt zur Erstellung notwendig. Die dritte Klasse von Diensten bilden schließlich die Applikationsdienste, welche als Clients und Server vom Entwickler programmiert und vom Anwender direkt angesprochen werden.

Innerhalb des vorliegenden Artikels soll einer der Basisdienste näher betrachtet werden, und zwar der CORBA Trading Service. Der Trading Service besitzt in einem komplexen Verteilten System die Aufgabe, Dienste zu vermitteln [Po95, RTL96]. Parallel zu den Aktivitäten der OMG hat sich bereits seit längerer Zeit die Standardisierungsgruppe des Open Distributed Processing (ODP) mit der Spezifikation dieses Dienstes auseinandergesetzt, so daß auf ein breites Wissen zurückgegriffen werden kann.

Im folgenden wird von einem unter dem CORBA-Produkt Orbix implementierten Trading Service ausgegangen [ORBIX]. Der an der RWTH Aachen entwickelte CORBA-Trader [MZP96] bietet im wesentlichen die vom CORBAservice für das Trading geforderte Funktionalität. Bei der Vermittlung kann jedoch nur dann ein Dienst angeboten werden, wenn er genau mit den vom Kunden angeforderten Charakteristiken übereinstimmt. Diese Einschränkung wird durch das hier vorgestellte Konzept aufgehoben, indem die Berücksichtigung von Nutzerinteressen ermöglicht wird. Hierzu geht man neben dem Diensttyp von Quality of Service (QoS)-Attributen aus, welche Leistungsmerkmale angebotener Dienste beschreiben [QoS95]. Der Kunde des Systems erhält dann die Möglichkeit, quantitativ anzugeben, welche QoS-Attribute er wie präferieren möchte. Daraufhin wird ihm der am besten geeignete Dienst empfohlen, bevor er selbst entscheiden kann, ob er diesen in Anspruch nehmen will oder nicht.

Die vorliegende Arbeit ist wie folgt gegliedert: Im nächsten Abschnitt wird auf die grundlegenden Konzepte des unter Orbix implementierten Traders eingegangen, während das dritte Kapitel ein Konzept zur Berücksichtigung von Nutzerinteressen für die Entscheidung des Traders skizziert. Der vierte Abschnitt gibt dann einen Überblick über die Modellierung der Entscheidungskomponente. Schließlich wird im fünften Kapitel auf die Implementierung dieser Ansätze eingegangen, bevor einige Meßergebnisse vorgestellt werden.

2 Trading im Kontext von CORBA

Der von der OMG vorgeschlagene Tradingservice ist von der OMG im Sommer 1995 übernommen und als OMG-Dokument verabschiedet worden [OMG 95]. In unserem Zusammenhang soll zunächst untersucht werden, wie sich der Trading Service in die CORBA-Architektur einordnet. Dazu ist die CORBA zugrundeliegende Architektur in Abbildung 1 dargestellt. Clients und Server ordnen sich in der Klasse der Application Objects ein. Die Serverobjekte exportieren dabei ihre Objektreferenz und geben zur Beschreibung der Semantik ihres Dienstes den Diensttyp und zugehörige Dienstattribute an, welche die Qualität des Dienstes im Sinne eines QoS-Merkmals beschreiben. Sucht ein Kunde nach einem Dienst bzw. benötigt ein Objekt eine entsprechende Referenz zur Laufzeit des Systems, so vermittelt der Trading Service die Objektreferenz, und der als geeignet ausgewählte Dienst wird dynamisch gebunden.

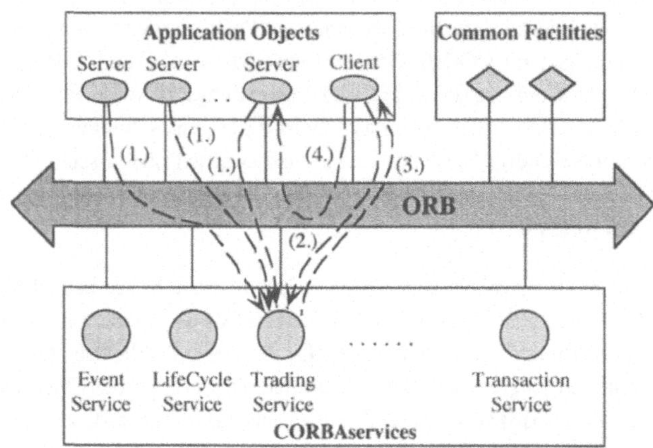

Abb. 1: Das Prinzip des Tradings in einer CORBA-Umgebung

Liegen Client- und Serverobjekte auf heterogenen verteilten Rechnern vor, so wird die Funktionalität des ORBs ausgenutzt. Er ermöglicht die Interoperabilität zwischen den verschiedenen Objekten. Dieses Prinzip des Tradings ist bereits seit einigen Jahren bekannt [SPM94]. Es beruht darauf, daß der dienstsuchende Kunde den benötigten Dienst exakt spezifiziert, indem er die gewünschten Eigenschaften des Dienstes genau beschreibt. Die Struktur des Dienstes läßt sich dadurch charakterisieren, daß zu einem Diensttyp verschiedene Dienstangebote existieren können. Diese Dienstangebote sind die konkrete Beschreibung der innerhalb des CORBA-Systems von den Objekten angebotenen Funktionalitäten.

Dienstangebote werden durch Eigenschaften oder Attribute charakterisiert. Eine Eigenschaft kann auf ein (Name, Typ, Wert)-Tripel zurückgeführt werden, wobei der Name der Eigenschaft in der Regel als bekannt vorausgesetzt wird. Dienste können nach verschiedenen Kriterien strukturiert und nach dem ODP-Konzept durch Föderationen bestehender Traderdienste in einem erweiterten Kontext angeboten werden. Wichtig ist dabei lediglich, daß im Service Directory, auf das die Trading-Funktion zugreift, Dienste vorhanden sind, welche die Anforderungen des Kunden erfüllen. Dazu muß der geforderte mit einem vorhandenen Diensttyp übereinstimmen und die Menge der spezifizierten QoS-Eigenschaften die Restriktionen der Anfrage erfüllen, wie Abbildung 2 verdeutlicht.

Die Importanfrage eines Traders kann prinzipiell auf zwei verschiedene Weisen formuliert werden. Eine Variante ist das sogenannte Search, das Suchen nach allen Dienstangeboten, die eine gegebene Spezifikation erfüllen. Die zweite Alternative ist das sogenannte Select, die Auswahl maximal eines Dienstes. Letzteres wird durch eine Superlativfunktion realisiert, welche – bezogen auf eine der QoS-Eigenschaften – einen maximalen oder minimalen Wert aussucht. Ferner ist es möglich, aus einer Menge von mehreren in Frage kommenden Dienstangeboten das erste,

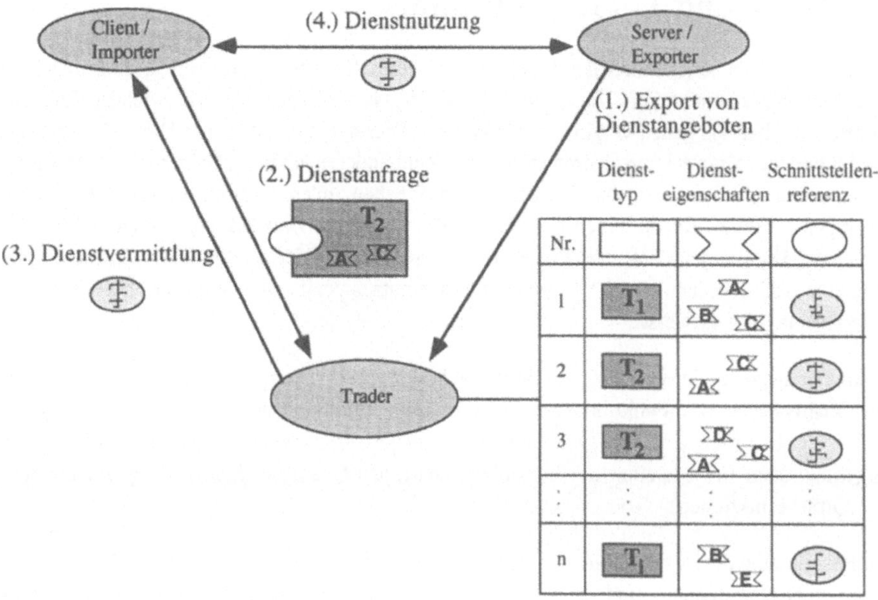

Abb. 2: Schnittstellenreferenzen angebotener und nachgefragter Dienste

letzte oder auch ein zufälliges Angebot auszuwählen. Bei dieser Realisierung der Dienstvermittlung werden jedoch alle Dienstangebote, die die Nutzeranforderungen erfüllen, als gleichwertig angesehen. Dies schränkt den Nutzer in seiner Dienstauswahl insofern ein, als er keine Möglichkeit hat, bestimmte Präferenzen zu setzen.

An dieser Stelle soll im folgenden angesetzt werden. Die im Standard spezifizierte Trading-Funktion wird erweitert, um dem Nutzer mehr Möglichkeiten für die Dienstsuche oder Dienstauswahl zur Verfügung zu stellen. Übernommen wird diese Funktionalität durch die im folgenden definierte Quality-of-*Service*-Funktion, die die numerische Bewertung eines Dienstangebots in Abhängigkeit von den Interessen des Nutzers erlaubt. Diese Funktion läßt sich zusammensetzen aus sogenannten Quality-of-*Service-Property*-Funktionen, deren jede die Charakterisierung einer einzelnen Diensteigenschaft des entsprechenden Dienstes hinsichtlich der Nutzerpräferenzen ermöglicht.

In der Literatur liegen bereits erste Ansätze vor, wie die im ursprünglichen Tradingkonzept vorgesehene exakte Übereinstimmung der Anfrage- mit den Angebotsattributen umgangen werden kann. In [Th96, TP96] wird ein geeigneter Abstand zwischen Dienstanfrage und -angeboten definiert, wobei dann das Angebot ausgewählt wird, dessen Abstand zur Anfrage am kleinsten ist. Der hier vorgestellte Ansatz bezieht zusätzlich die Präferenzen des Nutzers ein und stützt sich hierbei auf Konzepte der präskriptiven Entscheidungstheorie, die ursprünglich aus den Wirtschaftswissenschaften kommt (s. [KR76], [EW93]). Dabei wird vorausgesetzt, daß die in einem Dienstangebot spezifizierten Attribute im Falle einer Annahme auch tatsächlich eingehalten werden, während in [MLB93] mit der sogenannten Agency Theory eine Idee skizziert wird, wie man diesbezügliche "Unsicherheiten" modellieren könnte.

3   QoS- und QoSP-Funktionen

Nutzerpräferenzen hinsichtlich der Eigenschaften eines Dienstes lassen sich grundsätzlich in zwei Richtungen unterteilen. Zum einen kann der Nutzer festlegen, wie wichtig ihm eine Diensteigenschaft als ganze verglichen mit anderen Diensteigenschaften ist. Dadurch wird eine Gewichtung der Diensteigenschaften eingeführt. Zum anderen kann der Nutzer aber auch Präferenzen in Bezug auf jede einzelne Diensteigenschaft haben, indem bestimmte Ausprägungen des jeweiligen Attributes für ihn einen bestimmten Wert besitzen. Dies läßt sich durch eine für die betrachtete Diensteigenschaft spezifische Funktion charakterisieren, die jeder Attributausprägung eine Zahl zwischen 0 und 1 zuordnet, um den nutzerspezifischen Wert auszudrücken, den diese Ausprägung aufweist.

Abstrakter ausgedrückt wird also zur Berücksichtigung der Nutzerpräferenzen für jeden Dienst eine Quality-of-Service-Funktion (QoS-Funktion) eingeführt, anhand derer jedes Dienstangebot vom Trader bewertet wird. Die QoS-Funktion eines Dienstes setzt sich zusammen aus Bewertungsfunktionen für jede einzelne Diensteigenschaft, den Quality-of-Service-Property-Funktionen (QoSP-Funktionen).

Die Bestimmung dieser Funktionen erfolgt durch den importierenden Nutzer im Dialog mit einer Assessment-Komponente, und zwar bevor eine Dienstanfrage an den Trader gestellt werden kann. Die Anfrage beinhaltet dann neben den üblichen Einträgen zu jeder angefragten Diensteigenschaft d die entsprechende QoSP-Funktion P_d sowie ein Gewicht w_d. Aus diesen Angaben kann der Trader dann in einer neuen Evaluatorkomponente die verschiedenen ihm vorliegenden Dienstangebote nutzerspezifisch bewerten. Abbildung 3 verdeutlicht (im Schritt 2a) das Vorschalten der Assessment-Komponente vor die eigentliche Anfrage und die hieraus resultierende Bewertung der einzelnen Dienstangebote durch die Evaluator-Komponente des erweiterten Traders.

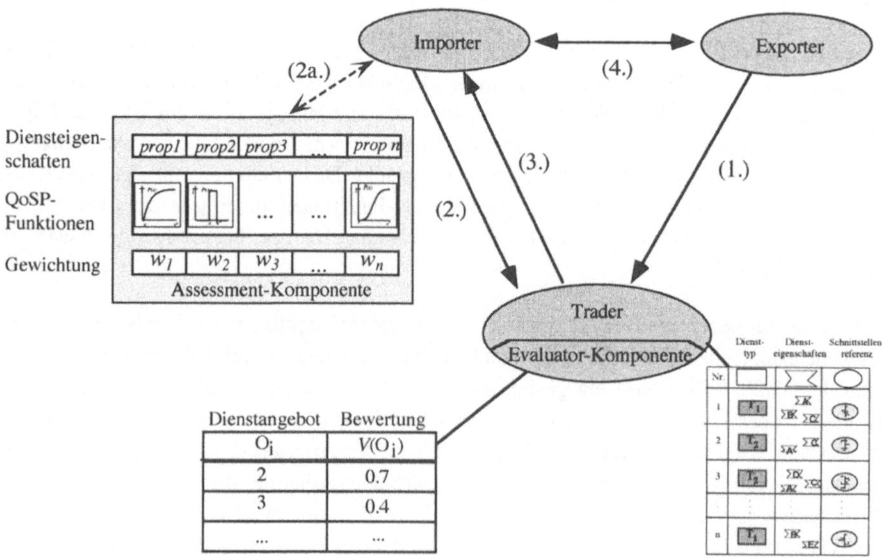

Abb. 3: Assessment-Komponente und Evaluator-Komponente

Dabei ist zwischen zwei verschiedenen Typen von Diensteigenschaften zu unterscheiden: Zum einen gibt es Attribute, für die der Nutzer genau einen Wert bzw. obere oder untere Schranken angeben kann, die dieses Attribut in jedem Fall einhalten muß. So sind etwa für den Ausdruck eines DIN-A3-Blatts alle Drucker, die lediglich DIN-A4 anbieten können, schlichtweg nutzlos. Solche K.o.-Kriterien lassen sich mit QoSP-Funktionen behandeln, die außerhalb des Zielwertes bzw. der Schranken identisch 0 sind. Man kann sie in der Anfrage aber auch wie bisher z.B. über die "conditional-selection-criteria" der Anfragesprache SRDL (vgl. [PM95]) formulieren. Der zweite Typ von Diensteigenschaften besteht aus den "evaluation-criteria", zwischen denen je nach Interessenlage des Nutzers ein Kompromiß gefunden werden muß.

Damit kann man eine Anfrage mit Hilfe einer erweiterten Version von SRDL folgendermaßen formulieren:

```
"SELECT" <service-type-identifier> "WITH"
"IF SUCCESS"
<conditional-selection-criteria>
"THEN"
<evaluation-criteria>
"ELSE END"


evaluation-criteria ::= <service-property-identifier> "WITH VALUE FUNCTION"
                        <value-vector> "AND WEIGHT" <weight>
                        |<evaluation-criteria> "AND" <evaluation-criteria>


value-vector ::=        <value-point> | <value-vector> "AND" <value-vector>
value-point ::="(" <real-number> "," <real-number> ")"
weight ::=              <real-number>
```

Im folgenden Abschnitt wird nun genauer darauf eingegangen, woher man die zu übergebenden Anfragevariablen value-vector und weight erhält.

4 Modellierung von Nutzerinteressen

Um eine Entscheidung zwischen verschiedenen Dienstangeboten treffen zu können, werden diese mit Hilfe der QoS-Funktion bewertet; die Entscheidung fällt dann auf das Angebot mit der höchsten Bewertung. Die QoS-Funktion hängt dabei von den einzelnen Diensteigenschaften und deren von Nutzer zu Nutzer unterschiedlichen Gewichtung ab. Außerdem ist zu berücksichtigen, daß auch die möglichen Ausprägungen der einzelnen Diensteigenschaften eine nutzerspezifische Bewertung besitzen.

Betrachten wir zur Veranschaulichung einen Dienst vom Typ *Printer*, der z.B. Druckgeschwindigkeit, Auflösung und räumliche Entfernung des Geräts als Diensteigenschaften aufweist. Dann sind Nutzer denkbar, die viel Zeit haben und denen es daher gleichgültig ist, wie schnell ein Druckvorgang erfolgt. Ein solcher Nutzer wird die verschiedenen möglichen Ausprägungen des Attributs Druckgeschwindigkeit gleich hoch bewerten, während ein eiliger Zeitgenosse eine hohe Druckgeschwindigkeit einer niedrigen vorziehen wird. Darüber hinaus wird jeder Nutzer individuelle Vorstellungen haben, wie wichtig ihm die Druckgeschwindigkeit als solche im Vergleich etwa zur räumlichen Entfernung des Gerätes sein wird.

Hieraus ergibt sich ein Vorgehen in zwei Schritten: Zunächst muß der Nutzer für jede relevante Diensteigenschaft d eine QoSP-Funktion P_d angeben. Im zweiten Schritt ist dann noch die Gewichtung der einzelnen QoSP-Funktionen zu ermitteln, mit der sie in die QoS-Funktion V eingehen sollen. Für beide Schritte werden im folgenden einige Verfahren beschrieben.

4.1 Ermittlung einer QoSP-Funktion

Ausprägungen einer Diensteigenschaft lassen sich mit Hilfe geeigneter *Attribute* darstellen. Typische Beispiele hierfür sind etwa die Geschwindigkeit eines Druckers mit dem Attribut "Seiten pro Minute" oder die Kapazität einer Netzverbindung in Mbps. Solche Attribute können grundsätzlich *quantitativ*, d.h. in Form einer ganzen oder reellen Zahl, oder *qualitativ*, d.h. in Form von Noten wie "sehr gut", "ausreichend", "ungenügend" etc., vorliegen.

Betrachten wir zunächst eine Diensteigenschaft, der ein quantitatives Attribut x zugeordnet werden kann. Dann läßt sich i.d.R. eine untere Grenze x^- und eine obere Grenze x^+ angeben, zwischen denen sämtliche möglichen Attributwerte liegen. Der Nutzer wird nun verschiedenen Attributwerten x_i unterschiedliche Bewertungen $P(x_i)$ zukommen lassen. Normiert man den Wertebereich der Funktion P auf das Intervall [0;1], und nehmen wir $P(x^-) = 0$ und $P(x^+) = 1$ an, d.h. x^- wird am niedrigsten und x^+ am höchsten bewertet, so ergibt sich typischerweise ein Kurvenverlauf wie in Abbildung 4a. Gibt der Nutzer eine Schwelle vor, die eine Diensteigenschaft überschreiten muß, so entspricht das einer stufenförmigen Funktion, analog läßt sich die Vorgabe einer unteren <u>und</u> oberen Schranke durch eine Rechteckfunktion darstellen (Abbildung 4b). Der Fall eines vom Nutzer vorgegebenen Zielwertes schließlich läßt sich näherungsweise durch eine Zackenfunktion wie in Abbildung 4c darstellen.

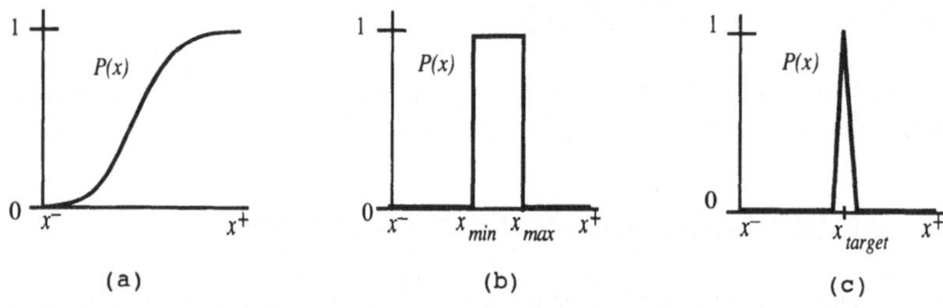

Abb. 4: Mögliche Kurvenverläufe einer QoSP-Funktion

Die Ermittlung von Funktionen zur Bewertung einzelner Diensteigenschaften durch den Nutzer ist zwar zentral für den hier vorgestellten Ansatz, aber dennoch oft nicht ganz einfach. Ein Blick in die einschlägige Literatur zeigt, daß derartige Fragestellungen dort breit diskutiert werden (vgl. [EW93], [KR76]). Wir stellen im folgenden die beiden Verfahren vor, die für unsere Fragestellung am vielversprechendsten erscheinen: das Direct Rating und die Midvalue Splitting Technique, auch unter dem Namen Halbierungsmethode (Bisection Method) bekannt. Die Verwendung des Direct Rating läuft im wesentlichen darauf hinaus, einige ausgesuchte Ausprägungen des Attributs quasi zu "benoten". Bei der Midvalue Splitting Technique hingegen werden die zu einzelnen "Noten" (also den jeweiligen Werten von P) gehörigen Attributausprägungen bestimmt. Damit lassen sich QoSP-Funktionen mit quantitativen wie auch qualitativen Attributen angeben.

Direct Rating

Das Direct Rating (Abbildung 5a) ist eine sehr einfache Methode zur Bestimmung einer Wertfunktion. Man wählt einige typische Ausprägungen x_i, die das entsprechende Attribut annehmen kann, und bewertet sie direkt mit einer Zahl y_i zwischen 0 und 1. Für diese Benotung kann man z.B. das aus der Schule bekannte sechsstufige Notensystem zugrunde legen (mit den Noten "sehr gut" = 1, "gut" = 0.8, "befriedigend" = 0.6, "ausreichend" = 0.4, "mangelhaft" = 0.2 und "ungenügend" = 0). Durch lineare Interpolation der so gewonnenen Stützstellen erhält man eine hinreichend gute Approximation der QoSP-Funktion (Abbildung 5b).

Midvalue Splitting Technique

Dieser Ansatz ist etwas umständlicher, kann aber dafür den Anspruch größerer "Objektivität" erheben. Hierbei werden zunächst $x^0 = x^-$ und $x^1 = x^+$ als die am schlechtesten bzw. am besten bewertete Attributausprägung ermittelt. In einem zweiten Schritt ist der "wertmäßige Mittelpunkt" $x^{0.5}$ des Intervalls $[x^0; x^1]$ anzugeben (s. Abbildung 5c); hierunter versteht man diejenige Attributausprägung, für die der Übergang (x^0 μ $x^{0.5}$) vom Nutzer genauso hoch bewertet wird wie der Übergang ($x^{0.5}$ μ x^1). Setzt man also $P(x^0) = 0$ und $P(x^1) = 1$, so ergibt sich $P(x^{0.5}) = 0.5$. Analog dazu kann man noch $x^{0.25}$ und $x^{0.75}$ ermitteln und die gewonnenen fünf Stützstellen wiederum durch lineare Interpolation zu einer QoSP-Funktion P fortsetzen.

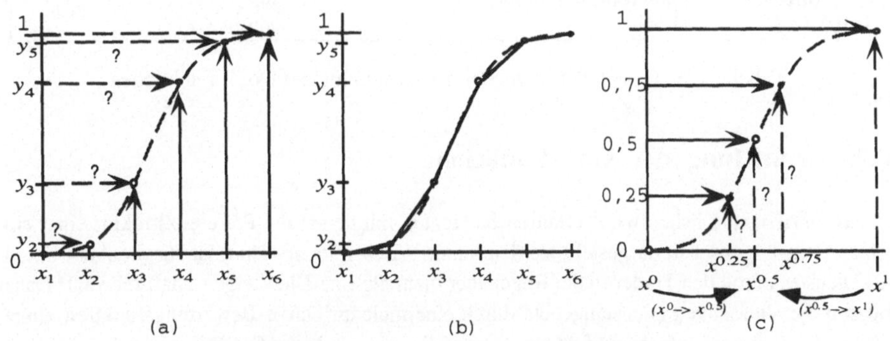

Abb. 5: Techniken zur Ermittlung der QoSP-Funktionen:
(a) Direct Rating (b) Lineare Interpolation (c) Halbierungsmethode

Vergleich der Methoden

Bewertungsfunktionen beruhen immer auf subjektiven Einschätzungen des Nutzers und sind daher nur schwer zu gewinnen. Unter den vielen Ansätzen gehören die beiden dargestellten Methoden zu den am weitesten verbreiteten. Welche der beiden Methoden zu bevorzugen ist, hängt einmal vom individuellen Typ des Nutzers ab. Denkt der Nutzer in erster Linie kostenorientiert, so empfiehlt sich die Halbierungsmethode, da sich hier die unterschiedlichen Bewertungen monetär interpretieren lassen: Ausgehend von Kosten 0 für x^- und 1 für x^+ hat der Nutzer den Wert $x^{0.5}$ anzugeben, bei dem er für den Übergang von x^- nach $x^{0.5}$ ebensoviel Geld investieren würde wie für den Übergang von $x^{0.5}$ nach x^+. Offensichtlich ist diese Methode allerdings nur für den Fall kontinuierlicher Attributausprägungen sinnvoll (im Fall eines Druckers z.B. für Druckgeschwindigkeit oder Entfernung). Sind dagegen Attribute von Natur aus eher diskret (wie beispielsweise Papiergröße bei einem Drucker) bzw. denkt der Nutzer eher qualitativ, so ist das Direct Rating wohl vorzuziehen.

Ferner ist zu bedenken, daß sich das bislang Gesagte nur auf quantitative Attribute bezieht, also Attribute, die in numerischer Form vorliegen. Die Erweiterung auf qualitative Attributausprägungen kann in verschiedener Hinsicht geboten sein. Einmal liegen manche Diensteigenschaften von vornherein in dieser Form vor. Außerdem erlaubt sie eine selbständige Ausweitung und Verbesserung des Dienstangebots im Trader, ohne daß eine Änderung der einmal durch den Nutzer ermittelten QoS-Funktionen notwendig wird. Hat der Nutzer nämlich einmal seine Präferenzen z.B. für die Diensteigenschaft Druckgeschwindigkeit ermittelt und dabei höchsten Wert auf eine schnellstmögliche Abwicklung gelegt, und befindet sich im Angebot des Traders plötzlich ein Drucker, der schneller ist als alle Drucker, die zum Zeitpunkt der Präferenzermittlung in Frage kamen, so wird dieser schnelle Drucker dem Nutzer bei der nächsten Anfrage zur Verfügung gestellt werden, ohne daß dieser erst einmal auf die erfolgte Änderung von x^+ mit der Ermittlung einer neuen QoS-Funktion reagieren müßte. Diesem Vorteil steht natürlich entgegen, daß die Einordnung der Druckgeschwindigkeit in die Notenskala eine reine Angelegenheit des Traders wird, dessen Einschätzung der Nutzer nicht unbedingt immer teilen muß.

Zusammengefaßt lassen sich also die beiden Methoden anhand folgender Tabelle vergleichen:

	Midvalue Splitting Technique	**Direct Rating**
Nutzertyp	quantitativ/kostenorientiert	qualitativ/vergleichend
Attribute	nur kontinuierliche	alle
Aufwand	hoch	gering

Tabelle 1: Vergleich der Methoden zur Ermittlung der QoSP-Funktionen

4.2 Ermittlung der QoS-Funktion

Im letzten Abschnitt haben wir Verfahren betrachtet, mit denen die Präferenzstruktur einer einzelnen Diensteigenschaft dargestellt werden kann. Wie bereits erwähnt, ist für die Auswahl eines Dienstes durch den Trader in der Regel aber mehr als eine Diensteigenschaft relevant. Daher müssen die alternativen Dienstangebote durch eine multiattributive Bewertungsfunktion eingeschätzt werden. Am einfachsten faßt man hierzu die verschiedenen QoSP-Funktionen mittels einer geeigneten Gewichtung zu einer linearen QoS-Funktion zusammen.

Betrachten wir also einen Dienst mit n Diensteigenschaften. Wenn wir zu jeder davon die entsprechende QoSP-Funktion sowie das Gewicht w_d kennen, das die jeweilige Eigenschaft im Vergleich zu den anderen Eigenschaften besitzt, dann ergibt sich die QoS-Funktion V in Abhängigkeit vom i-ten Dienstangebot O_i zu

$$V(O_i) = \sum_{d=1}^{n} w_d \cdot P_d(O_i)$$

Dieser Ansatz hat jedoch zur Voraussetzung, daß die einzelnen Diensteigenschaften sowohl wechselseitig präferenzunabhängig als auch wechselseitig differenzunabhängig sind. Detaillierte Ausführungen zu diesen Unabhängigkeitsbegriffen finden sich z.B. in [EW93]. Man kann aber annehmen, daß diese Voraussetzungen bei geeigneter Spezifikation der Diensttypen hinreichend gut erfüllt sind.

Ermittlung der Gewichte

Auch für die Ermittlung der Gewichte stehen mehrere etablierte Verfahren zur Verfügung, von denen hier kurz das Tradeoff- und das Swing-Verfahren vorgestellt werden sollen. Näheres findet man z.B. wiederum in [EW93].

Das *Tradeoff*-Verfahren beruht auf der Ermittlung des Tradeoffs zwischen zwei Dienstattributen. Vereinfacht ausgedrückt wählt man dazu zwei Attribute aus, läßt eines davon eine schlechter bewertete Ausprägung annehmen und fragt danach, um wieviel das andere besser sein müßte, damit die Gesamtbewertung des Dienstes gleich bleibt, wobei alle übrigen Attribute im Vergleich zu vorher nicht verändert werden. Dies führt man $(n-1)$mal durch. Genauer bedeutet dies: Es werden n-1 Alternativenpaare (a, b) bestimmt, die sich jeweils nur in zwei Attributausprägungen unterscheiden und vom Nutzer gleich bewertet werden. Zusammen mit der Normierungsbedingung für die Gewichte ergeben diese Indifferenzaussagen ein n-dimensionales lineares Gleichungssystem, durch dessen eindeutige Lösung wir die gesuchten Gewichte erhalten.

Das *Swing*-Verfahren geht üblicherweise von einer "Alternative" $a^- = (a_1^-, a_2^-, ..., a_n^-)$ aus, bei der alle Attribute jeweils den schlechtestmöglichen Wert annehmen. Relativ dazu werden sämtliche Alternativen der Form $b^r = (a_1^-, a_2^-, ..., a_{r-1}^-, a_r^+, a_{r+1}^-, ..., a_n^-)$ bewertet, die mit Ausnahme des r-ten Attributes identisch zu a^- sind, wobei das r-te Attribut nun aber seine am besten bewertete Ausprägung annimmt. Anders ausgedrückt entspricht dies also der Bestimmung der Kosten, die der Nutzer zu investieren bereit ist, um Alternative b^r anstatt Alternative a^- zu erhalten. Aus den entstehenden n Gleichungen lassen sich unter Ausnutzung der Linearitätsannahme sofort die gesuchten Gewichte ableiten.

Diskussion der Methoden

Ein spürbarer Nachteil des Tradeoff-Verfahrens ist, daß es nur auf kontinuierliche Attribute anwendbar ist, da Indifferenzaussagen zwischen diskreten Werten i.d.R. nur selten exakt sein werden. Dafür stehen allerdings für den Vergleich halbwegs realistische Alternativen zur Verfügung. Beim Swing-Verfahren hingegen werden zunächst ziemlich künstliche Alternativen konstruiert und diese anschließend durch einen Vergleich evaluiert, was eher ungesicherte Ergebnisse erwarten läßt. Andererseits läßt sich diese Methode auch bei diskreten Attributen anwenden, da es hierfür stets zumindest eine schlechteste und eine beste Ausprägung geben wird. Eine Möglichkeit, für das Swing-Verfahren realitätsnähere Alternativen zu erhalten, geht nicht von einer Alternative mit lauter pessimistischen Attributen a_r^-, sondern von mittelmäßigen a_r^o aus. Dadurch gewinnt man einerseits Realitätsnähe, andererseits verkleinert man aber den bewertungsmäßigen Spielraum zwischen den zu vergleichenden Alternativen.

Abschließend kann man also festhalten, daß man auch bei der Ermittlung der QoS-Funktion keine allgemeine Empfehlung für eine der Methoden geben kann. Die vorstehenden Überlegungen lassen sich kurz in folgender Tabelle zusammenfassen:

	Tradeoff-Verfahren	Swing-Verfahren
Exaktheit	hoch	mittel
Attribute	kontinuierliche	alle
Aufwand	gering	gering

Tabelle 2: Vergleich der Verfahren zur Ermittlung der QoS-Funktion

5 Implementierung und Ergebnisse

In diesem Kapitel wird eine Implementierung der bislang beschriebenen Ansätze vorgestellt. Hierbei erhält also der Trader also eine Anfrage nach einem bestimmten Diensttyp, wobei er die "conditional-selection-criteria" so behandelt, wie er dies im herkömmlichen Fall gewohnt ist. Die danach noch verbleibenden Angebote müssen nun anhand der vom Nutzer angegebenen QoS- und QoSP-Funktionen evaluiert werden. Der Einfachheit halber gibt der Importer die QoSP-Funktionen für die einzelnen Dienstattribute anhand von Stützstellen an, zwischen denen dann die Evaluatorkomponente linear interpoliert. Mittels der ebenfalls vom Importer spezifizierten Gewichtung wird dann die QoS-Funktion aus 4.2 berechnet und damit für jedes Angebot eine Bewertung ermittelt. Zuletzt kann dann der Trader dem Importer das am höchsten bewertete Angebot als optimal vorschlagen. Hieraus ergibt sich folgende Implementierung:

```
/* Die Angaben eines Importers zu einer Diensteigenschaft umfassen den
Namen der Diensteigenschaft, bis zu sechs Stützstellen der zugehörigen
QoSP-Funktion und die Gewichtung (Präferenz) der Diensteigenschaft.
*/
struct struct_property
{ iwt_types::NameType propertyName;
  pair p1;
...
  pair p6;
  CORBA::Double preference;
};
/* Die Klasse pet realisiert die Operationen zur Einbindung von Nutzer-
   präferenzen in die Dienstvermittlung. Dazu besitzt ein Objekt dieser
   Klasse zwei interne Zustände: einen evaluation_vector, der aus Elemen-
   ten struct_property besteht, und eine Liste aus Kriterien, die auf
   jeden Fall erfüllt sein müssen (K.o.-Kriterien). Die Funktion set_all
   belegt diese beiden Zustände mit den Importerspezifikationen. Die
   Funktion compute wird auf jedes Dienstangebot mit passendem Diensttyp
   angewendet und bewertet es bezüglich der internen Zustände.
*/
class pet
{ protected: iwt_types::RelationshipListType ko_criteria;
            evaluation_vector* evaluation_criteria;
                              :
                              :
  public: pet();
          ~pet();
          void set_all(iwt_types::RuleType& matchingConstraint,
                       iwt_types::RuleType& selectionPreference);
          CORBA::Double compute(iwt_types::PropertyValueListType& spv,
                                iwt_types::PropertyValueListType& sopv);
};

CORBA::Double pet::compute(iwt_types::PropertyValueListType& spv,
                           iwt_types::PropertyValueListType& sopv)
{
/* An dieser Stelle müssen die Sequenzen spv und sopv in eine Sequenz
   offer_prop einsortiert werden. Bei der beschleunigten Variante der
   Implementation geschieht dies bereits beim Export des Dienstes.
*/
...
  CORBA::Double ret=0;
  if(compute_ko(offer_prop))
    then ret=compute_cc(offer_prop);
  return ret;
};
```

Abb. 6: Einbindung der Nutzerpräferenzen in den Trading Service

Die vom Nutzer spezifizierten QoSP-Funktionen werden durch ein Objekt der Klasse `pet` realisiert. Ein Objekt dieser Klasse besitzt einen internen Zustand `compromize_criteria`, der QoSP-Funktionen aufnehmen kann, die durch bis zu sechs Stützstellen angegeben werden. Eine Stützstelle wird hierbei durch ein Paar aus reellen Zahlen beschrieben. Ein weiterer interner Zustand ist `ko_criteria`, der zur Aufnahme derjenigen Kriterien dient, die auf jeden Fall erfüllt sein müssen. Neben diesen beiden Zuständen enthält ein Objekt der Klasse `pet` gleichzeitig alle Operationen, die zur Evaluierung benötigt werden. Dies sind nur zwei öffentliche Funktionen. Die erste davon, `set_all`, dient zur Belegung der internen Zustände. Da der Standard zur Trading-Funktion fest definierte Schnittstellen vorsieht, können die QoSP-Funktionen und die zugehörigen Gewichte nicht direkt vom Importer an den Trader übergeben werden. Stattdessen stehen zwei Variablen zur Verfügung, die eine Policy-Struktur besitzen. Dies sind `matchingConstraint` und `selectionPreference`. Die QoSP-Funktionen werden im Importer in eine Policy umgewandelt und zusammen mit den K.o.-Kriterien in `matchingConstraint` abgelegt. Ebenso werden die Gewichte als Policy `selection Preference` übergeben. Die Funktion `set_all` dient dazu, `matchingConstraint` und `selectionPreference` in QoSP-Funktionen und K.o.-Kriterien rückzutransformieren. Dabei wird gleichzeitig zur Verbesserung der Effizienz eine alphabetische Sortierung der beiden Listen bezüglich der Diensteigenschaftsnamen vorgenommen. Die Umwandlung der Diensteigenschaften in die erforderliche Struktur erfolgt vor Beginn des Durchsuchens des Service Directory. Anstelle der Matching Constraints wird nun das Objekt verwendet, das die Beschreibung der QoSP-Funktionen erhält. Dieses Objekt wird an jedes Dienstangebot übergeben. Stimmt der Diensttyp der Anfrage mit demjenigen eines Dienstangebotes überein, wird dort die zweite öffentliche Funktion des Objektes, `compute`, aufgerufen. Diese Funktion realisiert die Bewertung des Dienstangebotes. Die Diensteigenschaften und Dienstangebotseigenschaften werden an das Objekt übergeben. An dieser Stelle existieren zwei mögliche Implementierungen. Die eigentliche Bewertung eines Dienstangebotes geht von einer sortierten Liste `offer_prop` von Eigenschaften des Dienstangebotes aus. Im ersten Fall (im folgenden als Version A bezeichnet) kann die Sortierung der Diensteigenschaften `spv` und der Dienstangebotseigenschaften `sopv` zu einer Liste `offer_prop` in der Funktion `compute` stattfinden. Diese Variante ist die zeitintensivere. Zur Beschleunigung des Auswahlvorgangs ist es alternativ auch möglich (Version B), die nötige Sortierung schon beim Export eines Dienstes vorzunehmen. Damit wird allerdings der Speicheraufwand pro Dienstangebot höher, da jede Eigenschaft des Dienstangebotes doppelt abgespeichert wird. Inwiefern sich dieser Mehraufwand an Speicher lohnt, soll später noch untersucht werden.

Die Bewertung eines Dienstangebotes geht nun davon aus, daß eine alphabetisch sortierte Liste `offer_prop` vorliegt, die alle Eigenschaften eines Dienstangebotes enthält. Die Variable `ret` dient zur Aufnahme der Bewertung. Zu Beginn ist sie mit Null initialisiert. Mittels einer geschützten Funktion `compute_kc` wird zuerst die Erfüllbarkeit der K.o.-Kriterien getestet. Sind sie nicht erfüllbar, bleibt die Bewertung Null. Andernfalls wird die geschützte Funktion `compute_cc` aufgerufen. Sie realisiert die in Kapitel 3 und 4 vorgestellte Berechnung einer Bewertung aufgrund von QoSP-Funktionen. Der berechnete Wert wird zurückgegeben. Innerhalb des Service Directory wird das Dienstangebot nun entsprechend seines Wertes in eine Ergebnisliste einsortiert. Nach Durchlaufen des gesamten Service Directory enthält diese Ergebnisliste alle passenden Dienstangebote nach Eignung sortiert. Ist nur eine SELECT-Operation gefordert, kann das erste Element dieser Liste als optimaler Dienst geliefert werden.

Abbildung 7 zeigt das Ergebnis eines Laufzeitvergleichs dieser Implementierung in den beiden beschriebenen Versionen A und B mit einem herkömmlichen Trader, wie er in [MZP96] vorgestellt wurde. Die Messung fand dabei auf einer SPARC 5 unter Verwendung von Orbix 2.0 bei geringer bis mittlerer Auslastung des Rechners statt.

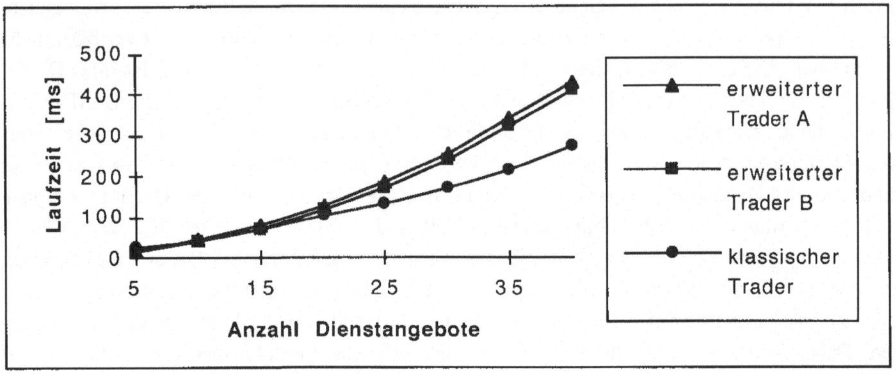

Abb. 7: Laufzeitvergleich der zwei Versionen des erweiterten Traders

Diesem Vergleich läßt sich entnehmen, daß der erweiterte Trader etwas länger braucht als sein klassischer Vorgänger. Dabei läßt sich das Ergebnis der Implementierungsversion A noch geringfügig verbessern, wenn man den höheren Speicherbedarf von Version B in Kauf nimmt. Als wesentliches Ergebnis aber kann man festhalten, daß sich der zeitliche Aufwand für die beschriebene Erweiterung der Funktionalität in vertretbaren Grenzen hält.

Abschließend soll noch der Frage nachgegangen werden, wie sich quantifizieren läßt, inwieweit der höhere Aufwand bei der Erstellung einer Anfrage dem Nutzer einen Vorteil bringt. Anders ausgedrückt: Wie oft würde der Trader ein für den Nutzer günstiges Angebot auch dann auswählen, ohne daß dieser seine Präferenzen derart detailliert spezifiziert?

Zur Beantwortung dieser Frage wurde ein Dienstanfrageszenario entwickelt und gegen zufällig gewählte Dienstangebote getestet. Die Dienstanfrage bestand aus der Spezifikation eines Dienstes mit fünf Diensteigenschaften, für die jeweils eine typische QoSP-Funktion (z. B. gem. Abbildung 4a) angegeben wurde; die Eigenschaften wurden mit den Gewichten 0.6, 0.15, 0.15, 0.05 und 0.05 versehen. In jeweils 100 Durchläufen wurden die Diensteigenschaften von m Dienstangeboten (für $m = 5, 10, 15, ..., 40, 50, 75, 100$) zufällig festgelegt. Sodann wurde mittels des beschriebenen erweiterten Traders ermittelt, welches der m Dienstangebote jeweils für den Nutzer optimal ist und welchen Wert die QoS-Funktion dafür annimmt. Die so ermittelten Referenzwerte entsprechen 100% in den Abbildungen 8 bzw. 9.

Im zweiten Schritt wurden zwei Varianten der Anfragespezifikation untersucht. Variante 1 spezifizierte die QoSP-Funktionen weiterhin exakt, verwendete aber identische Gewichte in Höhe von 0.2 für alle Diensteigenschaften. Variante 2 hingegen ließ die Gewichtung unverändert, verwendete aber anstatt exakter QoSP-Funktionen einfach lineare Funktionen, und zwar die Winkelhalbierenden. Für beide Varianten wurde ermittelt, in wieviel Prozent der Fälle der erweiterte Trader dasselbe Angebot als optimal auswählte wie vorher bzw. wie oft der Wert der

QoS-Funktion des jetzt ausgewählten Angebotes um höchstens 5% schlechter war als das im ersten Schritt ermittelte Optimum. Die Ergebnisse sind in Abbildung 8 und 9 wiedergegeben.

Zum Vergleich wurde auch noch der klassische Trader betrachtet. Die Dienstanfrage wurde hierfür in Form einer unteren Schranke für jede Diensteigenschaft formuliert, welche an der Stelle angesetzt wurde, an der die exakte QoSP-Funktion den Wert 0.5 überstieg, was sich dahingehend interpretieren läßt, daß der Nutzer mit einem solchen Dienst zumindest "halbwegs" zufrieden ist.

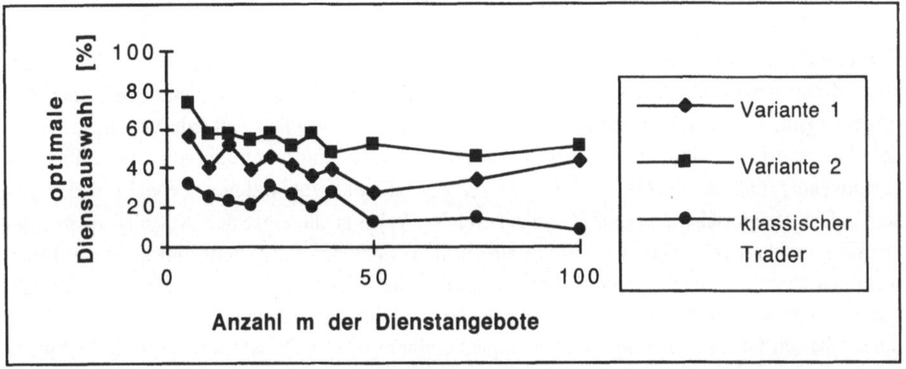

Abb. 8: prozentualer Anteil der Auswahl des optimalen Dienstes bei Wahl identischer Gewichte (Variante 1) bzw. linearer QoSP-Funktionen (Variante 2) sowie beim klassischen Trader

Abbildung 8 läßt sich entnehmen, daß sowohl die Verwendung identischer Gewichte als auch der Einsatz linearer QoSP-Funktionen bewirkt, daß für die meisten m der Trader höchstens in jedem zweiten Fall das tatsächlich optimale Angebot auswählt. Dabei ist es nicht überraschend, daß im Fall extrem weniger Dienstangebote ($m = 5$) die Häufigkeit aufgrund der begrenzten Auswahl noch etwas höher ist als für größere Werte von m. Der herkömmliche Trader schneidet hier wie auch in Abbildung 9 deutlich schlechter ab.

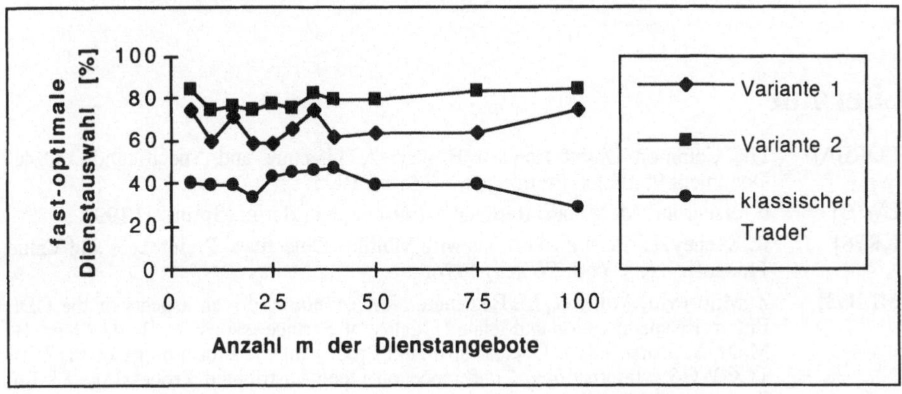

Abb. 9: prozentualer Anteil fast-optimal ausgewählter Dienste (Wert der QoS-Funktion höchstens 5 % schlechter als im optimalen Fall der Abb. 8)

Abbildung 9 zeigt die Häufigkeit, mit der der QoS-Funktionswert des ausgewählten Dienstangebots höchstens 95% des Optimums beträgt. Wie zu erwarten war, ist die Häufigkeit dafür deutlich höher als die für eine optimale Auswahl (wie in Abbildung 8 gezeigt), wenngleich auch in diesem Fall der durch den erhöhten Aufwand erzielte Vorteil signifikant bleibt. Diese Ergebnisse hängen natürlich vom verwendeten Anfrageszenario sowie von der Anzahl der Durchläufe ab. Die Standardabweichung für die einzelnen Meßpunkte liegt typischerweise in der Größenordnung von 8%, ist hier aber aus Gründen der Übersichtlichkeit nicht explizit eingezeichnet.

6 Zusammenfassung und Ausblick

Herkömmliche Trading Services unter CORBA bieten dem Nutzer nur dann einen Dienst an, wenn dieser genau die Diensteigenschaftsspezifikationen erfüllt, die der Nutzer in seiner Anfrage vorgibt. Das hier vorgestellte Konzept unterscheidet zwischen Anforderungen, die in jedem Fall zu erfüllen sind, und solchen, zwischen denen ein Kompromiß möglich ist. Hierzu ist es notwendig, daß der Nutzer in seiner Anfrage zusätzlich angibt, welches Gewicht er den einzelnen Diensteigenschaften beimißt und auf welche Weise er die einzelnen Ausprägungen jeder Diensteigenschaft präferiert. Es wurden ausführlich Methoden vorgestellt, um an diese Informationen zu gelangen. Sie ermöglichen es dem Trader, die einzelnen Dienstangebote nutzerspezifisch zu bewerten und dem Nutzer dasjenige Angebot vorzuschlagen, das individuell für ihn am besten ist. An der vorgestellten Implementierung läßt sich nachweisen, daß die hierfür benötigte zusätzliche Laufzeit nicht allzu groß ist. Andererseits zeigt sich, daß der durch die neue Funktionalität gewonnene Nutzen für den Anwender diesen zusätzlichen Aufwand durchaus rechtfertigt.

Mit dieser Arbeit ist ein erster Schritt zur Berücksichtigung detaillierter Nutzerinteressen im Rahmen des Trading Services getan. Damit dieser Ansatz praktische Bedeutung erlangen kann, wird es darauf ankommen, die Assessmentkomponente so benutzerfreundlich wie möglich zu gestalten. Darüber hinaus soll die hier vorgestellte Arbeit in Richtung auf Präferenzmodelle unter Unsicherheit erweitert werden. Hiermit läßt sich etwa der Fall berücksichtigen, daß die Attribute von Dienstangeboten bei der Dienstnutzung gewissen Schwankungen unterliegen können. Derartige Fragestellungen werden unter Verwendung weiterer Konzepte aus der Entscheidungstheorie, wie etwa Utility Theory oder Dempster-Shafer-Theorie, behandelt werden.

Literatur

[CORBA]   The Common Object Request Broker: Architecture and Specification. OMG Document 95.03.xx. Framingham (Mass.) 1995.

[EW93]   F. Eisenführ, M. Weber: Rationales Entscheiden. Berlin (Springer) 1993.

[KR76]   R. Keeney, H. Raiffa: Decisions with Multiple Objectives: Preferences and Value Tradeoffs. New York (Wiley) 1976.

[MLB93]   Z. Milosevic, A. Lister, M. Bearman: New economic-driven aspects of the ODP Enterprise specification and related Quality of Service issues. In: J. de Meer, B. Mahr, S. Storp (eds.): Open Distributed Processing II. Proceedings of the IFIP TC6/WG6.1 International Conference on Open Distributed Processing. Berlin, September 1993 (Chapman & Hall).

[MZP96]   B. Meyer, S. Zlatintsis, C. Popien: Enabling Interworking between Heterogeneous Distributed Platforms. Proceedings of ICDP'96. Dresden, February 1996 (Chapman & Hall)

[OMG 95]   [ISO/IEC JTC1/SC21 WG7 (ODP)] ODP Trader Document, OMG Document Number 95-07-06

[ORBIX]   Orbix – Programmer's Guide and Reference Manual. IONA Technologies Ltd., Release 2.0, 1996

[PM95]   C. Popien, B. Meyer: A Formal Approach to Service Import in ODP Trader Federations. In: D. Hogrefe, S. Leuer: Formal Description Techniques VII. Chapman & Hall 1995.

[Po95]   C. Popien: Dienstvermittlung in Verteilten Systemen. Teubner Texte zur Informatik. Stuttgart (Teubner) 1995.

[PSW96]   C. Popien, G. Schürmann, K.-H. Weiß: Verteilte Verarbeitung in Offenen Systemen. Stuttgart (Teubner) 1996.

[QoS95]   ISO/IEC JTC1/SC21/N9309: Open Systems Interconnection, Data Management and Open Distributed Processing – Quality of Service, Basic Framework. Working Draft, January 1995.

[RTL96]   P. Reichl, D. Thißen, C. Linnhoff-Popien: How to Enhance Service Selection in Distributed Systems. Proceedings of the International Conference on Distributed Computer Communication Networks DCCN'96. Tel Aviv, November 1996.

[SPM94]   O. Spaniol, C. Popien, B. Meyer: Dienste und Dienstvermittlung in Client/-Server-Systemen. Thomsons Aktuelle Tutorien. International Thomson Publishing 1994.

[Th96]   D. Thißen: QoS-basierte Optimierung der Dienstselektion in einem Orbix-Trader. Diplomarbeit am Lehrstuhl Informatik IV der RWTH Aachen. Aachen, Juli 1996.

[TP96]   D. Thißen, C. Linnhoff-Popien: Finding Optimal Services within a CORBA Trader. In: Trends in Distributed Systems. CORBA and Beyond. Aachen, October 1996 (Springer).

Ein werkzeugunterstützter Ansatz zur Gewinnung CORBA-konformer Managementagenten aus modularen SNMP-Implementierungen

Alexander Keller*
Fakultät für Informatik, Technische Universität München
c/o Institut für Informatik der
Ludwig Maximilians Universität München
Oettingenstr. 67, 80538 München
E-Mail: keller@informatik.uni-muenchen.de

Zusammenfassung

Mit der zunehmenden Verbreitung von CORBA für die Implementierung verteilter Anwendungen ergibt sich die Möglichkeit, diese objektorientierte Kommunikationsarchitektur auch zum Management dieser Applikationen und der Systeme, auf denen die verteilten Anwendungen laufen, einzusetzen. Es ist daher sinnvoll, CORBA-konforme Managementagenten bereitzustellen, die die Überwachung und Steuerung dieser Systeme auf effiziente Art gewährleisten. Während einerseits gegenwärtig keine solchen CORBA-konformen Agenten existieren, gibt es andererseits SNMP-Agenten, die diesen Zweck erfüllen. Gesucht ist daher ein Verfahren zur Gewinnung CORBA-konformer Managementagenten aus bestehenden SNMP-Implementierungen. Der Beitrag beschreibt ein Vorgehensmodell zur Migration bestehenden modularen SNMP-Agentencodes in eine CORBA-Umgebung und schildert dessen konkrete Anwendung anhand eines praxisnahen Beispiels. Es handelt sich hierbei um einen Agenten für das Management von UNIX-Endsystemen, der am Lehrstuhl entwickelt wurde und in der Praxis zum Einsatz kommt. Weiterhin wird skizziert, wie der Transformationsaufwand durch die Abstützung auf standardisierte Architekturen und Verfahren sowie am Markt erhältliche Werkzeuge in akzeptablen Grenzen gehalten werden kann.

1 Einführung

Durch die zunehmende Verbreitung vernetzter arbeitsteiliger Systeme sehen sich die Betreiber großer verteilter IV-Infrastrukturen steigenden Anforderungen an die Güte der von ihnen angebotenen Dienste ausgesetzt. Diese Situation wird durch das Vorhandensein stark heterogener Endbenutzersysteme sowie den in ihnen enthaltenen Objekten wie Anwendungsprogrammen, Betriebssystemen und Kommunikationsprotokollen noch weiter verschärft. Demgegenüber resultiert aus der hohen Konkurrenzsituation zwischen den Betreibern und dem dadurch entstehenden Kostendruck der Zwang, die Anzahl hochqualifizierten Personals zur Überwachung und Steuerung dieser interagierenden Komponenten zu reduzieren.

Der Brisanz der Situation, in der sich die Betreiber befinden, kann jedoch geeignet entgegengetreten werden, indem ihnen Werkzeuge zur Verfügung gestellt werden, die die zugrundeliegende Heterogenität verschatten und es ihnen somit ermöglichen, eine einheitliche Sicht auf die verteilten Systeme zu erhalten. Standardisierte Managementarchitekturen sind ein geeignetes Mittel, um dieses Ziel zu erreichen. Beispiele hierfür sind das ISO/OSI–Management Framework oder die Internet–Managementarchitektur (häufig auch als SNMP–Management bezeichnet), die jedoch per se nicht interoperabel sind.

---

*Diese Arbeiten wurden gefördert durch das IBM European Networking Center, Heidelberg

Beide Architekturen haben allerdings Gemeinsamkeiten, die unter anderem der Grund dafür sind, daß sich bis zum heutigen Tage keine dieser beiden Alternativen vollständig am Markt durchsetzen konnte: für die Beschreibung der zu steuernden Ressourcen wird ein eigenständiges Informationsmodell und damit eine spezielle Beschreibungssprache verwendet; zur Kommunikation zwischen Managementsystem und der zu überwachenden Infrastruktur existieren dedizierte Managementprotokolle. Die Handhabung dieser durch das Management zusätzlich eingeführten Heterogenität erweist sich im praktischen Betrieb jedoch oft als hinderlich und führt insbesondere dazu, daß die Hersteller einer verteilten Anwendung und der entsprechenden Managementapplikation nur in den seltensten Fällen identisch sind. Die Anforderungen der Betreiber an Managementsysteme werden daher in marktfähigen Produkten oft nur unzureichend berücksichtigt.

Auch im Bereich der Entwicklung von Managementsystemen macht sich die Fixierung auf eine spezielle Beschreibungsmethodik und ein eigenständiges Managementprotokoll bemerkbar: Allgemein verfügbare Modellierungs- und Implementierungswerkzeuge können entweder nicht oder nur mit hohem Anpassungsaufwand eingesetzt werden, da die Notation zur Beschreibung von Managementinformation oft nicht von den Herstellern dieser Werkzeuge unterstützt wird.

Demgegenüber verfolgt die im Rahmen der *Object Management Architecture (OMA)* von der *Object Management Group (OMG)* standardisierte *Common Object Request Broker Architecture (CORBA)* ([6]), die ursprünglich für verteilte objektorientierte Programmierung konzipiert wurde, einen anderen Ansatz: man fordert, daß *eine einzige* Architektur sowohl für die Entwicklung als auch für das Management einer verteilten Anwendung verwendet wird. Dies bedeutet, daß nicht nur die Beschreibung sowohl der Management- als auch der Anwendungsobjekte in einer identischen Notation (OMG IDL[1]) erfolgt, sondern ebenfalls Nutz- und Managementdaten einer Applikation mit demselben Kommunikationsmittel (einem sogenannten *Object Request Broker (ORB)*) übertragen werden. Management wird somit zu einem (zweifellos wichtigen) Teilaspekt verteilter Anwendungen. Somit kann das gesamte Spektrum verfügbarer Werkzeuge zur Softwareentwicklung genutzt werden, da Nutz- und Managementdaten identisch modelliert und implementiert werden.

Konzeptionelle Untersuchungen bezüglich der Mächtigkeit des CORBA-Objektmodells im Vergleich zu den Informationsmodellen etablierter Managementarchitekturen haben die prinzipielle Eignung von CORBA für das Management von Endsystemen und der auf ihnen ablaufenden Anwendungen nachgewiesen (siehe [12]). Einerseits sind aufgrund des geringen Alters von CORBA[2] momentan gerade erste Implementierungen auf dem Markt erhältlich; im Bereich des Managements sind derzeit noch keinerlei CORBA-konforme Managementsysteme und -agenten bekannt. Auf Seiten der Hersteller ist jedoch zunehmend die Tendenz erkennbar, solche Werkzeuge zu entwickeln ([15], [7]). Andererseits existiert gegenwärtig eine große Zahl an SNMP-fähigen Managementagenten und es stellt sich daher die Frage, wie bestehender SNMP-Agentencode nahtlos in die CORBA-Welt migriert werden kann. Ein so entstehender CORBA-Managementagent besteht aus verteilten kooperativen Managementobjekten, die mit Hilfe des Object Request Brokers interagieren.

Der Beitrag präsentiert ein Vorgehensmodell zur Migration bestehenden modularen SNMP–Agentencodes in eine CORBA–Umgebung und schildert die Schritte dessen konkreter Anwendung anhand eines praxisnahen Beispiels. Seine Struktur orientiert sich an dem in Abbildung 1 skizzierten Vorgehensmodell: Abschnitt 2 beschreibt die Eigenschaften des am Lehrstuhl entwickelten SNMP-Agenten zum Management von UNIX-Workstations und den JIDM-Algorithmus (siehe 2.2) zur Umsetzung des Internet-Informationsmodells in CORBA-Objektbeschreibungen. Das Ergebnis ist ein algorithmisch erzeugtes Objektmodell, das jedoch noch verbessert werden muß, um den Anforderungen gerecht zu werden. Die Gründe dafür sowie die Schritte und Werkzeuge zur Optimierung des vorhandenen Objektmodells sind in

---

[1]Die Interface Definition Language (IDL) ist die von der OMG standardisierte Beschreibungssprache für die Schnittstellen von CORBA-Objekten

[2]Der aktuelle Standard [2], der in der Version 2.0 vorliegt, wurde im Dezember 1994 verabschiedet

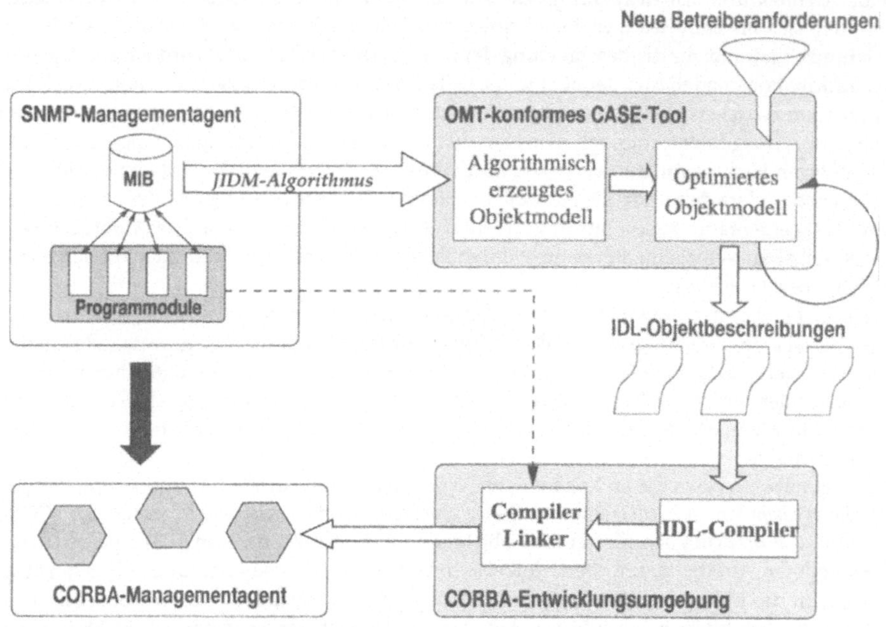

Abbildung 1: Vorgehensweise bei der Portierung des Agenten

Abschnitt 3 beschrieben. Hierbei ist es von großer Bedeutung, auf Werkzeuge wie CASE-Tools zurückgreifen zu können, die den zyklischen Prozeß der objektorientierten Analyse und des Designs geeignet unterstützen. Sie schaffen auch die Grundlage, um das bestehende Modell um neue Anforderungen von Seiten der Betreiber nahtlos zu erweitern. Nachdem die Modellierung abgeschlossen ist, kann die Implementierung erfolgen, die in Abschnitt 4 dargestellt wird. Hierbei hat sich bei unseren Arbeiten herausgestellt, daß die Schnittstellen zwischen den einzelnen Werkzeugen gegenwärtig noch verbesserungsbedürftig sind und man von einem reibungslosen Zusammenspiel aller am Entwicklungsprozeß beteiligten Komponenten noch etwas entfernt ist.

2 Ausgangssituation

2.1 Ein SNMP-Agent für das Management von UNIX-Workstations

Zum heutigen Zeitpunkt muß trotz zahlreicher Bemühungen der Hersteller die Problemstellung, integriertes Management von UNIX-Workstations sicherzustellen, noch immer als ungelöst betrachtet werden: Es existieren zwar Werkzeuge, die eine Vielzahl von Parametern eines Endsystems erfassen und mit Hilfe eines standardisierten Managementprotokolls an die Managementplattform weiterleiten ([5]); aktive Eingriffsmöglichkeiten durch den Administrator fehlen jedoch völlig. Andererseits existieren Produkte, die zwar Eingriffe zur Steuerung des Systems erlauben; die Kommunikation mit der Managementplattform geschieht jedoch lediglich auf der Grundlage eines herstellerspezifischen, proprietären Protokolls, dessen Schnittstellen nicht offengelegt sind ([9]). Zusätzlich sind beide Ansätze von einer Bottom-Up-Vorgehensweise geprägt, die nur selten die tatsächlichen Bedürfnisse der Netzbetreiber berücksichtigt. Von einer umfassenden, integrierten Managementlösung ist man daher noch weit entfernt.

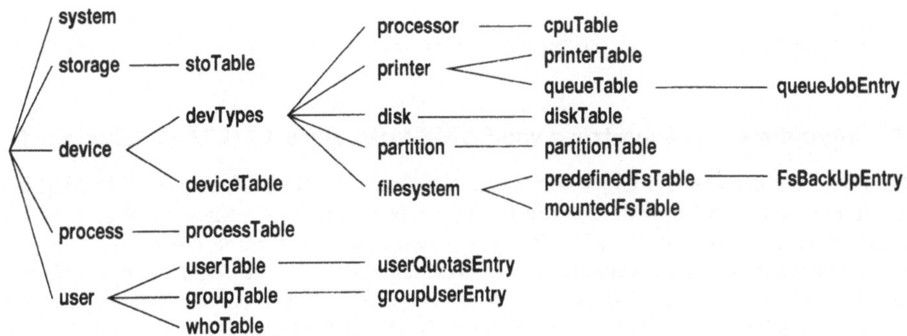

Abbildung 2: Eine MIB für das Management von UNIX-Workstations (nach [3])

Im Gegensatz zu kommerziell erhältlichen Werkzeugen haben wir in unseren Arbeiten [3] einen Top-Down-Ansatz verfolgt, der das typische Aufgabenspektrum eines UNIX-Systemadministrators abdeckt. Es wurden daher Möglichkeiten für das Einrichten und Löschen von Benutzerkennungen und -gruppen sowie deren Quoten für den Zugriff auf Betriebsmittel (Plattenplatz, Druckseiten) ebenso vorgesehen, wie Funktionen zum Erfassen und ggf. Stoppen der momentan aktiven Prozesse oder zum Mounten/Unmounten von Dateisystemen. Es ist somit nicht nur passives Monitoring von UNIX-Workstations möglich, sondern auch das aktive Eingreifen in den Betrieb des Systems. Als Managementprotokoll wird SNMP in der Version 2 verwendet.

Im Rahmen dieser Arbeiten wurde eine Systemmanagement-MIB entwickelt und der dazugehörige Agent auf verschiedenen Betriebssystemplattformen (IBM AIX, HP-UX, SunOS, Solaris) implementiert. Diese MIB ist in Abbildung 2 schematisch dargestellt; sie umfaßt 195 MIB-Variablen und 15 Tabellen und stellt (unter anderem) ein Modell folgender Komponenten eines UNIX-Systems zur Verfügung:

- Speicher (Hauptspeicher, Swap-Bereich)

- Geräte (Prozessoren, Drucker, Platten und deren Dateisysteme usw.)

- Prozesse

- Benutzer (Kenndaten, Gruppen, Quoten usw.)

Im Falle der Benutzer- und Gruppenverwaltung tritt jedoch durch eine Einschränkung des Internet-Informationsmodells unweigerlich folgendes Problem auf: in der Regel sind auf einem UNIX-System mehrere Benutzer eingetragen, die ihrerseits wieder zu mehreren Gruppen gehören. Tabellen innerhalb von Tabellen sind jedoch explizit durch den entsprechenden Internet-Standard [1] untersagt. „Zu den Internet-Standards konforme" Managementsysteme akzeptieren jedoch MIBs, die diese Anomalie aufweisen, klaglos.

Als sehr vorteilhaft für die Kapselung des SNMP-Agentencodes hat sich der modulare Aufbau des SNMP-Agenten erwiesen: Zum Zugriff auf die MIB-Variablen wurde jeweils eine Prozedur verwendet. Dies bedeutet, daß jede MIB-Variable in einem eigenen Modul implementiert worden ist und über eine bzw. zwei Schnittstellen verfügt, je nachdem, ob auf die Variable nur lesend oder auch schreibend zugegriffen werden kann. Die ausschließlich lesbare MIB-Variable sysName wird durch Aufruf der Prozedur get_sysName ermittelt; eine schreib- und lesbare Variable wie sysLocation wird durch die Prozeduren get_sysLocation und set_sysLocation implementiert. Der SNMP-Agent besteht daher insgesamt aus 195 get- und 150 set-Prozeduren. Der ursprüngliche Grund für diese Modularisierung lag in der besseren Erreichbarkeit von

Plattformunabhängigkeit, da man zwischen Betriebssystem-spezifischen Systemaufrufen und Aufrufen, die für alle unterstützten Betriebssysteme identisch sind, besser unterscheiden konnte.

2.2   Algorithmus zur Umsetzung von SNMP-MIBs in das CORBA-Objektmodell

Die Abbildung bestehender Objektbeschreibungen in das CORBA–Objektmodell bedingt die algorithmische Überführung der Spezifikationssprachen, in denen die Managementobjekte beschrieben sind. In unserem Fall handelt es sich um eine Übersetzung der in der Internet-Managementarchitektur verwendeten ASN.1–Templatesprache in die OMG *Interface Definition Language (IDL)*. Für diesen Zweck existiert ein Algorithmus [16], der im Rahmen der Aktivitäten der *Joint X/Open NM-Forum Inter-Domain Management Task Force (JIDM)* entworfen wurde und sich zur Zeit in der Standardisierungsphase befindet. Wichtigster Gesichtspunkt bei der Überführung von Agenten einer Managementarchitektur in eine andere Architektur ist die unterschiedliche Mächtigkeit der jeweiligen Informationsmodelle. Während das Internet-Informationsmodell sämtliche Aspekte eines Agenten (Parameter und Aktionen) in Form von skalaren Datentypen bzw. Tabellen beschreibt und – im Gegensatz zu CORBA – keine Mechanismen wie Vererbung und Polymorphie kennt, werden im CORBA-Objektmodell Agenten in Form von Objektklassen sowie deren zugehörigen Attributen und Methoden definiert. Die Transformation der in SNMPv2 vorhandenen Datentypen, Makros und asynchronen Ereignismeldungen in die CORBA–Entsprechungen geschieht folgendermaßen:

- Für jede Gruppe einer SNMP–MIB wird eine Objektklasse erzeugt; die darin enthaltenen einfachen skalaren Datentypen werden zu Attributen der Objektklasse. So werden zum Beispiel `Integer32` bzw. `TimeTicks` auf die IDL–Datentypen `long` bzw. `unsigned long` abgebildet; `DisplayString` und `IpAddress` werden einer Sequenz von Octets zugeordnet.

- SNMP–Tabellen werden durch den Algorithmus ebenfalls zu Objektklassen transformiert: Jede Zeile einer Tabelle wird damit zu einer Instanz einer Objektklasse, die durch eine IDL–Schnittstelle festgelegt ist. Ein Beispiel soll dies erläutern: Enthält ein System drei Festplatten, so wird dies auf der SNMP–Seite durch das Anlegen von drei Zeilen der Tabelle `stoTable` dargestellt. CORBA–seitig würden stattdessen drei Instanzen der Objektklasse `StorageDevice` erzeugt. Das CORBA-Objektmodell ist hierbei dem intuitiven Verständnis näher als das entsprechende Internet-Informationsmodell.

- Variablen, die einzelne Felder der Tabelle spezifizieren, werden im Falle einfacher Datentypen zu Attributen der entsprechenden Objektklasse.

- SNMP-Traps werden in CORBA-Events, asynchrone Ereignismeldungen, transformiert, die durch den *Object Event Service* ([8]) bereitgestellt werden.

Obwohl mit dem Übersetzungsalgorithmus dem Entwickler ein mächtiges Werkzeug zur syntaktischen Überführung von SNMP–Objektbeschreibungen in das CORBA–Objektmodell zur Verfügung steht, sind manuelle Eingriffe erforderlich, da Managementsemantik im Internet-Informationsmodell oft nur implizit definiert ist: So wird das Auslösen von Aktionen auf Managementobjekten, für das in der Internet-Managementarchitektur kein explizites Sprachmittel vorgesehen ist, durch das Setzen entsprechender MIB–Variablen (sogenannter *Pushbutton-*Variablen) simuliert. Das CORBA–Analogon hierzu besteht im Aufruf einer Methode auf dem jeweiligen Managementobjekt. Der Übersetzungsalgorithmus, der die Abbildung der SNMP-Datentypen in äquivalente IDL–Konstrukte vornimmt, müßte also eine Pushbutton–Variable auf eine Methode des Managementobjektes abbilden. Da Pushbutton–Variablen jedoch nicht syntaktisch erkennbar sind, muß diese Transformation manuell durch den Entwickler erfolgen. Eine MIB-Variable `stoFormat`, deren Setzen die Formatierung einer Festplatte veranlaßt, muß daher manuell auf eine Methode `storage_format` der Objektklasse `Storage` abgebildet werden, da sie ansonsten durch algorithmische Umsetzung zu einem einfachen Attribut würde.

257

2.3 Ergebnis der algorithmischen Transformation: Ein erstes Objektmodell

Der im vorigen Teilabschnitt beschriebene JIDM-Algorithmus bildet die Grundlage für die Gewinnung einer ersten Version des Objektmodells von UNIX-Endsystemen. Hierzu sind folgende Anmerkungen zu machen:

1. Der JIDM-Algorithmus dient in erster Linie dazu, Managementinformation für Managementgateways bereitzustellen; er soll einem CORBA-basierten Manager ermöglichen, SNMP-konforme Managementagenten durch ein dazwischen liegendes CORBA/SNMP-Managementgateway derart zu steuern, daß der Manager die SNMP-Agenten als CORBA-Agenten sieht. Dieses Szenario impliziert unter anderem, daß sämtliche zur Verwaltung der SNMP-Information notwendige Daten wie die Indizes der Tabellenzeilen in Attribute der CORBA-Objektklassen umgewandelt werden müssen. Während dies für Managementgateways zweifellos notwendig ist, ist ein solches Vorgehen für das objektorientierte Design des Agenten nicht wünschenswert, da beispielsweise die Indizes von SNMP-Tabellenzeilen bereits implizit in den Instanzenidentifikatoren der entsprechenden CORBA-Objektklassen enthalten sind.

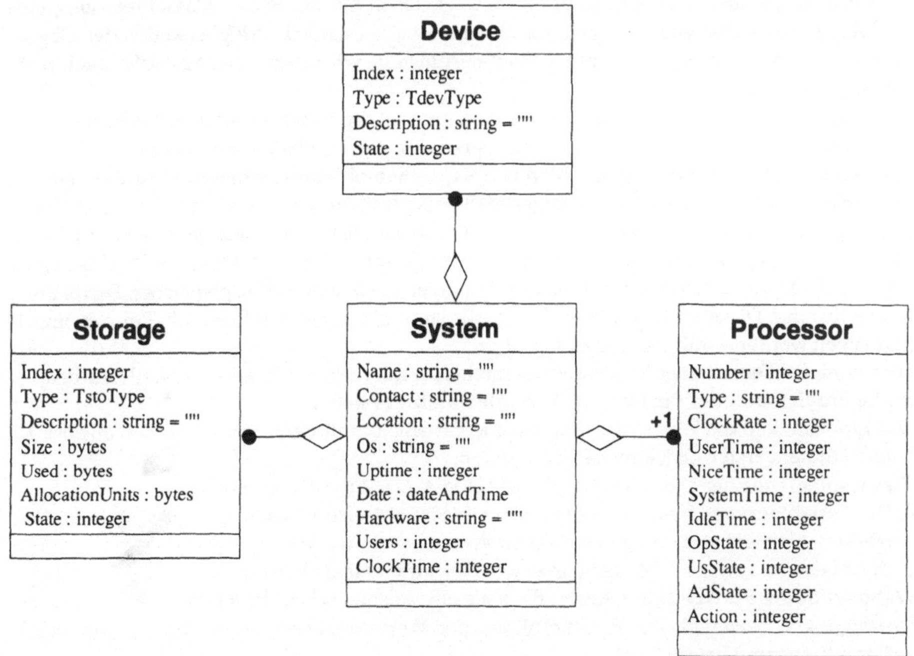

Abbildung 3: Algorithmisch erzeugtes Objektmodell in OMT-Notation (Teilansicht)

2. Die Zielsprache des JIDM-Algorithmus ist, wie oben erwähnt, OMG IDL. Für das weitere Design und die Erweiterung des UNIX-Managementagenten ist es jedoch zwingend erforderlich, die gewonnenen Objektbeschreibungen in eine Notation zu überführen, die es gestattet, die Beschreibungen mit kommerziellen CASE-Tools nachzubearbeiten. Das uns zur Verfügung stehende Werkzeug (beschrieben in Abschnitt 3.1) verwendet die *Object Modeling Technique (OMT)* nach Rumbaugh et al [11]. Die Umsetzung der IDL-Syntax in OMT mußte daher von Hand erfolgen. Dies war jedoch trotz des beachtlichen Umfangs der zugrundeliegenden MIB innerhalb kürzester Zeit machbar, da die Struktur und die Datentypen der Objektklassen bzw deren Attribute bereits durch den JIDM-Algorithmus festgelegt waren.

Ein weiteres Problem bestand darin, daß das Internet–Informationsmodell keine Angaben über die Kardinalität der Beziehungen zwischen einzelnen Objektklassen vorsieht, da es zwar objekt*basiert* ist, keinesfalls jedoch objekt*orientiert*. Demzufolge fehlen Angaben bezüglich vorhandener Enthaltenseinsbeziehungen vollständig, wurden jedoch bereits bei der Überführung in die OMT–Notation von Hand eingefügt. Abbildung 3 stellt einen Ausschnitt aus dem so gewonnenen Objektmodell dar.

3 Gewinnung eines geeigneten Objektmodells

Zusätzlich zu den im vorigen Abschnitt angesprochenen Konvertierungen gibt es natürlich noch eine Reihe offener und für das Design des CORBA–Agenten substantielle Kritikpunkte, die nachfolgend aufgezählt sind. Es sei an dieser Stelle daran erinnert, daß das Ziel der Arbeit darin besteht, einen Agenten zu erhalten, der *möglichst vollständig* objektorientierten Prinzipien entspricht.

1. Zwischen den einzelnen Klassen fehlt (bis auf die Enthaltenseinsbeziehung zur Systemklasse) jegliche Hierarchie

Eine Enthaltenseinshierarchie ist nur ansatzweise (eben mit der Systemklasse) realisiert, eine Vererbungshierarchie fehlt gänzlich. Damit sind zwei wesentliche Möglichkeiten der Objektorientierung noch nicht ausgeschöpft. Polymorphismus wird damit zwangsläufig auch nicht unterstützt.

Dies sind unmittelbare Konsequenzen aus dem Internet–Informationsmodell, das keinerlei Beziehungen zwischen Objektklassen (weder Vererbung noch Enthaltensein) kennt.

2. Die noch vorhandenen Typvariablen widersprechen objektorientierten Grundsätzen

Beispiele für solche Typvariablen in obigen MIB-Ausschnitten sind `Type` in der `Storage`-Klasse oder `Type` in der `Device`-Klasse. Damit ist es zwar möglich, verschiedene Arten der Objektklasse `Storage` (durch entsprechendes Setzen der Typvariablen) zu bilden, die Objektstruktur wäre aber für die unterschiedlichen Arten von Speicherobjekten (Hauptspeicher, Festplatten, Magnetbänder, Disketten) dieselbe gewesen; die stark differierenden Eigenschaften der einzelnen Typen werden somit nicht berücksichtigt.

Hier wird das Fehlen einer Vererbungshierarchie im Internet–Informationsmodell deutlich.

3. Die Problematik der Pushbutton-Variablen bleibt bestehen

Das Problem, daß die Wertzuweisung an eine Variable unmittelbar eine Operation auslöst, ist auch in diesem ersten Objektmodell vorhanden.

Dies resultiert aus der Tatsache, daß SNMP keine *Action*–Protokolldateneinheit kennt.

4. Die Variablentypen beschränken sich nur auf ASN.1-Grundtypen

Auch Variablen mit stark eingeschränktem Wertebereich, wie z.B. `OpState`[3] oder `AdState`[4] in der Klasse `Processor`, besitzen im ersten Objektmodell einen einfachen integer-Datentyp. Während dieser Punkt auf den ersten Blick als ein „kosmetisches" Problem erscheint, so sind Überlegungen bezüglich der Einschränkung der Wertebereiche von Attributen hinsichtlich späterer Konformitätstests wichtig.

Das objektorientierte Prinzip der Kapselung (*Encapsulation*) ist in diesem Stadium bereits berücksichtigt:

Wäre diese erste Version als Basis für die Implementierung herangezogen worden, so hätte der IDL-Compiler Rahmendateien erzeugt, in denen die einzelnen Attribute als private gekennzeichnet, also nur über spezielle get-/set-Operationen (deren Rahmen ebenfalls erzeugt würden) zugreifbar gewesen wären.

Es ist somit nicht möglich, auf die Attribute über andere als die bei der Implementierung vorgesehenen Wege zuzugreifen.

---

[3] `OpState` (Operational State) kann die Werte 1 (enabled) oder 2 (disabled) annehmen; ein Aufzählungstyp reicht hier aus.

[4] `AdState` (Administrative State) kann die Werte 1 (unlocked), 2 (locked) oder 3 (shutting down) annehmen; auch hierfür ist ein Aufzählungstyp besser geeignet.

3.1 Werkzeugunterstützung

Die im vorangehenden Abschnitt beschriebenen Mängel implizieren massive Eingriffe in die Struktur des ersten Objektmodells. Ebenso sollten zusätzliche neue Anforderungen von Seiten des Betreibers in die Konzeption des verbesserten Objektmodells einfließen. Die damit verbundenen Modifikationen sollten jedoch mit vertretbarem Aufwand für den Entwickler erfolgen; ebenso sollte die Einarbeitungszeit in akzeptablen Grenzen bleiben. Es fiel daher die Entscheidung, ein am Markt erhältliches CASE-Tool für das Re-Engineering des Managementagenten einzusetzen, das konform zur objektorientierten Analyse- und Designmethodik OMT ist. Ein weiteres Kriterium bestand darin, daß der Codegenerator des CASE-Tools in der Lage sein sollte, die Objektklassen in der OMG-Schnittstellenbeschreibungssprache *IDL (Interface Definition Language)* auszugeben, damit diese anschließend von der CORBA–Entwicklungsumgebung weiterverarbeitet werden können. Unsere Anforderungen konnten schließlich vom kommerziellen CASE-Tool *Software through Pictures* [14] erfüllt werden, mit dessen Unterstützung die Optimierungen am Objektmodell durchgeführt wurden. Hierbei ist hervorzuheben, daß für die unterschiedlichen Phasen der Softwareerstellung leistungsfähige Editoren bestehen, deren Navigationsmöglichkeiten den zyklischen Prozeß der Analyse und des Designs berücksichtigen ([10]). Die Erstellung graphischer Modelle und deren „Nachbearbeitung" in Tabellen wurde ebenso unterstützt wie die Dokumentation des Projektes. Features wie die Möglichkeit, Attributen bereits bei der Modellierung Eigenschaften wie „nur lesbar" oder Default-Werte zuzuweisen, haben sich beim Übergang zur Implementierung ebenfalls als vorteilhaft erwiesen. Insbesondere hilfreich war die übersichtliche Darstellung des vollständigen Objektmodells; die vergleichbare SNMP-MIB umfaßte demgegenüber 35 Seiten.

3.2 Optimierung des Objektmodells

Aus den am Anfang dieses Abschnitts gemachten Beobachtungen ließen sich folgende Regeln für die Optimierung des Objektmodells ableiten:

- In mehreren Klassen vorkommende identische Attribute und Operationen werden in einer (ggf. neu einzuführenden) Superklasse zusammengefaßt.

- Typenbezeichner werden entfernt. An die Stelle dieser Bezeichner treten neue Unterklassen.

- Pushbutton-Variablen werden zu Methoden der jeweiligen Klasse.

- Möglichst realitätsgetreue Modellierung von Objektbeziehungen; Einführung objektorientierter Hierarchien (Vererbung und Enthaltensein).

- Definition neuer Variablentypen für Attribute mit bestimmten Wertebereichen (z.B. Aufzählungstypen).

Die Konsequenzen der Anwendung dieser Regeln sind nachfolgend detailliert beschrieben.

3.2.1 Neue Superklassen für gemeinsame Attribute und Operationen

Auffällig an der ersten Version des Objektmodells ist, daß mehrere Klassen Attribute mit identischer Bedeutung (aber zum Teil abweichender Bezeichnung) hatten. Stattdessen bot es sich an, gemeinsame Attribute in eine Oberklasse aufzunehmen, betreffende Klassen von dieser Oberklasse abzuleiten und dafür in den Unterklassen die gemeinsamen Attribute zu streichen. Typische Beispiele für gemeinsame Attribute mehrerer Klassen sind Identifikatoren, Namensbezeichnungen und Statusvariablen. Diese traten u.a. in den Objekten `Printer`, `Storage` und `Processor` auf. Anstatt nun eine neue Oberklasse einzuführen, wurde der Klasse `Device` (umbenannt in `Generic Device`) die Rolle der Oberklasse zugewiesen. Damit wurde die

Aufgabe der `Device`-Klasse geändert. Sie dient nun als Wurzel der Vererbungshierarchie mehrerer Systemkomponenten. Dies erleichtert auch spätere Erweiterungen des Objektmodells, bei denen eine neue Systemkomponente von `Generic_Device` abgeleitet werden kann, wodurch schon eine gewisse Grundfunktionalität bereitgestellt werden kann (und zwar die, die in den meisten Komponenten gleich ist).

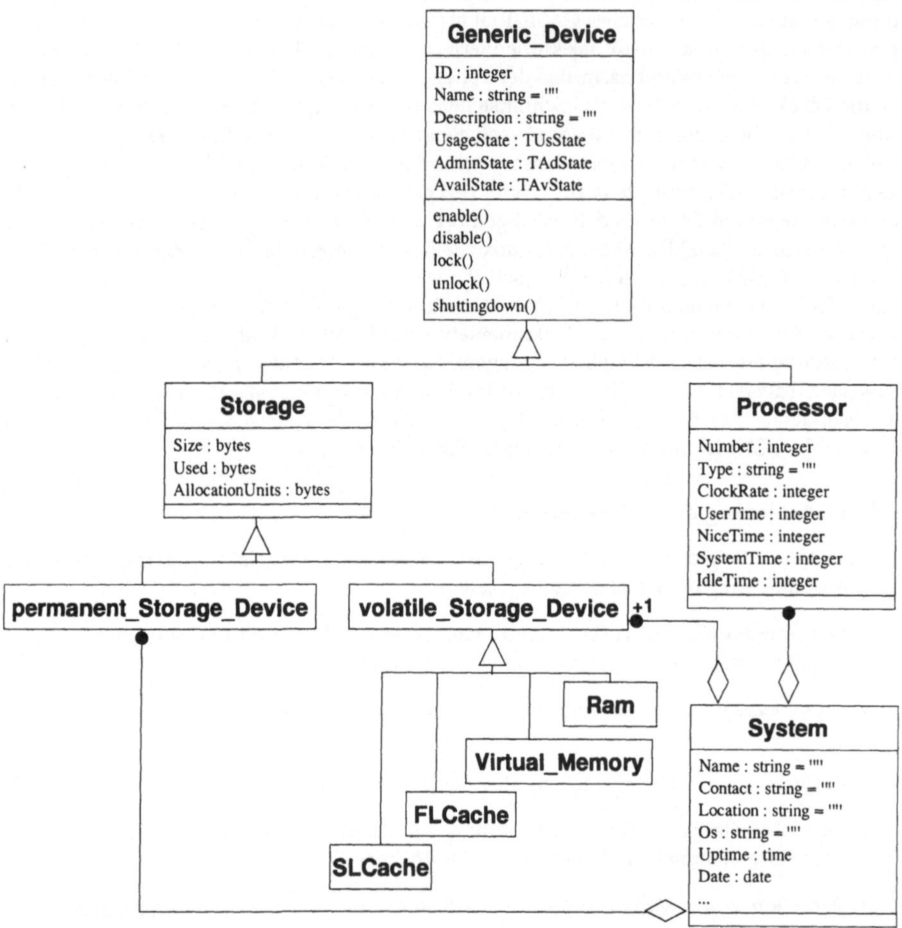

Abbildung 4: Optimiertes Objektmodell für das Workstation-Management (Ausschnitt)

3.2.2 Neue Unterklassen anstelle von Typvariablen

Dieser Optimierungsansatz ist die Antwort auf den zweiten Kritikpunkt an der ersten Version des Objektmodells. Durch vorhandene Typvariablen war es zwar möglich, Objekte verschiedener Typen einer Klasse zu instantiieren. Dies steht jedoch in klarem Widerspruch zum objektorientierten Klassenkonzept, wonach alle Instanzen einer Objektklasse dieselben Eigenschaften aufweisen sollten. Es war innerhalb des vorliegenden Objektmodells also nicht möglich, verschiedenen Typen einer Objektklasse unterschiedliche Eigenschaften (Attribute, Operationen etc.) zuzuweisen; jedes Objekt der Klasse (gleich welchen Typs) hätte den gleichen Aufbau gehabt. So konnte man zwar Objekte verschiedenen Typs der Klasse Device erzeugen (durch entsprechendes Belegen der Variablen Type); für jede dieser Komponenten hätten dann jedoch nur drei Variablen (Index, Description und State) zur Verfügung gestanden, die, separat betrachtet, nur über beschränkte Aussagekraft verfügen. Dies war ein weiterer Grund, weshalb die virtuelle d.h. nicht instantiierbare Klasse Generic_Device zur Wurzel des Vererbungsbaumes gemacht wurde (siehe auch 3.2.1). Soll nun ein Objekt für eine Systemkomponente erzeugt werden, so wird nicht die Generic_Device-Klasse instantiiert, die nun als Containerklasse für allgemeingültige Attribute dient, sondern eine entsprechende Subklasse.

Ähnlich verhielt es sich mit der Storage-Klasse. Hier konnten zwar die Typen Ram, VirtualMemory, FLCache und SLCache[5] erzeugt werden; es war jedoch nicht möglich, den einzelnen Typen auch unterschiedliche Eigenschaften zuzuordnen. Deshalb wurden die neuen Klassen permanentStorageDevice und volatileStorageDevice eingeführt. Dabei fielen unter die erste Subklasse Komponenten wie Festplatten, Magnetbänder oder Wechselfestplatten. Die zweite Subklasse sollte die Komponenten umfassen, die ursprünglich über die Storage-Klasse instantiiert wurden. Als Folge davon wurden die Subklassen Ram, VirtualMemory, FLCache und SLCache eingeführt.

3.2.3 Operationen anstelle von Pushbutton-Variablen

Das Problem der sogenannten Pushbutton-Variablen, welches in der SNMP-MIB bestand, wurde auch in die erste Version des Objektmodells (siehe Abbildung 3) übernommen: Eine Operation auf einem Objekt (und damit auf der entsprechenden Systemkomponente) mußte dadurch ausgelöst werden, daß einem entsprechenden Objektattribut ein Wert zugewiesen wurde. Hinsichtlich der Erkennbarkeit der Semantik einer Operation ist dies generell fragwürdig, da auf den ersten Blick nicht zwischen einem normalen Wertattribut und einem Pushbutton-Attribut unterschieden werden kann. Beim objektorientierten Ansatz ist dieses Problem jedoch sehr leicht zu lösen: An die Stelle der Pushbutton-Variablen traten Operationen. Für jeden möglichen Wert einer Pushbutton-Variablen wurde dabei eine eigene Operation eingeführt. Ein Beispiel hierfür ist das Attribut cpuAction der Processor-Klasse. Für die fünf Werte, die dieser Variable ursprünglich zugewiesen werden konnten, wurden die entsprechenden Operationen enable(), disable(), lock(), unlock() und shuttingdown() eingeführt. Die bisherige Wertzuweisung cpuAction:=1, ausgeführt durch das Senden einer SNMP set-Protokolldateneinheit an den Agenten, entspricht nun einem Aufruf der Operation enable(). Da diese fünf Operationen in vielen Komponenten eines Systems ebenfalls auftreten, wurden auch sie in die Klasse Generic_Device aufgenommen (siehe Abbildung 4).

3.2.4 Möglichst realitätsgetreue Modellierung der Objektbeziehungen

Hinsichtlich der Beziehungen zwischen Klassen weist die erste Version der Objektmodells dieselben Defizite auf, wie die SNMP-MIB: Es ist keinerlei Vererbungshierarchie vorhanden; Containment-Hierarchien sind nur ansatzweise vorhanden. Ein Grundgedanke des objektorientierten Paradigmas ist es jedoch, die reale Welt, d.h. die einzelnen Objekte sowie ihre Beziehungen zueinander, möglichst gut abzubilden. Die Einführung einer Vererbungshierarchie ist ein Modell für den Sachverhalt, daß eine Systemkomponente eine Spezialisierung einer anderen ist. So ist z.B. ein Mikroprozessor eine Spezialisierung eines Gerätes (Device).

Zur Wurzel des Enthaltenseins- oder Containment-Baumes wurde die Klasse System bestimmt. Dies entspricht auch der Realität: Ein (End-)System ist diejenige Hauptkomponente, die andere Teilkomponenten enthält. Dabei sollten Enthaltenseinsbeziehungen der Objektklasse System mit möglichst spezialisierten Klassen bestehen, also Klassen, die sich im Vererbungsbaum „unten" befinden. Damit können die einzelnen Beziehungen individuell gestaltet werden: So benötigt ein System mindestens einen Prozessor (hier also eine 1:n-Beziehung mit n≥1), jedoch kann es beliebig viele permanentStorageDevices besitzen (in diesem Fall eine 1:n-

---

Beziehung mit n≥0). Ein Drucker wiederum ist kein unmittelbarer Bestandteil eines Systems (im Sinne einer Workstation), sondern ein Peripheriegerät. Hier besteht also keine Aggregationsbeziehung, sondern eine einfache 1:n-Beziehung mit n≥0. Wäre die Beziehung zwischen System und „höher" liegenden Klassen modelliert worden, so wäre eine individuelle Gestaltung nicht möglich gewesen, da jede Subklasse dieselbe Beziehung zu System wie die entsprechende Oberklasse gehabt hätte. Abbildung 4 gibt einen Überblick über die Beziehungsstruktur eines Teils des optimierten Objektmodells.

Eine weitere Besonderheit findet sich in der Beziehung zwischen den Klassen Filesystem und Account (vormals die User-Klasse). Die Klasse Account enthielt in der SNMP-MIB Attribute, die benutzerspezifische Quoten für Betriebsmittel wie zum Beispiel Plattenplatz darstellen. Dies war semantisch eigentlich nicht korrekt, da eine Quota keine Eigenschaft eines Benutzers ist, sondern eine Eigenschaft der Beziehung zwischen einem Benutzer und einem Dateisystem. Aus diesem Grunde wurden die entsprechenden Attribute ausgelagert und unter der Assoziationsklasse Quota zusammengefaßt. Abbildung 5 veranschaulicht dies.

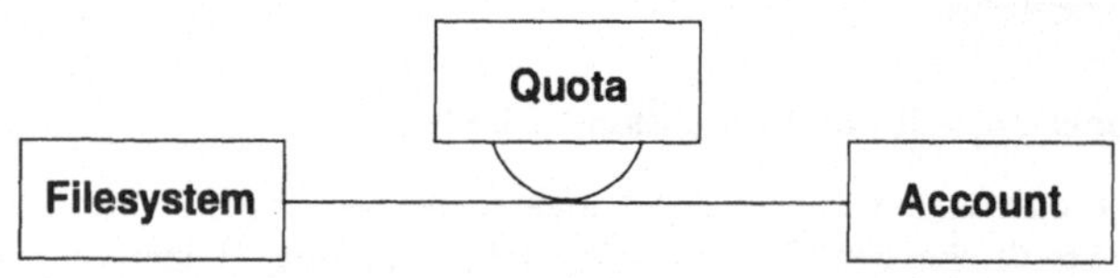

Abbildung 5: Anwendung von OMT-Assoziationsklassen

3.2.5 Neue Variablentypen für Variablen mit eingeschränktem Wertebereich

Die algorithmische Übersetzung der SNMP-MIB hatte nichts daran geändert, daß die meisten Attributtypen im Objektmodell einfache ASN.1-Grundtypen waren. Dies war in vielen Fällen problematisch: So hat die Variable OpState in der Objektklasse Processor den Datentyp integer, obwohl sie eigentlich nur die Werte 1 (für enabled) und 2 (für disabled) annehmen darf. Es wäre nun im Rahmen der Optimierung naheliegend gewesen, den Datentyp dieser Variablen auf boolean zu setzen. Es erwies sich jedoch als besser, einen (gleichwertigen) Aufzählungstyp zu definieren, der sofort erkennen läßt, in welchem Nutzungszustand sich ein Gerät befindet (enabled oder disabled).

Ein weiteres Beispiel für die Einführung eines neuen Datentyps ist die Variable AdminState (vorher AdState). Hier wurde (aus denselben Gründen wie oben) ein Aufzählungstyp definiert, der die Administrationszustände *unknown, unlocked, shutting down* und *locked* zuläßt.

4 Implementierung in CORBA

Da als Implementierungsarchitektur CORBA vorgesehen war, wurden zunächst die dem Objektmodell entsprechenden IDL-Schnittstellenbeschreibungen vom CASE-Tool generiert. Als Beispiel folgt in Listing 1 ein Auszug aus der Schnittstellenbeschreibung der Objektklasse System.

Die Ausgabe verdeutlicht, daß alle mit dem CASE-Tool angegebenen Einstellungen (readonly, Datentypen u.ä.) in die IDL-Ausgabe übernommen werden. An obiger Ausgabe ist auch gut zu erkennen, wie Beziehungen aus dem Objektmodell in IDL-Schnittstellenbeschreibungen abgebildet werden. Dabei stellte sich heraus, daß Beziehungen nur mangelhaft in IDL wiedergegeben werden.

```
{...}
// stp class definition 108
interface System
{
// stp class members
attribute string Contact;                      // einfache les-
attribute date Date;                           // und schreibbare
attribute string Hardware;                     // Attribute
attribute string Location;
attribute string Name;
readonly attribute string Os;                  // nur lesbare
readonly attribute time Uptime;                // Attribute
readonly attribute long maxProcessNumber;
readonly attribute long maxProcessSize;
attribute sequence<Printer> assnPrinter;       // 1:n Assoziation
attribute Process assnProcess;                 // einfache Assoz.
attribute sequence<Processor> aggrProcessor;   // 1:n Aggregation
...
};
```

Listing 1: IDL-Schnittstellenbeschreibung der Objektklasse `System` (Auszug)

4.1 Semantische Nachbesserungen bei der Generierung von IDL-Schnittstellen

Die Generierung gibt die Beziehungen zwischen Objektklassen zwar korrekt wieder; folgendes Problem ergibt sich jedoch durch die Beschreibung von Beziehungen durch Attribute: Wird ein Objekt einer Klasse instantiiert, welche in mehreren anderen Klassen durch entsprechende Attribute als assoziiert gekennzeichnet ist, kann es leicht zu Inkonsistenzen kommen, wenn das Objekt z.B. in der sequence eines Objektes zwar enthalten ist, in einem anderen Objekt jedoch nicht.

Außerdem mußten neue Methodenschnittstellen eingefügt werden, die die Gültigkeit der Beziehungen periodisch überwachen. So überprüft beispielsweise die Methode der `System`-Objektklasse update_Processes(), welche Prozesse momentan aktiv sind. Für die Methoden, die ausschließlich der Verwaltung von Beziehungen zwischen Objektklassen dienen, mußten daher neue Methoden entworfen und implementiert werden. Dies resultiert aus der Tatsache, daß der OMG *Object Relationship Service* [8] zwar spezifiziert wurde, aber noch nicht Bestandteil der CORBA-Entwicklungssysteme ist. Eine zukünftige Version des CORBA-Agenten wird diesen Dienst nutzen.

Bezüglich des Erzeugens und Löschens von Objekten bzw. der Objektverwaltung allgemein ergibt sich ein weiteres Problem: Es besteht keine zentrale Komponente (eine sogenannte *factory*), über die Objekte einer Klasse erzeugt, gelöscht oder zum Beispiel aufgelistet werden könnten. Eine Lösung für dieses und das obige Problem war die Einführung von Metaklassen. Zu jeder Klasse existierte damit eine weitere Klasse, von der allerdings nur ein einziges Objekt instantiiert wird und Funktionen bereitstellt, die der Verwaltung von Objekten der Hauptklasse dienen. Da diese Überlegungen rein implementierungsbedingt sind, wurde darauf verzichtet, die Metaklassen in das Objektmodell aufzunehmen.

Ein Fall, in dem der Nutzen von Metaklassen auf eine andere Art zum Vorschein kommt, trat im Zusammenhang mit der Prozeß-Klasse auf: Generell gilt, daß die CORBA-Systemmanagement-Objekte beim Systemstart instantiiert werden sollten. Bei statischen Objekten bzw. Objekten, die nur über eine geringe Änderungsdynamik verfügen (wie z.B. Prozessoren, Festplatten) ist dies auch kein Problem. Anders verhält es sich aber mit dynamischen Objekten, wie zum Beispiel bei der Überwachung von Prozessen. Es ist nahezu unmöglich, diese Objekte mit dem realen Systemzustand konsistent zu halten. Dazu hätte bei jedem Start eines Prozesses ein entsprechendes Prozeßobjekt instantiiert und bei Prozeßterminierung wieder gelöscht werden müssen. Durch den Zugriff auf die Prozeßobjekte über eine sogenannte „before/after"-Metaklasse MetaProcess, konnte dieses Problem gelöst werden. Sobald nun ein Zugriff auf die Metaklasse durchgeführt wird, wird der Bestand an Prozeßobjekten aktualisiert; das anfragende Objekt (in diesem Fall das Managementsystem) erhält also beim Zugriff immer den aktuellen Systemzustand.

4.2 Syntaktische Nachbearbeitung der generierten IDL-Schnittstellen

Als CORBA-Entwicklungsumgebung wird das IBM *SOMobjects Developer Toolkit* [4] eingesetzt; es umfaßt einen CORBA 1.2-konformen Object Request Broker, einen IDL-Compiler, die CORBA-Laufzeitumgebung und mehrere zu den OMG-Standards konforme Dienste [13]. Die vom CASE-Tool erzeugten IDL-Schnittstellenbeschreibungen konnten nicht unmittelbar als Eingabe für den SOM IDL-Compiler eingesetzt werden, da Nachbearbeitungen an folgenden Stellen erforderlich waren:

- **Definition von Attributtypen**
  Datentypen, die nicht zu den IDL-Grundtypen gehören, müssen, sofern sie nicht in der Attributdeklaration festgelegt sind, gesondert definiert werden. Weiter ist zu beachten, daß der SOM IDL-Compiler zwar Sequenzen kennt, oft jedoch nicht den Datentyp, über dem die Sequenz definiert wurde. Dem Auftreten von sequence(Processor) mußte die Definition der Objektklasse Processor vorangehen.

- **Ableitung aller IDL-Interfaces von SOMObject**
  Die Konventionen des SOM IDL-Compilers verlangen, daß alle auftretenden Schnittstellen von der Objektklasse SOMObject abgeleitet werden.

- **Ergänzung aller IDL-Dateien um eine „Implementation Section"**
  Hierbei mußte dem IDL-Compiler mitgeteilt werden, in welche DLL[6] die spätere Ausgabe geschrieben werden soll. Außerdem mußten noget- oder noset-Anweisungen für Nur-Lese- bzw. Schreib-Lese-Attribute eingefügt werden, um zu verhindern, daß der Compiler automatisch interne get- oder set-Operationen erzeugt, die den entsprechenden Attributwert liefern bzw. setzen. Dies war notwendig, da der bereits existierende Code eingebunden werden sollte.

4.3 Übernahme bestehenden Agentencodes

Nachdem die IDL-Beschreibungen der Objektklassen mit ihren Attributen und Methoden erzeugt und an das CORBA-Entwicklungssystem angepaßt waren, mußte nun in einem weiteren Schritt die Umsetzung der Funktionalität erfolgen, die die Nutzung der Managementinformation erst ermöglicht.

Dies ist gleichbedeutend mit der in zahlreichen Bereichen der Informatik auftretenden Fragestellung, wie bestehende Altsysteme (*legacy systems*) schonend in die objektorientierte Welt migriert werden können. Zentraler Gedanke ist hierbei, unter Zuhilfenahme sogenannter *Wrapper* bestehenden Code geeignet in Objektklassen zu kapseln und somit für neue objektorientierte Systeme zugreifbar zu machen. Der betrachtete SNMP-Agent ist in der Programmiersprache C implementiert worden und genügt damit keinesfalls objektorientierten Prinzipien. Dies ist jedoch für die Migration ohne Bedeutung, da für objektorientierte Applikationen der Begriff des „Perception is reality" gilt. Es ist also nicht erforderlich, daß ein System objektorientiert implementiert worden ist; maßgeblich ist jedoch, daß seine Bestandteile wie Objekte aussehen. Sehr wichtige Voraussetzungen für eine Kapselung in hinreichend feiner Granularität sind, daß das zu migrierende System genügend modular implementiert worden ist und die Schnittstellen seiner Prozeduren offengelegt sind bzw. die Prozeduren im Quellcode vorliegen. Beides war in

---

[6]DLL: Dynamic Link Library

unserem Fall gegeben (siehe 2.1).

Die IDL–Schnittstellenbeschreibungen werden nun einem IDL–Compiler übergeben, der zum einen die Schnittstellen der neu erstellten Objektklassen (hier: die *Wrapper* für die bereits bestehenden Prozeduren) innerhalb des ORB–Laufzeitsystems bekanntmacht und zum anderen die Datenstrukturen und Schnittstellen des CORBA–Agenten in einer herkömmlichen Programmiersprache (im betrachteten Fall: C) generiert. Momentan sind Algorithmen zur Übersetzung (sogenannte *Language Mappings*) der Quellsprache IDL in die Zielsprachen C, C++ und Smalltalk durch OMG–Standards spezifiziert; Abbildungen für ADA, COBOL und Java sowie die Skriptsprache Perl sind geplant.

Die so entstandenen C-Programmrümpfe des CORBA–Agenten können nun um die entsprechenden Aufrufe von Prozeduren des bestehenden SNMP–Agenten ergänzt werden, deren Aufgabe lediglich darin besteht, die erhaltenen Parameter auf die Parameter der bestehenden Agentenprozeduren abzubilden und anschließend diese Prozeduren aufzurufen. Hierbei ist es von großem Vorteil, daß der Agent modular aufgebaut ist und die Schnittstellen des Agenten sowohl zu den Ressourcen als auch zum Managementprotokoll hin klar definiert sind.

5 Zusammenfassung und Ausblick

Der Beitrag hat anhand eines praxisnahen Beispiels aufgezeigt, welche Schritte erforderlich sind, um aus bestehendem modularen Code eines SNMP-Agenten kooperierende CORBA-Managementobjekte zu gewinnen. Das in diesem Beitrag vorgestellte Vorgehensmodell stellt einen universell verwendbaren, systematischen Ansatz zum Re-Engineering bestehender Managementagenten dar. Drei kritische Erfolgsfaktoren konnten hierbei identifiziert werden: Der modulare Aufbau des zu portierenden Agenten, die Abstützung auf standardisierte Verfahren zur Transformation der Managementinformation sowie eine gute Werkzeugunterstützung durch CASE-Tools, die State-of-the-art–Modellierungstechniken (wie z.B. OMT) instrumentieren.

Die Tatsache, daß momentan noch syntaktische Divergenzen zwischen dem von CASE-Tools erzeugten und von CORBA-Entwicklungssystemen akzeptierten IDL-Schnittstellenbeschreibungen bestehen, ist angesichts des geringen Alters von CORBA verständlich; dies sind vielmehr natürliche Reibungsverluste bei der Kombination von frei am Markt erhältlichen Produkten, die sich zum Teil noch in einem sehr frühen Stadium befinden. Unter diese Kategorie fallen auch die angesprochenen Probleme bei der Überwachung der Gültigkeit von Beziehungen; sobald geeignete, bereits spezifizierte CORBAservices Bestandteil von kommerziell erhältlichen Entwicklungssystemen sind, wird sich eine zukünftige Version unserer Implementierung darauf abstützen können.

Ebenso konnte die Tragfähigkeit von CORBA für die Belange des Systemmanagements nachgewiesen werden, selbst wenn heutige CORBA-Entwicklungsumgebungen noch nicht die für den Produktionsbetrieb erforderliche Leistungsfähigkeit und Skalierbarkeit besitzen: Unzulänglichkeiten heutiger CORBA-Toolkits beruhen beispielsweise auf der Implementierung des *Interface Repository* in Form einfacher Dateien, deren Verzeichnisse von den Maschinen, auf denen der Object Request Broker läuft, wechselseitig über das *Network File System* exportiert bzw. gemountet werden müssen. Hierdurch entstehen massive Einbrüche der Performance.

Zweifellos sind mit dem derzeitigen Stand des Projektes noch nicht alle Möglichkeiten ausgeschöpft, die moderne OOA/OOD-Methoden bieten, da bisher das (statische) Objektmodell von Managementagenten im Mittelpunkt der Betrachtungen stand. Weitere Schritte bestehen daher in der Untersuchung und Modellierung der dynamischen Aspekte von Managementagenten sowie der Potentiale möglicher Delegierbarkeit von Managementaufgaben zur Laufzeit durch Managementsysteme an Managementagenten.

Danksagung
Der Autor dankt dem Münchner Netzmanagement Team für intensive Diskussionen zu früheren Versionen dieses Beitrags. Das MNM-Team, das von Prof. Hegering geleitet wird, ist eine Gruppe von Wissenschaftlern beider Münchner Universitäten und des Leibniz-Rechenzentrums der Bayerischen Akademie der Wissenschaften.

Literatur

[1] Case, J., McCloghrie, K., Rose, M., Waldbusser, S.: Structure of Management Information for version 2 of the Simple Network Management Protocol (SNMPv2). RFC 1902. IAB. (Januar 1996)

[2] The Common Object Request Broker: Architecture and Specification. OMG Specification Revision 2.0. Object Management Group. (Juli 1995)

[3] Gutschmidt, M., Neumair, B.: Integration von Netz- und Systemmanagement: Ziele und erste Erfahrungen. In: *Proceedings der 3. Fachtagung Arbeitsplatzrechensysteme (APS'95), Hannover*. Mai 1995

[4] SOMobjects: A Practical Introduction to SOM and DSOM. IBM Corporation, International Technical Support Organization. Research Triangle Park, NC 27709-2195, Juli 1994. Order Number: GG24-4357-00

[5] IBM Systems Monitor: Anatomy of a Smart Agent. IBM Corporation, International Technical Support Organization. Research Triangle Park, NC 27709-2195, Dezember 1994. Order Number: GG24-4398-00

[6] Mowbray, T. J., Zahavi, R.: The Essential CORBA - Systems Integration using Distributed Objects. John Wiley & Sons, Inc. 1995

[7] SunSoft's NEO Product Family. Product Overview. SunSoft Inc. (März 1996). http://www.sun.com/sunsoft/neo/external/whitepapers/FamilyNEO.ps

[8] CORBAservices: Common Object Services Specification, Volume 1. OMG Specification. Object Management Group. (März 1996)

[9] HP OpenView Operations Center Concepts Guide. User Manual. Hewlett Packard. (1993)

[10] Poston, R. M.: Automated from Object Models. Communications of the ACM, (September 1994)

[11] Rumbaugh, J., Blaha, M., Premerlani, W., Eddy, F., Lorensen, W.: Object-Oriented Modeling and Design. Prentice-Hall International, Inc. 1991

[12] Rutt, T.: Comparison of the OSI Management, OMG and Internet Management Models. A report of the Joint X/Open-NM Forum Inter-Domain Management Task Force. AT&T Bell Laboratories. (März 1994)

[13] SOMobjects Developer Toolkit Programmer's Guide Volume 2: Object Services. IBM Corporation. März 1996. First Edition

[14] Software through Pictures Technical White Paper. Interactive Development Environments. San Francisco, CA 94105, 1995

[15] Tivoli TME 10. IBM Announcement Letters (US) - Document '296-216. (Juni 1996). http://www1.ibmlink.ibm.com/PS/ALET/296216.PS

[16] Inter-Domain Management Specifications: Specification Translation (Final Sanity Check Draft). Preliminary Specification Pxxx. X/Open Ltd. (September 1996)

A Pattern Language for the Use of CORBA in Large Scale Business Applications

Fridtjof Toenniessen

sd&m
software design & management GmbH&Co.KG
Thomas-Dehlerstr. 27
81737 München

1.   Introduction

This paper describes the pattern language *Smart Proxy Decomposition*, an architectural pattern for the transport of large objects in a WAN using CORBA technology. It is designed for reuse in various contexts and shows the suitability of CORBA 2.0 for use in large scale business information systems. The pattern language considers high transaction rates combined with low bandwidth networks by

- transporting only these parts of the instances that are really requested

- offering flexible transport and caching strategies.

The Smart Proxy Decomposition is successfully used in the project DaRT (Database for railway carriages and locomotives) for the German Railway Company, in which two commercial available ORB products were brought into action to achieve interoperability between Smalltalk and C++. Although a number of important services specified in [COSS] have not yet been available, we already profit a lot by only using the product's message forwarding features.

It should be mentioned that the presented pattern language does not depend on the COSS services at all, not even on the usage of CORBA products. The communication mechanisms in the lower layers could also have been written with a TCP/IP library in C for example. However, using CORBA compliant products makes it much easier to deal with the problem.

2.   Description of the Pattern Language

The description of the patterns follows [Busch] as far as possible, using the original ideas of the building architect Christopher Alexander in [Alex].

2.1.   The Pattern Language Smart Proxy Decomposition

The Smart Proxy Decomposition describes the transport of large objects in distributed information systems using an architecture like CORBA. It allows flexible transmission of small packages of data. Thus it consideres high transaction rates and low bandwidth networks, which appear very often as restrictions in large scale business information systems. The pattern language will be motivated by an example:

Imagine you are designing an information system for a railway company, that allows to read and maintain the technical data of all the locomotives and waggons. There will be 500-1000 online users. It is proposed to use a two tier client/server architecture with one central server. This is because the vehicles move through the whole country and are maintained at the stations where they are at the moment. So distributed local servers would cause high redundancy and complexity.

During specification you are faced with vehicle objects that contain more than 400 technical attributes, some of them multivalued. Up to very distant stations your customer uses an older network technology with bandwidths down to 9,6 Kbaud. The clients and the server are implemented in two different object oriented languages (e.g. Smalltalk and C++).

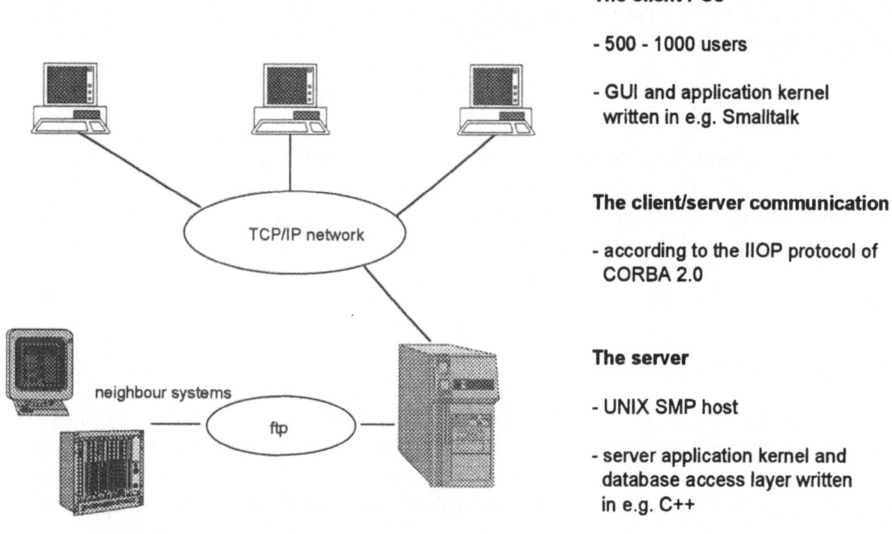

Fig 1: A possible client/server architecture in a distributed information system

Context and problem

You are designing an object oriented distributed information system, in which the data of large objects in a WAN are required by many users in parallel. A low bandwidth network makes it impossible to transmit complete objects for every user query. So how do you transport suitable parts of large objects with CORBA in a low bandwidth network?

Forces

The transmission of complete objects in a low bandwidth network from one node to the other will sometimes last a considerable amount of time. The experience shows that this time even increases if the network has high load. This is intolerable since the online users are very often interested in small parts of the objects only.

On the other extreme, the fine grained standard accessor methods for every attribute offered by CORBA interfaces don't work either: If we want to fill a window with 20 fields there would be the same number of server accesses. With this approach we would overload the dispatcher in the server nodes because of the high transaction rate caused by many users.

The next step is to assume that the truth lies in the middle: The large objects (as CORBA interfaces) should offer a special service for each window to fetch the data needed for filling it. But even this approach has disadvantages: In addition to being already monster objects, their interfaces get even more complex this way. This makes maintenance significantly harder. Furthermore, it seems suspicious to have too much functionality concentrated in only few objects of a large system.

So what advice do we get from CORBA?

The first problem that arises in our situation is the fact that CORBA is based upon remote *services* instead of what we actually need: remote *data*. All you get on the client side is a proxy of the object containing the data. Of course there is no reason to reproach CORBA with that! The CORBA philosophy stems from the pure object oriented principles of data abstraction, encapsulation and object identity while guaranteeing full location transparency. That means the data of the objects are not directly visible to the clients and no copies of objects should exist.

On the other side, CORBA offers a general mechanism for moving and copying objects between the network nodes (see the life cycle services in [COSS]). But unfortunately this mechanism is too expensive for our purposes: For every object to copy you first have to locate factory objects. In following steps you have to link these remote factories with the original object and tell the factory to instatiate a remote copy. So you will have a number of remote calls reducing performance significantly. Furthermore, the standard is rather generic at this point, so it seems that commercial products will at most offer a general framework and you have to code the important parts by yourself anyway.

All these considerations make it necessary to search for a pragmatic, flexible and light-weight solution. One possible architecture satisfying these requirements will be presented in the following sections.

Solution

First of all decompose your large classes on the server nodes so that you get smaller ones, whose data is transported in less than a second. The decomposition should be done in a way such that the data required in one dialog step corresponds roughly to the data contained in one object. Use weak coupling by references between the small objects.

Now use the same class model on the client and install a remote object reference (e.g. a CORBA reference) for each of these proxy classes to the corresponding class on the server. Being exactly doubled on the client, the proxy classes have the same instance variables as their counterparts on the server (including the local references to other proxies). This makes them *smart* proxies because their instance variables serve as a cache for the elementary data.

Every object on the server offers a remote service to transport its elementary data to the smart proxy on the client, which calls this service whenever its data should be displayed on the screen and is not already cached (smart pointer logic). The local references on the client side are used to navigate through the object graph and are part of the elementary data of an object. This makes it possible to instantiate every smart proxy dynamically during navigation when the data of an object is required that holds a reference to it.

This approach is shown in the figure below. It guarantees that only the really requested objects are allocated on the clients and no unnecessary data is transported by the network.

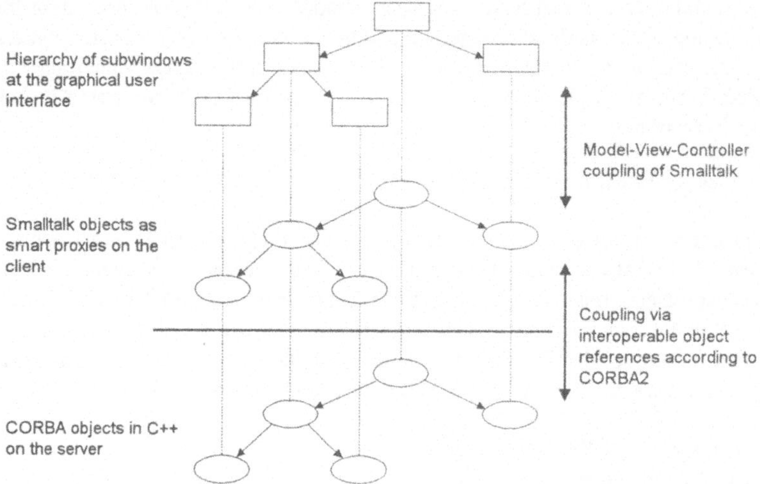

Fig 2: The smart proxies on the client copy the object hierarchy on the server

Structure

The Smart Proxy Decomposition as a pattern language consists of a number of design patterns. The following figure presents an overview. The important parts of the pattern language highlighted with shadows will be presented in the following chapters.

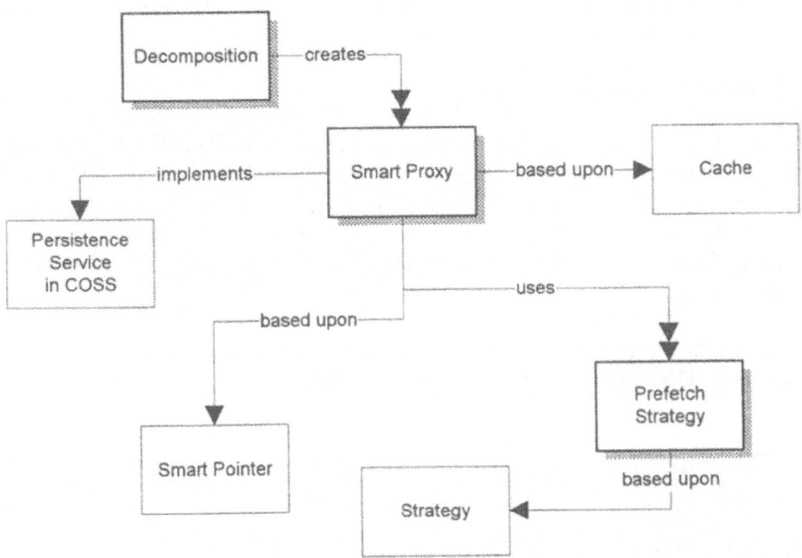

Fig 3: The components of the pattern language

Decomposition

This principle (it is rather a principle than a pattern) keeps you from transporting too much data and instantiating too much objects on the clients by using weak coupling through references. When the objects in your application are already fine grained enough and weakly coupled you don't need to apply this principle.

Smart Proxy

The objects on the client side fulfill two tasks: Primarily they serve as proxies and pass through the requests to the corresponding objects on the server (see [CORBA]). On the other hand, they extend the proxy functionality with the instance variables of their counterparts on the server. These variables can be divided into two categories:

- elementary variables serve as cache for the data to be displayed on the screen

- local references to other smart proxies enable the navigation through the object graph

Smart Pointer

This generally known pattern is used in e.g. almost every database access layer and is also mentioned in the standard ODMG-93 [ODMG] for object database systems. The smart proxies use the smart pointer mechanism for caching.

Persistence Service according to the standard COSS

As will be explained in the dynamics section, the smart proxies implement a two-step protocol according to the persistent objects in [COSS]. In that protocol you first establish a connection to the persistent object in form of a remote reference. Only when you really need the data they are fetched in a second step.

Prefetch Strategy

For reasons of performance it is very important to be flexible in the data transport logic. The smart proxies are therefore able to use different strategies which are connected via the well known *Strategy* pattern [Gamma]. A useful strategy could be for example transporting not only the elementary data of an object but also those of a whole subtree of objects under the actual object. Especially if you have very small objects or multivalued instance variables this will be rather useful.

The following three sections contain more detailed descriptions of the the three main patterns in this language: Decomposition, Smart Proxy and Prefetch Strategy.

2.2.   Decomposition

Context and problem

Your application entities resulting from analysis are huge aggregations of several hundred attributes. You don't want to instantiate them always completely on the clients. How can you manage to allocate and transport only these parts of the objects you are interested in?

Solution

Decompose your large analysis objects into smaller ones which form application specific units. Although this results semantically very often in a tree-like *aggregation*, you have to couple the parts weakly by *references*. By using references instead of embedding it is possible to allocate only these parts of the objects you are interested in. This minimizes network load and memory allocation on client and server.

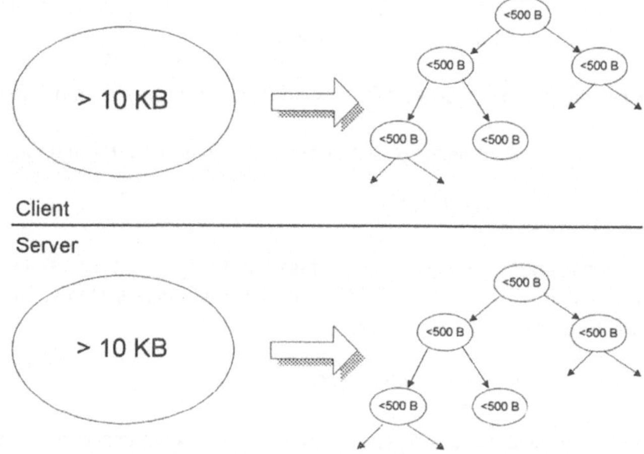

Fig 4: Decomposition of large objects causes smaller units of data to be transported

The class model on the client and server side are semantically equivalent. This can be done even when you use different languages on client and server. You only have to restrict yourself to a common denominator of the language features.

2.3. Smart Proxies

Context and problem

Imagine you are designing a distributed information system whose client nodes display the data of persistent objects spread all over the network. Clients and servers will be implemented in object oriented languages which suggest an architecture like CORBA to you. The system is based upon a low bandwidth network that does not allow too many parallel server accesses or the transport of large units of data. So how can you manage the transport of the object's data without overloading the servers and the network?

Solution

At first, use the *Proxy* pattern ([Busch], [Gamma]) as suggested in [CORBA] to have a handle to the remote objects whose data is to be displayed. The important difference to the standard proxy pattern consists of two aspects:

- The proxy contains as a cache all the instance variables of the object it is connected to.

- Every object on the server offers (beside others) a remote service `getElementaryData` to return its elementary data to the proxy.

Note that these elementary data comprise both data to be displayed on the screen *and* remote references of all objects referenced directly by the actual object. By this means you need to read objects by key only for the roots of object hierarchies. For further navigation all the handles are already available. The next sections will help the reader to understand this completely.

The first property makes a proxy 'smart'. It is therefore called a *smart proxy*. To summarize, a smart proxy contains four different kinds of instance variables:

- a reference to a pure proxy as specified in [CORBA]. This proxy represents the actual link to the corresponding server object

- some variables to maintain local information, e.g. cache state or dirty markers

- the elementary data of the server object to display on the screen, e.g. numbers, strings, characters

- local references to other smart proxies to fully imitate the object graph(s) on the server(s)

The first two kinds of instance variables should be inherited from an abstract superclass. Note that the smart proxies let the system appear to the client as a local one. They make it possible to transparently navigate through the object graph as if there were no remote server accesses at all.

An interesting fact is that the smart proxies are able to use different cache strategies to optimize performance (see the pattern *Prefetch Strategy* below).

Structure

A simplified and idealized part of a more comprehensive class model, containing a `Vehicle` and a `Motor`, will serve as an example for the following sections.

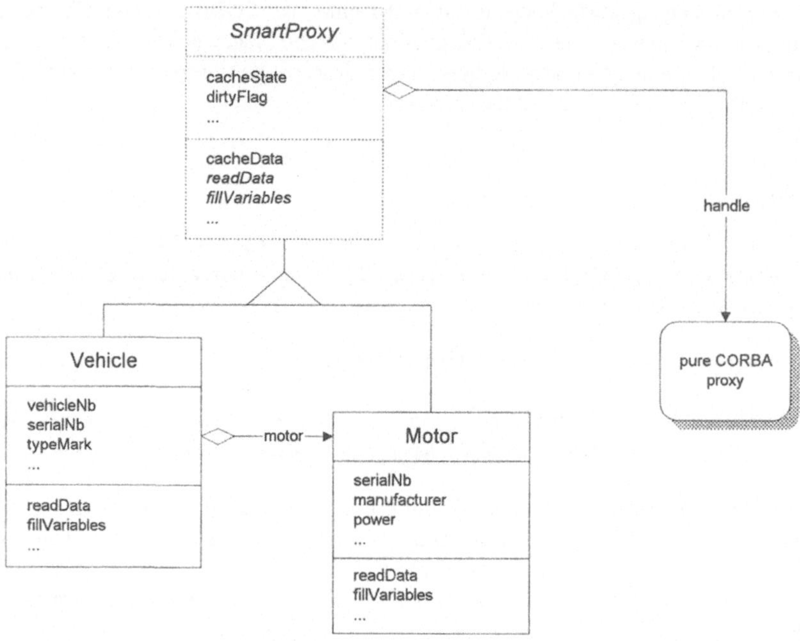

Fig 5: A small class model of smart proxies inheriting from `SmartProxy`

The `Vehicle` and `Motor` classes on the client side contain the same application specific attributes as their counterparts on the server. Further they inherit a `handle` to the pure CORBA proxy and some attributes to administer the cache state from an abstract class `SmartProxy`.

Dynamics

When the action for reading an instance `aVehicle` of class `Vehicle` is triggered from the user interface, the dialog control first calls the class method `readVehicle`. In a class variable of `Vehicle` we have a reference to `aVehicleFactory` on the client: this is a pure proxy (in the sense of CORBA) to the real object factory `aVehicleFactory` on the server. This CORBA connection is established during the start-up of the client processes. `aVehicleFactory` offers the interface method `readVehicle` taking an application key and returning a remote reference to the selected object (lying e.g. in a database). Finally the local copy `aVehicle` is instantiated, equipped with the reference `aVehicleReference` in the `handle` and with its cache state set to CONNECTED. (Later on this state will cause the reading of the elementary data when an instance variable is to be displayed for the first time.)

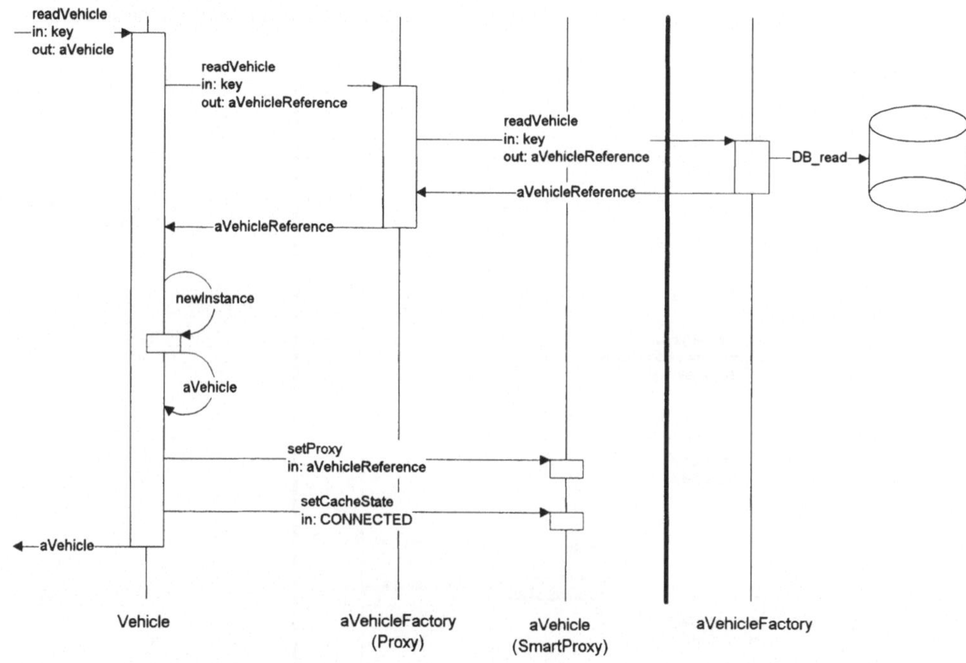

Fig 6: Scenario diagram for connecting the root of an object hierarchy

Here is a code example in Smalltalk for better understanding:

```smalltalk
Vehicle class >> readVehicle: key

    | aVehicle |

    "the remote call via CORBA"
    aVehicleReference := self factoryProxy readVehicle: key.

    "creating and connecting the smart proxy"
    aVehicle := Vehicle new.
    aVehicle setProxy: aVehicleReference.
    aVehicle cacheState: #CONNECTED.

    ^aVehicle
```

Now suppose that a widget is opened which shows some application specific data of `aVehicle`, e.g. the `vehicleNb`. The GUI framework calls the accessor method `vehicleNb`. Here the smart pointer mechanism recognizes the state CONNECTED and activates the template method `cacheData`. Now the method `readData` (implemented in the subclasses of `SmartProxy`) is called providing the caller with a class specific data structure `data`. This structure contains the elementary data for displaying and the remote reference to `aMotor` for further navigation. By this means `aMotor` needs no remote factory for itself because the handle is already available on the client. The next method `fillVariables` fills the elementary data of `aVehicle`, creates a local reference to a new smart proxy `aMotor` which on its part is connected to its counterpart on the server.

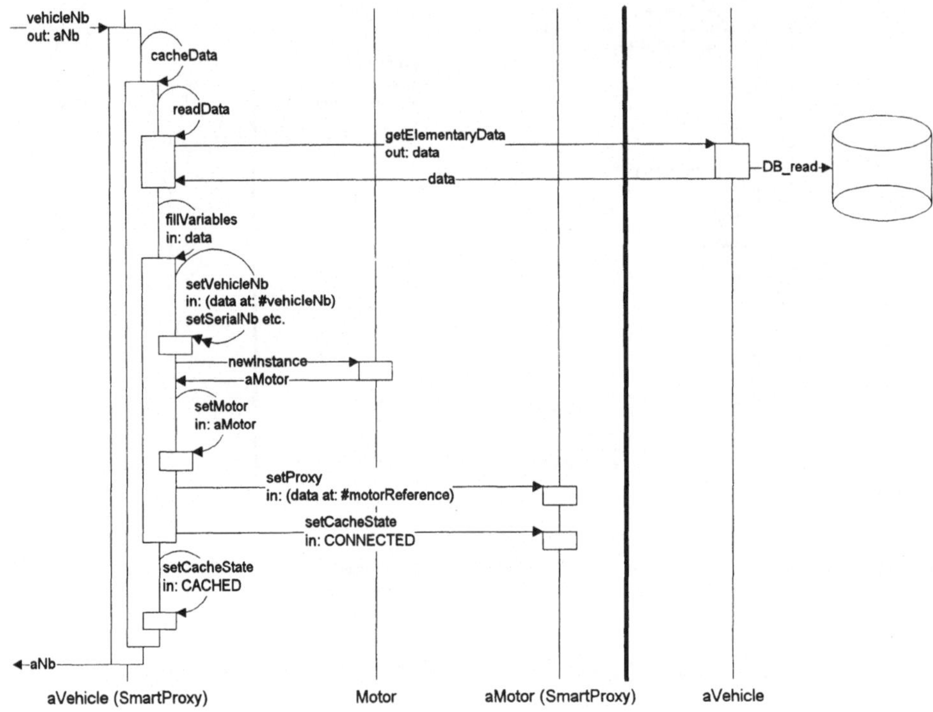

Fig 7: Scenario diagram for accessing an elementary attribute of the `Vehicle`

Note that the methods of the `SmartProxy` are structured according to the metapattern *Template Hook Unification* following [Pree]: The template method `cacheData` (see also the pattern *Template Method* in [Gamma]) calls the two virtual hook methods `readData` and `fillVariables` implemented in the concrete subclasses. In the Smalltalk example above the standard accessor to get the `vehicleNb` looks like:

```
Vehicle >> vehicleNb

    self isConnectedButNotCached ifTrue: [ self cacheData ].
    ^vehicleNb
```

Here the template method `cacheData` is implemented as:

```
SmartProxy >> cacheData

     | data |

     [ "getting the data stream via the handle"
       data := self readData.

       "filling all the instance variables of Vehicle"
       self fillVariables: data.

       "setting the own status"
       self cacheState: #CACHED
     ]
```

The hook methods or "Hot Spots" (Pree) `readData` and `fillVariables` look like:

```
Vehicle >> readData

     ^self handle getElementaryData


Vehicle >> fillVariables: data

     "first filling all the strings and chars..."
     self vehicleNb: (data at: #vehicleNb);
          serialNb:  (data at: #serialNb);
     ...

     "creating the smart proxy for Motor and connecting
      it to the corresponding server object"
     motor := Motor new.
     motor setProxy: (data at: #motorReference).
     motor cacheState: #CONNECTED.
```

If the user navigates to a widget containig data of `aMotor`, the same caching mechanism is triggered as before with `aVehicle`. In case of having still more references emerging from `aMotor`, the procedure would continue recursively.

Note that the methods `cacheData`, `readData` or `fillVariables` semantically belong to a seperate layer: the communication layer, a special case of access layer. Embedding these methods within the application class corresponds to the architectural pattern *Multilayer Class* (see [ARCUS]).

2.4.   Prefetch Strategies

Context and problem

Imagine you are building a client cache for an object graph containing a lot of fine grained objects with multivalued attributes on a server. Using e.g. the default two-step protocol as specified in [COSS] for persistent objects would be far too expensive. How do you implement different prefetch strategies to be able to read more than one object at once in a flexible way?

Solution

Use the well known *Strategy* pattern as described in [Gamma] and delegate the calls of the hook methods `readData` and `fillVariables` to separate strategy classes. This approach is also known as *Template-Hook 1:1-Connection* according to [Pree].

Structure

For keeping the network load as flexible as possible we extend the abstract class `SmartProxy` with a reference to an abstract strategy class `CacheStrategy` which works according to the *Strategy* pattern: At runtime every smart proxy is equipped with a special instance of a subclass of `CacheStrategy`. This subclass implements the hook methods `readData` and `fillVariables`.

Note that by delegating the hotspots to separate strategies we somehow leave the concept of the *Multilayer Class*.

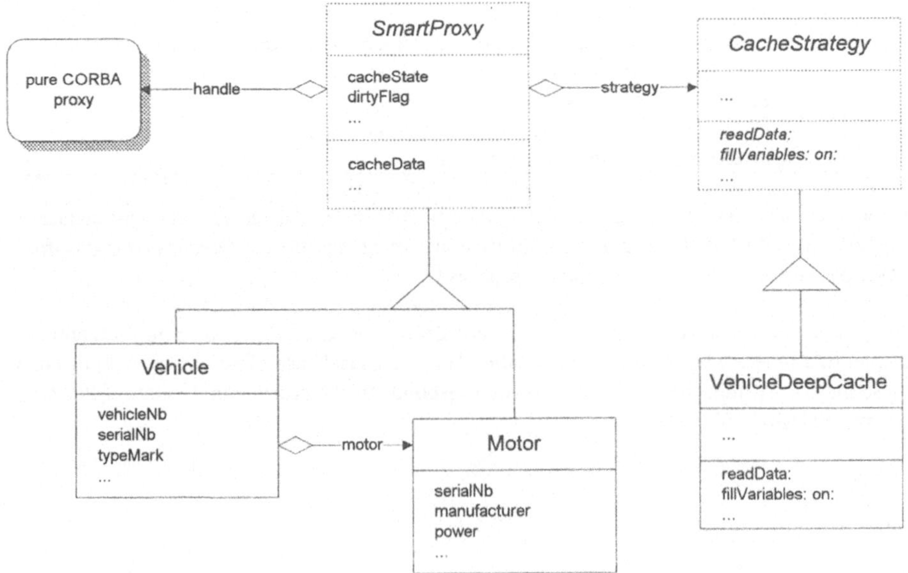

Fig 8: The above class model when using different transport strategies

The `VehicleDeepCache` can be plugged into a smart proxy for `Vehicle` to read the complete data of the `Vehicle` and the `Motor` at once when the first instance variable of the vehicle is needed. This is illustrated by the following code examples. Note that when using different strategies, the hook methods have to be equipped with an additional parameter for accessing the smart proxy objects.

```
SmartProxy >> cacheData

    | data |

      "getting the data stream via the handle"
      data := self strategy readData: self.

      self strategy fillVariables: data on: self.
      self cacheState: #CACHED


VehicleDeepCache >> readData: aSmartProxy

    | deepData |

      "getting the deep data stream via the handle"
      deepData := aSmartProxy handle getDeepData.
      ^deepData
```

Of course the method `fillVariables` will now be more complicated, because it has to (re)construct parts of an object graph from a flat data structure:

```
VehicleDeepCache >> fillVariables: data on: aVehicle

      "filling the strings and numbers of Vehicle"
      aVehicle vehicleNb: (data at: #vehicleNb);
             serialNb:  (data at: #serialNb);
             typeMark:  (data at: #typeMark);
      ...

      "creating and connecting the Motor smart proxy"
      aVehicle motor: Motor new.
      aVehicle motor setProxy: (data at: #motorReference).
      aVehicle motor cacheState: #CONNECTED.

      "filling the strings and numbers of Motor"
      aVehicle motor serialNb: (data at: #Motor_serialNb);
             motor manufacturer:
                            (data at: #Motor_manufacturer);
             motor power: (data at: #Motor_power);
      ...

      aVehicle motor cacheState: #CACHED
```

Note that the class `VehicleDeepCache` is a specific strategy suitable for `Vehicle` only. This restriction can be avoided in compilated languages only through the introduction of meta classes (see also the pattern *Reflection* in [Busch]), which hold information about the elementary instance variables and the relationships between objects. In Smalltalk however, meta information is available at runtime and the strategy classes can be implemented generally[1]. Several general strategies, valid for all classes, can now be implemented, e.g.

- `Default`, the standard case reading the elementary data only,

- `CacheToLevel_N`, reading a subtree of depth N starting from the actual object,

- `CacheMultiValued`, reading the multivalued attributes in addition to the elementary data.

---

[1] This is only a proposal for the future. It has not yet been implemented.

Literature

[Alex]   **C. Alexander**: *The Timeless Way of Building*, Oxford University Press 1979.

[ARCUS]   **J. Coldewey, W. Keller**: *Multilayer Class*, pre-print for the proceedings to the PLoP96.

[Busch]   **Frank Buschmann et al.**: *Pattern Oriented Software Architecture*, J. Wiley & Sons 1996.

[CORBA]   **OMG**: *The Common Object Request Broker: Architecture and Specification, Revision 2.0*, July 1995.

[COSS]   **OMG**: *CORBAservices: Common Object Services Specification, Revised Edition*, March 1995.

[Gamma]   **E. Gamma et al.**: *Design Patterns*, Addison Wesley 1995

[ODMG]   **Rick G. G. Cattell (Ed.) et. al.**: *Object Database Standard: ODMG-93 - Release 1.2* Morgan Kaufmann Publishers, San Mateo, California, 1996.

[Pree]   **W. Pree**: *Design Patterns for Object Oriented Software Development*, Addison Wesley 1994.

Zugriffsmodalitäten für objektintensive Anwendungen in verteilten Systemen[*]

Jörn Hartroth, Dietmar A. Kottmann, Arnd G. Grosse
Institut für Telematik, Universität Karlsruhe
Zirkel 2, 76128 Karlsruhe
Tel.: (+49) 721 608-[4045|4022|4026], Fax: (+49) 721 38 80 97
e-mail: [hartroth| kottmann| grosse]@ira.uka.de

Kurzfassung

Die Integration unabhängiger Anwendungen in einem verteilten System basiert zunächst auf der Nutzung eines gemeinsamen Datenbestandes. Aus Anwendungserfordernissen heraus hat sich dabei die objektorientierte Datenmodellierung und die Datenhaltung in objektorientierten Datenbanken durchgesetzt. Diese Vorgehensweise ist mit den heutigen Client-Server-Datenbanken dann geeignet, wenn die Anwendung komplett in einem homogenen Netz abläuft. Sind hingegen wie bei der standortübergreifenden Integration in Unternehmen oder der Integration mobiler Teilnehmer Netzgrenzen zu überwinden, so gerät diese starre Architektur an ihre Leistungsgrenze. Als Alternative wird in der vorliegenden Arbeit die systemtechnische Integration dreier Zugriffsmodalitäten vorgestellt, die neben der existierenden Architektur Konzepte aus Verteilungsplattformen wie OMG CORBA und aus aktuellen agentenbasierten Systemen ausnutzen. Damit wird unter Beibehaltung eines einheitlichen Entwicklungszyklusses die situationsgerechte Anpassung einer Anwendung an die aktuellen Netzgegebenheiten ermöglicht. Im folgenden werden die konzeptionellen und architekturellen Grundlagen dieser sogenannten *Stublet*-Lösung und ihre Umsetzung an unserem aktuellen Prototyp vorgestellt.

1　Einleitung

Die Integration unabhängiger Anwendungen in verteilten Systemen beginnt mit der Nutzung eines gemeinsamen Datenbestands. Dies zeigt schon ein Blick auf die Kernfunktionalität der heute verbreiteten Netzbetriebssysteme wie Novell Netware oder Banyan Vines [Zun94], die zunächst einen gemeinsamen Datenspeicher umfaßt. Werden erhöhte Anforderungen an die Datenintegrität, die Beherrschung nebenläufiger Zugriffe durch viele Nutzer oder die Fehlertoleranz gestellt, so sind Datenbanksysteme der geeignete Integrationskern. Beleg dafür ist der kommerzielle Erfolg der Datenbankschnittstelle ODBC [Ude93], die Schnittstelle MsqlJava [Col96] von Java [Sun95] zu der freien SQL-Datenbank Msql oder die aktuellen Bemühungen

---

[*] Diese Arbeit entstand im Rahmen des Sonderforschungsbereichs 346 „Rechnerintegrierte Konstuktion und Fertigung von Bauteilen" der Deutschen Forschungsgemeinschaft.

mit JDBC [Sun96] ein SQL-Interface für Java zu standardisieren. Viele moderne Anwendungsgebiete wie ingenieurwissenschaftliche Anwendungen oder Software-Engineering weisen zudem eine hohe strukturelle Komplexität auf, die am besten mit einem objektorientierten Datenmodell beherrscht werden kann [KeM94, HMN*95]. Folglich haben objektorientierte Datenbanken (ooDB) ein großes Potential, als Integrationsplattformen für unabhängige Anwendungen zu dienen.

Objektorientierte Datenbanken sind durch ihre Client/Server-Architektur [HMN*95] bereits für den Einsatz in verteilten Systemen vorbereitet. Da heutige Systeme Objektzugriffe auf die Übertragung unselektierter Daten vom Server zum Client abbilden, stellen sie hohe Anforderungen an die grundlegenden Netze, so daß ihr Einsatzbereich auf LAN-Umgebungen beschränkt ist. Auf der anderen Seite ergibt sich aus aktuellen Engpässen die Forderung nach der Modellierung, Optimierung und Integration von Abläufen, die sich auf Unternehmen als Ganzes beziehen [Jab95] oder gar die Unternehmensgrenze überschreiten [Sch93], was zwangsläufig die Überschreitung von LAN-Grenzen nach sich zieht. Verglichen mit LANs sind die dann zu verwendenden Netze langsamer oder zumindest kostenintensiver. Um auch dabei ooDBs als anwendungsadäquate Integrationsplattform verwenden zu können, muß die Möglichkeit geschaffen werden, andere Zugriffsmodalitäten zu unterstützen, um den Datenverkehr über Netzgrenzen hinweg zu minimieren. Einen vielversprechenden Ansatzpunkt bilden die agentenbasierte Systeme [CGH*95], da sie die dynamische Übertragung und Installation von Selektionsfunktionen ermöglichen. Erfordert dies aber die komplette Neuentwicklung von Anwendungen, so ist wenig gewonnen. Wünschenswert ist vielmehr ein integrierter Ansatz, der die Nutzung mehrerer Zugriffsmodalitäten je nach vorliegender Netzsituation ermöglicht.

Diese Arbeit beschreibt einen solchen Ansatz. Ausgehend von der Erörterung des Felds der objektintensiven Anwendungen und der bestehenden Technologie objektorientierter Datenbanken in Kapitel 2, werden in Kapitel 3 deren Anforderungen an eine Unterstützungstechnologie in verteilten Systemen abgeleitet. Aus dieser Diskussion präzisiert Kapitel 4 sinnvolle Zugriffsmodalitäten näher. Sie umfassen neben den bereits oben skizzierten eine dritte Modalität, die auf den Konzepten bekannter Verteilungsplattformen wie OMG CORBA [OMG92] basiert. Diese werden in einen gemeinsamen Entwicklungszyklus und in eine Systemarchitektur integriert. Erfahrungen mit dem aus diesem Konzept abgeleiteten Prototypen bilden dann den Gegenstand von Kapitel 5. Der Ansatz wird in Kapitel 6 mit alternativen Lösungen verglichen, bevor Kapitel 7 die Ergebnisse knapp zusammenfaßt und mit einem kurzen Ausblick schließt.

2 Objektintensive Anwendungen in verteilten Systemen

2.1 Integration unabhängiger Anwendungen

Erfolgt die Interaktion einer Anwendung mit anderen in erster Linie über den Austausch von Objekten, so wird von *objektintensiven Anwendungen* gesprochen. Dabei kann natürlich orthogonal eine Aktivierungskontrolle durch ein Workflow-Management-System [Jab95] erfolgen. Typische Fälle für derartige Anwendungen sind die Integration im Bürobereich oder in der rechnerintegrierten Konstruktion und Fertigung. In dieser Arbeit liegt der primäre Fokus auf dem zweiten Bereich, da er durch die Wechselwirkungen mit physikalischen Prozessen und die Zusammenhänge zwischen Informations- und physikalischen Materialflüssen generell größere Anforderungen stellt. Zudem ist die Komplexität der abzubildenden Objekte und Prozesse so hoch, daß sie zur Abbildung objektorientierte Konzepte erfordern [Hay93, KeM94].

Basis der Integration ist ein gemeinsames Objektschema, das die Struktur und Semantik der von den einzelnen Anwendungen verwendeten Daten festlegt. Beispiele für solche Schemata sind STEP [GAE*94], das allerdings nicht die volle Mächtigkeit der objektorientierten Modellierung ausnutzt, oder das im SFB 346 entwickelte voll objektorientierte Produkt-Produktionsmodell (PPM) [MeH95]. Ist das gemeinsame Schema dann in eine objektorientierte Datenbank abgebildet, so können unabhängige Anwendungen über das Schema interagieren, wobei evtl. noch eine Konvertierung von anwendungslokalen Beständen über Prä- und Postprozessoren erfolgen muß.

2.2 Architektur objektorientierter Datenbanken

Der Begriff objektorientierte Datenbank ist heute mit unterschiedlichen Belegung erfüllt, wie deutlich aus den Ansichten der drei maßgeblichen Manifeste [ABD*89, SRL*91, DaD95] hervorgeht. Im folgenden wird der Begriff in der oftmals als „C++-Datenbanken" bezeichneten Bedeutung verwendet, deren Architektur in Abb. 1 skizziert ist.

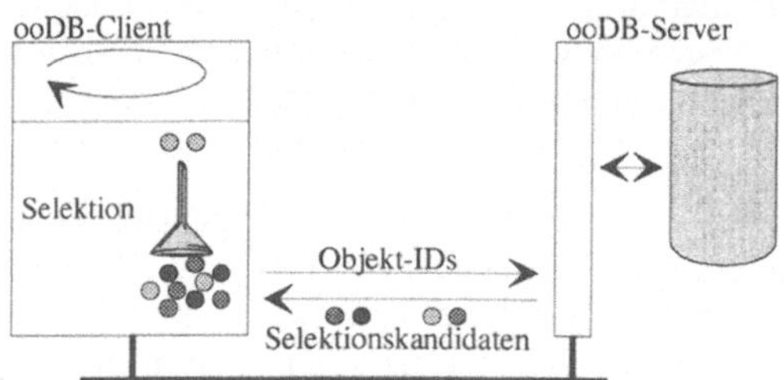

*Abb. 1: Prinzip objektorientierter
Datenbanken*

Eine objektorientierte Datenbank ist in einen ooDB-Server, der die persistente Ablage der Objekte übernimmt, und in viele ooDB-Clients, auf denen die zugreifenden Anwendungen ablaufen, unterteilt. Zum Zugriff auf persistente Objekte wird in den kommerziell verbreiteten Architekturvarianten des Datei-, Seiten- oder Objektservers [HMN*95] durch die Übermittlung der ID des gewünschten Objekts zum ooDB-Server die Übertragung der Inhalte des gewünschten Objekts zum ooDB-Client ausgelöst. Diese Übertragung beschränkt sich auf die Zustandskomponenten des Objekts. Die Methoden sind bereits in der Anwendung integriert, da das ooDB-Schema beim Übersetzen der Anwendung bekannt ist. Beispiele für derartige Datenbanken sind Objectivity (Datei-Server) [Obj90], Objectstore (Seiten-Server) [LLD*91] oder Ontos (Objekt-Server) [Ont91].

Das Kennzeichen objektorientierter Datenbanken ist es, daß die Selektion der für die Anwendung relevanten Informationen vollständig auf Seiten des ooDB-Clients erfolgt. Dies betrifft sowohl *mengenwertige Anfragen*, bei denen in Analogie zu SQL-Datenbanken aus einer Kandidatenliste passende Objekte ausgewählt werden, als auch *navigierende Anfragen*, wie beispielsweise die Frage nach einer bestimmten Ecke eines in BREP-Repräsentation abgelegten CAD-Körpers, bei der ausgehend von der Objekt-ID des Körpers zunächst auf das betroffene Flächenobjekt und dann auf die gewünschte Ecke navigiert wird. Damit ist i. allg. die Menge der über das Netz übertragenen Objekte weit größer als sie aus Anwendungsgesichtspunkten heraus nötig wäre. Diese Zugriffsmodalität wird im folgenden als *unmittelbarer Client* bezeichnet.

3 Anforderungen in unterschiedlichen Netzumgebungen

Aus der Diskussion der Architektur objektorientierter Datenbanken in Kapitel 2.2 läßt sich ableiten, daß der Ansatz auf der Annahme einer breitbandigen Verbindung zwischen ooDB-Client und ooDB-Server basiert. Diese Annahme ist bei der Verwendung von objektorientierten Datenbanken zur unternehmensweiten Integration nicht mehr haltbar, da nun standortübergeifend Objekte ausgetauscht werden müssen. Dabei ist es erforderlich, den Datentransfer über die auftretenden *Netzgrenzen* zu überwinden, da die dazu nötigen WANs verglichen mit LANs schmalbandig und teuer sind. Ein extremes Beispiel hierfür ist die Integration von Vertriebspersonal über Mobilnetze. So bietet beispielsweise das deutsche Datenfunknetz MODACOM eine Bandbreite von nur 9600 bit/s, wobei zudem die Übertragung von 1 MByte Daten zwischen 83 und 222 DM kostet [Bec96].

Unterscheidet man Netze gemäß den Netzgrenzen, über die Kommunikation vermieden werden soll, so resultieren aus Sicht eines ooDB-Clients die 5 prinzipiellen in Abb. 2 dargestellten Fälle. Relevant ist die Plazierung des ooDB-Clienten, des ooDB-Servers und der Entwicklung der Client-Anwendung in organisatorisch zusammenhängenden Netzen. Prinzipiell kann jede der Instanzen in einem eigenen Netz angesiedelt sein oder mit einer der anderen Funktionen kollokiert sein. Je nach Ausprägung dieser Anordnung sind die Funktionen somit auf ein bis drei Netze verteilt, die in der Abbildung durch Ziffern repräsentiert sind.

Typ	Entwicklung/ Installation	ooDB-Client	ooDB-Server
A	1	1	1
B	2	1	1
C	1	2	1
D	1	1	2
E	1	2	3

Abb. 2: Typen objektintensiver Anwendungen aus Sicht des ooDB-Client.

Für die Optimierung der Zugriffe ist dabei allein die Grenze zwischen ooDB-Client und ooDB-Server entscheidend. Ziel einer fortgeschrittenen Architektur sollte es hier sein, die Funktionen der Selektionskomponente aus Abb. 1 im Netz des ooDB-Servers auszuführen, um nur noch die für den Client relevanten Objekte über die Netzgrenze übertragen zu müssen. Das Netz, in dem eine Anwendung entwickelt oder installiert wurde, spielt nur insofern eine Rolle, ob die Selektionskomponente bereits im Netz des Servers bekannt ist oder nicht. Man beachte, daß die Typisierung aus Sicht des

Clients durchgeführt ist und folglich ein ooDB-Server gleichzeitig von Clients unterschiedlichen Typs genutzt werden kann.

Typ A&B – Standard-Datenbankanwendung: Die in Kapitel 2.2 vorgestellte Architektur objektorientierter Datenbanken ist für Anwendungen der Typen A und B geeignet. Beispiele finden sich bei den üblichen Anwendungen wie CAD. Deshalb beschränkt sich die folgende Diskussion auf die restlichen drei Typen, wobei zunächst mit konkreten Beispielen für fortgeschrittene Anwendungen dieser Typen aus dem Bereich der rechnerintegrierten Konstruktion und Fertigung begonnen wird.

Typ C – Diagnoseinformationen: Bei komplexen technischen Geräten tritt häufig der Fall auf, daß mit einer Erstauslieferung des Geräts die Häufigkeit auftretender Fehler ungewiß ist oder gar gewisse Fehler noch unbekannt sind. Letzteres ist vor allem dann die Regel, wenn die Fehler aus dem Zusammenspiel mit Komponenten von Drittherstellern resultieren, die erst nach Auslieferung entwickelt wurden. Werden folglich wie heute üblich Diagnoseinformationen nur in Form eines Handbuchs mitgeliefert, so bietet dieses zu wenig Hilfe bei der Suche nach häufigen Fehlern, da zum Druckzeitpunkt keine Häufigkeitsinformationen vorliegen. Zudem kann dieses Vorgehen nicht die zu diesem Zeitpunkt noch unbekannten Fehler abdecken. Auch ist die Nachlieferung neuer Fehler- und Diagnoseinformationen in Form einer Loseblattsammlung ungeeignet, da oft die Fehlerhäufigkeit zu gering ist. Einen besseren Weg stellt die Lieferung einer elektronischen Diagnoseinformationsbank dar, ergänzt um eine vom Gerätehersteller verwaltete Datenbank, in die aktuelle Informationen ergänzt sowie gehalten werden und auf die registrierte Kunden Zugriff erhalten. Bei Eintritt eines Fehlers kann sich dann die Diagnoseinformationsbank bedarfsgesteuert auf den aktuellen Stand bringen. Hier liegt die Entwicklung der Informationsbank und der ooDB-Server auf Seiten des Geräteherstellers und der ooDB-Client auf Seiten des Gerätenutzers. Ein weiteres typisches Anwendungsfeld für diesen Typ von Anwendungen ist das Mobile Computing, bei dem Anwendungsentwicklung/-installation als auch der Betrieb des ooDB-Servers auf dem Festnetz erfolgt, die ooDB-Clients aber mobil sind.

Typ D & E – Ferndiagnose: Da das Wissen über Fehlerhäufigkeiten und -arten bei komplexen technischen Geräten mit der Zeit zunimmt, hat dies nicht nur Auswirkungen auf die manuell durchgeführte Diagnose bei Typ C, sondern auch auf die Ferndiagnose. Ferndiagnose bedeutet, daß ein Gerätehersteller im Fehlerfall auf beim Kunden gespeicherte Betriebs- und Fehlerdaten zugreift und diese auswertet, um beispielsweise die richtig qualifizierten Servicemitarbeiter für die Reparatur vor Ort auszuwählen und ihnen die richtigen Ersatzkomponenten mitzugeben. Mit dem Wissen über neue Fehler ändern sich aber auch die Diagnoseprogramme. Damit sind die in einem Produktmodell abgelegten Fehlerdaten – also der ooDB-Server – vor Ort beim Kunden, während der ooDB-Client beim Gerätehersteller angesiedelt ist. Ob es sich dabei um Typ D oder E handelt hängt nun davon ab, ob der Gerätehersteller die Wartung von einer Zentrale aus betreibt oder mehrere Servicezentren unterhält. Der verallgemeinerte Fall von Typ E sind folglich nach dem Konzept des Netzcomputers strukturierte ooDB-Clients, die entfernte Daten benutzen.

4 Stublets: Systemtechnische Integration von Zugriffsmodalitäten

Im folgenden wird vorgestellt, wie die in Kapitel 2 identifizierten Anwendungstypen durch eine integrierte Nutzung mehrerer Zugriffsmodalitäten geeignet unterstützt werden können.

4.1 Alternative Zugriffsmodalitäten

Um die Kommunikation über Netzgrenzen zu optimieren, muß die Selektion von Objekten vom ooDB-Client in das Netz des ooDB-Servers verlegt werden können. Dazu ist es zunächst erforderlich, die Selektionsfunktionen in der Anwendung zu separieren. Dies führt zum in Abb. 3 dargestellten Aufbau von ooDB-Clients.

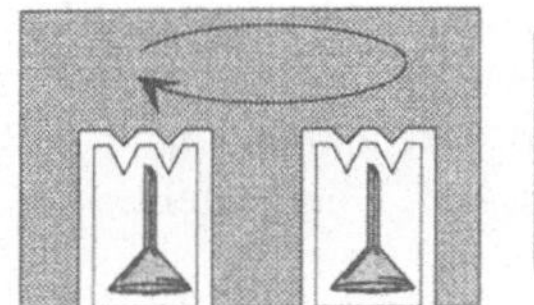
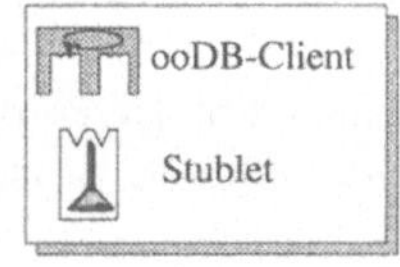

Abb. 3: Das Stublet als Teil von ooDB-Clients

Ein ooDB-Client nutzt folglich eine Menge von Selektionsfunktionen, die in eigene Module, sogenannte *Stublets* ausgelagert sind. Stublets können sowohl mengenorientierte Anfragen als auch navigierende Anfragen enthalten. Folglich reicht es nicht aus, für sie eine mengenbasierte Sprache im Stil von SQL oder deren objektorientierten Pendants [Cat94] zu verwenden. Vielmehr muß es möglich sein, beliebige Prozeduren zu kodieren. Ein Beispiel wäre die Berechnung eines Schnittkörpers zwischen zwei in der Datenbank abgelegten Körpern, da hierzu nicht nur Datenzugriffe, sondern auch prozedurale Algorithmen erforderlich sind. Die Integration von Stublets in den ooDB-Client entspricht der konventionellen Architektur objektorientierter Datenbanken aus Abbildung 1 und deckt damit die Anwendungstypen A und B mit der Zugriffsmodalität des unmittelbaren Clients ab.

Um die Anwendungstypen D und E zu unterstützen, ist es erforderlich, das im Netz des ooDB-Servers unbekannte Stublet dort dynamisch zu installieren. Damit kann die mengenorientierte oder navigierende Selektion vor dem Überwinden der Netzgrenze erfolgen, um die dort durchzuführende Kommunikation zu minimieren. Dieses Prinzip des *Delegate-Stublet* zeigt Abb. 4.

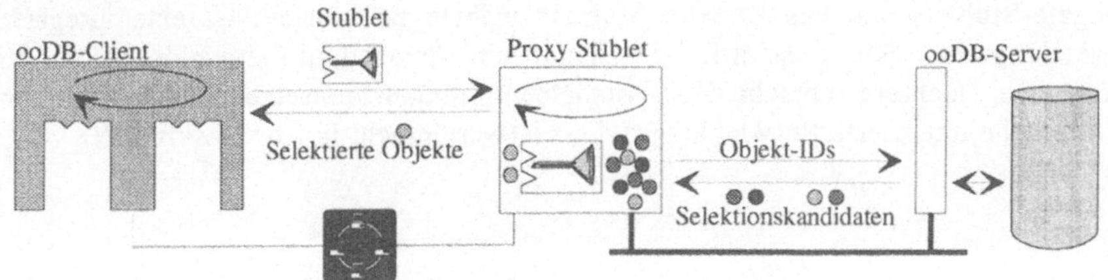

Abb. 4: Konzept der Delegate-Stublets

Zunächst wird das Stublet über die Netzgrenze übertragen, um auf einem Proxy-Stublet im Netz des ooDB-Servers dynamisch installiert zu werden. Der Proxy-Server kann sowohl zusammen mit dem ooDB-Server auf einem Rechner angesiedelt sein, als auch mit diesem über eine leistungsfähige Verbindung vernetzt sein. Aus der Anwendung wird auch klar, daß bei dieser Lösung zusätzlich die Übertragung des Stublets notwendig ist, so daß sich das Konzept erst dann lohnt, wenn die Selektivität des Stublets größer ist als dieser Zusatzaufwand. Möchte man beispielsweise die Kosten in einem nach real übertragenen Daten abrechnenden Mobilfunknetz minimieren und ist die ooDB als Seiten-Server konzipiert, wobei die Größe einer Datenbankseite die üblichen 4 KByte betrage [HMN*95], so lohnt sich die Übertragung für ein Stublet schon dann, wenn seine Größe kleiner als 4 KByte ist und es im Schnitt die Übertragung eines Objektes einspart.

Ist im Gegensatz zur bisherigen Diskussion das Stublet im Netz des ooDB-Servers bereits bekannt, so kann die beim Delegate-Stublet nötige Übertragung des Stublets eingespart werden. Dies ist in allen Anwendungen des Typs C gegeben. Dort ist es sinnvoll, Stublets in einem Stublet-Pool vorzuhalten und bei Bedarf zu aktivieren. Diese Konzept des *Remote-Stublets* ist in Abb. 5 dargestellt.

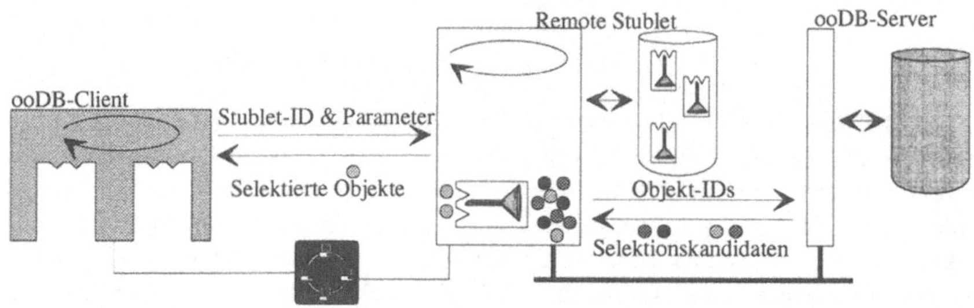

Abb. 5: Konzept der Remote-Stublets

Das Konzept des Remote-Stublet stimmt folglich weitgehend mit dem aus OMG CORBA bekannten Aktivierungsmodus des *persistent Servers* überein. Zur Laufzeit ist nur noch die Auswahl und Parametrisierung des Stublet erforderlich. Wiederum übernimmt das Stublet die Objektselektion. Insgesamt resultiert aus dieser Alternative der geringste Übertragungsaufwand über die Netzgrenze.

4.2   Integration in einen Entwicklungszyklus

Um je nach Bedarf zwischen den Zugriffsmodalitäten des unmittelbaren Clients, des Delegate-Stublets und des Remote Stublets wählen zu können, ist eine integrierte Anwendungsentwicklung erforderlich, damit ein Anwendungsentwickler nicht eine Aufgabe in mehrere verschiedene Implementierungen umsetzen muß. Der dazu erforderliche integrierte Entwicklungszyklus ist vereinfacht in Abb. 6 skizziert.

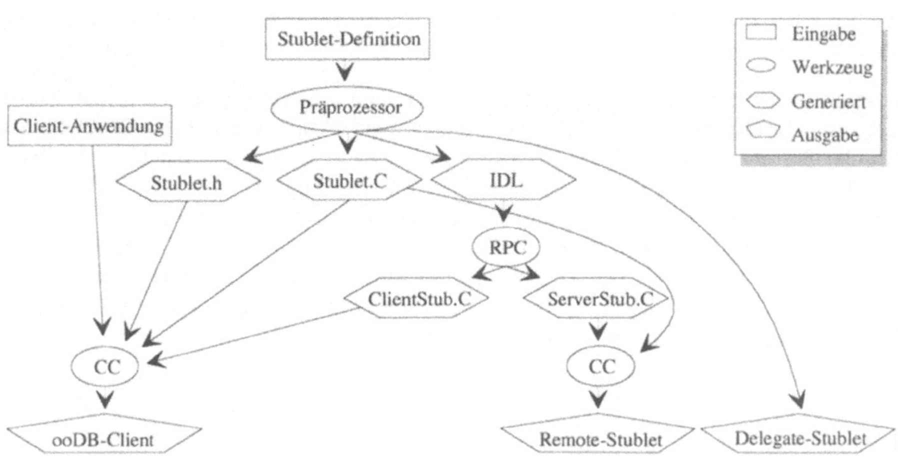

Abb. 6: Entwicklungszyklus

Die Aufgabe des Anwendungsentwicklers reduziert sich auf die Implementierung der Client-Anwendung und der Stublets. Aus einer Stublet-Definition werden durch einen Präprozessor die folgenden Dateien abgeleitet:

Stublet.h: Diese Datei enthält die Schnittstelle zum Stublet, die bei der Entwicklung der Client-Anwendung eingebunden wird, um eine typsichere Interaktion mit dem Stublet zu gewährleisten.

Stublet.C: Diese Datei enthält alle Funktionen, die an die Client-Anwendung gebunden werden müssen. Entsprechend der drei Zugriffsmodalitäten umfaßt der generierte Code die direkten Datenbankzugriffe (unmittelbarer Client), eine Schnittstelle zum Aufruf von Stublets übers Netz (Remote Stublet) und die Funktion zur dynamischen Übertragung des Stublets übers Netz (Delegate-Stublet).

IDL: Die Zugriffsmodalität Remote-Stublet kann direkt auf ein RPC-System abgebildet werden. Dazu dient die IDL-Datei, die vom RPC-Compiler in einen Client-Stub und einen Server-Stub übersetzt wird. Der Client-Stub wird von Stublet.C aufgerufen und bildet nach dem Binden den RPC-Client. Der Server-Stub wird hingegen zusammen mit den direkten Datenbankzugriffen in Stublet.C zum Remote-Stublet übersetzt. Da die Entwicklung im Netz des ooDB-Servers stattfindet, kann das Remote-Stublet direkt im Stublet-Pool abgelegt werden.

Delegate-Stublet: Das Delegate-Stublet schließlich ist der dynamisch übers Netz zu übertragende Code in Form eines Skripts. Er wird zusammen mit dem ooDB-Client installiert und bei Bedarf von den Funktionen in Stublet.C übertragen.

Insgesamt resultiert damit ein Entwicklungsprozeß, der im Vergleich mit der herkömmlichen Entwicklung von ooDB-Clients keine zusätzlichen Eingaben vom Entwickler erfordert und dennoch alle drei Zugriffsmodalitäten integriert unterstützt.

4.3   Resultierende Systemarchitektur

Die Laufzeitunterstützung für die Zugriffsmodalitäten des unmittelbaren Clients und des Remote-Stublet stimmen mit der herkömmlichen Architektur von ooDB-Clients nach Kapitel 2 bzw. der Architektur von RPC-Systemen überein. Demnach beschränkt sich die folgende Diskussion auf die Aspekte der Unterstützung des Delegate-Stublets.

Aufgabe der Laufzeitunterstützung ist die dynamische Entgegennahme, Installation und Ausführung der vom Client übertragenen in Skripten codierten Stublets. Da Stublet-Skripten prinzipiell beliebige Berechnungen codieren können, sind dabei spezielle Sicherheitsvorkehrungen zu treffen. Zudem ist es notwendig, Konvertierungen zwischen den internen Typrepräsentationen in der Laufzeitumgebung von Stublet-Skripten, den in der Datenbank verwendeten Typrepräsentationen und schließlich den zur externen Kommunikation verwendeten Repräsentationen vorzunehmen. Diese Aufgaben werden vom Proxy-Stublet wahrgenommen, dessen an [CGH*95] angelehntes Innenleben Abb. 7 zeigt.

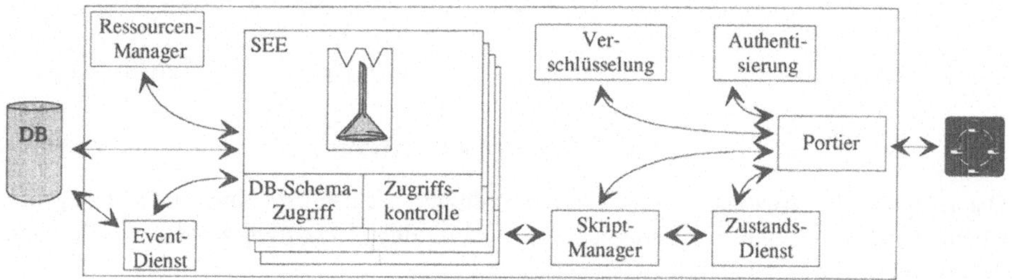

Abb. 7: Systemarchitektur des Proxy-Stublets

Die Aufgabe der einzelnen Architekturkomponenten gestalten sich wie folgt:

Portier: Der Portier nimmt eingehende Skripten entgegen, überprüft sie und installiert sie unter Rückgriff auf die anderen Architekturkomponenten.

Authentisierung: Über die Authentisierung wird der Client, der das Stublet-Skript verschickt identifiziert.

Verschlüsselung: Um dem Abhören oder Abgreifen übertragener Skripten und Objekte vorzubeugen kann die Kommunikation des Proxy-Stublets mit dem Client fakultativ verschlüsselt werden.

Zustands-Dienst: Dient zur Verwaltung des aktuellen Zustands des Skripts (z.B. aktiv, suspendiert, abgebrochen, beendet).

Skript-Manager: Verwaltet Hilfsskripten des Laufzeitsystems, die Funktionen zum Zugriff auf die Datenbank und auf die Systemmodule beinhalten.

Secure Execution Environment (SEE): Bildet ein virtuelles Laufzeitsystem, um den Proxy-Stublet gegen Fehler oder böswilligen Mißbrauch von Rechten in den Stublet-Skripten zu schützen. Zwei seiner wesentlichen Komponenten sind:

DB-Schema-Zugriff: Die Komponente, die die Typtransformation zwischen der Stublet-internen Typrepräsentation von persistenten Objekten und der Repräsentation im DB-Schema vornimmt.

Zugriffskontrolle: Die Komponente, die Zugriffe auf die Datenbank auf die Rechte des jeweiligen Stublet-Skripts beschränkt.

Event-Dienst: Regelt das Zusammenwirken des SEE mit datenbankspezifischen Events (z.B. abort) und weiteren Events, die bei der Programmierung des Stublets verwendet werden können (z.B. Timer).

Ressourcen-Manager: Überprüft eingehende Stublet-Skripten auf ihren Ressourcenbedarf und installiert die Zugriffskontrolle des SEE.

Für jedes eingehende Stublet wird sowohl aus Gründen der Fehlerisolation als auch zur Gewährleistung der Sicherheitsanforderungen hinsichtlich Verschlüsselung und Zugriffskontrolle ein eigenes SEE installiert.

5   Realisierung

Die Umsetzung in eine prototypische Implementierung der vorgestellten Konzepte ist weitgehend abgeschlossen und diente als Basis für die unten angegebenen Laufzeitmessungen. Als Datenbank findet das im Sonderforschungsbereich 346 entwickelte objektorientierte Datenbanksystem GOM [KMW*91] Verwendung, das die kommerzielle Datenbank Objectstore als Seiten-Server einsetzt. Bei der Basisprogrammiersprache für Stublets fiel die Wahl auf die Scriptsprache Tcl7.5 [Ous96], in der auch ein Teil des Proxy-Servers implementiert wurde. Der Zugriff der Stublets auf die Datenbank erfolgt über die GOMtcl-Schnittstelle. Die aktuelle Implementierung realisiert den Ansatz des Delegate-Stublets, indem das Stublet in Form eines Scripts beim Client entworfen wird und nach Übertragung auf den Proxy-Server ausgeführt wird.

Für die Realisierung mobiler Stublets erweist sich Tcl7.5 vor allem durch sein Programmformat und die neu hinzugekommenen *slave-interpreters* als besonders geeignet. Tcl-Scripten bestehen aus Textdateien, die interpretativ ausgeführt werden, und somit vollständig portabel und einfach auf Proxy-Stublets zu übertragen sind. Das Tcl-Laufzeitsystem erlaubt die Erzeugung von abhängigen Interpretern, sog. *slave-interpreters*, die den Zugriff des in ihnen ablaufenden Scripts auf Systemfunktionen, wie z.B. Dateizugriff und Ein-/Ausgabe, reglementieren können. Das innerhalb eines *slave-interpreters* ablaufende Script ist gegenüber anderen Scripten völlig gekapselt und kann nur auf seine eigenen Datenstrukturen und über explizit vereinbarte Funktionen auf die Außenwelt zugreifen. Damit sind wesentliche Voraussetzungen für die in der Architektur definierten SEEs erfüllt.

Für den Laufzeitvergleich wurde eine einfache Anwendung vorausgesetzt, die eine Auswertungsfunktion mit linearem Aufwand auf einem Datenbestand der GOM-Datenbank durchführt. Die Verbindung zwischen der Client-Anwendung und dem ooDB-Server bestand einmal aus einem schnellen lokalen Ethernet mit 10Mbit/s Übertragungsrate und zum anderen aus einer seriellen SLIP-Verbindung mit 9,6 kbit/sec Übertragungsrate zur Simulation eines schmalbandigen Weitverkehrsnetzes. Gemessen wurden die Laufzeiten für verschiedene Problemgrößen für direkten Zugriff in GOM, über die GOMtcl-Schnittstelle und aus einem Delegate-Proxy heraus. Die Auswertung erfolgte jeweils durch die im objektorientierten Schema enthaltene Implementierung der Anwendungsfunktion, bei GOMtcl und Delegate wurde zusätzlich die interpretative Ausführung derselben Funktion in Tcl gegenübergestellt.

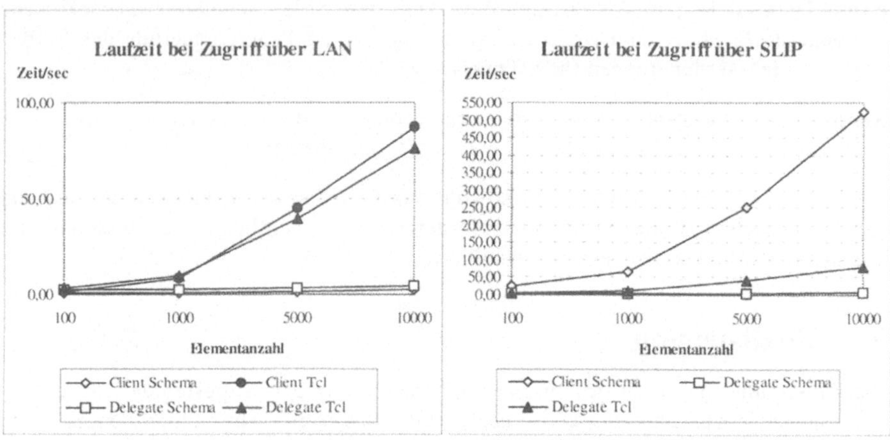

Abb. 8: Laufzeitmessungen für verschiedene Zugriffsmodalitäten

Wie die in Abbildung 8 im linken Teil dargestellten Ergebnisse zeigen, nimmt die langsame interpretative Ausführung der Tcl-Skripten gegenüber der ins Schema compilierten Funktion bei ansonsten gleichen Randbedingungen einen erheblichen Einfluß auf die Laufzeit. An dieser Stelle ist noch erhebliches Verbesserungspotential zu erkennen, das durch Compilierung der Skripten in ein effizienteres Format ausgeschöpft werden könnte. Erst bei vergleichbarer Codeeffizienz – also bei der einheitlichen Verwendung von in Tcl kodierten Funktionen (Client Tcl vs. Delegate Tcl) bzw. reiner Verwendung von ins Schema compilierten Methoden (Client Schema vs. Delegate Schema) – werden die prinzipiell erzielbaren Gewinne deutlich. Im Falle der schnellen Ethernet-Anbindung fällt der Aufwand für die Datenübertragung gegenüber der Funktionsauswertung kaum ins Gewicht. Hier können Delegate Stublets erwartungsgemäß keine Verbesserung erreichen, allerdings bedeutet die zusätzliche Installation des Stublets auch keinen signifikanten Zusatzaufwand. Bei Verwendung der langsamen seriellen Verbindung wird hingegen die Datenübertragung zum bestimmenden Faktor. Die Ausführungszeit des Delegates erhöht sich im SLIP-Szenario nur um einen konstanten Wert von etwa 2 Sekunden für die Übertragung des Skripts (unter 1 KB), die direkte Ausführung im Client wird hingegen durch die Übertragung des gesamten Datenbestands (maximal 200 KB für 10000 Elemente) deutlich verzögert. Der festgestellte Nachteil einer langsamen interpretativen Ausführung des Skripts wird hier bereits für moderate Problemgrößen durch den eingesparten Kommunikationsaufwand ausgeglichen.

Das gewählte Szenario gibt die im realen Weitverkehrsbereich herrschenden Verhältnisse leicht verzerrt wieder, da die SLIP-Verbindung eine wesentlich geringere Bandbreite, allerdings auch eine erheblich kleinere Latenzzeit aufweist. Die beobachtete Beschleunigung von bis zu 2 Größenordnungen im größten Beispiel übertrifft jedoch die modellbedingten Abweichungen und belegt somit die Eignung des Ansatzes für effizienten Datenzugriff in objektintensiven Anwendungen.

6   Verwandte Arbeiten

Die vorgestellte Integration mehrerer Zugriffsmodalitäten basiert auf den bekannten Ansätzen der C++-basierten objektorientierten Datenbanken, der entfernten

Prozedurausführung und auf agentenbasierten Systemen. Dabei liegt die wesentliche Neuerung auf der nahtlosen Nutzung von effizienter konventioneller Technologie und Agententechnologie. Durch den integrierten Entwicklungszyklus ist es damit möglich, je nach aktueller Situation die richtige Zugriffsmodalität auszuwählen. Im Gegensatz dazu haben bisherige Ansätze jeweils nur eine Modalität unterstützt, so daß die Nutzung einer anderen Modalität zwangsläufig mit Doppelimplementierungen verbunden war und zudem der weiter diskutierte Bruch zwischen verschiedenen Implementierungsparadigmen die Entwicklungsarbeit erschwert. Die vorgestellte Lösung konnte sich aber nicht auf die Übernahme existierender Technologie beschränken, da bisherige Agentensysteme keine direkte Zusammenarbeit mit objektorientierten Datenbanken ermöglichen [Whi96, Nwa96, CGH*95]. Deshalb verzichten wir an dieser Stelle auf eine Diskussion der Agententechnologie und verweisen statt dessen auf [CGH*95, HaK96].

Ein zweiter Bereich verwandter Ansätze sind objektorientierte Datenbanken, die nach dem Prinzip des Query-Servers strukturiert sind. Beispiels dafür wären der Coexistent Ansatz von Starburst [AGK*93], Persistence [KJA93], KRISYS [TMM*93] oder PENGUIN [LeW94]. Bei Query-Servern wird der Datenbankzugriff nicht durch den ooDB-Client durchgeführt, sondern in Analogie zu SQL durch die Übertragung einer Anfrage an den Server und die anschließende Übermittlung der selektierten Objekte an den Client. Bei allen diesen Ansätzen handelt es sich aber um Forschungsprototypen, so daß aus ihnen heraus kein Zugriff auf eine kommerzielle objektorientierte Datenbank wie Objectstore möglich ist [HMN*95]. Zudem sind die meisten hybride Mischungen aus relationalen und objektorientierten Datenbanken, was im Vergleich zu den heute kommerziell Verbreitung findenden Ansätzen eine Einschränkung an Mächtigkeit bedeutet. Bei heutigen kommerziellen Ansätzen wie OQL [Cat94] mangelt es hingegen an hinreichender Anfragemächtigkeit, so daß beispielsweise keine rekursiven Anfragen bearbeitet werden können. Eine solche Mächtigkeit ist erst für SQL3 geplant, wobei es sich aber wie bei den anderen Query-Servern um einen „one-size-fits-all"-Ansatz handelt, der im Vergleich zur hier vorgestellten Lösung gewichtige Nachteile aufweist. Zum einen kommt es zum Bruch zwischen der imperativen Programmierung der Client-Anwendung und der deklarativen Formulierung der Query, was die Anwendungsentwicklung erschwert. Zum anderen sind Queries auf mengenwertige Anfragen ausgelegt, so daß die speziell im Bereich der rechnerintegrierten Konstruktion und Fertigung auftretenden navigierenden Anfragen kaum unterstützt werden. Bei solchen Anfragetypen ist nur die ineffiziente Lösung der Abbildung jeder Navigation auf eine eigenständige Query möglich. Da andererseits in Stublets beliebige prozedurale Berechnungen codiert werden können und zudem ein direkte Weiterverarbeitung von Zwischenergebnissen auf Server-Seite möglich wird, weist der hier vorgestellte Ansatz i.allg. eine größere Reduktion der Kommunikation über Netzgrenzen auf. Des weiteren ermöglicht der Modalitätswechsel von Delegate-Stublets zum unmittelbaren Client oder dem Remote-Stublet die effizientere Unterstützung mehrerer Anwendungstypen.

7   Zusammenfassung und Ausblick

In dieser Arbeit wurde ein Ansatz zur Integration mehrerer Zugriffsmodalitäten auf objektorientierte Datenbanken vorgestellt. Ausgehend von einer Analyse der Defizite von objektorientierten Datenbanken in verteilten Systemen und der Typisierung von Anwendungen wurden drei Zugriffsmodalitäten abgeleitet. Diese wurden unter

Verwendung des Gedankenguts von Konzepten zur entfernten Prozedurausführung und der Agententechnologie in den Stublet-Ansatz umgesetzt. Neben den grundlegenden Konzepten dieses Ansatzes wurde ein Entwicklungszyklus präsentiert, der die effiziente Entwicklung von Anwendungen, die alle drei Zugriffsmodalitäten nutzen, ermöglicht und die notwendige Laufzeitarchitektur einschließlich Sicherheits- und Konvertierungsmechanismen diskutiert. Abschließend wurde mit Messungen an unserer aktuellen prototypischen Implementierung belegt, daß der Ansatz wesentliche Vorteile in Umgebungen mit Netzgrenzen aufweist, die bei der unternehmensweiten oder gar -übergreifenden Anwendungsintegration in verteilten Systemen üblicherweise auftreten.

Erweiterungen finden sich zunächst in der Ermöglichung eines nahtlosen Übergangs zwischen den Teilkonzepten des Remote- und des Delegate-Stublet. Durch das Caching von übertragenen Stublet-Skripten durch das Proxy-Stublet kann bei wiederholter Nutzung desselben Skripts die Kommunikation wesentlich reduziert werden. Dabei kann das Caching sowohl Client- als auch Server-initiiert erfolgen. Der erste Fall wäre für Anwendungen typisch, die wissen, daß sie analoge Funktionen mehrfach verwenden. Der zweite Fall ist hingegen dann sinnvoll, wenn zu erwarten ist, daß verschiedene Clients mit ähnlichen neuen Skripten auf einen Server zugreifen. Dies ist etwa beim Versionswechsel einer Anwendung der Fall. Aktuelle Arbeiten in diesem Bereich setzten in erster Linie bei der Suche nach geeigneten Sprachkonstrukten zur Beschreibung dieser anwendungsabhängigen Caching-Semantik an. In diesem Kontext stellt sich auch die Frage, ob es sinnvoll ist, über eine Kostenfunktion automatisch zwischen den Ausführungsmodalitäten zu wählen.

Ferner kann es in größeren Netzen auch sinnvoll sein, daß ein Stublet-Skript nicht von dem Client, sondern von einem anderen Proxy-Server übertragen wird, etwa da der Client ein teures Mobilfunknetz nutzt, während zwischen mehreren Proxy-Servern billigere Kommunikation möglich ist. Aktuell untersuchen wir Möglichkeiten hierzu einen Trading-Dienst zu verwenden.

Schließlich haben die Laufzeitmessungen gezeigt, daß wesentliche Effizienzgewinne beim Delegate-Stublet erzielbar wären, würde man von der interpretativen Skiptlösung zu compilierten Stublets übergehen. Hier versprechen wir uns weitere Verbesserungen durch die Nutzung von On-The-Fly-Compilern zur dynamischen Übersetzung von Skripten vor ihrer Ausführung durch das Proxy-Stublet. Da entsprechende Werkzeuge für Tcl nicht verfügbar sind, werden aktuell Möglichkeiten zur Nutzung von Java [Sun95] als Basislaufzeitsystem untersucht. Zusammen mit dem Caching so übersetzter Stublets würde im übrigen die Lücke zwischen Delegate- und Remote Stublets noch weiter geschlossen werden.

Dank

Unser Dank geht an Andreas Zachmann und Andreas Müller, die für wesentliche Teile der Implementierung verantwortlich sind.

Literatur

[ABD*89] M. Atkinson, F. Banclihon, D. J. DeWitt, K. R. Dittrich, D. Maier, S. Zdonik: *The Object-Oriented Database System Manifesto,* Int. Conf. on Deductive and Object-Oriented Databases, Kyoto, Dezember 1995, S. 40-57.

[AGK*93] R. Ananthanarayanan, V. Gottemukkala, W. Käfer, T. J. Lehmann, H. Pirahesh: *Using the coexistence Approach to achieve combined functionality of object-oriented and relational systems,* ACM SIGMOD Conference, Washington, Mai 1993, S. 109-118.

[Bec96] C. Beckmann: *Tarifierungsstrukturen in Mobilkommunikationsnetzen,* Studienarbeit, Institut für Telematik, Universität Karlsruhe, 1996.

[Cat94] R. G. G. Cattell: *ODMG-93: A Standard for Object-Oriented DBMs,* ACM SIGMOD Conference, Minneapolis, Mai 1994.

[CGH*95] D. Chess, B. Grosof, C. Harrison, D. Levine, C. Parris, G. Tsudnik: *Itinerant Agents for Mobile Computing,* IEEE Personal Communications, 2(5), Oktober 1995, S. 34-49.

[Col96] D. Collins: *MsqlJava Release 1.1.0,* März 1996, http://www.minmet.uq.oz.au/msqljava/index.html.

[DaD95] H. Darween, C. J. Date: *The Third Manifesto,* SIGMOD Records 24(1), März 1995.

[GAE*94] H. Grabowski, R. Anderl, J. Erb, A. Polly: *STEP-Grundlage der Produktdatentechnologie: Aufbau und Entwicklungsmethodik,* CIM Management, 10(4), 1994, S. 45-51.

[HaK96] J. Hartroth, D. Kottmann: *Mobile Softwareagenten: Entwicklungsstand und Einsatzperspektiven,* HMD - Theorie und Praxis der Wirtschaftsinformatik, Heft 190, Vol. 33, Juli 1996, S. 91-107.

[Hey93] H. Hayashi: *Manufacturing - A Preview of the 21st Century,* IEEE Spectrum, September 1993, S. 82-85.

[HMN*95] T. Härder, B. Mitschang, U. Nink und N. Ritter: *Workstation/Server-Architekturen für datenbankbasierte Ingenieuranwendungen,* Informatik Forschung und Entwicklung, 10(1), 1995, S. 55-72.

[Jab95] S. Jablonski: *Workflow-Management Systeme. Motivation, Modellierung, Architektur,* Informatik.Spektrum, 18(1), 1995, S. 13-24.

[KeM94] A. Kemper, G. Moerkotte: *Object-Oriented Database Management: Applications in Engineering and Computer Science,* Prentice Hall, Englewood Cliffs, NJ, 1994.

[KMW*91] A. Kemper, G. Moerkotte, H.-D. Walter, A. Zachmann: *GOM: A Strongly Typed Persistent Object Model With Polymorphism,* Datenbanksysteme in Büro, Technik und Wissenschaft, GI Fachtagung, Kaiserslautern 1991, S. 198-217.

[KJA93]   A. Keller, R. Jensen, S. Agrawal: *Persistence Software: Bridging Object-Oriented Programming and Relational Databases*, ACM SIGMOD Conference, Mai 1994, S. 523-528.

[LeW94]   B. Lee, G. Wiederhold: *Outer Joins and Filters for Instantiating Objects from relational Databases:* IEEE Knowledge and data Engineering, 6, 1994, S. 108-119.

[LLD*91]   C. Lamb, G. Landis, J. Orenstein, D. Weinreb: *The Objectstore Database System*, CACM 34(10), Oktober 1991, S. 50-63.

[MeH95]   E. Meis, K. Hain: *Integriertes Produkt- und Produktionsmodell*, it&ti, 37(5), 1995, S. 32-38.

[Nwa96]   H. S. Nwana: *Software Agents: An Overview*, Erscheint in: Knowledge Engineering Review, 1996.

[Obj90]   Objectivity Onc.: *Objectivity Database System Overview*, Menlo Park, CA, 1990.

[OMG92]   Object Management Group: *Object Management Architecture Guide, Revision 2.0*, OMG Document No. 92.11.1, 1992.

[Ont91]   Ontologic Inc.: *ONTOS Developers Guide*, Billercia, MA, 1991.

[Ous96]   J. Ousterhout: *The Tcl 7.5 and Tk 4.1 releases*, URL: http://www.sunlabs.com/research/tcl/4.1.html.

[Sch93]   A. Schaafsma: *Global Competition demands High Performance*, Logistics Technology International, 1993.

[SRL*91]   M. L. Stonebraker, L. A. Rowe, B. Lindsay, J. Gray, M. Carey, M. L. Brodie, P. Bernstein, D. Beech: *Third-Generation Database Systems Manifesto*, in: R. A. Meersmann. W. Kent, S. Kohla (Hrsg.): DS-4: Object-Oriented Databases: Analysis, Design and Construction, Elsevier, 1991, S. 495-511.

[Sun95]   Sun Microsysteme: *The Java Language Environment - A White Paper*, Sun Microsystems, Mountain View, CA., Mai 1995.

[Sun96]   Sun Microsystems: *JDBC: A Java SQL API Version 1.01*, White Paper, Sun Microsystems, Mountain View, CA. Augsut 1996.

[TMM*93]   J. Thomas, B. Mitschang, N. M. Mattos, S. Deßloch: *Enhancing Knowledge Processing in Client/Server-Environments. 2nd Conf. on Information and Knowledge Management, Washington, 1993, S. 324-334.*

[Ude93]   J. Udell: *Beyond DOS: Connecting Windows to Data with ODBC*, Byte Magazine, 18(1), Januar 1993, S. 271-278.

[Whi96]   J. E. White: *Mobile Agents*, In: Jeffrey Bradshaw (Ed.): Software Agents, AAAI Press, Menlo Park, California, 1996.

[Zun94]   A. Zunk: *Lokale Netze - Kommunikationsplattform der 90er Jahre*, 3. Aufl, Addison-Wesley, 1994.

Session 7:
Gruppenkommunikation

Die ITU Standard-Familie T.120 als
Basis für verteilte Mehrbenutzeranwendungen

Tobias Helbig
Philips Forschungslaboratorien
Weißhausstr. 2
D-52066 Aachen

Email: helbig@pfa.research.philips.com

Dirk Trossen
RWTH Aachen
Ahornstr. 4
D-52056 Aachen

Email: dirk@i4.informatik.rwth-aachen.de

Zusammenfassung. Telekonferenz-Anwendungen erlauben die Kommunikation und Kooperation von räumlich entfernten Benutzern. Ihr praktischer Einsatz in der täglichen Arbeit wird durch Fortschritte in der Kommunikationstechnik immer besser möglich. Zunehmender Kostendruck und räumliche Verteilung von Behörden und Unternehmen führt zur verstärkten Verbreitung von Telekonferenz-Anwendungen als effizientes Werkzeug zur Zusammenarbeit.
Von der ITU wurde zur Realisierung interoperabler Konferenzanwendungen eine Reihe von Standards definiert. Die Standards wurden in der Standard-Familie T.120 zusammengefaßt. Das Papier gibt einen Überblick über die im T.120 standardisierte Funktionalität. Es bewertet die vorgeschlagenen Konzepte und Algorithmen, um Aussagen über die unterstützten Anwendungsbereiche zu gewinnen. Unter anderem werden zwei wesentliche konzeptuelle Schwachstellen aufgezeigt: Durch das Aufsetzen der Mehrpunkt-Kommunikation auf Punkt-zu-Punkt-Verbindungen wird das Ausnutzen effizienter Multicast-Fähigkeiten von Netzwerken unterbunden. Desweiteren wird die Verwaltung der Konferenzdatenbank auf eine Weise definiert, die den Standard als ungeeignet für Konferenzen mit vielen Teilnehmern erscheinen läßt.

1 Einleitung

Durch Telekonferenz-Anwendungen wird die Kommunikation und Kooperation von räumlich entfernten Benutzern unterstützt bzw. überhaupt erst möglich. Fortschritte in der Kommunikationstechnik und ein besseres Verständnis für die Techniken zur Realisierung von Konferenzanwendungen zählen zu den aus technischer Sicht treibenden Faktoren für diese Klasse von Anwendungen. Gleichzeitig resultiert aus wachsendem Kostendruck und zunehmender räumlicher Verteilung von Behörden und Unternehmen von Anwenderseite her der verstärkte Wunsch, Telekonferenz-Anwendungen als effizientes Werkzeug für Kommunikation und Zusammenarbeit einzusetzen.

Eine der wesentlichsten von Telekonferenz-Anwendungen angebotenen Funktionen ist die Unterstützung der Kommunikation beteiligter Benutzer untereinander. In der Mehrzahl der Anwendungsszenarien bildet diese Kommunikation das Mittel zum Zweck: der gemeinsamen Arbeit an Dokumenten, dem gemeinsamen Spiel, usw. Aus den gemeinsamen, in Zusammenhang stehenden Aktivitäten ergibt sich für Telekonferenz-Anwendungen die Notwendigkeit zur Koordination und Synchronisation konkurrierender Programme und Benutzer. Ebenso werden Funktionen benötigt, die es Benutzern oder Programmen erlaubt, Wissen über existierende Konferenzen zum Zwecke der eigenen Teilnahme zu erfragen, andere Teilnehmer einzuladen und eine effektive Zugangskontrolle zu realisieren, um ungebetene Teilnehmer ausschließen zu können.

Da wesentliche Charakteristika von Telekonferenz-Anwendungen unabhängig vom spezifischen Anwendungsszenario immer wieder realisiert werden müssen, erscheint es sinnvoll, solche Funktionen generisch bereitzustellen. Mittels geeigneter Systemunterstützung kann die Implementierung von Telekonferenz-Anwendungen beschleunigt und vereinfacht werden.

Überdies bildet die Standardisierung von Abläufen die wesentliche Voraussetzung dafür, daß Systeme unterschiedlicher Hersteller untereinander interoperieren.

Von der ITU wurde zur Realisierung interoperabler Konferenzanwendungen eine Reihe von Standards definiert. Diese wurden in der Standard-Familie T.120 zusammengefaßt. Der T.120 definiert sowohl Basisfunktionen wie auch anwendungsorientierte Protokolle und Dienste. In den Bereich der Basisfunktionen fallen Spezifikationen für Mehrpunkt-Datenkommunikation, die Token-Verwaltung zur Synchronisation konkurrierender Anwendungsbausteine, die Verwaltung von Strukturinformationen über aktive Konferenzen und deren internen Aufbau. Zu den anwendungsorientierten Protokollen zählen die Spezifikation von kooperativen Zeichenprogrammen ("shared whiteboard") und binärem Mehrpunkt-Dateitransfer.

Mit den im T.120 zusammengefaßten Standards bietet die ITU eine Bündel von aufeinander abgestimmten Konzepten und Funktionen an, auf die Telekonferenz-Anwendungen aufgesetzt werden können. Ziel dieses Papiers ist es, die im Kern des T.120 befindlichen Basiskonzepte für die Realisierung von Mehrpunkt-Kommunikation und Konferenzverwaltung näher zu analysieren. Damit soll eine Bewertung erreicht werden, inwieweit der Standard als Basis für verschiedene Konferenzszenarien geeignet ist bzw. unter welchen Bedingungen davon auszugehen ist, daß die festgelegten Abläufe nicht ausreichend sind. Unter anderem werden dabei zwei wesentliche konzeptuelle Schwachstellen aufgezeigt: Durch das Aufsetzen der Mehrpunkt-Kommunikation auf Punkt-zu-Punkt-Verbindungen wird das Ausnutzen effizienter Multicast-Fähigkeiten von Netzwerken unterbunden. Desweiteren wird als Teil der generischen Funktionalität zur Konferenzsteuerung die Verwaltung der Konferenzdatenbank auf eine Weise definiert, die den Standard als ungeeignet für Konferenzen mit vielen Teilnehmern erscheinen läßt.

Das weitere Papier gliedert sich wie folgt. In Abschnitt 2 wird ein Überblick über einige Arbeiten der IETF (Internet Engineering Task Force) aus dem Bereich der Unterstützung für Telekonferenz-Anwendungen gegeben. Der Abschnitt 3 stellt die wesentlichen Konzepte und Abläufe der im T.120 definierten Basisfunktionalität und die generelle Softwarestruktur von Endsystemen vor. Die bei unserer Implementierung der im T.120 definierten Mehrpunkt-Kommunikationsprotokolle verwendete Architektur und die ersten damit gemachten Erfahrungen werden in Abschnitt 4 dargestellt. Weiterhin werden die zur Verwaltung der Konferenzdatenbank vorgeschlagenen Abläufe hinsichtlich des damit realisierbaren Anwendungsspektrums analysiert. Abschnitt 5 fast die Ergebnisse zusammen und beschreibt weitergehende Arbeiten.

2 Verwandte Arbeiten

Arbeiten, in deren Fokus die Systemunterstützung für Konferenz-Anwendungen liegt, werden von zwei großen Standardisierungsgremien vorangetrieben. Dies ist einerseits die IETF (*Internet Engineering Task Force*), welche die Festlegung von Internet-Standards verwaltet. Andererseits ist dies die ITU (*International Telecommunication Union*), die für Standards im Telekom-Umfeld verantwortlich ist. Bevor in diesem Papier eine ITU-Standard-Familie genauer betrachtet wird, soll im weiteren ein kurzer Überblick über die Pendants der IETF gegeben werden.

Der Ansatz der IETF stellt ein *simple conference control protocol* ([18]), basierend auf einem Multicast Transport Protokoll (wie z.B. RTP), zur Verfügung. Das Einladen der Konferenzteilnehmer geschieht über Applikationsprotokolle wie z.B. *simple invitation protocol* ([19]). Die bereitgestellten Dienste des Konferenzprotokolls stellen Funktionen vergleichbar zu den entsprechenden T.120 Protokollen zur Verfügung. Gleichzeitig soll eine höhere Skalierbarkeit und Robustheit als bei ITU Protokollen gegeben sein. Die Unterstützung von IP Multicast für Realzeit- und Kontrolldaten ist gegeben. Der Konferenzkontext wird als verteilte Datenbank gehalten. Token Management und Konferenzleitung werden ebenfalls unterstützt. Die Applikationsprotokolle (APEs) nutzen den bereitgestellten Dienst der Konferenzkontrolle und des Multicastprotokolls.

Das Konferenzprotokoll der IETF basiert auf einem Multicast Transportprotokoll. Verschiedene Ansätze für Multicast im Internet existieren. Eine Audiokonferenz im März 1992 auf dem Treffen der IETF in San Diego, USA bildete den Anfang umfangreicher Multicast Entwicklungen im Internet. Daraus resultierte das MBone (*Multicast Backbone*), welches Multicast-Fähigkeiten im Internet zur Verfügung stellt. Als Ziel wird die Multicast-Verteilung innerhalb von Konferenzen mit vielen Teilnehmern und großer Ausdehnung gesehen. MBone wird dabei als virtuelles Netzwerk oberhalb des eigentlichen Internets aufgefaßt. Es ist unterteilt in einzelne Unternetze, die die Multicast-Fähigkeiten zur Verfügung stellen. Die einzelnen Unternetze sind durch Unicast-Verbindungen, sog. *Tunnel*, verbunden. Diese dienen dazu, Subnetze, die die Multicast-Fähigkeit nicht bieten, zu überbrücken. Dazu wird ein Multicast-Paket durch einen speziellen Router so verpackt, daß es wieder als IP-Packet einer Unicast-Verbindung weitergeleitet wird. Am Router des Ziel-Subnetzes angelangt, wird die ursprüngliche Multicast-Adresse wieder hergestellt und das Paket weitergeleitet. Abbildung 1 zeigt eine mögliche MBone-Topologie. Die drei Teilnetze sind über die Router M1 bis M3 durch das Internet verbunden. Innerhalb der Teilnetze werden Pakete direkt mittels Multicast übertragen.

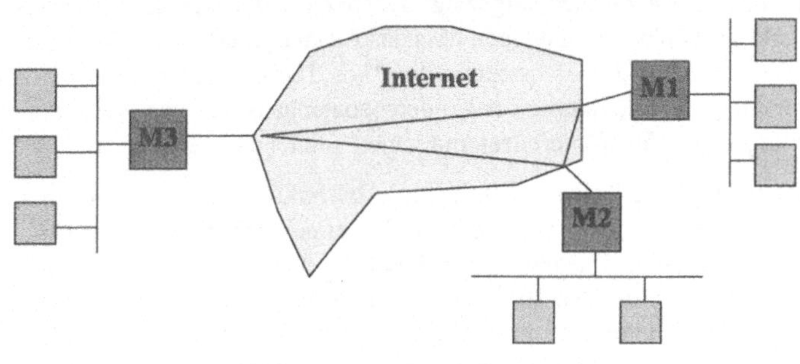

Abbildung 1: MBone-Topologie

Das Multicast-Routing innerhalb eines Subnetzes geschieht durch einen speziellen Routing-Daemon (*multird*). Als Weiterentwicklung zum Transport von Echtzeitströmen wurde das *Realtime Protocol* (RTP) von der Audio-Video Transport Working Group der IETF entworfen, welches auf UDP/IP aufsetzt. Dabei werden die Pakete zusätzlich mit Zeit- und Reihenfolgeinformationen gekennzeichnet, um Verzögerungen und Vertauschungen besser zu verarbeiten.

Die Funktionalitäten des Multicastprotokolls werden von verschiedenen Tools im Internet-Bereich ausgenutzt, wie z.B. *vat* für Audio-, *nv* für Videokonferenzen und *wb* für Whiteboard-Funktionen. Für weitere Informationen zu MBone siehe [1] und [2].

Der Ansatz der ITU, der in die Standard-Familien T.120 und T.130 mündet, ist oberhalb der Transportschicht angesiedelt. Die Konferenzinitiierung und -verwaltung geschieht durch die *Generic Conference Control* (GCC) im Standard T.124 ([7]), die auf dem *Multipoint Communication Service* (MCS) des Standards T.125 ([5]) aufsetzt, der eine Mehrpunkt-Kommunikation unabhängig von der Netzwerkschicht anbietet. Dieser Dienst bildet die Mehrpunktverbindungen auf sichere Punkt-zu-Punkt Verbindungen auf Transportebene ab und bietet Token- und Kanalmanagement und Datenverkehr zwischen Benutzergruppen. Die Umsetzung auf die Netzwerkschicht geschieht durch *Network Specific Data Protocol Stacks*, die für PSDN, PSTN, ISDN, ATM und TCP/IP im Standard T.123 ([6]) definiert sind. Die Kontrolle von Echtzeitströmen und die Aushandlung von Dienstgüte-Parametern wurde mittlerweile aus der Standard-Familie T.120 herausgelöst und als eigene Standard-Familie T.130 definiert.

Zur Anbindung der Funktionalitäten des MCS und GCC an Applikationsprotokolle hat die IMTC (*International Multimedia Teleconferencing Consortium*) APIs (*Application Programmers Interfaces*) definiert ([20],[21]) und ein Implementor's Guide für den T.120 entworfen ([22]).

Im folgenden Kapitel wird auf die einzelnen Konzepte der Standard-Familie T.120 näher eingegangen.

3 Übersicht über die Konzepte der Standard-Familie T.120

Die Standard-Familie T.120 (Abbildung 2) beschreibt Standards für (Daten-)Kommunikation zwischen Terminals und *Multipoint Communications Units* (MCU), sowie die Verwaltung der bestehenden Kommunikationbeziehungen. Die Standard-Familie umfaßt sowohl Basisfunktionen zur Verwaltung der Multipunkt-Kommunikationsinfrastruktur wie auch Anwendungsfunktionen. Als konzeptionelles Modell eines T.120 Applikationsmodells wurde der T.121 ([4]) entworfen, welcher Entwicklern als Leitfaden eines einheitlichen Ansatzes zur Entwicklung von Anwendungsprotokollen dienen soll.

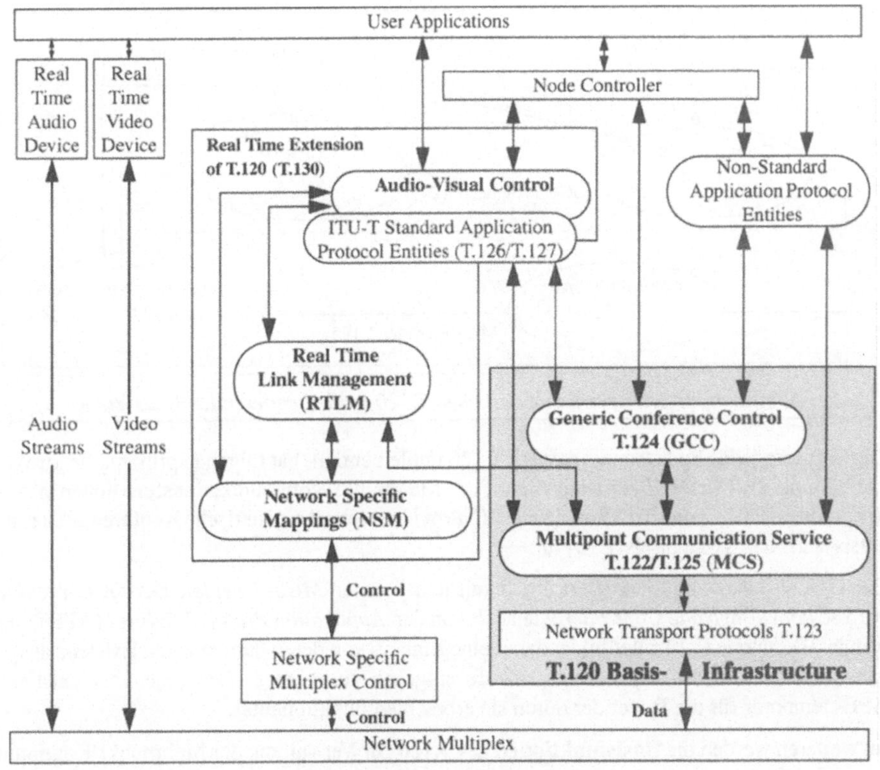

Abbildung 2: Standard-Familie T.120

Einen zentralen Bestandteil der **Basisfunktionen** stellen die Standards T.122 ([5]) und T.125 ([8]) dar, die den *Multipoint Communication Service* (MCS) definieren. Der MCS bietet einen allgemeinen Dienst zur Durchführung interaktiver Multimedia-Anwendungen. Es werden vollduplex Mehrpunktverbindungen zwischen Benutzern über einer Vielzahl verschiedener Netzwerke unterstützt. Die Anbindung an verschiedene Netzwerke wird im Standard T.123 ([6]) beschrieben. Der MCS bietet Multicast-Verbindungen, die über sichere Unicast-Verbindungen realisiert werden. Weiterhin wird ein Token- und Kanalmanagement zur Verfügung gestellt. Zur Realisierung von Mehrpunktkonferenzen wurde der T.124 definiert ([7]), der die *Generic Conference Control* (GCC) aufgesetzt auf dem MCS anbietet. Im GCC findet eine Abbildung der Mehrpunktverbindungen in den Konferenzkontext statt. Außerdem werden mittels einer Datenbank die Konferenz- und Anwendungsdaten verwaltet.

Als **Anwendungsfunktionen** wurden der *Still Image Transfer* im Standard T.126 ([9]) und der *Multipoint Binary File Transfer* im Standard T.127 ([10]) entwickelt. Diese ermöglichen den Austausch von Bildern und Dateien innerhalb der Mehrpunkt-Kommunikationsumgebung des T.120. Um auch den Austausch von Echtzeitdaten zu ermöglichen, enthielt die Standard-Familie T.120 ursprünglich den T.128-Standard. Dieser wurde jedoch mittlerweile in die Standard-Familie T.130 ([11]) ausgegliedert. Darin wird das *Real Time Link Management* im Standard T.132 ([12]) sowie die Anbindung an die Netzwerkschicht (*Network Specific Mappings*, NSM) definiert. Infolge dieser Ausgliederung ist die Echtzeit-Kommunikation inklusive der hierfür notwendigen Dienstgüteaushandlungen völlig aus dem T.120 ausgelagert. Der T.120 deckt somit *nicht* den Bereich der Audio-/Video-Kommunikation in Konferenz-Anwendungen ab.

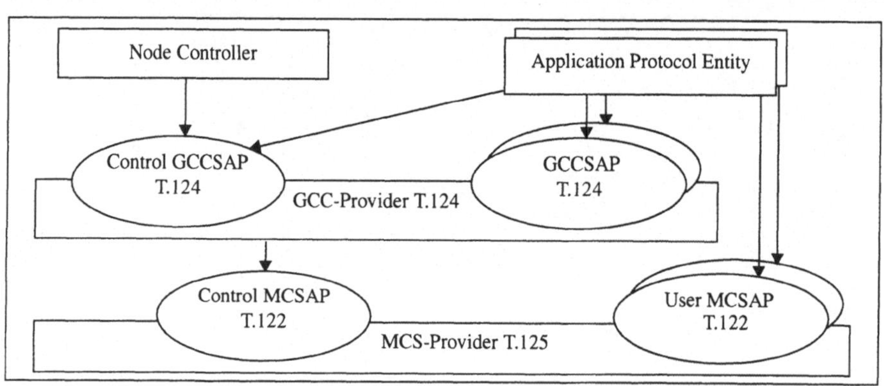

Abbildung 3: Systemstruktur eines den T.120 implementierenden Endsystems

Die Software jedes Endsystems, das den T.120 implementiert, hat folgende prinzipielle Struktur (Abbildung 3): Der MCS-Provider bietet die Mehrpunkt-Kommunikationsfunktionen gemäß der Standards T.122 und T.125 an. Der GCC-Provider bietet die generische Konferenzsteuerung entsprechend des Standards T.124 an.

Der *GCC-Provider* kommuniziert direkt mit dem lokalen *MCS-Provider*. Der GCC-Provider wird sowohl vom *Node Controller* wie auch von den *Application Protocol Entities* (APEs) verwendet. Der Node Controller bildet dabei eine Einheit, von deren permanenten Existenz ausgegangen wird, z.B. um asynchrone Aufrufe entgegen zu nehmen. Demgegenüber existieren APEs temporär für die Dauer der durch sie erbrachten Funktionalität.

Im weiteren werden die **Basisfunktionen** des T.120 zur Verwaltung der Mehrpunkt-Kommunikationsinfrastruktur, d.h. der MCS und der GCC, detaillierter vorgestellt, bevor in Abschnitt 4 auf Implementierungserfahrungen und Bewertungen eingegangen wird.

3.1 T.122/T.125: Mehrpunkt-Kommunikationsdienst

In diesem Abschnitt werden die Konzepte des *Multipoint Communication Service* (MCS) beschrieben und die wichtigsten Begriffe der Standards T.122 und T.125 erläutert.

Der *MCS-Provider* stellt die Funktionalität des Mehrpunkt-Kommunikationsdientes auf einem Endsystem (Terminal oder MCU) zur Verfügung. Die Kommunikation mit dem MCS-Provider erfolgt über einen Control MCSAP und mehrere User MCSAP (siehe Abbildung 3).

Mehrere MCS-Provider können in einer Baumstruktur zu einer *Domain* verbunden werden. Der für die Verwaltung eines Endsystems zuständige *Node Controller* kreiert oder löscht *Domains*. *Application Protocol Entities* können sich mit einer Domain verbinden (*Attachment*). Domains werden lokal über einen *Domain Selector* identifiziert. Innerhalb einer Domain gelten beim Verbindungsaufbau ausgehandelte *Domain Parameter*. Darin sind die maximal zu vergebenden Kanal- und Tokennummern, maximal zu verbindende Benutzer u.ä. enthalten. Die MCS-Provider werden mittels MCS-Verbindungen hierarchisch miteinander verbunden. Der oberste Provider innerhalb des Baums wird als *Top Provider* bezeichnet. Werden zwei Domains über eine MCS-Verbindung zwischen zwei Providern verbunden, so findet ein *Merging* der Domains statt. Dabei werden Kanal-, Token- und Benutzerkonflikte aufgelöst. Abbildung 4 zeigt ein Beispiel einer MCS-Topologie mit der Baumstruktur einer Domain.

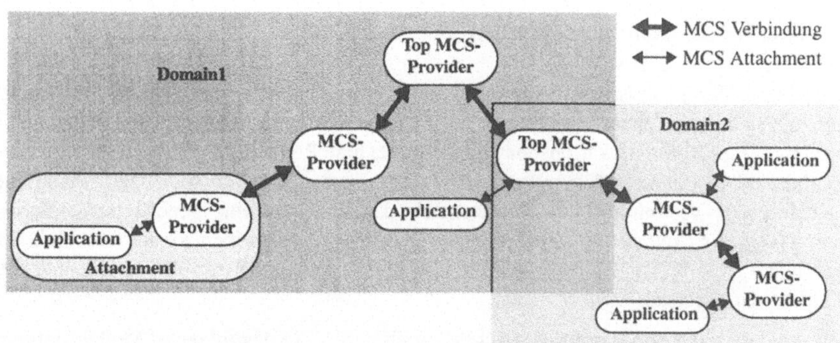

Abbildung 4: Beispiel einer MCS-Topologie

Nach dem Aufbau der Verbindungen zwischen den MCS-Providern und dem Verbinden von Applikationen mit einer Domain kann der Datenaustausch zwischen den Anwendungen über Kanäle (*Channels*) durchgeführt werden. Kanäle bieten ein sehr flexibles Konzept zur Adressierung von Gruppen von Empfängern innerhalb einer Domain. Der MCS stellt vier verschiedene Kanaltypen zur Verfügung, die *Benutzer-Identifikator-Kanäle*, die *statischen*, die *zugewiesenen* und die *privaten* Kanäle. Der Bereich der Kanalnummern ist limitiert, reicht von 1 bis 65535 und ist in feste Unterbereiche für die verschiedenen Kanaltypen unterteilt. Benutzer werden mittels eines Benutzer-Identifikators, der einer eindeutigen Kanalnummer entspricht, verwaltet. Dem Identifikator ist ein Kanal zugeordnet, über den Daten an den Benutzer verschickt werden. *Statische Kanäle* bilden einen zweiten Kanaltyp. Diese Kanäle können von jeder Applikation belegt werden. Daten auf diesen Kanälen können nur empfangen werden, wenn der Kanal vorher beim MCS-Provider belegt wurde. Dies gilt auch für die *zugewiesenen Kanäle* (*assigned channels*). Diese Kanäle werden vom MCS-Provider vergeben, wenn als zu belegende Kanalnummer eine Null angegeben wurde. *Private Kanäle* werden auf Anforderung eines Kanalverwalters vergeben. Ein Belegen des Kanals durch andere Benutzer ist nach voriger Einladung des Kanalverwalters möglich. Dem Kanalverwalter hat die Möglichkeit zur Ausladung von Benutzern und zur Freigabe des Kanals.

Zur Verwaltung von Ressourcen und zur Synchronisation von Anwendungszuständen bietet der MCS die Nutzung von *Token* an. Die Token können exklusiv (*grabbed tokens*) oder nicht-exklusiv (*inhibited tokens*) belegt werden. Der Status eines Tokens kann erfragt werden. Ebenso ist die Übergabe des (exklusiven) Besitzrechtes eines Tokens möglich. Dies kann durch eine vorangegangene Anfrage initiiert werden.

MCS bietet ein einfaches Prioritätenmodell bei der Übertragung von Daten über Kanäle an. Kontrolldaten zur Kanal-, Benutzer- oder Tokenverwaltung werden mit der höchsten Priorität übertragen. Drei weitere Prioritäten sind möglich. Die genaue Anzahl wird beim Aufbau einer Domain ausgehandelt.

Die Übertragung von Benutzerdaten von einem Endsystem zu anderen geschieht auf zwei verschiedene Arten. Die einfachste ist die *Non-Uniform*-Übertragung, bei der Daten auf dem kürzesten Weg in der Baumstruktur übertragen werden. Als Erweiterung dient die *Uniform*-Übertragung. Dabei wird eine einheitliche Reihenfolge der Datenpakete bei allen Empfängern gewährleistet. Bei dieser Datenübertragung werden die Pakete zum Top Provider der Domain geschickt, der dann für die reihenfolgegetreue Aussendung an alle Empfänger sorgt. Außerdem kann der Sender seine eigenen Nachrichten empfangen, sofern er den entsprechenden Kanal belegt hat. Eine Quittierung empfangener Pakete durch den Provider oder den empfangenden Nutzer ist nicht vorgesehen.

3.2 T.124: Generische Konferenzsteuerung

In einer Telekonferenz existieren Kommunikationsbeziehungen zwischen Teilen von Anwendungen, die sich i.a. auf unterschiedlichen, voneinander entfernten Endsystemen befinden. Die Verwaltung dieser Kommunikationsbeziehungen setzt eine Reihe Funktionen voraus, die durch den Standard T.124 generisch bereitgestellt werden. Dieser Standard spezifiziert Funktionen und Abläufe zur Verwaltung von Konferenzen, d.h. er bietet eine generische Konferenzsteuerung (*Generic Conference Control* - GCC) an. Im weiteren wird ein kurzer Überblick über das durch den GCC bereitgestellte Modell von Konferenzen und die zur Verwaltung angebotenen Funktionen gegeben.

Für die Modellierung von Konferenzen wird durch den GCC das folgende Modell definiert: Jedes Endsystem, d.h. ein Terminal oder eine MCU, kann an einer oder mehreren *Konferenzen* beteiligt sein. Dabei ist eine Konferenz eindeutig mit einer Domain des MCS assoziiert. Jede Konferenz kann aus mehreren *Sessions* bestehen, in die logisch zusammengehörige Anwendungsbausteine, die *Application Protocol Entities* (APE), gruppiert werden. Eine APE, die gemäß ihres Namens die eigentliche, auf dem GCC aufgesetzte Anwendungsfunktionalität realisiert, ist höchstens einer Session zugeordnet.

Zur Verwaltung der logischen Struktur von Konferenzen bietet der GCC eine Reihe von Funktionen an. So können existierende Konferenzen erfragt, neue Konferenzen erzeugt und andere Endsysteme zu existierenden Konferenzen eingeladen werden. Es wurden Signallisierungsmechanismen definiert, mit denen Informationen über Änderungen an der Struktur von Konferenzen wie z.B. das Hinzukommen oder Entfernen von Endsystemen oder APE's mitgeteilt werden.

Der GCC unterstützt die Aushandlung von Fähigkeiten (*Capabilities*) der an einer Konferenz beteiligten APE's, paßwort-gesicherten Zugang zu Konferenzen und die generische Verwaltung von Ressourcen wie z.B. den belegten Kanälen und Tokens im MCS sowie anwendungsspezifischer Parameterwerte.

Die logische Struktur von Konferenzen spiegelt sich in der Implementierung des GCC in einer Datenbank wider. Diese Datenbank wird *auf jedem beteiligten Endsystem* einer Konferenz gehalten. Für jede Konferenz hält ein GCC-Provider

- den *Conference Roster* (Informationen darüber, an welchen Konferenzen ein Endsystem beteiligt ist und welche Endsysteme an einer bestimmten Konferenz beteiligt sind),

- den *Local Application Roster* und den *Conference Application Roster* (Informationen darüber, welche APE's auf einem Endsystem erzeugt wurden, welche APE's an einer Konferenz beteiligt sind, in welche Sessions die APE's organisiert wurden, welche Fähigkeiten APE's haben),

- die *Application Registry* (eine Ablage für die in einer Konferenz benutzten Ressourcen, wie z.B. Kanäle des MCS, Tokens oder generische Parameter, die für die spezielle Anwendung interpretierbar sind),

- einige weitere Hilfsstrukturen.

Für den *Conference Roster* und den *Conference Application Roster* werden überdies zwei verschiedene Versionen gehalten: Die als *full* bezeichnete Version enthält die komplette Information über alle Endsysteme, Sessions und APE's einer Konferenz. Demgegenüber wird in der *subhierachy* Version nur die Information über die in der Subhierarchie eines Endsystems befindlichen Endsysteme und deren Sessions und APE's gehalten. Diese Unterscheidung resultiert aus den Abläufen, die für den Austausch den Konferenzdatenbank in MCU-Hierarchien vorgeschrieben werden. Dieser Austauschprozeß beeinflußt in entscheidendem Maße die Leistungsfähigkeit des GCC und damit auch seine potentielle Einsetzbarkeit für unterschiedliche Szenarien. Er wird deshalb in Abschnitt 4.2 detailliert dargestellt und bewertet.

4 Implementierungserfahrungen und Leistungsbewertung von MCS und GCC

In diesem Abschnitt wird das Design von MCS und GCC hinsichtlich ihres Einsatzspektrums und ihrer Effizienz bewertet. Dabei werden für den MCS die ersten Erfahrungen aus seiner Implementierung über TCP/IP beschrieben. Die Bewertung des GCC basiert auf einer Analyse der zur Verwaltung der Konferenzdatenbank im T.124 festgelegten Abläufe.

4.1 Implementierungserfahrungen für MCS über TCP/IP

Die vorzustellenden Ergebnisse für die Realisierung des MCS resultieren aus einer Implementierung des MCS über TCP/IP unter Zuhilfenahme eines SDL-Entwicklungswerkzeugs. Zuerst wird ein kurzer Abriß über die Architektur der Implementierung gegeben. Dann folgt ein Abschnitt mit festgestellten Bottlenecks der Implementierung und deren Behebung. Ein kurze Leistungsbewertung schließt den Abschnitt ab.

4.1.1 Architektur der Implementierung des MCS über TCP/IP

In diesem Kapitel soll die Architektur der Implementierung des MCS über TCP/IP beschrieben werden. Die einzelnen funktionellen Einheiten werden vorgestellt. Die Codeentwicklung wurde unter Sun Solaris durchgeführt.

Die Funktionalität des MCS wurde im T.125 mittels der *Specification and Description Language* (SDL, [17]) definiert. Diese SDL-Spezifikation wurde für unsere Implementierung verwendet und gemäß der im Standard T.123 vorgegebenen Abbildung via X.224 (OSI TP0, [16]) an TCP/IP angebunden. Einige Optimierungen und Änderungen wurden durchgeführt (siehe Abschnitt 4.1.2).

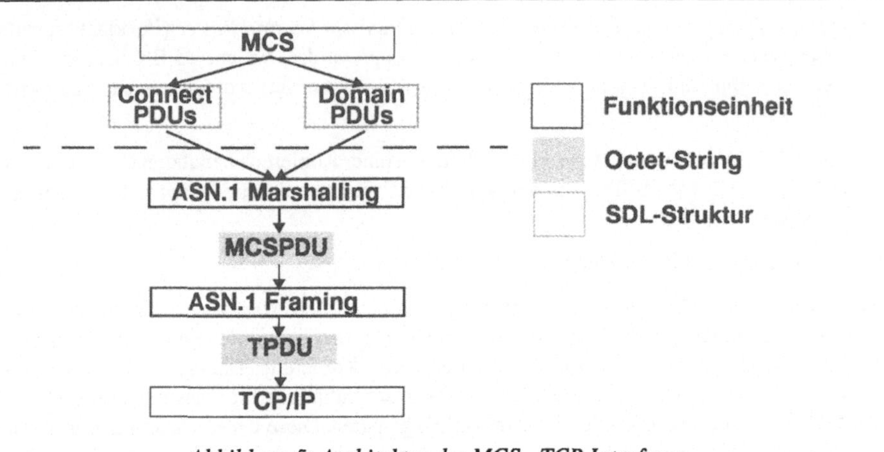

Abbildung 5: Architektur des MCS - TCP Interfaces

Abbildung 5 zeigt die einzelnen Funktionseinheiten der MCS-Implementierung und die zwischen ihnen ausgetauschten Protokolldateneinheiten. Die Übertragung der Protokolldateneinheiten des MCS ist, wie im Standard T.123 definiert, mittels X.224 in der ASN.1-Notation [14] vorgesehen. Dazu ist eine Umsetzung der SDL-Datenstrukturen mittels der *Basic Encoding Rules* ([15]) in ASN.1 notwendig. Zur Realisierung von X.224 über TCP/IP ist ein weiteres Marshalling der Pakete nötig, da TCP/IP streamorientiert arbeitet im Gegensatz zum paketorientieren Ansatz von X.224. Für dieses Umsetzen werden ebenfalls ASN.1-Routinen verwendet.

Die Protokolldateneinheiten von MCS werden vor der Weitergabe an die Transportschicht in der Funktionseinheit *ASN.1 Marshalling* mittels der *Basic Encoding Rules* in die ASN.1 Notation übersetzt. Dies geschieht durch entsprechende Kodierungs- und Dekodierungsroutinen, die mit Hilfe des Public Domain Tools *snacc* erstellt wurden.

Das MCS-Protokoll setzt ein OSI-konformes Transportprotokoll der Klasse 0 voraus. Durch die streamorientierte Übertragung von TCP/IP wird deshalb eine weitere Umsetzung der Protokolldateneinheiten notwendig, da das OSI-Transportprotokoll paketorientiert arbeitet. Die Umsetzung geschieht in der Funktionseinheit *ASN.1 Framing* mittels ASN.1 Kodierroutinen, die ebenfalls durch das Tools *snacc* erzeugt werden.

Wie bereits erwähnt, wurde der MCS in SDL mit Hilfe eines kommerziellen Tools (SDT von Telelogic) entworfen. Die Anbindung des MCS und der TCP-Routinen geschah durch Entwerfen geeigneter Umgebungsroutinen für SDL. Diese sind nicht im Standard T.125 spezifiziert und werden mittels C-Code implementiert. Die Routinen umfassen neben der Funktionalität des MCS auch die oben beschriebenen Routinen zur Umsetzung der PDU's (*Marshalling*) und die Sende- und Empfangsroutinen von TCP. Dazu wird beim Start des Systems ein Socket eingerichtet, an dem auf ankommende Pakete gewartet wird. Diese Pakete werden dann wie oben beschrieben weiterverarbeitet. Die vom MCS-Prozeß gesendeten Signale werden dabei erweitert und an die Umgebung weitergeleitet. Dort findet das Verpacken der Pakete mittels der jeweiligen Marshalling-Routinen statt, bevor das Paket dann über TCP versendet wird.

4.1.2 Leistungsbewertung und Verbesserungen der Implementierung

Das folgende Kapitel zeigt eine Leistungsbewertung und Verbesserung der MCS Implementierung. Bottlenecks und deren Beseitigung werden aufgezeigt.

Bei der Implementierung des MCS fiel das (unnötige) Kopieren von Daten als besonderer Engpaß ins Auge. Dies geschieht sowohl bei der Kommunikation von SDL-Prozessen untereinander, als auch beim Marshalling der Protokolldateneinheiten an der Schnittstelle zu SDL. Zur Optimierung der MCS-Implementierung wurde deshalb nach Wegen gesucht, das Umkopieren von Daten weitestgehend zu vermeiden.

Das Problem bei der Kommunikation von SDL-Prozessen untereinander wurde durch die Referenzierung von Daten anstatt des Kopierens umgangen. Dazu wurden die im T.125 definierten Datentypen (Mengen, Queues) als C-Code implementiert. Da in SDL keine Zeiger auf Datentypen vorgesehen sind, wurde der Standard so abgeändert, daß dieser mit den (zeigerorientierten) Datentypen in C zusammenarbeitet.

Ein weiteres Problem stellt die Weitergabe der Benutzerdaten bei Übertragungen zwischen Anwendungen dar. Die ursprüngliche Spezifikation im T.125-Standard sieht eine Implementierung als Octet-String vor. Dadurch werden die Daten bei der Kommunikation über SDL-Signale und beim Aufruf von Funktionen als Ganzes kopiert. Auch hier konnte durch die Einführung eines zeigerorientierten Datentyps und der entsprechenden Weiterreichung des Zeigers bis zur Transportschicht unnötiges Kopieren gespart werden. Sogar bei der Segmentierung durch MCS wird kein Datenbereich kopiert, sondern nur der Speicher referenziert. Nach Übertragung des letzten Segments wird der Speicher durch die Transportschicht freigegeben.

Weiterhin wird das Marshalling von Multicast-Verbindungen dahingehend geändert, daß die Daten in einem Endpoint übersetzt und für andere referenziert werden. Dadurch wird das n-fache Marshalling beim n-Multicast in den einzelnen Endpoints auf 1 Marshalling reduziert.

Das Marshalling kann zu weiterer Geschwindigkeitssteigerung in homogenen Netzwerkumgebungen komplett abgeschaltet werden. Dabei wird anstatt eines zweimaligen Umsetzens der Daten ins ASN.1-Format lediglich eine C-Struktur beschrieben, die dann übertragen wird. Das Abschalten des Marshalling wird während des Verbindungsaufbaus innerhalb der Parameter der Domain ausgehandelt.

4.1.3 Bewertung der Implementation

Diese ersten Optimierungen wurden in Testläufen untersucht. In einem ersten Testlauf (Abbildung 6) wurde die Geschwindigkeit des MCS Protokolls resultierend aus der Auffrischung der Datenbank in jedem Provider untersucht. Primitive, die Ressourcen benutzen (Tokens, Kanäle), werden bis zum Top Provider gesendet und passieren jeden Zwischenprovider. Eine einfache Topologie aus drei Providern, angeordnet in einer Kaskade, wurde gewählt. Diese kann auf Baumhierachien skaliert werden. Beim Testlauf wurde eine Ressource belegt, die von keinem anderen Nutzer benutzt wurde. Dadurch wird die Anforderung in jedem Falle bis zum Top Provider durchgereicht. Abbildung 6 zeigt, daß sich die Primitive in der Abarbeitungszeit kaum unterscheiden. Sie durchlaufen die gleichen internen MCS Prozeduren und unterscheiden sich nur in der aufzufrischenden Datenbank. Ca. 90 Prozent der Abarbeitungszeit wird im MCS Code aufgewendet. Daher sind hier weitere Performanceverbesserungen sinnvoll.

Weiterhin wurde der Aufbau einer MCS Verbindung und eines Attachments untersucht (Abbildung 7). Der Aufbau einer Domain ist der aufwendigste Prozeß innerhalb des Protokolls. Es

werden dabei drei Transportverbindungen geöffnet und eine Vielzahl interner Mengenstruktu-
ren eingerichtet. Da der Aufbau eines Attachment das Einrichten eines SDL-Prozesses erfordert, benötigt das Attach-Primitiv eine um ca. 80 Prozent höhere Abarbeitung als andere Res-
sourcenprimitive.

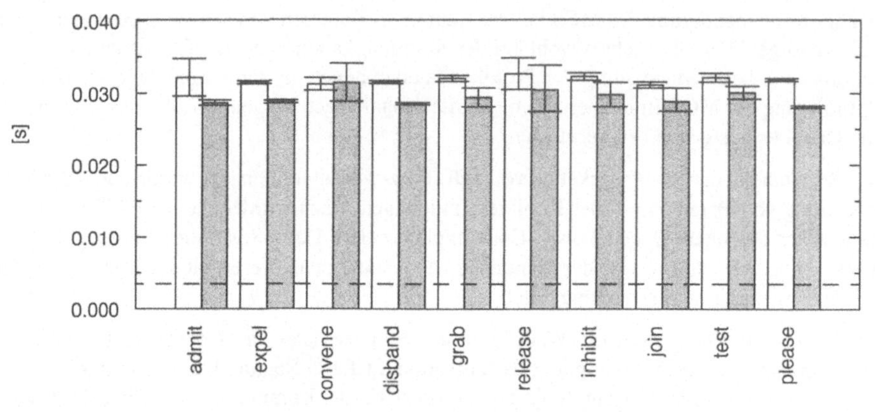

Abbildung 6: Meßergebnisse der MCS Primitive

Die Abbildungen zeigen die Ergebnisse der beiden Testläufe mit den 95%-Konfidenzinterval-
len. Die rechten Balken zeigen jeweils die Ergebnisse bei ausgeschaltetem Marshalling. Die
Testläufe wurden auf SparcStation 5 (End- und Zwischenprovider) und einer SparcStation 20
(Top Provider) unter Sun Solaris durchgeführt. Der Overhead der TCP Verarbeitung wurde mit
ca. 3.8 ms ermittelt, dargestellt durch die gestrichelten Linien. Beim Einrichten von MCS Verbindungen ist der Overhead für den Aufbau der Transportverbindungen nicht mit eingerechnet.

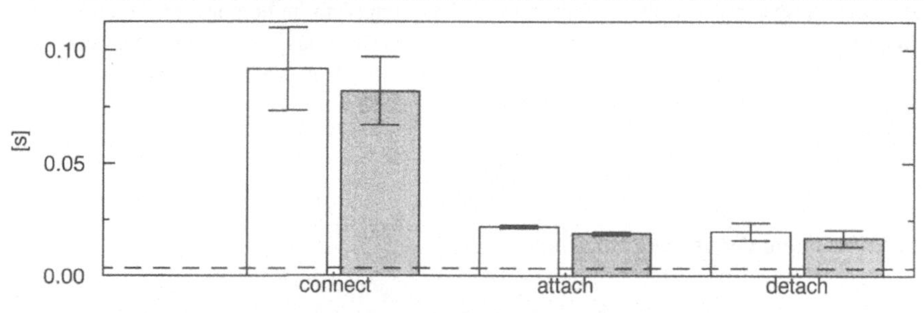

Abbildung 7: Meßergebnisse Verbindungs- und Attachementaufbau

4.1.4 Einsatzbereiche und Restriktionen des MCS

Die Standard-Familie T.120 mit der Hierarchie von Multipoint Communications Units (MCU's)
ist für Mehrpunkt-Kommunikation im Weitverkehrsbereich entwickelt worden. Die Mehrpunkt-Kommunikation des MCS wird umgesetzt auf sichere Punkt-zu-Punkt-Verbindungen.
Diese Entwicklungsvorgaben des Standards können im Hinblick auf Geschwindigkeit und
Nützlichkeit zu Schwierigkeiten führen, wenn man andere Umgebungen als typische Weitver-
kehrs-(telefon-)netze betrachtet:

- Die Multicast-Fähigkeiten von lokalen Netzen werden nicht genutzt. Eine Integration *echten* Multicasts in MCS ohne Einführung neuer Konzepte ist nur schwer möglich. Ein Weg wäre über die Einführung spezieller Adressgruppen, wie dies z.B. im MBone durch eigene Multicast-Adressen geschieht. Dies würde aber in weiten Teilen ein neues Design der MCS-Implementierung verlangen. Ansätze wie [23] versuchen, das X.224 Protokoll durch ein spezielles T.120 Multicast-Transportprotokoll (T.MT) zu ersetzen. Dabei sollen keine Änderungen des MCS notwendig werden.

- Der MCS stellt zusammen mit den anderen Teilen des T.120 lediglich einen Mehrpunkt-*Daten*verkehr zur Verfügung. Eine Unterstützung von Echtzeit-Datenströmen wie z.B. Audio und Video mit einer zu vereinbarenden Dienstgüte wird im Rahmen des T.120 nicht erreicht. Allerdings werden solche Funktionalitäten im Rahmen der Standard-Familie T.130 momentan diskutiert. Dabei wird ein Protokoll-Stack parallel zum T.120-Stack aufgebaut, der sich teilweise der MCS- und GCC-Funktionalität bedient.

- Aufgrund der hierarchischen Struktur einer Domain und der Auswahl eines Top Providers für diese Struktur ist das Weitersenden von Anforderungen (Token, Channels) bis hin zum Top Provider notwendig. Dieser wird in einer Konferenz automatisch zum "Single-Point-of-Failure" und mit hoher Wahrscheinlichkeit auch zum Engpaß.

- Mit der Festlegung der Nummernbereiche für Kanäle und Tokens wurden Obergrenzen für Anwendungsgrößen fest vorgeschrieben.

4.2 Verwaltung der Konferenzdaten durch den GCC-Provider

Im Kern der vom GCC angebotenen Funktionalität sitzt die Verwaltung und Manipulation der Konferenzdatenbank. Dafür werden im T.124 Datenstrukturen festgelegt, in denen ein GCC-Provider eine Reihe von Informationen über eine Konferenz ablegt. Dabei wird die zu einer Konferenz gehörige Information auf *jedem* an der Konferenz beteiligten Endsystem repliziert gehalten. Die Algorithmen zur Verwaltung des Konferenzkontexts bestimmen entscheidend das Einsatzspektrum des T.120.

4.2.1 Algorithmus zur Verwaltung der Konferenz-Informationen

Alle Informationen über eine Konferenz (Abschnitt 3.2) werden zwischen den an einer Konferenz beteiligten Endsystemen in einer einzigen Nachricht, der *RosterUpdateIndication PDU*, ausgetauscht. Die Regeln für die Handhabung dieser Nachricht beschreibt das Replikationsprotokoll für die Konferenzdatenbank. In Abhängigkeit von den Werten einiger Flags dient die *RosterUpdateIndication PDU* zur Weitergabe von Änderungen an der Konferenzdatenbank als voller Refresh (Weitergabe der kompletten Datenbank) oder als "Delta"-Meldung (Weitergabe von veränderten Teilen). Der Austausch von Änderungsmeldungen wird angestoßen, wenn

- ein Endsystem zu einer Konferenz hinzukommt oder daraus ausscheidet,

- ein APE auf einem Endsystem zu einer Konferenz hinzukommt oder ausscheidet,

- ein APE seine Eigenschaften ändert.

Die Weitergabe von Änderungsmeldungen zwischen Endsystemen erfolgt in einem zweiphasigen Protokoll: In der ersten Phase wird eine Änderung aufwärts durch die Hierarchie von Endsystemen in einer Konferenz weitergegeben. Jeder GCC Provider, der eine solche Änderungsmeldung erhält, aktualisiert seine Informationen über die unter ihm liegende Subhierarchie von Endsystemen und reicht die Änderungsmeldung nach oben weiter. Sobald sie beim Top-GCC-Provider, d.h. bei der Wurzel des Baumes, eintrifft, wird von diesem der nun gültige Inhalt der Konferenzdatenbank bestimmt. Sollte die Änderungsmeldung entstanden sein, weil ein neues Endsystem in die Konferenz eingetreten ist, wird der *komplette* Inhalt der Konferenzdatenbank als voller Refresh an *alle* beteiligten Endsysteme gemulticastet. Dadurch wird erreicht, daß das eine, neu hinzugekommene Endsystem eine gültige Konferenzdatenbank erhält (Man beachte, daß der MCS den Multicast auf Punkt-zu-Punkt-Übertragungen abbildet!). In allen anderen Fällen wird vom Top-GCC-Provider nur eine "Delta"-Meldung an alle Endsysteme der Konferenz gemulticastet.

4.2.2 Bewertung und Folgerungen

Beim Design des GCC wurde die Entscheidung gefällt, Strukturinformationen über Konferenzen intern in einer Datenbank zu halten. Deren Implementierung wurde so vorgeschrieben, daß der Overhead zum Lesen von Daten minimal ist, da jede Leseanfrage lokal durch einen GCC-Provider beantwortet werden kann. Demgegenüber ist der Änderungsaufwand maximal, da jede Kopie der Datenbank auf jedem Endsystem konsistent gehalten werden muß. Zusätzlich zu dieser Design-Entscheidung, die für einige Anwendungsszenarien vertretbar ist, wurde jedoch ein sehr ineffizientes Replikationsprotokoll definiert, insbesondere unter dem Aspekt, daß bessere Protokolle seit geraumer Zeit bekannt sind.

Die mögliche Ineffizienz der Datenverwaltung des T.124 resultiert aus dem Vorgehen, jedesmal beim Eintreten eines neuen Endsystems in eine Konferenz die komplette Konferenzdatenbank an alle Endsysteme zu schicken, obwohl bei allen bis auf dem neu hinzugekommenen der größte Teil der Informationen schon richtig vorliegt. Daraus ergeben sich folgende Konsequenzen für die Einsetzbarkeit des T.120:

* Da die Konferenzdatenbank auf jedem Endsystem gehalten wird, ist der T.120 ungeeignet für Endsysteme, die (z.B. aus preislichen Überlegungen) mit beschränktem Speicher ausgestattet sind. Ein Beispiel hierfür sind Set Top Units.

* Der T.120 erscheint als ungeeignet für Konferenzen mit großen Teilnehmerzahlen.[1] Dies resultiert wesentlich aus dem definierten Replikationsprotokoll, durch das beim Anmelden neuer Teilnehmer enorme Datenmengen verschickt werden und mit langen Verzögerungen zu rechnen ist. Überdies stellt der Top-GCC-Provider als zentrale Instanz einen Engpaß dar.

5 Schlußfolgerungen und weitere Arbeit

Mit der ITU Standard-Familie T.120 werden Funktionen und Abläufe für die Erzeugung und Verwaltung von Telekonferenz-Anwendungen spezifiziert. Ziel dieses Papiers war eine Analyse der Basisfunktionen dieser Standard-Familie hinsichtlich ihrer Verwendbarkeit für beliebige Konferenzszenarien. Dabei zeigte sich, daß die als Dienste der Standards angebotenen Abstraktionen und Modelle sehr nützlich für die Implementierung von Telekonferenz-Anwendungen sind. Sowohl die vom MCS gebotenen Mittel zur Mehrpunkt-Kommunikation wie auch die vom GCC verfügbar gemachten Konzepte zur Konferenzverwaltung decken weite Bereiche der in

---

1. Die exakte Grenze hängt wesentlich von der Leistungsfähigkeit des Top-GCC-Providers und der Bandbreite der Verbindungen ab.

Anwendungen immer wiederkehrenden Anforderungen ab. Somit könnten die Standards eine echte Hilfe bei der Realisierung von Telekonferenz-Anwendungen sein.

Bei der Analyse der Abläufe, über welche die definierten Konzepte tatsächlich realisiert werden sollen, zeigen sich jedoch eine Reihe von Restriktionen, durch welche die direkte Verwendbarkeit der Standards für einige Anwendungsbereiche ausscheidet. Mit den beschriebenen Abläufen erscheinen die Standards im wesentlichen für kleinere Konferenzen von bis zu (einigen) 10 Benutzern geeignet.

Der MCS bietet Konzepte zur Mehrpunkt-Kommunikation an, die intern auf sichere Punkt-zu-Punkt-Verbindungen abgebildet werden. Damit wird die direkte Nutzung effizienter Multicast-Funktionen ausgeschlossen. Gleichzeitig schränkt dieses Vorgehen die ursprünglich angestrebte Unterstützung der Übertragung von Audio-und Video-Daten über den T.120 ein, da die Echt-zeit-Eigenschaften dieser Ströme nicht genügend berücksichtigt werden. Als Folge wurde für den letzteren Bereich begonnen, eine weitere Standard-Familie, den T.130, zu definieren.

Bei der Verwaltung von Konferenzen mittels des GCC wurde die Entscheidung gefällt, die Konferenzdatenbank für jedes beteiligte Endsystem zu replizieren. Damit ergibt sich zwangsläufig eine Obergrenze für die Größe der realistisch unterstützbaren Konferenzen. Jedes Anmelden eines neuen Benutzers führt zu einer Flut von Aktualisierungsnachrichten, die überdies nicht als bloße Änderungsmeldungen, sondern durch das Verschicken der kompletten Konferenzdatenbank realisiert werden. Ein enormes Datenaufkommen und lange Aufsetzzeiten von Konferenzen sind die Folge. Anwendungen wie z.B. Town-Meetings mit einigen 1000 Teilnehmern sind kaum vorstellbar. Ebenso ist die Implementierung von Anwendungsszenarien schwierig, wenn Endsysteme wie beispielsweise Set Top Units zum Einsatz kommen, deren Speicher (aus preis-lichen Gründen) klein dimensioniert ist.

So generisch wie die von MCS und GCC gebotenen Konzepte und die Vielzahl von Alternativen für die Gestaltung und Verwaltung von Konferenzen sind, sie haben auch eine Kehrseite: Sie resultieren in einem hohen Implementierungsaufwand hinsichtlich der zu realisierenden Protokolle und Datenstrukturen für die regulären Abläufe und die aufgrund der Vielzahl von Optionen auftretenden Sonderfälle.

In unserer weiteren Arbeit werden wir uns auf zwei Bereiche konzentrieren. Einerseits soll untersucht werden, wie die Abbildung der Funktionen des MCS auf die Multicast-Funktionen erreicht werden kann, welche durch das in den Philips Forschungslaboratorien Aachen entwik-kelte ATM-Netz geboten werden. Andererseits soll der GCC in einer Weise umgestaltet werden, die eine bessere Anpassung der Datenverwaltung an verschiedene Anforderungen und Größen von Konferenzen zulassen.

6 Literatur

[1]   Stephen Casner, Stephen Deering, First IETF Internet Audiocast, ACM SigCOMM

[2]   Hans Eriksson, MBONE: The Multicast Backbone, Communications of the ACM, Vol.37, No.8, August 1994

[3]   ITU-T Study Group 8, ITU-T Recommendation T.120 (Draft, März 1995): Data Protocols for Multimedia Conferencing

[4]   ITU-T Study Group 8, ITU-T Recommendation T.121 (Draft, Februar 1995): Generic Application Template

[5]   ITU-T Study Group 8, ITU-T Recommendation T.122 (1993): Multipoint Communication Service for Audio Graphics and Audiovisual Conferencing

[6] ITU-T Study Group 8, ITU-T Recommendation T.123 (Draft, Juni 1994): Protocol Stack for Audiographic and Audiovisual Teleconference Applications

[7] ITU-T Study Group 8, ITU-T Recommendation T.124 (Draft, März 1995): Generic Conference Control for Audiographic and Audiovisual Teleconference Applications

[8] ITU-T Study Group 8, ITU-T Recommendation T.125 (Draft, 1993): Multipoint Communication Service Protocol Specification

[9] ITU-T Study Group 8, ITU-T Recommendation T.126 (Draft, 1995): Still Image Transfer Protocol Specification

[10] ITU-T Study Group 8, ITU-T Recommendation T.127: Multipoint Binary File Transfer Protocol

[11] ITU-T Study Group 8, ITU-T Recommendation T.130 (Draft, 1996): Real Time Architecture for Multimedia Conferencing

[12] ITU-T Study Group 8, ITU-T Recommendation T.132 (Draft, 1996): Real Time Link Management

[13] ITU-T Study Group 8, ITU-T Recommendation T.133 (Draft, 1995): Audio Video Control Application Protocol

[14] CCITT Recommendation X.208 (1988): Specification of Abstract Syntax Notation One (ASN.1)

[15] CCITT Recommendation X.209 (1988): Specification of Basic Encoding Rules for Abstract Syntax Notation One (ASN.1)

[16] CCITT Recommendation X.224 (1988): Transport Protocol Definitions for Open Systems Interconnection for CCITT Applications

[17] CCITT Recommendation Z.100 (1988): Specification and Description Language (SDL)

[18] Carsten Borman, Joerg Ott, Christoph Reichert (1996): Simple Conference Control Protocol, ftp://ftp.ietf.org/internet-drafts/draft-ietf-mmusic-sccp-00.txt

[19] Schulzrinne (1996): Simple Conference Invitation Protocol, ftp://ftp.ietf.org/internet-drafts/draft-ietf-mmusic-scip-00.ps

[20] IMTC (1996): IMTC MCS API, ftp://ftp.imtc-files.org/imtc-site/AP-AG/TECH/CD/MCS-API

[21] IMTC (1996): IMTC GCC API, ftp://ftp.imtc-files.org/imtc-site/AP-AG/TECH/CD/GCC-API

[22] IMTC (1996): Implementor's Guide, ftp://ftp.imtc-files.org/imtc-site/IMPGUIDE/impguid4.zip

[23] ITU-T Study Group 8 Contribution (1996): T.120 Multicast Concept Description

Resource Reservation in Advance (ReRA) in heterogenen Netzen

Alexander Schill, Frank Breiter, Sabine Kühn, Janko Oeser
Technische Universität Dresden, Fakultät Informatik,
01062 Dresden; Telefon: 0351/463 8352
schill/breiter/kuehn/oeser@ibdr.inf.tu-dresden.de

Zusammenfassung
Die Einführung von Mechanismen für die Reservierung im voraus (ReRA) ermöglicht die Reservierung und Verwaltung von Netzwerkressourcen vor der eigentlichen Datenübertragung. Für Ereignisse, die längere Zeit im voraus terminlich festgelegt werden, kann somit die Verfügbarkeit der erforderlichen Ressourcen für den gewünschten Zeitpunkt garantiert werden. Aktuelle Reservierungsprotokolle führen Reservierungen entweder kurz vor oder zeitgleich mit dem Verbindungsaufbau für die Übertragung der Daten durch. Ein Nachteil, der mit dieser „immediate reservation" verbunden ist, kann in der teilweisen Ablehnung der Anwendungsanforderungen liegen, die auf mangelnde Ressourcen zurückzuführen ist.
Dieses Papier beschreibt eine mögliche Umsetzung von Vorabreservierungsstrategien für heterogene Netze. Grundlage für die laufenden Implementierungsarbeiten bildet eine RSVP/IPng/ATM Umgebung. Entsprechend werden zunächst Erfahrungen verbunden mit der Bereitstellung dieses Protokollstacks dargelegt sowie weiterführend die wesentlichen Grundgedanken des ReRA - Konzeptes. Der Diskussionsschwerpunkt liegt dabei hauptsächlich auf der Realisierung der Kommunikation mit RSVP als auch auf einer sich daraus ergebenden Problemanalyse.

Schlagworte: ATM, TCP/IP, IPng, RSVP, Dienstgüte, Reservierung im voraus

1 Einleitung

Mit dem Vorstoß der ATM - Technologie in die lokale Netzwelt wird nicht nur den Ansprüchen bezüglich hoher Bandbreiten, sondern auch der Skalierbarkeit der Bandbreite, dem Transport unterschiedlicher Dienste wie Sprache und Bild und der Gewährleistung einer qualitätsgerechten Übertragung gerecht. Mit der Gründung des ATM Forums als ein Herstellergremium werden Spezifikationen (ATM 1993), (ATM 1995) derart erarbeitet, daß eine schrittweise Implementierung der komplexen ATM Technologie sowohl im LAN als auch im WAN ermöglicht wird.

Da die meisten Netze jedoch nicht ausschließlich auf Netztechnologien wie z.B. ATM oder FDDI basieren, sondern auf dem Zusammenschluß unterschiedlichster Netze, werden Protokolle benötigt, die eine Interoperabilität in einem heterogenen Netz ermöglichen (Alles 1995).

Im Bereich der heterogenen Netze sind noch einige Aspekte offen. So stellt sich die Frage, wie sich der Ansatz garantierter Dienstqualitäten in einer heterogenen Netzlandschaft sicherstellen läßt. Ein Ansatz wie LAN Emulation (LAN) sieht die Möglichkeit, diesen Anforderungen Rechnung zu tragen, nicht vor. Auch in der nach RFC 1577 (Laubach 1994) vorgestellten Architektur eines reinen IP Protokollstacks über ATM ist die Unterstützung einer mit Dienstgüte behafteten Kommunikationsbeziehung nicht integriert.

In Hinblick auf die Weiterentwicklung und Verbesserung des Internet Protokolls wurden in den letzten Jahren Anstrengungen von der IETF für den Entwurf eines neuen Internet Protokolls IP (Version 6) unternommen, um den limitierten Adreßraum des IP zu überwinden (Hinden 1995) und neue Konzepte (Narten 1995) und Eigenschaften (verbesserte

Unterstützung von Optionen, Multimedia-Unterstützung) in dieses Protokoll zu integrieren. Die Entwicklung von IPv6 hat weitere Betrachtungen über die Anpassung dieses Protokolls an unterliegende Systeme wie z.B. an ATM (Schulter 1995) zur Folge. Mit der Entwicklung einer integrierten Dienstumgebung für das Internet entstanden Reservierungsprotokolle, die für die Abbildung der geforderten Dienste auf die jeweilige Link Layer geeignet erscheinen. Das Resource ReServation Protocol (RSVP) (Braden 1996) wurde speziell für die Unterstützung der Reservierung von Ressourcen für verbindungslose Datenübertragungen entwickelt.

Die derzeitigen Reservierungsprotokolle innerhalb der ATM Schichten und in den darüberliegenden Schichten ermöglichen eine „unverzügliche" Reservierung: Ressourcen können nur zu dem Zeitpunkt der eigentlichen Datenübertragung belegt werden. Ein entscheidender Nachteil ergibt sich dabei im Fall einer Ablehnung in Ermangelung der geforderten, mit entsprechender Dienstgüte behafteten Ressourcen. Mechanismen wie Vorab - Reservierungen sind eine Variante zur Behebung dieses Problems. Im Rahmen eines Forschungsprojektes der TU Dresden werden auf der Basis eines allgemeinen Modells Mechanismen für die Integration von ReRA entwickelt, die sowohl für Reservierungen im voraus in ATM selbst als auch innerhalb heterogener Netze mit teilweiser ATM - Infrastruktur Gültigkeit besitzen sollen.

Diese Arbeit ist wie folgt gegliedert: In Kapitel 2 wird zunächst ein Konzept für Vorab - Reservierungen vorgestellt, welches die Basis sowohl für die Abbildung auf ATM als auch auf RSVP im Internet - Bereich darstellt.

Zur besseren Verständlichkeit wird zu Beginn des Kapitels 3 der aktuelle Entwicklungsstand traditioneller Reservierungsmechanismen anhand einer Implementierung des RSVP/IPng/ATM - Protokollstack aufgezeigt. Mit Hilfe dieser Umgebung war zunächst möglich, erste Erfahrungen und Leistungsmessungen mit RSVP und IPng über ATM zu sammeln, um somit über eine geeignete Basis für die Erweiterung um ReRA-Mechanismen zu verfügen.

Aufbauend auf den Kapiteln 2 und 3 wird in Kapitel 4 eine mögliche Umsetzung von ReRA in RSVP diskutiert und diesbezüglich Lösungen für zu erwartende Probleme aufgezeigt.

Kapitel 5 schließt mit einer Zusammenfassung und einem Ausblick auf weitere zukünftige Forschungsaspekte diese Arbeit ab.

2 Allgemeines Konzept von ReRA

Der ständig zunehmende Einsatz von Echtzeit - Multimedia - Anwendungen, wie Videokonferenzsysteme, verteiltes Lehren und Lernen oder Video on Demand, führen zu einem erhöhten Datenaufkommen mit gleichzeitig steigenden Forderungen an die zu erbringende Dienstgüte. Diesen Forderungen kann einerseits durch den Einsatz von Hochleistungsnetzen und andererseits durch Reservierungen von entsprechenden Ressourcen nachgekommen werden. Derzeitige Reservierungsprotokolle belegen die Ressourcen kurz vor der eigentlichen Datenkommunikation. Signalisierungsprotokolle wie z.B. RSVP belegen die Ressourcen vor dem Verbindungsaufbau (bei der Nutzung von verbindungsorientierten Transportprotokollen), während andere Signalisierungsprotokolle z.B. die des ATM die Ressourcen mit dem Verbindungsaufbau reservieren. Daraus ergibt sich der Nachteil, daß Netzwerkressourcen nur dann reserviert werden können, wenn sie zur Verfügung stehen und nicht von anderen Anwendungen benutzt werden. Im ungünstigsten Fall erfolgt, auf Grund begrenzter Ressourcen, eine Ablehnung der Reservierung. Gegebenenfalls muß die Anwendung zu einem späteren Zeitpunkt, unter Umständen mit reduzierten Anforderungen, die Anfrage wiederholen, die wiederum abgelehnt werden kann.

Um dem entgegenzuwirken, ist es sinnvoll, Mechanismen einzuführen, die eine langfristige Reservierung erlauben. Anwendungen haben somit die Möglichkeit, über einen längeren Zeitraum betrachtet, Reservierungen vor der eigentlichen Datenübertragung vorzunehmen. Die wesentlichen Vorteile liegen dabei in einer nahezu 100 %igen Garantie der Verfügbarkeit der Ressourcen, sowie einer besseren Planung bei der Vergabe bzw. Verwaltung der Ressourcen, das nach unserer Meinung zu einer effizienteren Ausnutzung der Bandbreite führen sollte, jedoch erst mit Simulationen bzw. Tests nachgewiesen werden kannn.

Ein konkreter Anwendungsfall wird am Beispiel (Abbildung 1) einer Videokonferenz verdeutlicht. Dabei ist der Termin für den Beginn der Konferenz bereits festgelegt und die Teilnahme vom Sender S und den Empfänger 1-3 gefordert. Um die Ressourcen für diesen festgelegten Termin garantieren zu können, sollte entsprechend im voraus geplant und reserviert werden. Tritt während der Reservierung dennoch ein Mangel an Ressourcen auf, so

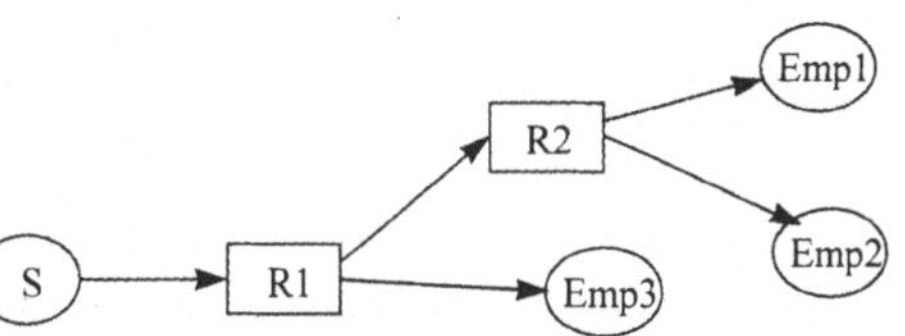

Abbildung 1: Szenario einer Videokonferenz

können aufgrund der Empfehlungen vom Netz entweder Teilreservierungen (unterschiedliche Reservierungszeiten) oder gar Neuaushandlungen für den empfohlenen Beginn wahrgenommen werden. Bei der erfolgreichen Aushandlung der Reservierungen werden diese in den einzelnen Switches/Routern (R1, R2) verwaltet und erst mit der Aktivierung zu Beginn der Videokonferenz auch physisch reserviert.

Der Abgrenzung zu anderen Arbeiten folgend, werden die erforderliche Kommunikation für den Austausch der Reservierungsinformationen, die Eigenschaften von Vorabreservierungen anhand eines zeitlichen Verhaltens als auch die Spezifika der Zugangskontrolle (Admission Control) zum Netz aufgezeigt. Für die Abbildung auf RSVP, als Hauptbestandteil dieser Arbeit, ist im Unterschied zur Integration des ReRA Modells in ATM, die Betrachtung der Admission Control von geringerer Bedeutung.

2.1 Abgrenzung zu anderen Arbeiten

Die Ressourcen Reservierung im Voraus ist eine Thematik, die aufgrund der fortschreitenden Entwicklung der Reservierung in Hochleistungsnetzen an Bedeutung gewinnt. Die zu diesem Thema veröffentlichten Papiere sind aufgrund der Komplexität des Themas meist spezieller Art wie beispielsweise (Degermark 1995) mit der Erweiterung des Internet Dienstes Predictive Service (Shenker 1995) um ReRA Mechanismen.

(Ferrari 1995) beschäftigt sich mit der Erarbeitung einer Zugangskontrolle für ReRA. Als Ergebnis von Simulationen wurde für eine Multipartyumgebung festgestellt, daß die Akzeptanz für das Partitionieren der Ressourcen höher ist als für ein Teilen (resource sharing). Diese Betrachtungen erfolgten im Rahmen der Tenet Protokoll Suite, wobei für die notwendige Kommunikation Probleme wie beispielsweise Topologieänderungen oder Routing nicht diskutiert wurden. (Reinhardt 1994, 1995) diskutiert allgemeine Fragen und Probleme von ReRA und untersucht die Eignung der Reservierungsprotokolle ST-II und RSVP für die Aushandlung von Reservierungen im Voraus. Als Ergebnis dieser Untersuchungen favorisiert er ST-II, da RSVP durch das Verwenden von Soft States weniger geeignet erscheint. Er diskutiert die Nützlichkeit des Einsatzes von ReRA anhand einiger Anwendungsbeispiele. Im Unterschied zu diesen Arbeiten faßt (Wolf 1995) die Grundzüge der „advance reservation" zusammen.

Hinsichtlich der Bedeutung von RSVP als Bestandteil des diensteintegrierten Internet erscheint uns dieses Reservierungsprotokoll geeignet. Da RSVP eine Ergänzung des IP-Stacks darstellt (im Gegensatz dazu ist ST-II eine Weiterentwicklung von IP und ersetzt somit die gesamte Netzwerkschicht), sowie frei verfügbare Implementierungen in Form eines im *user space* realisierten Daemon-Prozesses vorliegen, können die von uns vorgeschlagenen zusätzlichen Reservierungmechanismen problemlos integriert und getestet werden. In den folgenden Kapiteln soll nun ein detaillierter Ansatz für die Integration von ReRA in RSVP gegeben, auftretende Probleme erörtert sowie Lösungen aufgezeigt werden. Das im folgenden kurz beschriebene allgemeine Modell ist als ein Ergebnis bisheriger Arbeiten anzusehen (Schill 1997).

2.2 Parameter

Im Unterschied zur Aushandlung traditioneller Reservierungen wird für ReRA-Verbindungen die Angabe zusätzlicher Parameter notwendig. In Verbindung mit der Durchführung einer Zugangskontrolle ist die Angabe des Startzeitpunktes und die geschätzte Verbindungsdauer anzugeben, um Überschneidungen mit anderen Reservierungen erkennen zu können. Obwohl die Spezifizierung der Gesamtdauer einer Verbindung von Anwendungsseite sicherlich nicht immer einfach ist, wird aus Gründen einer effektiven Ressourcenauslastung in diesem Ansatz das Wissen um die Verbindungsdauer vorausgesetzt.

Die Bekanntgabe der Werte Dauer und Startzeit an die beteiligten Rechner und Zwischenknoten muß über die in Abschnitt 2.4. eingeführten Nachrichten erfolgen. Für die Darstellung der Zeiten stehen 2 Varianten zur Diskussion:

- als relative Zeitangabe, d.h. die Angabe des Startes erfolgt relativ zum aktuellen Zeitpunkt
- und als absolute Zeitangabe.

Da die Reservierung von Ressourcen für einen bestimmten Zeitraum in der Zukunft auf mehreren Rechnern vorgenommen werden muß, spielt die Synchronisation eine wichtige Rolle. Konkret bedeutet das, daß mit Verwendung einer absoluten Zeit bezogen auf das lokale System, die Uhrensynchronität der Rechner unerläßlich ist. Dabei genügen moderne Protokolle zur Zeitsynchronisation wie NTP und DTS (DCE) den Ansprüchen ohne weiteres.

In Zusammenhang mit der Verwendung der absoluten Zeit ist auch die Einführung einer Granularität sinnvoll, die ein effektives zeitliches Zusammenfassen von Reservierungen erlaubt, da Anfangs- und Endzeiten verschiedener Reservierungen zugunsten eines geringeren Verwaltungsaufwandes zusammenfallen. Ein Nachteil der Einführung einer Granularität ist beispielsweise die innere Fragmentierung der Reservierungsdauer. Der in Kapitel 4 beschriebene Vorschlag für die Integration von ReRA in RSVP sieht die Übertragung einer Granularität noch nicht vor, allerdings ist mit wenig Aufwand eine derartige Erweiterung möglich.

2.3 Zeitliches Verhalten

Mit dem in (Abbildung 2) dargestellten Modell werden einige zeitbezogene Begriffe eingeführt, die, in Zusammenhang mit den nachfolgend beschriebenen Dienstprimitiven, der Darlegung der zeitlichen Abfolge des Kommunikationsablaufes dienen.

Der Sender eines Datenstromes gibt zum Zeitpunkt t_{DB} die Startzeit t_{DS}, das voraussichtliche Ende t_{DE} des angebotenen Dienstes und gegebenenfalls weitere Parameter[1] bekannt. Das kann explizit durch eine Anfrage des Nutzers oder auch durch ein- oder mehrmalige Bekanntgabe geschehen, z.B. durch Senden von PATH Nachrichten in RSVP. Eine Reservierung von Ressourcen zu diesem Datenstrom kann jetzt von einem Nutzer zum Zeitpunkt t_{RA} angefordert werden. Dabei müssen Startzeit t_{RS} und Ende t_{RE} der Reservierung nicht notwendigerweise

---

[1] z.B. Beschreibung eines Senderdatenstroms hinsichtlich seiner Verkehrscharakteristik

mit den Zeiten des Datenstromes übereinstimmen, jedoch im Intervall $[t_{DS}, t_{DE}]$ liegen. Ist die Reservierung erfolgreich, so erfolgt innerhalb eines bestimmten Zeitraumes $[t_{RA}, t_{RB}]$ eine Reservierungsbestätigung.

Die Reservierung wird zum Zeitpunkt t_{RI} durch eine Aktivierungsnachricht initialisiert. Die maximal erlaubte Startzeitüberschreitung wird durch $T_Ü$ gekennzeichnet, danach werden die reservierten Ressourcen freigegeben. Eine Verlängerung über das eigentliche Reservierungsende hinaus ist bei verfügbaren Ressourcen bis zum Zeitpunkt t_{RV} möglich. Der Zeitraum I_{ReRA} zwischen

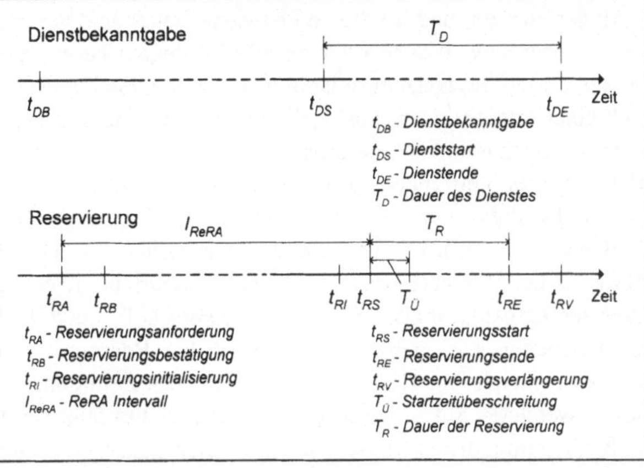

Abbildung 2: Zeitliches Verhalten

der Reservierungsanforderung und der Inanspruchnahme der Reservierung ist im Gegensatz zu $[t_{RA}, t_{RB}]$ und $[t_{RI}, t_{RS}]$ sehr groß. Reservierungen über einen Zeitraum von Wochen oder sogar Monaten sind denkbar. Ein ReRA-System könnte jedoch aus verwaltungstechnischen Gründen ein maximales ReRA Intervall $I_{ReRA,max}$ festlegen.

2.4 Dienstprimitive und Kommunikation

Das Kommunikationsmodell und die zugehörigen Dienstprimitive (Abbildung 3) sind so allgemein gehalten, daß es sowohl für eine sender- als auch eine empfängerorientierte Reservierung Gültigkeit besitzt. Dementsprechend wurde auf die Einführung eines Dienstprimitivs zur Bekanntgabe eines Dienstangebotes verzichtet, da im

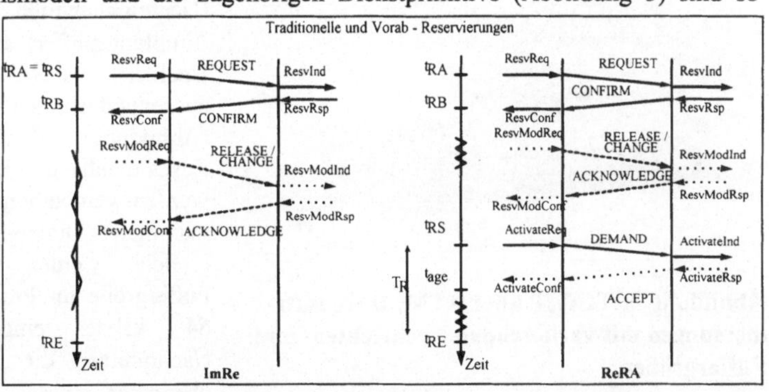

Abbildung 3: Kommunikationsmodell mit Primitiven

Fall eines senderorientierten Ansatzes dieses mit dem Primitiv der Reservierungsanforderung zusammenfällt.

Die Spezifikation der geforderten Ressourcen erfolgt durch das Senden einer REQUEST Nachricht durch einen Nutzer. Zusätzlich enthält diese Nachricht den Übertragungsbeginn und die gewünschte Dauer. Nach einer erfolgreichen Aushandlung und Call Admission Control, sendet der korrespondierende Nutzer bzw. Diensterbringer eine Bestätigung CONFIRM. Im Fall einer Ablehnung sendet der Diensterbringer eine RELEASE Nachricht. In Verbindung mit einer solchen Ablehnung erfolgt die Übermittlung von Empfehlungen über alternative Reservierungen:

• die Dauer wird ermittelt, für die eine Reservierung der geforderten Ressourcen möglich ist.

- Eine weitere Möglichkeit ist die Übermittlung einer neuen Startzeit, ab der die gewünschten Ressourcen für die vorgegebene Dauer zur Verfügung stehen.
- Ab der Startzeit und für die vorgegebene Dauer sind nur begrenzt Ressourcen nutzbar.

Die Entscheidung, welche oder ob alle Strategien bereitgestellt werden sollten, liegt in der Verantwortung des Netzadministrators oder Bereitstellers.

Nach einer erfolgreichen Aushandlung der Reservierung hat der Nutzer die Möglichkeit, die Reservierungsparameter zu ändern. Das umfaßt das Entfernen der Reservierung, aber auch die Erhöhung oder Verminderung der geforderten Ressourcen. Solche Änderungen betreffen nicht nur die Qualitäts- und Verkehrsparameter, sondern auch die Parameter Startzeit und Dauer. (Startzeit nur bis t_{rs}). Um eine flexiblere Handhabung der Änderungen zu erreichen, werden Policy Data innerhalb der CHANGE Nachricht übertragen, um anzuzeigen, ob die Reservierung gelöscht oder beibehalten werden soll, wenn die Modifikation fehlschlägt.

Der Übergang zur expliziten Nutzung der Ressourcen wird durch das Senden einer Aktivierungsnachricht DEMAND innerhalb des Zeitraums $T_Ü$ geregelt, die in Abhängigkeit vom verwendeten Signalisierungsprotokoll auch bestätigt werden kann.

Die Realisierung dieses Modells in einer heterogenen Netzumgebung erfolgt auf der Basis von RSVP (Kapitel 4), dessen Grundlagen im Kapitel 3 dargelegt werden.

3 Ressourcenreservierung: Grundlagen

3.1 Untersuchung herkömmlicher Protokolle

Untersuchungen über das Verhalten konventioneller Protokolle wie TCP/IP über ATM haben gezeigt, daß ohne eine entsprechende Anpassung der Protokollparameter (Nachrichtengröße, Sende-/Empfangspuffer) die Vorteile der Hochleistungsnetze nicht vollständig ausgenutzt werden können. Messungen (Abbildung 4), die in diesem Zusammenhang von uns durchgeführt wurden, verdeutlichen, daß nur dann ein maximaler Durchsatz von 135 Mbit/s erreicht werden kann, wenn die Puffergröße im Protokoll auf mehr als 64 kByte eingestellt und die Nachrichten, die an das Protokoll übergeben werden, entsprechend groß

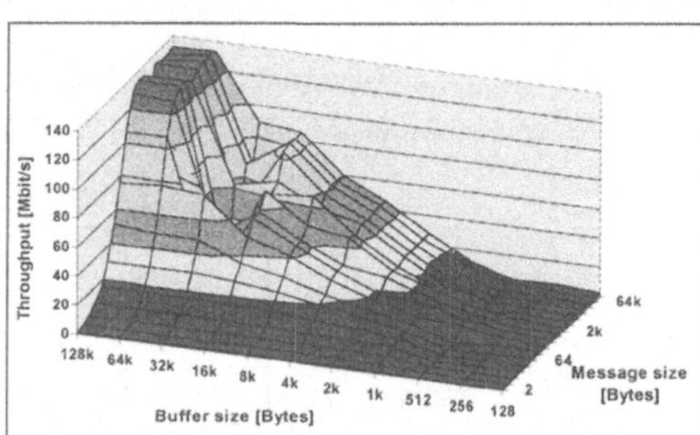

Abbildung 4: TCP/IP über ATM: Durchsatzmessungen mit variierenden Nachrichten- und Puffergrößen

gewählt werden. Grundsätzlich kann jedoch gesagt werden, daß herkömmliche Protokolle wie TCP/IP in Hinblick auf den erzielbaren Durchsatz mit einem entsprechenden Tuning der Parameter auch für den Einsatz in Hochleistungsnetzen geeignet sind.

Um die Eigenschaften eines QoS-basierten Netzes, die beispielsweise durch die Lösung des klassischen IP über ATM weitestgehend verborgen sind, auch Anwendungen zur Verfügung zu stellen, können Reservierungsprotokolle wie RSVP genutzt werden. Damit ist zum einen die Aushandlung der Reservierung in einem heterogenen Netz gegeben, zum anderen die Kommunikation mit dem unterliegenden System für die Übermittlung der angeforderten Reservierungsparameter. In diesem Zusammenhang stehen Arbeiten, die sich mit der Abbildung der Kommunikationsmechanismen und der Parameter auf die der ATM Technologie beschäftigen (Berger 1996), (Borden 1996), (Schill 1996).

3.2 Grundideen des Reservierungsprotokolls - RSVP

Im Rahmen des Modells des diensteintegrierenden Internet wurde das Reservierungsprotokoll RSVP (*ReSerVation Protocol*) entwickelt. Mit Hilfe von RSVP wird es Anwendungen ermöglicht, die Charakteristik eines Datenstromes einer Gruppe von möglichen Empfängern bekanntzugeben, so daß diese entlang des Übertragungsweges Ressourcen entsprechend der benötigten QoS reservieren können.

Da die Reservierung der Ressourcen von den Empfängern initiiert wird, bezeichnet man RSVP als ein empfängerorientiertes Reservierungsprotokoll. Es werden nur die Ressourcen belegt, welche die Empfänger tatsächlich benötigen. Außerdem erlaubt dieses Prinzip eine effektivere Verwaltung größerer Gruppen, dynamische Gruppenmitgliedschaft und heterogene Empfänger (Braden 1996).

3.3 Architekturmodell und Schnittstellen von RSVP

Als ein wesentlicher Bestandteil des diensteintegrierenden Internet gliedert sich RSVP in dessen Architekturmodell ein (Braden 1994). Innerhalb der RSVP-Architektur wird zwischen einem Host- (Abbildung 5) und einem Router-Modell unterschieden. Voraussetzung für eine erfolgreiche Reservierung ist die Unterstützung des RSVP-Protokolles auf allen beteiligten Netzknoten entlang der Übertragungsstrecke.

RSVP setzt auf dem *Internet Protocol* auf und beansprucht dabei den Platz eines Transportprotokolls im Protokollstack (Braden 1996). Da aber keine Anwendungsdaten von RSVP transportiert werden, ist es eher den Steuerprotokollen zuzurechnen. RSVP ist kein Routingprotokoll, sondern konsultiert die lokale Routingdatenbank, um die benötigten Weginformationen zu erhalten.

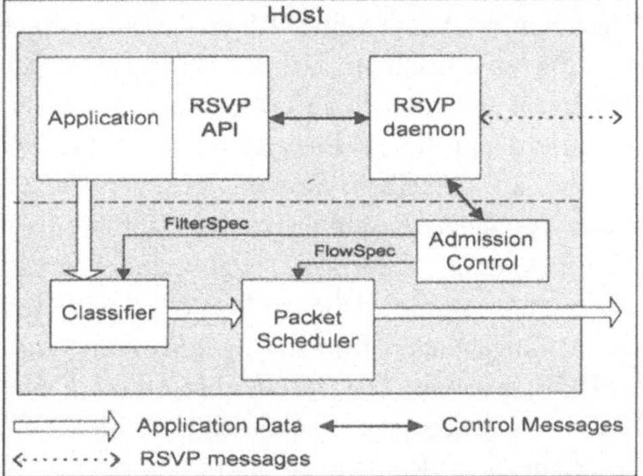

Abbildung 5: RSVP Host-Architektur

Das *ReSerVation Protocol* wird in einem RSVP-*Daemon* Programm implementiert, welches auf *User*-Ebene läuft. Eine Anwendung greift über eine RSVP-*Client Library*, die zur Übersetzungszeit an die Anwendung gebunden wird, auf diesen *Daemon* zu. Die RSVP-*Client Library* stellt der Anwendung Funktionen zur Registrierung, Reservierung, und Beendigung zur Verfügung und gestattet es dem RSVP-*Daemon* über asynchrone Rückrufe (*Upcalls*), die Anwendung über Fehler und Reservierungsereignisse zu informieren. Diese Funktionen bilden das RSVP *Application Programming Interface* (RAPI).

Die Hauptaufgabe von RSVP ist die Signalisierung der Ressourcenanforderungen, das eigentliche Reservieren der Ressourcen geschieht jedoch durch die Bausteine *Admission Control*, *Packet Classifier* und *Packet Scheduler* der diensteintegrierenden Internetarchitektur. Demzufolge ist ebenfalls eine Schnittstelle zu diesen in ihrer Gesamtheit als *Traffic Control* bezeichneten Modulen erforderlich.

3.4 Das RSVP Reservierungsmodell

Eine Anwendung kann als Sender oder Empfänger in einer RSVP-*Session* teilnehmen, nachdem eine Anmeldung zu dieser erfolgte. Eine RSVP-*Session* ist gekennzeichnet durch ein Transportprotokoll[2], eine (*Multicast*) IP-Zieladresse und gegebenenfalls einen Zielport. Sie beschreibt eine Gruppe von Empfängern, welche zu einem an diese Adresse gesendeten Datenstrom Reservierungen vornehmen dürfen. Jede einzelne *Session* wird von RSVP unabhängig behandelt. Nach der Anmeldung kann ein Sender die Charakteristik seines Datenstromes an die *Session* bekanntgeben, und die Empfänger können Ressourcen zu diesem Datenstrom anfordern. Eine Modifizierung bereits bestehender Reservierungen durch den Empfänger ist ebenfalls möglich. Mit der Beendigung einer *Session* gibt der Empfänger die reservierten Netzwerkressourcen wieder frei.

Die Reservierungsinformationen werden entlang des Übertragungsweges in veränderlichen Zustandsinformationen, den sogenannten *Soft States*, gehalten, deren periodische Auffrischung (*Refresh*) die benachbarten Netzknoten übernehmen. Erfolgte bis zum Ablauf eines *Cleanup-Timers* keine Auffrischung, so werden diese *Soft States* gelöscht. RSVP unterscheidet zwei Arten von *Soft States*; *Path States* kennzeichnen den Übertragungsweg und *Reservation States* repräsentieren eine Reservierung bezogen auf diese Übertragung. Ändert sich der Weg der Daten, z.B. durch den Ausfall eines Netzknotens, so werden die RSVP-Nachrichten entlang der geänderten Route geschickt und es wird versucht, die Reservierung dort neu aufzubauen.

Nachdem ein Sender einer RSVP-*Session* beigetreten ist, beginnt RSVP mit der Übertragung von *Path*-Nachrichten. Dabei wird in jedem Zwischenknoten entsprechend den in der *Path*-Nachricht enthaltenen Informationen ein neuer *Path State* eingerichtet. Erreicht die *Path*-Nachricht ein RSVP-Endsystem, so benachrichtigt der RSVP-*Daemon* jede Anwendung, welche zu derselben *Session* wie der Sender gehört. Der Empfänger kann jetzt eine Reservierung zu diesem Datenstrom anfordern.

RSVP überträgt diese Reservierungsanforderung mit Hilfe von *Resv*-Nachrichten. Die *Resv*-Nachrichten werden dabei entlang des durch die *Path States* gebildeten Pfadbaumes jeweils an den vorangehenden Router (*previous hop* - PHOP) gesendet. Die *Admission Control* jedes Netzknotens überprüft, ob ausreichend Ressourcen für die gewünschte Dienstgüte zur Verfügung stehen. Ist das der Fall, wird ein neuer *Resv State* eingerichtet. Konnte die Reservierung entlang der gesamten Übertragungsstrecke bis zum Sender erfolgreich eingerichtet werden, so informiert der RSVP-*Daemon* die Senderanwendung von der Reservierung (Abbildung 6). Erwartet der Empfänger

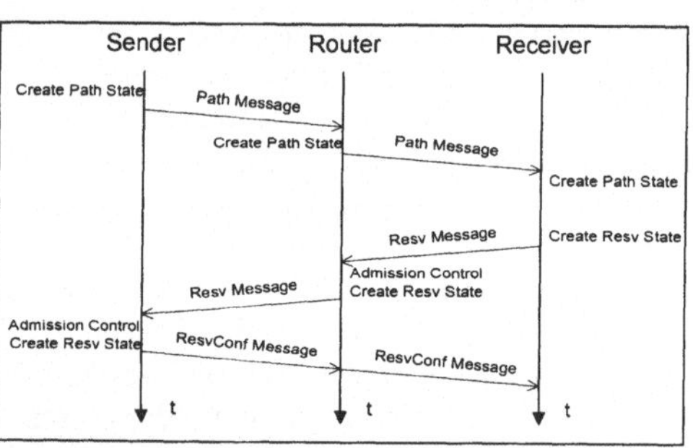

Abbildung 6: Erfolgreiche Reservierung

eine Bestätigung für eine gelungene Reservierung, so wird eine *ResvConf*-Nachricht an ihn gesendet und die entsprechende Anwendung benachrichtigt.

Neben den bereits erwähnten *Path-*, *Resv-* und *ResvConf*-Nachrichten stellt RSVP auch *PathTear-*, *ResvTear-*, (zusammengefaßt als *Teardown*) sowie *PathErr-* und *ResvErr-* (*Error*) Nachrichten zur Verfügung. Dabei dienen die *Teardown*-Nachrichten zum hostinitiierten Abbau des Pfadbaumes bzw. der Reservierung. Die *Error*-Nachrichten weisen auf aufgetretene Fehler hin.

Als Grundlage für die folgenden Erweiterungen dient im Rahmen dieses DFG-Forschungsprojektes zunächst eine Public Domain Implementierung, die auf einem IPng/ATM Protokollstack, als Bestandteil des Digital Unix Betriebsystems, aufsetzt. Dabei

---

[2] Momentan werden UDP, TCP sowie deren Versionen für das neue Internet Protokoll IPv6 unterstützt.

wurde die entsprechende Anpassung für die Abbildung der RSVP Parameter und Nachrichten auf die des ATM von uns bereits als Bestandteil des Digital Unix Betriebssystem (ATM Subsystem) implementiert.

4 Integration von ReRA in RSVP

4.1 Untersuchung zur Eignung von RSVP

Im Gegensatz zu dem herkömmlichen Verfahren bei der Reservierung von Ressourcen (*Immediate Reservation* - ImRe) erfolgt bei der *Resource Reservation in Advance* die Aushandlung der Reservierung weit vor deren Inanspruchnahme. Die Reservierung muß über den Zeitraum der *Intermediate Phase* hinweg aufrechterhalten werden, Änderungen bzw. ein Wiederauflösen der Reservierung sind zulässig. Die Zuteilung der Ressourcen zum Startzeitpunkt erfolgt automatisch oder durch eine Aktivierungsnachricht.

Aufgrund dieser Besonderheiten ergeben sich für eine Erweiterung des Reservierungs-protokolls RSVP zur Unterstützung von ReRA eine Reihe von Erfordernissen:

- Abbildung der ReRA Dienstprimitive auf RSVP Nachrichten
- Bestimmung zusätzlicher Parameter
- Gewährleistung der Reservierung in der Intermediate Phase
- Aktivierung der reservierten Ressourcen

Eine weitere Voraussetzung ist die Unterstützung von ReRA durch die *Traffic Control* Komponenten, welche die eigentliche Reservierung der Ressourcen vornehmen (Schill 1997).

4.1.1 Abbildung der ReRA Dienstprimitive auf RSVP Nachrichten

In Ergänzung des vorgestellten allgemeinen ReRA Modells (siehe Kapitel 2) ist die Einführung eines neuen ReRA Primitives notwendig. Bevor in einem empfängerorientierten System der Empfänger eine Reservierung anfordern kann, müssen ihm Informationen über zukünftige Datenströme und deren Charakteristik zur Verfügung stehen. Dies wird durch das neu eingeführte Primitiv AnnounceReq erreicht. Ändert sich die voraussichtliche Charakteristik des Datenstromes während der *Intermediate Phase*, so kann der Empfänger durch AnnModReq über die Modifikation informiert werden und darauf reagieren. Ebenso ist eine Anpassung der Reservierungsanforderung (ResvReq) jederzeit mit Hilfe eines ResvModReq möglich. Die Bestätigung einer erfolgreichen Reservierung erfolgt mit ResvCnf bzw. ResvModCnf. In Abbildung 7 wird gezeigt, daß alle bisher beschriebenen ReRA Dienstprimitive auf die bereits vorhandenen RSVP Nachrichten abbildbar sind. Auch die Aktivierung der Reservierung zum Beginn der *Usage Phase* ist, wie in 4.1.4 beschrieben, mit Hilfe einer *Resv*-Nachricht möglich. Der vorzeitige Abbau einer Reservierung kann sowohl von Sender- als auch Empfängerseite durch die RSVP *Teardown*-Nachrichten realisiert werden. Das Einführen eines neuen RSVP Nachrichtentyps ist daher nicht notwendig.

4.1.2 Bestimmung zusätzlicher Parameter

In Abschnitt 2.2 wurde gezeigt, daß für eine Vorabreservierung von Ressourcen der Startzeitpunkt (*ResvStart*) und die Dauer bzw. das Ende (*ResvEnd*) der beabsichtigten Ressourcennutzung erforderlich sind. Diese beiden Parameter sind daher in die *Resv*-Nachricht eines erweiterten RSVP zu integrieren. Analog dazu ist in der *Path*-Nachricht die Angabe des Datenstromstarts (*FlowStart*) und das voraussichtliche Ende (*FlowEnd*) notwendig. Die Start- und Endzeiten von Datenstrom und Reservierung müssen dabei jedoch nicht unbedingt identisch sein, da auch eine zeitlich eingeschränkte Reservierung zu einem bestimmten Datenstrom denkbar ist[3]. Desweiteren ist auch das Senden mehrerer zeitlich aufeinanderfolgender Datenströme durch ein und denselben Sender während einer RSVP *Session* zu unterstützen.

Die Zugehörigkeit einer Reservierung zu einem bestimmten Datenstrom eines Senders kann mit der folgenden Bedingung geprüft werden:

FlowStart ≤ *ResvStart* < *FlowEnd* und *FlowEnd* ≥ *ResvEnd*

Bietet ein Sender mehrere zeitlich versetzte Datenströme an, so reicht diese Identifizierung für eine mittelfristige Reservierung nicht aus.

Ein Datenstrom innerhalb einer *Session* ist dann durch den Empfänger eindeutig bestimmbar mit *<SrcAddr, SrcPort, FlowStart>*, da ein Sender zu einer bestimmten Zeit nur jeweils einen Datenstrom je Port sendet. Für den dadurch gekennzeichneten Datenstrom können die Empfänger einer *Session* verschiedene, auch zeitlich versetzte, Reservierungen tätigen. Wenn mehrere Reservierungen zu einem Datenstrom zu demselben Zeitpunkt vorliegen, ist zusätzlich die Dauer bzw. der Endzeitpunkt (*ResvEnd*) der Reservierung für eine Unterscheidung notwendig. Eine Reservierung innerhalb einer *Session* wird demzufolge durch *<SrcAddr, SrcPort, ResvStart, ResvEnd>* bestimmt.

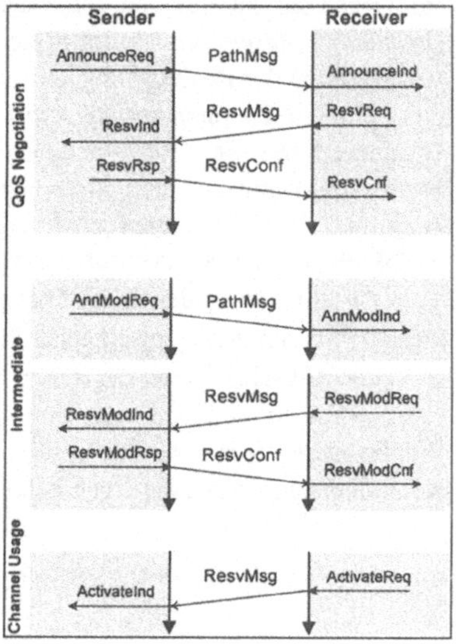

Die für die Aktivierung der Reservierung relevanten Para-meter Startzeitüberschreitung und Aktivierungsflag werden in 4.1.4 beschrieben. Weitere mögliche Erweiterungen sind die Angabe einer Verlängerungsoption oder die Verwendung von Wildcards für Beginn und Ende einer Reservierung in bezug auf einen bestimmten Datenstrom. Diese zusätzlichen Parameter werden in unserer jetzigen Implementation jedoch noch nicht berücksichtigt.

Abbildung 7: ReRA Dienstprimitive und RSVP Nachrichten

4.1.3 Gewährleistung der Reservierung in der Intermediate Phase

Die Aufrechterhaltung einer Reservierung in RSVP während der Datenübertragungsphase wird durch das zyklische Versenden von *Path*- und *Resv*-Nachrichten zur Auffrischung der *Soft States* der Nachbarknoten realisiert. Dabei gibt die *Refresh*-Zeit *R* an, in welchen Zeitabständen eine Aktualisierung durch den Nachbarknoten erwartet wird, und die Lebenszeit *L* bestimmt die Dauer, nach der ein *State* gelöscht wird, falls er keine Auffrischung erhält. Damit kein vorzeitiger Verlust an *States* auftreten kann, muß *L* die folgende Bedingung erfüllen: $L \geq (K+0.5) * 1.5 * R$

K ist dabei ein ganzzahliger Wert, wobei *K-1* aufeinanderfolgende Nachrichten verloren gehen können, ohne daß ein *Soft State* gelöscht wird.

---

[3] man denke z.B. an die Übertragung einer Videokonferenz, bei der nur ein bestimmter Beitrag interessiert.

Ein gängiger Wert für R in herkömmlichen RSVP Implementationen beträgt 30 Sekunden, als Wert für K wird 3 vorgeschlagen (Braden 1996). Für eine *Resource Reservation in Advance* bedeutet das:

1. Bei einem Ausfall eines Netzknotens auf der Reservierungsstrecke wird innerhalb kurzer Zeit die gesamte Reservierung auf den restlichen Routern abgebaut, da keine Auffrischung der *Path States* in Richtung Empfänger bzw. der *Resv States* in Richtung Sender mehr erfolgt.
2. Die auszutauschenden *Refresh*-Nachrichten während der *Intermediate Phase* stellen einen nicht vernachlässigbaren *Overhead* dar[4].

Um die Lebenszeit der zu einem ausgefallenen Router benachbarten *States* zu verlängern, bietet sich ein Erhöhen von R und/oder K an. Ein größerer Zeitabstand zwischen den *Refresh*-Nachrichten reduziert dabei gleichzeitig den *Overhead*. Es ist denkbar, die *Refresh*-Zeit in Abhängigkeit von der bis zur Inanspruchnahme der Reservierung verbleibenden Zeit schrittweise bis auf den Standardwert für ImRe zu verringern.

Genauere Werte für R und K werden in Zukunft am Beispiel unserer experimentellen Umgebung ermittelt.

4.1.4 Aktivierung der reservierten Ressourcen

Die Aktivierung der Reservierung kann automatisch bei Erreichen der Startzeit *ResvStart* durch das Systemmanagement ausgelöst werden, oder auf eine explizite Aufforderung durch den Empfänger. Wir bevorzugen die zweite Variante, da Ressourcen nur bei einer tatsächlichen Inanspruchnahme durch den Empfänger zugeteilt werden. Unsere Lösung sieht vor, daß der Empfänger zum Startzeitpunkt eine *Resv*-Nachricht mit einem gesetzten Aktivierungsflag sendet, welche die Freigabe der Ressourcen an die Verbindung auslöst. Wird die Reservierung nicht innerhalb eines bestimmten Zeitraumes $T_Ü$ in Anspruch genommen, so wird die Reservierung aufgehoben. Der Wert für diese erlaubte Startzeitüberschreitung $T_Ü$ könnte entweder explizit vom Empfänger festgelegt und bei der Reservierungsanforderung als weiterer Parameter angegeben werden, oder er wird vom Provider in der RSVP-Implementation fest vorgegeben.

4.2 Spezielle Probleme

4.2.1 Routing

In RSVP ist die Routingentscheidung unabhängig von der Reservierung. Ändert der Routingalgorithmus in der *Intermediate Phase* wegen veränderter Lastsituation im Netz die Route, so würde das einen Neuaufbau der Reservierung auslösen, obwohl die Dienstgüte zum Reservierungszeitraum nicht gefährdet ist.

Ein zustandsabhängiges Routingprotokoll müßte für die Berücksichtigung von ReRA den Zeitraum, zu dem eine Reservierung angefordert wird, mit in die Routingentscheidung einbeziehen. Ein solches Protokoll ist jedoch noch nicht verfügbar. Zur Vereinfachung gehen wir deshalb davon aus, daß der Routingalgorithmus lediglich auf den Ausfall von Netzkomponenten bzw. Topologieänderungen mit einer veränderten Wegewahl reagiert

---

[4] Angenommen, auf einem Router liegen 100 verschiedene Vorabreservierungen vor. Bei der gegenwärtig vorgeschlagenen *Refresh*-Zeit von 30 Sekunden bedeutet das 12000 *Resv-Refresh*-Nachrichten in einer Stunde bzw. ein Abarbeiten der *Refresh*-Routine ungefähr alle 300 ms.

(lastunabhängig). Die Anpassung der Reservierung wird in diesen Fällen durch den nächsten *Refresh* initiiert.

4.2.2 Verfügbarkeit der Endsysteme

Moderne Arbeitsplatzcomputer ermöglichen aufgrund ihrer hohen Rechenleistung und hochwertiger Peripheriegeräte die Verarbeitung von Multimediadaten in hoher Qualität. Typische ReRA-Anwendungen, wie z.B. Videokonferenzen, bleiben nicht nur leistungsfähigen Workstations vorbehalten, sondern sind auch auf PCs realisierbar.

Es ist daher wahrscheinlich, daß ein Endknoten mehrmals für längere Zeit ausgeschaltet wird, bevor der Startzeitpunkt einer mittelfristigen Reservierung überhaupt erreicht ist. Die Auffrischung der *Soft States* des benachbarten Routers ist nicht mehr gewährleistet und nach Ablauf der Lebenszeit *L* (siehe 4.1.3) werden diese gelöscht. Dieser Vorgang wiederholt sich für den jeweils nächsten Router, bis die Reservierung vollständig aufgelöst ist.

Die von uns vorgeschlagene Lösung besteht darin, die *Soft States* der direkt benachbarten Router (Router 1 und 3 in Abbildung 8) bei einem Ausbleiben der Auffrischung durch die Endknoten **nicht** zu löschen. Diese Router senden weiterhin die *Path-* bzw. *Resv-Refresh*-Nachrichten und übernehmen dadurch eine gewisse „Stellvertreter"-Funktion. Im folgenden werden

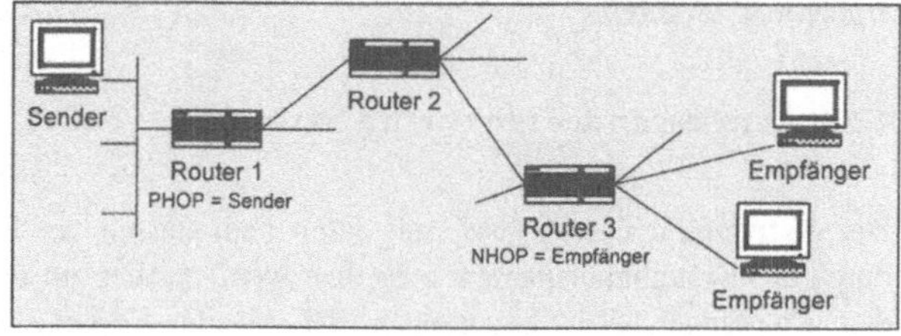

Abbildung 8: Konzept der Proxy-Router

diese direkt mit einem Endknoten verbundenen Router als *Proxy*-Router bezeichnet.

Bei jedem Ablauf der Lebenszeit *L* wird vor dem Löschen eines *Soft States* geprüft, ob eine Auffrischung durch einen Endknoten erwartet wurde. Das trifft zu

- für Resv States: wenn NHOP = Empfänger *(ReceiverAddr* aus RESV_CONFIRM)
- für Path States: wenn PHOP = Sender *(SrcAddr* aus SENDER_TEMPLATE)

Befindet sich die Reservierung zu diesem Zeitpunkt außerdem noch in der *Intermediate Phase*, d.h. ist die aktuelle Zeit kleiner der in den *States* enthaltenen Startzeit, so bleiben die *States* erhalten. Ein Löschen dieser *States* ist somit nur durch *Teardown*-Nachrichten möglich. Durch den soeben beschriebenen Lösungsansatz ist die Auffrischung der *Soft States* trotz zeitweiser Nichtverfügbarkeit der Endknoten in der *Intermediate Phase* gewährleistet. Auch ein zeitlich befristeter Ausfall eines auf der Übertragungsstrecke liegenden Routers wird toleriert. Da die *Soft States* der *Proxy*-Router nicht wie die anderen *Soft States* nach Ablauf ihrer Lebenszeit gelöscht werden, ist eine automatische Regenerierung der Reservierung bei Ausfall von Netzknoten gewährleistet.

Nach dem Wiedereinschalten werden Endsysteme durch die *Refresh*-Nachrichten des *Proxy*-Routers über neu hinzugekommene *Path*-Nachrichten anderer Sender oder inzwischen eingetretene Modifikationen an Reservierungen zu ihrem Datenstrom informiert.

Damit ein problemloses Wiedereintreten des Endsystems in den Reservierungsprozeß möglich ist, müssen die beim Beenden des RSVP-*Daemon* vorhandenen *Soft States* mit einer Endzeit größer der aktuellen Zeit gesichert werden. Das geschieht durch eine Sicherungsroutine, welche die *States* in einem festgelegten Format in eine Datei schreibt. Ist beim Start des RSVP-*Daemon* eine solche Datei vorhanden, so werden alle *Soft States* in den Speicher geladen, deren Endzeit größer als der Startzeitpunkt des *Daemons* ist. Dasselbe Vorgehen ist auch bei Routern denkbar, wenn diese zu Wartungszwecken außer Betrieb gesetzt werden müssen.

4.2.3 Multicasting

Ein wesentlicher Vorteil von RSVP gegenüber anderen Reservierungsprotokollen ist die konsequente *Multipoint-to-Multipoint* Ausrichtung (Mitzel 1994). Eine Voraussetzung dafür ist, daß durch das Senden der *Path*-Nachrichten an eine *Multicast*-Gruppe ein Pfadbaum für alle Mitglieder dieser Gruppe aufgebaut wird.

Die Mitgliedschaft in einer *Multicast*-Gruppe nach IGMP (Internet Group Management Protocol) ist jedoch dynamisch. Reagiert der Host nicht auf periodische Anfragen des Routers nach bestehenden Gruppenmitgliedschaften, so stoppt der Router das Bekanntgeben dieser Gruppenadresse an andere Router und erhält folglich keine an den Host adressierten Pakete mehr. Das bedeutet für RSVP, daß *Path*-Nachrichten nicht mehr in Richtung Empfänger weitergeleitet werden, wenn dieser vom Netz getrennt ist. Der durch die *Path States* gebildete Pfadbaum verfällt und alle Reservierungen zu diesem Datenstrom werden zerstört.

Das Bestimmen der Ausgangsports für *Path*-Nachrichten wurde daher dahingehend erweitert, daß diese nicht nur an die aktuellen Mitglieder einer *Multicast*-Gruppe gesendet werden, sondern auch an Empfänger, welche der Gruppe zu einem früheren Zeitpunkt angehörten.

RSVP befragt den Routingdaemon nach den *Outgoing Interfaces* für die in der *Path*-Nachricht angegebene Zieladresse des Datenstroms (Gruppe von Empfängern). Im Gegensatz zum herkömmlichen RSVP werden die *Path*-Nachrichten jetzt nicht nur an diesen Schnittstellen gesendet, sondern auch an allen in der Vergangenheit benutzten. Zu diesem Zweck wird eine Liste mit allen bisher ermittelten *Outgoing Interfaces* dieser Zielgruppe in den *Path States* eingeführt.

Die Wegewahl für die Pakete des Datenstromes zur Übertragungszeit basiert weiterhin nur auf den aktuellen Mitgliedern einer RSVP *Session*.

4.3 Realisierung

Die Grundlagen für die laufende Implementierung, die unter Verwendung der RSVP public domain Implementierung (ISI: Version 3.2) auf Digital Unix 3.2 basierten Alpha Workstation durchgeführt wird, sind in den folgenden Punkten zusammengefaßt:

- die erweiterten RSVP Message Processing Rules, die als Bestandteil einer Detailkonzeption in (Oeser 1996) beschrieben sind,
- die in 4.3.1 beschriebene Möglichkeit der Übertragung der neuen Parameter,
- die in 4.3.2 erwähnte umfangreiche Schnittstellenerweiterung als auch für eine weiterführende Impelementierung
- noch zu erarbeitende Detailkonzepte der vorhergehend diskutierten Lösungsansätze.

4.3.1 ReRA Objekt

Eine Integration der im Zusammenhang mit ReRA gefundenen neuen Parameter (4.1.2) wird durch die Einführung einer Objektklasse für die RSVP Nachrichten realisiert. Neben der Start- und Endzeit des Datenstromes (in *Path*-Nachricht) bzw. der Reservierung (*Resv*-Nachricht) enthält diese neue Klasse (Abbildung 9) Felder für Flags und Optionen. Das Feld Flags beinhaltet das Aktivierungsflag, welches in einer *Resv*-Nachricht den Beginn der Ressourcennutzung anzeigt. Der jeweilige Inhalt

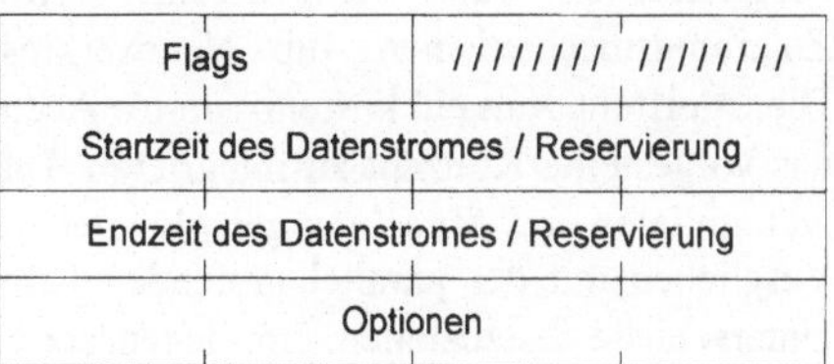

Abbildung 9: ReRA-Klasse

des Optionenfeldes (z.B. eine Verlängerungsoption) wird durch weitere entsprechend gesetzte Flags widergespiegelt.

Dieses neue ReRA Objekt muß in allen *Path-*, *Resv-*, *ResvConf-*, *Teardown-* und *Error-*Nachrichten enthalten sein, welche sich auf eine Vorabreservierung beziehen.

4.3.2 Schnittstellenerweiterung

Neben der Einführung eines neuen Objektes ist auch die Erweiterung der Schnittstellen von RSVP zur Anwendung und zur *Traffic Control* notwendig. Dabei wurde die in (Braden 1996) beschriebene Implementation als Grundlage benutzt. Um die Semantik der bereits vorhandenen Funktionen der RSVP API zu erhalten, wurden zwei neue Funktionen eingeführt. Mit der LEAVE Funktion meldet sich eine Anwendung vom RSVP-*Daemon* ab, ohne wie bei der RELEASE Funktion auch die RSVP Session zu beenden. Die neue TEARDOWN Funktion ermöglicht das Löschen einzelner Reservierungen bzw. eines durch die *Path-*Nachrichten errichteten Pfadbaumes. Die Funktionen der RSVP API bzw. der RSVP / *Traffic Control* wurden außerdem um die beschriebenen ReRA Parameter erweitert, um neben der *Immediate Reservation* auch eine *Reservation in Advance* unterstützen zu können. Zusätzlich müssen die die *Soft States* widerspiegelnden *State Blocks* (Path-, Rerservation- and Traffic Control State Blocks) um die neuen Parameter erweitert und die Nachrichtenbehandlungsregeln des RSVP-*Daemons* an die neue Funktionalität angepaßt werden. Da Ergänzungen jedoch sehr komplex sind, ist eine ausführliche Diskussion im Rahmen dieses Betrages nicht möglich.

5 Abschliessende Betrachtungen

Das Ziel dieser Arbeit bestand in der Konzeption und Implementierung einer funktionalen Erweiterung des Reservierungsprotokolls RSVP fuer eine „Resource Reservation in Advance". Ein allgemeines Modell wurde vorgestellt und ReRA Dienstprimitive eingeführt. Durch die Abbildung der Parameter und Dienstprimitive auf RSVP sowie die Entwicklung geeigneter Lösungen zu den aufgetretenen Problemen konnte ein implementierungsnahes Konzept zur Erweiterung von RSVP erarbeitet werden. Das Konzept toleriert dabei sowohl kurzzeitige Ausfälle der Zwischenknoten auf der Übertragungsstrecke als auch Toplogieänderungen. Ein neu eingeführtes Prinzip der *Proxy-Router* gestattet, daß Endsysteme nach der Aushandlung der Reservierung vom Netz getrennt werden können. Voraussetzung für das vorgeschlagene Konzept sind Zeitsynchronität aller beteiligten Netzknoten und die Verwendung eines lastunabhängigen Routingprotokolls.

Es wurde verdeutlicht, daß aufgrund des verwendeten Soft State Konzeptes in RSVP Probleme in der Intermediate Phase einer mittelfristigen Reservierung auftreten. Bestandteil dieser Arbeit war die Erarbeitung eines Lösungsvorschlages für dieses Problem, das jedoch aufgrund des Single Points of Failures der Proxy Router überdacht werden muß.

Möglichkeiten für weiterführende Arbeiten bestehen in der Untersuchung von Zuteilungsmechanismen für Netzwerkressourcen hinsichtlich der Abrechnung dieser Dienstleistung, um ein kostenbasiertes Accounting Management für ReRA einzuführen und in das vorgestellte Konzept zu integrieren. Damit wäre es möglich, die Anwendung von ReRA zu regulieren und Abrechnungen globaler Netzanbieter zu überprüfen.

Verglichen mit der parallel laufenden Umsetzung des allgemeinen Modells auf ATM sind Unterschiede festzustellen. Im Gegensatz zu RSVP, als ein Protokoll zur Aushandlung von Reservierungsinformationen in heterogenen Netzen, stellt ATM ein QoS-basiertes Netz dar, bei dem die Reservierung von Ressourcen und deren Signalisierung, aber auch die

Zugangskontrolle zum Netz eine Rolle spielt. Die Integration von ReRA in ATM wird im Rahmen unseres DFG-Forschungsprojektes an der TU-Dresden derart realisiert, daß zusätzlich zur Erweiterung der Signalisierung auch die Admission Control erweitert wird. Im Vergleich zur IP-Signalisierung ist die ATM-Signalisierung komplexer, da mit der Reservierung auch der Verbindungsaufbau verbunden ist.

Literatur

Alles, A. (1995) ATM Internetworking, Cisco Systems Inc.

ATM (1993) ATM UNI Specification Version 3.0, ATM-Forum: Specification, Prentice Hall

ATM1 (1995) ATM-Forum: Technical Committ; ATM Forum 94-1018R5: UNI Signaling 4.0, ATM Forum 95-0013R6: Traffic Managment Spec. Version 4.0, Work in Progress

Berger, L. (1996) RSVP Over ATM: Framework and UNI 3.0; Work in Progress

Borden, M.; Crawley, E.; KrawczykIssues, J. (1996) Issues for RSVP and Integrated Services over ATM; draft-crawley-rsvp-over-atm-00; Work in Progress

Braden, R.; Clark,D.; Shenker, Z. (1994) Integrated Services in the Internet Architecture: an Overview, RFC 1633

Braden, R.; Zhang, L. (1996) Resource ReSerVation Protocol (RSVP); Work in Progress

DCE: Distributed Computing Environment An Overview; Open Software Foundation

Degermark, M., Köhler, T., Pink, S., Schelén, O. (1995) Advance Reservation for Predictive Service, 5th International Workshop on Network and Operating System Support for Digital Audio and Video, Durham

Delgrossi, L., Herrtwich, R.G., Hoffmann, F. (1994) An Implementation of ST-II for the Heidelberg Transport System; Internetworking: Research and Experience, Vol. 5

Ferrari, D., Gupta A., Ventre, G. (1995) Distributed advance Reservation of real-time connections, 5th International Workshop on NOSSDAV, Durham

Hinden, R.; Deering, S. (1995) IP Version 6 Addressing Architecture,Work in Progress

LAN (1995) LAN Emulation over ATM Specification-Version 1, ATM Forum

Laubach, M. (1994) Classical IP and ARP over ATM; RFC 1577

Mitzel, D., Estrin, D., Shenker, S., Yhang, L. (1994) An Architectural Comparison of ST-II and RSVP, Proceedings of IEEE INFOCOM ´94

Narten, T.; Nordmark, E. (1995) Neighbor Discovery for IP Version 6 (IPv6)

Schill, A., Kühn, S., Breiter, F. (1996) Internetworking over ATM: Experiences with IP/IPng and RSVP, 7th Joint European Networking Conference, Budapest, Hungary, 1996

Schill, A., Kühn, S., Breiter, F. (1997) Resource Reservation in Advance in Heterogeneous Networks with Partial ATM Infrastructures, eingereicht zur Infocom 97, Kobe, Japan

Schulter, P. (1995) A Framework for IPv6 Over ATM; Work in Progress, DEC

Shenker, S., Partridge, C. (1995) Specification of Predictive Quality of Service, draft-ietf-intserv-predictive-svc-00, Work in Progress

Reinhardt, W. (1994) Advance Reservation of Network Resources for Multimedia Applications, Proceedings of the 2nd IWACA94, Heidelberg

Reinhardt, W. (1995) Advance Resource Reservation and its Impact on Reservation Protocols, Technical Report

Wolf, L.C., Delgrossi, L., Steinmetz, R., Schaller, S., Wittig, H. (1995) Issues of Reserving Resources in Advance, IBM European Network Center Heidelberg, Technical Report 43.9503

Hierarchische Strukturierung globaler Kommunikationsgruppen im Internet

Markus Hofmann
Institut für Telematik, Universität Karlsruhe
Zirkel 2, 76128 Karlsruhe, Deutschland
Tel.: +49 (0)721/608-3982, Fax: +49 (0)721/388097
E-Mail: m.hofmann@ieee.org

Kurzfassung: Moderne Anwendungen in verteilten Umgebungen erfordern in zunehmendem Maße vom zugrundeliegenden Kommunikationsdienst eine leistungsfähige Unterstützung für den Datenaustausch innerhalb einer Gruppe von Teilnehmern. Dabei stellt das Problem der Skalierbarkeit hinsichtlich der Anzahl der Kommunikationsteilnehmer eine große Herausforderung dar. Der vorliegende Artikel beschreibt ein Verfahren zur hierarchischen Strukturierung von Kommunikationsgruppen im Internet, wodurch ein effizienter Datenaustausch auch innerhalb sehr großer Empfängermengen ermöglicht wird.

1 Einleitung

Die Arbeit innerhalb von Projektteams nimmt in der internationalen Wirtschaft sowie in der weltweiten Forschung und Wissenschaft einen immer größer werdenden Stellenwert ein. Arbeitsgruppen, die über den gesamten Erdball hinweg verteilt sind, werden zur Bearbeitung eines gemeinsamen Projektzieles zusammengestellt. Ein schneller und zuverlässiger Informationsaustausch zwischen allen Beteiligten ist die Grundvoraussetzung für ein erfolgreiches Arbeiten im Team. Dabei müssen sowohl zeitliche als auch räumliche Grenzen überwunden werden. Neben der verteilten Teamarbeit rückt die globale, rechnergestützte Informationsverteilung immer mehr in den Mittelpunkt des Interesses. Sie ermöglicht eine extrem schnelle und kostengünstige Verteilung von Nachrichten jeglicher Art. So können beispielsweise komplette Zeitungen oder aktuelle Börseninformationen innerhalb kürzester Zeit allen Abonnenten über Rechnernetze weltweit zugestellt werden. Die Zahl der Empfänger kann dabei durchaus im Bereich von mehreren tausend oder gar mehreren hunderttausend liegen.

Bedingt durch die prinzipiell beliebig große Anzahl von Informationsempfängern treten bei der Gruppenkommunikation neuartige Probleme auf. Diese können mit den Mechanismen der klassischen Zwei-Parteien-Kommunikation nicht zufriedenstellend gelöst werden [13]. Vielmehr gilt es, neuartige Protokollarchitekturen zu entwerfen, die der erweiterten Kommunikationsform Rechnung tragen. Einer besonderen Bedeutung kommt hierbei der sogenannten *Multicast*-Kommunikation zu, bei der ein Sender die Daten an mehrere Empfänger übermittelt. Mit der Standardisierung und der allgemeinen Verfügbarkeit von Multicast im Internet (IP-Multicast) [7] wurde erstmals die Grundlage geschaffen, auch in Weitverkehrsnetzen einen effizienten Datenaustausch innerhalb von Anwendergruppen zu realisieren. Multicast-Routingprotokolle, wie das *Distance Vector Multicast Routing Protocol (DVMRP)* [8] oder das *Multicast Open Shortest Path First (MOSPF)* [17], reduzieren deutlich die globale Netzwerklast und vereinfachen die Nutzung von Multicast-Diensten durch Unterstützung von Gruppenadressen. Häufig genügt jedoch der von IP bereitgestellte, unzuverlässige Basisdienst nicht den Anforderungen der Anwender. So ist zur Verteilung bestimmter Nachrichten, wie beispielsweise Börseninformationen, ein absolut zuverlässiger Übertragungsdienst erforderlich. Auch Anwendungen zum verteilten Arbeiten, wie etwa das im Internet häufig eingesetzte *whiteboard (wb)* [14], erfordern eine fehlerfreie Übertragung der Daten an alle Teilnehmer. Aus diesem Grunde muß der von IP bereitgestellte, unzuverlässige Basisdienst um Mechanismen zur Fehlerbehebung und Fehlererkennung ergänzt werden. Ebenso sind in einigen Anwendungsfeldern Verfahren zur Fluß- oder Ratenkontrolle sinnvoll anwendbar. Diese erweiterte Funktionalität wird gemäß der Internet-Philosophie auf Ende-zu-Ende Ebene von Transportprotokollen erbracht [4]. Ein wesentliches Problem ist hierbei das in großen Gruppen erhebliche Aufkommen von Quittungen und Statusmeldungen im Falle einer zuverlässigen Multicast-Kommunikation und die Realisierung einer effizienten Fehlerkorrektur.

Der vorliegende Artikel beschreibt, basierend auf dem *Local Group Concept (LGC)* [10], mehrere Protokollmechanismen zur skalierbaren Fehler- und Verkehrskontrolle für Multicast-Kommunikation in heterogenen Netzen. Eine einführende Erläuterung der behandelten Problematik und ein Überblick über den derzeitigen Forschungsstand wird in Abschnitt 2 gegeben. Abschnitt 3 stellt aufbauend darauf die Grundprinzipien des Local Group Concept (LGC) vor. Diesem liegt eine hierarchische Strukturierung der globalen Kommunikationsgruppe zugrunde, welche in Abschnitt 4 näher betrachtet wird. Abschnitt 5 gibt schließlich eine kurze Bewertung des neu entwickelten Konzeptes, bevor in Abschnitt 6 mit einem Ausblick auf weitere Arbeiten abgeschlossen wird.

2 Verfahren zur Kontrolle von Multicast-Datenströmen

Mit der allgemeinen Verfügbarkeit und der zunehmenden Akzeptanz von Anwendungen im *Multicast Backbone (MBone)* [15] nimmt die Größe der Kommunikationsgruppen und deren räumliche Verteilung beständig zu. So kann beispielsweise die Anzahl der Empfänger einer Konferenzübertragung durchaus im Bereich mehrerer hundert oder tausend weltweit verteilter Rechnersysteme liegen. Auch die Anzahl der Abonnenten einer elektronischen Zeitung kann sich durchaus in diesem Bereich bewegen. In einem solchen Szenario ist die Realisierung eines zuverlässigen Multicast-Dienstes besonders problematisch. Ein (all-) zuverlässiger Multicast-Dienst garantiert die fehlerfreie Übertragung der Daten an alle Kommunikationsteilnehmer. Insbesondere kann hierbei der Ausfall einzelner Empfänger erkannt und dem Benutzer des Kommunikationsdienstes mitgeteilt werden. Hierzu muß die sendende Protokollinstanz stets über den Zustand jedes einzelnen Empfängers Kenntnis haben. Dies erfolgt durch das Senden von Statusanfragen mit anschließender Auswertung der erhaltenen Statusmeldungen. Ein solcher Austausch von Statusinformationen ist nicht nur zur Fehlerkontrolle, sondern auch zur Durchführung einer Fluß- oder Ratenkontrolle notwendig.

Bei einem rein *Sender-orientierten* Ansatz, wie er in den meisten traditionellen Kommunikationsprotokollen definiert ist, ergeben sich dadurch erhebliche Skalierungsprobleme. Die Überflutung mit Statusnachrichten, auch als *Implosionsproblem* bezeichnet, führt rasch zu einer Überlastung des Senders. Der erhöhte Bearbeitungsaufwand führt zu deutlichen Durchsatzeinbußen. Zudem steigt mit der Anzahl zu sendender Quittungen auch der Bedarf an zusätzlicher Bandbreite und an Pufferspeicher. Dies führt zu einer erheblichen Mehrbelastung des Netzwerkes, was insbesondere im Falle weltweit verteilter Empfängergruppen als kritisch anzusehen ist.

Zur Vermeidung des Implosionsproblems werden sogenannte *Empfänger-orientierte* Verfahren vorgeschlagen [18]. Hierbei sind die Empfänger selbst für die Erkennung und die Behebung von Fehlern verantwortlich. Dadurch besteht keine Notwendigkeit, dem Multicast-Sender in regelmäßigen Abständen den Status der einzelnen Empfänger mitzuteilen. Lediglich bei Auftreten eines Übertragungsfehlers fordern die Empfänger fehlende Daten durch eine negative Quittung direkt bei der sendenden Instanz an. Mit solchen Verfahren kann jedoch kein (all-) zuverlässiger Kommunikationsdienst erbracht werden, da der Sender beispielsweise den Ausfall eines Empfängers nicht erkennen kann. Darüber hinaus sind Statusmeldungen zur Durchführung einer Fluß- oder Ratenkontrolle auch bei einer Empfänger-orientierten Fehlerbehandlung notwendig, was wiederum zu einer Überflutung des Senders führt.

Neben dem Implosionsproblem stellt eine effiziente Fehlerkorrektur einen weiteren wichtigen Aspekt im Hinblick auf die Skalierbarkeit von Kommunikationsprotokollen dar. Gemäß herkömmlicher Protokolle fordern Empfänger fehlende Dateneinheiten stets direkt beim Multicast-Sender an. Dabei wird weder die aktuelle Netzlast noch die Struktur der Kommunikationsgruppe berücksichtigt. Im Falle der Gruppenkommunikation können Datenlücken im Empfangsstrom jedoch meist auch mit Hilfe benachbarter Empfänger geschlossen werden. So kann eine fehlende Dateneinheit von einem unmittelbar benachbarten Gruppenmitglied fehlerfrei empfangen worden sein. In diesem Fall sollte zur Behebung des Fehlers nicht der unter Umständen weit entfernte Sender zur Übertragungswiederholung aufgefordert werden. Vielmehr kann die Datenlücke durch einen lokalen Datenaustausch mit dem benachbarten Empfänger geschlossen werden. Im optimalen Fall wird eine fehlende Dateneinheit stets beim nächstgelegenen Gruppenmitglied angefordert. Jedoch ist ein solch optimales Verfahren mit einer nicht unerheblichen Steigerung der Protokollkomplexität verbunden. Aus diesem Grunde sind auch suboptimale Heuristiken zur Verbesserung der Skalierbarkeit in Betracht zu ziehen.

Entsprechend der jeweiligen Einsatzgebiete wurden bereits mehrere Multicast-Protokolle entwickelt [3]. Das *Multicast Transport Protocol (MTP)* [1] zielt vor allem auf die Realisierung einer ordnungserhaltenden Multipeer-Übertragung ab. Dabei werden die Daten mehrerer Sender bei allen Gruppenmitgliedern in derselben Reihenfolge ausgeliefert. Ein ausgezeichnetes Gruppenmitglied, der sogenannte *Master,* kontrolliert den Datenfluß durch die Vergabe spezieller Marken (sogenannter Token). Nur der Besitzer des Tokens darf an die Kommunikationsgruppe Daten übertragen. Somit ist sichergestellt, daß zu einem Zeitpunkt stets nur ein Sender aktiv ist. Dies ermöglicht eine global gültige Numerierung der Dateneinheiten. Die Fehlerbehebung beruht auf einer negativen Quittierungsstrategie, weshalb von MTP bei endlichem Sendepuffer kein (all-) zuverlässiger Dienst erbracht werden kann.

Das in [21] vorgestellte *Reliable Multicast Protocol (RMP)* erbringt einen zuverlässigen Multicast-Dienst. Es basiert auf einer Modifikation des Token-Passing-Protokolls [5] und kann zur Realisierung eines total geordneten Multipeer-Dienstes genutzt werden. Das Protokoll sieht vor, Übertragungswiederholungen über Unicast-Verbindungen durchzuführen.

Fehlende Daten werden ohne Berücksichtigung der aktuellen Netzlast und der Gruppenstruktur stets beim vorhergehenden Token-Halter angefordert. Falls eine bestimmte Dateneinheit jedoch von mehreren Empfängern zur Übertragungswiederholung angefordert wurde, kann dieses auch unter Nutzung der Multicast-Verbindung erneut übertragen werden. Bei der Entscheidungsfindung muß die entstehende Netzwerklast gegen die Anzahl redundanter Datenübertragungen bei der Multicast-Variante abgewägt werden.

Das *Xpress Transport Protocol (XTP)* [20] bietet dem Anwender sowohl einen unzuverlässigen als auch einen zuverlässigen Multicast-Dienst an. Die Protokolltechniken zur Unterstützung der Gruppenkommunikation leiten sich mit wenigen Modifikationen aus den Prozeduren für Unicast-Verbindungen ab. Die Fehlerkorrektur beruht auf der Durchführung von Übertragungswiederholungen, wobei fehlende Dateneinheiten stets beim Sender angefordert werden. In der Version 3.6 von XTP [6] wurde zur Vermeidung des Implosionsproblems der sogenannte Damping- und Slotting-Algorithmus definiert. Dabei werden die Quittungen von den Empfängern nach Erhalt einer Statusanfrage mit einer zufälligen Verzögerung gruppenweit gesendet ("Slotting"). Somit wird den restlichen Gruppenmitgliedern die Möglichkeit gegeben, redundante Quittungen zurückzuhalten ("Damping") und auf diese Weise das Netz und den Multicast-Sender zu entlasten. In globalen Netzen führt das gruppenweite Senden von Quittungen bei einer großen Empfängerzahl zu einer nicht unerheblichen Belastung des Netzes. Aus diesem Grunde wurden die beschriebenen Algorithmen nicht mehr in die Version 4.0 übernommen. Auch bei XTP werden alle Übertragungswiederholungen durch den Sender ausgeführt und an alle Empfänger adressiert. Wiederholt gesendete Dateneinheiten durchlaufen demnach den gesamten Verbindungsbaum zwischen Sender und Empfängern. Die neuesten Änderungen an der Protokollspezifikation [2] betreffen das Key-Management bei Multicast-Verbindungen. Sie erlauben eine schnellere und effizientere Zuordnung empfangener Dateneinheiten zu dem entsprechenden Kontext, verbessern jedoch nicht die Skalierbarkeit des Protokolls.

Eine erweiterte Form des Damping- und Slotting-Algorithmus von XTP 3.6 wird im *Scalable Reliable Multicast (SRM)* [9] zur Vermeidung der Senderimplosion eingesetzt. SRM ist weniger als ein eigenständiges Protokoll, sondern eher als eine Sammlung von Mechanismen und Algorithmen zum Erbringen eines halb-zuverlässigen Multicast-Dienstes anzusehen [3]. Die grundlegenden Konzepte von SRM wurden bereits in der MBone-Anwendung *whiteboard (wb)* [14] implementiert. Im Falle eines Übertragungsfehlers sendet ein Empfänger mit der Verzögerung T_1 eine negative Quittung (*Request-Paket*) an die gesamte Gruppe. Empfänger, die eine negative Quittung erhalten und über die angeforderten Daten verfügen, leiten nach einer Zeitspanne T_2 eine Übertragungswiederholung (*Repair-Paket*) an die gesamte Gruppe ein. Erkennt ein Empfänger vor Ablauf von T_2 die Übertragungswiederholung eines weiteren Gruppenmitgliedes, so stoppt er seinen eigenen Zeitgeber und unterdrückt die Durchführung einer redundanten Übertragungswiederholung. Die Zeitintervalle T_1 und T_2 werden basierend auf der Entfernung des Empfängers zu dem jeweiligen Erzeuger der Daten bestimmt. Während der Kommunikation werden die Zeitgeberwerte entsprechend der erkannten Request- und Repair-Pakete angepaßt. Eine zufällige Komponente in der Berechnung der Zeitintervalle soll das zeitgleiche Senden identischer Anforderungen vermeiden. Die Effizienz des Verfahrens hängt vor allem von einer optimalen Berechnung der Zeitgeberwerte ab, was in dynamischen Netzen mit ständig wechselnder Netzlast und Gruppenzusammensetzung keine triviale Aufgabe darstellt. Zur Realisierung eines zuverlässigen Übertragungsdienstes oder einer Flußkontrolle müssen die Empfänger weiterhin ihren aktuellen Status dem Sender mitteilen. In diesem Fall ergibt sich wiederum das Problem der Senderimplosion.

Weitere Protokollentwürfe verfolgen einen hierarchischen Ansatz, bei dem die globale Kommunikationsgruppe in einer geordneten Struktur organisiert wird. Beim *Log-Based Receiver-Reliable Multicast (LBRM)* [12] werden die Nachrichten der Empfänger an statisch festgelegte Server gesendet. Diese Server bearbeiten die Quittungen und führen notwendige Übertragungswiederholungen durch. Ein ähnlicher Ansatz wird auch im *Reliable Multicast Transport Protocol (RMTP)* [16] verfolgt. Allen Ansätzen ist gemeinsam, daß normale Empfänger nicht in die Fehlerkorrektur einbezogen werden. Ein Server fordert fehlende Dateneinheiten immer beim jeweils übergeordneten Server oder direkt beim Sender an. Dies ist auch dann der Fall, wenn ein unmittelbar benachbarter Empfänger die fehlende Dateneinheit bereits fehlerfrei erhalten hat. Das im folgenden Abschnitt überblickartig vorgestellte *Local Group Concept (LGC)* [10] löst sich von der starren Definition einer hierarchischen Ordnung und bezieht alle Gruppenmitglieder in die Fehlerbehandlung ein.

3 Das Local Group Concept (LGC)

Das Local Group Concept· (LGC) [10] bietet einen Multicast-Dienst, der in heterogenen Weitverkehrsnetzen auch bei sehr großen Empfängerzahlen eine effiziente Kommunikation erlaubt. Im Unterschied zu bekannten Multicast-Protokollen werden beim Local Group Concept Übertragungswiederholungen auch zwischen Empfängern durchgeführt. Dieser Ansatz ermöglicht eine zur Datenübertragung des Senders parallele Fehlererkennung und Fehlerbehandlung. Das Local Group Concept ist gemäß der Internet-Architektur [4] auf Ebene der Ende-zu-Ende Kommunikation angesiedelt. Es setzt lediglich einen unzuverlässige, multicastfähigen Netzwerkdienst voraus. Obwohl diese Anforderungen von IP-Multicast erfüllt werden und die derzeitige Realisierung von LGC auf IP aufsetzt, ist das beschriebene Konzept nicht auf die Internet-Protokollfamilie beschränkt. Vielmehr können die grundlegenden Mechanismen von LGC auch in eine erweiterte ATM-Adaptionsschicht (AAL) integriert werden.

3.1 Das Prinzip der hierarchischen Strukturierung

Die grundlegende Idee des Local Group Concept besteht in der Zusammenfassung nahe beieinander gelegener Kommunikationsteilnehmer zu lokalen (Unter-) Gruppen. Diese werden wiederum hierarchisch angeordnet. Jede lokale Gruppe schließt genau ein ausgezeichnetes Endsystem, den *lokalen Gruppenverwalter*, ein. Dieser wird nicht statisch festgelegt, sondern kann während der Lebenszeit der lokalen Gruppe dynamisch wechseln. Der Verwalter ist für die korrekte Übertragung der Daten an die Mitglieder der lokalen Gruppe verantwortlich und tritt gegenüber dem Multicast-Sender oder einem übergeordneten Gruppenverwalter als deren Repräsentant auf. Dem Verwalter ist die Identität aller Mitglieder der ihm zugeordneten lokalen Gruppe bekannt. Prinzipiell ist jedes Endsystem in der Lage, die Rolle eines Gruppenverwalters zu übernehmen. Somit ist der Aufbau und die Unterhaltung spezieller Kommunikationsknoten zur Verwaltung der Untergruppen nicht notwendig. Insbesondere müssen auch keine Änderungen an netzinternen Vermittlungssystemen vorgenommen werden. Die Gruppierung der Kommunikationsteilnehmer und die Wahl geeigneter Gruppenverwalter erfolgt dynamisch.

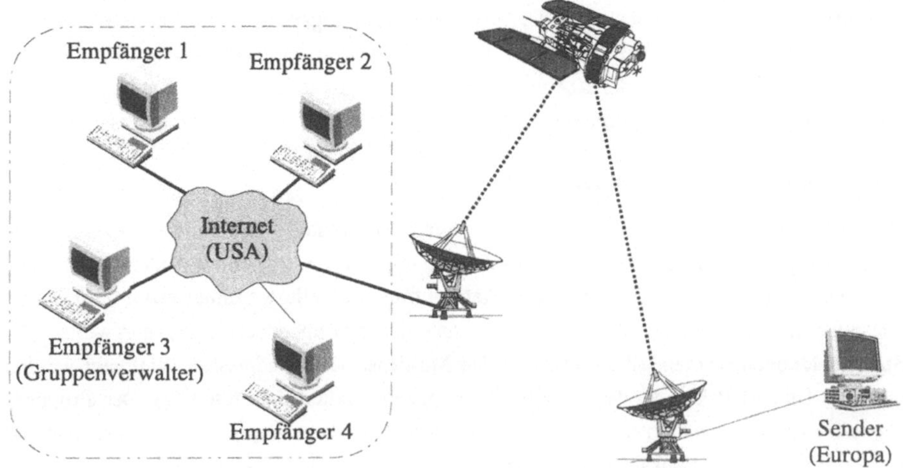

Abbildung 1: Beispiel zur Bildung lokaler Gruppen

Ein Beispiel für die Aufteilung einer globalen Kommunikationsgruppe in lokale Untergruppen ist in Abbildung 1 gegeben. In dem dargestellten Szenario sind mehrere Empfänger in den USA zu einer lokalen Gruppe zusammengefaßt. Die Empfänger müssen nicht an ein und dasselbe lokale Netz angeschlossen sein. Vielmehr können sie über ein Regional- oder ein Weitverkehrsnetz miteinander verbunden sein. Empfänger 3 agiert in dem dargestellten Beispiel zugleich als lokaler Gruppenverwalter. Treten innerhalb des amerikanischen Netzbereiches Paketverluste auf, so müssen die fehlenden Daten nicht notwendigerweise erneut über die teure Satellitenstrecke übertragen werden. Wurden die fehlenden Daten von mindestens einem der Empfänger korrekt erhalten, so können die Datenlücken durch lokale Übertragungswiederholungen innerhalb der USA geschlossen werden.

3.2 Etablierung lokaler Gruppen

Möchte ein Endsystem an der Gruppenkommunikation teilnehmen, so muß es sich zunächst einem geeigneten Gruppenverwalter und damit einer lokalen Gruppe zuordnen. Dazu bedient es sich der in Abschnitt 4 beschriebenen Dienste des *Group Distance Service (GDS)*. Wird keine geeignete lokale Gruppe gefunden, gründet das Endsystem eine neue lokale Gruppe und ernennt sich selbst zu deren Verwalter. Die Eignung einer lokalen Gruppe bzw. der Begriff der "Nähe" einer lokalen Gruppe wird bei LGC durch die Anwendung beeinflußt. Sie definiert die der Distanzbestimmung zugrundegelegte Metrik, wie z.B. die Übertragungsverzögerung zum Verwalter der lokalen Gruppe, den Durchsatz auf der Verbindung zum Verwalter, die geographische Distanz oder die Fehlerwahrscheinlichkeit des Verwalters. Auch die Kombination und unterschiedliche Gewichtung mehrerer Metriken wird von LGC unterstützt. Dadurch kann für jede Anwendungsklasse eine geeignete Entfernungsfunktion festgelegt werden. Beispielsweise wird sich bei gleicher Gruppenzusammensetzung die optimale

Gruppenhierarchie für eine interaktiven Anwendung von der optimalen Anordnung für einen Multicast-Dateitransfer unterscheiden. Im ersten Fall ist oberstes Ziel die Minimierung der Übertragungsverzögerung, wohingegen im zweiten Anwendungsszenario eher der Durchsatz oder die Leitungskosten im Vordergrund stehen. Entsprechend sollte beim Aufbau einer Gruppenhierarchie im ersten Fall die Übertragungsverzögerung zwischen den einzelnen Systemen und im zweiten Fall der Durchsatz oder die Kosten verwendet werden. Die Eignung unterschiedlicher Metriken, deren Abhängigkeiten vom zugrundeliegenden Routing-Protokoll und Möglichkeiten zur Erfassung unterschiedlicher Metriken werden derzeit untersucht.

3.3 Datentransfer und Fehlerbehebung

Der Datentransfer gestaltet sich wie in Abbildung 2 dargestellt. Der Sender übermittelt die Datenpakete unter Nutzung der Multicast-Verbindung an alle Gruppenmitglieder (1). In regelmäßigen Zeitabständen stellt der Sender Statusanfragen an alle Kommunikationsteilnehmer. Diese werden von allen Empfängern, mit Ausnahme der Gruppenverwalter, beantwortet. Die Statusmeldungen werden jedoch nicht an den Multicast-Sender adressiert. Vielmehr werden diese als Unicast-Pakete an den jeweiligen Gruppenverwalter übermittelt (2). Der Gruppenverwalter sammelt die eintreffenden Quittungen innerhalb einer vorgegebenen Zeitspanne und wertet diese unter Berücksichtigung seines eigenen Status aus. Dadurch erhält er Kenntnis über die korrekt empfangenen Datenpakete der einzelnen Mitglieder. Ihre Vereinigung ergibt die von der lokalen Gruppe korrekt empfangene Datenmenge. Schließlich quittiert der lokale Gruppenverwalter noch den Erhalt der Daten beim Multicast-Sender oder beim übergeordneten lokalen Gruppenverwalter (3).

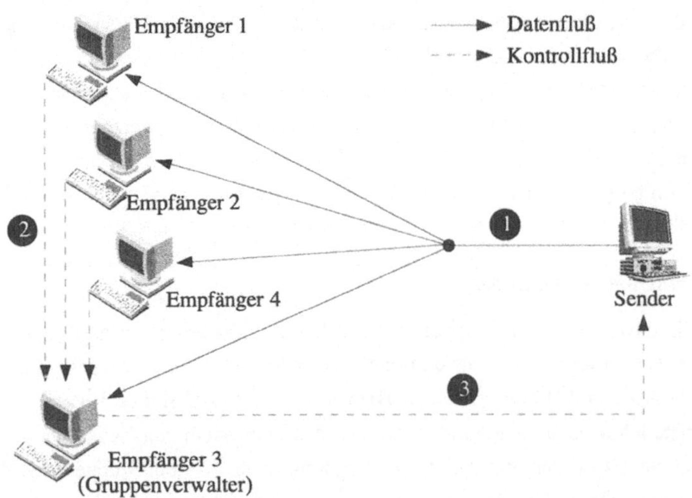

Abbildung 2 : Datenfluß

Hat ein Gruppenverwalter negativ quittierte Datenpakete fehlerfrei erhalten, so sendet er diese sofort nach Erhalt der ersten negativen Quittung per Multicast an die gesamte lokale Gruppe. Mit der Durchführung lokaler Übertragungswiederholungen wird nicht auf das Eintreffen der Kontrollnachrichten aller Mitglieder gewartet. Vielmehr werden bei Erhalt der ersten negativen Quittung alle angeforderten Übertragungswiederholungen sofort eingeleitet, was die durchschnittliche Übertragungsverzögerung verringert. Um redundante Übertragungswiederholungen desselben Datenpaketes zu vermeiden, müssen die bereits durchgeführten lokalen Übertragungswiederholungen mit später eintreffenden Quittungen abgeglichen werden. Dazu wird ein Mechanismus basierend auf *sync/echo*-Werten, wie in [11] beschrieben, eingesetzt.

Erhält ein Gruppenverwalter eine positive Quittung über ein von ihm selbst nicht korrekt empfangenes Datenpaket, so fordert er den Absender dieser Quittung zur Durchführung einer lokalen Übertragungswiederholung auf. Dieser übermittelt die angeforderten Dateneinheiten per Multicast an die gesamte lokale Gruppe. Somit werden ausschließlich diejenigen Datenpakete, die kein Mitglied der lokalen Gruppe korrekt empfangen hat, direkt beim Sender oder bei einem übergeordneten lokalen Gruppenverwalter angefordert.

Weitere Informationen zum Local Group Concept können [10] entnommen werden. Darüber hinaus sind aktuelle Informationen zum LGC-Projekt im World Wide Web unter "http://www.telematik.informatik.uni-karlsruhe.de/~hofmann/LocalGroups.html" verfügbar.

4 GDS - Ein Dienst zum Aufbau von Gruppenhierarchien

Die Leistungsfähigkeit von Konzepten, die wie LGC eine hierarchische Strukturierung der globalen Kommunikationsgruppe vornehmen, hängt maßgeblich von der angelegten Gruppenhierarchie ab. Entscheidend ist hierbei sowohl die Aufteilung der Gesamtgruppe in mehrere Untergruppen und Hierarchiestufen als auch die Plazierung der Verwaltungseinheiten (d.h. der lokalen Gruppenverwalter). Dabei sind zunächst folgende Fragen zu klären:

- In welche Typen von Kommunikationsknoten sollen die Verwaltungseinheiten integriert werden? Dies können zum einen reguläre Endsysteme, Vermittlungssysteme oder spezielle Kommunikationsknoten sein.

- In welche Instanz eines Kommunikationssystems sollen die Verwaltungseinheiten plaziert werden? Hierbei ist zu klären, in welches der real vorhandenen Kommunikationssysteme der Verwalter zu plazieren ist. Dabei ist auch zu klären, ob eine solche Auswahl statisch vorgenommen wird oder ob sie zur Laufzeit dynamisch an die Netzlast und die Gruppenzusammensetzung angepaßt werden kann.

Die Integration der Verwalterfunktionalität in Vermittlungssysteme bringt sowohl Vorteile als auch Nachteile mit sich. Zum einen ermöglicht dieses Verfahren das Zwischenspeichern von Dateneinheiten entlang des Multicast-Routingbaumes. Lokale Gruppenverwalter, die in Vermittlungssystemen plaziert sind, befinden sich stets auf dem Pfad zwischen Sender und Empfängern. Dadurch puffern die lokalen Gruppenverwalter alle Dateneinheiten, die von den restlichen Mitgliedern der lokalen Gruppe korrekt empfangen werden. Eine lokale Übertragungswiederholung in Richtung von den Empfängern hin zum Gruppenverwalter ist demnach nicht mehr notwendig.

Andererseits skaliert dieser Ansatz nur sehr schlecht hinsichtlich der Anzahl unterschiedlicher Multicast-Verbindungen. Für jede Multicast-Assoziation muß in den Vermittlungssystemen ausreichend Pufferspeicher und Verarbeitungskapazität vorhanden sein. Durch die Verwaltung zahlreicher lokaler Gruppen unterschiedlicher Multicast-Verbindungen und die damit verbundene Bearbeitung von Quittungen bzw. der Durchführung lokaler Übertragungswiederholungen wird ein Vermittlungssystem schnell zum Engpaß bei der Datenübertragung. Vorzugsweise sollte die Last der Gruppenverwaltung und das Puffern von Dateneinheiten für unterschiedliche Multicast-Assoziationen auf mehrere Kommunikationssysteme verteilt werden.

Die Einführung spezieller Kommunikationssysteme zur Übernahme der Verwalter-Funktionalität erfordert zusätzlichen Aufwand zur Installation und Wartung dieser Systeme. Zudem ist diese Lösung äußerst statisch und verhindert eine Anpassung der Gruppenstruktur an die aktuelle Netzlast oder Gruppenzusammensetzung. Auch die Skalierbarkeit hinsichtlich der Anzahl unterschiedlicher Multicast-Verbindungen stellt, wie bei der Integration in Vermittlungssysteme, bei diesem Ansatz ein Problem dar.

Aus den genannten Gründen wurde das Local Group Concept flexibel gestaltet. Es erlaubt die Integration lokaler Gruppenverwalter in beliebige Kommunikationssysteme. Prinzipiell ist jedes Endsystem in der Lage, diese Funktion wahrzunehmen. Dadurch kann die Last der Gruppenverwaltung für unterschiedliche Multicast-Assoziationen auf mehrere Kommunikationssysteme verteilt werden. Durch die Installation entsprechender Protokoll-Software können lokale Gruppenverwalter bei Bedarf auch in Vermittlungssysteme integriert werden.

Die Auswahl geeigneter Kommunikationssysteme zur Übernahme der Gruppenverwalter-Funktionalität und deren Konfiguration kann zunächst manuell durch einen Systemverwalter erfolgen. Dies bringt jedoch zusätzlichen Verwaltungsaufwand mit sich und erfordert bei Ausfall eines lokalen Gruppenverwalters den Eingriff eines Operators. Gemäß der Internet-Philosophie sollte das Verfahren zum Aufbau der lokalen Gruppenhierarchie jedoch selbstorganisierend und fehlertolerant ausgelegt sein [4]. Zu diesem Zweck wurde der *Group Distance Service (GDS)* entworfen. Er unterstützt den Dienstbenutzer beim Aufbau einer lokalen Gruppenhierarchie und reorganisiert die Struktur automatisch bei Ausfall eines lokalen Gruppenverwalters.

4.1 Die Architektur einer GDS-Instanz

Jeder Teilnehmer an einer Multicast-Kommunikation muß sich gemäß dem Local Group Concept zunächst einer geeigneten lokalen Gruppen zuordnen. Der Group Distance Service, ein verteilter Mehrwertdienst, unterstützt den Kommunikationsteilnehmer hierbei. Er erfaßt zunächst existierende lokale Gruppen und bestimmt deren Entfernung vom Teilnehmer gemäß der vorgegebenen Gewichtung. Dazu sendet die lokale GDS-Instanz eines beitrittswilligen Empfängers einen `Search-Request` an die Adresse der globalen Multicast-Gruppe. Der `Search-Request` wird von den GDS-Instanzen aller aktiver Gruppenverwalter einer Multicast-Assoziation durch ein `Search-Answer` beantwortet. Die Antworten identifizieren die vorhandenen lokalen Gruppen und werden zur Distanzberechnung herangezogen. Der GDS übergibt dem Dienstnutzer schließlich eine nach Entfernung geordnete Liste der existierenden Gruppenverwalter einschließlich der gewichteten Distanz.

Der GDS ist als Komponente des Protokollautomaten in jedem Kommunikationssystem vorhanden. Er umfaßt sowohl eine passive als auch eine aktive Komponente. Das passive Element unterstützt entfernte GDS-Instanzen, indem es deren Anfragen (`Search-Request`) beantwortet und ihnen die benötigten Informationen zur Distanzberechnung

(Search-Answer) zukommen läßt. Die Architektur der aktiven GDS-Komponente ist in Abbildung 3 skizziert.

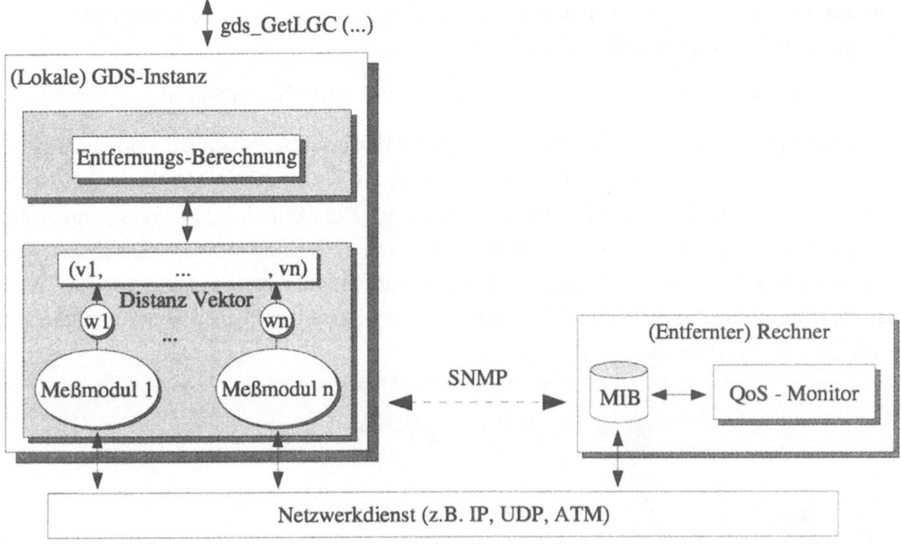

Abbildung 3: Architektur der aktiven GDS-Komponente

Die aktive GDS-Komponente besteht aus mehreren Meßmodulen. Jedes dieser Meßmodule bestimmt die Entfernung zu bereits existierenden lokalen Gruppen gemäß einer bestimmten Metrik. So ist beispielsweise ein Meßmodul realisierbar, welches die Anzahl der Zwischensysteme auf dem Weg zum Verwalter einer lokalen Gruppe durch einen Expanded Ring Search vornimmt. Ein weiteres Meßmodul kann durch Messung der Paketumlaufzeit die Übertragungsverzögerung abschätzen. Der modulare Aufbau der aktiven Komponente ermöglicht die einfache Hinzunahme weiterer Meßmodule, sobald zusätzliche Metriken im Netzwerk erfaßbar sind. So kann zu einem späteren Zeitpunkt beispielsweise ein Modul hinzugefügt werden, das mittels SNMP-Abfrage eines Service-Switches die finanziellen Kosten für die Nutzung einer Übertragungsstrecke ermittelt. Wie in Abbildung 3 dargestellt, wird für den Zugriff auf die Management Information Base (MIB) eines entfernten QoS-Monitors ein eigenes Meßmodul realisiert werden. Der QoS-Monitor des Kommunikationssystems speichert in einer solchen MIB alle QoS-relevanten Daten ab [19]. Diese sind über SNMP von außen zugänglich. Auf diese Weise kann das Meßmodul einer entfernten GDS-Instanz beispielsweise die aktuelle Fehlerrate eines lokalen Gruppenverwalters ermitteln und diese als weiteres Auswahlkriterium in die Entscheidungsfindung einbeziehen.

4.2 Gewichtung unterschiedlicher Metriken

Die von den Meßmodulen ermittelten Entfernungen $d(i)$ werden mit einem Metrik-spezifischen Gewicht $w(i)$ multipliziert. Diese Gewichtung wird vom Benutzer gemäß seiner Anforderungen festgelegt. Ist ein Anwender beispielsweise an der Minimierung der Übertragungsverzögerung interessiert, so wird er diese Metrik gegenüber den restlichen Metriken relativ hoch gewichten. Um lediglich eine einzelne Metrik $m(i)$ bei der Auswahl einer geeigneten lokalen Gruppe zu berücksichtigen, wird allen Gewichten $w(j)$ mit $i \neq j$ der Wert "0" zugeteilt. Die gewichteten Entfernungen definieren einen Distanzvektor $v = [v(1), ..., v(n)]$, wobei $v(i) = d(i) * w(i)$ und n die Anzahl der unterstützten Metriken ist. Die aktive GDS-Instanz berechnet für jede vorhandene lokale Gruppe einen solchen Distanzvektor. Diese Vorgehensweise entspricht einer Abbildung

$$\ell: \ell(S) = v = [v(1), ..., v(n)] \quad \forall\, S \in \{\text{Menge der realen Kommunikationssysteme}\}$$

des realen Netzwerkes auf einen n-dimensionalen Vektorraum. Prinzipiell sind auch anders definierte Abbildungen denkbar. In Abbildung 4 ist mit ℓ eine Abbildung des realen Netzes auf einen 3-dimensionalen Vektorraum dargestellt. Die Achsen des Vektorraumes entsprechen den im Beispiel berücksichtigten Metriken "Paketumlaufzeit", "Durchsatz" und "Anzahl Zwischensysteme". Der neu hinzukommende Empfänger, welcher die Distanzwerte ermittelt und somit die Abbildung vornimmt, ist in der Abbildung 4 als Anker bezeichnet und wird auf den Ursprung abgebildet.

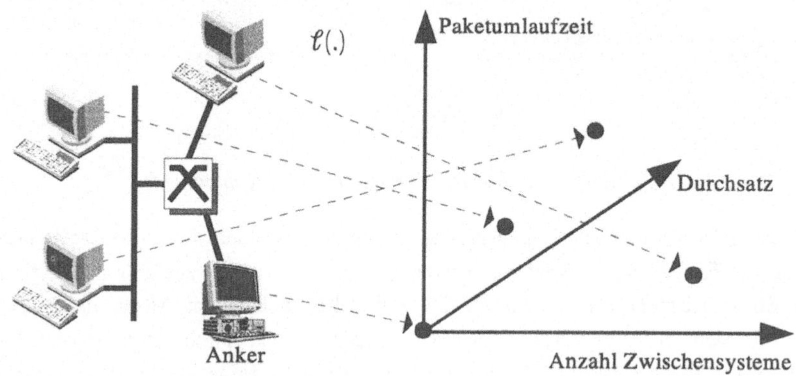

Abbildung 4: Abbildung eines realen Netzes auf einen Vektorraum

Zur Auswahl eines geeigneten Gruppenverwalters berechnet die GDS-Instanz den euklidischen Abstand[1] $d(0,v(i))$ aller Distanzvektoren vom Ursprung. Die Distanzvektoren werden daraufhin gemäß der folgenden Ordnungsrelation '$\leq$' geordnet:

$$v \leq w \quad \Leftrightarrow \quad d(0,v) \leq d(0,w) \quad \forall\, v, w \in \{\text{Menge der Distanzvektoren}\}$$

Ist die Abbildung ℓ injektiv, liefert die Umkehrabbildung ℓ^{-1} angewendet auf den ersten Distanzvektor der geordneten Vektorenliste den nächstgelegenen Gruppenverwalter. Ist die Abbildung ℓ nicht injektiv, können mehrere Kommunikationssysteme den gleichen Distanzvektor besitzen. In diesem Fall kann aus der Menge der Gruppenverwalter, deren Distanzvektor an erster Stelle der geordneten Liste steht, ein beliebiger ausgewählt werden.

Ein Beispiel zur Abhängigkeit zwischen Metrik-Gewichtung und der Auswahl eines geeigneten Gruppenverwalters ist in Abbildung 5 gegeben.

Die Entfernung von Gruppenverwalter A beträgt gemäß der Metrik $m(1)$ den Wert 1 und gemäß der Metrik $m(2)$ den Wert 2. Die Entfernung des Gruppenverwalters B beträgt (2,1).

---

1 Hier können auch Metriken unterschiedlich vom euklidischen Abstand gewählt werden.

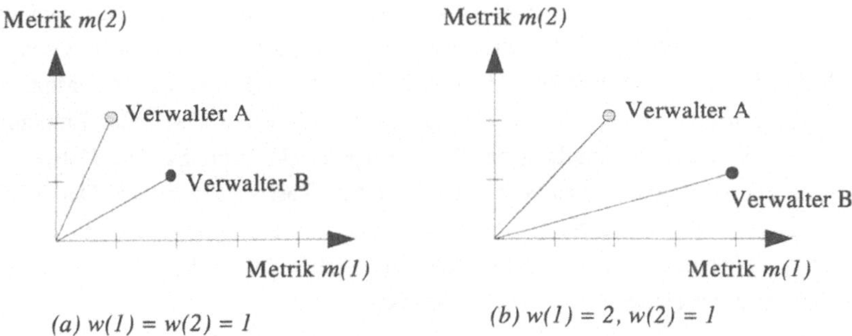

Abbildung 5: Einfluß der Gewichtung auf die Distanzvektoren

Ordnet der Dienstnutzer beiden Metriken die gleiche Gewichtung $w(1) = w(2) = 1$ zu, so beträgt der euklidische Abstand beider Distanzvektoren den Wert sqrt(5) (siehe Abbildung 5 (a)). Somit könnten beide Gruppenverwalter vom GDS als Ergebnis zurückgegeben werden. Bevorzugt der Dienstnutzer eine Minimierung der Metrik $m(1)$, so kann er beispielsweise die Gewichtung $w(1) = 2$ und $w(2) = 1$ vorgeben. Wie in Abbildung 5 (b) dargestellt, resultiert dies in einem kleineren euklidischen Abstand für den Distanzvektor des Gruppenverwalters A. Der GDS wird als Ergebnis demnach die Identität des lokalen Gruppenverwalters A zurückgeben. Gemäß der Anforderung des Dienstbenutzers ist dies der Gruppenverwalter mit dem kleineren Abstand gemäß Metrik $m(1)$.

Der Anwender hat die Möglichkeit, beim Aufruf des GDS zu jeder der unterstützen Metriken $m(i)$ eine maximal akzeptable Entfernung $Th(i)$ anzugeben. Ist die ungewichtete Entfernung $d(i)$ eines Gruppenverwalters gemäß der Metrik $m(i)$ größer als der vorgegebene Maximalwert $Th(i)$, so wird dieser Gruppenverwalter nicht in die Ergebnisliste aufgenommen. Gibt der Anwender als obere Schranke für die Metrik "Anzahl Zwischensysteme" beispielsweise den Wert "2" an, so werden vom GDS alle Gruppenverwalter ignoriert, die mehr als zwei Zwischensysteme entfernt sind. Wird vom GDS kein Gruppenverwalter gefunden, der den Anforderungen des Benutzers genügt, so etabliert der hinzukommende Empfänger eine neue lokale Gruppe und ernennt sich zu deren Verwalter. Dabei ist zu beachten, daß der Sender während des Suchvorganges per Definition wie ein lokaler Gruppenverwalter behandelt wird.

Der Group Distance Service (GDS) wird derzeit aufbauend auf UDP und IP implementiert. In einer ersten Version werden Meßmodule zur Erfassung der Paketumlaufzeit und der Anzahl von Zwischensystemen realisiert. Ein weiteres Modul zur SNMP-basierten Abfrage entfernter QoS-Monitore befindet sich momentan in der Entwurfsphase.

5 Simulationsergebnisse

Um eine Leistungsbewertung des Local Group Concept vorzunehmen, müssen die entworfenen Protokollmechanismen im Rahmen einer Multicast-Kommunikation mit mehreren hundert oder tausend von Empfängern eingesetzt werden. Da über eine solch große Anzahl von Testpartnern in der Praxis meist nicht verfügt werden kann, kommt der Simulation des Protokolls eine entscheidende Rolle zu.

Zur Bewertung der Leistungsfähigkeit von LGC wurden mehrere Simulationen mit dem Netzwerksimulator BONeS (Block Oriented Network Simulator) von »The Alta Group of Cadence Design Systems« durchgeführt. Als Vergleich diente ein Sender-basiertes Multicast-Protokoll, wie es derzeit in der Praxis eingesetzt wird. Dabei quittiert jeder Empfänger explizit die von ihm korrekt empfangene Datenmenge direkt beim Sender. Notwendige Übertragungswiederholungen werden vom Sender per Multicast vorgenommen. Der Einfluß der Empfängerzahl auf die durchschnittliche Übertragungsverzögerung und die globale Netzlast ist in [10] dargestellt. Es zeigen sich deutliche Vorteile für das Local Group Concept gegenüber rein sender-basierten Multicast-Protokollen.

Um den Einfluß der aufgebauten Gruppenstruktur auf das Verhalten eines LGC-basierten Protokolls zu untersuchen, wurde das in Abbildung 6 skizzierte reale MBone-Szenario modelliert und mit den in [22] gemessenen Werten parametrisiert.

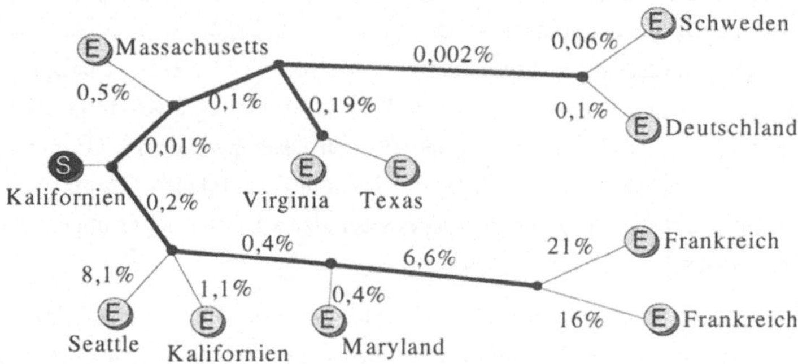

Abbildung 6: MBone-Szenario (Abbildung entnommen aus [22])

In Abbildung 6 sind zu den Übertragungsabschnitten jeweils die gemessenen Paketverlustraten aus [22] eingetragen. Auffallend sind hierbei die relativ geringen Paketverlustraten im Backbone-Bereich, welcher in der Abbildung durch fette Linien gekennzeichnet ist. Im Simulationsmodell generiert der Sender Dateneinheiten mit einer konstanten Rate von 2 Mbps. Das Auftreten von Übertragungsfehlern wird durch einen Markov'schen Prozeß modelliert, dem als Parameter die Paketverlustrate und die Burstlänge übergeben wird. Die Burstlänge beschreibt hierbei die durchschnittliche Länge von Bündelfehlern und wurde auf 5 Dateneinheiten festgelegt. Weitere Simulationsparameter betreffen die Verzögerung durch das Bearbeiten einer Dateneinheit und die Statusanforderungsrate. Die Bearbeitungsverzögerung wurde auf 100 µs festgesetzt. Eine Statusanfrage wird vom Sender alle 100 Dateneinheiten gestellt. Um die Gesamtzahl der Empfänger zu erhöhen, wurden im Modell anstelle eines realen Empfängers jeweils 20 Empfänger eingesetzt. Die Empfängermenge wurde schließlich in unterschiedliche Gruppenhierarchien eingeteilt, die sich sowohl in ihrer Tiefe als auch in der Größe ihrer Untergruppen und deren Anordnung unterscheiden. Zur Strukturierung der Empfängermenge wurde dabei ausschließlich die Metrik "Anzahl Zwischensysteme" herangezogen. Abbildung 7 stellt zu verschieden Gruppenstrukturen die jeweils resultierende durchschnittliche Übertragungsrate dar, wobei der Sender als weißer Punkt und die lokalen Gruppen jeweils als schwarze Punkte gekennzeichnet sind. Auf die Darstellung der exakten Gruppeneinteilung kann aus Platzgründen nicht eingegangen werden.

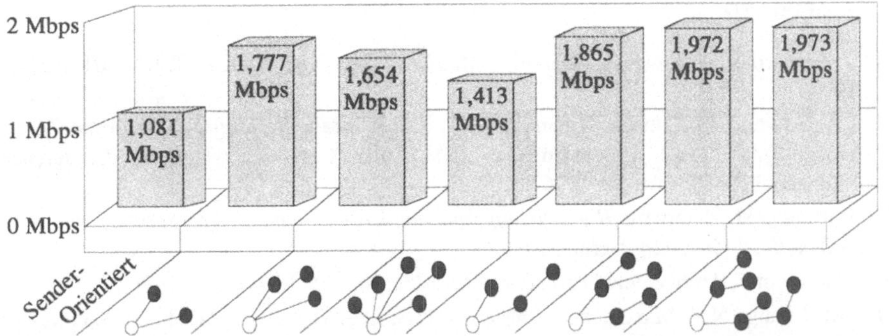

Abbildung 7: Durchschnittliche Übertragungsrate in Abhängigkeit von der Gruppenstruktur

Auffallend sind zunächst die verbesserten Durchsatzwerte bei Anwendung des Local Group Concept. Diese begründen sich vor allem in der Entlastung des Senders durch eine parallele Quittungsbearbeitung und der Durchführung lokaler Übertragungswiederholungen. Mit zunehmender Anzahl der lokalen Gruppen verringert sich in einer flachen Hierarchie jedoch der Durchsatz, da hierbei auch der Verwaltungsaufwand beim Sender zunimmt. Abhilfe schafft die Etablierung weiterer Hierarchieebenen, wodurch auch bei einer größeren Anzahl lokaler Gruppen die Last der Quittungsbearbeitung und der Durchführung von Übertragungs-wiederholungen gleichmäßig verteilt werden kann. Insgesamt bleibt jedoch festzuhalten, daß die optimale Gruppenstruktur maßgeblich von der Topologie und den Merkmalen des zugrun-deliegenden Netzwerkes abhängt. Ebenso beeinflußt die Zusammensetzung der Empfänger-menge das Kommunikationsverhalten, was insbesondere bei Unterstützung dynamischer Gruppen zu berücksichtigen ist. Die Ermittlung und der Aufbau einer geeigneten Gruppen-hierarchie sollte demnach dynamisch unter Berücksichtigung der Gegebenheiten zur Laufzeit erfolgen.

6 Ausblick

Neben einer Vertiefung der simulativen Bewertung werden derzeit sowohl der Group Distance Service als auch das Local Group Concept implementiert. Dazu wurde das Local Group Concept auf die Mechanismen von XTP abgebildet und in eine vorhandene Implemen-tierung des Xpress Transport Protokoll eingearbeitet. Zusätzlich wird derzeit ein eigenständi-ges Protokoll entworfen und implementiert, welches im Hinblick auf die in LGC definierten Mechanismen optimiert ist. Eine komfortablen Testumgebung zur Vermessung von Multicast-Protokollen im Internet schafft die Voraussetzung für eine spätere Bewertung von LGC im realen Betrieb.

Danksagung

Dank gebührt vor allem den studentischen Mitgliedern der LGC-Arbeitsgruppe. Des weiteren gilt der Dank Herrn Prof. Dr. Dr. h.c. Gerhard Krüger, der zeitlich und organisatorisch die Arbeiten an diesem Forschungsprojekt ermöglicht hat. Ebenso sei Herrn Prof. J.W. Atwood von der Concordia University in Montreal und der Forschungsgruppe um Frau Prof. Dr. Martina Zitterbart an der TU Braunschweig gedankt, die durch kritische Anmerkungen zur Verbesserung der Konzeptentwürfe beigetragen haben.

7 Referenzen

[1] S. Armstrong, A. Freier, K. Marzullo: *Multicast Transport Protocol*. RFC 1301, Februar 1992.

[2] J.W. Atwood, O. Catrina, J. Fenton, W.T. Strayer: *Reliable Multicasting in the Xpress Transport Protocol*. Proceedings of 21st Local Computer Networks Conference, Minneapolis, MN, Oktober 1996.

[3] T. Braun. M. Zitterbart: *Hochleistungskommunikation, Band 2: Transportdienste und - protokolle*. Oldenbourg Verlag, 1996.

[4] B. Carpenter: *Architectural Principles of the Internet*. RFC 1958, Juni 1996.

[5] J.M. Chang, N.F. Maxemchuck: *Reliable Broadcast Protocols*. ACM Transactions on Computer Systems, 2 (3), August 1994.

[6] G. Chesson, ed.: *Xpress Transfer Protocol Specification, Revision 3.6*. Protocol Engines, Inc., erhältlich vom XTP Forum, Santa Barbara, 1993.

[7] S. Deering, D. Cheriton: *Multicast Routing in Datagram Internetworks and Extended LANs*. ACM Transactions on Computer Systems, 8(2):85-110, Mai 1990.

[8] S. Deering, C. Partridge, D. Waitzman: *Distance Vector Multicast Routing Protocol*. RFC-1075, November 1988.

[9] S. Floyd, V. Jacobson, S. McCanne, C. Liu, L. Zhang: *A Reliable Multicast Framework for Light-weight Sessions and Application Level Framing*. Computer Communication Review, Vol. 25, No. 4, Tagungsband, ACM SIGCOMM'95, August 1995.

[10] M. Hofmann: *A Generic Concept for Large-Scale Multicast*. In: B. Plattner (Hrsg.), Broadband Communiations, Proceedings of International Zurich Seminar on Digital Communications (IZS'96), LNCS No. 1044, Springer Verlag, Februar 1996.

[11] M. Hofmann: *Design und Implementierung von Multicast-Erweiterungen in XTP-Lite*. Arbeitsbericht zum Berkom-II Projekt, Teilbereich MMT, DeTeBerkom GmbH, 1995.

[12] H. Holbrook, S. Singhal, D. Cheriton: *Log-Based Receiver-Reliable Multicast for Distributed Interactive Simulation*. Computer Communication Review, Vol. 25, No. 4, Tagungsband, ACM SIGCOMM'95, August 1995.

[13] C. Huitema: *Routing in the Internet*. Prentice Hall, New Jersey, 1995.

[14] V. Jacobson: *A portable, public domain network whiteboard*. Xerox Parc, viewgraphs, April 1992.

[15] V. Kumar: MBone*: Interactive Multimedia on the Internet*. New Riders Publishing, Indianapolis, USA 1995.

[16] J.C. Lin, S. Paul: *RMTP: A Reliable Multicast Transport Protocol*. Proceedings of IEEE INFOCOM'96, 1996.

[17] J. Moy: *Multicast Extensions to OSPF*. RFC-1584, März 1994.

[18] S. Pingali, D. Towsley, J.F. Kurose: *A Comparison of Sender-Initiated and Receiver-Initiated Reliable Multicast Protocols,* Proceedings of ACM SIGMETRICS, 1994.

[19] C. Schmidt, R. Bless: *QoS Monitoring in High Performance Environments*. 4th International IFIP Workshop on Quality of Service, Paris, Frankreich, März 1996.

[20] W.T. Strayer, ed.: *Xpress Transport Protocol Specification, Revision 4.0*. Erhältlich vom XTP Forum, Santa Barbara, USA, März 1995.

[21] B. Whetten. T. Montgomery, S. Kaplan: *A High Performance Totally Ordered Multicast Protocol*. Theory and Practice in Distributed Systems, LCNS 938, Springer Verlag, 1995.

[22] M. Yajnik. J. Kurose, D. Towsley: *Packet Loss Correlation in the MBone Multicast Network*. UMASS CMPSCI Technical Report # 96-32, University of Massachusetts at Amherst, 1995.

Session 8:
Mobilkommunikation

Temporäre Einbindung mobiler Clienten
und Optimierung der Dienstauswahl in einem verteilten System

Rudolf, Steffen / Richter, Klaus / Irmscher, Klaus
TU Bergakademie Freiberg, Institut für Informatik
Bernhard-von-Cotta-Straße 1, D-09596 Freiberg
E-Mail: [rudolflrichterlirmscher]@informatik.tu-freiberg.de

Zusammenfassung

Ausgehend von der Integration mobiler Clienten in die Client-Server-Kooperation heterogener verteilter Systeme wird ein Szenarium untersucht, mit dem eine von der Mobilregion losgelöste Arbeitsweise des Festnetzes in bestimmten Verarbeitungsphasen möglich wird. Der Architekturentwurf des verteilten Systems enthält neben der dynamischen Dienstverwaltung einen neuen Traderservice zur optimalen Dienstauswahl im Festnetz. Eine zur Datenvermittlung und zur Unterbrechungsbehandlung eingeführte zusätzliche Mediatorinstanz ermöglicht im Zusammenwirken mit der Typ- und Schnittstellenverwaltung des Traders die Bearbeitung unterschiedlich strukturierter Verarbeitungsflüsse. Eine prototypische Implementation der Architektur belegt die Realisierbarkeit des Vorhabens und dient als Basis für Systemmessungen.

1   Einleitung

Kennzeichnend für die moderne Informationsgesellschaft ist neben dem gestiegenen Informationsbedarf vor allem die Forderung nach einem sicheren Zugriff auf Informationen an jedem Ort, zu jeder Zeit und unter Nutzung unterschiedlicher Übertragungsmedien. Die Umsetzung der Mobilität innerhalb der Informationsbereitstellung führt zu neuen Anfordrungen an die Rechentechnik und Kommunikationssoftware (s.[1], [10]). Besonderheiten der Mobilkommunikation folgen aus den erhöhten Übertragungskosten (z.B. GSM), der schwankenden bzw. eingeschränkten Dienstgüte der Übertragung (QoS), Störungen sowie der zeitweilig fehlenden Erreichbarkeit mobiler Netzkomponenten.

Gegenstand der Arbeit ist die Architektur eines verteilten Systems, die das sichere Einbinden mobiler Clienten, eine dynamische Dienstverwaltung, die gezielte Auswahl konkurrierender Dienste im Festnetz und die problembezogene Realisierung unterschiedlich stukturierter Arbeitsabläufe zum Ziel hat. Zu diesem Zweck werden zwei zusätzliche Instanzen ins Festnetz integriert. Durch einem Trader werden die Schnittstellen, Diensttypen und Leistungsparameter bereitgestellter Dienste erfaßt. Die grundlegende Arbeitsweise eines Traders wird als bekannt vorausgesetzt (s.[2], [4], [11]). Nach einer Dienstanforderung mobiler Clienten beim Trader wird in der vorliegenden Arbeit ein neuer, intelligenter Traderdienst ausgelöst: auf der Basis eines im Abschnitt 4 beschriebenen Auswahlalgorithmus werden aus dem konkurrierenden Dienstangebot Dienstschnittstellen ausgewählt. Zielstellung der Auswahl ist es, günstige Verarbeitungszeiten zu erreichen und damit Einfluß auf die Kosten zu nehmen. Als Vermittler der Datenströme zwischen Mobilregion und Festnetz sowie zwischen einzelnen Servern im Festnetz wurden durch die Autoren in [6], [7] und [8] Mediatoren eingeführt. Eine erste Aufgabe der Mediatoren besteht in der Vermittlung der Daten zwischen der Mobilregion und den Servern. Zweitens übernehmen die Mediatoren die Behandlung von Störungen auf den mobilen Übertragungsstrecken bzw. die definierte Weiterführung von Aufgaben nach gezielt herbeigeführten Unterbrechungen. Darüber hinaus wird die Cachefunktion der Mediatoren genutzt, um Daten im Festnetz entsprechend einer vorgegebenen Verarbeitungsstruktur zu vermitteln. Die Realisierung komplexer Arbeitsabläufe durch die Inanspruchnahme unterschiedlicher oder auch gleicher Dienste innerhalb einer Aufgabe wird möglich. Die als kritisch eingeschätzte

Mobilanbindung bleibt bei dieser Herangehensweise auf die Bereitstellung der Ausgangs-informationen und das Abfordern der Resultate beschränkt.

Die Architektur wurde in der vorgebenen Weise als Prototyp auf der Grundlage von Sockets implementiert und auf heterogener Technik erprobt. Zielstellung war es, die Umsetzbarkeit der Architektur nachzuweisen und Aussagen zum Laufzeitverhalten zu gewinnen.

2 Architektur des verteilten Systems mit mobilen Stationen

Im folgenden wird stets davon ausgegangen, daß mobile Clienten zeitlich versetzt oder auch parallel über einen Trader Dienste eines oder auch mehrerer geeigneter Server anfordern, dazu Eingangsdaten an die Server übermitteln und Resultatdaten von den Servern zurückerhalten. Dabei sind Probleme zu beachten, die mit den besonderen Bedingungen bei einer Dienst-vermittlung für mobile Clienten auftreten, wobei stets von einem Austausch größerer Mengen von Eingangs- und Resultatdaten zwischen mobilen Clienten und Servern ausgegangen wird.

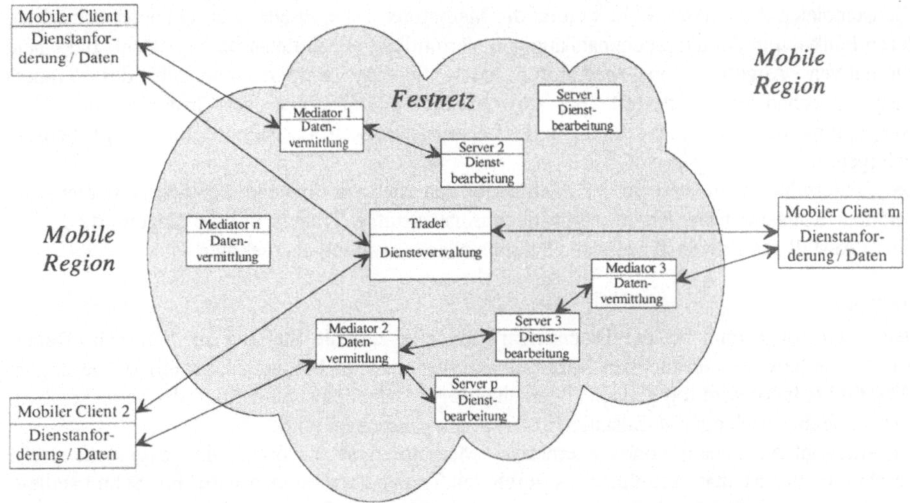

Abb.1: *Architektur eines verteilten Systems mit mobilen Clienten (Beispielszenario)*

Die in der Abb.1 dargestellte Architektur eines verteilten Systems besteht im Festnetz aus einem Trader, n Mediatoren und p Servern (Dienstanbietern). In der Mobilregion können Dienstanforderungen ausgelöst werden, die aufgabenspezifisch einen Teil der oder auch alle p Server in Anspruch nehmen. Die parallele Nutzung der Dienste bei unterschiedlichen Anforde-rungen ist möglich. Weiterhin vermittelt die Abbildung einen ersten Eindruck des Daten- und Steuerflusses zwischen den Instanzen. Neben der Spezifikation der angeforderten Dienste sind die Schnittstellen der genutzten Instanzen, die bereitgestellten Eingangsinformationen, die Resultatdaten, die Steuerinformationen für die Auswahloptimierung und die Kontrolle des Arbeitsfortschritts zu vermitteln. Die Cachefunktion der Mediatoren bildet dabei die Voraussetzung für ein zeitweilig losgelöstes Arbeiten der Instanzen im Festnetz und in der Mobilregion.

Nachfolgend wird die Funktionalität der Instanzen beschrieben.

Mobiler Client

Unter softwaretechnologischem Aspekt wird eine Unterteilung des Clients in eine nutzerspezifische Komponente und eine Vermittlungskomponente vorgenommen. Im Nutzerteil werden problemabhängig die Eingangsdaten (z.B. Datenbankabfragen, arithmetische Werte für Berechnungen) bereitgestellt und die empfangenen Resultatdaten aufbereitet. Die in Files gepufferten Eingangs- und Resultatdatenströme bilden die clientinterne Schnittstelle zur Vermittlungskomponente. Alle Steuerungs- und Übertragungsoperationen zwischen Client und Trader bzw. Mediator werden im Vermittlungsteil realisiert, so daß aus Nutzersicht eine Transparenz gegenüber Trader, Mediator und Servern besteht. Im Vermittlungsteil des Clients werden die Mediator- und Serverschnittstellen vom Trader abgefordert und die Eingangsdaten zum Mediator gesendet bzw. die Resultatdaten empfangen. Nach einem Abbruch übernimmt der Vermittlungsteil des Clients das Handling zum Fehlerbehebungsdienst des Mediators.

Trader

Die Aufgaben eines Traders innerhalb eines verteilten Systems bestehen in der diensttypbezogenen Erfassung, Verwaltung, Auswahl und Bereitstellung von Schnittstellen potentieller Dienstanbieter. Aus dieser Sicht werden die Mediatoren als spezielle Dienstanbieter betrachtet, deren Funktion in der aufgabenunabhängigen Vermittlung von Datenströmen besteht. Bei einem alternativen Angebot von Mediatoren oder Servern werden innerhalb des Traders Auswahlmechanismen aktiviert, die sowohl die Lokalisierung der Instanzen im Netz (Wegoptimierung) als auch die aktuelle Leistungsfähigkeit (Leistungsoptimierung) berücksichtigen.

Die Traderschnittstelle stellt in der Architektur den einzigen Fixpunkt dar. Mit dem Ziel einer erhöhten Robustheit werden in zukünftigen Ausbaustufen Traderreplikate eingeführt, die bei einem Ausfall des aktiven Traders die Schnittstellenverwaltung übernehmen.

Mediator

Dem Mediator kommt bei der Datenvermittlung eine zentrale Stellung zu. Sämtliche Datenströme von bzw. zu den mobilen Netzstationen werden vom Mediator kontrolliert übertragen. Mit dem Mediator wird folglich ein allgemeingültiger Datendienst eingeführt, der beim Auslösen einer Aufgabe durch eine Mobilstation in Anspruch genommen wird.

Die Auswahl aus einem Fonds alternativer Mediatoren setzt voraus, daß eine dynamische Verwaltung der Mediatorschnittstellen durch den Trader übernommen wird. Ein Schnittstellenexport zum Trader in Analogie zu den Serverdiensten ist ein Bestandteil der Dienstbereitstellung.

Aus Sicht der Datenvermittlung werden vom Mediator drei Hauptaufgaben erfüllt:

- Der Vermittlungsdienst des Mediators realisiert auf der Basis der vom Trader importierten Serverschnittstellen die Datenübertragung zwischen den mobilen Clienten und den Servern. Ein Protokollieren des Verarbeitungsstandes und eine Pufferung der Daten ist in den Vermittlungsdienst integriert.

- Nach einem Abbruch analysiert der Fehlerbehebungsdienst unter Bezug auf die Protokolldatenbank den bereits erreichten Verarbeitungsstand, um eine definierte Weiterführung der Aufgabe vornehmen zu können. Nach einer Unterbrechung im Mobilbereich leitet der Fehlerbehebungsdienst eine Fortführung der Datenübertragung exakt an der Abbruchstelle ein.

- Eine Erweiterung des Vermittlungsdienstes stellt der Serveransteuerungsdienst dar, der Daten zwischen den Servern im Festnetz entsprechend einer vorgegebenen Verarbeitungsstruktur vermittelt. Zwischenergebnisse können damit zur weiteren Bearbeitung nachfolgenden Servern zugeführt werden.

Ein gezielter Abbruch der Verbindung zur Mobilstation nach der Bereitstellung der Eingangsdaten wird für das untersuchte Szenarium den Normalfall darstellen und unterscheidet sich vom Fehlerfall nur durch die exakte Definition des Abbruchzeitpunktes. Im Fall eines

Mediatorausfalls wird ein Neustart aller vom betreffenden Mediator vermittelten Aufgaben notwendig. Dieses Herangehen ist vertretbar, da die Auswirkungen auf die vom betreffenden Mediator vermittelten Aufgaben beschränkt bleiben und die Ausfallwahrscheinlichkeit im Festnetz relativ gering ist.

Server

In Analogie zum mobilen Client wird auch bei den Servern eine Unterteilung in einen Nutzer- und Vermittlungsteil vorgenommen. Das interne Zusammenwirken der Komponenten erfolgt über den Austausch von Datenströmen. Einen unmittelbaren Problembezug weist der Nutzerteil auf, da hier die Serverleistung erbracht wird.

Der allgemeingültige Vermittlungsteil schließt den Export der Schnittstellen- und Typinformationen zum Trader ein, die den Ort und die Art der potentiellen Serverleistung charakterisieren. Weiterhin wird der eingangs- und ausgangsseitige Datenaustausch zum Mediator realisiert.

Die von der Architektur umgesetzten Funktionen können wie folgt zusammengefaßt werden:

- Vom mobilen Client aus ist ein Zugriff auf Dienste im Festnetz möglich, die dynamisch verwaltet werden.

- Der Vermittlungs- und Fehlerbehebungsdienst des Mediators unterstützt neben der Behandlung von Störungen im Bereich der mobilen Übertragungsstrecke den gezielt herbeigeführten Abbruch der Verbindung zu definierten Zeitpunkten. Eine Reduzierung der Übertragungskosten wird damit möglich.

- Die dynamische Schnittstellenverwaltung des Traders schließt einem Mechanismus für die Auswahloptimierung konkurrierender Mediatoren und Dienstangebote ein.

- Im Zusammenwirken der Trader- und Mediatorinstanzen wird von der Architektur die Abarbeitung unterschiedlich strukturierter Arbeitsflüsse umgesetzt. Während der Trader die Schnittstellen potentieller Dienstanbieter bereitstellt, werden vom Mediator die Datenströme auch zwischen verschiedenen Servern vermittelt.

3 Dienstverwaltung und Unterbrechungsbehandlung

Ausgehend von der Funktionalität der einzelnen Instanzen wird in Abb.2 eine Gliederung des Gesamtablaufes in Phasen vorgenommen.

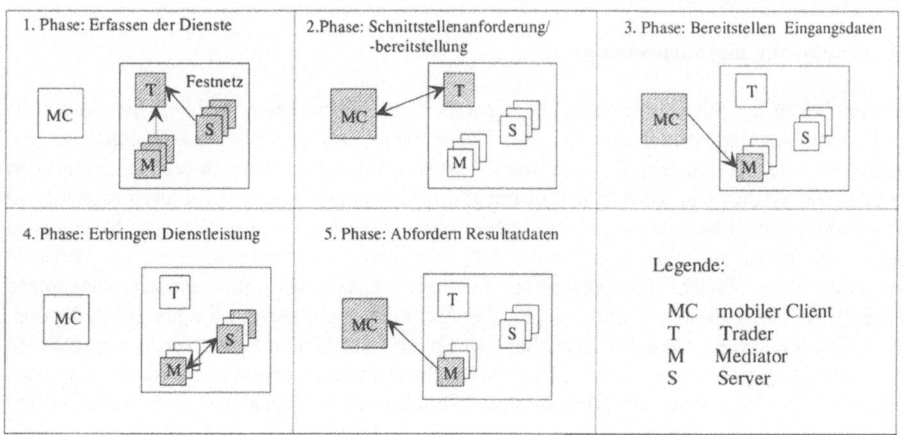

Abb.2: *Zusammenwirken der Instanzen bei einer Aufgabenbearbeitung*

Im folgenden werden vorrangig die Bereitstellung der Dienste, die Vermittlung der Steuerflüsse und Datenströme sowie die Unterbrechung der Mobilanbindung behandelt. Die Auswahloptimierung und die Realisierung komplexer Verarbeitungsstrukturen bleiben aus Gründen der Übersichtlichkeit zunächst unberücksichtigt.

Voraussetzung für eine dynamische Dienstevermittlung ist das diensttypbezogene Erfassen der Server- und Mediatorschnittstellen (Phase 1). Jeder Dienst verfügt über eine Komponente, die beim Start die aktuelle Hostadresse selbständig ermittelt und zum Trader überträgt. Der Trader stellt innerhalb des verteilten Systems einen Fixpunkt dar und ist in der Lage, Dienstangebote entgegenzunehmen und deren Schnittstellen einschließlich des Diensttyps zu speichern (Interface- und Type-Repository). Die Aktualisierung der Dienstangebote ist ein Prozeß, der sich über den gesamten Lebenszyklus des Systems erstreckt. Dienstanforderungen werden vom mobilen Client ausgelöst (Phase 2) und vom Trader bearbeitet. Die bereitgestellten Serverschnittstellen sind von der Art der Dienstanforderung abhängig. Gleichzeitig wird ein Datenvermittler (Mediator) ausgewählt, der eine zeitgünstige Vermittlung der Datenströme zwischen Client und Server ermöglicht. In einer 3. Phase werden vom mobilen Client Steuerinformationen und die aufgabenbezogenen Eingangsinformationen zum vorher ausgewählten Mediator übertragen. Dieser Vorgang wird als kritisch eingeschätzt, setzt er doch eine Verbindung von der Mobilregion zum Festnetz voraus. Durch das Ablegen der empfangenen Informationen in einem Cachespeicher des Mediators und ein Protokollieren des Übertragungsverlaufs ist nach Störungen eine definierte Weiterführung des Transfers an der Abbruchstelle möglich. Diese Eigenschaft des Mediators kann nach dem vollständigen Empfang der Eingangsinformationen bewußt genutzt werden, um die Verbindung zur Mobilkomponente während der Festnetzarbeit gezielt zu unterbrechen. Die unmittelbare Dienstleistung wird im Zusammenwirken des ausgewählten Mediators und der benötigten Server erbracht (Phase 4). Mögliche Abläufe der Dienstbereitstellung werden im Abschnitt 5 näher untersucht. Dem Abrufen der Resultatdaten durch den mobilen Client geht dann ein erneuter Aufbau der Verbindung zwischen der Mobilstation und dem Festnetz voraus. Nach einer Identifikation der Aufgabe wird eine Statusmeldung des Mediators ausgewertet, die den Stand der Aufgabenrealisierung charakterisiert. Eine Übertragung der Bearbeitungsergebnisse zum Client wird eingeleitet, wenn die Resultatdaten am Mediator vorliegen (Phase 5). Die Behandlung von Übertragungsstörungen erfolgt in Analogie zur Phase 3.

4 Optimierung der Dienstauswahl

4.1 Einführung und Zielstellung

Die Architektur des Systems ermöglicht den parallelen Zugriff mehrerer mobiler Clienten auf die im Festnetz bereitgestellten Dienste. Die Folge kann eine parallele Inanspruchnahme von Mediatoren und Servern sein. In [7] wurde der Mediatordienst von den Autoren eingeführt und zunächst ein Mediator in die Architektur integriert. Messungen an einem Prototyp zeigten, daß die parallele Vermittlung umfangreicher Datenströme durch nur einen verfügbaren Mediator zu unvertretbar hohen Bearbeitungszeiten der Aufgaben führen kann und somit eine Schwachstelle der Architektur bildet. Entsprechende Aussagen gelten für nur einfach angebotene Serverdienste. Aus diesem Grunde enthält die Architektur gemäß Abb.1 mehrere Mediatoren sowie die Möglichkeit, spezielle Serverdienste mehrfach anzubieten. Die in Tab. 1 angegebenen Taskbearbeitungszeiten für verschiedene Architekturvarianten untermauern diese Aussagen quantitativ. Die Messungen erfolgten an einem Prototyp mit n Mediatoren, m mobilen Clienten und p festen Servern gleichen Typs (n, m, p = 1, 2, 3). Es wurde eine unterbrechungsfreie Verarbeitung sowie eine ständige Verfügbarkeit der mobilen Clienten simuliert. Jeder Client sendete und jeder Server erhielt die gesamte Eingangsdatenmenge. Andererseits erzeugte jeder der p Server nur den 1/p-ten Teil der Resultatdaten. Die gemessenen Bearbeitungszeiten zeigen, daß im Falle nur eines verfügbaren Mediators die Taskbearbeitungszeiten für eine steigende Anzahl von Dienstanforderungen mobiler Clienten stark wachsen. Andererseits führt die Integration mehrerer Mediatoren im Falle paralleler Clientzugriffe zu einem deutlichen Leistungszuwachs. Entsprechende Aussagen lassen sich aus Tab. 1 für mehrfach angebotene Serverdienste ableiten.

Anzahl		Anzahl Server			Struktur am Bsp. von 2 Servern
M	MC	1	2	3	
1	1	218	160	153	$MC - M <^S_S$
	2	305	223	209	$\begin{matrix} MC \\ MC \end{matrix} > M <^S_S$
	3	392	375	334	$\begin{matrix} MC \\ MC \\ MC \end{matrix} M <^S_S$
2	2	227	173	163	$\begin{matrix} MC-M \\ MC-M \end{matrix} \times \begin{matrix} S \\ S \end{matrix}$
3	3	238	180	172	$\begin{matrix} MC-M \\ MC-M \\ MC-M \end{matrix} \}^S_S$

Tab.1 *Taskbearbeitungszeit bei paralleler Auftragsbearbeitung für eine unterschiedliche Anzahl von Mediatoren (M), mobilen Clienten (MC) und Servern [in Sekunden]*

Die im Experiment benutzte Aufgabe erforderte die Vermittlung umfangreicher Datenströme und im Vergleich dazu nur einen geringen Verarbeitungsaufwand der Server. Deshalb belegen die Messungen die oben genannte Schlußfolgerung insbesondere für Mediatoren.

Mit der Integration mehrerer Mediatoren und mehrerer Server gleichen Typs in die Architektur muß der Trader zwangsläufig für jede Dienstanforderung mobiler Clienten eine Auswahl unter den konkurrierenden Mediatoren und Servern vornehmen. Dabei hängt die Auswahl sowohl von der Performance und der aktuellen Arbeitslast der Server und Mediatoren als auch von der Breite und der aktuellen Auslastung der Kommunikationslinien ab. Dieser Aufgabe wurde in der Literatur bisher wenig Aufmerksamkeit gewidmet. Ziel des im folgenden beschriebenen intelligenten Traderdienstes zur Auswahl von Mediator- und Serverschnittstellen ist es, die totale Taskbearbeitungszeit unter Beachtung der anfallenden Gesamtkosten zu minimieren.

Für praktische Anwendungsfälle ist davon auszugehen, daß mehrere konkurrierende Server bzw. Mediatoren verfügbar sind, aber auch Server unterschiedlichen Typs zur Realisierung der Aufgabe benötigt werden. In Abb.3 werden ausgewählte Szenarien in vereinfachter Form dargestellt.

Ziel der optimierten Dienstauswahl ist es, aus einem Angebot konkurrierender Server und Mediatoren eine Auswahl zu treffen, um

- die Übertragungszeiten zwischen mobilem Client und dem ausgewählten Mediator gering zu halten.

- die Gesamtverarbeitungszeit zu minimieren, so daß die Zeitdifferenz zwischen der Bereitstellung der Eingangs- und Resultatdaten herabgesetzt wird.

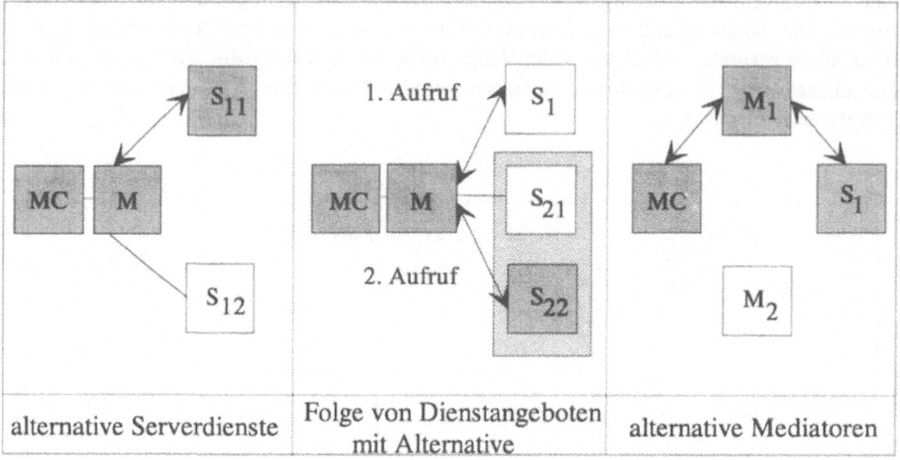

Abb.3: *Vereinfachte Auswahlszenarien der Server- und Mediatorauswahl*

Es wird davon ausgegangen, daß die Vielzahl der Einflußfaktoren keine hinreichend genaue Berechnung der Verarbeitungszeiten auf der Basis theoretischer Leistungsmerkmale zuläßt. Mit dem Auswahlverfahren wird daher ein Vergleich möglicher Mediator-/Serverkombinationen auf der Basis von Bewertungsfaktoren durchgeführt, ohne eine Berechnung exakter Bearbeitungszeiten anzustreben. Für die Bewertung werden Leistungsparametern herangezogen, die im Verlauf der Verarbeitung gewonnen und aktualisiert werden. Das Verfahren berücksichtigt neben den Zeitaufwendungen, die für die Übermittlung der Datenströme zwischen den Instanzen erforderlich sind, die benötigten Verarbeitungszeiten des Mediators und der Server. Durch die Mehrstufigkeit des Verfahrens wird insbesondere der Wirtschaftlichkeitsaspekt berücksichtigt. Die Unterscheidung in eine Vorbereitungs- und Auswahlphase ermöglicht die Trennung der zeitintensiven Bereitstellung von Leistungsdaten und der unmittelbaren Dienstauswahl nach einer Anforderung.

4.2 Phasen des Auswahlverfahrens

4.2.1 Vorbereitungsphase

Die Vorbereitungsphase läuft im Vorfeld einer konkreten Auftragsbearbeitung mit dem Ziel ab, Informationen für eine spätere Dienstauswahl zur Verfügung zu stellen. Zum Zeitpunkt der Bereitstellung eines Mediators bzw. Serverdienstes werden die Schnittstellen- und Typinformationen vom Trader erfaßt (Type- und Interface-Repository). Die dynamische Dienstverwaltung gehört zur Grundfunktionalität eines Traders. Daneben werden Leistungsfaktoren der genutzten Maschinen durch einen im Server bzw. Mediator integrierten Algorithmus ermittelt und dienst- und maschinenbezogen vom Trader gespeichert (Abb.4).

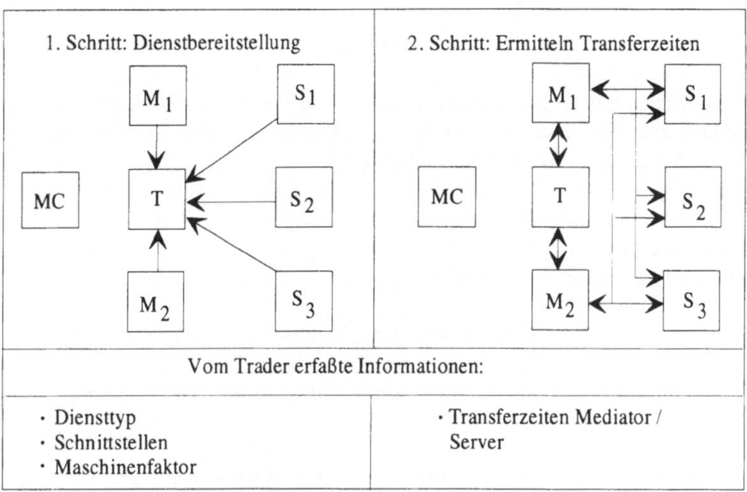

Abb.4: *Bereitstellung von Leistungsdaten in der Vorbereitungsphase*

Mit einem höheren Aufwand ist das empirische Bereitstellen der Transferzeiten verbunden, da die Vorgehensweise auf der Messung von Pollzeiten zwischen allen verfügbaren Mediatoren und Servern beruht. Veränderungen der aktuellen Netzbelastung führen zu Unsicherheiten, die durch eine periodische Wiederholung der Messungen zu vorgegebenen Zeitpunkten abgebaut werden können. Die Leistungsfähigkeit der einzelnen Maschinen hängt u.a. von der aktuellen Belastung ab. Wird der auf einer Maschine laufende Mediator oder Serverdienst mehrfach in Anspruch genommen, muß die damit verbundenen Verzögerung der Auftragsbearbeitung im Auswahlprozeß berücksichtigt werden. Das Verfahren sieht vor, daß die Schnittstellen der genutzten bzw. auch freigegebenen Serverdienste vom vermittelnden Mediator in Form des Belegungsstatus an den Trader übertragen werden. Die zentrale Stellung der Mediatoren innerhalb der Datenvermittlung rechtfertigt, daß in Analogie zu den Servern auch der Belegungsstatus der Mediatoren im Auswahlprozeß Berücksichtigung findet. Eine Fremdbelastung der Maschinen nimmt auf die gemessenen Leistungsparameter Einfluß. Unkontrollierte Veränderungen während der Bearbeitung einer Aufgabe sollten bei zeitkritischen Aufgabenstellungen durch organisatorische Maßnahmen beschränkt werden.

4.2.2 Auswahlphase

Die unmittelbare Auswahlphase wird durch eine Dienstanforderung eines mobilen Clienten beim Trader aktiviert. Vom Trader wird unter Bezugnahme auf die gespeicherten historischen Daten (Leistungsfaktoren, Transferzeiten) und die aktuellen Maschinenbelastungen (Belegungsstatus) eine *Vorauswahl* vorgenommen, die bei einem entsprechenden Dienstangebot zu mehreren möglichen Mediator-/Serverkombinationen führen kann. Eine *Präzisierung der Auswahl* ist notwendig, wenn die Vorauswahl zu keinem eindeutigen Ergebnis führt. Die schrittweise Bewertung der potentiellen Server und Mediatoren erfolgt auf der Basis dimensionsloser Faktoren, die Werte zwischen 0 und 1 annehmen können.
Der Auswahlvorgang kann in folgende Arbeitsschritte unterteilt werden:
1. Aus der Sicht potentieller Mediatoren werden typbezogen die einzelnen konkurrierenden Server bewertet. Für jeden der Mediatoren wird darauf aufbauend der günstigste Server ausgewählt.

2. Erfordert die Realisierung der Aufgabe die Bereitstellung mehrerer Dienste, schließt sich wiederum aus Sicht der konkurrierenden Mediatoren eine Bewertung der Gesamtheit benötigter Serverdienste an.

3. Unter Berücksichtigung der Leistungsparameter der einzelnen Mediatoren wird eine Gegenüberstellung der Mediator-/Serverfolgen vorgenommen. Eine Aussonderung möglicher Varianten erfolgt auf der Basis eines Grenzwertes.

4. Durch ein Bewerten des Datentransfers Client/Mediator wird die Verbindung des mobilen Clients zum Festnetz beurteilt, so daß eine Präzisierung der Auswahl auch dann möglich wird, wenn die Vorauswahl zu keinem eindeutigen Ergebnis führte. Ein differenziertes Herangehen in Abhängigkeit vom Übertragungsszenarium wird nachfolgend diskutiert.

Tab.2 enthält eine Aufstellung der Arbeitsschritte unter Berücksichtigung der Berechnungsgrößen. Die funktionalen Zusammenhänge zur Bewertung der Auswahlvarianten wurden in [9] dargestellt. Im Experiment gewonnene Meßwerte und berechnete Faktoren sind aus Ab- schnitt 7 dieser Arbeit ersichtlich.

Auswahl-phase		Ziel	Herkunft der Berechnungsgrößen			Ablauf
			Vorb.-phase	akt. Ablauf	vorgegebene Faktoren	
Vorauswahl	1	Bewertung Mediator/ Serverkombination — · — · — · — Ermitteln optimale Server	-Pollzahl Mediator/ Server (Transfer) - normierte Maschinenleistung Server	- Belegungs- status des Servers	- Verzögerungs- faktor Mehr- fachnutzung - Wichtungsfaktor Transfer/ Masch.-leistung	Berechnung des Bewertungsfaktors am Trader
	2	Bewertung der Gesamtheit der benötigten Dienste				Berechnung auf Basis der in Phase 1 ermittelten optimalen Server
	3	Berücksichtigung der Mediatoren- leistung	- normierte Maschinenleistung Mediator	- Belegungs- status des Mediators	- Verzögerungs- faktor Mehr- fachnutzung	Berechnung auf Basis Phase 2 am Trader
		Aussondern von Angeboten			- Grenzwert	Vergleich potentieller Folgen
Präzisierung	4	Bewerten Erreichbarkeit der Mediatoren vom mobilen Client	- Pollzahl Agent/ Mediator	- Pollzahlen Client/ Mediatoren	- mediator- bezogener Faktor	Anpollen potentioneller Mediatoren vom Client

Tab.2: *Phasen im Auswahlprozeß*

Während die Maschinenleistung und die Pollzahlen als Maß für den Datentransfer in der Vorbereitungsphase empirisch gewonnen werden, charakterisiert der Belegungsstatus die aktuelle Belastung der Maschinen. Veränderungen sind eine Folge der unmittelbaren Aufgabenbearbeitung und werden zu diesem Zeitpunkt an den Trader gemeldet. In die Berechnung der Bewertungsfaktoren gehen weiterhin Wichtungsfaktoren ein, die den Einfluß der Datenvermittlung im Vergleich zum Verarbeitungsanteil charakterisieren. Die derzeitige Vorgabe der Faktoren berücksichtigt nur ungenügend die Spezifik des jeweiligen Serverdienstes und die Größe des zu vermittelnden Datenvolumens, so daß eine Erweiterung des Auswahldienstes mit einer Korrekturkomponente notwendig wird. Für die Korrektur können in Abhängigkeit vom Serverdienst und Datenvolumen die gemessenen Zeitanteile herangezogen werden. Berechnungsgrundlage für die Verzögerungsfaktoren, die eine Mehrfachbenutzung von Diensten berücksichtigen, sind gegenwärtig die am Prototyp gemessenen Verarbeitungszeiten (siehe Tab. 3). Auch hier ist eine Abhängigkeit von der Art des Serverdienstes und der genutzten Maschine zu erwarten.

Führte die in den Auswahlphasen 1-3 vorgenommene Vorauswahl zu keiner eindeutigen Aussage, wird in einem weiteren Schritt eine Präzisierung der Auswahl vorgenommen. Kriterium ist dabei die Erreichbarkeit der Mediatoren durch den mobilen Client. Unter Berücksichtigung der im mobilen Übertragungsbereich entstehenden Kosten wird ein differenziertes Herangehen in Abhängigkeit vom genutzten Szenarium erforderlich sein:

- Werden die Aufgaben auf unterschiedlichen Rechnern des Festnetzes ausgelöst, ist ein Anpollen potentieller Mediatoren zum Bearbeitungszeitpunkt vertretbar. Diese Form ist auf Grund der eingeschränkten Mobilität als Sonderfall zu betrachten.
- Erfolgt ein Zugang der Mobilkomponente zum Festnetz über ein lokales Funknetz, werden in der Regel keine zusätzlichen Kosten anfallen. Ein Bestimmen der aktuellen Erreichbarkeit der Mediatoren durch Anpollen ist möglich.
- Werden für die Realisierung der Mobilität ein Weitverkehrsfunknetz (für die Untersuchungen am Prototyp D2) oder auch eine Modemanbindung genutzt, stehen die anfallenden hohen Kosten dieser Verfahrensweise entgegen. In diesem Fall ist der Umstand zu nutzen, daß der Festnetzzugang an einem oder mehreren definierten Stellen erfolgt. Die Installation eines Agenten am Zugangspunkt, der bereits in der Vorbereitungsphase durch Anpollen eine Erreichbarkeit der Mediatoren bewertet, vermeidet zusätzliche Aufwendungen im Mobilbereich.

5 Strukturierte Dienstbearbeitung

5.1 Prinzipielles Vorgehen

Die Integration von Mediatoren in die Architektur wurde mit dem Ziel vorgenommen, eine zeitweilig separate Arbeit der Instanzen im Festnetz zu ermöglichen. Zu diesem Zweck enthält der Mediator für die bereitgestellten Eingangsdaten und anfallenden Resultatdaten einen Cachespeicher. Eine Erweiterung dieses Prinzips stellt die sequentielle bzw. parallele Vermittlung zwischengespeicherter Daten zu Servern gleichen oder unterschiedlichen Typs dar. Die Ansteuerung von Diensterbringern nach einer vorgegebenen Struktur in Abhängigkeit von der Aufgabenspezifik (Verarbeitungsstrukturen) erfordert eine Funktionserweiterung im Zusammenwirken der Instanzen:

- Vom Client werden die Schnittstellen für die Gesamtheit der zu erbringender Dienste angefordert. Die Struktur der Dienstbearbeitung ist für den Auswahlprozeß wesentlich, so daß vom Client die Verarbeitungsstruktur zum Trader übertragen werden muß.
- Der beschriebene Auswahlalgorithmus des Traders berücksichtigt bei der Bewertung die Gesamtheit benötigter Dienste einschließlich ihres Zusammenwirkens.
- Vom Mediator sind schließlich die Diensterbringer in Abhängigkeit von der Aufgabenstruktur anzusteuern, Zwischenergebnisse zu speichern und an Folgedienste weiterzuleiten. Der erreichte Verarbeitungsstand ist zu protokollieren.

Die eingangs genannten Vorteile des Herangehens bleiben nach dieser Funktionserweiterung erhalten, da die kritische Verbindung zur Mobilkomponente auch bei der Abarbeitung von Verarbeitungsstrukturen zeitweise aufgehoben werden kann. Die komplexe Bearbeitung von Aufgaben führt zu einer verminderten Transparenz beim Verfolgen des Verarbeitungsablaufs. Es ergibt sich die Notwendigkeit, den erreichten Verarbeitungsstand der Dienstbearbeitung dem Mobilnutzer bei Anforderung zugänglich zu machen, durch den Ausfall von Servern bedingte Störungen anzuzeigen bzw. bereits zum Zeitpunkt der Dienstanforderung einen Abbruch herbeizuführen, wenn ein unzureichendes Dienstangebot keine korrekte Bearbeitung zuläßt.
Das derzeitig vom Prototyp umgesetzte Konzept sieht die Verarbeitung von zwei unterschiedlichen Grundstrukturen vor, wobei beliebige Kombinationen der Grundtypen möglich sind. Der

erste Ablauftyp realisiert die Abarbeitung einer rein sequentiellen Folge von Diensten. Vom Mediator wird eine Vermittlerrolle übernommen, die in der Bereitstellung der Eingangs- und Zwischenspeicherung der Resultatdaten besteht. Störungen im Arbeitsfluß (z.B. Ausfall eines Servers) können behandelt werden, indem in Analogie zur Arbeitsweise des mobilen Clients nach der Beseitigung der Fehlerursache durch Zugriff auf die gespeicherten Zwischenergebnisse eine definierte Weiterführung der Festnetzarbeit eingeleitet wird. Im vorliegenden Prototyp ist diese Leistung noch nicht enthalten. Ein zweiter Ablauftyp sieht die parallele Inanspruchnahme aller verfügbaren Server des geforderten Typs vor (z.B. Recherchen in verteilten Datenbeständen). Um verbesserte Verarbeitungszeiten zu erreichen, wird vom Mediator eine Parallelisierung des Datentransfers zu und von den genutzten Servern vorgenommen. Eine Fortsetzung des Verarbeitungsablaufs, d.h. auch eine Übermittlung der Ergebnisse zum mobilen Client, erfolgt erst nach Eingang sämtlicher Resultatdaten. Eine weitere Spezifizierung möglicher Ablaufstrukturen, insbesondere nach Störungen, wird notwendig sein.

5.2 Realisierung des Verarbeitungsablaufs

Eine detaillierte Darstellung des Zusammenwirkens der Instanzen unter dem Aspekt der Bereitstellung und Realisierung strukturierter Ablauffolgen ist aus Abb.5 ersichtlich.

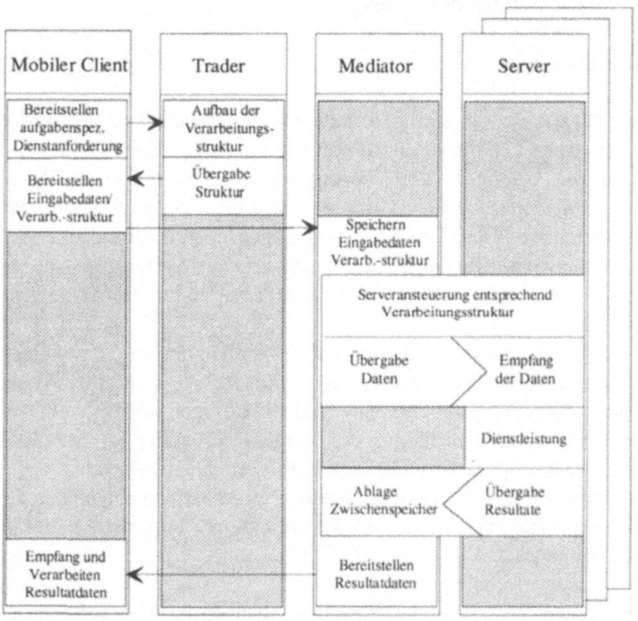

Abb. 5: *Realisierung von Ablauffolgen*

Im vorliegenden Architekturkonzept wird mit dem Auslösen einer Aufgabe am Client eine fest vorgegebene Verarbeitungsstruktur abgefordert, d.h. im nutzerspezifischen Teil des Clients wird die zu lösende Gesamtaufgabe durch Angabe der geforderten Diensttypen und der Struktur des Zusammenwirkens der Dienste beschrieben. Die Schnittstellenanforderung vom Trader setzt eine Verbindung des mobilen Clients zum Festnetz voraus. Auf Grund des geringen Datenvolumens und der kurzen Bearbeitungszeit des Traders ist diese Mobilanbindung als unkritisch einzuschätzen. Die Dienstanforderung am Trader ist mit einer Auswahloptimierung verbunden, wenn alternative Dienstangebote vorliegen. Gleichzeitig werden Abhängigkeiten von der geforderten Verarbeitungsstruktur berücksichtigt und unvollständige Dienstangebote erkannt. Das Ergebnis des Auswahlprozesses sind ein oder mehrere Angebote von Verarbeitungs-strukturen, die neben den Serverschnittstellen jeweils die Schnittstellen eines Mediators enthalten. Eine Präzisierung der Auswahl erfolgt in der im Auswahlverfahren beschriebenen Weise durch den Client, wenn mehrere Mediatoren als Datenvermittler in Betracht kommen. Eine aufgabenbezogene Abspeicherung des Auswahlergebnisses einschließlich der bereit-gestellten Schnittstellen wird mit der Zielstellung vom Client vorgenommen, nach Unter-brechungen die ausgewählten Instanzen erneut ansteuern zu können. Über einen Identifikator wird eine Eindeutigkeit der Aufgabenzuordnung erreicht.

Nach der Übertragung der um die Schnittstellen erweiterten Verarbeitungsstruktur zum ausge-wählten Mediator und der Zwischenspeicherung der vom Client gelieferten Eingangsdaten ist ein vorübergehender Abbruch der Mobilanbindung möglich. Der Mediator übernimmt in Abhängigkeit von der Verarbeitungsstruktur die Ansteuerung der Server und übermittelt die Eingangsdaten. Am Mediator eingehende Resultatdaten werden zwischengespeichert, wobei nach einer parallelen Serveransteuerung die Kontrolle und Zusammenfassung des Resultatdaten-stromes vom Mediator übernommen wird. Auf Grund der Allgemeingültigkeit der Datenvermit-tlung des Mediators ist eine weitere Aufbereitung der Resultatdaten (z.B. Filterfunktion) an dieser Stelle nicht vorgesehen. In Abhängigkeit von der Verarbeitungsstruktur können die Resultatdaten des n-ten Verarbeitungsschrittes die Eingangsdaten des (n+1)-ten Schrittes sein. Ein managementseitiger Ausbau der Architektur sollte verstärkt Unterbrechungen des Arbeitsflusses im Festnetz berücksichtigen und eine administrative Einflußnahme ermöglichen. Die Resultatdaten können von Client nach der Realisierung der Gesamtaufgabe abgefordert werden.

6 Erprobung und Bewertung an einem Prototyp

Die beschriebene Architektur wurde als Prototyp implementiert und auf heterogener Rechen-technik erprobt. Ein erstes Ziel war es, einen Beleg für die Umsetzbarkeit des Konzepts und Aussagen zum Laufzeitverhalten zu gewinnen. Für einen zukünftigen praktischen Einsatz ist insbesondere die Nutzung heterogener Technik von Bedeutung. Die Implementierung der In-stanzen erfolgte deshalb auf unterschiedlichen UNIX-Systemen und Windows NT. Mit der Implementation des Clients unter Windows 3.1 sollte darüber hinaus ein weiteres Einsatzgebiet erschlossen werden. Für das Einbinden der Mobilregion wurden verschiedene physikalische Medien (Modem, FunkLan, Mobilfunk) genutzt. Die in dieser Arbeit ausgewerteten Meßergebnisse wurde auf Basis einer Socket-Implementierung gewonnen. Eine Weiterführung stellt eine derzeitig in Bearbeitung befindliche Lösung auf der Basis von CORBA-Middleware dar. Die Auswahl des CORBA-Produktes ORBIX ist mit ersten guten Erfahrungen und der Verfügbarkeit auf unterschiedlichen Hardwareplattformen zu begründen.

Ein erster Untersuchungsschwerpunkt war auf die separate Arbeitsweise der Mobilstationen und der Instanzen im Festnetzes gerichtet. Bereits in [8, 9] wurden Meßergebnisse ausgewertet, die die Funktionalität und das Zeitverhalten der Lösung bei einer gestörten Mobilanbindung belegen. Durch Überwachung des Arbeitsfortschritts nach periodischen Verbindungsabbrüchen zwischen Client und Festnetz konnte nachgewiesen werden, daß das Konzept auch dann eine Bearbeitung verteilter Aufgaben zuläßt, wenn die Zahl der Störungen eine Bearbeitung ohne Unterbrechungsbehandlung verhindert. Die Messungen ergaben, daß der für die Weiterführung der Aufgaben erforderliche Overhead im Vergleich zur Gesamtbearbeitungszeit gering ist. Die von der Architektur vorgesehene gezielt herbeigeführte Unterbrechung der Mobilanbindung stellt daher einen vertretbaren Weg dar, Kosten im Mobilbereich zu senken, ohne einen unzumutbaren Mehraufwand der Bearbeitungszeit in Kauf nehmen zu müssen.

Ein zweiter Untersuchungskomplex befaßt sich mit der Überprüfung des Auswahlalgorithmus für die im Festnetz installierten konkurrierenden Dienste. Durch das parallele Auslösen gleicher Aufgaben wurden Meßwerte gewonnen, die Rückschlüsse auf die verarbeitungsbedingten Verzögerungen bzw. eine Wichtung der benötigten Teilzeiten zulassen. Um vergleichbare Ergebnisse erzielen zu können, wurde die in Tab.3 dargestellte Versuchsanordnung im Rahmen dieser Meßreihe auf homogener Rechentechnik installiert.

Die Versuchsanordnung sieht die Bereitstellung genau eines Mediator und eines Server vor. In den Versuchsreihen wurden diese Instanzen von einer unterschiedlichen Anzahl von Clients parallel in Anspruch genommen. Tab. 3 enthält nach ihrer Herkunft gegliederte Meßwerte und Berechnungsgrößen sowie Aussagen zur weiteren Verwendung der Ergebnisse.

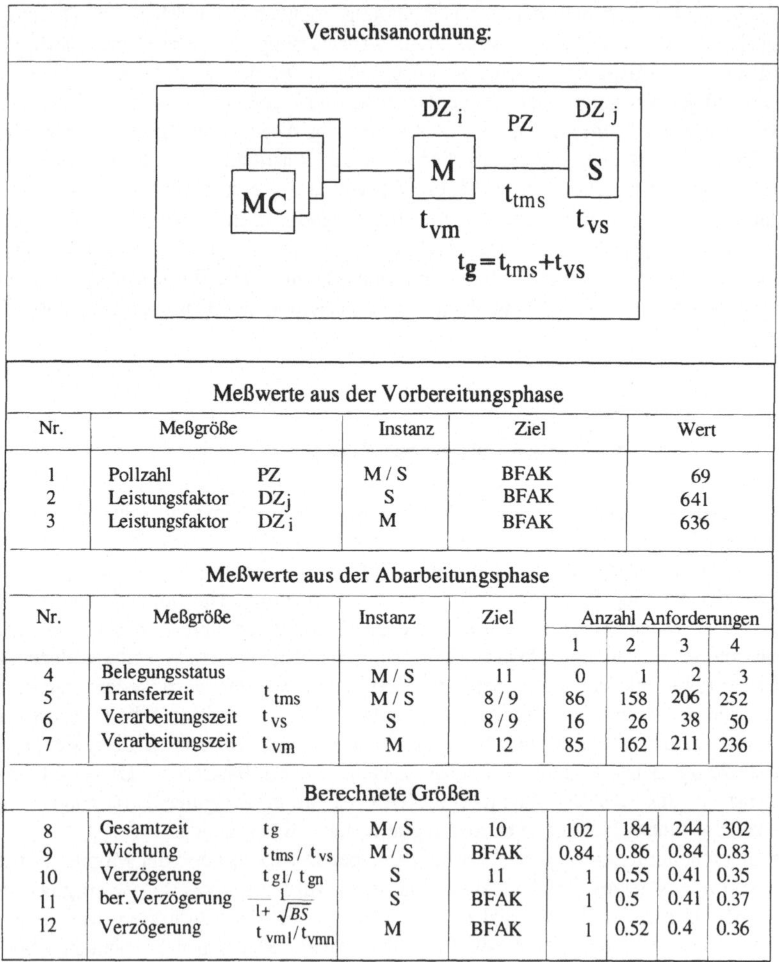

Meßwerte aus der Vorbereitungsphase				
Nr.	Meßgröße	Instanz	Ziel	Wert
1	Pollzahl $\quad$ PZ	M / S	BFAK	69
2	Leistungsfaktor $\quad DZ_j$	S	BFAK	641
3	Leistungsfaktor $\quad DZ_i$	M	BFAK	636

Meßwerte aus der Abarbeitungsphase							
Nr.	Meßgröße	Instanz	Ziel	Anzahl Anforderungen			
				1	2	3	4
4	Belegungsstatus	M / S	11	0	1	2	3
5	Transferzeit $\quad t_{tms}$	M / S	8 / 9	86	158	206	252
6	Verarbeitungszeit $\quad t_{vs}$	S	8 / 9	16	26	38	50
7	Verarbeitungszeit $\quad t_{vm}$	M	12	85	162	211	236

Berechnete Größen							
8	Gesamtzeit $\quad t_g$	M / S	10	102	184	244	302
9	Wichtung $\quad t_{tms} / t_{vs}$	M / S	BFAK	0.84	0.86	0.84	0.83
10	Verzögerung $\quad t_{gl} / t_{gn}$	S	11	1	0.55	0.41	0.35
11	ber. Verzögerung $\quad \dfrac{1}{1 + \sqrt{BS}}$	S	BFAK	1	0.5	0.41	0.37
12	Verzögerung $\quad t_{vml} / t_{vmn}$	M	BFAK	1	0.52	0.4	0.36

Tab.3: *Messungen zur Auswahloptimierung*

Zum Zeitpunkt der Dienstbereitstellung, d.h. in der Vorbereitungsphase, werden die Leistungsfaktoren der genutzten Maschinen DZ und die Pollzahl PZ ermittelt. Da diese Meßwerte als Vergleichszahlen zur Berechnung des Faktors BFAK herangezogen werden, ist deren absolute

Größe von untergeordneter Bedeutung. In einem zweiten Komplex wurden die während der Aufgabenbearbeitung am Mediator bzw. Server in Abhängigkeit vom Belegungsstatus gemessenen Zeiten zusammengefaßt. Die Transferzeiten beinhalten den Zeitbedarf für die Datenübertragung zwischen Mediator und Server. Die Verarbeitungszeiten stellen den unmittelbaren Zeitbedarf für das Erbringen der Dienstleistung dar. Für die Untersuchung steht die Bereitstellung von Vergleichszahlen im Vordergrund, wobei zwei Zielstellungen verfolgt werden. Die Berechnung der Bewertungsfaktoren BFAK dient der Beurteilung konkurrierender Dienstangebote und ist folglich eine Leistung, die auch im Auswahlalgorithmus des Traders integriert ist. Darüber hinaus werden vom Auswahlalgorithmus Faktoren benötigt, um z.B. den Einfluß der Mehrfachnutzung zu berücksichtigen. Zur Abschätzung der Größen werden die in den Versuchsreihen gewonnenen Werte herangezogen. Eine Wichtung der Zeitaufwendungen für Datentransfer und Verarbeitung wird durch Gegenüberstellung der Positionen 5 und 6 möglich. Die Unabhängigkeit des Wichtungsfaktors in Position 9 vom Belegungsstatus ist erkennbar, jedoch wird ein Einfluß des Datenvolumens und des Diensttyps zu erwarten sein. Die derzeitige statische Vorgabe des Wichtungsfaktors genügt daher den Anforderungen einer allgemeingültigen Diensteauswahl nur ungenügend. Durch die Gegenüberstellung der Gesamtbearbeitungszeit (Position 8) in Abhängigkeit vom Belegungsstatus wurden empirisch Verzögerungsfaktoren ermittelt, die Rückschlüsse auf die funktionale Abhängigkeit zwischen Verzögerung und Belegungsstatus ermöglichen. Die weitgehende Übereinstimmung der berechneten und experimentell ermittelten Werte ist durch weitere Messungen zu belegen.

Die im Rahmen einer weiteren Versuchsreihe durchgeführten Messungen hatten eine Überprüfung des Auswahlalgorithmus für konkurrierende Dienstangebote bei unterschiedlich strukturierten Dienstanforderungen zum Ziel. Meßergebnisse liegen beispielsweise für die parallele Inanspruchnahme gleicher Dienste vor und zeigen den erhöhten Zeitbedarf für die vom Mediator vorgenommene Synchronisation der eingehenden Resultatdaten. Eine qualitative Aussage zur Funktionsweise des Auswahlalgorithmus stellt die im Experiment nachgewiesene korrekte Dienstauswahl dar, wenn zeitlich verschoben bei einem konkurrierenden Dienstangebot gleiche Aufgaben ausgelöst werden. Eine Berücksichtigung des Belegungsstatus wird erst möglich, wenn die entsprechenden Steuerinformationen des Mediators am Trader eingegangen sind.

7 Schlußfolgerungen und Ausblick

Mit der in der Arbeit untersuchten Architektur wurde die Zielstellung verfolgt, mobile Stationen so in heterogene verteilte Systeme einzubinden, daß in bestimmten Verarbeitungsphasen ein Abkoppeln der Mobilrechner vom Festnetz möglich wird. Die im Festnetz eingeführten Mediatoren lösen das Problem in effektiver Weise und übernehmen darüber hinaus die Vermittlung der Datenströme im Festnetz, wenn mehrere unterschiedliche oder auch gleiche Dienste entsprechend einer vorgegebenen Ablaufstruktur in Anspruch genommen werden. Mit einer Erweiterung der Traderfunktionalität ist die Integration einer Auswahloptimierung für konkurrierende Mediatoren und Server verbunden. Das Ziel dieser Auswahl besteht in einem verbessertes Laufzeitverhalten im Festnetz, wenn durch eine steigende Anzahl von Dienstanforderungen Performanceverluste zu unvertretbaren Bearbeitungszeiten führen.

Die implementierte Prototyplösung zeichnet sich durch hohe Robustheit aus und diente dem Nachweis der Realisierbarkeit der Architektur. Gleichzeitig wurden die Messungen für eine Beurteilung des Laufzeitverhaltens herangezogen und der Einfluß bestimmter Leistungsparameter bewertet.

Eine weitere, komfortablere Prototypimplementation der Architektur, die auf eine CORBA-Plattform aufsetzt, ist gegenwärtig in Entwicklung. Auf der Basis dieser Middleware wird die Ausdehnung des Geltungsbereiches auf mehrere Namensräume und ein verbesserter Sicherheitsdienst erreicht.

Ansätze für mögliche Verbesserungen der Architektur wurden an verschiedenen Stellen der Arbeit genannt. Beispielsweise wird eine dynamische Korrektur der Wichtungs- und Verzögerungsfaktoren unter Berücksichtigung der zu vermittelnden Datenstöme und der Diensttypen zu einer qualitativen Verbesserung der Auswahlergebnisse führen. Die Intelligenz des Auswahlverfahrens beruht auf einer Auswertung aktueller Teilzeiten in Analogie zu Abschnitt 6, so daß mit korrigierten Bewertungsfaktoren eine Berücksichtigung aktueller Bedingungen erreicht wird. Aus der Möglichkeit, komplexe Dienstleistungen im Festnetz verarbeiten zu können, ergeben sich managementseitige Anforderungen. Die Unterbrechung des Arbeitsflusses, z.B. durch Serverausfall, erfordert Maßnahmen zur Überwachung des Arbeitsablaufs und eine Einflußnahme auf die Weiterführung bzw. einen kontrollierten Abbruch.

Literatur

[1] Haas, Z.J. / Alonso, R. / Duchamp, D. / Gopinath, B. / Cheung, N.K.: Mobile and Wireless Computing Networks; IEEE Journal on Selected Areas in Communications 13(1995)5, 836 - 837

[2] Irmscher, K.: Simulation eines erweiterten Trader-Konzepts zur Dienstevermittlung in verteilten Systemen; in: Kampe, G. / Zeitz, M. (Hrsg.), Simulationstechnik, 9.Symposium in Stuttgart (ASIM94), Oktober 1994, Vieweg Verlag, Braunschweig / Wiesbaden, 1994, 253 - 258

[3] Irmscher, K.: Stochastic Modelling of Mobile Distributed Systems, in: Breitenecker, F. / Husinsky, I. (Eds.), Proceedings of the EUROSIM Simulation Congress, EUROSIM 1995, Vienna, Austria, 11-15 Sept. 1995, Elsevier Science Publishers B.V., Amsterdam, 1995, 553 - 558

[4] Mittasch, Ch. / Irmscher, K.: On the Way to Competitive Market of Services in Heterogeneous Networks; IFIP Congress 94, Hamburg, 28.08.-02.09.94, in: Brunnstein, K. / Raubold, E. (Eds.), 13th World Computer Congress 94, Vol. 2, Elsevier Science B.V., Amsterdam, 1994, 57 - 62

[5] Richter, K.: Modellierung und Simulation von Client-Server-Rechnernetzen mit Blockierungen; in: Sydow, A. (Hrsg.), Simulationstechnik, 8.Symposium in Berlin (ASIM93), September 1993, Vieweg Verlag, Braunschweig / Wiesbaden, 1993, 417 - 420

[6] Richter, K. / Rudolf, St.: Client-Server Networks: Modelling, Simulation, Measurement, and Analytical Solution, in: Breitenecker, F. / Husinsky, I. (Eds.), Proceedings of the EUROSIM Simulation Congress, EUROSIM 1995, Vienna, Austria, 11-15 Sept. 1995, Elsevier Science Publishers B.V., Amsterdam, 1995, 511 - 516

[7] Rudolf, St. / Richter, K. / Irmscher, K.: Handling mobiler Clienten in heterogenen verteilten Systemen; in: Mittasch, Ch. (Hrsg.), Anwendungsunterstützung für heterogene Rechnernetze, Tagungsband des Workshops an der TU Bergakademie Freiberg, 30.-31.03.95, Freiberg, 1995, 135 - 144

[8] Rudolf, St. / Richter, K.: Mediatoren zur Vermittlung von Serverdiensten für mobile Clienten; in: 40.Internationales Wissenschaftliches Kolloquium, TU Ilmenau, 18.-21.09.95, Proceedings, Band 1, Ilmenau, 1995, 188 - 193

[9] Rudolf, St. / Richter, K. / Irmscher, K.: Ein Traderdienst zur Auswahl von Servern und Mediatoren in mobilen verteilten Systemen; in: Cap, C. (Hrsg.), Workstations und ihre Anwendung, SIWORK'96, Universität Zürich, 14.-15.5.96, Proceedings, 1996, 349 - 360

[10] Schill, A. / Kümmel, S.: Design and Implementation of a Support Platform for Distributed Mobile Computing; Distrib. Syst. Engng. 2 (1995), 128 - 141

[11] Spaniol, O. / Popien, C. / Meyer, B.: Dienste und Dienstvermittlung in Client/Server-Systemen; Intern. Thomson Publ., Bonn, 1994.

Off-Line Verteilung multimedialer Daten in mobilen Systemen

D. Gollnick, S. Kümmel, A. Schill , T. Ziegert
Technische Universität Dresden, Fakultät Informatik, 01062 Dresden
e-Mail: {gollnick, kuemmel, schill, ziegert}@ibdr.inf.tu-dresden.de

Zusammenfassung

Der vorliegende Beitrag beschäftigt sich mit der Off-Line Verteilung multimedialer Daten in mobilen Systemen. Es werden die Problematiken der Themenfelder *multimedialer Datenaustausch*, *Verteilung von Informationen* und *Anforderungen durch Nutzermobilität* unter diesem Gesichtspunkt analysiert. Daran anschließend werden aus den spezifizierten Problemen die Anforderungen an ein System zur multimedialen Informationsverteilung herausgearbeitet. Es wurde ein adaptiver Transportdienst zur Verteilung von multimedialen Informationen in mobilen Umgebungen konzipiert. Die Implementierung des Systems ermöglichte praktische Untersuchungen, die zur Validierung herangezogen wurden.

Schlüsselwörter: mobile computing, Multimedia, Informationsverteilung

1 Einführung

Forschungen im multimedialen Umfeld betrachten in erster Linie einen kontinuierlichen Datenstrom (z.B. Videokonferenzen, Teleteaching, Videoverteildienste) [STN95, WOH95]. Andererseits bildet der Austausch multimedialer Informationen in Form von Dateien und die damit verbundenen Aspekte einen weiteren Forschungsschwerpunkt [CAG95].
Der vorliegende Beitrag setzt sich zum Ziel, multimedialen Datenaustausch in Form einer Off-Line Verteilung in mobilen Systemen zu betrachten. Die notwendigen Grundlagen werden zunächst im Abschnitt 2 analysiert. Kapitel 3 informiert über das zugrunde liegende Systemkonzept (GISMO Projekt). Die an sich konträren Lösungsmöglichkeiten werden im Kapitel 4 vorgestellt und in ein Gesamtkonzept integriert, das in die Schaffung einer dedizierten Komponente zur Datenverteilung mündet. Aufbauend auf dieser Komponente wird in Abschnitt 5 ein konkretes Anwendungsbeispiel vorgestellt. Das abschließende Kapitel 6 enthält eine Leistungsanalyse der in Kapitel 4 und 5 vorgestellten Systeme.

2 Grundlagen

Der Off-Line Austausch multimedialer Daten erfordert einen integrierten Lösungsansatz, der die Aspekte des *multimedialen Datenaustausches*, der *Verteilung von Informationen* und die *Anforderungen durch Nutzermobilität* mit berücksichtigt.
Der Begriff Multimedia wird in Veröffentlichungen und in der einschlägigen Literatur vielfach unterschiedlich definiert bzw. interpretiert [FEG93, FLU95, MIK94, VAU94]. Für die Betrachtungen in diesem Beitrag ist es ausreichend, Multimedia als Integration verschiedener diskreter (Text, Grafik, Bild) und kontinuierlicher Medien (Audio, Video) aufzufassen, die zusammengefaßt ein *Multimedia Dokument* bilden. Folgende Aspekte sind bei der Off-Line Übertragung multimedialer Daten zu beachten:

> **Datenumfang multimedialer Dokumente:** Im Gegensatz zu Dokumenten ohne Integration multimedialer Elemente, ist das Datenvolumen multimedialer Dokumente groß.

Redundanzanteil multimedialer Daten: Multimediale Dokumente weisen in unkomprimierter Form eine hohe Redundanz auf.

Formatvielfalt multimedialer Dokumente: Es existieren viele unterschiedliche Formate für Multimedia Dokumente, für deren Darstellung die entsprechenden Hardware- und Softwarevoraussetzungen notwendig sind.

Ein- und Ausgabegeräte: In der Praxis ist durch die große Heterogenität der Ein- und Ausgabegeräte die Darstellung multimedialer Informationen auf dem Endsystem nur möglich, wenn die Formate auch tatsächlich unterstützt werden.

Die effiziente Verteilung von Informationen im mobilen Umfeld gewinnt zunehmend an Bedeutung. Zusätzliche Anforderungen ergeben sich hierbei aus der Komplexität des *Mobile Computing*. Im Detail handelt es sich um die nachfolgend beschriebenen Problemstellungen:

Dynamische Konfiguration: Das Senden von Informationen an einen mobilen Nutzer ist nicht bzw. nur eingeschränkt . (*Mobile IP*, [MYS93]) möglich, wenn die Adressierung des Ziels (Nutzer, Applikation, etc.) auf einen Rechner (Netzwerknoten) bezogen ist (nutzer@station.domain.de). Es besteht die Notwendigkeit der Schaffung einer vom Rechner unabhängigen Adressierung, ähnlich einer URN.
Durch die Mobilität ändert sich gleichzeitig das Ressourcenangebot für die mobile Station.

Netzunterbrechung: Bei der Verwendung von lokalen Funknetzen oder zellulären Weitverkehrsnetzen (GSM[1]) ist eine zeitweilige Verbindungsunterbrechung bzw. ein ungewollter Verbindungsabbau möglich. Datenverlust oder die Notwendigkeit einer erneuten vollständigen Übertragung sind häufig die Folge.

Netzabkopplung: Befindet sich eine mobile Station im Zustand der Abkopplung, so ist eine Datenübertragung in keine Richtung möglich. Zum einen liegen keine Adreßinformationen bezüglich der mobilen Station vor, zum anderen kann die mobile Station keine Verbindung zu einem Kommunikationspartner aufbauen. Existierende Protokolle erreichen bereits nach kurzer Zeit (i.d.R. liegen diese Zeiten im Minutenbereich) ihren *time-out*, so daß diese Protokolle in mobilen Systemumgebungen nur eingeschränkt nutzbar sind.
In Abhängigkeit des Kontextes der zu übertragenden Daten sollte das Einstellen der Daten in eine *queue* möglich sein, die bei späterer Netzankopplung die Auslieferung der Daten vornimmt.

Qualität der Kommunikationsmedien: In mobilen Systemumgebungen schwankt die Qualität der Kommunikationspfade erheblich. Derzeitige Netze weisen große Unterschiede in bezug auf Verzögerungszeiten, Zuverlässigkeit und Fehlertoleranz auf. In GSM - Netzen, wie beispielsweise e plus, wird auf Grund der hohen Verzögerungszeiten des Mediums, bei Protokollen wie TCP/IP, die verfügbare Bandbreite nicht voll genutzt.

Wechselnde Bandbreite: Einen speziellen Aspekt der Qualität der Kommunikationsmedien stellt die Bandbreite dar. Durch die Mobilität der Nutzer, die damit verbundenen Subnetzwechsel und die verschiedenen Möglichkeiten der Ankopplung an ein Netz (Ethernet, GSM), kann die verfügbare Bandbreite variieren. Eine schmalbandige GSM - Verbindung eignet sich auf Grund der maximalen Übertragungsgeschwindigkeit von 9600 bit/s nur bedingt zur multimedialen Datenübertragung.

---

[1] Global System for Mobile communication, maximale Übertragungsgeschwindigkeit 9600 bit / s

Sicherheit: Der Aspekt der Sicherheit spielt gerade im Bereich der mobilen Datenkommunikation eine wichtige Rolle. Hierbei stehen nicht so sehr kryptographische Probleme im Vordergrund, sondern vielmehr die Anforderung an Authorisierung und Authentisierung von mobilen Nutzern.

Aus Sicht der Verteilung von Informationen sollten leistungsfähige Informationsverteilsysteme folgenden Anforderungen genügen:

gesicherte Übertragung der Informationen: Die Notwendigkeit der Gewährleistung einer transaktionalen Datenübertragung stellt in vielen Anwendungsfällen eine zwingende Voraussetzung für den Einsatz dar. Systeme zur transaktionalen Verteilung von Informationen, wie *ENCINA* [ENC92, ENC93] oder DEC *Message Queue*, berücksichtigen jedoch mobile Aspekte nicht.

effektive Nutzung der Speicherkapazität: Bei der Informationsverteilung erfolgt in den der Übertragung dienenden Stationen vielfach eine Zwischenspeicherung der Informationen. Große Datenmengen können die Effizienz dieser Systeme negativ beeinflussen. Bei *Punkt - zu - Mehrpunkt* Übertragungen ist die Effizienz eines Verteilsystems vom Ort der Informationsvervielfältigung abhängig.

hoher Durchsatz: Darunter ist einerseits die Übertragung großer Datenmengen zu verstehen. Viele Systeme sind in Abhängigkeit der zur Verfügung stehenden Bandbreite in der Lage, diese Forderung zu erfüllen. Andererseits bedeutet ein hoher Durchsatz die Übertragung einer hohen *Anzahl* von Informationen. Bei einer transaktionalen Übertragung einer sehr hohen Anzahl kleiner Informationsmengen kann die transaktionale Sicherung schnell zum Flaschenhals des Systems werden.

Zusammenfassend kann die Aussage getroffen werden, daß ein System zur effektive Off-Line Verteilung multimedialer Daten in mobilen Systemen folgenden Ansprüchen genügen sollte:

- schnelle Übertragung multimedialer Daten
- Anpassung der Daten an das verfügbare Medium
- Unterstützung möglichst vieler Datenformate und ihre Anpassung an das Endsystem
- Verteilung *Punkt - zu - Punkt* und *Punkt - zu - Mehrpunkt*
- Versenden der Informationen auf Grundlage einer Zielbeschreibung (im Gegensatz zu einer auf den Endknoten bezogenen Adressierung)
- Lokalisierung des Empfängers (i.d.R. Lokalisierung des *Nutzers*)
- Stabilität gegenüber Verbindungsunterbrechungen

3 Systemlösungen im mobilen Umfeld

In jüngster Zeit sind nicht nur im wissenschaftlichen Umfeld Bestrebungen zur Lösung dieser Probleme erkennbar. Durch die Europäischen Union wurde das ACTS Programm (*Advanced Communications Technologies and Services*) initiiert. Den Schwerpunkt der einzelnen Teilprojekte bilden Untersuchungen zur Breitbandkommunikation und der Schaffung einer globalen Informationsinfrastruktur. Im Rahmen von ACTS beschäftigen sich die beiden Projekte *On The Move* und *Moments* (*Mobile Media and Entertainment Services*) mit Problemen im mobilen Umfeld [OTM95, MOM95]. Die Bestrebungen des *On The Move* Projektes richten sich letztendlich auf die Entwicklung einer mobilen API im multimedialen Umfeld.
Auch das MONET (*Mobile interNET*) Projekt zielt auf eine Unterstützung von Nutzern im mobilen Umfeld ab. [MON96].

Bereits seit 1994 existiert am Lehrstuhl Rechnernetze der TU Dresden eine Arbeitsgruppe *Mobile Computing*, die sich mit den Problemen im mobilen Umfeld in ihrer Gesamtheit be-

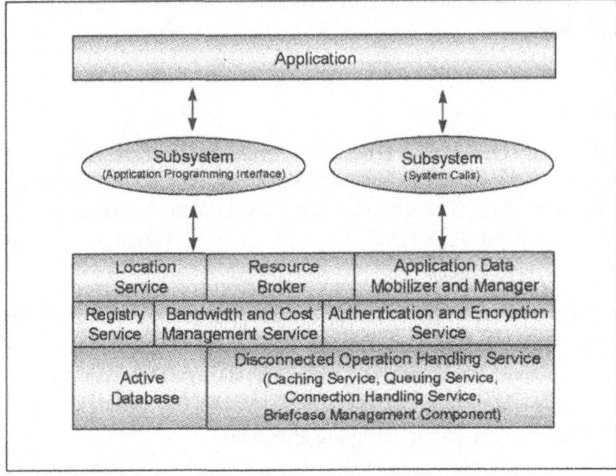

Abbildung 1 - Architekturmodell Stationsmanager

schäftigt und deren Ergebnisse in das GISMO[2] Projekt eingehen. Die konzeptionelle Arbeit befindet sich in einem fortgeschrittenen Stadium. Im Rahmen des GISMO Projektes werden Netze und Rechner in Domänen untergliedert, die durch einen *Domänenmanager* verwaltet werden. Jede Station verfügt über eine dedizierte Komponente *Stationsmanager*, die die mobile Systemunterstützung gewährleistet. Abbildung 1 zeigt das Architekturmodell des Stationsmanagers. Der Schwerpunkt der nachfolgenden Betrachtungen richtet sich

auf den *Queuing Service (QS)*, dem adaptiven Transportsystem des GISMO Projektes. Er arbeitet eng mit dem *Application Data Mobilizer and Manager (ADMM)* zusammen, der den QS bei der Wegewahl unterstützt. Der *Bandwidth and Cost Management Service (BCM)* stellt dem QS Topologieinformationen zur Verfügung, die dieser für eine optimale Datenübertragung nutzt [SCK95].

4 Adaptiver Transportdienst

Die Notwendigkeit neuer generischer Transportdienste geht aus den oben erläuterten Problemen im mobilen Umfeld

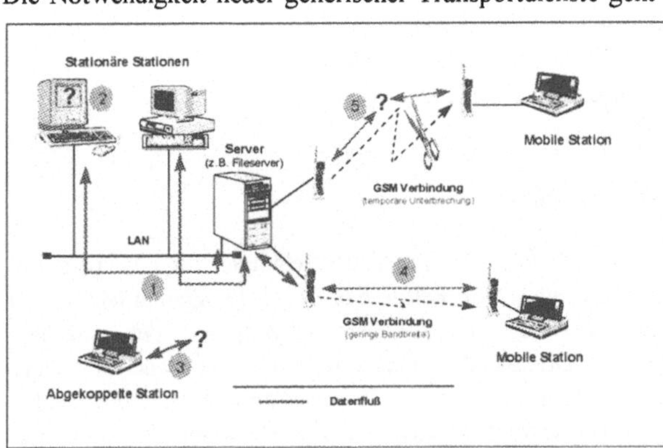

Abbildung 2 - Konventionelle Datenübertragung

hervor. Zur Veranschaulichung ist in Abbildung 2 der Verlauf eines konventionellen Datenaustausches zwischen zwei Anwendungen dargestellt. Eine Anwendung baut zum Kommunikationspartner eine logische Verbindung auf. Im lokalen Umfeld, unter Verwendung konventioneller lokaler Netztechnologien und Protokolle, erfolgt der Austausch von multimedialen Dokumenten

in einem akzeptablen Zeit- und Kostenrahmen (1). Die Übertragung der Daten stellt nicht die

---

[2] Generic Infrastructure Support for Mobile Objects

Möglichkeit ihrer Darstellung sicher (2). Verbindungsunterbrechungen (5), wie sie bei der Verwendung lokaler Funknetze oder zellulärer Weitverkehrsnetze auftreten können, bedeuten die Beendigung der Datenübertragung. In der Regel muß die Anwendung dafür Sorge tragen, daß nach der Verbindungsunterbrechung die Datenübertragung fortgesetzt wird. Existierende Anwendungen sind jedoch oftmals darauf angewiesen, daß der Nutzer den Datenaustausch erneut initiiert, dabei gehen in vielen Fällen die bereits übertragenen Informationen verloren.

Die Voraussetzung für einen Informationsaustausch ist die Erreichbarkeit des Kommunikationspartners. Befindet sich der Kommunikationspartner in einem abgekoppelten Zustand und ist somit nicht lokalisierbar(3) ist in konventionellen Systemen eine Initiierung des Datenaustausch nicht möglich. Ist ein Kommunikationspartner nur über eine schmalbandige Verbindung (GSM - Verbindung, WAN) erreichbar (4), ist die Übertragung multimedialer Daten auf Grund des enormen Zeit- und Kostenaufwandes nahezu unmöglich.

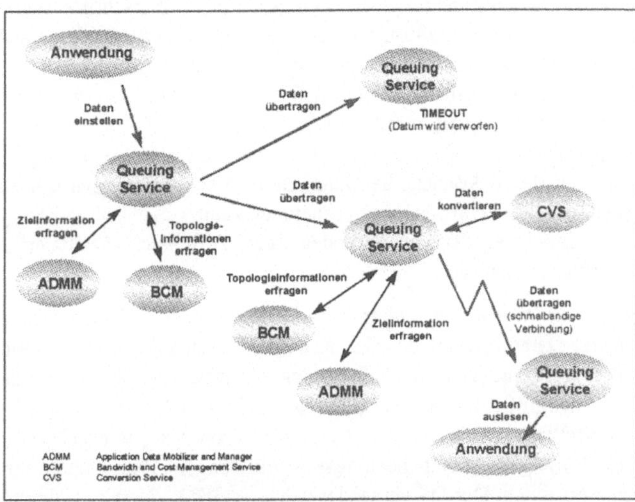

Abbildung 3- Queuing Service

Im Rahmen des GISMO Projektes wurde deshalb eine dedizierte Komponente entwickelt, die Lösungsansätze für die genannten Probleme enthält. Der *Queuing Service* (QS) ist das Transportsystem innerhalb der GISMO Architektur [SKZ96b].

Abbildung 3 ist die Verteilung multimedialer Dokumente unter Verwendung des *Queuing Service* dargestellt. Die Anwendung sendet die Daten nicht mehr direkt, sondern stellt sie unter Angabe des Ziels in den *Queuing Service* ein. Zielbeschreibungen können sehr einfach, z.B. aus einer Nutzer- und Anwendungskennung, aufgebaut sein oder aus komplexen Ausdrücken bestehen, die durch boolsche Algebra verknüpft sind. Die Adressierung der Daten kann beispielsweise durch eine Zielbeschreibung, die aus dem Nutzer und der Anwendung besteht, erfolgen. Die Eindeutigkeit der Zielbeschreibungen wird durch Tag UUIDs[3] erreicht. Eine Tag UUID besteht aus einem 32bit Wert der die Klasse[4] des Objekts kennzeichnet und einer UUID, die seine eindeutige Identifizierung ermöglicht. Die Tag - UUID eines Nutzers setzt sich beispielsweise aus der Klassen ID *Nutzer* sowie einer für jeden Nutzer verschiedenen UUID zusammen. Nach dem Einstellen der Daten in den QS wird der *Application Data Mobilizer and Manager* (ADMM) nach der Lokalität des Empfängers befragt. Ist die Lokalität bekannt, können die Daten zum Ziel weitergeleitet werden, andererseits gibt der ADMM unter Angabe von Wahrscheinlichkeiten mögliche Lokalitäten des Empfängers an. Entsprechend dieser Informationen werden die Daten dann an verschiedene Lokalitäten gesendet. Die Vervielfältigung der Informationen erfolgt dabei jeweils beim letzten gemeinsamen QS, um die Netzbelastung so gering wie möglich zu halten.

---

[3] Universal Unique Identifier

[4] Für die mobilen Objekte existiert eine Klassenhierarchie, in der für die einzelnen Klassen Identifikatoren vergeben wurden.

Bevor ein QS Daten an den nächsten sendet, werden beim *Bandwidth and Cost Management Service* (BCM) Topologieinformationen über den Transportweg eingeholt. Entsprechend dieser Informationen werden die Sendeparameter (Blockgröße, Anzahl der Threads zur parallelen Datenübertragung[5]) dynamisch konfiguriert.

Bei besonders geringen Bandbreiten sind in Abhängigkeit der beim Einstellen der Daten angegebenen Übertragungsparameter verschiedene Szenarien denkbar.

Wurde die Datenübertragung mit dem Flag *TRANSFER_ALWAYS* gekennzeichnet, so werden die Daten in jedem Falle übertragen. Das Flag *TRANSFER_AND_CONVERT* bewirkt, daß der QS bei einem lokalen bzw. nahegelegenen *Konvertierungsdienst* (CVS), die (verlustbehaftete) Konvertierung der Daten in Auftrag gibt. Durch die Konvertierung reduziert sich die Größe eines Datums, so daß eine beim Einstellen gesetzte Übertragungszeit nicht überschritten wird. Wird keines dieser Flags gesetzt, so stellt der QS die Daten in ein *postponed repository* und teilt dem nachfolgenden QS lediglich mit, daß Daten vorliegen. Letztendlich ist somit die Endanwendung bzw. der Nutzer verantwortlich, die Auslieferung der Daten zu initiieren, wobei hier ebenfalls die Möglichkeit der Konvertierung der Daten existiert.

Ein weiterer Vorteil bei der Verwendung des CVS besteht darin, daß die Datenformate an das Endgerät angepaßt werden können. Dazu können die Daten unter Verwendung des QS zu einem CVS transportiert werden, der diese Umwandlung vornehmen kann.

Nachfolgend wird der QS entsprechend der im vorangegangen Abschnitt spezifizierten Anforderungen an ein Transportsystem analysiert.

Optimierte Übertragung multimedialer Daten über verschieden Medien: Eine optimierte Übertragung von Daten erreicht der QS durch die Zusammenarbeit mit dem BCM. Durch die zur Verfügung gestellten Topologieinformationen kann er die Sendeparameter, wie die Blockgröße, an das Übertragungsmedium anpassen. Für GSM - Verbindungen hat sich in Meßreihen eine optimale Blockgröße von 4 Kbyte ergeben. In Netzwerken mit großer Verzögerungszeit beeinflussen die langen Wartezeiten auf Quittungen den Durchsatz erheblich. Der QS versendet daher in GSM - Netzen während der Wartezeit weitere Datenblöcke. Im Gegensatz zu einer Fenstersteuerung werden hierbei parallele Threads verwendet, die unabhängig voneinander wirken und sich somit nicht beeinflussen [SKV96].

Die zu versendenden Daten können mit Prioritäten versehen werden. Ein starres Versenden entsprechend der Prioritäten kann aber unter Umständen fatale Folgen haben. Eine optimierte Datenübertragung geht einher mit der effizienten Nutzung der verfügbaren Medien. Es ist zu beachten, daß ein QS mehrere logische Verbindungen zu anderen QS aufgebaut haben kann, wobei die Verbindungen über verschiede Medien bestehen können.

Die Anzahl der maximal möglichen logischen Verbindungen ist begrenzt. Ist der Durchsatz, bezogen auf die logische Verbindung, gering (GSM etc.), so stellt die Ressource *„logische Verbindung"* den Flaschenhals des Systems dar. Das kann im Zusammenhang mit einer Prioritätssteuerung dazu führen, daß ein System durch eine Vielzahl logischer Verbindungen blockiert ist, ohne das die Systemleistung vollständig ausgeschöpft ist. Notwendig ist hierbei eine dynamische Zuteilung und Überwachung der Verbindungen, wobei ebenfalls berücksichtigt werden kann, ob Daten niedrigerer Priorität für die selbe Station vorliegen.

Diese Betrachtungen beziehen sich bisher nur auf die sendenden QS. Es besteht weiterhin das Problem, daß ein empfangender QS nur eine begrenzte Anzahl von Threads zur Bearbeitung der eingehenden Anfragen (Verbindungen) hat. Es kann hierbei zu Überlastsituationen kommen, die abgefangen werden müssen. Das wird durch den

---

[5] Die Auswirkungen der Parallelität der Übertragung wird an späterer Stelle behandelt.

empfangenden QS geregelt, der jedem sendenden QS eine Anzahl von Verbindungen zuteilt und auch die Zuteilung dynamisch anpassen kann. Überlastsituationen treten beim QS häufiger auf als in anderen Systeme, da hier zur Kompensation der Übertragungsverzögerungen massiv parallel übertragen wird. Daraus leitet sich die Forderung an ein komplexes *und* schnelles *Scheduling* ab, das die Lastsituation der Sender und Empfänger, die Qualität der logischen Verbindungen und den Kontext der zu übertragenden Daten sowie ihre Prioritäten dynamisch berücksichtigt. Die Konzeption einiger Prinzipien ist noch nicht vollständig abgeschlossen. Hier bieten sich für die zukünftige Arbeit interessante Themenbereiche an.

Anpassung der Daten an das verfügbare Medium: Die Anpassung der Daten erfolgt mit Hilfe des CVS. Bei schmalbandigen Netzverbindungen kann der QS die (verlustbehaftete) Konvertierung der Daten in Auftrag geben und das Datenaufkommen reduzieren. Somit können multimediale Informationen zeit- und kosteneffektiv übertragen werden.

Unterstützung vieler Datenformate, Anpassung an das Endsystem: Auch hierbei erfolgt eine Zusammenarbeit mit dem CVS. Der QS selbst ist nicht in der Lage, Datenformate zu ändern. Er ist allerdings in der Lage, diese Anpassungen zu veranlassen.

Versenden von Informationen auf Grundlage einer Zielbeschreibung: Das Versenden von Informationen erfolgt beim QS nicht mehr unter Angabe des Zielrechners. Statt dessen wird der Empfänger durch eine Zielbeschreibung angegeben. Zielbeschreibungen können sehr komplex sein, i.d.R. enthalten sie einen Nutzer- und (mindestens) eine Anwendungskennung. Die Wegbeschreibung, d.h. das Mapping der logischen Zielbeschreibung auf eine Adresse übernimmt der ADMM. Existierende Verzeichnisdienste (DNS, X.500) eignen sich für mobile Systeme aufgrund der periodischen Änderung der Abbildung Nutzer - Maschine nur bedingt.
Da der ADMM anhand von Nutzerprofilen Wegbeschreibungen zu wahrscheinlichen Aufenthaltsorten eines Nutzer geben kann, ist ein „*Voraussenden*" von Informationen an verschiedene Orte möglich.

Verteilung Punkt - zu - Punkt und Punkt - zu - Mehrpunkt: Die Punkt - zu - Mehrpunkt Verteilung erfolgt durch entsprechende Zielbeschreibungen. Die Informationen werden am letzten gemeinsamen QS dupliziert.

Lokalisierung des Empfängers: Die Lokalisierung des Empfängers erfolgt nicht durch den QS. Er ist jedoch in der Lage, mit einer dedizierten Komponente (ADMM) zusammenzuarbeiten, von der er eine Wegbeschreibung zum Empfänger erhält.

Stabilität gegenüber Verbindungsunterbrechungen: Die Datenübertragung des QS erfolgt transaktional. Längere Verbindungsunterbrechung haben i.d.R. den Verlust der logischen Verbindung zur Folge. Der QS ist jedoch in der Lage, eine neue logische Verbindung aufzubauen und die Datenübertragung fortzusetzen.

Zusammenfassend kann die Aussage getroffen werden, daß der QS als Verteildienst konzipiert wurde, der eine effiziente Verteilung von Daten in mobilen Systemen realisiert. Die zentrale Aufgabe besteht in der transaktional gesicherten Übertragung von Daten. Dem *Queuing Service* sind die Problemfelder der mobiler Kommunikation bekannt. Die Lösungen erfolgen durch externe Komponenten (ADMM, BCM, CVS). Diese Aufgabenteilung hat sich als notwendig erwiesen, um die Komplexität der Problematik zu beherrschen und führte gleichzeitig zu einer Vielzahl universeller, wiederverwendbarer Komponenten.

5 Beispielanwendung Mobile X.400

Zur Validierung der im Rahmen des GISMO Projektes konzipierten und realisierten Komponenten werden Beispielanwendungen geschaffen. Im folgenden wird die Erweiterung eines X.400 Message Handling Service um mobile verteilte Aspekte vorgestellt.

Abbildung 4 stellt der konventionellen Nachrichtenauslieferung die Nutzung des *Mobile Enhanced Message Handling Systems* (MEMHS) gegenüber.

Bei der Verwendung des MEMHS erfolgt die Übertragung vom MS zum UA nicht mehr direkt. Hier kommt das *Client - Agent - Server* Prinzip zur Anwendung, das die Auftrennung der direkten Client - Server Kommunikation bewirkt. Das P7 - Protokoll wird zwischen dem MS und dem UA Proxy einerseits, und einem *Subsystem* und dem *User Agent* andererseits verwendet. Die Auftrennung des Protokolls bleibt sowohl dem MS als auch dem UA verborgen. Die Nachrichten werden durch den UA Proxy aus dem MS gelesen (1) und gelangen dann unter Verwendung des *Queuing Service* zum Subsystem (4), das die Verwaltung der Nachrichten übernimmt, den mobilen Mailzugriff unterstützt und dem Nutzer das Eintreffen neuer Nachrichten signalisiert.Abbildung 5 zeigt die Architektur des MEMHS im Detail.

Um die Akzeptanz des MEMHS zu erhöhen, wurde der X.400 Standard nicht erweitert. Der Einsatz von MEMHS beschränkt sich lediglich auf mobile Nutzer, alle anderen Nutzer können ihre X.400 Anwendungen weiterhin ohne Änderungen verwenden.

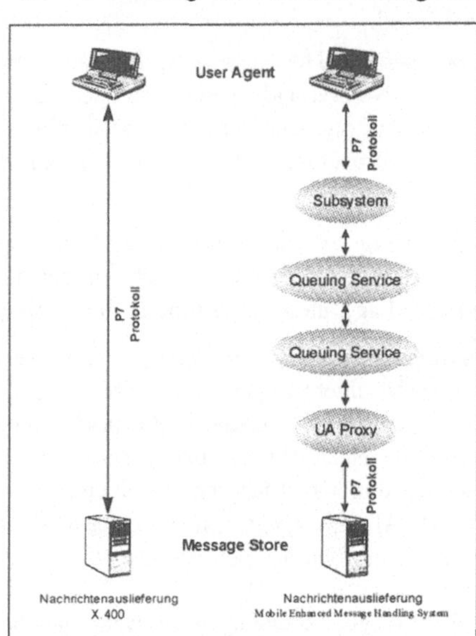

Abbildung 4 -
Vergleich der Nachrichtenauslieferung

Den Ansatzpunkt des Systems stellt der X.400 *Message Store* dar. Stellvertretend für den *User Agent* liest der UA Proxy unter Verwendung eines *Fileinterfaces*[6] die Nachrichten aus dem *Message Store*. Nach dem Auslesen der Nachrichten werden diese in den *Queuing Service* eingestellt. Die Adressierung erfolgt durch die Beschreibung des Ziels, in Form der Identifikatoren (*Tag - UUIDs*) des Nutzers und der Zielanwendung; in diesem Falle dem X.400 Subsystem. Der *Queuing Service* befragt den *Application Data Mobilizer and Manager* (ADMM), ob die Zielinformation aufgelöst werden kann (3). Ist das der Fall, werden entsprechend der verfügbaren Bandbreite die Daten übertragen (*direkter* Nachrichtenempfang) bzw. zurückgehalten (*indirekter* Nachrichtenempfang).

Bei einer schmalbandigen Verbindung stellt der *Queuing Service Bodyparts*, die eine bestimmte Dateigröße überschreiten in ein *postponed repository*. Dem Subsystem wird das Eintreffen der Daten in einem vorgelagerten *Queuing Service* mitgeteilt (3a). Das Subsystem erfragt beim Queuing Service relevante Informationen zu den *Bodyparts*, wie Dateityp und Dateigröße. Es generiert aus diesen Informationen Ersatzdateien die eine Beschreibung der *Bodyparts* enthalten und übergibt diese dem *User Agent*. Durch die Ersatzdateien wird beim Anwählen der *Bodyparts* ein externes Programm, der *X.400 Viewer*, gestartet (Abbildung 6).

---

[6] Zur Anwendung kommt hier das Fileinterface des X.400 *User Agent* der Firma *Maxware*, Version 2.2.

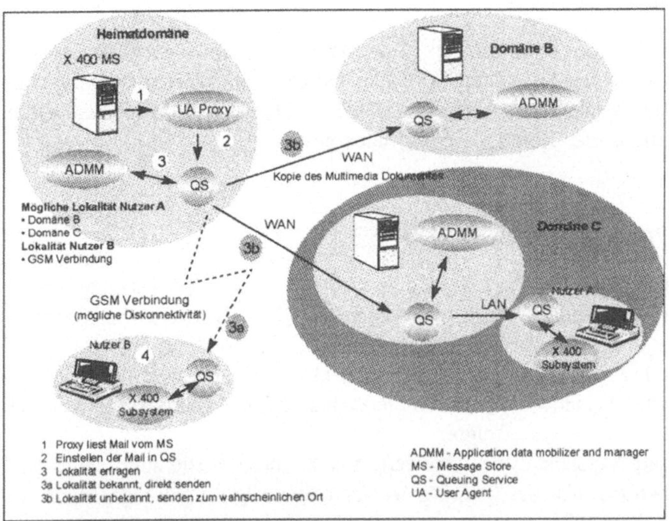

Abbildung 5 - Mobiles X.400 Mailsystem

Dem Nutzer werden, ausgehend von der Originaldatei, verschiedene Konvertierungsstufen angeboten, die die Qualität der Originaldatei verändern, wodurch die zu übertragende Dateigröße und somit Zeit und Kosten verringert werden.

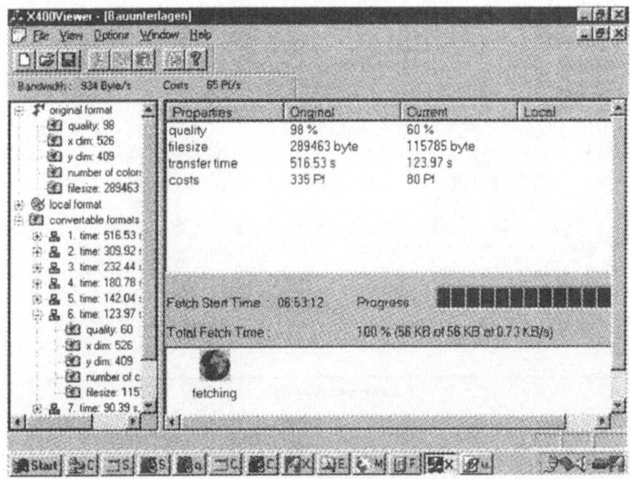

Abbildung 6 - X.400 Viewer

Kann die Zielinformation nicht aufgelöst werden, so wird an Hand von Nutzerprofilen, diese enthalten mögliche bzw. häufige Aufenthaltsorte des Nutzer, die Nachricht in diese Domänen weitergeleitet (3b). Meldet sich der Nutzer später in einer solchen Domäne an, werden die Nachrichten auf seinen Rechner übertragen [SKZ96a].

Die Beispielanwendung wurde in C++ implementiert. Auf den stationären Rechnern wird Windows NT 3.51 verwendet. Die mobilen Rechner werden auf Grund der guten Unterstützung der PCMCIA Karten mit Windows 95 betrieben.

6 Leistungsmessungen

Zur Validierung der Leistungsfähigkeit des Transportdienstes *Queuing Service* erfolgten verschiedene Leistungsuntersuchungen. Dabei wurden zum einen der Durchsatz des *Queuing Service* in Abhängigkeit verschiedener Parameter untersucht, zum anderen wurde das MEMHS einem konventionellen X.400 MHS gegenübergestellt.

6.1 Leistungsuntersuchung Queuing Service

Die Übertragungsleistung des *Queuing Service* wurde unter Verwendung eines 100VG Netzes und einer GSM - Verbindung (e plus) untersucht. Die Hardwarevoraussetzung bildeten zwei Pentium 133 Computer (64 MB Hauptspeicher) unter Windows NT (100VG Messung) bzw. ein Pentium 133 Computer / Windows NT und ein Pentium 120 Notebook (40 MB Hauptspeicher)[7] unter Windows 95, dessen Netzanbindung über eine e plus Verbindung mit einer *Nokia Cellular Data Card* erfolgte.

Für das bessere Verständnis der Meßwerte sind an dieser Stelle noch einige Ausführungen zur internen Funktionsweise des *Queuing Service* notwendig. Im vorangegangen Abschnitt wurde die parallele Sendefähigkeit des *Queuing Service* kurz vorgestellt. Der *Queuing Service* arbeitet intern auf zwei Ebenen parallel. Abbildung 7 stellt den internen Aufbau der Sendelogik des QS dar.

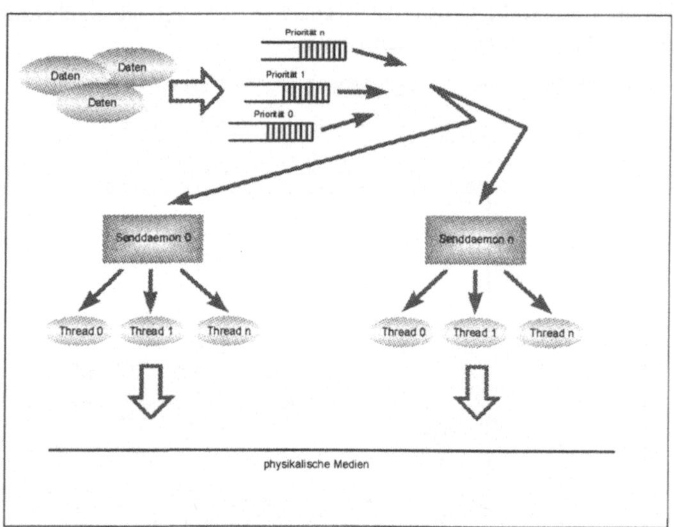

Abbildung 7 - Interne Funktionsweise eines QS

Zunächst werden die Daten ihrer Priorität entsprechend in die entsprechende Warteschlange eingestellt.

Das Auslesen der Daten (QS-Elements) aus den *queues* übernehmen sogenannte *senddaemons*. Da mehrere *senddaemons* existieren, werden die Daten parallel gelesen. Die gegenwärtige Implementierung erlaubt bisher nur eine statische Anzahl von *senddaemons*. Übersteigt die Größe eines Datums die vom BCM vorgegebene optimale Blockgröße, so erfolgt die Übertragung durch parallele *sendthreads*.

---

[7] Äquivalente Leistungsdaten ergeben sich auch mit leistungsschwächeren Notebooks. Minimale Systemvoraussetzungen für die mobilen Komponenten ist eine Notebook mit DX2/66 und 8MB Hauptspeicher.

Die maximale Anzahl der *sendthreads* ist hierbei, genau wie ihre Zuordnung zu den einzelnen *Daemons*, ebenfalls statisch vorgegeben. Diese statische Zuordnung hat sich in großen Szenarien als nicht optimal erwiesen. Vielmehr ist in zukünftigen Implementierungen ein dynamisches *Scheduling* notwendig, welches auf einer last- und kontextabhängigen Zuordnung der einzelnen *Daemons* und *Threads* basiert. Diese interne Problematik des *Queuing Service* ist allerdings hinreichend komplex. Gegenwärtig wird untersucht, wo bei verschiedenen Netzwerktypen die „*optimalen Parameter*" liegen.

Die Vergleichsmessungen in den Grafiken 1 und 2 verdeutlichen, daß verschiedene Faktoren die Übertragungszeit beeinflussen und stellen die Auswirkungen der parallelen Arbeitsweise dar.

Grafik 1 zeigt Übertragungszeiten von Daten unterschiedlicher Blockgrößen über ein lokales 100 VG Netzwerk. Die Messung vergleicht einen sequentiellen *Queuing Service* (1 *sendthtread* / 1 *senddaemon*) und einen parallelen QS (5 *senddaemon* mit je 3

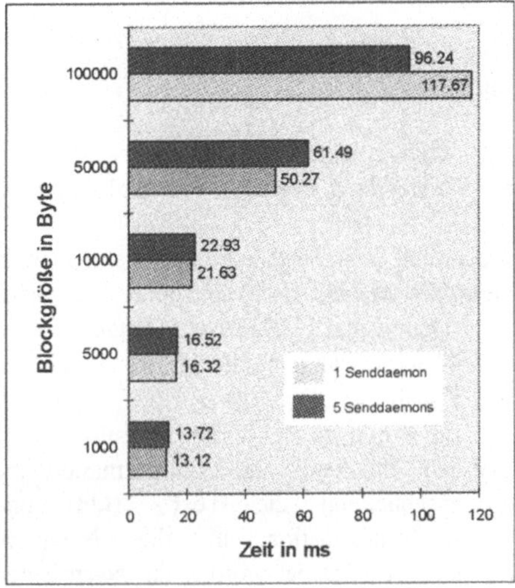

Grafik 1 - Meßwerte 100 VG

sendthreads). Es wurden jeweils 100 Dateneinheiten mit der angegebenen Blockgröße übertragen. Die Zeiten stellen den Mittelwert der Übertragungszeit für ein Datum dar. Hierbei waren zwischen sendender und empfangender Anwendung zwei QS geschaltet.

Wie Grafik 1 zeigt, sind die Unterschiede zwischen den verschieden konfigurierten Varianten im LAN nur sehr gering, da die Verzögerungszeiten hinreichend klein sind. Es kommt eher zu einem etwas ungünstigeren Leistungsverhalten des parallelen QS. Jede Übertragung verläuft transaktional gesichert. Da beim parallelen QS viele Threads wenige Daten übertragen, beeinflußt das schlechte Verhältnis Nutzdaten zu internem Verwaltungsoverhead die Übertragunsleistung im Vergleich leicht negativ. Erst bei großen Datenmengen (100 000 Byte) wirkt sich die Parallellisierung des QS auch im LAN positiv aus. Vergleichende Untersuchungen auf Mehrprozessormaschinen haben ergeben, daß bei einer echt parallelen Ausführung aller beteiligten Komponenten (incl. der Treiber für Plattencontroller und Netzwerkkarten) durch den parallelen QS auch eine deutliche Leistungssteigerung im LAN möglich ist.

Die Messungen verdeutlichen, daß für eine effiziente Informationsverteilung die Kenntnis des Übertragungsweges notwendig ist. Dies wird auch durch die in Grafik 2 dargestellten Meßergebnisse verdeutlicht. Hier wurden die

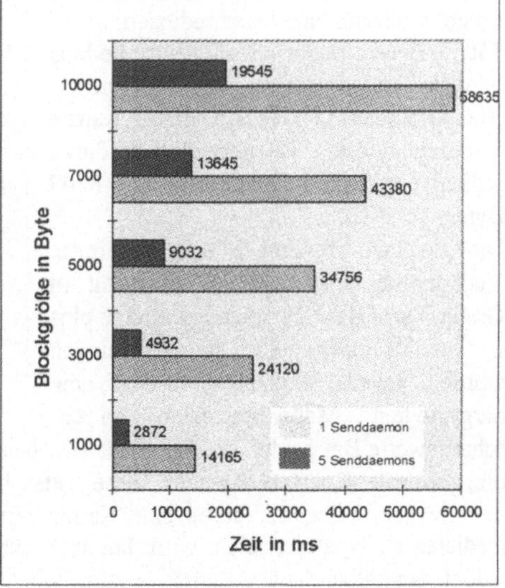

Grafik 2 - Meßwerte GSM Verbindung

selben Messungen unter Verwendung einer GSM Verbindung durchgeführt. Es ist eine deutlich geringere Übertragungszeit für den parallelen QS erkennbar. Im Gegensatz zum LAN werden hier die lange Antwortzeit und die diesbezüglichen Gegenmaßnahmen im parallelen QS auf die Übertragungsleistung deutlich erkennbar.

6.2 Leistungsvergleich MEMHS - P7 Protokoll

Zum Vergleich mit anderen Informationsverteilungssystemen wurde das Leistungsverhalten bei der Übertragung multimedialer Nachrichten unter Verwendung des P7 - Protokolls und der MEMHS Architektur gegenübergestellt.

Den Ausgangspunkt bildete eine multimediale Nachricht, bestehend aus einer Textnachricht (Dateigröße 5238 Byte), einem JPEG Bild (Dateigröße 289463 Byte) und einer Wavedatei (Dateigröße 132356 Byte, Abtastfrequenz 44 KHz, Samplingrate 16 Bit, Anzahl der Kanäle 2).

Es wurde zunächst die Textinformation, dann die Text- und Bildinformation und abschließend die Text-, Bild- und Audioinformation in die Nachricht integriert. Dabei wurden die Nachrichten zunächst über eine konventionelle Modemverbindung[8] und anschließend über eine GSM - Verbindung[9] übertragen. Grafik 3 vergleicht beim Einsatz des Modems die Übertragungszeiten bei Verwendung des P7 Protokolls und den direkten Nachrichtenempfang bei

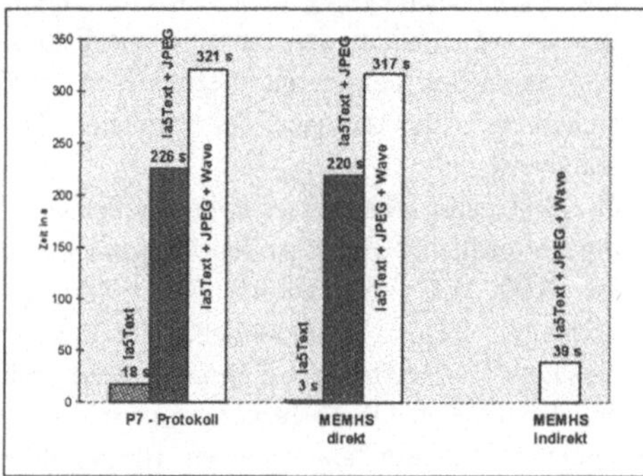

Grafik 3 - Übertragungszeiten Modemverbindung

Verwendung des MEMHS und stellt diese Zeiten der Übertragungszeit des indirekten Nachrichtenempfanges gegenüber. Die Konvertierung der Bilddatei in diesem Fall hat eine Verringerung der JPEG Qualität auf 25% zur Folge, wodurch eine Datenreduzierung auf 25055 Byte erreicht wird. Die Audiodatei wird in eine Datei mit den Parametern Abtastfrequenz 11 kHz, Anzahl der Kanäle 1, Samplingrate 8 Bit überführt. Dadurch reduziert sich die Dateigröße auf 8269 Byte.

Die gleichen Messungen erfolgten unter Verwendung einer GSM - Verbindung. In Grafik 4 sind die Übertragungszeiten e plus zu e plus dargestellt. Die Messungen wurden jeweils fünfmal wiederholt, die dargestellten Meßwerte sind Durch-

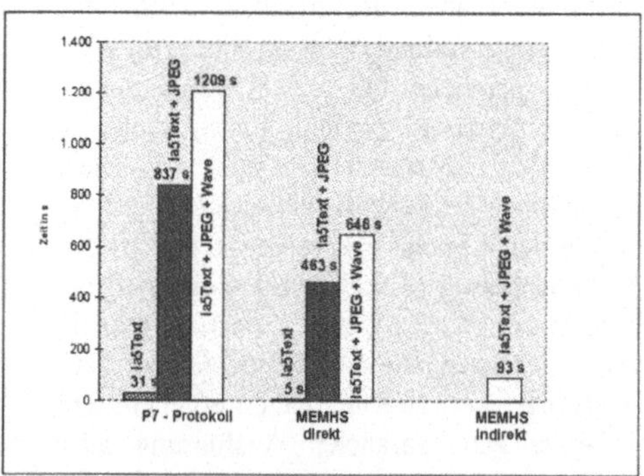

Grafik 4 - Übertragungszeiten GSM - Verbindung

schnittswerte. Bei beiden Medien zeigt sich beim Einsatz des indirekten Nachrichtenempfangs die geringste Übertragungszeit. Diese Tatsache liegt in dem bedeutend geringeren Datenumfang begründet, der durch eine Verminderung der qualitativen Eigenschaften der multimedialen Bodyparts erreicht wird. Für viele Einsatzgebiete ist eine Verringerung der Qualität jedoch eine akzeptable Alternative zum hohen Zeit- und Kostenaufwand. Im Gegensatz zur

---

[8] Micro Link, PCMCIA, Übertragungsrate 14400 bit/s
[9] E Plus, Nokia Cellular Data Card, Übertragungsrate 9600 bit/s

konventionellen Modemverbindung ist bei der GSM - Verbindung auch ein deutlicher Unterschied zwischen den Übertragungszeiten des P7 Protokolls und des direkten Nachrichtenempfangs durch das MEMHS ersichtlich.

Der *Queuing Service* berücksichtigt im Unterschied zum P7 Protokoll die große Verzögerungzeit bei der GSM - Verbindung. Es hat sich gezeigt, daß die im *Queuing Service* verwendeten Übertragungsmechanismen auch in der realen Anwendung eine deutliche Einsparung an Übertragungszeit und damit auch -kosten erbringen. In der Diskussion mit Anwendern hat sich ebenfalls ergeben, daß häufig nicht der finanzielle Aspekt im Vordergrund steht, sondern die Akzeptanz eines Systems mehr durch die erreichbaren Antwort bzw. Übertragungszeiten im mobilen Umfeld beeinflußt wird.

7 Zusammenfassung und Ausblick

In dem vorliegenden Papier wurden die Probleme bei der Off-Line Übertragung multimedialer Informationen diskutiert und die Notwendigkeit neuer Systeme für diesen Bereich begründet.

Als Ergebnis dieser Schlußfolgerungen wurde die Konzeption und Realisierung eines adaptiven Transportsystems vorgestellt, auf dessen Grundlage Leistungsmessungen vorgenommen wurden. Anhand einer Beispielanwendung wurde die Verwendbarkeit des System nachgewiesen.

Die zukünftigen Arbeiten am Lehrstuhl sind durch eine Vertiefung des erreichten Forschungsstandes gekennzeichnet. Weiterhin ist geplant, die Implementierungen anderer Forschungsgruppen über das Internet zugänglich zu machen, um somit Rückschlüsse für die weitere Arbeit zu erhalten.

Speziell für den *Queuing Service* steht zunächst die Portierung auf das Betriebssystem Digital Unix an. Die Portierung des Systems geht mit der Erweiterung und Effizienzsteigerung des *Queuing Service* einher. Letztendlich ist dann eine umfangreiche Testreihe zu den Übertragungseigenschaften des *Queuing Service* und daraus folgend die Ableitung von Schedulingstrategien geplant, welche nicht nur in der konkreten Implementierung des GISMO - Projektes zur Anwendung kommen können.

Danksagung

Diese Forschungsarbeiten sind nur durch tatkräftige Unterstützung von verschiedenen Seiten möglich. Besonderen Dank gilt der Firma *Digital Equipment Corporation* (EARC Karlsruhe), die durch ihre Zuwendungen und technische Unterstützung dieses Projekt erst ermöglichte. Weiterhin sind wir der Firma „e plus" zu Dank verpflichtet, die durch die zur Verfügungstellung von Mobiltelefonen und Modemkarten die kostenfreien Nutzung ihres zellularen Weitverkehrsnetzes zu umfangreichen Meßzwecken ermöglichte. Nicht zu vergessen sind die studentischen Mitarbeiter, die durch ihr Engagement einen hohen Beitrag zur Forschungsarbeit leisten.

Literatur

[CAG95]   Carrier, S., Georganas, N.: Practical Multimedia Electronic Mail on X.400, IEEE Multimedia, Vol. 2, No. 4, 1995, pp. 12-23

[ENC92]   Dietzen, S.: Distributed Transaction Processing with ENCINA and the OSF DCE; Transarc Corporation, 1992

[ENC93]   Transarc Corporation: ENCINA Transaction Processing, 1993

[FEG93]   Fetterman, R.L., Gupta, S.K.: Mainstream Multimedia, Van Nostrand Reinhold, New York, 1993

[FLU95]   Fluckiger, F.: Understanding networked multimedia : applications and technologie; Prentice Hall, 1995

[MIK94]   Minoli, D., Keinath, R.: Distributed Multimedia Through Broadband Communications Services, Artech House, Norwood, Massachusetts, 1994

[MOM95]   AC002: MOMENTS - Mobile Media and Entertainment Services; http://veppi.ncscst.fi:443/, 1995

[MON96]   MONET Project, http://fury.nosc.mil/, 1995

[MSS93]   Moeller, E., Scheller, A., Schürmann. G.: Der BERKOM-Teledienst , Multimedia-Mail', 1993

[MYS93]   Myles, A., Skellern, D.: Comparison of Mobile Host Protocols for IP, Internetworking: Research and Experience, Vol. 4, pp. 175-194, 1993

[OTM95]   AC034: On The Move; http://www.sics.se/~onthemove/, 1995

[PLA93]   Plattner, B.: X.400, elektronische Post und Datenkommunikation : Die Normen und ihre Anwendung; Addison-Wesley. Bonn, Paris [u.a.], 1993

[SCK95]   Schill, A., Kümmel, S.: Design and Implementation of a Support Platform for Distributed Mobile Computing;
Mobile Computing Special Issue of Distributed Systems Engineering; Sept. 1995

[SKV96]   Schill, A., Kümmel, S., Volkmann, G.: RPC over Advanced Network Technologies: Evaluation and Experiences; in Proceedings SDNE'96, 1996

[SKZ96a]   Schill, A., Kümmel, S. and Ziegert, T.: Mobility aware Multimedia X.400 email: A Sample Application Based on a Support Platform for Distributed Mobile Computing, in Proceedings of the IMC '96 Workshop for Information Visualization & Mobile Computing, 1996

[SKZ96b]   Schill, A., Kümmel, S., Schumann, K., Ziegert, T.: An adaptive data distribution system for mobile environments; in Proceedings IFIP96 World Computer Congress, Canberra, Australia, September 1996

[STN95]   Steinmetz, R.; Nahrstedt, K.: Multimedia Computing, Communications and Applications; Prentice Hall, Englewood Cliffs, NJ, 1995

[VAU94]   Vaughan, T.: Multimedia: Making It Work; Osborne McGrew-Hill, Berkley, California, 1994

[WOH95]   Wolf, B.; Hall, W.: Multimedia Pedagogues: Interactive Systems for Teaching and Learning; IEEE Computer, Vol. 28, No. 5, May 1995, pp 74 - 80

[X400]   CCITT Recommendation X.400 Series: Data Communication Networks, Message Handling Systems, 1988

Überblick über die europäische Standardisierung von Funk-LANs [1]

W.Franz, M.Aldinger, M.Wolf

Daimler-Benz AG, Forschung und Technik, F3K/K

Wilhelm-Runge-Str. 11

89081 Ulm

Tel. :   (0731) 505-2125   Fax.:   (0731) 505-4110

email: (franz, aldinger, michael.wolf)@dbag.ulm.DaimlerBenz.COM

Zusammenfassung

Dieser Beitrag gibt einen Überblick über den Stand der europäischen Standardisierung von Funk-LANs. Es wird auf die HIPERLAN-Familie eingegangen, die derzeit vom ETSI spezifiziert wird. Der HIPERLAN 1-Standard wird ausführlich in seiner Konzeption und Architektur erläutert. Mittels Simulationsergebnissen wird eine Leistungsabschätzung des Systems vorgenommen und begründet, warum sich dieser Standard nicht für die Übertragung von ATM-Zellen eignet. Für die HIPERLAN Typen 2, 3 und 4, die als mobiles Zugangsnetz zu ATM-Netzen, Wireless Local Loop bzw. für die breitbandige Übertragung von ATM-Zellen konzipiert werden, wird der derzeitige Stand der Standardisierung erläutert.

1 Einführung

Seit 1992 arbeitet das ETSI[2] an der Spezifikation von Standards für Funk-LANs unter dem Titel „High Performance Radio Local Area Network" (HIPERLAN). Die Ausrichtung auf diese Thematik ist nach Abschluß der Arbeiten für zellulare Mobiltelefonnetze (GSM[3], [1], [2]) und privat betriebener, auf Sprachübertragung ausgelegter Funksysteme (DECT[4], [3]) eine folgerichtige Weiterentwicklung der Funktechnologie. Dies gilt umsomehr, als im lokalen Bereich die klassischen Endgeräte der LANs mit dem Aufkommen leistungsstarker Notebooks und tragbarer Rechner immer stärker mobil werden. Hinzu kommt der allgemeine Trend zur multimedialen Kommunikation, welcher auch die LAN-Technologien beeinflussen wird. Dies wird nicht zuletzt mit dem Aufkommen der ATM[5]-Technologie, der ansteigenden multimedialen Kommunikation im ISDN[6] und der Durchdringung des Internets mit dem „World Wide Web" sichtbar. Daher wurde bei der HIPERLAN-Standardisierung durch die ETSI Arbeitsgruppe RES[7] 10 die Unterstützung von zeitkritischen Diensten von Beginn an mitverfolgt.

Wesentliches Ziel der HIPERLAN-Aktivitäten ist die Spezifikation universeller Funk-LANs, die die heutigen lokalen Netze ergänzen und mobile Endgeräte verbinden bzw. an Festnetze anbinden. Parallel zu den Arbeiten zu HIPERLAN wurde von der IEEE[8]-Arbeitsgruppe

---

[1] Diese Arbeit ist gefördert im Rahmen des BMBF-Förderschwerpunktes „Breitbandige Mobilkommunikation für Multimedia auf ATM-Basis"

[2] European Telecommunications Standards Institute
[3] Global Systems for Mobile Communications
[4] Digital European Cordless Telecommunications
[5] Asynchronous Transfer Mode
[6] Integrated Services Digital Network
[7] Radio Equipment and Systems
[8] Institute of Electrical and Electronic Engineers

802.11 ebenfalls ein drahtloses LAN unter dem Titel „Wireless LAN" spezifiziert ([12], [16]), was die Aktualität dieser Thematik unterstreicht.

Im Laufe der Arbeiten zu HIPERLAN wurde erkannt, daß es unter Berücksichtigung wirtschaftlicher Aspekte nur schwer möglich ist, ein Funk-LAN zu realisieren, das wirklich universell und in den verschiedensten Anwendungsgebieten gleich gut einsetzbar ist und zudem günstige Kostenstrukturen für Entwicklung und Produktion erlaubt. Daher wurde Anfang 1996 nach Erarbeitung des ursprünglichen HIPERLAN-Standards (Typ 1) beschlossen, für verschiedene Anwendungszenarien verschiedene HIPERLAN-Spezifikationen zu definieren. Für diese wurden die Bezeichnungen HIPERLAN Typ 1, 2, 3 bzw. 4 eingeführt.

Alle diese Funk-Systeme werden die in Europa ausgewiesenen HIPERLAN-Frequenzbänder verwenden. Im Vergleich zum ursprünglichen HIPERLAN-Draft wird neuerdings insbesondere der aufkommenden ATM-Technologie Rechnung getragen. So werden HIPERLAN Typ 2, 3 und 4 ATM-Netze ergänzen, indem sie für verschiedene Einsatzszenarien die verbindungsorientierte Übertragung von ATM-Zellen bzw. den Zugang von mobilen Endgeräten zu ATM-Netzen ermöglichen. Diese Ausrichtung auf die Ergänzung der ATM-Technologie um drahtlose Netze erfolgte parallel zum Aufkommen neuer europäisch geförderter Forschungsprojekte wie „WAND"[9], oder dem Nachfolger des RACE II-Projekts „MBS"[10] ([15]) namens „SAMBA"[11], welche Grundlagenforschung für drahtlose ATM-Systeme betreiben. Eines der Ziele dieser Projekte ist das Einbringen der Ergebnisse in die HIPERLAN-Standardisierung. Auf nationaler Ebene wird seit 1996 das Projekt „ATMmobil" vom „BMBF"[12] gefördert, das ebenfalls die Weiterentwicklung der drahtlosen ATM-Technologie verfolgt. Die Ergebnisse von „ATMmobil" werden auch in die Standardisierung der HIPERLAN-Familie eingebracht. In diesem Projekt wird neben der Ausrichtung auf lokale Netze auch die Weiterentwicklung von öffentlichen zellularen Netzen und des drahtlosen Teilnehmerzugangs zu öffentlichen Netzen erforscht. Nicht zuletzt hat auch das ATM-Forum mit der Gründung einer neuen Arbeitsgruppe zur Standardisierung von Schnittstellen für drahtlose ATM-Systeme diese Thematik aufgegriffen.

Die Arbeiten der ETSI RES 10-Gruppe im Jahr 1996 umfaßten einerseits die Fertigstellung und Verabschiedung des HIPERLAN 1-Standards ([5], [6]) und hierbei insbesondere die Festlegung einer Spezifikation für den „Conformance Test" dieser Systeme. Für die anderen HIPERLAN Typen wurde an der Definition der Anwendungsszenarien und Systemarchitekturen ([4]) gearbeitet, welche die technischen Randbedingungen dieser Systeme festlegt.

Im weiteren Verlauf dieses Beitrags werden in Kapitel 2 der derzeitige Stand (4. Quartal 1996) in der Erarbeitung der Anwendungsfelder der verschiedenen HIPERLAN-Ausprägungen dargestellt. Im dritten Kapitel wird der HIPERLAN 1-Standard beschrieben. In Kapitel 4 werden Simulationsergebnisse zur Leistungsabschätzung von HIPERLAN 1 vorgestellt. Der Beitrag schließt mit einer Zusammenfassung in Kapitel 5.

2 Eigenschaften der HIPERLAN-Familie

In diesem Abschnitt werden die Eigenschaften und Anwendungsgebiete der einzelnen HIPERLAN-Typen beschrieben. Während der Standard für HIPERLAN 1 mittlerweile verabschiedet ist, wurde für die anderen Typen des HIPERLAN-Standards eine Richtlinie spezifiziert, welche die Anforderungen und die prinzipielle Architektur dieser Systeme festlegt ([4]). Diese Richtlinie dient als Basis für die weitere Entwicklung funktioneller Standards und

---

[9] Wireless ATM Network Demonstrator
[10] Mobile Broadband System
[11] System for Advanced Mobile Broadband Application
[12] Bundesministerium für Bildung, Wissenschaft, Forschung und Technologie

Spezifikationen. Tabelle 1 gibt die darin charakterisierten Anwendungsfelder der vier HIPERLAN-Typen wieder.

Typ	Anwendung:	Beschreibung:
1	Drahtloses LAN	Drahtlose Ergänzung bzw. Erweiterung von LANs
2	„Short Range Wireless ATM Access"	Zellulares Zugangsnetz zu leitungsgebundenen ATM-Systemen. Unterstützung von ATM-Diensteklassen.
3	„Remote Wireless Access to ATM"	Punkt-zu-Mehrpunktverbindungen auf ATM-Basis. Unterstützung von ATM-Diensteklassen.
4	„Wireless Interconnection"	ATM-kompatible drahtlose Verbindungen von Kommunikationsnetzen und Endgeräten

Tabelle 1. Klassifizierung der Typen der HIPERLAN-Familie.

Im weiteren Verlauf dieses Kapitels werden in Abschnitt 2.1 die für HIPERLAN in Europa zur Verfügung stehenden Frequenzbereiche vorgestellt. Anschließend werden prinzipielle Problemfelder für die Erweiterung der ATM-Technologie auf Funksysteme angesprochen. Die Abschnitte 2.3 bis 2.6 beschreiben die Eigenschaften der einzelnen Typen der HIPERLAN-Familie. In der Tabelle in Abschnitt 2.7 werden diese Eigenschaften zusammengefaßt.

2.1 Frequenzbereiche

Die von der CEPT empfohlenen Frequenzbereiche für HIPERLAN-Systeme liegen bei 5 und 17 GHz. Das HIPERLAN 1 zugeordnete Frequenzband beginnt bei 5,15 GHz und endet bei 5,30 GHz ([9]). Das 150 MHz breite Band im 5 GHz-Bereich wurde in 5 Trägerfrequenzkanäle unterteilt. Die unteren drei Trägerfrequenzkanäle zwischen 5,15 und 5,25 GHz sind für HIPERLAN-Systeme in Europa prinzipiell nutzbar, das restliche Band hingegen ist nicht in allen europäischen Ländern verfügbar. Ursprünglich war vorgesehen, daß die vier HIPER-LAN-Typen dieselben Frequenzbänder nutzen sollten. Dies kann zu unerwünschten Interferenzen zwischen den Systemen führen. Um dies zu vermeiden, bemüht sich ETSI RES10 um eine Erweiterung der zugeteilten Frequenzen oberhalb 5,30 GHz. Der Frequenzbereich bei 17 GHz umfaßt insgesamt 200 MHz zwischen 17,1 und 17,3 GHz. Der jetzige Entwurf ([4]) sieht vor, daß HIPERLAN 1, 2 und 3 das Frequenzband bei 5 GHz verwenden und HIPERLAN 4 das Band bei 17 GHz nutzt.

2.2 Zur Problematik von drahtlosen ATM-Systemen

Wie aus Tabelle 1 entnommen werden kann, werden die HIPERLAN-Typen 2, 3 und 4 drahtlose Erweiterungen von ATM-Netzen realisieren, d.h. sie werden standardisierte ATM-Schnittstellen verwenden und Dienstgüteanforderungen der ATM-Diensteklassen „Constant Bitrate" (CBR), „Realtime Variable Bitrate" (RT-VBR), Non-Realtime Variable Bitrate (NRT-VBR), „Available Bitrate" (ABR) und „Unspecified Bitrate" (UBR) erfüllen. Eine prinzipielle Problematik hierzu ist in den Abbildungen 1 und 2 dargestellt. Während die Dienstgütegarantien in herkömmlichen ATM-Netzen in den Adaptionsschichten und spätestens auf der ATM-Schicht berücksichtigt werden, müssen Dienstgüteparameter auch auf Ebene des Funkkanalzugriffs zur Verfügung stehen und umgesetzt werden. In leitungsgebundenen ATM-Systemen wird unterhalb der ATM-Schicht keinerlei Vermittlung und Vielfachzugriff durchgeführt, da dedizierte Punkt-zu-Punkt-Verbindungen zwischen den ATM-Vermittlungen und den Endgeräten zur Verfügung stehen. Im Falle einer Übertragung auf einem Funkanal jedoch muß unterhalb der ATM-Schicht ein Vielfachzugriff zwischen verschiedenen drahtlos angebundenen ATM-Systemen durchgeführt werden. Hinzu kommt, daß die für eine Verbindung vereinbarten Dienstgüten auch im Falle mobiler Endgeräte und entsprechend zeitvarianter Netztopologien aufrecht erhalten werden müssen. Dieses erfordert ein leistungsfähiges Mobilitätsmanagement mit entsprechenden Handover- und Roamingmechanismen.

Weitere Problemfelder ergeben sich aus den, verglichen mit leitungsbasierten Systemen, hohen Bitfehlerraten und dem daraus entstehenden Zwang zur Wiederholung fehlerhafter Zellen unter engen Randbedingungen der Übertragungszeiten. Weiterhin stellen die ATM-Zellen mit der Länge von 53 Byte für Funkkommunikation eine relativ kleine Größe dar. In herkömmlichen Systemen erfordert jeder Kanalzugriff wegen der Sende/Empfangs-Umschaltzeiten bzw. den Präambeln zur Kanalausmessung und Synchronisation des Empfängers einen Overhead. Je kleiner das Paket ist, desto ungüstiger wird der Nutzungsgrad. Am Beispiel von HIPERLAN 1 wird in Kapitel 3 die Leistungseffizienz bei verschiedenen Paketgrößen beschrieben.

Neben diesen wesentlichsten Problemfeldern zur Protokollarchitektur ergeben sich eine Vielzahl von Fragestellungen aus der Übertragungstechnik, auf die hier nicht eingegangen wird. Eine ausführlichere Diskussion hierzu findet man z.B. in [13] und [14].

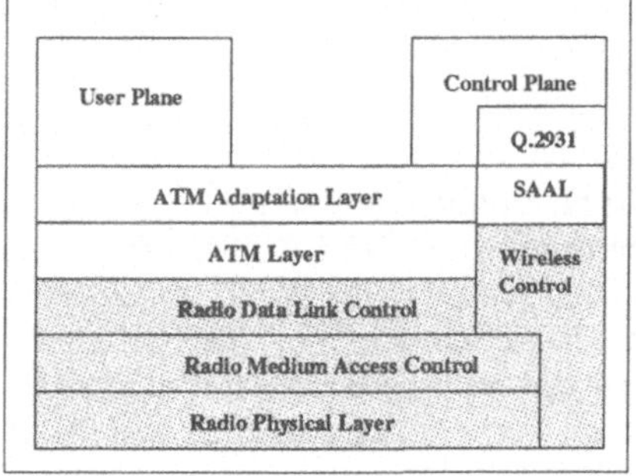

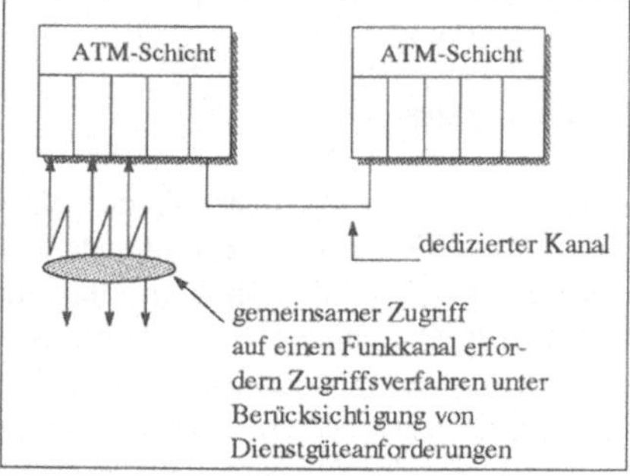

Abbildung 1. Schichtenstruktur von WATM-Systemen. Die Garantie von Dienstgütekriterien auf dem Funkanal erfordert die Übertragung von Signalisierungsinformationen in die Schichten des Funksystems.

Abbildung 2. Zugriffsproblematik auf den Funkkanal. Während in leitungsgebundenen ATM-Systemen jede ATM-Instanz über einen dedizierten Kanal verbunden ist, müssen bei Funksystemen mehrere solcher physikalischer Verbindungen gemultiplext werden. Dabei müssen die Dienstgüten der virtuellen ATM-Verbindungen mit berücksichtigt werden.

2.3 HIPERLAN 1 (ETS 300 652)

HIPERLAN Typ 1 ist ein privat betriebenes drahtloses LAN, das einerseits unabhängig von jeglicher fester Infrastruktur als „Ad-Hoc"-Netz betrieben werden kann. Andererseits unterstützt HIPERLAN 1 auch den Zugang zu herkömmlichen leitungsgebundenen lokalen Netzen. Mehrere HIPERLAN 1 können räumlich parallel betrieben werden. Dabei wird die zur Verfügung stehende Bandbreite zwischen diesen Systemen ohne Koordination durch die Nutzer aufgeteilt.

Es wird sowohl Punkt-zu-Punkt, als auch Punkt-zu-Mehrpunkt-Kommunikation unterstützt. Das Zugriffsverfahren ist dezentral, unterstützt Prioritäten in den Paketen und arbeitet auch wenn versteckte Stationen auftreten. Es zeigt gute Leistungsergebnisse, unabhängig von der Anzahl der am Zugriffsverfahren beteiligten Stationen. Forwarding (siehe Abschnitt 3.1) ist standardisiert und erlaubt Datenübertragung auch in teilvermaschten Topologien.

HIPERLAN 1 kennt keine Verbindungen. Alle Daten werden verbindungslos, d.h. auf Paketbasis übertragen. Zeitkritische Dienste werden unterstützt, indem die Paketlebenszeit und Nutzerpriorität beim Kanalzugriff berücksichtigt werden. Die verbindungslose Struktur bietet keine Abbildung von Dienstgüteanforderungen einzelner Anwendungen oder isolierter Verbindungen auf die Prioritätsvergabe. Daher sind für Dienstgüteanforderungen von Verbindungen oder Anwendungstypen keine garantierten Größen, sondern nur stark vom Anwendungsszenario abhängige statistische Aussagen möglich.

HIPERLAN 1-Endgeräte sind im allgemeinen mobil. Die Funkreichweite von bis zu 50 m wird mit omnidirektionalen Antennen erreicht. Der HIPERLAN 1-Standard wurde im November 1996 verabschiedet ([5]). Die Spezifikation zur Durchführung von „Conformance Tests" liegt derzeit (November 1996) den ETSI-Mitgliedsländern zur Kommentierung vor.

2.4 HIPERLAN 2 („Short Range Wireless ATM Access")

HIPERLAN Typ 2 wird ein Zugangsnetz für mobile und stationäre Terminals zu ATM-Infrastrukturen über Basisstationen („Access Points") realisieren. Dieses Zugangsnetz verbindet mobile Endgeräte mit der leitungsgebundenen Infrastruktur. Ziel ist es, die Übertragung von ATM-Zellen über HIPERLAN 2 aus Sicht der Anwender transparent zu realisieren. Das heißt, die Dienste und Dienstgütegarantien, die leitungsgebundenen ATM-Netze derzeit und zukünftig bieten, müssen auch von HIPERLAN 2 garantiert werden. HIPERLAN 2 wird zentral organisiert sein. Wesentliche Protokollelemente, insbesondere der Kanalzugriff werden von den Basisstationen zentral gesteuert. Somit wird dieser Standard Merkmale von zellularen Netzen aufweisen, wie z.B. Funktionalitäten wie Handover oder Roaming beinhalten. Die notwendigen Erweiterungen in der Signalisierung hierzu werden durch die neu gegründete Wireless-Gruppe des ATM-Forums spezifiziert. Als Bitraten werden Raten von über 20 MBit/s angestrebt. Bei der Funkreichweite wird von einer Größenordnung von 50 m ausgegangen. Diese soll mit omnidirektionalen Antennen erreicht werden.

2.5 HIPERLAN 3 („Remote Wireless Access to ATM")

Dieser Standard wird eine ATM-basierte Punkt-zu-Mehrpunkt-Kommunikation zwischen stationären Endgeräten spezifizieren. Ein typisches Anwendungsfeld hierfür sind funkbasierte Anschlußnetze, die die Verbindung zwischen lokalen und öffentlichen Netzen herstellen („Wireless Local Loop"). Aufgrund des Aufkommens der leitungsgebundenen ATM-Technologie und der steigenden Nachfrage nach Diensten mit hohen Bitraten wird für diese Systeme ein großer Markt prognostiziert. Die Netzstruktur entspricht der von HIPERLAN 2 mit einigen wesentlichen Unterschieden. Die Funkreichweite von bis zu 5 km wird durch den Einsatz gerichteter Antennen auf Kosten der Mobilität der Endgeräte erreicht. Die Endgeräte werden im Gegensatz zu HIPERLAN 2 als stationär bzw. quasistationär angenommen. Die Datenrate von größer 20 MBit/s kann von den auf einen einzigen Konzentrationspunkt zugreifenden Nutzern geteilt werden.

2.6 HIPERLAN 4 („Wireless Interconnection")

Als Einsatzfeld von HIPERLAN 4-Systemen wird die Kommunikation zwischen drahtgebundener Infrastruktur bzw. festen Endgeräten mittels dedizierten Punkt-zu-Punkt-Verbindungen angesehen. Benötigt werden hierzu hohe Bitraten und große Kanalkapazitäten. HIPERLAN 4 bietet Punkt-zu-Punkt-Verbindungen mit Datenraten bis zu 155 MBit/s über Entfernungen von bis zu 150 m. Hierzu werden direktionale Antennen verwendet. Die Endsysteme werden als stationär oder quasistationär angenommen. Als Endgeräte werden einzelne ATM-Arbeitsstationen oder Schnittstellensysteme zu Festnetzen angestrebt. HIPERLAN 4-Systeme werden das Frequenzband bei 17 GHz nutzen.

2.7 Tabellarische Zusammenfassung der Eigenschaften der HIPERLAN-Familie

	HIPERLAN 1	HIPERLAN 2	HIPERLAN 3	HIPERLAN 4
Anwendung	drahtloses LAN	Zugangsnetz zu ATM-Festnetz	Punkt-zu-Mehrpunkt ATM-Verb.	Punkt-zu-Punkt ATM-Verb.
Trägerfrequenz	5,15-5,25 (5,3) GHz (eine Erweiterung wird derzeit geprüft)			17,2-17,3 GHz
Topologie	dezentral organisiertes Adhoc-Netz	zellulare, zentrale Struktur	Punkt-zu-Mehrpunkt	Punkt-zu-Punkt
Antenne	omnidirektional	omnidirektional	direktional	direktional
Funkreichweite	50 m	50 - 100 m	5000 m	150 m
Dienstgütegarantien	keine, statistisches Verhalten	ATM Diensteklassen RT-VBR, NRT-VBR, CBR, ABR, UBR		
Betreiber	privat	privat/öffentl.	privat/öffentl.	privat
Mobilität	< 10 m/s	< 10 m/s	stationär, quasistationär	
Schnittstellen	konventionelle LAN	ATM-Netze	ATM-Netze	ATM-Netze
Datenrate	< 20 MBit/s	>20 MBit/s	> 20 MBit/s	155 MBit/s
Power Conservation	ja	ja	nicht zwingend	nicht zwingend
Verzögerung von Zellen (Varianz)	-	< 5 ms, (< 1ms)	< 5 ms, (< 1ms)	< 5 ms, (< 1ms)
Zellenrate mit nicht detektierten Fehlern		$< 5x\ 10^{-14}$	$< 5x\ 10^{-14}$	$< 5x\ 10^{-14}$
Produktreife	1998	2000 (geschätzt)	nach 2000	nach 2000

Tabelle 2. Eigenschaften der HIPERLAN-Typen

3 HIPERLAN 1

3.1 Grundprinzipien

Der wesentliche Leitgedanke beim Entwurf von HIPERLAN 1 war die Vorstellung, bestehende lokale Netze um ein Funknetz zu erweitern und den Nutzern des Funk-LANs dabei heute gängige Leistungsmerkmale zu bieten. Darüber hinaus sollte HIPERLAN 1 als „Ad Hoc"-Netz betrieben werden können, d.h. unabhängig von bestehenden Infrastrukturen und ohne planerische Vorleistung. Dieser Ansatz führte zu dem Konzept der direkten Kommunikation der Endgeräte ohne Basisstation und zu einer völlig dezentralen Struktur für die Netzorganisation und insbesondere für den Kanalzugriff. Eine Konsequenz dieses Ansatzes ist, daß keine Vollvermaschung des Kommunikationsnetzes vorausgesetzt werden kann. In dezentral organisierten Netzen müssen die Datenpakete an Stationen, die sich nicht in direkter Reichweite befinden über andere Mobilstationen, die mit Relaisfunktionalität ausgestattet sind, weitergegeben werden („Forwarding"). Dabei wird zwischen Knoten, die diese Relaisfunktion unterstützen („Forwarder") und anderen („Non-Forwarder") unterschieden. Die Forwarder bauen durch den Austausch von Steuernachrichten, den sogenannten „Topology Change PDU[13] („TC-PDU"); eine Datenbank auf, anhand derer die Wegefindung durchgeführt wird. Diese TC-PDU werden ausgetauscht, wenn ein Forwarder eine Topologieänderung in seiner Umgebung detektiert. Jeder Knoten, der seinen Kommunikationspartner nicht direkt sieht, sendet sein Datenpaket an einen Forwarder, der das Paket dann weitervermittelt.

Die netzweite Kommunikation wird somit auf zwei Ebenen realisiert. Direkte Kommunikation zwischen zwei Knoten, wenn sich diese in Kommunikationsreichweite befinden und Weitergabe der Pakete an einen in Funkreichweite befindlichen Forwarder. Dieser reicht dann das Paket innerhalb der Forwarder-Ebene solange weiter, bis ein Forwarder Verbindung zum letztendlichen Adressaten besitzt. Damit die HIPERLAN 1-Knoten die anderen Stationen in Funkreichweite kennenlernen, werden sogenannte „Hello"-Pakete periodisch an alle Funknachbarn im Broadcast-Modus gesendet.

Wie bereits in Kapitel 1 angedeutet, unterstützt HIPERLAN neben dem für heutige LANs typischen asynchronen Datenaustausch auch zeitkritische Datenübertragungen. In Anlehnung an die verbindungslose Übertragungsstruktur in den meisten der heute eingesetzten LAN-Technologien, wie z.B. dem Ethernet, arbeitet auch HIPERLAN 1 verbindungslos. Um die zeitlichen Randbedingungen zu erfüllen, wird den Datenpaketen eine Lebenszeit zugeordnet, welche die Priorität der Übertragung bestimmt.

Da das Medium Funk gegenüber Abhören nicht gesichert ist, sieht der Standard einen Verschlüsselungsmechanismus vor, der zumindest ein zu leitungsgebundenen lokalen Netzen vergleichbares Sicherheitsniveau gewährleisten soll.

HIPERLAN 1 verwendet zwei Verfahren zur Verringerung des Leistungsverbrauchs. Diese zielen daraufhin ab, die Zeitintervalle, in denen die empfangenen Signale dekodiert und entzerrt werden müssen, zu verringern. Unter Entzerren versteht man die Kompensation von Signalverzerrungen durch Mehrwegeempfang. Die hierzu eingesetzten Algorithmen sind rechenintensiv und energieaufwendig, da sie ständig beim Empfang durchgeführt werden müssen.

Im ersten Verfahren werden Zeiten definiert, in denen eine Station nicht empfangsbereit ist. Diese „Schlafzeiten" werden den Nachbarstationen mitgeteilt. Sendende Stationen halten solange ihre Daten zurück, bis der Empfänger wieder empfangsbereit ist. Dieser optionale Algorithmus wird als Schlafmodus bezeichnet.

Das zweite Verfahren, zur Reduktion des Energieverbrauchs, zielt darauf ab, daß aktive Stationen nur dann Pakete entzerren, wenn diese für sie bestimmt sind. Die HIPERLAN 1-Stationen können mit diesem Verfahren erkennen, ob ein Paket an sie adressiert ist, ohne den Inhalt des Datenpaketes zu dekodieren und die Schicht 2-Adresse zu bestimmen. Hierzu sieht der HIPERLAN-Standard vor, zu Beginn eines jeden Datenpakets in einem sogenannten „Low Bitrate Header" (LBH) mit einer niedrigeren Datenrate (LBR) einen Indikator zu senden, anhand dessen die Stationen mit sehr großer Wahrscheinlichkeit ohne Entzerren bestimmen können, ob das Paket an sie adressiert ist . Ist dies der Fall, so wird das Paket entzerrt und dekodiert, ansonsten jedoch nicht. Dann wird der Entzerralgorithmus nicht durchlaufen und Energie gespart. Die niedrige Bitrate kann ohne Entzerren genügend sicher dekodiert werden. Sie beträgt 1,4704 MBit/s im Vergleich zu den 23,5294 MBit/s der Standard-Bitrate. Als Indikator für die Empfangsstation sind 9 Bit im LBR-Paketkopf reserviert. In dem Adreß-

---

[13] Protocol Data Unit

raum von 512 Stationen ist eine eindeutige Zuordnung nicht möglich, so daß eine Restwahrscheinlichkeit bleibt, daß eine Station ein nicht an sie gerichtetes Paket dekodiert. Anhand der für den Empfänger maßgeblichen Schicht 2-Adressierung stellt die Station in diesem Fall fest, daß das Paket nicht für sie ist und verwirft es. Den Großteil der Pakete wird die Station jedoch nicht dekodieren und somit ihren Leistungsverbrauch senken.

Die Kanalkodierierung in HIPERLAN Typ1 erfolgt durch einen Blockcode (31,26 BCH) mit Interleaving zum Auseinanderbrechen von Fehlerbündeln. Auf die Charakteristik der Übertragungsschicht und das Format der Daten- und Steuerpakete wird an dieser Stelle nicht weiter eingegangen und auf [5] verwiesen. Die wichtigsten Parameter sind in Tabelle 3 zusammengefaßt.

Frequenzbereich	5,15 ... 5,3 GHz (in einigen Ländern: ...5,25 GHz)
Sendeleistung	max. 1 Watt, Standard spezifiziert drei Sende- und Empfangsklassen mit unterschiedlicher Leistung bzw. Empfindlichkeit
Funkreichweite	ca. 50 m
Stationsgeschwindigkeit	max. 10 m/s
Modulationsverfahren	GMSK, Bandbreite-Zeitprodukt 0,3
Entzerrung	ja, das Verfahren ist nicht standardisiert.
„Carrier Sense"-Grenzwert	adaptiv, wird anhand der empfangenen Energie durchgeführt.
Bitrate (Funkschnittstelle)	23,5294 Mbit/s (Übertragung von Nutz- und Steuerdaten)
„Low Bitrate"	1,4706 MBit/s (für LBR-Header und Quittierung)

Tabelle 3. Zusammenfassung von Daten zur Übertragungsschicht von HIPERLAN 1

3.2 Architektur

Um die Anbindung von HIPERLAN-Systemen an die vorhandene Rechner- und Kommunikationsinfrastruktur so einfach wie möglich zu gestalten, wurde die Architektur von HIPERLAN 1 an das Referenzmodell der heutigen klassischen lokalen Netze angegliedert. Dieses umfaßt die Übertragungs- und Datensicherungsschicht des OSI-Referenzmodells ([7]). Die Datensicherungsschicht ist dabei unterteilt in die sogenannte „Logical Link Control"- Schicht (LLC) und die „Medium Access Control"-Schicht (MAC). Die MAC-Schicht unterscheidet heute gängige LANs wie Ethernet-, Token Ring- oder FDDI-Netze. Die LLC-Schicht ist für alle LAN-Typen definiert. HIPERLAN orientiert sich an diesem Konzept, indem die Standardisierung sich auf die Übertragungsschicht und die klassische MAC-Schicht beschränkt und die standardisierte Schnittstelle zur LLC-Schicht beibehält.

Um die im vorigen Abschnitt genannten Funktionen wie Forwarding, Verschlüsselung bzw. Energiesparfunktionalitäten, die eigentlich in höheren Schichten anzusiedeln sind, trotzdem unterstützen zu können, wurde die Funktionalität der MAC-Schicht erweitert und in eine HIPERLAN-MAC- und HIPERLAN-„Channel Access"-Schicht unterteilt. In Abbildung 3 ist diese Systemarchitektur von HIPERLAN 1 dargestellt.

3.2.1 Datentransfer und Kanalzugriff zeitkritischer bzw. nichtzeitkritischer Pakete

Wie zu Beginn dieses Artikels dargestellt, wird HIPERLAN sowohl asynchronen Datenverkehr, als auch die Übertragung von Diensten, die zeitliche Anforderungen an die zu übertragenen Datenpakete stellen, unterstützen. Zu diesem Zweck wurden im HIPERLAN-Architekturmodell Regeln zum Datentransfer eingeführt. Dabei werden zwei Schwerpunkte unterschieden. Dies ist einmal die Definition eines Priorisierungsalgorithmus, der bestimmt, mit welcher der 5 Prioritäten Pakete auf den Funkkanal zugreifen. Zum zweiten ist dies die Durchführung des Kanalzugriffs, bei dem diese Prioritäten berücksichtigt werden.

Um dies zu ermöglichen, wurde keine feste Vergabe der Prioritäten zu definierten Anwendungen vorgesehen, die Prioritäten werden vielmehr dynamisch vergeben. Prinzip der Zuordnung der Prioritäten ist, daß die Priorität umso höher wird, je näher die Pakete an ihrer Verfallszeit sind. Zu diesem Zweck wird für jedes Paket individuell von der Anwendung eine Lebenszeit vorgegeben. Innerhalb der Datenpakete wird die Restlebenszeit vermerkt und mit übertragen. Unter der normalisierten Restlebenszeit („Normalized Residual MSDU Lifetime, NRL") wird die Restlebenszeit des Pakets dividiert durch die Anzahl der Übertragungen (bei Forwarding) verstanden. Dieser Wert bildet die Grundlage zur Bestimmung der Priorität des Kanalzugriffs. Weiterhin kann der HIPERLAN-Nutzer die sogenannte „Benutzerpriorität" des Paketes als „Normal" oder „Hoch" kennzeichnen. Die Kanalzugriffspriorität ergibt sich aus den Parametern normalisierte Restlebenszeit und Benutzerpriorität anhand der in Tabelle 4 dargestellten Zuordnungsvorschrift. Man kann aus dieser Tabelle erkennen, daß alle Pakete, unabhängig von den Anforderungen der Anwendungen, die jeweils höchste Priorität in Abhängigkeit von der Benutzerpriorität erlangen können. Dies bedeutet, daß einerseits aufgrund des verbindungslosen Ansatzes nicht zwischen Dienstgüteanforderungen einzelner Verbindungen unterschieden werden kann. Zum anderen werden bei hohen Systemlasten und den dann auftretenden Wartezeiten in den HIPERLAN-Stationen alle Pakete der Benutzerpriorität „Hoch" untereinander gleichberechtigt konkurrieren, so daß mit diesem Verfahren keine festen Dienstgütekriterien garantiert werden können. Auch für zeitkritische Anwendungen tritt ein „Best-Effort"-Verhalten auf.

Hält eine Station zu Beginn eines Zugriffszyklus mehrere Pakete, so wählt sie dasjenige mit der kleinsten NRL in der höchsten Prioritätsklasse aus und konkurriert mit den anderen HIPERLAN-Stationen um den Kanalzugriff. Es ist zu bemerken, daß die Station bis auf die Namen der in Reichweite befindlichen Stationen keinerlei Informationen über die anderen

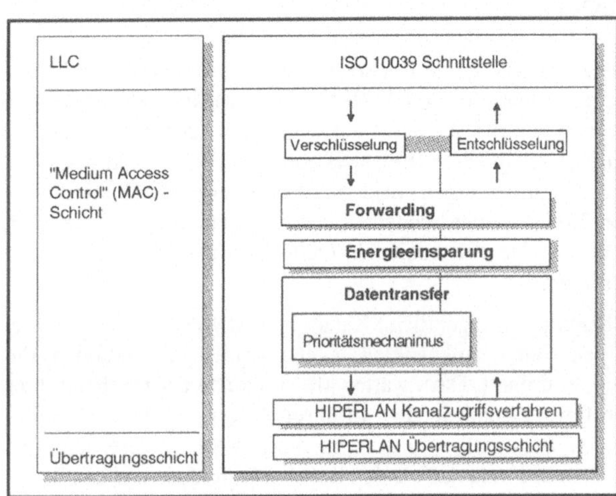

Abbildung 3. Systemarchitektur von HIPERLAN. Im Vergleich zur MAC-Schicht konventioneller LANs umfaßt HIPERLAN 1 (rechts) eine Reihe von zusätzlichen Funktionalitäten.

Stationen hat. Sie hat insbesondere keine Kenntnis davon, wieviele Stationen sich an der Konkurrenz um den Kanalzugriff beteiligen und welche Prioritäten die Pakete der anderen Stationen besitzen.

3.2.2 Kanalzugriff in HIPERLAN 1

Als Kanalzugriffsverfahren für HIPERLAN wurde das sogenannte „Elimination Yield Non-Preemptive Priority Multiple Access"-Verfahren („EY-NPMA") entwickelt. Dieses erlaubt ausschließlich einen konfliktbasierten Zugriff auf den Funkkanal nach vorherigem „Carrier Sense". Das EY-NPMA-Verfahren ist anhand eines Beispiels von 5 Stationen in Abbildung 4 beschrieben. Als Abszisse ist die Zeit aufgetragen. In dem Beispiel überträgt Station 1 zu Beginn ein Datenpaket an Station 2. Nach einer Schutzzeit bestätigt Station 2 den korrekten Empfang des Datenpakets, indem sie eine entsprechende Quittung unter Verwendung der niedrigen Datenrate an Station 1 sendet.

Nach einer weiteren Schutzzeit beginnt der eigentliche Kanalzugriffszyklus, wobei die drei Stationen „3", "4" und „5" um den Kanal konkurrieren. Zuerst werden die Stationen, die nicht die höchste Priorität besitzen, eliminiert. Dazu warten alle Stationen entsprechend ihrer Priorität, bis sie den sogenannten Prioritätspuls senden. In unserem Beispiel haben alle drei Stationen die Priorität 2 und senden demzufolge im dritten Prioritätsslot. Andere Stationen mit niedrigerer Priorität erkennen dies dadurch, daß sie den Kanal ständig überwachen.

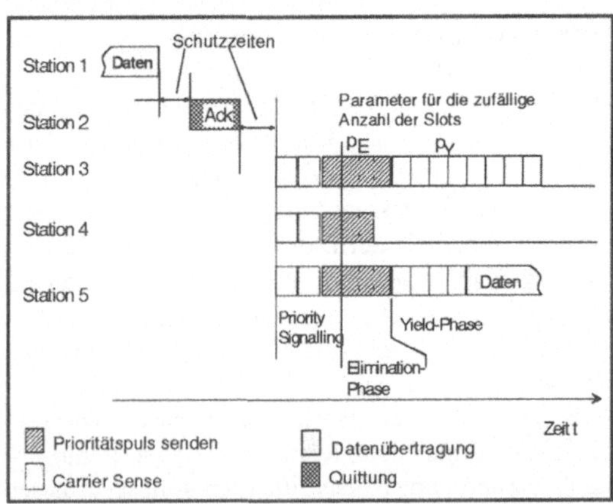

Abbildung 4. Kanalzugriffsverfahren EY-NPMA. Durch das Aussenden des Prioritätspulses erlaubt dieses Verfahren die Signalisierung der Priorität eines Paketes und zwei Ausscheidungsphasen für den Kanalzugriff.

	Benutzer-priorität	
	Hoch	Normal
NRL < 10ms	0	1
10ms ≤ NRL < 20ms	1	2
20ms ≤ NRL < 40ms	2	3
40ms ≤ NRL < 80ms	3	4
80ms ≤ NRL	4	4

Tabelle 4. Zuordnungsvorschrift zwischen normalisierter Restlebenszeit (NRL), Benutzer-Priorität und Kanalzugriffspriorität. Dabei bedeutet für den Kanalzugriff „0" die höchste und entsprechend „4" die niedrigste Prioritätsstufe.

Nach dem Signalisieren der Priorität treten die Stationen in eine erste Ausscheidungsphase, der sogenannten „Elimination-Phase", ein. Dazu wird der Prioritätspuls um eine zufällig ausgewählte Zahl von Slots verlängert. Diejenige Stationen, die den Prioritätspuls am längsten senden, gewinnen. Alle anderen erkennen dies, indem sie nach dem Senden des eigenen Pulses schnellstmöglich den Kanal detektieren und die noch sendenden Stationen hören. Diejenigen Stationen, die nach Ende des verlängerten Prioritätspulses den Kanal als frei detektieren, hören nun über die Zeitdauer einer zufällig gewählten Anzahl von sogenannten „Yield-Slots", ob der Kanal weiterhin frei bleibt. Dieses wird als die „Yield-Phase" bezeichnet. Ist dies der

Fall, so sendet die übriggebliebene oder die übriggebliebenen Stationen ihr Datenpaket. In unserem Beispiel ist dies die Station 5. Sendet mehr als eine Station, so tritt eine Kollision auf. Die Dauer der Prioritäts-, Elimination- und Yield-Slots können der Tabelle 5 entnommen werden. Diese Zeiten leiten sich aus den Umschaltzeiten zwischen Senden und Empfangen bzw. Empfangen und Senden ab. Beim Entwurf des Standards wurde von realisierbaren Umschaltzeiten von einigen µs ausgegangen.

Das EY-NPMA-Verfahren weist eine Reihe von interessanten Eigenschaften auf. Zum einen ermöglicht es, die Prioritätsausscheidung und zwei weitere Ausscheidungsphasen mit nur einem Signalisierungspuls durchzuführen. Andererseits ist es nachteilig, daß in der „Elimination-Phase" genau diejenigen Knoten überleben, die am längsten signalisieren und somit am meisten Overhead verursachen. In der anschließenden Yield-Phase ist dies vorteilhafter gelöst, da die Station mit der kürzesten Wartezeit die Ausscheidung gewinnt.

Von wesentlicher Bedeutung für das Verfahren sind die Zufallsverteilungen für die Auswahl der Anzahl der Elimination- bzw. Yield-Slots. Diese sind in Abbildung 5 dargestellt. Durch Analyse und Simulation läßt sich zeigen, daß die Kollisionswahrscheinlichkeit dieses Verfahrens nur sehr schwach von äußeren Parametern abhängt. Insbesondere ist die Kollisionswahrscheinlichkeit von der Anzahl der konkurrierenden Stationen nahezu unabhängig. Die in Abbildung 5 und Tabelle 5 dargestellten und im HIPERLAN-Standard spezifizierten Parameter führen zu einer Kollisionswahrscheinlichkeit von 3.5%. Diese konstante Kollisionsrate ist für den Betrieb des Funk-LANs von Vorteil. [11] beschreibt die Leistungseinbußen bei variierender Anzahl von konkurrierenden Stationen bei Zugriffsverfahren mit nicht konstanten Kollisionswahrscheinlichkeiten. Als Beispiel wird das „CSMA/CA[14]"-Zugriffsverfahrens herangezogen, das das „IEEE 802.11 Wireless LAN" verwendet.

3.2.3 Versteckte Stationen

Wie bereits in Abschnitt 3.1 angedeutet, arbeiten die Protokolle von HIPERLAN 1 dezentral und verbindungslos. Dies wird dadurch deutlich, daß jedes Paket für sich alleine und unabhängig von Folgepaketen, die untereinander in einem zeitlichen Zusammenhang stehen, bearbeitet wird. Die dezentrale, verbindungslose Struktur führt jedoch dazu, daß HIPERLAN 1-Netze im allgemeinen nicht vollvermascht sind. Dies bedeutet, daß sich nicht alle Stationen gegenseitig in Kommunikationsreichweite befinden.

Der „Carrier Sense"-Mechanismus von HIPERLAN 1 stellt fest, ob auf dem Funkkanal eine andere Station sendet oder ob der Kanal frei ist. Dies wird durch Messen der Empfangsfeldstärke an der Empfängerantenne ermittelt. Der Grenzwert, der für die Detektion von Übertragungen definiert wurde, ist adaptiv und paßt sich an Hintergrundinterferenzen an. Er ist jedoch so dimensioniert, daß auch sendende Stationen, die sich in größeren Entfernungen als die Kommunikationsreichweite aufhalten, noch detektiert werden können. Dies bedeutet, daß Stationen, deren Sendesignal zu schwach ist, um korrekt dekodiert werden zu können, in einem gewissen Bereich zumindest noch detektiert werden können. Diese Detektionsreichweite reicht allerdings nicht weit genug, um versteckte Stationen gänzlich zu eliminieren ([8]).

Zudem treten bei teilvermaschten HIPERLAN-Netzen zusätzlich Interferenzen durch eigentlich nicht versteckte Stationen auf, da Quittungen ohne vorherigen „Carrier Sense" vom Empfänger gesendet werden („Versteckte Stationen zweiter Ordnung") und unter Umständen mit Steuersignalen der Elimination-Phase oder Datenpaketen anderer Stationen kollidieren ([10]).

---

[14] Carrier Sense Multiple Access / Collision Avoidance

Versteckte Stationen führen zu unkontrollierbaren Kollisionen und zu einer Erhöhung der Kollisionswahrscheinlichkeit, da sich versteckte Stationen aus Sicht der gestörten Stationen nicht an die Regeln des Kanalzugriffs halten.

HIPERLAN 1 spezifiziert einen Mechanismus, der den leistungsmindernden Einfluß solcher versteckter Stationen verringert. Dabei überprüft jeder Knoten, der sich an einem Kanalzugriffszyklus beteiligt und verliert, ob er die Datenübertragung des Gewinners des Zugriffszyklus detektiert. Wenn nicht, so schließt er auf eine versteckte Station und begibt sich für 500 ms in einen sogenannten „Hidden Station Mode". In diesem Modus verzögert er seine Beteiligung an einem Kanalzugriff zufällig um 1 bis 5 sogenannte Kanalsperrslots mit einer Zeitdauer von jeweils 1 ms. Somit konkurriert der Knoten nicht in jedem Zugriffszyklus um den Kanal, sondern verschiebt seine Übertragung um eine zufällige Zeitdauer. Er reduziert damit die Wahrscheinlichkeit mit dem aus seiner Sicht versteckten Gewinner des Zugriffszyklus zu kollidieren. Die Zeit von 500 ms, in der sich ein Knoten im „Hidden Station Mode" befindet wird immer dann neu gestartet, wenn der Knoten erneut in einem Zugriffszyklus keine Übertragung oder keine Quittung detektiert.

$$P_E(n) = \begin{cases} p_E^{\,n} \cdot (1 - p_E) & \text{für } 0 \le n < m_{ES} \\ p_E^{\,m_{ES}} & \text{für } n = m_{ES} \end{cases}$$

$$P_y(n) = \frac{1}{m_{ys} + 1} \quad \text{für } 0 \le n \le m_{ys}$$

m_{ES} und m_{YS} sind die maximale Anzahl der Elimination bzw. Yield-Slots. p_E und p_y sind Parameter der Zufallsverteilungen $P_E(n)$ und $P_Y(n)$.

Für HIPERLAN 1 wurde festgelegt:

$$m_{ES} = 12 \qquad m_{YS} = 9 \qquad p_E = 0{,}5$$

Abbildung 5 Parameter für das EY-NPMA-Kanalzugriffsverfahren. $P_E(n)$ und $P_y(n)$ beschreiben die Wahrscheinlichkeiten, daß in der Elimination- bzw. Yield-Phase n Slots lang gesendet bzw. gewartet wird.

In [10] wird die Leistungsfähigkeit dieses Algorithmus bei zeitkritischer Übertragung von paketierter Sprache in Szenarien, in denen versteckte Stationen zweiter Ordnung auftreten, untersucht.

4 Leistungsabschätzungen von HIPERLAN 1

4.1 Simulationsmodell

Als Simulationsmodell wird ein HIPERLAN 1-Netz mit 16 vollvermaschten Knoten verwendet, d.h. alle Knoten können einander detektieren und miteinander kommunizieren. Versteckte Stationen treten in diesem Modell nicht auf. Simuliert wurde speziell das Kanalzugriffsverfahren. Der Overhead, der durch die Codierung und durch die Paketstrukturen der Schicht 1 und 2 verursacht wird, wurde wie unten beschrieben mit berücksichtigt. Ziel der Simulation ist es, die Abhängigkeit des maximal erzielbaren Durchsatz von HIPERLAN 1-Systemen in Abhängigkeit von der Paketgröße zu zeigen.

Alle Stationen besitzen im gewählten Simulationsmodell einen unendlich großen Eingangspuffer, in dem sie ankommende Datenpakete zwischenspeichern und für jeden Kanalzugriff dasjenige Datenpaket auswählen, das die höchste Priorität nach den in Kapitel 3 beschriebenen Regeln besitzt. Jedes Paket hat eine Lebenszeit von 512 ms. Wird die Lebenszeit eines Pakets überschritten, so wird es von der sendenden Station, wie im HIPERLAN 1-Standard vorgesehen, verworfen. Die Simulationen wurden mit HMSDU[15]-Paketgrößen von 64, 512, 1024 und 1536 Byte durchgeführt. Diese Pakete repräsentieren die zu übertragene Nutzlast. Bezüglich der Bitfehlerraten wurde ein idealer Kanal angenommen.

Von wesentlicher Bedeutung für die Leistungsfähigkeit des Systems ist neben dem Overhead durch das Kanalzugriffsverfahren die Größe der auf dem Funkkanal gesendeten Datenblöcke (HPPDU[16]) im Verhältnis zur Größe der Nutzdaten (HMSDU).

Parameter des HIPERLAN 1 Standards ([5])	Werte
Anzahl der Kanalprioritäten	5
p_E (siehe Abbildung 5)	0,5
m_{ES} (siehe Abbildung 5)	12
m_{YS} (siehe Abbildung 5)	9
Zeitdauer eines Prioritätssignalisierungsslots	168 Bit (7,14 µs)
Zeitdauer eines Eliminationsslots	212 Bit (9,01 µs)
Zeitdauer des Eliminationskontrollslots	256 Bit (10,88 µs)
Zeitdauer eines Yieldslots	168 Bit (7,14 µs)
Schutzzeit zwischen Daten und Quittung	512 Bit (21,76 µs)
Schutzzeit zwischen Quittung und neuem Kanalzyklus	256 Bit (10,88 µs)
Dauer einer Quittung	33 µs
Dauer des „Hidden Station Mode"	500 ms
Zeitdauer eines Kanalsperrslots im „Hidden Station Mode"	1 ms
Maximale Anzahl von Kanalsperrslots	5
Bitrate (Standardbitrate der Luftschnittstelle)	23,5294 MBit/s
„Low Bitrate" (Low Bitrate Header)	1,4706 MBit/s

Tabelle 5. HIPERLAN 1-Parameter. Die Zeitdauer der Slots ist in Bits der Standardbitrate angegeben.

Eine HPPDU setzt sich unter anderem zusammen aus einem LBR-Paketkopf, aus einer Trainingssequenz von 450 Bits, aus Adressierungs- und Steuerinformation der HIPERLAN MAC-Schicht und der eigentlichen Nutzinformation (HMSDU). Rechnet man die spezifizierten Größen dieser Felder um und berücksichtigt die Kanalkodierung [5], so erhält man die in Tabelle 6 in der zweiten Zeile angegebenen HPPDU-Größen zur korrespondierenden Nutzdatengröße (HMSDU, erste Zeile). Für die Simulationen, die den Zugriff auf den Kanal und die Übertragung auf dem Funkkanal nachvollzieht, wurden die entsprechenden HPPDU-Größen als Eingangsparameter verwandt. Die weiteren Parameter wurden nach dem HIPERLAN 1-Standard ([5]) gewählt. Diese sind in Tabelle 5 dargestellt.

4.2 Simulationsergebnisse

In Abbildung 6 sind die Ergebnisse der Simulation dargestellt. Man erkennt, daß bei kleinen Paketgrößen sich der maximal erzielbare Durchsatz deutlich verringert. Verwendet man nun die Nutzanteile einer HPPDU und multipliziert diese mit dem Nutzanteil beim Kanalzugriff, so erhält man die Effizienz der Übertragung in HIPERLAN 1 in Abhängigkeit von der Paketgröße. Diese ist in der vierten Zeile in

HMSDU (Byte)	64	512	1024	1536
HPPDU (Bit)	2498	6962	11426	16386
Max.Durchsatz (Simulation)	0,395	0,642	0,741	0,80
Effizienz	0,081	0,378	0,531	0,6
Nutzbitrate (MBit/s)	1,90	8,89	12,50	14,12

Tabelle 6. Leistungsfähigkeit von HIPERLAN 1-Systemen.

---

[15] HIPERLAN MAC Service Data Unit
[16] HIPERLAN Physical Protocol Data Unit

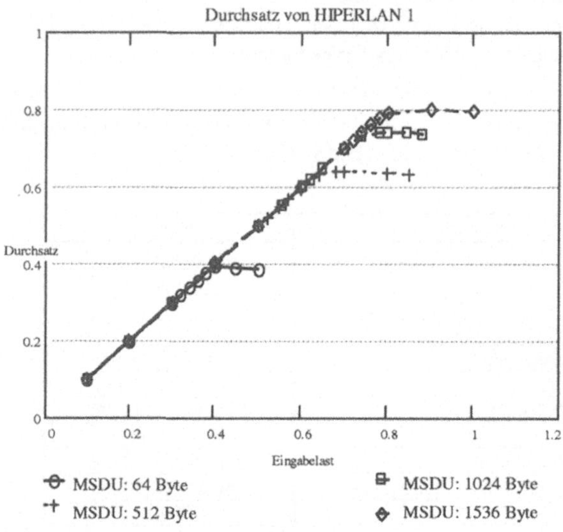

Abbildung 6. Simulationsergebnisse. Der maximale Durchsatz hängt stark von der Größe der Datenpakete ab.

Tabelle 6 dargestellt. Die Bitrate, die ein HIPERLAN-System nun seinen Nutzern in der gewählten Topologie mit 16 vollvermaschten Stationen maximal zur Verfügung stellt, ist in Zeile 5 der Tabelle 6 eingetragen. In der Simulation wurde wie erwartet eine Kollisionsrate von ca. 3,5% festgestellt.

Während bei großen Paketgrößen Datenraten von bis zu 14 MBit/s erreicht werden, fällt die nutzbare Datenrate bei kleinen Paketen aus oben genannten Gründen stark ab. Dieses Verhalten, das letztendlich auf das dezentrale Grundprinzip, dem „Ad-Hoc"-Netz-Ansatz und den daraus folgenden Konsequenzen von Verbindungslosigkeit und konfliktbasiertem Kanalzugriff von HIPERLAN 1 zurückzuführen ist, war nicht zuletzt der Grund dafür, weitere HIPERLAN-Standards speziell für nicht dezentrale und verbindungsorientierte Übertragung zu fordern.

5 Zusammenfassung

Der HIPERLAN 1-Standard, der im November 1996 verabschiedet wurde, spezifiziert ein dezentral organisiertes Funknetz, das eine verbindungslose Datenübertragung ermöglicht. Aufgrund dieser Eigenschaften eignet er sich sehr gut zur Übertragung von asynchronen Datenströmen, wie sie in heute gängigen LANs bevorzugt auftreten. Bei der Übertragung von kurzen Datenpaketen können jedoch mit diesem System nur geringere Übertragungsraten erzielt werden. Verbindungsspezifische Dienstgüteanforderungen, wie sie z.B. von zukünftigen ATM-Systemen unterstützt werden, werden in HIPERLAN 1 nicht definiert und von HIPERLAN 1 nicht unterstützt.

Dies war der Grund, die HIPERLAN-Standardisierung auch auf andere Anwendungsfelder auszudehnen, insbesondere auf die effiziente verbindungsorientierte Übertragung von kurzen zeitkritischen Datenblöcken bzw. ATM-Zellen. Derzeit wird an drei weiteren HIPERLAN-Standards gearbeitet, die unter anderem einen mobilen Zugang zu ATM-Systemen, Punkt-zu-Mehrpunkt-Verbindungen im Netzzugangsbereich und hochbitratige Punk-zu-Punkt-Verbindungen ermöglichen werden. Ein erstes Dokument hierzu ([4]), das die Anforderungen und Architekturen dieser neuen HIPERLAN-Typen beschreibt, wurde Ende 1996 fertiggestellt. Die neuen Typen der HIPERLAN-Familie basieren auf der ATM-Technologie und werden die ATM-Diensteklassen „RT-VBR", „NRT-VBR", „CBR", ABR" und „UBR" unterstützen.

6 Literatur

[1]   ETSI, GSM-Standard, Global Systems for Mobile Communications

[2]   R. Eberhardt, W. Franz, Mobilfunknetze - Technik, Systeme, Anwendungen,Vieweg, Wiesbaden, 1993

[3]   ETSI, Radio Equipment and Systems, ETS 300 175, Digital European Cordless Tele-communications

[4]   ETSI, Radio Equipment and Systems, High Performance Radio Local Area Networks (HIPERLANs), Requirements and Architecture, Draft Version Oct. 1996, Work Item No.: Res 10-07

[5]   ETSI, Radio Equipment and Systems, pr ETS 300 652, High Performance Radio Local Area Network (HIPERLAN), Type 1, Functional Specification, 1996

[6]   W. Franz, HIPERLAN - Der ETSI-Standard für lokale Funknetze, ntz, 9/1995, S. 10-17

[7]   A. Tanenbaum, Computer Networks, Prentice Hall, 1988

[8]   K. C. Chen, Medium Access Control of Wireless LANs for Mobile Computing, IEEE Network, September/October 1994, pp.50-63

[9]   CEPT, Rec. T/R 22-06

[10]   M. Wolf, W. Franz, Reduction of Hidden Node Interference in HIPERLAN, Proceedings of Second Workshop on Personal Wireless Communications (Wireless Local Access), December 1996, Frankfurt, IFIP TC 6

[11]   G. Bianchi, L. Fratta, M. Oliveri, Performance Evaluation and Enhancement of the CSMA/CA MAC Protocol for 802.11 Wireless LANs, Proceedings Seventh IEEE International Symposium on Personal, Indoor and Mobile Radio Communications PIMRC '96, Taipei, October 1996, pp. 392-396

[12]   IEEE 802.11, P802.11 IEEE Draft Standard - Wireless LAN, Jan. 1996

[13]   B. Walke, D. Petras, D. Plassmann, Wireless ATM: Air Interface and Network Protocols of the Mobile Broadband System, IEEE Personal Communications Magazine, Aug. 1996

[14]   WATM-Tutorial, ATM-Forum, Wireless ATM Working Group, Oktober 1996

[15]   Mobile Broadband System - System Description Document, CEC RACE II, Deliverable R2067/UA/WP215/DS/P/068.61

[16]   R. O. LaMaire, A. Krishna, P. Bhagwat, J. P. Panian, Wireless LANs and Mobile Networking: Standards and Future Directions, IEEE Communications Magazine, August 1996

Session 9:
Netzwerkmanagement

Dynamisches Sicherheitsmanagement
mit Hilfe regelbasierter Vorverarbeitungsprozesse

Monika Horak & Markus Trommer
Lehrstuhl für Datenverarbeitung
Technische Universität München
D-80290 München
{Horak,Trommer}@e-technik.tu-muenchen.de

Zusammenfassung

Die Administratoren eines Rechnernetzes benötigen Unterstützung durch ein Werkzeug, um die vorhandenen Sicherheitsmechanismen korrekt einzusetzen, zu konfigurieren und in ihrer Wirksamkeit zu überwachen. Das sich laufend ändernde Umfeld stellt besondere Anforderungen an ein Sicherheitsmanagementsystem. Dieses muß an Änderungen der Rechnerkonfiguration oder der Sicherheitsvorgaben flexibel angepaßt werden und daher dynamisch erweiterbar sein. Die Beschreibung von Sicherheitsvorgaben auf höheren Abstraktionsebenen und die Strukturierung der zu verwaltenden Parameter bilden die Grundlage für eine dynamische Erweiterbarkeit. Diese wird durch einen regelbasierten Ansatz gewährleistet, der Managementfunktionen in Form von Bedingungen und Aktionen definiert. Die vorgestellten Konzepte werden mit Hilfe einer erweiterten SNMP-Standardarchitektur realisiert. Diese beinhaltet spezifische Vorverarbeitungsprozesse, sogenannte Security-MAgICs, die in einer speziellen "Rule-MIB" die Regeln zur Verwaltung der Managementobjekte bereitstellen.

1.   Einleitung

Die zunehmende Vernetzung von Systemen ermöglicht neue Formen der Zusammenarbeit zwischen Firmen. Daneben findet vermehrt eine Auslagerung von Teilarbeiten bzw. eine Verlagerung des Arbeitsplatzes in den Privatbereich ("Teleworking") statt.

In dem Maße, in dem Absprachen, gemeinsames Bearbeiten sensibler Daten, Verträge etc. auf elektronischem Wege getätigt werden, nimmt auch die Bedeutung der Sicherheit zu. Eine Reihe von Sicherheitsmechanismen steht zur Verfügung, um Daten sowohl innerhalb eines Firmennetzes, als auch bei ihrer Übertragung über unsichere Kommunikationswege vor Angriffen auf die Vertraulichkeit, Verfügbarkeit, Integrität und Verbindlichkeit zu schützen.

Die vorhandenen Sicherheitsmechanismen bieten aber nur dann einen ausreichenden Schutz, wenn sie richtig konfiguriert und eingesetzt werden. Außerdem sollte ihre Wirksamkeit, auch im Hinblick auf das Zusammenspiel der einzelnen Mechanismen untereinander, regelmäßig überwacht werden. Es sind einige Werkzeuge für spezielle Auswertungen verfügbar, beispielsweise "Cops" [FaSp90] oder "Satan" [Hugh96]. Diese Tools sind jedoch nicht flexibel erweiterbar und bieten keine Möglichkeit zur Interaktion mit anderen Werkzeugen.

Durch eine Integration des Sicherheitsmanagements in das vorhandene Netz- und Systemmanagement können die Nachteile von einzelnen, nicht interaktionsfähigen Überwachungstools vermieden werden. Es ist auf diese Weise möglich, vorhandene Ressourcen und Informationen, die auch für andere Managementbereiche benötigt werden, gemeinsam zu nutzen. Ferner wird eine Kooperation der unterschiedlichen Managementbereiche möglich.

Im Umfeld TCP/IP-basierter Rechnernetze hat sich das "Simple Network Management Protocol" (SNMP) als Standard etabliert. Es wird von den meisten Herstellern von Netzkomponenten unterstützt und ist deswegen weit verbreitet. Am Lehrstuhl für Datenverarbeitung der Technischen Universität München wurde ein verteiltes, hierarchisches Sicherheitsmanagementsystem entwickelt, das auf einer erweiterten SNMP-Standardarchitektur basiert.

In diesem Beitrag erörtern wir ein Konzept, das es ermöglicht, die Funktionalität des Sicherheitsmanagementsystems dynamisch zu erweitern. Kapitel 2 erläutert dieses Konzept und stellt insbesondere den regelbasierten Ansatz vor, der die Basis für die dynamische Erweiterbarkeit bereitstellt. Kapitel 3 beinhaltet die Realisierung mit Hilfe einer erweiterten SNMP-Standardarchitektur. Ein Szenario in Kapitel 4 soll die Anwendung der vorgestellten Konzepte veranschaulichen. Kapitel 5 enthält eine kurze Zusammenfassung und gibt einen Ausblick auf weitere Arbeiten.

2. Konzept für ein dynamisches Sicherheitsmanagement

2.1 Anforderungen

Ein Sicherheitsmanagementsystem muß eine Reihe von Anforderungen erfüllen. Beispielsweise ist neben der Integrationsfähigkeit in bestehende Netz- und Systemarchitekturen [HeAb93] auch die Anpassung an vorhandene Unternehmensstrukturen wichtig. Die Heterogenität der Netze bringt eine Vielzahl von unterschiedlichen Sicherheitsaspekten mit sich. Das Sicherheitsmanagementsystem sollte ferner eine Aufgabenverteilung ermöglichen und Sicherheitsmechanismen möglichst automatisch verwalten und überwachen. Als Grundvoraussetzung für ein wirksames Sicherheitsmanagement muß natürlich die Sicherheit des Managementsystems selbst gewährleistet sein.

Besondere Anforderungen ergeben sich dadurch, daß das Sicherheitsmanagementsystem in einem Umfeld agiert, das ständigen Änderungen unterworfen ist. Nicht nur die Restrukturierung der Organisationsstruktur des Unternehmens oder der Aufgaben einzelner Abteilungen haben eine Veränderung der Rechnerkonfiguration zur Folge. Auch im laufenden Betrieb werden Rechner aus einem Teilnetz entfernt und zu neuen Subnetzen zusammengestellt, bzw. neue Rechner hinzugefügt. Wenn neue Versionen von System- oder Anwendungsprogrammen eingespielt werden, sind die sicherheitsrelevanten Parameter dieser Programme so einzustellen, daß die vorgegebenen Sicherheitsanforderungen erfüllt werden. Gleichzeitig ändern sich oftmals auch die Anforderungen an das System in Bezug auf einzuhaltende Sicherheitslevels. Wenn eine Abteilung eine Aufgabe zugewiesen bekommt, die eine höhere Vertraulichkeitsstufe erfordert als die vorhergehenden, so ist auch die Konfiguration der Sicherheitsmechanismen dementsprechend zu ändern. Bei einem UNIX-System könnten beispielsweise *Access Control* - Listen für eine feingranulare Zugriffskontrolle eingerichtet werden, ferner ist die Sperrung von Rechnerzugängen ohne Paßwort über den „.rhost"-Mechanismus denkbar.

Das Sicherheitsmanagementsystem muß den Administrator dabei unterstützen, auf aktuelle Eindringversuche in das System oder auf Informationen über bekanntgewordene Sicherheitslücken rasch zu reagieren. Solche Sicherheitslücken können durch fehlerbehaftete Programme entstehen, aber auch durch veraltete Sicherheitsmechanismen, die den aktuellen Anforderungen nicht mehr genügen. Das Managementsystem muß laufend um das Wissen über neue Bedrohungen erweitert werden, damit es in der Lage ist, auch diese neuen Sicherheitslücken im System aufzuspüren.

2.2 Politikbasiertes Management

Ein Sicherheitsmanagementsystem beinhaltet alle Parameter und Merkmale von Sicherheitsmechanismen und sicherheitsrelevanten Programmen, die eingestellt und überwacht werden können. Dabei ergibt sich rasch eine schwer zu überblickende Vielzahl von unterschiedlichen Parametern, die mit Hilfe von Managementfunktionen verwaltet werden müssen. Um eine flexible Änderungs- und Erweiterungsfähigkeit des Managementsystems zu gewährleisten, ist es sinnvoll, die Parameter in geeigneter Weise zu strukturieren. Die Ansätze des politikbasierten Netz- und Systemmanagements erscheinen hierfür als geeignet. Diese Ansätze werden im Rahmen der Forschung vielfach diskutiert. Sie zielen darauf ab, höhere Abstraktionsebenen einzuführen. Der Manager soll sich nicht um Details kümmern müssen, sondern abstrakte Managementziele vorgeben, die das System automatisch in konkrete Aktionen umsetzt. Allgemeine Erläuterungen finden sich beispielsweise in [AlPl95] und [Wies95].

Unser Ansatz für ein politikbasiertes Sicherheitsmanagement beinhaltet eine Beschreibung von Sicherheitsvorgaben auf hoher Abstraktionsebene. Als Abstraktionen werden die Konzepte der OSI-Sicherheitsarchitektur [ISO7498-2] verwendet, die Sicherheitsdienste und Mechanismen beinhalten. Die zu verwaltenden Parameter werden, soweit möglich, den einzelnen Diensten und Mechanismen zugeordnet.

Der Administrator führt eine Bedrohungs- und Risikoanalyse durch, um die bedrohten Objekte seines Systems zu identifizieren (siehe Abbildung 1). Als Anleitung hierfür kann das Verfahren des Bundesamtes für Sicherheit in der Informationstechnik dienen [BSI92]. Anschließend erstellt er ein Sicherheitskonzept, das aus einzelnen Sicherheitspolitiken besteht. Als Beispiel sollen hier Zugriffskontroll-, Integritäts- oder Verfügbarkeitspolitiken genannt werden.

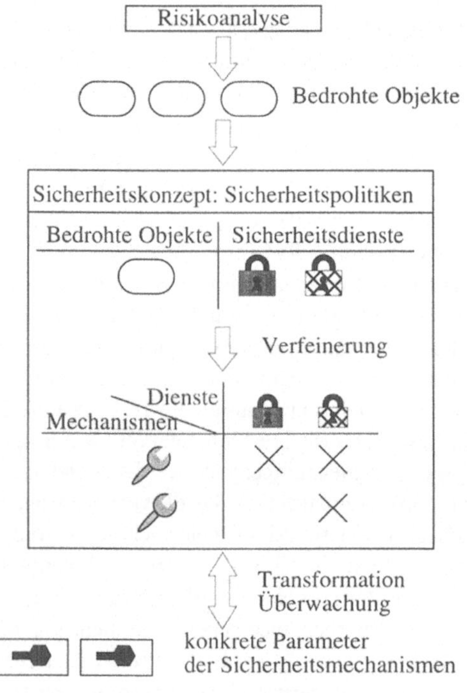

Abbildung 1 : Von Sicherheitspolitiken zu den konkreten Parametern der Mechanismen

Es werden Sicherheitsdienste definiert, um die sicherheitsrelevanten Objekte vor den identifizierten Bedrohungen zu schützen. Dann werden geeignete Mechanismen ausgewählt, um die geforderten Dienste zu realisieren. Es erfolgt eine Verfeinerung, bis eine möglichst automatische Transformation in die einzustellenden und zu überwachenden Parameter des Systems vorgenommen werden kann.

Zur allgemeingültigen, systemübergreifenden Definition und Verwaltung von Sicherheitsdiensten und -mechanismen werden übergeordnete Modelle (Meta-Konstrukte) bereitgestellt. Dabei wird versucht, soweit möglich, die Grundkonzepte einzelner Sicherheitsmechanismen zu extrahieren. Als Beispiel sollen hier die Zugriffskontrollmechanismen für Unix- bzw. WindowsNT-Systeme genannt werden. Die zugehörigen übergeordneten Modelle beinhalten sogenannte „virtuelle Rechte", die eine weitgehend einheitliche Verwaltung der unterschiedlichen Parameter der beiden Ausprägungen des Zugriffskontrollmechanismus erlauben. Weitere Gruppierungskonstrukte dienen dazu, eine mögliche Vielzahl von Einzelobjekten wie Dateien oder Benutzer zu handhaben. Beispielsweise werden die Dateien eines Systems nach ihrer Funktionalität zu sogenannten „virtuellen Ressourcen" zusammengefaßt. Die virtuelle Ressource "WWW-Server" beispielsweise enthält die Dateigruppen "ausführbare Dateien", "Konfigurationsdateien", "Protokolldateien" und weitere.

2.3 Funktionen

Die Funktionen des Managementsystems können gemäß dem oben beschriebenen Konzept unterschiedlichen Abstraktionsebenen zugeordnet werden.

Auf hoher Abstraktionsebene finden sich Funktionen, die Gruppen von Parametern und Meta-Konstrukten verwalten: Funktionen zur Verwaltung der Sicherheitspolitiken beinhalten deren Erzeugung, Aktivierung, Deaktivierung, Löschung und Änderung. Nach der Definition neuer oder der Änderung bestehender Sicherheitsvorgaben müssen diese auf Plausibilität und auf Widersprüche zu den übrigen Politiken geprüft werden. Die anfallenden Aufgaben sind eventuell auf mehrere Managementinstanzen wie auch auf mehrere Administratoren zu verteilen. Zu diesem Zweck werden unterschiedliche Zuständigkeitsbereiche definiert und verwaltet (siehe auch [TrKo96]).

Die Überwachung der Sicherheitsvorgaben findet auf mehreren Ebenen statt. Es werden die konkreten sicherheitsrelevanten Parameter ermittelt, die den Ist-Zustand des Systems repräsentieren. Soweit möglich, wird dann auf höheren Abstraktionsebenen analysiert, ob der aktuelle Zustand den Sicherheitsvorgaben entspricht. Wo eine Abstraktion nicht möglich ist, werden Analysen direkt auf Basis der einzelnen Parameter durchgeführt.

Die Transformation zwischen unterschiedlichen Abstraktionsebenen wird von einer weiteren Gruppe von Managementfunktionen durchgeführt. Diese setzen die abstrakten Sicherheitsvorgaben in die konkreten Parameter der Sicherheitsmechanismen um. Analog dazu werden konkrete sicherheitsrelevante Vorfälle abstrahiert, um sie leichter auswerten zu können.

Grundfunktionen wie das Abfragen oder Einstellen von Parametern, mathematische Funktionen oder Auswertefunktionen wie Schwellwertberechnungen und andere können von Managementfunktionen auf allen Ebenen genutzt werden. Daneben sind noch Funktionen für eine Benutzerschnittstelle und Steuerungsfunktionen zu nennen.

Die Funktionen zur Überwachung und Transformation sind besonders wichtig im Hinblick auf eine dynamische Erweiterbarkeit des Systems. Deshalb sollen sie im folgenden anhand einiger Beispiele näher betrachtet werden.

2.3.1 Transformationsfunktionen

Gruppierungskonstrukte

Ein Beispiel für Gruppierungskonstrukte ist die Zusammenfassung einzelner Dateien zu virtuellen Ressourcen, um ihre Verwaltung handhabbar zu gestalten. Für eine Analyse der zugehörigen Sicherheitseigenschaften müssen vom Managementsystem die konkreten Parameter der zu einer Gruppe gehörenden Dateien abgefragt werden. Dies können beispielsweise Zugriffsrechte oder kryptographische Prüfsummen zur Integritätssicherung sein. Funktionen zur Transformation von virtuellen Ressourcen in reale können in zwei Fälle unterschieden werden:

1. Die Abbildungsfunktion ist systemabhängig fest vorgegeben. Die zum Dienst „E-Mail" gehörenden ausführbaren Dateien werden z. B. bei einem bestimmten Betriebssystem immer unter einem festen Pfadnamen abgelegt. Für weitere Dateiarten gilt entsprechendes. Es handelt sich also um eine direkte Zuordnung von virtuellen Ressourcen zu realen Pfadnamen, abhängig von festen Parametern wie der Art des Betriebssystems, der Systemversion und ähnlichen Bedingungen.

2. Der Administrator „weiß", wie die Abbildung von virtuellen in reale Ressourcen vorzunehmen ist, beispielsweise weil er selbst die Installation der Dateien vorgenommen hat. In diesem Fall werden die systembedingt vorgegebenen Abbildungsfunktionen um die vom Administrator festzulegenden ergänzt.

Transformation von übergeordneten Modellen

Übergeordnete Modelle zur Verwaltung von Zugriffskontrollmechanismen beinhalten z. B. virtuelle Rechte, die in die realen Zugriffsrechte der zugrundeliegenden Mechanismen umgesetzt werden müssen. Dabei kann unterschieden werden zwischen grundlegenden Rechten und benutzerdefinierten Rechten. Zu den grundlegenden Rechten gehören „Dateien Anzeigen", „in Verzeichnis Wechseln" oder „Dateien Löschen". Diese werden gemäß einer systembezogenen Abbildungsmatrix in die realen Rechte transformiert. Beispielsweise sind im Unix-Dateisystem alle Dateien eines Directories löschbar, wenn Schreib- und Ausführungsrecht auf dieses Directory vorhanden sind. Bei NT kann eine Datei gelöscht werden, wenn auf das betreffende Verzeichnis das Recht "Ändern" oder explizit "Löschen" gesetzt ist und wenn für die Datei dieselben Rechte gesetzt sind.

Die Abbildungsmatrix für die Umsetzung benutzerdefinierter Rechte muß vom Administrator festgelegt werden. Ein Beispiel für eine derartige Abbildung soll am virtuellen Recht „Konfigurieren" erläutert werden. Wenn ein Benutzer eine virtuelle Ressource konfigurieren darf, dann soll daraus folgen, daß er die zugehörigen ausführbaren Dateien lesen, die Konfigurationsdateien lesen und schreiben und die Protokolldateien lesen darf.

Allgemeine Abstraktion bzw. Detaillierung von Parametern

Zur Abstrahierung von einzelnen sicherheitsrelevanten Parametern auf Dienste und Mechanismen muß festgelegt werden, welche Parameter einzustellen und zu überwachen sind, um einen bestimmten Dienst bzw. Mechanismus zu verwalten. Ferner ist eine Interpretation der einzelnen Parameter in Bezug auf die Bedeutung für den zugehörigen Dienst/Mechanismus notwendig. Wenn beispielsweise bei einem Unix-System in der Datei /etc/hosts.equiv ein

"+" steht, werden alle anderen Systeme als vertrauenswürdig ausgewiesen. Ein User mit dem gleichen Benutzernamen auf einem anderen System kann sich von dort aus ohne Authentifikation einloggen. Der Authentifikationsmechanismus, der beim Unix-System durch eine Paßwort-Abfrage realisiert ist, wird dann für diese Fälle ausgeschaltet.

2.3.2 Überwachungsfunktionen

Zu den Überwachungsfunktionen gehören einfache Auswertungen anhand mathematischer oder logischer Operationen. Als Beispiele sollen Soll-Ist-Vergleiche oder Schwellwertüberwachungen genannt werden. Falls höhere Sicherheitslevels eingehalten werden müssen, reichen diese einfachen Überwachungsfunktionen eventuell nicht aus. Oftmals gibt es systembedingte oder durch das Zusammenwirken unterschiedlicher Verfahren entstehende indirekte Wege, um vorhandene Sicherheitsmechanismen zu umgehen. Diese müssen aufgespürt werden. Beispielsweise kann eine Zugriffsbeschränkung auf eine Datei im Unix-Dateisystem umgangen werden, wenn es einem Benutzer gelingt in eine Gruppe zu wechseln, die Zugriff auf diese Datei hat.

Eine weitere Aufgabe ist die Suche nach bekannten Sicherheitslücken wie einem Fehler in einer Software-Version (vgl. sendmail-bug) oder bestimmte Konfigurationen des Betriebssystems, die nicht direkt Sicherheitsmechanismen betreffen, aber indirekt zu Schwachstellen werden können. Wenn erfolgreiche Angriffe gegen einen Sicherheitsmechanismus bekannt werden, ist zu prüfen, ob diese Schwachstelle auch für das zugrundeliegende System relevant ist.

Auch die Auswirkungen von erkannten Fehlkonfigurationen oder sicherheitsrelevanten Ereignissen sind zu ermitteln. Hierzu ist es notwendig, die Beziehungen zwischen einzelnen Sicherheitsdiensten und -mechanismen zu beschreiben. Ein Beispiel für eine Wirkungskette ist ein falsch konfigurierter Hash-Mechanismus, der dazu führt, daß auch alle darauf aufbauenden Mechanismen wie digitale Signatur oder Integritätsmechanismen nicht mehr sicher arbeiten.

2.4 Regelbasierter Ansatz

Wie bereits in Kapitel 1 beschrieben, zeichnet sich ein leistungsfähiges Sicherheitsmanagement durch eine leichte Anpaßbarkeit und Erweiterbarkeit aus. Die periodische Installation neuer Versionen von Softwaresystemen, wie sie verteilte Sicherheitsapplikationen darstellen, ist aufgrund des hohen Aufwandes oft nicht durchführbar. Außerdem handelt es sich dabei zwangsläufig um einen herstellerspezifischen Ansatz, der sich nur schwer mit den Anforderungen an ein integriertes Netzmanagement in Einklang bringen läßt.

Um flexibel auf Änderungen des Umfelds (neue Systeme, neue Sicherheitslücken,...) reagieren zu können, sind unterschiedliche Ansätze denkbar:

- Parameterisierte Funktionen
  Das Verhalten der Managementinstanz wird von fest vorgegebenen Abläufen bestimmt. Diese enthalten Parameter, über die eine Beeinflussung in gewissen Grenzen möglich ist. So kann beispielsweise die Zuordnung von realen Dateien zu einer virtuellen Ressource geändert werden. Die Regeln, nach denen dann diese Dateien überwacht werden, sind dagegen fest vorgegeben.

- Verteilte Applikationen
  Dieser Ansatz stellt sicher einen Schwerpunkt in der augenblicklichen Forschung dar. Es gibt eine ganze Reihe von Vorschlägen für die Verteilung und Ausführung von Programmteilen auf entfernten Rechnern ("mobiler Code"), sei es in Form von Assembleranweisungen für eine Art virtueller Stackmaschine [SiTr95], der Definition von Skript-Sprachen oder gar Java als universelle, plattformunabhängige Programmiersprache. Diese für das Netz- und Systemmanagement sicher interessanten Ansätze weisen aber, abgesehen von der fehlenden Standardisierung, speziell für das Sicherheitsmanagement Nachteile auf. So haben beispielsweise Java-Implementierungen im Augenblick noch große Sicherheitslücken. Außerdem ergibt sich durch die große Anzahl von Freiheitsgraden bei der Verwendung mächtiger Programmiersprachen auch ein erhöhter Konfigurations- und Fehlerbehandlungsaufwand.

- Dynamische Regeln
  Regelbasierte Ansätze werden häufig in Expertensystemen verwendet. Dabei führt eine sogenannte Inferenz-Maschine die Regeln aus [GiRi89]. Diese Maschine hat zwar auch eine interpretierende Aufgabe, die aber durch den systematischen Aufbau der Regeln vereinfacht wird. Die Struktur der Regeln erleichtert die Einbindung in bestehende Netzmanagementumgebungen, da in diesem Umfeld übliche Datenstrukturen (MIB-Tabellen) verwendet werden können. Damit ist auch gleichzeitig der Weg vorgegeben, über den sich bestehende Regeln verändern, bzw. neue hinzufügen lassen, ohne neue Protokolle einführen zu müssen.

Da dynamisch veränderbare Regeln bezüglich Aufwand und Flexibilität einen Kompromiß darstellen, wurde der regelbasierte Ansatz als Ausgangspunkt für die Entwicklung der Sicherheitsarchitektur verwendet.

Regeln lassen sich im allgemeinen auf einfache Weise gruppieren und kapseln. Diese Eigenschaft soll genutzt werden, um die Menge an Regeln in einem umfangreichen Sicherheitsmanagementsystem handhabbar zu machen. Deshalb werden Regeln nach verschiedenen Gesichtspunkten klassifiziert.

Grundsätzlich lassen sich drei Wissensbasen unterscheiden: *Systemwissen* ist in Abhängigkeit von dem zu Grunde liegenden System (Betriebssystem, Hardware-Revision, Programmversion) definiert. *Administratorwissen* befaßt sich mit den lokalen Besonderheiten (benutzer-, abteilungs- oder organisationsspezifisch). *Krypto-Wissen* bezieht sich auf bekannte Sicherheitsmechanismen bzw. Applikationen.

Neben dieser generellen Einteilung können die Regeln zusätzlich nach dem Abstraktionsgrad der zugehörigen Sicherheitspolitik klassifiziert werden. Am unteren Ende dieser Skala befinden sich die sogenannten Basisregeln, die sich keiner Politikbeschreibung zuordnen lassen.

Ein drittes Klassifizierungsmerkmal ist die Problemstellung, die von der Regel bearbeitet wird. Einfache Beispiele hierfür sind Regeln zur Initialisierung der Managementumgebung, zur Konfiguration von Abfragemechanismen oder zur Auswertung von einfachen Sicherheitsproblematiken.

Die Gruppierung der Regeln, die sich aus diesen Kriterien ergibt, sollte durch das Sicherheitsmanagementsystem unterstützt werden, um die Verwaltung und Versionskontrolle zu erleichtern.

3. Realisierung

Um die in Kapitel 2 angeführten Aufgaben und Probleme bewältigen zu können, entstand im Rahmen der Forschungsarbeit am Lehrstuhl für Datenverarbeitung der TU-München eine Architektur, die ein verteiltes Sicherheitsmanagement ermöglicht und auf die Bedürfnisse umfangreicher, heterogener Netze eingeht. Die Umsetzung des Konzepts für einen dynamischen, regelbasierten Ansatz gemäß Kapitel 2.4 erfolgt durch die Einführung spezieller Vorverarbeitungsprozesse innerhalb dieser Architektur.

3.1 Sicherheits-Architektur mit Security-MAgICs

Die vorgestellte Architektur beruht auf den Prinzipien des sog. Internet-Managements. In diesem Umfeld hat sich das Simple Network Management Protocol (SNMP) als ein Standard etabliert. Er definiert nicht nur das Protokoll für den Austausch von Daten, sondern auch die grundsätzliche Struktur der Managementinformation (Management Information Base, MIB). Obwohl speziell auf dem Sektor des Systemmanagements auch andere Lösungen, wie z.B. das OSI-Management [ISO7498-4] oder verteilte Funktionsaufrufe (DCE-RPC [ISO9072-1]) existieren, so kann dennoch SNMP aufgrund seiner weiten Verbreitung als eine, auch auf einfachen Komponenten verfügbare, gemeinsame Basis für das Netzmanagement in einem heterogenen Umfeld angesehen werden.

Da sich das Sicherheitsmanagement nicht immer exakt von den übrigen Funktionsbereichen des Netzmanagements (Fehler-, Leistungs-, Abrechnungs- und Konfigurationsmanagement) trennen läßt, ist es für ein integriertes Netz- und Systemmanagement sinnvoll, auf einen einheitlichen Kommunikationsmechanismus zurückzugreifen. Im Zusammenhang mit der Verwaltung der Sicherheit ist ein besonderes Augenmerk auf die Sicherung der Managementvorgänge selbst zu legen. Nachdem die erste Version von SNMP mit einer, durch den Austausch unverschlüsselter Paßwörter nur sehr schwachen, Sicherung versehen wurde, sollte für sicherheitskritische Managementoperationen der als "User-based Security" bezeichnete Erweiterungsvorschlag ([SNMP2] mit [RFC1909] und [RFC1910]) der zweiten Version von SNMP (genannt SNMPv2u) verwendet werden. Er bietet optional eine benutzerbezogene Authentifizierung und Verschlüsselung. Eine weitergehende Betrachtung hierzu findet sich in [Rose96].

Bei einer SNMP-Kommunikationsbeziehung handelt es sich um ein klassisches Client-Server-Prinzip. Eine Management-Instanz (Manager = Client) schickt eine Anfrage oder einen Befehl an einen Agenten (Server), der den gewünschten Dienst, z.B. Auslesen eines Wertes aus der internen Konfiguration der zu verwaltenden Komponente, erbringt. Der Agent liefert den entsprechenden Wert oder eine Fehlermeldung. Außerdem besitzt er die Möglichkeit, Manager von außergewöhnlichen Ereignissen durch Meldungen informieren zu können. Manager und Agent besitzen eine einheitliche Sicht auf die Managementinformation einer MIB, die die von einem Agenten verwalteten Managementobjekte in einer Baumstruktur zusammenfaßt. Die Managementobjekte sind allerdings nicht im strengen Sinne objektorientiert, sondern sind eher mit Variablen der klassischen Programmiertechnik vergleichbar.

Um verteiltes Management zu ermöglichen, wurde der von SNMP verfolgte zweistufige Ansatz (Manager-Agent) um eine weitere Stufe ergänzt: Managing Agents for Information Control (MAgICs - vgl. Abbildung 2). Diese Prozesse, die teilweise oder sogar völlig selbständig agieren können, beinhalten sowohl eine Manager-, als auch eine Agenten-Schnittstelle. Über die Manager-Schnittstelle ist es einem MAgIC-Prozeß möglich, sich Information aus dem zu verwaltenden System zu beschaffen bzw. konkrete Einstellungen vorzunehmen. Über die Agenten-Schnittstelle kann das Verhalten des MAgICs mittels einer eigens definierten Management Information Base kontrolliert werden. Durch diese Konzepte wird die Basis für die Einführung höherer Abstraktionsebenen bei gleichzeitiger Reduktion der benötigten Informationsmenge geschaffen (siehe auch [KoTr95]).

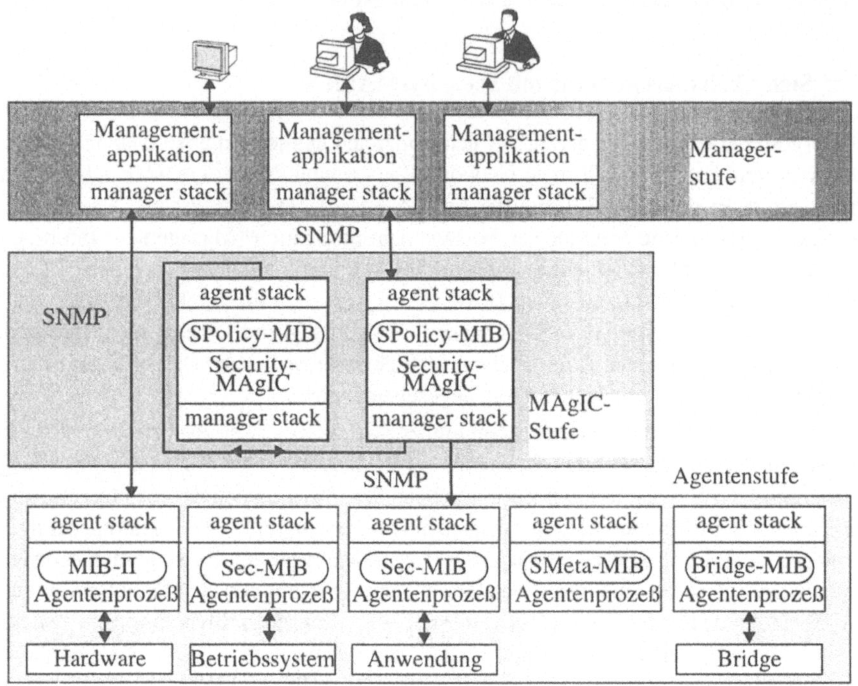

Abbildung 2 : Prinzip der mehrstufigen Sicherheitsarchitektur

Somit lassen sich die am Lehrstuhl entwickelten Komponenten der verwendeten Sicherheitsarchitektur folgenden Stufen zuordnen (vgl. Abbildung 2). Für weitere Informationen siehe [HoTr96].

- Agentenstufe
  Zu dieser Stufe zählen die sog. Sec-MIB-Agenten, die den Zugriff auf sicherheitsrelevante Managementinformation der zu verwaltenden Komponenten einschließen. Sie erlauben die Konfigurierung und Überwachung der betriebssystemeigenen Sicherheitsmechanismen. Auch Sicherheitsapplikationen und Netzdienste können über die Sec-MIB verwaltet werden. Selbstverständlich lassen sich auch alle weiteren für das Sicherheitsmanagement nützlichen Agenten mit ihren MIBs (sowohl herstellerspezifische, als auch standardisierte) einbinden. Besonders soll an dieser Stelle auf die SMETA-MIB hingewiesen werden. Diese erlaubt die dezentrale Definition und Verwaltung von Sicherheitsdomänen (nach [Scha95]).

- MAgIC-Stufe
Zentraler Bestandteil dieser Stufe ist der sog. Security-MAgIC. Dieser Prozeß transformiert die abstrakten Vorgaben von Sicherheitspolitiken in Managementoperationen innerhalb einer festgelegten Menge von Komponenten. Ziel dieser Operationen können sowohl beliebige Agenten der Agentenstufe, als auch weitere, untergeordnete Security-MAgICs sein. Diese Prozesse können beliebig im System verteilt werden, um ein dezentrales, hierarchisches Sicherheitsmanagement zu ermöglichen. Vorgaben und Verhalten der Prozesse lassen sich über eine sogenannte SPolicy-MIB steuern. Sie enthält die abstrakte Beschreibung des Sollzustandes eines Systems von Komponenten (Sicherheitspolitik), der von einer zentralen Stelle vorgegeben und von einem lokalen Sicherheitsadministrator in definierbaren Grenzen verfeinert werden kann.

- Managerstufe
Diese Kategorie umfaßt Managementanwendungen, die die domänenübergreifende Festlegung von Sicherheitspolitiken und die Überwachung des Gesamtsystems zum Ziel haben. Anwendungen, die an diese Architektur angepaßt sind, können auch innerhalb von Managementplattformen realisiert werden. Da das Konzept der Sicherheitsarchitektur vorsieht, daß sich Security-MAgIC-Prozesse flexibel hierarchisch verschalten lassen, ist es möglich, diese als reine Managementapplikation zu betreiben.

3.2   Dynamische Erweiterung

Wie bereits in Kapitel 3.1 erwähnt, erlaubt die SPolicy-MIB eines Security-MAgICs eine parameterorientierte Definition der Sicherheitspolitik einer Domäne. Da die in Kapitel 2.3 angesprochenen Funktionen, die der MAgIC erfüllen muß, einen zum Teil sehr hohen Komplexitätsgrad besitzen und ein hohes Maß an Expertenwissen erfordern, wurde die Integration einer kommerziellen Expertensystementwicklungsumgebung [Stei95] vorgenommen. Auf diese Weise können Expertensysteme für spezielle Aufgaben realisiert und in das Sicherheitsmanagementsystem eingebunden werden. Obwohl eine solche Lösung auch die Einbindung der Konzepte anderer Überwachungswerkzeuge (z.B. COPS [FaSp90]) erleichtert, so ergeben sich dennoch einige Nachteile. Neben dem großen Resourcenverbrauch eines Expertensystems ist vor allem die mangelnde Flexibilität ein Hindernis. Das Ändern und Hinzufügen von Regeln ist nicht ohne weiteres zur Laufzeit möglich. Das Ziel sollte jedoch stets aus einer Menge 'schlanker', skalierbarer Managementprozesse bestehen, die sich auf einfache Weise verteilen und konfigurieren lassen.

Aus diesem Grund wurde der Security-MAgIC in seinem Aufbau um einen dynamischen, regelbasierten Anteil erweitert. Die Regeln und Regelsätze sind ebenfalls über SNMP konfigurier- und abfragbar. Dazu wurde die Information Base des MAgICs um Tabellen zur Verwaltung von Regeln erweitert. Die Abarbeitung der Regeln kann auf eine vereinfachte Weise erfolgen, ist aber für komplexe Problemstellungen auch über eine, in Expertensystemen übliche, Inferenz-Maschine realisierbar.

Aufbau von Regeln und Regelsätzen

Die Struktur der Regeln ist an die der regelbasierten Expertensysteme angelehnt. Sie gliedert sich in zwei Bestandteile: Bedingungs- und Aktionsteil.

Der *Bedingungsteil* enthält eine durch logische Operationen (AND, OR, ...) verknüpfbare Menge von Vergleichen. Mögliche Vergleichsoperatoren sind:

$$> \quad < \quad \geq \quad \leq \quad != \quad =$$

Gegenstand von Vergleichen können Konstanten, Werte von Managementobjekten oder ein aus diesen Elementen bestehender mathematischer Ausdruck sein. Sind alle Bedingungen erfüllt, so wird die Regel als "aktiviert" bezeichnet.

Der *Aktionsteil* einer Regel wird nur im Fall der Regelaktivierung ausgeführt. Er enthält eine Liste von auszuführenden Einzelaktionen. Die für ein proaktives Management gebräuchlichste Aktion ist das Setzen eines Objektwertes. Dies kann Objekte in den MIBs der zu verwaltenden Komponenten betreffen, aber auch Werte in der SPolicy-MIB des Security-MAgICs selbst. Außerdem ist es möglich, Botschaften an übergeordnete Managementinstanzen zu versenden. Ebenso kann eine aktivierte Regel die Abarbeitung weiterer Regelsätze anstoßen.

Ein Regelsatz ist eine Gruppe von Regeln zur Behandlung eines Problemfeldes, z.B. der Transformation virtueller Rechte in reale Zugriffsrechte. Die Abarbeitung eines Regelsatzes kann gezielt angeregt oder unterbunden werden. Somit läßt sich der Ressourcenverbrauch durch eine räumlich und zeitlich verteilte Bearbeitung auf dem jeweiligen MAgIC einschränken.

Regelbasierter Security-MAgIC

Neben der Agenten- und der Managerschnittstelle beinhaltet ein Security-MAgIC stets auch eine SPolicy-MIB. Zur Realisierung des regelbasierten Ansatzes wurde diese MIB um Tabellen zur Speicherung und Verwaltung von Regelsätzen erweitert (siehe Abbildung 3). Dieser Teilbereich der Management Information Base wird als Rule-MIB bezeichnet. Die Steuerung der Abläufe innerhalb des MAgIC-Prozesses erfolgt durch eine sogenannte Abarbeitungseinheit. Die Reihenfolge, in der diese die einzelnen Regeln eines Regelsatzes bearbeitet, ist von der konkreten Realisierung dieser Steuereinheit abhängig. Eine einfache Implementierung kann die Regeln entsprechend der Eintragsreihenfolge in den Rule-MIB-Tabellen abarbeiten. Wird eine aufwendigere Inferenzmaschine verwendet, so können auch andere Prinzipien (z.B. Zufall) zum Tragen kommen.

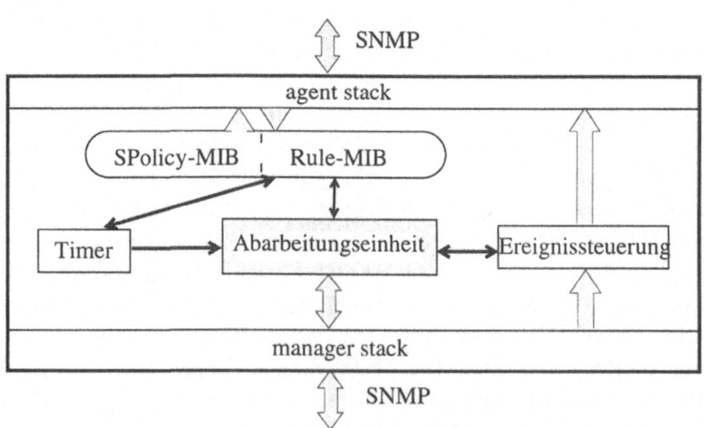

Abbildung 3 : Grundstruktur des Security-SMAgICs

Der MAgIC muß ankommende Botschaften untergeordneter Managementinstanzen empfangen und speichern können. Außerdem soll er die Möglichkeit besitzen, gewonnene Schlußfolgerungen, beispielsweise erkannte Sicherheitslücken, selbständig an den übergeordneten Sicherheitsmanager weiterleiten zu können. Deshalb ist eine Ereignissteuerung vorgesehen, die diese Funktionalität besitzt. Für zeitabhängige Vorgänge, z.B. das Anstoßen von Regeln zur periodischen Integritätssicherung, ist ein Timer vorhanden.

Die Interaktion zwischen den beteiligten Modulen des Security-MAgICs basiert auf dem Prinzip von Verweisen mittels sogenannter Objektidentifikatoren. Diese adressieren in eindeutiger Weise einzelne Managementobjekte im System. So kann beispielsweise die Bearbeitung von Ereignismeldungen auf einen anderen Security-MAgIC ausgelagert werden.

Die Rule-MIB

Die Rule-MIB ist, wie aus Abbildung 4 ersichtlich, in fünf Bereiche gegliedert. Der erste Bereich enthält Information über die allgemeine Konfiguration des MAgICs. Neben Objekten für die Initialisierung und Versionskontrolle ist die RegistrationTable(4) von besonderer Bedeutung. In dieser Tabelle werden alle Regelsätze, die der MAgIC verwaltet, registriert. Dies erleichtert das Definieren, Auffinden, Ändern, Aktivieren, Deaktivieren und Löschen von Regelsätzen. Außerdem wird ein Vermerk hinterlegt, über den sich die Managementinstanz identifizieren läßt, die den Eintrag angelegt hat. Zusätzlich kann die Menge der Komponenten, auf die ein Regelsatz angewendet werden soll, mit Hilfe der TargetTable(6) definiert werden.

Die einzelnen Regeln der Regelsätze sind im Knowledge(2)-Bereich der Rule-MIB untergebracht. Die zweigeteilte Struktur der Regeln (Bedingungsteil und Aktionsteil) bewirkt die getrennte Unterbringung dieser Teile in einer Bedingungs- (Condition Table) und in einer Aktions-Tabelle (Action Table). Die einzelnen Vergleichsoperationen bzw. Aktionen werden über einen gemeinsamen Index in Beziehung gebracht, der sich aus Regelsatznummer, Regelnummer und einer Bedingungs- bzw. Aktions-Nummer zusammensetzt. Auf diese Weise kann eine beliebige Menge von Vergleichsoperationen mit einer ebenso frei zu wählenden Anzahl von Aktionen verknüpft werden.

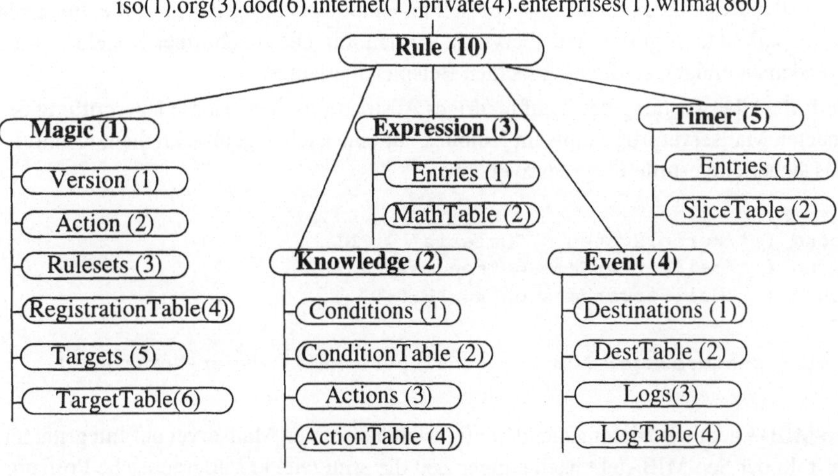

Abbildung 4 : Schematische Struktur der Rule-MIB

Um mathematische Ausdrücke verwenden zu können, wurde der Expression(3)-Teilbaum definiert. Dort lassen sich zweiwertige Operationen definieren, die zusätzlich über den Tabellenindex rekursiv verkettet werden können, um auch komplexere Berechnungen auszuführen. So kann ein mathematischer Ausdruck in einer Regel als Objektidentifikator angegeben werden, der seinerseits auf den entsprechenden Eintrag in der MathTable(2)-Struktur verweist. Mit diesem Ansatz ist es somit möglich, aufwendigere Funktionen, wie z.B. Verfügbarkeitsprognosen, in eigene Vorverarbeitungsprozesse auszulagern und als Entscheidungsgrundlage innerhalb von Regeln heranzuziehen.

Im Event(4)-Bereich werden ankommende Botschaften (SNMP-Traps oder Inform-Requests) in der Log-Tabelle (LogTable(4)) aufgezeichnet. Um Botschaften verschicken zu können, werden in der Zieltabelle (DestTable(2)) die Adressen derjenigen Managementstationen zu einer "Destination" zusammengefaßt, an die eine Botschaft versendet werden soll.

Die Zeitbereiche, die ein Regelsatz aktiv sein soll, werden im Timer(5)-Bereich festgelegt. Dabei sind absolute, relative, einmalige und periodische Zeitangaben möglich.

4. Szenario

Die Anwendung der vorgestellten Konzepte soll anhand eines exemplarischen Szenarios verdeutlicht werden. Die Verwaltung der Sicherheit einer Firmenfiliale wird mit Hilfe eines Security-MAgICs durchgeführt, in dessen Rule-MIB bereits eine Grundmenge von Regeln definiert wurde. Auf den einzelnen Komponenten wie Hosts und Router sind Agenten installiert, die über eine Sec-MIB sicherheitsrelevante Parameter zur Verfügung stellen. Der E-Mail-Dienst wird bisher nicht als bedrohtes Objekt vom Sicherheitsmanagementsystem verwaltet.

Nun wird der E-Mail-Dienst verstärkt zur Kommunikation sowohl mit Kunden als auch mit der Zentrale genutzt. Aus diesem Grund nimmt die Bedeutung dieses Dienstes zu. Die Zentrale paßt die allgemeine Sicherheitspolitik diesbezüglich an. Von einer Managementinstanz der Zentrale werden auf den Security-MAgIC der Filiale die entsprechenden neuen Sicherheitspolitiken und zugehörigen Regelsätze geladen. Die Politik umfaßt die Definition einer virtuellen Ressource "Email", die speziell im Hinblick auf Zugriffskontrolle, Integrität und Verfügbarkeit konfiguriert und überwacht werden soll. Die zugehörigen Regeln werden im folgenden an einigen stark vereinfachten Beispielen erläutert.

Eine einfache Überwachungsregel auf niedriger Abstraktionsebene ist die Überprüfung des verwendeten Mailserverprogramms im Hinblick auf eine nach augenblicklichem Kenntnisstand als sicher eingestufte Programmversion.

```
IF
    cond ( */kernelSystem = "Solaris" ) AND
    cond ( */mailServerName = "sendmail") AND
    cond ( */mailServerVersion <= "8.8.0" )          .

THEN
    act ( sendMessage; Admin1; "unsichere Mail-Server-Version" )
```

Der Sec-MIB-Agent wird dahingehend konfiguriert, daß er den Mailserver auf Integrität hin überprüft. In der Sec-MIB steht nach einiger Zeit die ermittelte kryptographische Prüfsumme über die zum Mailserver gehörenden Filesets zur Verfügung. In der SPolicy-MIB ist der zugehörige Sollwert abgelegt (Systemwissen). Bei einer Abweichung der beiden Werte wird ein entsprechender Vermerk in der Logtabelle der SPolicy-MIB angelegt.

```
IF
    cond ( */SEC_MIB.integrityConfName = "/usr/lib/sendmail" ) AND
    cond ( */SEC_MIB.integrityTestError = noerror(0)) AND
```

```
    cond ( */SEC_MIB.integrityTestHashValue != \
           SecurityMagic/SPOLICY_MIB.configResourceAuthDigest)
THEN
    act ( setObject; SecurityMagic/SPOLICY_MIB.logMessageText; \
          "Integrität des Sendmail-Servers verletzt")
```

Abschließend ein Beispiel für eine Regel auf hoher Abstraktionsebene:

```
IF
    cond ( SecurityMagic/SPOLICY_MIB.logMessageText = \
           "Hash-Algorithmus wird als unsicher eingestuft" )
THEN
    act ( startRule; checkSecurityServices; )
```

Wenn der zur Integritätsprüfung verwendete Hash-Mechanismus als unsicher erkannt wird (kryptographisches Wissen), so wird ein weiterer Regelsatz aktiviert. Dieser führt eine Überprüfung der Sicherheitsdienste auf Verwendung dieses Hash-Mechanismus durch.

5. Stand der Arbeiten und Ausblick

Am Lehrstuhl für Datenverarbeitung wurden Werkzeuge erstellt, um die Realisierung von Managementinstanzen zu unterstützen. Ein MIB-Compiler wandelt MIB-Beschreibungen in C-Strukturen, das SNMP-Toolkit dient zur Implementierung von Managementapplikationen. Desweiteren stehen ein Agentensimulator für Testzwecke, ein MIB-Browser zum Auslesen und Visualisieren von MIBs sowie weitere Tools zur Verfügung (siehe auch [Rose96, Seite 242-243]).

Es wurden die wesentlichen Bestandteile der verteilten Sicherheitsmanagementarchitektur realisiert. Die Anwendung dieser Architektur wurde exemplarisch anhand ausgewählter Szenarien untersucht. Security MAgICs stellen in der SPolicy-MIB abstrakte Sicherheitsvorgaben und -ziele zu einigen Sicherheitsdiensten wie z.B. Zugriffskontrolle, Integrität und Verfügbarkeit bereit. Die Sec-MIB enthält die zu verwaltenden Parameter dieser Mechanismen und Informationen in Bezug auf die Sicherheit von Unix-Systemen. Von den Managementfunktionen wurden Transformations- und Überwachungsfunktionen in Form von Regeln in der Rule-MIB definiert. Dadurch ist die Funktionalität des Sicherheitsmanagementsystems über die SNMP-Schnittstelle dynamisch veränderbar und erweiterbar.

Für zukünftige Arbeiten ist eine Erweiterung der Wissensbasis vor allem im Hinblick auf kryptographisches Wissen geplant. Die Funktionalität des Sicherheitsmanagementsystems soll um Regeln zur Plausibilitäts- und Konsistenzprüfung von Sicherheitspolitiken ergänzt werden.

Ein Teil der entstandenen Software ist für die nicht kommerzielle Nutzung über den FTP-Server des Lehrstuhls für Datenverarbeitung beziehbar (ftp://ftp.ldv.e-technik.tu-muenchen.de/dist/WILMA/).

Literatur

[AlPl95]   B. Alpers, H. Plansky: Policybasiertes Management - Konzepte und Anwendungen, Tagungsband der 'Kommunikation in Verteilten Systemen', 22.-24.02.95 in Chemnitz, Springer Verlag, 1995

[BSI92]   Bundesamt für Sicherheit in der Informationstechnik: IT-Sicherheitshandbuch, Handbuch für die sichere Anwendung der Informationstechnik; Version 1.0, BSI 7105, Bonn 1992

[FaSp90]   D. Farmer, E. Spafford: The COPS security checker system, in USENIX Conference Proceedings, Anaheim, CA, Summer 1990

[GiRi89]   J.C. Giarratano, G. Riley: Expert Systems: Principles and Programming, PWS-KENT Publishing Company, Boston, 1989

[HeAb93]   H.-G. Hegering, S. Abeck: Integriertes Netz- und Systemmanagement, Addison-Wesley, Bonn Paris, 1993

[HoTr96]   M. Horak, M. Trommer: Architektur für ein dezentrales, hierarchisches Sicherheitsmanagement; Proceedings der Fachtagung SIS '96, VDF Hochschulverlag, Zürich, 1996

[Hugh96]   L. J. Hughes: Actually useful Internet Security Techniques, New Riders Publishing, Indianapolis, Indiana, 1995, p. 273-291

[ISO7498-2] Information processing systems - Open Systems Interconnection - Basis Reference Model - Security Architecture (Part 2), ISO 7498-2/CCITT x.700

[ISO7498-4] Information processing systems - Open Systems Interconnection - Basis Reference Model - OSI Management Framework (Part 4), ISO 7498-4/CCITT X.700

[ISO9072-1] Information processing systems - Text Communication - Remote Operations - Part 1: Model, Notation and Service Definition, 1989, ISO/IEC 9072-1

[KoTr95]   R. Konopka, M. Trommer: A Multilayer-Architecture for SNMP-Based, Distributed and Hierarchical Management of Local Area Networks, Proceedings of the 'Fourth International Conference on Computer Communications and Networks', September 20-23, Las Vegas, 1995

[RFC1909]   K. McCloghrie: An Administrative Infrastructure for SNMPv2, February 1996

[RFC1910]   G. Waters: User-based Security Model for SNMPv2, February 1996

[Rose96]   M. T. Rose: The Simple Book - An Introduction to Networking Management, revised second edition; Prentice-Hall Inc., Upper Saddle River, 1996

[Scha95]   H.N. Schaller, A concept for a hierarchical, decentralized management of the physical configuration in the Internet, in: K. Franke, U. Hübner, W. Kalfa, Kommunikation in Verteilten Systemen, GI/ITG-Fachtagung, Springer-Verlag, Berlin, 1995

[SiTr95]   M. R. Siegl, G. Trausmuth: HIERARCHICAL NETWORK MANAGEMENT: A Concept and its Prototype in SNMPv2, Proceedings of the 'Joint European Networking Conference (JENC)', 1995

[SNMP2]   J. Case, K. McCloghrie, M. Rose & S. Waldbusser: Version 2 of the Simple Network Management Protocol (SNMPv2), SNMPv2 Working Group, RFCs 1902 to 1908, January 1996.

[Stei95]   A. Stein: Einbindung von Managementobjekten in eine Expertensystementwicklungsumgebung und beispielhafte Realisierung eines Sicherheitsexpertensystems, Diplomarbeit, Lehrstuhl für Datenverarbeitung, TU München, 1995

[TrKo96]   M. Trommer, R. Konopka: Verteilung von Netzmanagementaufgaben mit Hilfe einer dezentralen hierarchischen Mehrschichtenarchitektur; in Proceedings der Fachtagung STAK '96, ITG-Fachbericht 137, VDE-Verlag Berlin, 1996, Seite 253 - 265

[Wies95]   R. Wies: Using a Classification of Management Policies for Policy Specification and Policy Transformation; Integrated Network Management, Proceedings of the fourth intern. symposium on integrated netmanagement, Santa Barbara, Chapman & Hall, London, 1995

Interoperable Architekturen als Basis eines integrierten Managements

*Alexander Keller** *Bernhard Neumair*

Münchner Netzmanagement Team
Institut für Informatik, Universität München
Oettingenstrasse 67, 80538 München, Germany
E-Mail: {keller|neumair}@informatik.uni-muenchen.de

Zusammenfassung

Managementarchitekturen stellen die Basis für integriertes Management von heterogenen verteilten
Systemen und Kommunikationsnetzen dar. Derzeit existieren mehrere standardisierte Architekturen,
die teilweise in Konkurrenz zueinander stehen. Da sich vermutlich nicht eine einzige Architektur
für alle Einsatzbereiche durchsetzen wird, wird es wohl zu einem Nebeneinander von verschiedenen
Ansätzen kommen. Für wirklich integriertes Management müssen also Übergänge geschaffen werden, die eine nahtlose Kombination der Architekturen erlauben. Der Beitrag wird die grundlegenden
Alternativen für solche Übergänge darstellen und anschließend eine Analyse der prinzipiellen Unterschiede der Architekturen skizzieren. Auf dieser Basis werden dann konkrete Projekte vorgestellt,
die zum einen eine Integration von CORBA-konformen Managementanwendungen in eine vorhandene, CMIP- bzw. SNMP-basierte Plattform und zum anderen Management-Gateways zwischen
verschiedenen Architekturen prototypisch realisiert haben.

1 Einführung und Motivation

Die zunehmende Komplexität und Heterogenität verteilter Systeme stellt für ihre Betreiber eine große
Herausforderung dar. Heutige umfangreiche DV-Infrastrukturen können nur noch dann mit vertretbarem
Aufwand administriert werden, wenn man integrierte Managementlösungen einsetzt. Solche Lösungen
auf der Basis standardisierter Managementarchitekturen ([3, 14]) sollen die Betreiber dabei unterstützen,
eine optimale Versorgung der Benutzer mit akzeptablem Aufwand sicherzustellen.

In letzter Zeit trat auf dem Weg zum integrierten Management allerdings eine zusätzliche Komplika-
tion auf: neben proprietären Ansätzen wurden *mehrere* Managementarchitekturen standardisiert, die teilweise in Konkurrenz zueinander stehen. So ist das bekannte Internet-Management (*SNMP-Management*)
im Bereich des LAN-Managements weit verbreitet, während im Bereich der Telekommunikationsnetze vor allem auf das OSI-Management gesetzt wird. Mit dem *Desktop Management Interface* (DMI)
der DMTF wird derzeit versucht, für das Management von Endsystemen wie PCs oder Workstations
einen weiteren Standard zu etablieren. Neuerdings werden auch die Arbeiten der OMG (*Object Management Architecture - OMA, CORBA*) für die Bereiche des Endsystem- und Anwendungsmanagements
zunehmend beachtet. Dem OMG-Ansatz werden heute gute Chancen auf große Verbreitung für die
Entwicklung verteilter Anwendungen eingeräumt. Bewahrheitet sich dies, wird er auch für *integriertes* Management sehr wichtig werden, obwohl er nicht wie die anderen Architekturen speziell auf das
Management einer DV-Infrastruktur ausgerichtet, sondern prinzipiell für alle verteilten Anwendungen
gedacht ist.

In verteilten und heterogenen Systemumgebungen ist das Management natürlich eine verteilte Anwendung, deren Komponenten von verschiedenen Herstellern stammen. Zentraler Bestandteil einer
Managementarchitektur ist damit die Definition eines Beschreibungsrahmens für die zu Managementzwecken ausgetauschte Information. Diese Information wird heute meist objektorientiert modelliert.

---

*Die Arbeiten des Autors wurden gefördert durch das IBM European Networking Center, Heidelberg

Der Informationsaustausch findet also z.B. durch Lesen oder Setzen von Attributen sogenannter Managementobjekte oder durch Anwendung von Methoden auf diesen Objekten statt. Je detaillierter diese Information festgelegt ist, desto effizienter ist Management auf der Basis der jeweiligen Architektur möglich. Weiterhin ist offensichtlich ein Kommunikationsprotokoll für diesen Austausch – ein sogenanntes Managementprotokoll – festzulegen.

Vermutlich wird sich nicht eine einzige Managementarchitektur durchsetzen; es wird wohl zu einem Nebeneinander von verschiedenen Architekturen kommen. Wirklich integriertes Management setzt also voraus, daß Übergänge geschaffen werden, die eine nahtlose Kombination der Architekturen erlauben (siehe auch [1, 9]). Prinzipiell gibt es hier *3 Alternativen*:

- *„Management-Gateway"*: Der Übergang wird durch ein Zwischensystem realisiert, das sowohl eine Übersetzung der Managementinformation als auch die Umsetzung der Managementprotokolle vornimmt. Zuerst müssen also die verschiedenen Spezifikationssprachen, in denen die Managementobjekte beschrieben sind, algorithmisch ineinander überführt werden. Besonders interessant ist die Abbildung der Sprachen des OSI- und des Internet-Managements auf den OMG-Ansatz, da in den beiden erstgenannten Fällen umfangreiche Objektspezifikationen speziell für Managementzwecke existieren, die für CORBA-basiertes Management übernommen werden können. Dieser statische Aspekt der Kooperation von Managementarchitekturen, die sogenannte *Specification Translation*, wird mit Hilfe von Spezifikations-Compilern behandelt. Zur Laufzeit müssen dann noch die Protokolle bzw. deren Elemente umgesetzt werden, was als *Interaction Translation* bezeichnet wird. Abb. 1 zeigt ein mögliches Szenario.

- *„Multiarchitekturelle Plattform"*: Hier erfolgt der Übergang innerhalb der Managementplattform, also des managenden Systems, das damit mehrere oder alle „Management-Sprachen spricht". Damit ist auch keine direkte Umsetzung der Protokolle notwendig, sondern jeweils nur eine Abbildung auf das entsprechende Kommunikations-API der Plattform. Häufig findet die Übersetzung der Managementinformation nicht in der Infrastruktur der Plattform statt, sondern muß in den Anwendungen durchgeführt werden. Damit schlagen dann die Unterschiede der Architekturen bis in die Anwendungen durch; es bleibt häufig bei einem bloßen Nebeneinander der Architekturen unter einer gemeinsamen Oberfläche.

- *„Multiarchitektureller Agent"*: In diesem Fall erfolgen die notwendigen Abbildungen im Agenten, also im zu administrierenden System; hier „spricht" der Agent mehrere oder alle „Management-Sprachen" (siehe auch [11, 6]). Bei dieser Alternative fällt allerdings der höchste (Implementierungs-)Aufwand an, da naturgemäß die Anzahl an Agenten die der Managementsysteme bei weitem übersteigt. Insbesondere für einfache Komponenten ist eine solche Mehrsprachigkeit nicht sinnvoll realisierbar. Für den Betreiber einer DV-Infrastruktur ist dieser Ansatz irrelevant, da der Quelltext des Agenten vorliegen muß. Dies ist jedoch in der Regel nicht der Fall. Das Papier wird sich deshalb im folgenden auf die ersten beiden Alternativen beschränken.

Ziel ist bei allen Varianten, die Existenz verschiedener Managementarchitekturen für Benutzer, also die Betreiber einer DV-Infrastruktur, und die Managementanwendungen möglichst weitgehend zu verschatten. Man möchte dem Benutzer eine möglichst einheitliche Sicht auf alle zu administrierenden Systeme bieten und die Implementierung der Anwendungen effizient gestalten.

Im weiteren werden in Abschnitt 2 skizzenhaft die Managementarchitekturen verglichen und die grundsätzlichen Möglichkeiten für Übergänge gezeigt. Anschließend werden konkrete Projekte vorgestellt, die zum einen prototypisch Teile einer multiarchitekturellen Plattform implementiert (Abschnitt 3) und zum anderen Gateways zwischen CORBA und SNMP bzw. zwischen CMIP und SNMP (Abschnitt 4) realisiert haben.

2 Vergleich der Managementarchitekturen

Der folgende Vergleich der verschiedenen, heute definierten Managementarchitekturen (siehe auch ([5, 4]) soll die Basis legen für die Beschreibung der möglichen Architekturübergänge. Der Schwerpunkt

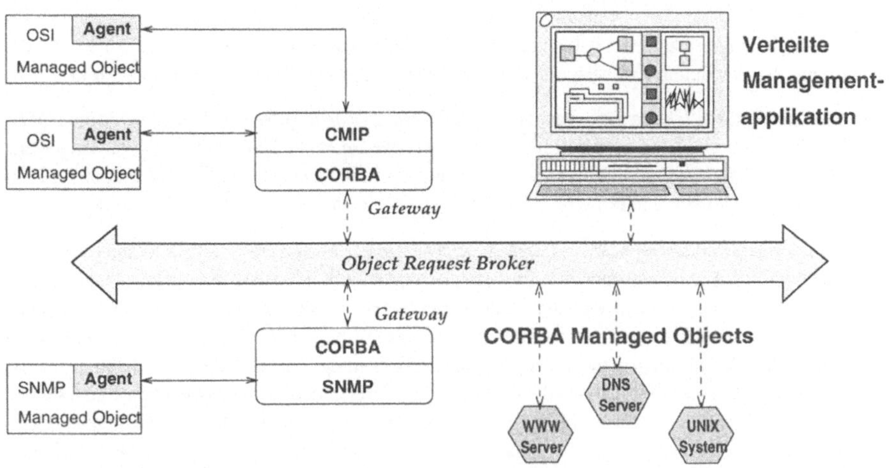

Abbildung 1: Interoperabilitätsszenario für Managementarchitekturen

wird dabei nicht auf einem Vergleich bekannter Architekturen wie dem OSI-Management oder dem Internet-Management liegen, sondern auf einer Gegenüberstellung mit dem neueren CORBA-Ansatz der OMG als Architektur für das Netz- und Systemmanagement.

2.1 Ziel und Inhalt einer Managementarchitektur

Wie in jeder Architektur für verteilte Systeme müssen auch für die verteilte Anwendung *Management* die grundlegenden Interaktionsprinzipien und die ausgetauschte Information festgelegt werden. Managementarchitekturen müssen deshalb u.a. die folgenden Bereiche abdecken:

- *Zu Managementzwecken auszutauschende Information:* Wie in der Einleitung erwähnt, wird derzeit zur Spezifikation der Information der objektorientierte Ansatz favorisiert. Es muß also ein Beschreibungsrahmen für die zu definierenden Managementobjekte festgelegt werden. Dabei ist grundsätzlich zu entscheiden, ob und wie weit dieser Rahmen bereits speziell auf das Management oder sogar auf spezifische Managementbereiche zugeschnitten wird oder eher allgemein gehalten werden soll (Abschnitt 2.3).

- *Kommunikationsprotokoll:* Bei der Festlegung eines Managementprotokolls, die ja in verteilter Umgebung offensichtlich nötig ist, ist grundsätzlich die Entscheidung zu treffen, ob für die beim Management auftretenden Kommunikationsvorgänge (Abfragen von Information über Ressourcen, Austausch von Steuerinformation, (asynchrone) Ereignismeldungen) ein komplett neues Protokoll definiert werden soll, für das dann natürlich eigene Protokollinstanzen zu implementieren sind. Alternativ dazu könnten auch vorhandene Mechanismen und Protokolle (z.B. RPCs etc.) angepaßt werden, indem z.B. die ausgetauschte (Protokoll-)Information verfeinert und mit einer speziellen Semantik versehen wird. Im RPC-Beispiel würde sich dies z.B. auf die aufrufbaren Prozeduren und deren Semantik beziehen (Abschnitt 2.4).

- *Infrastruktur-Dienste:* Neben den reinen Kommunikationsdiensten sind noch weitere Dienste zu definieren, die für deren effektive und effiziente Nutzung unbedingt notwendig sind. Darunter fallen z.B. Dienste für die Namensverwaltung und für das Ereignismanagement. Solche Dienstdefinitionen können, da sie bei hinreichend genauer Spezifikation ja in verschiedenen Systemen realisiert werden können, auch die Skalierbarkeit des Managements verbessern. Dies gilt z.B. für Überwachungsdienste, die bei Bedarf delegiert werden können (Abschnitt 2.5).

2.2 Grundsätzliche Architektur-Varianten

Die in der Einleitung erwähnten existierenden Architekturen unterscheiden sich grundsätzlich, was die im Abschnitt 2.1 skizzierten Kriterien und Entscheidungen anbelangt. Man kann sie einteilen in:

- *Managementarchitekturen im engeren Sinn: OSI-Management, Internet-Management* und *DMTF DMI* sind von vornherein speziell für Managementzwecke entwickelt worden. Es wurden jeweils praktisch von Grund auf ein eigenes Managementinformationsmodell, ein eigenes Protokoll nur für das Management und teilweise auch managementspezifische Infrastrukturdienste definiert.

- *Managementarchitekturen im weiteren Sinn:* Die *Object Management Architecture (OMA)* der OMG für verteilte objektorientierte Programmierung erlaubt in erster Linie ortsungebundene Ko- operation von Objekten in verteilter Umgebung. Sie ist, im Gegensatz zu den bisher genannten Architekturen, nicht speziell auf das Management der DV-Infrastruktur ausgerichtet, sondern prin- zipiell für alle verteilten Anwendungen gedacht. Neuerdings gewinnt sie an Bedeutung für das integrierte Management, da vor allem Produkte im Bereich des Managements von Endsystemen auf OMG-Technologie aufsetzen bzw. aufsetzen werden. Soll sie in heterogener Umgebung ein- setzbar sein, müssen die allgemein gehaltenen Konzepte und Methoden spezialisiert und verfeinert werden. Man setzt dabei allerdings auf einem höheren Niveau auf als bei den vorigen Ansätzen. Die *X/Open Systems Management Working Group (XoTGsysMan)* sowie die *OMG Telecom Spe- cial Interest Group* befassen sich u.a. speziell mit Infrastrukturdiensten, die auf das Management zugeschnitten sind. Stützt man sich, wie hier vorgesehen, weiter als bei den Managementarchi- tekturen im engeren Sinn auf eine vorhandene Infrastruktur ab, bestehen zum einen natürlich Aussichten auf Einsparungen bei SW- und Installationskosten für den Anwender. Zum anderen können Entwickler von Managementsoftware dann Werkzeuge benutzen, die nicht ausschließ- lich für Managementapplikationen einsetzbar sind. Die Einarbeitungszeit, z.B. bezogen auf die Modellierung von Information, wird deutlich kürzer.

2.3 Ausgetauschte Information

Im Rahmen eines sogenannten Informationsmodells muß für jede Architektur festgelegt werden, wie Syntax und Semantik der auszutauschenden Managementinformation definiert werden. Grundsätzlich muß entschieden werden, ob aus Gründen der Interoperabilität die allgemein denkbaren Möglichkeiten objektorientierter Spezifikationen weiter einzuschränken und zu spezialisieren sind oder ob aus Gründen der Flexibilität des Ansatzes darauf verzichtet werden soll. Zusätzlich ist festzulegen, ob man es bei einem Beschreibungsrahmen belassen möchte oder auf dieser Basis dann zur Förderung der Interoperabilität bereits konkrete Information spezifiziert werden soll. Dabei können folgende Eigenschaften der Modelle unterschieden werden:

- *Struktur der Information:* Hierzu existieren die beiden folgenden grundsätzlich verschiedenen Alternativen.

    - Der OMG-Ansatz definiert (bisher) ausschließlich eine Schnittstellen-Beschreibungssprache, die *Interface Definition Language (IDL)*. Mit dieser C++-ähnlichen Sprache werden keiner- lei weitere, managementspezifische Annahmen über die Struktur von Managementobjekten getroffen; es erfolgen keine weiteren Einschränkungen der denkbaren Objektwelt.

    - Die managementspezifischen Ansätze sind hier (vor allem aus Gründen der Interoperabi- lität) sehr viel restriktiver; es werden wesentliche Annahmen über die Struktur der Objekte gemacht. So legt das OSI-Informationsmodell z.B. fest, daß ein Managementobjekt durch Attribute, Aktionen und Notifikationen zu charakterisieren ist und gibt sehr detailliert soge- nannte Templates vor. Im Internet-Management und bei DMI sind Managementobjekte nur einfache Variable oder Tabellen, die ebenfalls über spezielle Templates beschrieben sind.

- *Datentypen:* Wie bei anderen Spezifikationssprachen sind Basis-Datentypen festzulegen, die für die Charakterisierung der Objekte bzw. der Attribute verwendet werden können. Die management- spezifischen Ansätze geben hier teilweise bereits eine große Zahl an Typen vor, die für Managementzwecke nützlich sind. Beispiele hierfür sind Zähler, Schwellwerte, Pegel etc., die z.B. aus `integer`-Typen abgeleitet sind. Solche Festlegungen fehlen beim OMG-Ansatz völlig.

- *Semantik der Zugriffe:* Hier ist die Frage zu klären, welche Objektzugriffe die Architektur unterstützt. Die managementspezifischen Ansätze legen die Semantik möglicher Zugriffe von vornherein sehr detailliert fest. Die Basis dafür findet man in den obigen Restriktionen der Struktur von Objekten.

  Der OMG-Ansatz macht naturgemäß weniger Vorgaben an mögliche Objektzugriffe, was seinen Grund im allgemeiner gehaltenen Objektmodell hat. Um problemlose Interoperabilität in heterogener Umgebung für das Management sicherzustellen, sind dann noch weitergehende Festlegungen nötig.

- *Semantik der Objekte selbst:* Integriertes Management in heterogener Umgebung ist nur dann sinnvoll möglich, wenn auch an die Semantik der Objekte selbst Vorgaben gemacht werden. Einfache Beispiele hierzu sind die Semantik von Statusvariablen (`operational, up` etc.) und Statusübergängen (`restarting, rebooting` etc.) oder die Parameter von Ereignismeldungen (`coming up, going down` etc.).

  Derartige Vorgaben werden i.a. durch generische, nicht instantiierbare Objektklassen bzw. Interfaces realisiert, deren Eigenschaften weitervererbt werden können, was Einheitlichkeit und damit Interoperabilität fördert. In diesem Bereich ist das grundsätzliche Vorgehen beim OSI-Management und beim OMG-Ansatz sehr ähnlich: Im Rahmen bestimmter sogenannter *Systems Management Functions* bzw. *CORBA-Services* und *-Facilities* (siehe auch Abschnitt 2.5) werden nicht getrennt implementierbare Dienste bzw. Funktionen spezifiziert, sondern Vorgaben bezüglich der Semantik bestimmter Attribute, Methoden oder Object Interfaces gemacht. Diese sollen bei der Definition instantiierbarer Objektklassen bzw. Interfaces ererbt bzw. importiert werden.

  Internet-Management bzw. DMI liefern weniger Vorgaben. Hier baut man eher darauf, daß Informationsspezifizierer erkennen, wenn Gleiches schon einmal anderswo festgelegt wurde, und sich dann entsprechend daran ausrichten.

Insgesamt liefern die Definitionen der managementspezifischen Ansätze (vgl. Abschnitt 2.2) naturgemäß eine Interoperabilität des Managements in heterogener Umgebung, die beim OMG-Ansatz trotz der Arbeit von Gruppen wie der XoTGsysMan noch nicht gegeben ist. Andererseits hat dieser Ansatz den Vorteil, daß für ihn, weil er eben für viele andere verteilte Anwendungen ebenfalls einsetzbar ist, zukünftig eine größere Auswahl an Entwicklungs- bzw. Modellierungswerkzeugen als bei den anderen Architekturen zur Verfügung stehen wird.

Eine Möglichkeit zur Kombination der Vorteile beider Ansätze könnte darin bestehen, die weitergehenden Festlegungen der „klassischen" Managementarchitekturen in OMG-IDL zu übersetzen bzw. zu übernehmen (siehe auch Abschnitte 3.2 und 4.1). Damit könnte man einerseits die allgemein verwendbare Infrastruktur und die Entwicklungswerkzeuge für Managementzwecke nutzen, würde aber andererseits die bei den spezifischen Ansätzen erreichte Interoperabilität auch nicht aufgeben.

2.4   Kommunikationsprotokoll

Analog zu den Informationsmodellen stehen auch bei den Kommunikationsprotokollen mehrere hochspezialisierte Protokolle einem sehr allgemein gehaltenen Protokoll gegenüber. CMIP, das Managementprotokoll des OSI-Managements, und das bekannte SNMP sind extrem abgestimmt auf Managementinteraktionen und auf die jeweiligen Informationsmodelle. Die in Abschnitt 2.3 dargestellten möglichen Zugriffe auf Objekte werden direkt auf PDU-Strukturen abgebildet. Spezifika dieser Kommunikationsprotokolle und -dienste wie *Scoping & Filtering* und die protokolltechnische Behandlung des Allomorphiekonzepts bei CMIP bzw. der `GETNEXT`-Operator bei SNMP sind kaum auf andere Einsatzbereiche übertragbar.

Dem stehen die ORB-Dienste bzw. ein Inter-ORB-Protokoll gegenüber, das „nur" einen „objektorientierten RPC" definiert, also die Übertragung vollkommen beliebiger Methodenaufrufe und der zugehörigen Ergebnisse.

Genau wie bei den Informationsmodellen ist die Allgemeinheit des OMG-Protokolls aus Managementsicht hinderlich im Hinblick auf Interoperabilität in heterogener Umgebung. Übersetzt man aber die managementspezifischen Informationsdefinitionen aus der OSI- und Internet-Welt in IDL, schränkt man die mit ORB-Dienstaufrufen auf Managementobjekten aufrufbaren Methoden ein; die skizzierten Interoperabilitätsprobleme können nicht auftreten. Man kann dann relativ einfach vorhandene CORBA-Infrastrukturen für Managementkommunikation im engeren Sinn nutzen.

2.5 Infrastruktur-Dienste

Wie in Abschnitt 2.1 erwähnt, muß für jede Managementarchitektur eine Infrastruktur aus Basisdiensten definiert werden, die die Nutzung der Kommunikationsdienste erleichtern oder überhaupt erst möglich machen.

Führend in diesem Bereich ist das OSI-Management, das im Rahmen diverser Systems Management Functions umfangreiche derartige Basisdienste[1] definiert. Beispiele sind Dienste für die Handhabung asynchroner Ereignismeldungen, für die Schwellwertüberwachung oder für die Vorverarbeitung großer Datenmengen.

Auch die OMG hat in Form diverser *CORBA Services* solche Dienste definiert und erweitert diese laufend um neue. Die XoTGsysMan und die OMG Telecom SIG arbeiten nun daran, diese nicht managementspezifischen Dienste in Form sogenannter *CORBA Facilities* auf Managementzwecke abgestimmt zu verfeinern, wobei einige Konzepte aus dem OSI-Management hier wiederzufinden sind ([10]). Dies soll an zwei Beispielen erläutert werden:

- *Gruppieren von Objekten und Definition von Zielvorgaben:* Der *Managed Set Service* erlaubt es, zu Managementzwecken zusammengehörige Objekte zu gruppieren und diese Gruppen zu administrieren. Darunter fallen Tätigkeiten wie die Aufnahme und Streichung von Mitgliedern oder das Einholen von Informationen über Mitglieder einer bestimmten Gruppe. Mit dem *Policy Management Service* können dann Zielvorgaben (*Policies*) zu solchen Objektgruppen definiert und ihre Einhaltung überwacht werden. Er soll Administratoren dabei helfen, das Verhalten eines Managementsystems ihrer spezifischen Umgebung anzupassen. Diese Dienste sind weitgehend vergleichbar mit der *Management Domain and Management Policy Management Function* (ISO 10164-19) des OSI-Managements. Im Internet-Management sind keine derartigen Funktionen vordefiniert; Domains und Policies sind Sache der Anwendung.

- *Handhabung asynchroner Ereignismeldungen:* Das OSI-Management liefert mit der *Event Report Management Function* (ISO 10164-5) sehr flexible Mechanismen, mit denen eine Anwendung z.B. Ereignisse eines bestimmten Typs abonnieren oder Ereignismeldungen nach frei wählbaren Kriterien filtern lassen kann. Ähnliche Funktionalität innerhalb der OMA stellt der *Object Event Service* bereit, allerdings ohne (managementrelevante) Filtermöglichkeiten. Letzteres ist für Managementanwendungen ein schwerwiegender Nachteil. Die OMG Telecom SIG plant deshalb, hier mit dem *Notification Service* eine Erweiterung vorzunehmen. Einfache Funktionen zum Ereignismanagement, allerdings ebenfalls ohne Filtermöglichkeiten, finden sich im Rahmen der *Remote Network Monitoring MIB* (RFC 1757) auch im Internet-Management.

Managementdienste wie z.B. die entfernte Überwachung von Schwellwerten, zu denen im OSI-Management flexible und komplexe Mechanismen existieren (*Metric Objects and Attributes*, ISO 10164-11), werden im Rahmen der OMA bisher nicht behandelt. Da diese Dienste aber alle mit Hilfe des Management-Informationsmodells definiert wurden, könnte man aus diesen Beschreibungen IDL-Schnittstellen generieren, evtl. vorhandene Implementierungen damit kapseln und so OSI-Managementfunktionen auch per CORBA verfügbar machen (siehe auch Abschnitt 3.2).

---

[1] In diesen SMFs strebt man also im Gegensatz zu den in Abschnitt 2.3 erwähnten SMFs nicht die Verfeinerung der Semantik von Managementobjekten, sondern die Definition abgesetzt implementierbarer Dienste an.

2.6   Fazit

CORBA als gemeinsame Infrastruktur für viele Anwendungen incl. Management ist aus heutiger Sicht sehr zukunftsträchtig. Noch fehlen allerdings viele Festlegungen, die speziell für die verteilte Anwendung *Management* unbedingt notwendig sind, obwohl bereits CORBA-basierte Managementprodukte wie z.B. IBM TME 10 am Markt verfügbar sind. Dies gilt nicht nur für die fehlende Definition vieler konkreter Managementobjekte, wie sie im OSI-Management oder im Internet-Management zu finden sind. Es gilt auch, wie in den vorigen Abschnitten ausgeführt, für die Verfeinerung und Spezialisierung der Semantik der Zugriffe auf Objekte, für das Managementprotokoll zwischen den verschiedenen Akteuren des Managements und für die Basisdienste der Infrastruktur.

Würde man viele managementspezifische Spezifikationen aus der Internet- und OSI-Welt in die CORBA-Welt übertragen, würde man nicht nur die Interoperabilität von CORBA-basierten Managementsystemen und Komponenten in heterogener Umgebung verbessern bzw. sicherstellen, sondern auch die Übergänge zu Managementkomponenten, die auf den „klassischen" Managementarchitekturen basieren, ermöglichen bzw. erleichtern.

Dies könnte dann technisch mit den oben erwähnten und in Abschnitt 3 bzw. 4 noch genauer ausgeführten multiarchitekturellen Plattformen oder Management-Gateways realisiert werden. Man würde damit einerseits vorhandene Investitionen retten (z.B. die große Zahl an SNMP-Agenten), und andererseits gleichzeitig neue CORBA-Investitionen auch für das Management nutzen.

3   Multiarchitekturelle Plattform

Managementplattformen (wie z.B. *IBM TME 10 NetView for AIX* oder *HP OpenView*) haben sich seit geraumer Zeit als praktikabler Weg für integriertes Management etabliert und bilden den Kern heutiger Managementlösungen. Sie sind die Basis, auf der die eigentlichen Managementapplikationen (wie z.B. *Cisco Works*, eine Anwendung für das Router-Management) ablaufen. Typische Plattformfunktionalitäten sind die Kommunikation mit den zu managenden Ressourcen über ein standardisiertes Managementprotokoll, die Verwaltung der Datenbank, in der die Netztopologie sowie Informationen zu den Ressourcen gehalten werden, sowie die Bereitstellung einer graphischen Benutzerschnittstelle, die flexibel anpaßbar ist. Eine weitere grundlegende Eigenschaft von Plattformen ist die Fähigkeit, asynchrone Ereignismeldungen von den Agenten entgegenzunehmen und zu verarbeiten. Wir zeigen in den folgenden Abschnitten am Beispiel von *IBM TME 10 NetView for AIX*, wie eine am Markt erhältliche SNMP-Managementplattform um Fähigkeiten für das Ereignis– und Topologiemanagement CORBA-konformer Agenten erweitert werden kann, was einen wichtigen Schritt auf dem Weg zu einer multiarchitekturellen Plattform darstellt.

Als CORBA-Entwicklungssystem kam das *IBM SOMobjects Developer Toolkit* zum Einsatz; es umfaßt einen IDL-Compiler, die CORBA-Laufzeitumgebung sowie mehrere zu den OMG-Standards konforme Dienste [15].

3.1   Erweiterung von *IBM TME 10 NetView* zu einer multiarchitekturellen Plattform

Sollen Plattformen als Basis für die Integration unterschiedlicher Managementarchitekturen verwendet werden, ist es naheliegend, unmittelbar an der Kommunikationsschnittstelle der Plattform anzusetzen, um so die Heterogenität verschiedener Managementprotokolle so weit „unten" wie möglich abzuhandeln. Ein typischer Vertreter dieses Gedankens ist XMP/XOM (X/Open Management Protocol, X/Open OSI-Abstract-Data Manipulation), dessen Zielsetzung darin besteht, eine einheitliche Programmierschnittstelle für die Managementprotokolle CMIP und SNMP bzw. die Darstellung von ASN.1-Datentypen in C bereitzustellen, um einheitliches Management unabhängig von der verwendeten Managementarchitektur zu erlauben. Dieser Versuch der Vereinheitlichung muß jedoch aus heutiger Sicht als gescheitert betrachtet werden, da sich die Heterogenität der Managementprotokolle nicht verbergen ließ. Das sehr komplexe XMP wird daher in heutigen Produkten (wie zum Beispiel der *IBM NetView TMN Support*

412

Facility, einem auf NetView basierenden OSI-Managementsystem) ausschließlich als CMIP-API[2] eingesetzt; SNMP-konforme Ressourcen werden in bestehenden Produkten über ein separates einfaches SNMP-API angesteuert.

Wir haben uns für unsere Implementierung aus folgenden Gründen gegen eine auf XMP/XOM basierende Lösung entschieden:

- Der XMP-Stack wird bei NetView durch den sog. *Postmaster*-Dämon verwaltet. Eine CORBA-Ereignismeldung ist, im Gegensatz zu SNMP oder CMIP, keine Protokolldateneinheit mit festgelegter Struktur, sondern ein beliebiger Methodenaufruf auf einem *Consumer*-Objekt. Im vorliegenden Falle würde der Postmaster in der Rolle des Consumers (s.u.) agieren; es folgt, daß er um jede neu eingeführte Ereignismeldung erweitert werden müßte. Aufgrund des zu erwartenden Aufwands ist dies nicht praktikabel, da eine solche Erweiterung beim Einbringen jeder neuen CORBA-Ressource erfolgen müßte.

- Um solche Erweiterungen vornehmen zu können, hätte der Quellcode des *Postmaster*-Dämons und einiger anderer NetView-Komponenten vorliegen müssen; diese Forderung ist bei kommerziellen Produkten natürlich illusorisch.

Eine Alternative zu XMP ist der unmittelbare Zugriff auf die plattformspezifischen Infrastrukturdienste, wie z.B. Topologiedatenbank, Ereignisfilter oder Ressourcenverwaltung; jede dieser Komponenten verfügt über ein eigenes API. Die Nutzung dieser produktspezifischen und nicht standardisierten Funktionen impliziert allerdings den Verlust der Unabhängigkeit von bestehenden Plattformimplementierungen: die Lösung ist damit nur unter vermutlich hohem Aufwand auf andere Plattformen zu portieren. Die oben beschriebenen Argumente ließen jedoch keine andere Wahl zu.

Beide Alternativen haben durch die Heterogenität der Informationsmodelle die Einschränkung, daß auf Managementobjekten einer Protokolldomäne nur die durch das entsprechende Protokoll erlaubten Funktionen anwendbar sind; *Scoping* und *Filtering*, essentieller Bestandteil des OSI–Modells, kann nicht für das Management von SNMP–Ressourcen verwendet werden (vergleiche dazu Abschnitt 4.3). Auf multiarchitekturellen Plattformen wird daher bereits an oberster Stelle der Topologiehierarchie zwischen beiden Protokollwelten unterschieden. Das in der Einleitung beschriebene Problem des Fortlebens unterschiedlicher Architekturen unter einer gemeinsamen Oberfläche bleibt bei diesem Integrationsansatz bestehen (siehe auch [9]).

Der Schwerpunkt des Integrationskonzeptes liegt auf einem möglichst hohen Verfügbarkeitsgrad von Infrastruktur-Diensten, wie sie in Abschnitt 2.5 beschrieben wurden. Dies kann auf zweierlei Arten geschehen:

- Falls die *Dienste* der einen Architektur *keine Entsprechung* in der anderen betrachteten Architektur haben, kann man (siehe Abschnitt 2.6) durch die Überführung der Beschreibungen dieser Dienste in das entsprechende Informationsmodell die Managementfunktionalität einer Architektur von einer anderen Managementarchitektur aus nutzen. Damit könnte man z.B. in der OSI-Architektur existierende Mechanismen zur Schwellwertüberwachung von CORBA-Objekten aus verwenden. Dieser Weg hin zu Interoperabilität von Infrastruktur-Diensten wird in Abschnitt 4 ausführlicher beschrieben. Es sei hier nur kurz erwähnt, daß die Beschreibungen der Dienstschnittstellen algorithmisch in das Informationsmodell der Zielarchitektur überführt werden müssen (vgl. Abschnitt 2.3). Dort werden Proxy-Objekte erzeugt, die die Dienstaufrufe innerhalb der einen Architektur auf die Dienstimplementierungen der anderen transparent für den Dienstnutzer weiterleiten.

- Liegen *vergleichbare Infrastruktur-Dienste* in beiden Architekturen vor, müssen sie aufeinander abgebildet werden. Dies gilt für die in den folgenden Abschnitten betrachteten Applikationen, die die Topologie von CORBA-Agenten ermitteln (siehe Abschnitt 3.3) bzw. die von ihnen ausgesendeten CORBA-Events auf SNMP-Traps (und umgekehrt) abbilden (siehe Abschnitt 3.2). Hierbei werden ebenfalls Infrastruktur-Dienste genutzt, die die Managementplattform bereitstellt, um die ermittelten Informationen einer CORBA-konformen Managementapplikation (siehe auch

---

[2]In der Tat war XMP das bisher einzige standardisierte CMIP-API; ein C++ API für CMIP befindet sich momentan in der Standardisierungsphase (siehe dazu Abschnitt 4.3)

[16]) zur Weiterverarbeitung anzubieten. Die Plattform fungiert dabei als Brücke zwischen den CORBA-Agenten und einer CORBA-Managementapplikation (siehe Abbildung 2).

3.2 Nutzung von Infrastruktur-Diensten für ein integriertes Ereignismanagement

Die Verarbeitung asynchroner Ereignismeldungen durch eine Managementplattform geschieht i.w. in folgenden Schritten:

- Von den Agenten der überwachten Systeme werden (im Fehlerfalle oder bei Überschreitung vorher definierter Schwellwerte) Ereignismeldungen an die Managementplattform gesandt, die diese empfängt und nach festgelegten Regeln filtert. Hauptaufgabe der Filterung ist es also, aus den eingehenden Ereignis-Rohdaten Managementinformation zu gewinnen. Filterkriterien sind beispielsweise die Art der Ressource, der Typ und der Zeitpunkt der Ereignismeldung oder die Häufigkeit des Auftretens.

- Die gefilterte Managementinformation wird anschließend der Managementapplikation bzw. dem Administrator zur Verfügung gestellt. Die durch den Administrator ausgelösten Aktionen werden über die Plattform an die Ressourcen zur Ausführung übermittelt.

Die Aufgabe bestand nun darin, die vorhandenen NetView-Dienste für das Management von Ereignissen so zu erweitern, daß sowohl SNMP-Traps als auch CORBA-Events von einer zentralen Stelle empfangen werden können. Unser Ansatz basiert auf dem CORBA Event Service [13], der Mittel für die asynchrone Kommunikation zwischen verteilten Objekten spezifiziert. Hierbei wird zwischen Objekten, die Ereignisse erzeugen (sog. *Supplier*) und empfangenden Objekten (sog. *Consumer*) unterschieden. Die Kommunikation zwischen diesen Objektarten erfolgt durch Aufruf einer Methode des Consumers durch den Supplier; zur Entkopplung der beiden werden sogenannte *Event Channels* eingesetzt, die ihrerseits sämtliche Ereignisse, die von Suppliern kommen, an diejenigen Consumer weiterleiten, die sich für die betreffenden Events registriert haben. Man erhält somit die Möglichkeit, durch „Multiplexing" ein Ereignis mehreren Consumern bzw. die Ereignisse sämtlicher Supplier einem Consumer zuzustellen. Letzterer Fall spiegelt unsere Anwendung der Event Channels wider.

Da NetView selbst nicht in der Lage ist, CORBA-Events zu verarbeiten, mußten diese im *ersten Schritt* in SNMP-Traps umgewandelt werden. Es wurde also ein Event-Gateway implementiert, das die NetView-Ereignisdienste kapselt[3]. Nachdem die Ereignismeldungen empfangen wurden, können sie nun ebenso wie SNMP-Traps durch die NetView-Dienste gefiltert, protokolliert und an der graphischen Benutzerschnittstelle angezeigt werden. Es hat sich gezeigt, daß durch die Abstützung auf vorhandene Plattformdienste bereits mit geringem Aufwand gute Ergebnisse erzielt werden konnten.

Der *zweite Schritt* bestand darin, einer CORBA-Managementapplikation die bereits von NetView gefilterten Ereignisse zuzustellen, um diese geeignet weiterverarbeiten zu können. Hierbei agiert nun die Plattform als Event-Supplier und die CORBA-Applikation als Consumer, die wiederum durch Event Channels entkoppelt sind. Das entsprechende Objekt, das den NetView-Dienst kapselt, wurde in Anlehnung an die OSI Event Report Management Function EFD_Supplier genannt, da seine Funktionalität identisch zu der eines OSI *Event Forwarding Discriminator (EFD)* ist: Die Managementapplikation registriert sich beim EFD_Supplier-Objekt für den Empfang gefilterter Ereignismeldungen einer bestimmten Art durch das Setzen eines Attributs des EFD_Suppliers auf den gewünschten Filterstring. Als Filterstring können alle in NetView erlaubten Filterregeln verwendet werden. Für jede Filterart kann ein EFD_Supplier-Objekt nach Bedarf erzeugt werden, an dem beliebig viele Consumer über Event Channels angeschlossen sein können.

3.3 Verwaltung der Topologie von CORBA-Managementagenten

Die Topologieverwaltung überwachter Ressourcen zählt zu den Kernaufgaben von Managementplattformen. Sie gliedert sich in folgende Teilschritte: Information über vorhandene Systeme und deren momentanen Zustand (up, down, usw.) wird ermittelt und in der Plattformdatenbank abgespeichert

---

[3] Das Kapseln von nicht CORBA-konformen Modulen ist der gebräuchlichste Weg, um bestehenden Programmcode für neue objektorientierte Systeme zugreifbar zu machen.

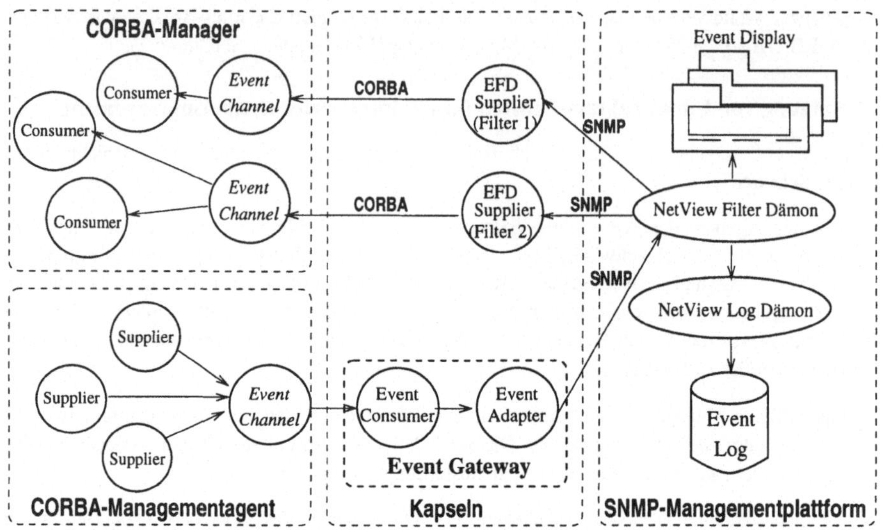

Abbildung 2: Verarbeitung von CORBA-Events bei einer multiarchitekturellen Plattform

(Discovery-Funktion). Ein übersichtliches Modell dieser Information (die Zustände der Ressourcen werden durch farbliche Kennzeichnung der entsprechenden Symbole dargestellt) wird anschließend an der graphischen Benutzeroberfläche der Plattform angezeigt. Um der Dynamik der überwachten Ressourcen gerecht zu werden, wiederholt sich dieser Prozeß in regelmäßigen Zeitabständen, der gewöhnlich durch die Plattform initiiert wird (*Polling*). Um der dadurch entstehenden hohen Netzlast zu begegnen, haben wir bei unserer Entwicklung einen ereignisgesteuerten Ansatz verfolgt, der nur dann Meldungen an die Plattform verschickt, wenn sich Änderungen an der Topologie ergeben haben.

Wir werden uns im folgenden auf die Beschreibung der Implementierung einer Discovery-Applikation für CORBA-Managementobjekte (dies können sowohl Anwendungen als auch Systeme sein) beschränken und aufzeigen, wie die Anbindung an den Topologiedienst von *NetView for AIX* erfolgte. Die Datenbank der Plattform wird somit zu einer integrierten Informationsbasis für SNMP– und CORBA–Managementobjekte.

Die Discovery-Applikation basiert auf dem NetView *Generalized Topology Manager (GTM)*, der abstrakte Datenobjekte zur Darstellung von Ressourcen bereitstellt und über ein API zugänglich ist. Dieses API wurde, analog zu unserem Vorgehen beim Ereignismanagement, durch CORBA-Interfaces gekapselt, um seine Nutzung durch die CORBA-basierte Discovery-Applikation überhaupt erst zu ermöglichen. Damit der GTM CORBA-Objekte geeignet darstellen kann, benötigt er von der Discovery-Applikation folgende Angaben: die insgesamt existierenden Applikationen oder Dienste, die Systeme (Hosts) und die Server (bzw. die Referenzen der Objektklassen, aus denen sie bestehen), die auf den Systemen laufen, sowie die Objektinstanzen, die auf einem Server aktiv sind. Diese Informationen wurden folgendermaßen ermittelt: das CORBA *Implementation Repository* enthält Angaben über verfügbare Systeme, auf ihnen laufende Server und eine Liste der durch letztere unterstützten Objektklassen. Die zu den jeweiligen Objektklassen existierenden Objektinstanzen werden durch den CORBA LifeCycle Service bereitgestellt. Über die Methoden der `Naming Context` Objekte (spezifiziert im CORBA Naming Service) können alle darin enthaltenen `Name Bindings` abgefragt werden; man kann damit die Namen und Objektreferenzen aller registrierten Objektinstanzen ermitteln.

Unsere Erfahrungen bei der Implementierung haben gezeigt, daß durch die Abstützung auf standardisierte bzw. von der Plattform zur Verfügung gestellte Infrastruktur-Dienste mit akzeptablem Aufwand eine brauchbare Lösung zur Topologieverwaltung erstellt werden konnte.

4 Management-Gateways

Management-Gateways, auch als *Proxies* bezeichnet, befinden sich an den Grenzen von Protokoll-domänen und haben die Aufgabe, die Unterschiede zwischen den beteiligten Managementarchitekturen zu überbrücken. Es handelt sich dabei keinesfalls nur um reine Konverter für Protokolldateneinheiten; es muß insbesondere auch eine Abbildung von Managementinformation vorgenommen werden (siehe Abschnitt 1).

Im Gegensatz zu den beiden anderen in der Einleitung beschriebenen Integrationsansätzen verfolgt der Gateway-basierte Ansatz das Ziel, Koexistenz und Kooperation zwischen unterschiedlichen Architekturen zu gewährleisten, ohne Modifikationen an Plattformen oder Agentensystemen vornehmen zu müssen. Die Vorteile der Integration durch multiarchitekturelle Plattformen gelten somit auch für Management-Gateways. Man erreicht sogar einen höheren Grad an Flexibilität, da weder Abhängigkeiten zu konkreten Plattform-Implementierungen (siehe Abschnitt 3), noch Eingriffe auf Agentenseite (wie im Fall der multiarchitekturellen Agenten) erforderlich sind. Management-Gateways spielen eine Doppelrolle: aus der Sicht des Managers erscheinen sie als ein Agent, der sich in der gleichen Protokollwelt befindet; für Agenten sieht das Gateway wie ein Manager aus.

Wir werden im folgenden auf derzeit standardisierte, vielversprechende Ansätze zur Spezifikation von Management-Gateways eingehen und über Erfahrungen aus eigenen Projekten zur Implementierung von CORBA/SNMP und CMIP/SNMP–Gateways berichten. Wir beschränken uns auf diese Gateway-Prototypen, da sie wegen der weiten Verbreitung von SNMP-Agenten besonders wichtig sind. Die Prinzipien sind jedoch auch im Fall von Gateways zwischen CORBA und der OSI–Managementarchitektur gültig und ohne weiteres auf diese übertragbar.

4.1 Entwurfshilfen für Management-Gateways

Die Spezifizierung von Algorithmen zur Implementierung von Management-Gateways ist das Ziel eines von X/Open und dem NM Forum gemeinsam durchgeführten Projektes, das den Titel *Joint Inter Domain Management (JIDM)* trägt. Das Projekt behandelt beide in Abschnitt 1 beschriebenen Phasen des Übergangs zwischen unterschiedlichen Managementarchitekturen: die *Specification Translation* und die *Interaction Translation*. In der ersten Phase soll die Darstellung eines Objekts aus einer Architekturdomäne in einer anderen möglich gemacht werden. Das Ergebnis der zweiten Phase sind architekturtransparente Datenaustauschmechanismen zwischen Objekten, die sich in unterschiedlichen Domänen befinden. Während sich die Specification Translation gegenwärtig am Ende der Definitionsphase befindet (siehe [17]), haben die Arbeiten an der Interaction Translation erst vor kurzem begonnen. Zweifellos existieren Parallelen zur IIMC (*ISO–Internet Management Coexistence*) Initiative, jedoch ist das Spektrum von JIDM breiter angelegt: während IIMC auf die Interoperabilität zwischen OSI– und Internet–Management abzielte, wird hier die Kopplung der OSI– und Internet–Architekturen mit CORBA betrachtet; man will die Stärken einer Architektur für die jeweils anderen verfügbar machen, um zu einer umfassenden integrierten Managementlösung zu kommen.

In der Literatur unterscheidet man zwischen zwei Designvarianten für Management-Gateways ([1]): Ein Gateway ist *stateless* (zustandslos), wenn in ihm keine Werte von Attributinstanzen der jeweiligen Managementobjektklassen gespeichert werden. Andernfalls handelt es sich um ein *stateful* (zustandsbehaftetes) Gateway. Aus dieser Definition folgt unmittelbar, daß stateless Gateways per se nicht über Cachingmechanismen für Attribute verfügen. Sie stellen die einfacher zu implementierende Gateway-Variante dar, da sie die Daten, die sie von Managern oder Agenten erhalten, lediglich an die entsprechenden Stellen weiterleiten.[4] Wir haben uns für die beschriebenen CORBA/SNMP– und CMIP/SNMP–Gateways jeweils für die zustandlose Variante entschieden, wobei jedoch das Gateway Kenntnis über die SNMP-MIBs derjenigen Ressourcen haben muß, die über das Gateway angesteuert werden. Dies impliziert, daß diese MIBs zuerst in das Informationsmodell des jeweiligen Managers durch die oben beschriebenen JIDM– bzw. IIMC–Algorithmen überführt und anschließend dem Gateway bekanntgemacht werden müssen.

---

[4]Neben diesen Einteilungen gibt es natürlich noch weitere (feinere) Abstufungen. Dies hängt mit der grundlegenden Designentscheidung zusammen, welche Funktionalität zur Umsetzung der Informations- und Kommunikationsmodelle an welcher Stelle (Manager oder Gateway) angesiedelt wird.

4.2 CORBA/SNMP-Gateway

Das Gateway für den Übergang von der CORBA– in die SNMP–Managementarchitektur muß folgende Anforderungen erfüllen:

1. Darstellung der SNMP–MIBs für den Manager in dessen eigenem Informationsmodell

2. Modifikationen weder am Manager noch an den Agenten, d.h. *vollkommen transparenter* Übergang aus Sicht dieser Systeme (Das Gateway muß daher Proxy-Objekte für sämtliche SNMP–Agenten vorhalten, damit ein CORBA-Request eines Managers an ein Proxy-Objekt durch einen entsprechenden Reply beantwortet wird).

3. Operationen, die der Manager durch Requests an den Proxy-Objekten durchführt (lesen, schreiben, erzeugen, löschen), müssen durch das Gateway interpretiert und an die entsprechenden SNMP-Agenten weitergeleitet werden. Umgekehrt müssen von den SNMP-Agenten stammende asynchrone Ereignismeldungen (sog. *Traps*) in CORBA-Events umgesetzt werden.

Abbildung 3 gibt einen Überblick über das Gateway. Jedes Proxy-Objekt repräsentiert eine Instanz der

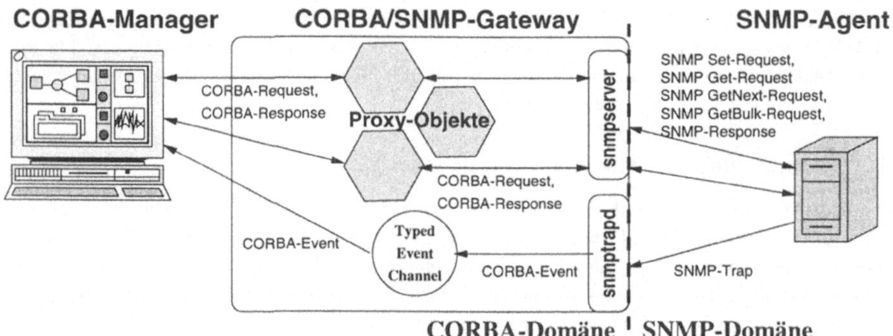

Abbildung 3: Ablauf der Kommunikation beim CORBA/SNMP-Gateway

nach dem JIDM–Algorithmus erzeugten Objektklasse, die SNMP-spezifische Informationen zu diesem Objekt bereithält (UDP-Socket, Object ID, Community String). Sobald ein Manager einen Request an ein Proxy-Objekt verschickt, ruft dieses eine entsprechende Methode auf dem `snmpserver`-Objekt unter Hinzufügen der SNMP-spezifischen Parameter auf. Das `snmpserver`-Objekt kann mit den mitgelieferten Parametern eine vollständige SNMP-PDU erzeugen, die anschließend durch den SNMP-Agenten beantwortet wird. Das Ergebnis wird nun als Response-Message vom `snmpserver`-Objekt zum aufrufenden Proxy-Objekt weitergeleitet, welches das Ergebnis nun seinerseits als Response zum Manager zurückschickt.

SNMP-Traps werden auf dem UDP-Port 162 des Gateways durch das `snmptrapd`-Objekt angenommen und an einen (für jede Art von Trap spezifischen) typisierten Event-Channel in Form eines CORBA-Requests weitergeleitet. Wie in Abschnitt 3.2 beschrieben, kann ein Event-Channel-Objekt den erhaltenen Event an diejenigen CORBA-Objekte (d.h. Manager) weiterleiten, die sich für die Zustellung solcher Ereignisse registriert haben.

Der Ansatz ist daher auch für die Verwendung mehrerer CORBA-Managementsysteme ausgelegt. Die Erfahrungen haben gezeigt, daß die gewählte Lösung unter Rückgriff auf bestehende Infrastruktur-Dienste elegant implementierbar ist ([7]); allerdings bleibt die Skalierbarkeit dieses Ansatzes durch das Vorhandensein der transformierten MIBs sämtlicher SNMP-Agenten im Gateway fraglich. Es ging uns jedoch primär darum, die prinzipielle Machbarkeit eines solchen Gateways aufzuzeigen.

4.3 CMIP/SNMP-Gateway

Das CMIP/SNMP-Gateway nutzt die IIMC-Erkenntnisse zur Interoperabilität zwischen den OSI– und Internet–Architekturen und soll Internet–Managementagenten in ein OSI–basiertes Management integrieren. Als OSI–konformes Managementsystem wurde die *IBM NetView TMN Support Facility* eingesetzt; die Implementierung des Gateways selbst geschah mit der *IBM TMN Workbench*, einem Entwicklungssystem für OSI-Agenten, das detailliert in [2] beschrieben ist. Zur Kommunikation zwischen Manager und Gateway wird CMIP eingesetzt; das Protokoll zwischen Gateway und den Agenten ist SNMP in der Version 2. Der herausragende Vorteil der IBM TMN-Entwicklungsumgebung liegt in der Verwendung eines neuartigen CMIP-API, das zur Zeit vom NM Forum genormt wird [12]: es ist damit möglich, OSI–Agenten unter Umgehung von XMP und dessen Komplexität zu implementieren. Der Entwickler wird vollständig vom Managementprotokoll abgeschirmt und kann aus den ihm in der OSI–Notation vorliegenden Beschreibungen der Managementschnittstellen direkt Schnittstellen in der Programmiersprache C++ generieren. Die eigentliche Managementfunktionalität wird in die Rümpfe sog. *Callbacks* eingetragen. Der Einarbeitungsaufwand sinkt durch den Komfort des CMIP-API erheblich.

Allgemein lassen sich Übergänge für Protokollelemente, für die es in beiden Architekturen Entsprechungen gibt, relativ einfach aufeinander abbilden. Schwierig ist jedoch beispielsweise die Umsetzung von CMIP-Action Diensten, da es in SNMP hierzu keine äquivalente Protokolldateneinheit gibt. Dies ist ein klassisches Beispiel für die enge Verzahnung der Informations- und Kommunikationsmodelle (siehe Abschnitte 2.3 und 2.4): Funktionalität, die das OSI-Kommunikationsmodell bietet, muß in der Internet-Welt durch das Internet-Informationsmodell nachgebildet werden. Tatsächlich geschieht das Ausführen von Aktionen auf SNMP-Managementobjekten durch das Belegen von MIB-Variablen mit einer Zahl durch eine SNMP-set Protokolldateneinheit.

Ein weiteres Problem stellen die sehr leistungsfähigen *Scoping–* und *Filtering–*Operationen der OSI–Managementarchitektur da, die es gestatten, Managementoperationen auf ganzen Teilbäumen einer MIB durchzuführen. In früheren Gateway-Projekten [1, 8] lag das Hauptproblem oft darin, die get-, set- oder action-Protokolldateneinheiten auf die richtigen Objekte anzuwenden. Diese Arbeit wurde uns vom Entwicklungssystem abgenommen, da zu jedem entwickelten Agenten automatisch ein Dämon erzeugt wird, der „scoped und filtered" Operationen in einzelne get-, set- bzw. action-PDUs auflöst, die einfacher auf SNMP-PDUs abgebildet werden können.

Insgesamt kann mit dem entwickelten Gateway das gesamte Spektrum der OSI-Protokollfunktionalität (insbesondere *Scoping* und *Filtering*) auf SNMP-Managementobjekte angewendet werden. Es ist damit möglich, SNMP-Ressourcen mit dem vollen OSI-Funktionsumfang zu überwachen und zu steuern, da sie aus der Sicht des Managers OSI-konform erscheinen. Dies bedeutet, daß ein Administrator, der SNMP-Agenten von einem über ein Management-Gateway verbundenen OSI-Manager aus überwacht, komfortablere und leistungsfähigere Operationen zur Verfügung hat, als ein Administrator, der dieselben SNMP-Agenten unmittelbar mit einem SNMP-Manager steuert.

Die vorgestellte Lösung ist vollkommen produktunabhängig, da sie sich auf standardisierte Managementarchitekturen abstützt. Sie funktioniert mit jedem OSI-konformen Managementsystem und allen SNMP-Agenten, sofern deren MIBs dem Gateway mit Hilfe des Specification Translation Algorithmus bekanntgegeben wurden. Allerdings ist die Lösung bisher nicht skalierbar: momentan verwaltet der Gateway-Prototyp die MIB-II und eine am Lehrstuhl entwickelte MIB für UNIX-Systemmanagement, die 195 Variablen und 15 Tabellen umfaßt. Der ausführbare Code des Gateway-Prototypen hat eine Größe von ca. 4 Megabyte.

Bei unseren Arbeiten hat sich der Gateway-basierte Ansatz zur Integration heterogener Managementarchitekturen als die tragfähigste der eingangs vorgestellten drei Integrationsalternativen herausgestellt. Wir vertreten daher die Auffassung, daß der Gateway-basierte Ansatz derjenige ist, mit dem man dem Ziel integrierten Managements in heterogenen Systemen am nächsten kommt.

5 Zusammenfassung und Ausblick

Der Beitrag hat gezeigt, daß es durchaus möglich und aussichtsreich ist, Übergänge zwischen Managementarchitekturen zu schaffen. Diese Übergänge können allerdings, auch das hat sich bei den Projekten gezeigt, wegen der Unterschiedlichkeit der Architekturen zwangsläufig nicht vollständig nahtlos sein. Es wird aber möglich sein, die relativen Meriten der einzelnen Architekturen jeweils weitgehend zu nutzen, ohne „Management-Inseln" zu bilden. Man ist dann also einen Schritt weiter auf dem Weg zu einem integrierten Management. Gleichzeitig bedeutet dies, einerseits vorhandene Investitionen zu retten (z.B. die große Zahl an SNMP-Agenten), und andererseits neue CORBA-Investitionen auch für das Management (mit) zu nutzen. Die notwendige „Management-Spezialisierung" von CORBA könnte, wie dargestellt wurde, in einer Übernahme und Übersetzung von MIBs aus der SNMP und CMIP-Welt bestehen. „CORBA-Facilities" für das Systemmanagement könnten via Specification-Translation aus OSI Systems Management Function mit entsprechender Kapselung evtl. vorhandener Implementierungen erzeugt werden.

Danksagung

Die Autoren danken dem Münchner Netzmanagement Team für intensive Diskussionen zu früheren Versionen dieses Beitrags. Das MNM-Team, das von Prof. Hegering geleitet wird, ist eine Gruppe von Wissenschaftlern beider Münchner Universitäten und des Leibniz-Rechenzentrums der Bayerischen Akademie der Wissenschaften.

Literatur

[1] Abeck, S., Clemm, A., Hollberg, U.: Simply Open Network Management: An Approach for the Integration of SNMP into OSI Management Concepts. In: *Proceedings of the 3rd IFIP/IEEE International Symposium on Integrated Network Management*. North-Holland, April 1993

[2] Feridun, M., Heusler, L., Nielsen, R.: Implementing OSI Agents for TMN. IBM Research Report RZ 2759. IBM Research Division, Zurich Research Laboratory. (1995)

[3] Hegering, H.-G., Abeck, S.: Integrated Network and System Management. Addison-Wesley 1994

[4] Hegering, H.-G., Neumair, B., Gutschmidt, M.: Architekturen und Konzepte für ein integriertes Management von verteilten Systemen. Informatik Spektrum *18*(5), (Oktober 1995)

[5] Hegering, H.-G., Neumair, B., Gutschmidt, M.: Cooperative Computing and Integrated System Management — A Critical Comparison of Architectural Approaches. Journal of Network and Systems Management *2*(3), 283–316 (1994)

[6] Heilbronner, S., Keller, A., Neumair, B.: Integriertes Netz- und Systemmanagement mit modularen Agenten. In: *Proceedings of SIWORK'96, Zurich, Switzerland.* Mai 1996

[7] Höller, T.: Konzeption und Realisierung eines CORBA / SNMP Gateways. Diplomarbeit. Technische Universität München. August 1996

[8] Kalyanasundaram, P., Sethi, A.: An Application Gateway Design for OSI-Internet Management. In: *Proceedings of the 3rd IFIP/IEEE International Symposium on Integrated Network Management.* North-Holland, April 1993

[9] Kalyanasundaram, P., Sethi, A.: Interoperability Issues in Heterogeneous Network Management. Journal of Network and Systems Management *2*(2), (1994)

[10] Keller, A., Neumair, B.: Systems Management Middleware: Verteilte objektorientierte Technologien für das Systemmanagement. In Wall, D. (Hrsg.): *Organisation und Betrieb von DV-Versorgungsstrukturen.* Deutscher Universitäts-Verlag, November 1995

[11] Mazumdar, S., Brady, S., Levine, D.: Design of Protocol Independent Management Agent to Support SNMP and CMIP Queries. In: *Proceedings of the 3rd IFIP/IEEE International Symposium on Integrated Network Management.* North-Holland, April 1993

[12] TMN C++ Application Programming Interface). Issue 1.0, Draft 5 - For Public Comment NMF xxx. Network Management Forum. (Januar 1996)

[13] CORBAservices: Common Object Services Specification, Volume 1. OMG Specification. Object Management Group. (März 1996)

[14] Sloman, M. S. (Hrsg.): Network and Distributed Systems Management. Addison Wesley 1994

[15] SOMobjects Developer Toolkit Programmer's Guide Volume 2: Object Services. IBM Corporation. März 1996. First Edition

[16] Vogs, T.: Entwurf und Implementierung eines Konzepts zur Anbindung von Object Request Brokern an eine Netzmanagementplattform. Diplomarbeit. Technische Universität München. Februar 1996

[17] Inter-Domain Management Specifications: Specification Translation (Final Sanity Check Draft). Preliminary Specification Pxxx. X/Open Ltd. (September 1996)

Verteilte Ereignisanalyse in paketvermittelnden Netzen

Ingo Bürger
Andreas Fasbender
Bernd Meyer
Ingo Rulands

Informatik IV, RWTH Aachen, Ahornstr. 55, 52056 Aachen
E-Mail: {fasbender, meyer} @i4.informatik.rwth-aachen.de

Kurzfassung

Der Artikel stellt einen neuen Ansatz zum verteilten Monitoring in paketvermittelnden Netzwerken, insbesondere dem Internet, vor. Im Gegensatz zu existierenden Ansätzen wird dabei nicht nur die Aufzeichnung sondern auch die Ereignisanalyse verteilt realisiert. Um eine vollständige Ereignisanalyse durchführen zu können, müssen die beobachteten Ereignisse aller beteiligten Rechnerknoten total geordnet werden. Das ist jedoch nur möglich, wenn die Uhren aller beteiligten Hosts synchron laufen. Da dies in der Regel nicht vorausgesetzt werden kann, haben wir in den Ereignismonitor ein neues Verfahren zur Uhrensynchronisation integriert. Es handelt sich dabei um einen zweistufigen Ansatz: Zunächst wird die relative Abweichung des Drifts je zweier Uhren bestimmt, bevor mit einem zweiten Verfahren der absolute Offset zwischen den Uhren berechnet wird. Im Gegensatz zu bestehenden Verfahren geht dieses Verfahren nicht davon aus, daß die Paketlaufzeiten symmetrisch, d.h. in beiden Übertragungsrichtungen gleich sind. Ein weiteres netzspezifisches Problem der verteilten Ereigniserkennung in paketvermittelnden Netzen sind die unterschiedlichen Nachrichtenlaufzeiten. Dadurch kann es zu Fehlentscheidungen bei der Erkennung komplexer Ereignisse kommen. Das hier entwickelte Uhrensynchronisationsverfahren erlaubt je-doch eine genaue Bestimmung von unidirektionalen Ereignislaufzeiten, mit deren Hilfe das Problem verspäteter Ereignisse behoben wird.

1. Einleitung

Die fortschreitende Verbindung isolierter lokaler Netze zu regionalen oder sogar internationalen Inter- und Intranets erfordert es, daß bestehende Anwendungen verteilt realisiert werden müssen. In diesem Kontext werden Middleware-Plattformen wie CORBA, DCE oder ANSAware immer populärer, weil sie es Programmierern ermöglichen, Anwendungen weitgehend unabhängig von dem Grad der Verteilung zu entwickeln. Die so gewonnene Verteilungstransparenz wird jedoch durch einen erhöhten Verbrauch an Rechenleistung erkauft. Die bestehenden Plattformen ermöglichen es dem Programmierer nicht, die Performance der Anwendung für zeitkritische Applikationen zu steuern, was für einige Informationssysteme schwere Nachteile mit sich bringt. Beispielsweise für die Investmentabteilung einer großen Bank stellt nicht nur der Gehalt einer Information einen Wert dar, sondern insbesondere deren rechtzeitige Verfügbarkeit. So kann die Kursschwankung einer Devise in Tokio an der dritten Stelle hinter dem Komma für eine Bank in London einen Gewinn bzw. Verlust in Millionenhöhe bedeuten. Existierende Middleware-Plattformen erlauben zur Laufzeit keine Änderungen an der Konfiguration oder der Lastverteilung der

Anwendungsobjekte. Dieses Manko kann durch ein geeignetes Managementsystem kompensiert werden. Kern solcher Systeme ist ein Monitor, der für die Überwachung des Systemzustands eingesetzt wird und vordefinierte Ereignisse wie beispielsweise den Empfang einer Nachricht oder den Ablauf eines Timers erkennt und an den Manager weiterleitet.

Das Kernproblem bei der Realisierung verteilter Monitore stellt die fehlende globale Systemzeit dar, d.h. die Rechneruhren weichen sowohl im Offset als auch in der Oszillatorfrequenz voneinander ab. Um die verteilt aufgezeichneten Ereignisse in eine Totalordnung bringen zu können, müssen die Uhren aller beteiligten Rechner synchronisiert werden. Das derzeit einzige verbreitete Protokoll zur Uhrensynchronisation im Internet ist das Network Time Protokol (NTP). NTP nimmt jedoch an, daß die Laufzeiten eines Pakets, das von Quell- zu Zielhost und zurückgeschickt wird, symmetrisch, d.h. in beide Richtungen identisch sind. Diese Annahme läßt sich in lokalen Netzen begründen, in paketvermittelnden Weitverkehrsnetzen wie dem Internet jedoch gilt sie nicht mehr. Daher müssen neue Verfahren zur Uhrensynchronisation entwickelt werden, wozu diese Arbeit beiträgt. Durch unterschiedliche Paketlaufzeiten kann auch die Reihenfolge der aufgezeichneten Ereignisse umgekehrt werden, was zu Fehlern bei der Ereignisanalyse führen kann. Im Beispiel aus Bild 1 ist die reale Reihenfolge der Ereignisse durch *a b c d* gegeben, ohne nachfolgende Korrektur würde jedoch vom Monitor die Folge *c b a d* protokolliert.

Zunächst geben wir in Kapitel 2 einen Überblick über das Monitoring Verteilter Systeme. Ein neues Uhrensynchronisationsverfahren wird in Kapitel 3 vorgestellt, das im Gegensatz zu bestehenden Verfahren nicht von der Symmetrie der Paketlaufzeit zwischen Rechnern ausgeht. Mit Hilfe diese Verfahrens wird in Kapitel 4 ein neuer, verteilter Ansatz zur Ereignisanalyse präsentiert, der in dem System DERS (Distributed Event Recognition System) realisiert worden ist.

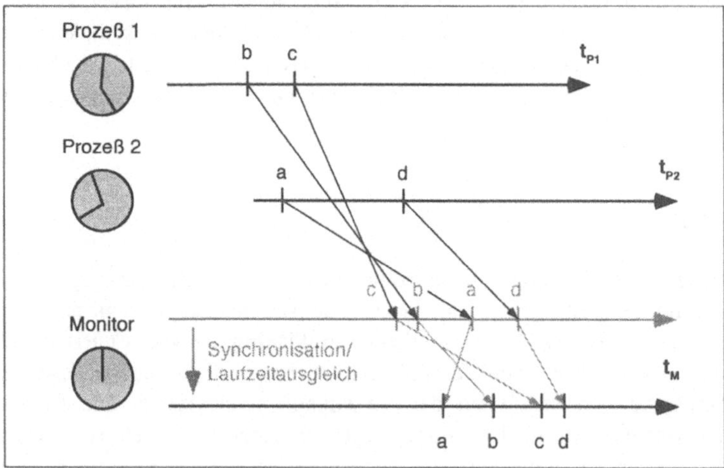

Bild 1. Motivation

2. Stand der Forschung

2.1 Monitoring Verteilter Systeme

Die Durchführung von Messungen eines Rechensystems - auch Monitoring genannt - ist neben der Analyse und Simulation von mathematischen Modellen des betreffenden Systems eine geeignete Möglichkeit der Leistungsbewertung, siehe [7], [11], [13] oder [14]. Der Vorgang des Monitorings Verteilter Systeme läßt sich in mehrere Phasen teilen, siehe Bild 2. Zunächst werden die relevanten Ereignisse aufgezeichnet, was mit Hilfe sogenannter Sensoren geschieht. Abhängig davon, wo die Aufzeichnung erfolgt, unterscheidet man zwischen Hardware- und Software-Monitoren. Während Hardware-Monitore Ereignisse direkt an der Hardware, also z.B. an Speicherbausteinen, Netzwerkkarten oder am Systembus abgreifen, werden sie bei Software-Monitoren durch die System- oder Anwendungssoftware ausgelöst. Bei Software-Monitoren bestehen Sensoren entweder aus Programmcode, der in das beobachtete System eingefügt wird, oder es handelt sich um eigenständige Objekte, die periodisch den Systemzustand aufzeichnen. Dabei bleibt das beobachtete System unverändert, allerdings muß die Adresse im Speicher bekannt sein, an der die relevanten Daten gehalten werden. Im ersten Falle spricht man von ereignisgesteuertem, im zweiten Fall von zeitgesteuertem Monitoring.

Da nicht alle aufgezeichneten Ereignisse für jedes Experiment relevant sind, kann während der Ereignisanalyse entschieden werden, welche Ereignisse unterdrückt werden sollen. Im Falle eines verteilten Monitors müssen die Ereignisse von den Sensoren verschickt und von der nachgeschalteten Analyse eingesammelt werden. Für einige Anwendungen ist jedoch nicht unbedingt der Zeitpunkt des Eintretens von Ereignissen von Bedeutung, sondern nur deren kausale Ordnung wichtig. In diesem Fall spricht man von logischer Zeit. In den meisten Fällen, insbesondere bei Laufzeitmessungen, ist die reale (oder physikalische) Zeit von

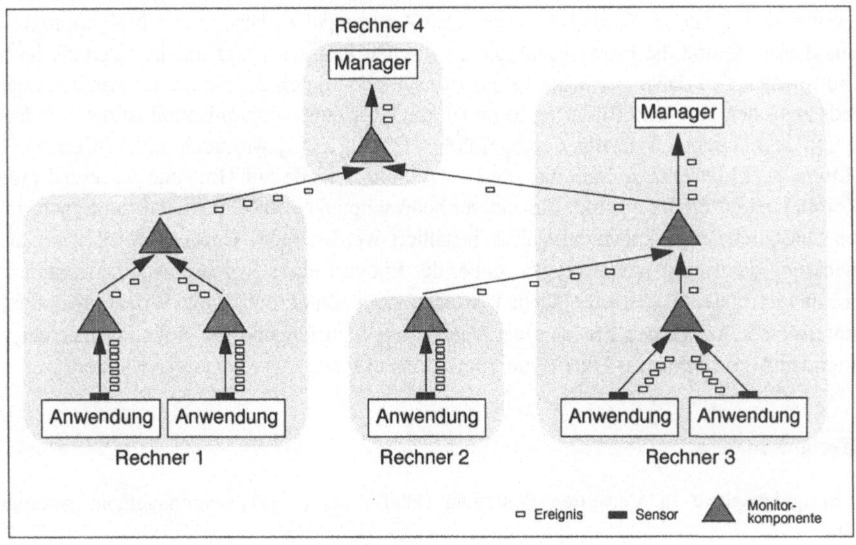

Bild 2. Beispielszenario für verteilte Ereignisanalyse

Bedeutung. Weiterhin unterscheiden sich Monitore darin, daß die Analyse der aufgezeichneten Ereignisse zur Laufzeit, d.h. on-line geschieht, oder post-mortem, d.h. nach Ablauf des Experiments durchgeführt wird. Konventionelle Netzmangementsysteme beispielsweise besitzen nur eine zentrale Managementinstanz, die die Analyse der aufgezeichneten Ereignisse durchführt. Sollen jedoch große Verteilte Systeme verwaltet werden, so ist eine verteilte Analyse notwendig. Die bei der Analyse gewonnenen Informationen werden entweder gespeichert oder direkt präsentiert. Es sind eine Vielzahl von Monitoren für Verteilte Systeme entwickelt worden, beispielsweise JEWEL [15], ZM4 [9] oder das Distributed Measurement System [6].

2.2 Uhrensynchronisation

Das Network Time Protocol (NTP) ist das am weitesten verbreitete Protokoll zur Synchronisation von Uhren innerhalb des Internet. Es wird seit ungefähr 10 Jahren von D. Mills an der Universität von Delaware, USA entwickelt und existiert zur Zeit in der Version 3 [19]. Die Software zum NTP ist kostenlos erhältlich und stellt daher eine kostengünstige Alternative im Vergleich zur hardwareorientierten Synchronisation mit Hilfe des Global Positioning Systems (GPS) oder anderen Empfängern dar. Durch den Einsatz von NTP ist eine Genauigkeit der Uhren in der Größenordnung von 50 Millisekunden bis hin zu einigen wenigen Millisekunden zu erreichen [18]. Der allgemeine Ablauf einer Synchronisation mittels NTP sieht folgendermaßen aus: Zwischen dem zu synchronisierenden Rechner und einer definierbaren Anzahl von Zeitgebern werden Zeitstempel ausgetauscht. Diese Zeitstempel werden unter Anwendung verschiedener Selektions- und Filterungsalgorithmen dazu benutzt, Differenzen in den absoluten Uhrzeiten und auf dieser Basis auch Unterschiede in den Frequenzraten der Uhren zu bestimmen. Die lokale Uhrzeit wird dann entsprechend den zu den Referenzzeitgebern gemessenen Abweichungen adaptiert.
Problematisch ist, daß im Gegensatz zu leitungsvermittelnden Netzen die Paketlaufzeiten im Internet nicht im voraus feststellbar sind. Es ist also insbesondere nicht möglich, den exakten Uhrenunterschied auf der Basis der versendeten Zeitstempel zu bestimmen. NTP approximiert aus diesem Grund die Einwegelaufzeiten zwischen Zeitserver und -client durch die halbe Roundtrip-Zeit. Der dabei gemachte Fehler ist nach oben durch die Hälfte des Laufzeitunterschieds zwischen Hin- und Rückweg begrenzt, die Güte der Synchronisation ist damit jedoch last- und zeitabhängig. Von uns durchgeführte Messungen [5] wie auch andere Berichte in der Literatur [2] belegen zudem, daß die Laufzeitunterschiede auf Hin- und Rückpfad einer IP-Verbindung oft erheblich sind. Ein anderer Schwachpunkt von NTP ist, daß zur Synchronisation zusätzliche Protokollfunktionalität installiert werden muß. Unser erstes Ziel bei der Entwicklung des Ereignismonitors war daher der Entwurf eines Synchronisationsverfahrens, das in den normalen Paketfluß eingebaut werden kann. Zusätzlich sollte Wissen über Laufzeitunterschiede auf beiden Pfaden einer Verbindung aquiriert und für einen lastunabhängig arbeitenden Algorithmus zur Uhrensynchronisation ausgenutzt werden (siehe Kapitel 3).

2.3 Ereignisanalyse

Die Ereignisanalyse in Verteilten Systemen (häufig auch Ereignismanagement genannt) umfaßt
- das Zusammenfassen bzw. Verdichten von Ereignissen zu abstrakteren Ereignissen,
- das Unterdrücken nichtrelevanter Ereignisse,

- das Erkennen kausaler Ordnungen auf der Menge der beobachteten Ereignisse sowie
- die Ereigniskorrelation, d.h. Erkennen des Zusammenhangs zwischen Ereignissen und ihren Ursachen.

Oft sind Ereignisse, die Sensoren verschicken, zu speziell als daß der Manager sie interpretieren kann. In anderen Fällen kann ein Ereignis erst erkannt werden, wenn eine bestimmte Folge von Ereignissen aufgetreten ist. Beispielsweise sollen Replikate eines Objekts zu jeder Zeit den gleichen Zustand haben. Die Konsistenz aller Replikate ist jedoch nur vorhanden, wenn nach einer Modifikation eine Aktualisierung auf allen Replikaten durchgeführt wird. Bisherige Ansätze zur Ereigniserkennung unterschieden sich primär bezüglich

- des Typs der erkannten Ereignisse sowie
- des Modells, das zur Erkennung komplexer Ereignisse eingesetzt wird.

Der Typ der zu erkennenden Ereignisse kann sehr unterschiedlich sein. Im einfachsten Fall bestehen zusammengesetzte Ereignisse aus einer Kombination elementarer Ereignisse, die mittels aussagenlogischer Operatoren verknüpft werden. Temporale Operatoren erlauben es zusätzlich, eine kausale Ordnung bezüglich des Auftretens von Ereignissen zu erkennen. In der Regel werden so Halbordnungen auf Ereignismengen beschrieben. Im Gegensatz dazu erfordert die Verwendung von Echtzeit, die sich sowohl auf Zeitpunkte wie auch auf Intervalle beziehen kann, eine totale Ordnung der Ereignisse. Voraussetzung für Totalordnungen ist jedoch, daß alle Uhren synchron laufen. Da dies in der Regel nicht der Fall ist, müssen Uhrensynchronisationsverfahren eingesetzt werden. Eine weitere wichtige Klasse stellt die Verdichtung von Ereignissen dar. Damit lassen sich beispielsweise Ereignisse unterdrücken, wenn eine bestimmte Bedingung erfüllt ist, oder es wird erst das n-te Eintreten eines Ereignis gemeldet. Zur Erkennung komplexer Ereignisse werden üblicherweise endliche Automaten, Baum- oder Graphstrukturen, und Petri-Netze eingesetzt.

Im folgenden sollen einige Ansätze zur Ereigniserkennung in Verteilten Systemen vorgestellt werden, die insbesondere aus dem Bereich des Netz- und Systemmanagements kommen: Der Schwerpunkt der Ereigniserkennung bei Kilger et al [21] liegt auf der Korrelation zwischen beobachtbaren Ereignissen und ihren Ursachen. Diese Ursachen können andere beobachtbare oder nicht beobachtbare Ereignisse sein. Die Informationen werden in einem Korrelationengraph gespeichert. Basierend auf diesem Graph wird ein sogenanntes „codebook" erstellt, das für jedes beobachtbare Ereignis einen Code speichert. Dieses Codewort enthält Informationen, welche Ursachen für dieses Ereignis zutreffen. Kilger et al stellen fest, daß diese Tabellen ein großes Maß an redundanter Informationen enthalten, so daß eine minimale Tabelle erstellt werden sollte, um die Ursachenbestimmung zu erleichtern. Jordaan et at beschreiben in [12] ein Ereignisanalysesystem, das im Gegensatz zu allen anderen beschriebenen Ansätzen die Abhängigkeiten zwischen verschiedenen Ereignissen zur Laufzeit herleitet. Die notwendige Information dazu befindet sich in der Management Information Base, welche das Informationsmodell des OSI-Netzmanagements benutzt. Verwendung finden dabei sowohl Managed Objects sowie Beziehungen zwischen Managed Objects, die in einem Graphmodell gespeichert werden. Jordaan et al beschreiben eine prototypische Implementierung für ein Netzmanagementsystem, welches eine zentrale Managerkomponente besitzt. Möller et al [20] beschreiben einen Filter, mit dessen Hilfe Ereignisse verdichtet werden können, die mittels einer regelbasierten Sprache beschrieben werden. Diese Filter können generell angewendet werden, wenn sie auch bisher nur im Bereich des SDH-Managements einsetzt wurden. Bei diesem Ansatz wird kein spezielles Informationsmodell definiert, sondern das Modell des jeweiligen Anwendungsgebiets übernommen. In [20] ist es das Informationsmodell des SDH-Managements gemäß G.774.

Weitere Ansätze im Bereich des Netz- und Systemmanagements sind z.B. in [16] sowie [10] beschrieben. Die Erkennung komplexer Ereignisse ist auch zentraler Bestandteil aktiver Datenbanksysteme, wo sie Teil sogenannter ECA-Regeln sind, siehe beispielsweise [8]. Dort werden Ereignisse jedoch immer zentral analysiert.

3. Uhrensynchronisation

In Abschnitt 2.2 wurde NTP als Protokoll zur Synchronisation von Uhren im Internet vorgestellt und auf dessen Schwachpunkte hingewiesen. Wir haben daher ein neues Verfahren entwickelt, mit dem ein Rechner auf der Basis der Messung von unidirektionalen Paketlaufzeiten seine Systemuhr zu der Referenzuhr eines beliebigen anderen Rechners anpassen kann. Hierzu wird zunächst der Frequenzunterschied zwischen den beiden Uhren gemessen und ausgeglichen, wonach auf der Basis der resultierenden empirischen Laufzeitverteilungen der Uhrenunterschied geschätzt werden kann.

Die Uhrensynchronisation wird wie bei NTP auf der Basis von Meßpaketen durchgeführt, die in den normalen Paketfluß eingestreut werden. Dies kann sowohl von höheren Ebenen aus angestoßen als auch innerhalb der IP-Ebene selbst geregelt werden, etwa auf der Basis zukünftiger Netzmanagementsoftware. Momentan nutzen wir die sogenannte Timestamp-Option des Internet Control Message Protokolls [3] dazu, in regelmäßigen, vom aktuellen Synchronisationsgrad abhängigen Abständen ein Meßpaket zwischen Quell- und Zielhost auszutauschen. Der Sender (Zeitnehmer) generiert die Meßpakete und trägt den Absendezeitpunkt in die Nachrichten ein. Beim Zielrechner (Zeitserver) werden die Nachrichten geechot und erhalten so wie in Bild 3 dargestellt insgesamt vier Zeitstempel.

Bei den weiteren Beschreibungen verwenden wir folgende Bezeichnungen: Seien i die Nummer des aktuellen Meßpakets und $t_{i,j}$ die vier Zeitstempel, die für das i-te Paket ($j = 0,...,3$) berechnet werden. δ_i und Δ_i definieren die Zeitdifferenz zwischen Ankunft eines Pakets und Abgang des nächsten Pakets beim Sender bzw. beim Empfänger. RTT_i bezeichnet die Roundtrip-Zeit abzüglich der Aufenthaltsdauer δ_i beim Zielrechner. $OWDF_i$ (one-way delay forward) und $OWDB_i$ (one-way delay backward) sind die Laufzeiten von Paket i für eine Übertragung in eine Richtung. θ_i beschreibt die tatsächliche Uhrendifferenz zwischen Client und Server zum Zeitpunkt $t_{i,0}$, d.h. beim Aussenden des i-ten Paket auf Clientseite.

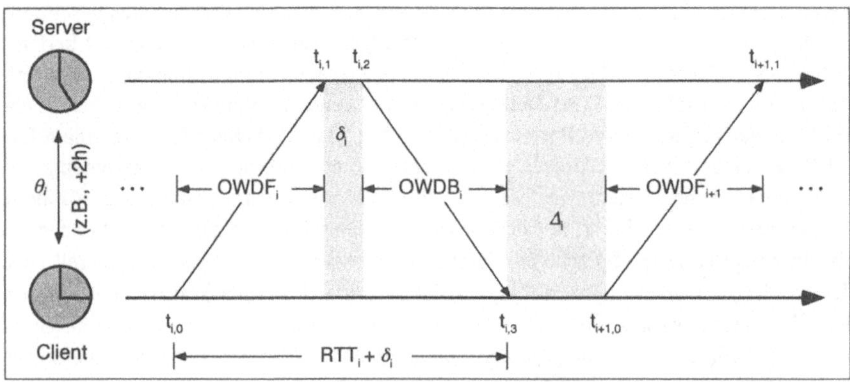

Bild 3. Meßaufbau und Bezeichnungen

3.1 Bestimmung des relativen Frequenzdrifts

Nach Erhalt der Antwort werden auf Senderseite die Laufzeiten $OWDF_i = t_{i,1} - t_{i,0}$ für den Hinweg und $OWDB_i := t_{i,3} - t_{i,2}$ für den Rückweg berechnet. Bild 4 zeigt das Ergebnis einer Messung zwischen einem Rechner in Aachen und einem in Dresden. Während der Messung wurden 10000 Pakete mit einer festen Zwischenabgangszeit von einer Sekunde erzeugt. Dies entspricht einem Meßintervall von annähernd drei Stunden. Die graue Kurve stellt die Gesamtlaufzeiten RTT_i dar, bei denen per Definition kein Drift festgestellt werden kann, da alle Zeitmessungen $t_{i,0}$ bzw. $t_{i,3}$ auf der lokalen Uhr durchgeführt werden. Im Gegensatz dazu sind die schwarze und die graue Kurve, die die unidirektionalen Laufzeiten darstellen, offensichtlich von einem linearen Faktor beeinflußt. Beide Kurven wurden zu Darstellungszwecken auf den halben Roundtrip-Wert des ersten Pakets normalisiert. Da im Meßintervall keine Inhomogenitäten bezüglich der Gesamtlaufzeiten auftreten, ist der einzige plausible Grund für die konstanten linearen Änderungen der Hin- und Rückweglaufzeiten die unterschiedliche Driftrate der beiden Uhren. Beide Kurven zeigen einen Driftwert von etwa 22 ms in 10000 Sekunden, was einem relativen Frequenzdrift von 2.2 ppm („parts per million") zwischen den Uhren entspricht.

Die zugehörigen Laufzeitverteilungen sind in Bild 5 dargestellt. Auf der linken Seite sind die Verteilungen entsprechend den Ergebnissen aus Bild 4 aufgetragen, auf der rechten Seite wurde der geschätzte Drift herausgerechnet. Zur vollständigen Beschreibung der Laufzeitverteilungen fehlt nun also nur noch die Bestimmung der korrekten Startwerte auf der x-Achse. Diesem Problem wenden wir uns im nächsten Abschnitt zu.

Im restlichen Teil dieses Abschnitts zeigen wir auf, wie eine Regressionsanalyse, so wie sie in obigem Beispiel benutzt wurde, zur exakten und effizienten Berechnung des vorliegenden Drifts herangezogen werden kann: Bild 4 legt die Vermutung nahe, daß die Steigung der Kurven am besten bestimmt werden kann, wenn die Meßreihe zuvor einem Minimum-Filter unterzogen wird, der innerhalb eines vorgegebenen Fensters angewendet wird. Neben warteschlangentheoretischen Überlegungen[1] spricht auch die folgende Beobachtung für diesen

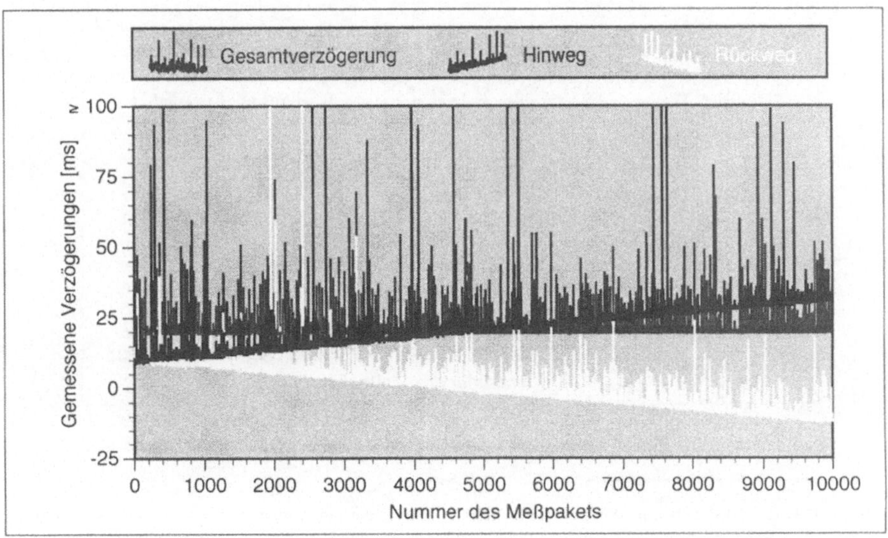

Bild 4. Messung zu einem Rechner in Dresden und Einfluß des Drifts auf die OWDs

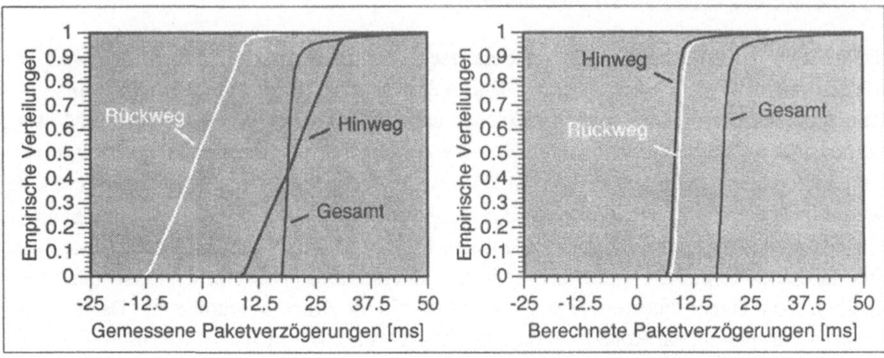

Bild 5. Laufzeitverteilungen vor (links) und nach (rechts) Beseitigung des Drifts

Ansatz: Unsere Messungen zu Rechnern überall auf der Welt lieferten empirische Laufzeitverteilungen, die einen starken Anstieg von ihrem Minimum zu ihrem Modalwert besaßen und anschließend langsam bis zum Maximalwert („heavy-tail"-Verteilungen) anstiegen. Der Median lag immer unterhalb des Erwartungswerts, siehe [4]. Das bedeutet, daß ein hoher Prozentsatz der Pakete Übertragungszeiten nahe dem Minimum ihrer Verteilungsfunktion erfährt, siehe auch Bild 5 rechts. Der Ansatz eines gleitenden Minimums filtert daher kurzzeitige Laufzeitschwankungen besser heraus als der Ansatz eines gleitenden Durchschnitts (vgl. Bild 6) und wurde daher von uns für die weiteren Analysen herangezogen.

Bei Anwendung der linearen Regression wird eine Menge von Meßpunkten durch eine lineare Regressionsfunktion approximiert [1]. Wir haben die Methode der kleinsten Fehlerquadrate gewählt, die eine Funktion liefert, deren summierte (quadrierte) Differenzen zwischen den Meßpunkten und der resultierenden Gerade minimal sind. Liefert diese Technik eine sehr genaue Abschätzung für den tatsächlich aufgetretenen Drift. Der für obiges Beispiel kalkulierte Drift beträgt 2.207 ppm. Der Verlauf der Minima muß jedoch nicht notwendig so gleichmäßig aussehen. Insbesondere bei gravierenden Laufzeitänderungen

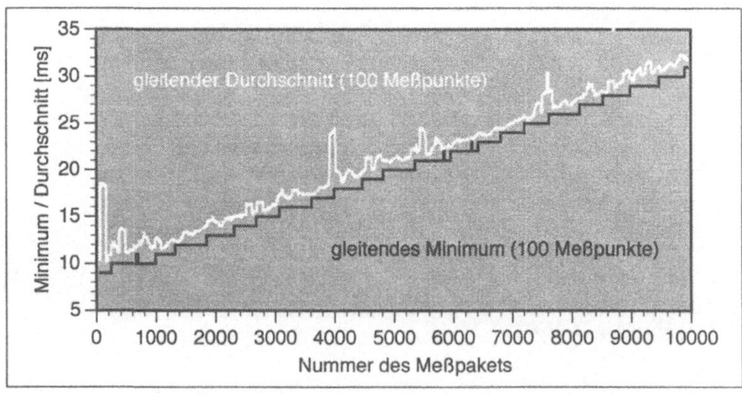

Bild 6. Gleitender Durchschnitt vs. gleitendes Minimum

---

1. In einem G/G/1-System beträgt die Wahrscheinlichkeit, daß ein neu ankommender Kunde ein leeres System vorfindet, $1-\rho$. Je kleiner also die Systemlast ist und je öfter die minimale Bedienzeit gewürfelt wird (je steiler also die Bedienzeitverteilung ist), desto häufiger wird die minimale Systemzeit (bei Wartezeit 0) angenommen.

innerhalb des Meßintervalls, wie sie z.B. bei einem Wechsel des Routingpfades auftreten können, sind nicht-lineare Meßergebnisse möglich. Die Auswirkungen auf die Genauigkeit der Regressionsanalyse sind umso größer, je näher die Laufzeitwechsel am Rand des Meßintervalls auftreten. In unseren Messungen zeigte sich, daß solche Effekte nur im internationalen Weitverkehrsbereich auftreten, in nationalen WANs konnten wir keine derartigen Einflüsse nachweisen. Es zeigte sich zudem, daß temporäre Erhöhungen der Netzlast nur zu einer Verdichtung höherer Laufzeiten führen, die Laufzeitminima jedoch davon unbeeinflußt bleiben (vgl. Bild 4). Wir gehen davon aus, daß gemäß der oben angedeuteten warteschlangentheoretischen Hintergründe die aktuell möglichen minimalen Verzögerungen auf einer Strecke auch mit relativ hoher Rate angenommen werden.

Falls es dennoch zu Laufzeitwechseln kommt, liefert die Regressionsanalyse dann brauchbare Resultate, wenn sich Verbesserungen und Verschlechterungen der Verzögerungen über der Zeit ausgleichen. In diesem Fall vergrößert sich zwar der Fehlerkoeffizient der Approximation, die Steigung der Regressionsgeraden bleibt aber unverändert. Treten Laufzeitwechsel am Rand der Meßperiode auf, muß das Meßintervall entsprechend verkleinert werden. Diese Entscheidung kann auf der Basis der Gesamtverzögerungen getroffen werden, da es in hohem Maße unwahrscheinlich ist, auf einem der Pfade steigende Laufzeiten zu beobachten, die auf dem anderen Pfad in gleichem Maße kompensiert werden. Man kann also das Meßintervall insofern einschränken, daß sich zu Beginn und am Ende der Meßperiode gleiche minimale Gesamtverzögerungen zeigen. Wir arbeiten zur Zeit an einer ausführlichen Beschreibung und Leistungsbewertung dieser Techniken, u.a. über Messungen zwischen zeitsynchronisierten Stationen im Internet [5].

3.2 Bestimmung der Verteilungsoffsets

Im vorhergehenden Abschnitt haben wir einen neuen Algorithmus zur Bestimmung der Form unidirektionaler Laufzeitverteilungen zwischen unsynchronisierten Hosts in paketvermittelnden Netzen eingeführt. Wir stellen nun eine Technik vor, mit deren Hilfe der letzte noch fehlende Parameter, der Startpunkt der Verteilungen auf der x-Achse und damit der tatsächlichen Uhrenoffset θ, abgeschätzt werden kann. Hierbei zeigt sich ein weiterer Vorteil des Verfahrens: Der Offset θ_i muß nur für ein einziges Paket i so genau wie möglich bestimmt werden. Der für dieses Paket berechnete Offset kann dann dazu benutzt werden, die Verteilungen entlang der x-Achse auf ihren korrekten Startpunkt zu verschieben.
Wir definieren hierzu:

$$OWDF_i = OWDF_{min} + F_i \quad \text{and} \quad OWDB_i = OWDB_{min} + B_i$$

F_i und B_i beschreiben also die Differenz zwischen den gemessenen Laufzeiten für Paket i und der minimalen Laufzeit auf beiden Pfaden. Dann gilt für jede gemessene Roundtrip-Zeit RTT_i:

$$RTT_i \stackrel{\text{Def.}}{=} OWDF_i + OWDB_i - \delta_i \stackrel{\text{Def.}}{=} OWDF_{min} + F_i + OWDB_{min} + B_i - \delta_i$$

$$\Leftrightarrow \quad OWDF_{min} + OWDB_{min} = RTT_i - F_i - B_i + \delta_i \qquad \oplus$$

Da die linke Seite der Gleichung $\oplus$ konstant sein muß, liefern jeweils zwei Messungen das gleiche Ergebnis und alle so abgeleiteten Gleichungen sind äquivalent (innerhalb einer Genauigkeit von 1 ms bedingt durch Rundungsfehler auf den Zeitstempeln). Deswegen münden alle Meßwerte in einer Gleichung $OWDF_{min} + OWDF_{min} = c$ mit zwei Unbekannten, wobei c eine (berechenbare) Konstante ist.

Wie bereits in Abschnitt 2.2 besprochen, setzt NTP auf die Annahme isotroper Laufzeiten. Messungen zu verschiedenen Rechnern, die mittels NTP zu UTC (Coordinated Universal Time) synchronisiert waren, bestätigten jedoch unsere Zweifel an der Richtigkeit dieser Annahme. Wir fanden heraus, daß die Laufzeiten eines Pakets auf Hin- und Rückweg in fast allen Fällen teilweise bemerkenswerte Unterschiede aufwiesen, und dies galt selbst für Pakete mit den kleinsten Roundtrip-Zeiten, die bei NTP aufgrund des niedrigeren Fehlers präferiert werden (Tabelle 1). Hierfür können statische und dynamische Effekte verantwortlich sein: Beispielsweise werden Pakete in die USA oft auf dem Hinweg über Satellit und auf dem Rückweg über Tiefseekabel geroutet, wodurch sich eine feste Laufzeitdifferenz von etwa 200 ms ergibt. Solche Einflüsse sind in nationalen Weitverkehrsnetzen vernachlässigbar. Dort kommt es allerdings durch hochdynamische Änderungen der Pufferfüllgrade in den Zwischensystemen zu lokal bedingten Differenzen in den Paketlaufzeiten. Da sich die Wartezeiten in den Routern für bis zu 80% der Paketlaufzeiten verantwortlich zeigen, ändern sich diese dynamisch und meist unabhängig für beide Richtungen einer IP-Verbindung.

Wenn allerdings die Pakete auf Hin- und Rückweg eine annähernd gleiche Anzahl an Routern passieren und über vergleichbare Entfernungen transportiert werden, müssen sich die minimalen Laufzeiten auf beiden Wegen in derselben Größenordnung bewegen. Wir nehmen daher für unser Verfahren an, daß die minimalen Einwegelaufzeiten auf beiden Übertragungspfaden gleich sind, daß diese aber nicht notwendigerweise im selben Paket auftreten müssen. Es ist offensichtlich, daß diese Annahme allgemeingültiger und daher realistischer als die von NTP getroffene ist.

Messung	NTP			eigener Ansatz	
	RTT_{min}	OWDF	OWDB	$OWDF_{min}$	$OWDB_{min}$
Aachen <-> Aachen (LAN)	3	1	2	1	1
Aachen <-> Aachen (MAN)	7	5	2	1	1
Aachen <-> Köln (WAN nat.)	5	1	4	1	1
Aachen <-> USA (WAN intern.)	185	94	91	89	90

Tabelle 1. Vergleich der Ergebnisse von NTP und eigenem Ansatz

In Tabelle 1 sind die Werte, die der NTP-Ansatz liefert, den Ergebnissen unseres Verfahrens gegenübergestellt. Dargestellt sind die kleinsten Gesamtlaufzeiten und die zugehörigen Laufzeiten für Hin- und Rückweg für Messungen im LAN-, MAN- und WAN-Bereich, bei denen insgesamt 50000 Pakete ausgetauscht wurden. Zusätzlich sind die minimalen Laufzeiten für Hin- und Rückweg aufgeführt. Es ist erkennbar, daß unser Ansatz die genaueren Ergebnisse liefert, d.h. zu einer besseren Synchronisation der beiden Uhren führen muß.

$OWDF_{min}$ und $OWDB_{min}$ werden also über eine Verschiebung der beiden Laufzeitverteilungen auf einen gemeinsamen Startwert geschätzt. Zur Auswertung von Gleichung $\oplus$ kann dann ein beliebiges Paket innerhalb des Meßintervalls ausgewählt und die lokale Uhr der Referenzuhr angepaßt werden, indem die lokale Zeit um den gemessenen Wert $t_{i,3} - t_{i,2}$ abzüglich der wie oben kalkulierten korrekten Laufzeit $OWDB_i$ korrigiert wird. Zur Ereignisanalyse werden allerdings nur die gemessenen Zeitstempel angepaßt (vgl. Abschnitt 4).

4. Ereignisanalyse mit DERS

Für die Realisierung automatischer Management- bzw. Steuerungssysteme ist es von Bedeutung, daß die Erkennung der Ereignisse zur Laufzeit, d.h. on-line geschieht. Dem Manager wird so die Möglichkeit gegeben, zur Laufzeit des Systems beispielsweise Fehler oder Leistungsengpässe zu erkennen und sofort steuernd einzugreifen. Die Ereignisse, die dabei erkannt werden sollen, werden in einer formalen Notation beschrieben und sind entweder elementar oder setzen sich aus mehreren Ereignissen zusammen. Im folgenden wird das System DERS vorgestellt, das an der RWTH Aachen entwickelt wurde. Dabei wurden Konzepte und Erfahrungen verwendet, die mit dem ebenfalls in Aachen entwickelten ANSAmon gemacht wurden, vgl. [17]. Es handelt sich dabei um einen ereignisgesteuerten Software-Monitor, mit dessen Hilfe komplexe Ereignisse verteilt analysiert werden können. Das System ist zunächst auf der Plattform ANSAware implementiert worden. Der Entwurf des System ist jedoch so gestaltet, daß er sich ohne große Änderungen auf ein CORBA-System übertragen läßt.

4.1 Ereignisbeschreibung

DERS kann neben elementaren Ereignissen, d.h. Ereignissen, die direkt durch die Instrumentierung der Anwendung oder der Middleware initiiert werden, auch komplexe Ereignisse erkennen. Komplexe Ereignisse können durch Kombination mehrerer Ereignisse mittels aussagenlogischer Operatoren oder temporallogischen Operatoren definiert werden. Mit Hilfe der Verlängerung von Ereignissen und Vergleichsoperatoren kann der relative Abstand zwischen zwei Ereignissen spezifiziert werden, siehe Tabelle 2.

Aufgezeichnete Ereignisse werden in dem Datentyp `Event Record` gespeichert. Alle Ereignisse besitzen einen Typ, der widerspiegelt, welche Systemaktion gerade beobachtet worden ist. Zusätzlich wird der Initiator eines Ereignisses mittels seiner Kennungen der Anwendung, des Rechnerknotens, des Prozesses sowie des Threads identifiziert. Neben diesen Informationen, die vom Typ des aufgezeichneten Ereignisses unabhängig sind, sind auch ereignisspezifische Daten vorgesehen, deren Semantik vom Ereignistyp abhängig ist. Es handelt sich dabei um ein statisches Feld von Integer-Werten. Diese Festlegung ist notwendig, damit die Puffer bei der Initialisierung allokiert werden können. DERS erlaubt es, Ereignisse nur unter bestimmten Bedingungen aufzuzeichnen. Innerhalb einer solchen Bedingung können die Informationen des Datentyps `Event Record` verwendet werden, beispielsweise könnten nur Ereignisse relevant sein, die von einem bestimmten Knoten erkannt werden.

Ereignis	Bedeutung
$E\,/\,\neg E$	Ereignis E tritt ein/ tritt nicht ein
$E_1 \vee E_2$	mindestens eines der beiden Ereignisse muß eintreten
$E_1 \wedge E_2$	beide Ereignisse müssen eintreten
$E_1 \sqsubset E_2$	Ereignis E_1 tritt zeitlich vor dem Ereignis E_2 ein
$E_1 \sqsupset E_2$	Ereignis E_1 tritt zeitlich nach dem Ereignis E_2 ein
$E + t\,ms$	Verlängerung der Ereignisdauer von E um t ms

Tabelle 2. Ereignistypen, die DERS erkennt

Beispiel

Angenommen, ein Dokument wird von zwei Benutzern auf unterschiedlichen Rechnern bearbeitet. Auf jedem Rechner ist eine Kopie des Dokuments vorhanden. Der Systemmanager soll benachrichtigt werden, wenn die Änderung eines Benutzer nicht rechtzeitig an den anderen Benutzer übertragen werden kann.

event DisconnectedReplika ::=
(Doc<-write **at** Node1)= (Doc<-write **at** Node2) = (Doc<-Update **at** Node2)

4.2 Konfiguration des verteilten Monitors

Verteilte Monitore lassen sich mit Hilfe der von DERS unterstützten Komponenten beliebig konfigurieren. Als Komponenten stehen aktive und passive Erkenner sowie Puffer zur Verfügung, über die Ereignisse von Sensoren zu Managern gelangen, siehe auch Bild 2. Voraussetzung ist jedoch, daß auf jedem zu beobachteten Rechnerknoten mindestens ein Erkenner eingerichtet ist. Zusätzlich ist auf jedem Rechner ein Zeitdienst installiert, der Drift und Offset zu einem ausgezeichneten Rechner mit Hilfe des in Kapitel 3 vorgestellten Verfahrens bestimmt. Dabei werden jedoch nicht die lokalen Systemuhren angepaßt, sondern bei der Erzeugung eines Ereignisses wird die globale Zeit aus der lokalen Systemzeit, dem Offset und dem Drift errechnet. Zwischen jeweils zwei Komponenten wird außerdem ein Puffer geschaltet. Bild 7 zeigt eine Beispielkonfiguration eines verteilten Monitors.

Passive Erkenner erhalten Ereignisse entweder von Sensoren oder anderen Erkennern. Sie sind in der Lage, alle Ereignistypen zu erkennen, ohne jedoch selbst aktiv zu werden. Erkannte komplexe Ereignisse werden an einen oder mehrere Erkenner oder einen Manager weitergeleitet. Aktive Erkenner zeichnen sich dadurch aus, daß sie beim Eintreten eines bestimmten Ereignisses in der Lage sind, Aktionen anzustoßen oder weitere Informationen mittels eines RPCs anzufordern, um die Ursache eines Ereignisses genauer festlegen zu kön-

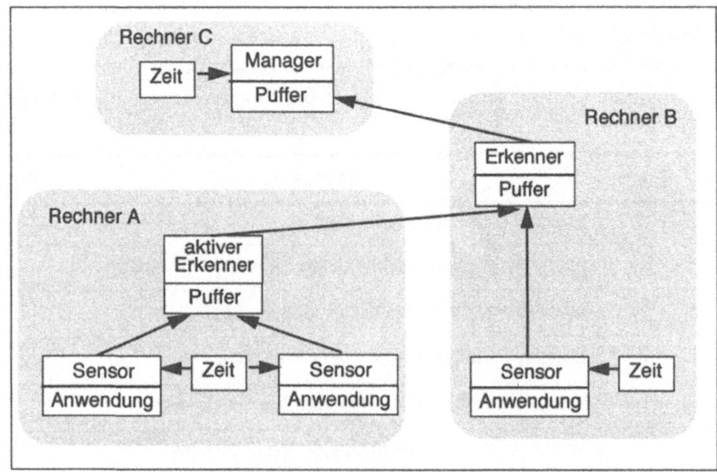

Bild 7.   Beispielkonfiguration eines verteilten Erkennungssystems

nen. Meldet beispielsweise die Middleware einem Client einen `RPC Failure` an seiner Schnittstelle, so ist entwe-der der Server-Prozeß nicht verfügbar oder die Nachrichtenübertragung ausgefallen. Es ist beispielsweise durch ungünstige Einstellung eines RPC-Timers möglich, daß ein `RPC Failure` gemeldet wird, obwohl der Server auf Transportebene erreichbar ist. Tritt ein `RPC Failure` auf, so kann ein aktiver Erkenner eine `Alive`-Nachricht an den Server schicken. Ist diese erfolgreich, so ist es besser, die RPC-Parameter anzupassen als einen neuen Server zu suchen.

Da sich die Komponenten eines verteilten Monitors auf verschiedenen Rechnern befinden können, muß die Kommunikation gesondert betrachtet werden. Ziel ist es, daß Sensoren oder Erkenner die Ereignisse, die sie erkannt haben, möglichst schnell weitergeben können. Jedoch sollen sie nicht blockiert werden, wenn der empfangende Erkenner gerade analysiert und keine Ereignisse empfangen kann. Daher wird ein Puffer zwischen jeweils zwei Monitorkomponenten geschaltet. Ereignisse werden per unidirektionaler Nachricht (Notifikation genannt) an den Puffer gesendet. Da auch dieser nicht weiß, wann der empfangende Erkenner neue Ereignisse empfangen kann, dient der Puffer als Server für den (empfangenden) Erkenner, der sich Ereignisse per RPC holt. Ereignisse werden nicht einzeln sondern in Gruppen verschickt, mit Ausnahme der Sensoren, die jedes Ereignis sofort weiterleiten. Weiterhin haben Puffer den Vorteil, daß sie die Monitorkomponenten entkoppeln, was eine dynamische Rekonfiguration des Monitors erleichtert.

4.3 Verteilte Ereignisanalyse

Für die Erkennung komplexer Ereignisse wird deren Beschreibung in eine Baumstruktur transformiert. Der Baum kann aus mehreren Teilbäumen bestehen, die jeweils von einem Erkenner ausgewertet werden, siehe Bild 8.

Für jedes komplexe Ereignis wird bei der Initialisierung eines Erkenners ein Baum angelegt, wobei in den Blättern die Ereignisse und in den Knoten die Operatoren stehen. Die Struktur des Baumes ist dabei fest durch das komplexe Ereignis vorgegeben. Wird ein relevantes Ereignis erkannt, so wird der Wert des entsprechenden Blatts aktualisiert. Nachfolgend wird der gesamte Teilbaum erneut ausgewertet. Wird bei der Auswertung die Wurzel erreicht, so sendet der Erkenner das erkannte komplexe Ereignis an einen oder mehrere Erkenner oder an einen Manager. Bei der Erkennung von Ereignissen, die Reihenfolgeoperationen wie ⊏ oder ⊐ enthalten sowie Ereignisse, deren Dauer verlängert wurde, ist es wichtig, daß die tatsächliche Reihenfolge, in der die Ereignisse eintreten, von den Erkennern äquivalent erkannt wird.

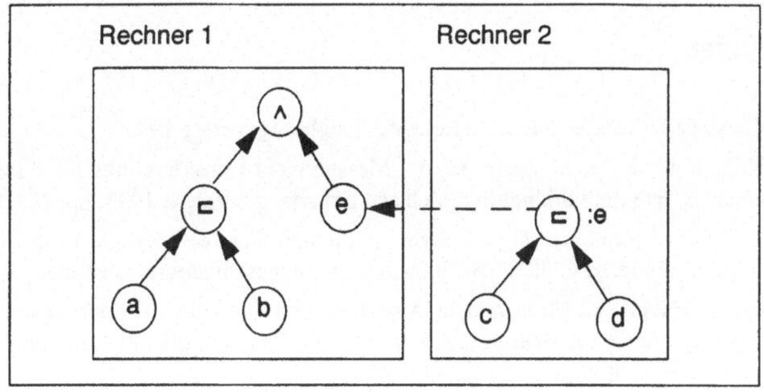

Bild 8. Beispiel eines verteilten Analysebaums

Beispiel

Es soll das komplexe Ereignis $((a \sqsubset d) \wedge (b \sqsubset c))$ erkannt werden. Die Ereignisse treten real in der Reihenfolge $a\ b\ c\ d$ auf. Obwohl die Uhren der beteiligten Hosts nun als synchronisiert angenommen werden können, kann es durch Laufzeitverzögerungen dazu kommen, daß die Ereig-nisse in der Reihenfolge $a\ c\ b\ d$ beim Erkenner an (vgl. Bild 1). In diesem Fall würde das komplexe Ereignis nicht erkannt, obwohl es tatsächlich eingetreten ist.

Das Problem verspäteter Teilereignisse kann gelöst werden, indem nach Erkennung eines Ereignisses dessen Weitergabe so lange verzögert wird, bis mit sehr hoher Wahrscheinlichkeit keine verspäteten Ereignisse eines zugehörigen komplexeren Ereignisbaumes mehr eintreffen können. Dazu kann auf der Basis der für die Uhrensynchronisation protokollierten unidirektionalen Laufzeiten eine empirische Verteilungsfunktion gebildet werden. Mit Hilfe fester Verteilungsquan-tile (1-α-Perzentile) kann dann sichergestellt werden, daß 1-α Prozent der Übertragungen innerhalb der vorgegebenen Zeit abgeschlossen sind.

Im Gegensatz zu einem zentralen Ansatz müssen in verteilten Analysesystemen alle Komponenten, die an der Erkennung eines komplexen Ereignis beteiligt sind, zurückgesetzt werden, wenn ein Ereignis erkannt worden ist. Durch das Rücksetzen der Erkenner wird verhindert, daß ein neues komplexes Ereignis fälschlich Ereignisse doppelt verwendet. Nur wenn das gesamte Ereignis erkannt wurde, wird es nötig, den (gesamten) Baum zurückzusetzen. Der oberste Erkenner schickt dann `Reset`-Meldungen an alle Teilbäume unter ihm. Wird jeder `Reset`-Meldungen eine laufende Nummer mitgegeben, die angibt, zum wievielten Mal das Ereignis erkannt wurde, so brauchen die untergeordneten Erkenner nicht auf verspätete `Reset`-Meldungen warten, weil der übergeordnete Erkenner immer weiß, welche Ereignisse er schon zurückgesetzt hat und daher ungültig erkannte Ereignis herausfiltern kann.

5. Schlußbemerkungen

Kernprobleme der verteilten Ereignisanalyse in paketvermittelnden Netzen sind das Fehlen einer globalen Systemzeit einerseits sowie die unterschiedlichen Laufzeiten der Notifikationen. Der in diesem Bericht vorgestellte verteilte Monitor basiert daher auf einem speziell auf variable Nachrichtenlaufzeiten ausgelegten Uhrensynchronisationsverfahren. Dadurch wird es insbesondere ermöglicht, unidirektionale Laufzeitverteilungen zu bestimmen, mittels derer das Problem verspätet eintreffender Ereignisse effizient gelöst werden kann. Zukünftige Messungen der Reaktionszeiten des Monitors bei der Erkennung komplexer Ereignisse sollen seine Eignung für den Einsatz in reaktiven Management- und Steuersystemen belegen.

Literaturreferenzen

[1] Bosch, K.: Statistik-Taschenbuch, 2. Auflage, Oldenbourg-Verlag 1993

[2] Claffy, K.C., Polyzos, G.C., Braun, H.-W.: Measurement Considerations for Assessing Unidirectional Latencies, Internetworking: Research and Experience, Vol. 4, 1993, pp. 121-132

[3] Defense Advanced Research Projects Agency: Internet Control Message Protocol, DARPA Networking Group Report RFC-792, USC Information Sciences Institute, September 1981.

[4] Fasbender, A., Davids, P.: Measurement, Modelling and Emulation of Internet Round-Trip Delays, 8th GI/ITG Conference on Measuring, Modelling and Evaluating Computing and Communication Systems, LNCS 977, Springer 1995, pp. 401-415

[5]   Fasbender, A.; Rulands, I.: On Assessing Unidirectional Latencies in Packet-Switched Networks, Eingereicht bei: ICC´97, Montreal, Juni 1997

[6]   Friedrich, R.; Rolia, J.: Performance evaluation of a distributed application performance monitor, In: Schill, A., Mittasch, C.; Spaniol, O. et al (eds.): Distributed Platforms, Chapman & Hall 1996, pp. 259-271

[7]   Ferrari, D.; Serazzi, G.; Zeigner, A.: Measurement and Tuning of Computer Systems, Prentice Hall 1983

[8]   Gehani, N.; Jagadish, H.; Shmueli, O.: Composite Event Specification in Active Databases: Model & Implementation. Proceedings of International Conference on Very Large Databases (VLDB) 1992, pp. 327-338

[9]   Hofmann, R.; Klar, R.; Mohr, B.; Quick, A.; Siegle, M.: Distributed Performance Monitoring: Methods, Tools and Applications, IEEE Transactions on Parallel and Distributed Systems, Vol. 5, No. 6, June 1994

[10]   Jakobson, G.; Weissmann, M.: Real-Time Telecommunication Network Management: Extending Event Correlation with Temporal Constraints, In: Sethi, A.; Raynaund, Y.; Faure-Vincent, F. (eds.): Integrated Network Management IV, Chapman & Hall 1995, pp. 290-301

[11]   Jain, R.: The Art of Computer Systems Performance Analysis, Wiley 1991

[12]   Jordaan, J.; Paterok, M.:Event Correlation in Heterogeneous Networks Using the OSI Management Framework, In: Hegering, H.; Yemini, Y. (eds.): Intergrated Network Management III, North-Holland 1993, pp. 683-695

[13]   Klar, R.; et al: Messung und Modellierung paralleler und verteilter Rechensysteme, Teubner 1995

[14]   Langendörfer, H.: Leistungsanalyse von Rechensystemen, Hanser 1992

[15]   Lange, F.; Kröger, R.; Gergeleit, M.: JEWEL: Design and Implementation of a Distributed Measurement System, IEEE Transactions on Parallel and Distributed Systems, Vol. 3, No. 6, November 1992, pp. 657-671

[16]   Mansouri-Samani, M.; Sloman, M.: GEM: A Generalized Event Monitoring Language for Distributed Systems, Imperial College Research Report No. DoC 95/8

[17]   Meyer, B.; Heineken, M.; Popien, C.: Performance Analysis of Distributed Applications using ANSAmon, In: Raymond, K.; Armstrong, L. (eds.): Open Distributed Proecssing - Experiences with distributed environments, Chapman & Hall 1995, pp. 309-320

[18]   Mills, D.L.: Precision Synchronization of Computer Network Clocks, ACM Computer Communication Review, Vol. 24, No. 2, April 1994, pp. 28-42

[19]   Mills, D.L.: Network Time Protocol (Version 3), Specification, Implementation and Analysis, RFC 1305, March 1992

[20]   Möller, M.; Tretter, S.; Fink, B.: Intelligent Filtering in Network Management Systems, In: Sethi, A.; Raynaund, Y.; Faure-Vincent, F. (eds.): Integrated Network Management IV, Chapman & Hall 1995, pp. 304-315

[21]   Yemini, S.; Kliger, S.; Mozes, E.; Yemini, Y.; Ohsie, D.: High Speed and Robust Event Correlation, IEEE Communications Magazin, Vol. 34, No. 5, May 1996, pp. 82-90

Session 10:
Preisträger

Shared Window Systems

Thomas Gutekunst
Swiss Bank Corporation
Business Technology Center
4002 Basel, Switzerland
<thomas.gutekunst@mhs.swissbank.com>

1 Introduction and Motivation

Today, the technical environment for high-speed data interchange enables people around the world to interact with each other. They may attend virtual meetings without even having to leave their offices, being able to access information from their personal or corporate information systems. This might lessen the need for travelling and increase the value of real meetings, which will be reserved then to situations where it is vital to meet face-to-face.

Forthcoming developments in the field of workgroup computing will probably have a far greater impact on the interaction habits of tomorrow. This is motivated by the expectation that new means will allow for occasional and spontaneous interaction that has not been practical or affordable yet.

In the area of computer-supported cooperative work, we currently find two major approaches: workflow management and workgroup computing, the latter of which is in our interest. Workflow management focuses on processes that may span an entire organization, i.e., this can involve a large number of actors. Furthermore, coordination is usually based on the established communication relationships and the decision competences described by organizational rules. Workflow management systems are suitable to support well-structured routine tasks with a high repetition rate [18].

In contrast, the aim of workgroup computing is to support small groups performing non-routine tasks, which are not a priori coordinated by organizational rules. Workgroup computing supports the self-organization of cooperative work. The members of the group are allowed to interact freely, i.e. without being constrained by prescribed procedures or established conversational conventions, through the provision of facilities enabling them to cooperate via joint construction of a common information space [22].

A number of workgroup computing systems have implemented the notion of a "shared view", where multiple users perceive the same object in the same state and perceive any changes in the state of the object concurrently. Any changes to the object by one user will immediately be perceivable to the other users.

The shared view allows the members of a group, each on his/her own workstation, to simultaneously create, administer, share, and revise information. A possible solution is to build a new set of collaboration-aware applications that explicitly support this facility. Though representing the emerging generation of CSCW applications, such an approach has several problems. Perhaps the most critical of these is that users are limited to the use of special-purpose collaboration-aware applications. Considering the diversity of existing computer applications, this requirement appears very limiting.

Shared window systems are another solution for providing shared views. They exploit properties of a base window system to allow joint usage of unmodified single-user applications, also referred to as "collaboration-transparent" applications. This "application sharing" approach has several advantages. Firstly, users are not required to use new applications—they can share the applications already in place. Secondly, the system does not need to be modified to support new applications or changes to existing applications.

Although application sharing is a useful concept, there are serious limitations that can only be overcome with "collaboration-aware" applications. In particular, it is not possible to let users have different roles. In contrast, collaboration-aware applications explicitly support the collaborative situation. They may offer richer interfaces and, therefore, have the potential to enhance group work.

The development of such applications, however, is currently not supported to the same extent as single-user applications. Collaboration-aware applications either have to be constructed from scratch or with specialized user interface toolkits.

Actually, shared window systems may also offer true multi-user support at the user interface level. An elegant solution would even allow collaboration-aware applications to be constructed using existing user interface toolkits, i.e. toolkits already in use for the development of single-user applications.

2 The Notion of Shared Window Systems

Window systems offer the functionality required to display windows, to render to these windows, and to receive input from the user. Although some window systems (e.g. the X Window System) allow applications to serve multiple displays simultaneously and thus allow for building multi-user applications, there is no support that simplifies the construction of these. The application must be built from scratch or with considerable additional effort. The application still has to open connections to each user's display, create windows on these displays, render to these windows, and handle the input originating from each user. This is exactly where shared window systems may be useful. For the construction of multi-user applications, they can simplify the application developer's task.

Some authors look at shared window systems as being the same as application sharing [5] [16]. Garfinkel et al. [15] define "application sharing" as displaying a view of an application on multiple displays and updating those displays simultaneously. Often, the sharing of collaboration-transparent applications and the provision of collaboration-aware applications are seen as orthogonal concepts.

Although the distinction between collaboration-transparency and collaboration-awareness as defined by Lauwers and Lantz [16] is a valid one from the perspective of the application in question, collaboration-transparency and collaboration-awareness are not competing but complementary concepts. We propose a somewhat broader view and define the notion of a shared window system as follows:

A window system that allows existing single-user applications to be viewed and interacted with on multiple users' workstations simultaneously, and that provides features that simplify the task of constructing multi-user applications, is referred to as a "shared window system".

The term originates from the fact that shared window systems support the sharing of applications among multiple users at the window system interface. When a shared window system is built on top of an existing window system, the underlying window system is called the "base window system".

3 Requirements to Shared Window Systems

In order to provide a generic service, a shared window system must address a number of issues. This section deals with the issues that we believe to be crucial. Some of these issues have already been discussed previously. However, as far as we know, there is currently no shared window system that addresses all of them.

3.1 Sharing Metaphor

One principal functionality of a shared window system is to allow collaboration-transparent, single-user applications to be displayed and interacted with on multiple users' workstations simultaneously. The terms "collaboration-transparent" and "single-user" denote that the applications were actually constructed for a single-user environment and hence are not aware of being run in a collaborative environment.

A principal requirement to a shared window system is that such applications need not be modified in order to be sharable. This allows even "off-the-shelf" applications to be shared. The possibility to share applications the users are already familiar with is very important since having to learn new interfaces for sporadic tasks discourages many users [5].

A shared window system has to be transparent for the applications that are to be shared, i.e., the applications should not notice any difference between the shared window system and the base window system. Also, users should be able to run applications under the shared window system without taking special preparations. Even more important, the run-time behavior of applications should not be affected by the shared window system, neither in quality nor in performance.

3.2 Relaxed WYSIWIS

"WYSIWIS" stands for "What You See Is What I See" and denotes interfaces in which the shared context is guaranteed to appear the same to each user [8]. Stefik et al. [23] define an interface to be "strictly WYSIWIS" when all users "see exactly the same thing and where the others are pointing". On the one hand this means that all users have the same image on their respective displays, on the other hand the cursors of all users are visible for all users. In practice, strict WYSIWIS was found to be too limiting. The shared focus of strict WYSIWIS makes concurrent operation with different applications by different users impossible.

With "relaxed WYSIWIS", only portions of the screen are shared by distinguishing shared windows from private windows [3, 8, 16, 23]. Shared windows are visible to each user while private windows are displayed locally only. Furthermore, relaxed WYSIWIS allows the users to rearrange private as well as shared windows as desired and to pursue independent activities on their workstation.

Shared window systems are based on the notion of shared windows that are visible on each users' workstation. Changes in the contents of a shared window are immediately reflected in all users' shared window instances. Relaxed WYSIWIS distinguishes shared window systems from display sharing systems where the whole screen content is replicated to all users in a conference [9, 11]. However, as far as the contents of shared windows is concerned, shared window systems strictly adhere to the WYSIWIS concept.

Even relaxed WYSIWIS may be too restrictive, especially when users have widely differing roles, knowledge, and abilities [12]. The sharing of collaboration-transparent applications does not allow for personalized views. This limitation is fundamental and can only be overcome with collaboration-aware applications, as will be discussed in Section 3.8.

3.3 Activity Awareness

To achieve successful cooperation, there is a clear requirement that group members are aware of individual and group activities [7, 8, 19, 23]. Dourish and Bellotti [7] define "awareness" as the "understanding of the activities of others, which provides a context for your own activity".

In cooperative work, users wish to be aware of what other users are doing. This requires the propagation of each user's activity to the other users [19]. There are several mechanisms for this propagation. Dourish and Bellotti [7] distinguish informational and role-restrictive approaches from the approach to present shared feedback. Systems following the informational approach provide explicit facilities through which the collaborators inform each other of their activities.

The role-restrictive approach arises from explicit support for roles in cooperative work. Ellis et al. [8] define a role as "a set of privileges and responsabilities attributed to a person, or sometimes to a system module". The purpose of roles is to achieve a greater awareness of the actions a user might take, however, this kind of awareness provides information only about the character of the activity, but not the content.

Though both the information and the role-restrictive approach provide an awareness of progress and joint activity, they also have some problems [7]. With the informational approach, the individual is required to supply the information. Firstly, this causes extra work from which he/she does not directly benefit. Secondly, it is not clear whether the others will benefit at all. They may benefit, but this is by no means guaranteed since they receive the information that its creator deemed to be appropriate. Whether or not the given information is appropriate, can only be determined in the context of the other users' activities. As for the role-restrictive approaches, the observation that roles are often negotiated and reassigned dynamically during the course of a cooperative activity indicates a major flaw of explicit support for roles.

The approach to present "shared feedback", as Dourish and Bellotti [7] refer to it, makes information about individual activities apparent to the other users by presenting feedback on operations within the shared workspace. Shared feedback resembles the mechanisms that is already known from natural cooperation. It allows the users to adopt different working styles and to vary their activities dynamically in response to the changing state of affairs.

By its nature, the sharing of collaboration-transparent applications provides shared feedback and achieves awareness for the collaborative situation—changes in the contents of a shared window are immediately reflected in all users' shared window instances.

3.4 Workspace Management

The workspace management is responsible for visualizing cooperative work in an appropriate way. A user wants to know which items are private and which are subject of cooperation. Furthermore, it is important that the user is able to associate shared items to a cooperative activity and to understand the relationships among them.

Under a shared window system, a user should be able to distinguish private windows from shared ones [16]. For shared windows, the user should also be able to see with whom they are shared or from which user they come from, respectively, and whether or not he/she may provide input to the underlying applications. This may be achieved by visual cues. Crowley et al. [5] argue that the workspace management should not provide a visible "shared workspace" on the workstation's display, but rather allow to easily mix and arrange shared and private windows as desired in order to allow the users to pursue independent activities on their workstation. Finally, a shared window system should allow users to make private windows shared and vice versa.

3.5 Concurrency and Floor Control

Single-user applications that run under a shared window system are not aware of being run in a group context. They are not prepared to interacting with multiple users. Thus, the shared window system must provide mechanisms that handle concurrent access by multiple users.

Many of the approaches to handling concurrency in database applications rely on the concept of atomic transactions and are often based on the use of locks. These approaches give the impression of shared access being carried out in isolation from other users and hence do not meet the awareness requirement [4]. Furthermore, it is not clear which granularity should be used with transaction-oriented approaches [4]. For example, in joint editing applications, transactions may be applied at a granularity of sections, paragraphs, sentences, or even words or characters. Finally, such an approach is not applicable for the sharing of collaboration-transparent applications since the shared window system is not aware of application-specific abstractions such as paragraphs and sentences.

Ellis et al. [8] highlight the importance of responsiveness, which requires a short response time, i.e. the time it takes for a user's own interface to reflect his/her actions, and a short notification time, i.e. the time required for these actions to be propagated to the other users' interfaces. The responsiveness of a shared window system is crucial for the cohesiveness of a cooperative activity, which would get lost if users were presented slightly different or out-of-date views.

From the above, one can conclude that transaction-oriented approaches are not suitable for handling concurrency control in shared window systems. Instead, concurrency control is achieved by "floor control", which determines at any given point in time which user is allowed to direct input to an application [8]. The right to generate input is denoted by the "floor", the user currently allowed to do so is referred to as "floor holder". There is only one floor holder at any given point in time.

Crowley et al. [5] separate the concept of floor control into mechanisms and policy. The floor control mechanisms handle the low-level activities of passing the floor and maintaining a synchronized event stream for all users. The floor control policy comprises a set of rules governing floor control, i.e. determining how users request and are granted the floor.

Lauwers and Lantz [16] characterize and discuss floor control policies along three dimensions:

- the scope of the floor (per conference, application, or window),
- the number of users that can concurrently hold a floor, and
- how the floor is passed.

The first dimension, the scope of the floor, determines the amount of concurrent activity to be permitted. A floor per application allows for concurrent activity with multiple applications while with a floor that is valid for an entire conference, concurrent activity within the conference is not possible. Thus, a floor per application provides more flexibility than a floor per conference. A floor per window could make sense for applications that present multiple windows. However, single-user applications have only one input focus and therefore do not permit concurrent activity within multiple windows belonging to the same application.

The second dimension, the number of users that can concurrently hold a floor, also has an impact on concurrent activity. Having more than one user holding the floor for a given application allows concurrent activity of multiple users with that application, however, the input focus is the same for all these users. Strictly speaking, it is not possible that multiple users are floor holder at the same point in time since the purpose of floor control is to serve for concurrency control. Though there is only one floor holder at any given point in time, a floor control policy may provide the illusion of concurrent floor holders.

Finally, the third dimension leads to a discussion of floor control policies, which determine how the floor is passed. Greenberg [12] gives four examples of how users might acquire and release the floor:

- *Ring-passing:*
  The current floor holder must explicitly release the floor before anyone else can acquire it.
- *Preemptive:*
  Any user can grab the floor at any time.
- *Time slices and timeouts:*
  A user has the token for a given time slice, after which the floor is taken away from him/her. Alternatively, the floor may be taken away after the current floor holder has been inactive for a given period of time.
- *Moderated:*
  A designated user acts as a chairperson who is responsible for passing the floor to and taking the floor away from other users.

Floor control policies may support explicit floor passing, where the floor moves from one user to another by an explicit assignment, as well as implicit floor passing, where the floor is implicitly assigned to a user as soon as he/she generates input events. Implicit floor passing corresponds to the concept of having no floor at all. However, low-level mechanisms within the shared window system then have to take care of avoiding inconsistent input events being sent to the application.

As observed by Crowley et al. [5], implicit floor passing works best in conjunction with voice interaction. High-quality audio links between the participants may provide for such (see also Section 3.7). Control of the cooperative activity is then mediated by social protocols that conform to the group's social etiquettes, which are mutually understood and agreed upon, but not enforced by the system [8].

The fact that users need not perform an explicit operation to request or grant the floor, constitutes an enormous advantage of implicit floor passing. However, while being reasonable for small groups, it is not sufficient to solely rely on social protocols. This is especially important for larger groups and in high-delay environments [16].

The preferred floor control policy for a given situation is depending on the group task, the size of the group, the politics of the group's interactions, and the application itself [12]. Since any given policy will not be able to satisfy all groups in all situations, a shared window system should not enforce specific floor control policies. It is better to provide simple mechanisms that allow various floor control policies to be built on top of them.

A fundamental limitation of the sharing of collaboration-transparent applications is that it does not allow concurrent, independent input to the same shared application because there is only one input focus per application. As with personalized views, collaboration-aware applications are required to handle this situation. Section 3.9 will deal with this topic. However, the possibility of concurrent, independent input brings new demands on users to stay informed about what other users are doing [23]. They can less easily interpret sudden display changes resulting from others' actions [8].

3.6 User Management

Schmidt and Bannon [22] point out that membership in a group of cooperating users is not stable and often even not determinable. Many cooperative activities do not occur in the context of scheduled meetings, but rather spontaneously and unplanned. Users cannot always anticipate with whom they will be cooperating, nor which items will be subject of cooperative work [16]. In order to support spontaneous interaction, it must be possible to initiate cooperative activities in a "light-weight" fashion. It is desirable—especially for longer-term cooperation—that users are able to join and leave a cooperative activity at any time [12].

A related aspect is admission control. It determines which users are allowed to participate in a cooperative activity as well as how they join. As with floor control, different policies for handling admission control may be appropriate depending on a given setup. As cooperative groups typically intersect [22], a user should also be able to participate in multiple cooperative activities simultaneously.

Dynamic user participation is a key requirement for a shared window system since cooperative activities often evolve in unexpected ways. A shared window system, therefore, should provide mechanisms that support dynamic user participation and allow various admission policies to be realized.

3.7 User Interaction

Providing only a shared visual space is not meaningful enough for carrying out desktop conferences. The observation that people coordinate their activities by their explicit interaction brings the demand for additional support [8].

Explicit interaction allows the users to discuss the contents of shared windows and to coordinate their work. Computer-based facilities such as audio links or desktop videophones may be used for that purpose. Often, applications are shared between two persons only. In this case, a telephone call may suffice. Experience indicates that the quality of the audio link is much more important for successful collaboration than the provision of a video link.

In many desktop conferencing systems, we also find telepointing facilities that provide pointing tools visible in all instances of the same shared window. There are two classes of telepointers: firstly shadow cursors, which track the floor holder's cursor movement and mirror this movement on the other users' displays, and secondly movable markers, which are not coupled to cursor movement. Both classes have proven useful to draw attention to a particular object within a shared window [12, 16, 20].

As with telepointing facilities that serve gesturing purposes, graphical annotation facilities may also be useful in many situations [16, 20]. Graphical annotation enables users to draw on top of shared windows in a way that is transparent to the underlying applications.

In our opinion, a shared window system should not offer telepointing and annotation facilities directly, but rather provide mechanisms that support the construction of these. The reason for this is, as with admission and floor control, that the shared window system should not impose a specific policy for the behaviour of these facilities.

3.8 Personalized Views

As pointed out in Section 3.2, relaxed WYSIWIS may be too restrictive for several cooperative activities. With the sharing of collaboration-transparent applications, all users are presented the same set of windows with identical contents, i.e., all users have the same view of the application. Collaboration-transparent applications do not allow for personalized views since this requires the applications to be collaboration-aware [12].

Bentley et al. [3] define "interface coupling" as the extent to which multi-user interfaces support sharing through the propagation of activities. The closer the coupling, the more the users will be aware of what the other users are doing. Bentley et al. identify three levels of sharing that correspond to "different degrees of interface coupling:

- *Presentation-Level Sharing (tight coupling):*
  Each user is presented with the same display of the same information from a common information space. When this presentation is changed in any way, all display screens are updated. This level of sharing is also known as 'what-you-see-is-what-I-see' (WYSIWIS).
- *View-Level Sharing (medium coupling):*
  Each user has presentations of the same information, but the presentations may differ. For example, different users may simultaneously interact with tabular or graphical displays of the same data.
- *Object-Level Sharing (loose coupling):*
  Each user has presentations of different information. For example, several users may edit different sections of the same document".

The sharing of collaboration-transparent applications belongs to the class of presentation-level sharing. With the concept of personalized views, collaboration-aware applications may provide multi-user interfaces based on view-level or object-level sharing, respectively. Cooperative activities cannot always be assigned to a single level of sharing. Often a mixture of different sharing levels makes sense.

In the context of shared window systems, the concept of personalized views includes the capability of an application to create both shared and private windows [6]—and further—the possibility to personalize the contents of shared windows. The latter may be achieved by allowing for private widgets within shared windows. Widgets are user interface components provided by user interface toolkits such as the Motif toolkit. Buttons, check boxes, menus, and scrolled lists are examples for widgets.

Personalized views are an important feature of collaboration-aware applications. A shared window system that claims to support collaboration-aware applications must allow for personalized views.

3.9 Concurrent, Independent Input

Collaboration-transparent applications have only one input focus. This is enforced by the fact that such applications only allow one user to provide input at a time [23]. With collaboration-aware applications introducing personalized views, the limitation to one input focus is no longer useful. The reason for this is that a single focus, which is shared among all users, could never enter private windows or private widgets as these are not present in all users' views. The solution is to allow each user to have his/her own focus.

Having more than one focus implies that collaboration-aware applications may also support parallel user interaction. This is possible by allowing for concurrent, independent input, i.e. enabling each user to concurrently follow his/her input focus and to provide input to the application independently of what the other users are doing.

The ability to interact in parallel brings with it potential for conflict [23]. However, floor control is not applicable here as it is a concurrency control mechanism that guarantees only one user to provide input at any given point in time, and thus, is incompatible with parallel user interaction. Though allowing for user interaction that seems to happen in parallel, floor control produces side effects that are caused by its obligation to forward a consistent stream of input events to collaboration-transparent applications.

Collaboration-aware applications have to be prepared to handle concurrent input originating from multiple users. Thus, a shared window system may offer the possibility to disable floor control and leave it up to the applications to interpret series of input events that would be invalid for collaboration-transparent applications.

4 Architectural Issues

The major issues with respect to the architecture of a shared window system concern the application execution, the topology of the system, and the separation of control.

4.1 Single-Execution vs. Replicated Architecture

For the sharing of collaboration-transparent applications, a primary issue is whether to choose a replicated or a centralized architecture with respect to application execution. In a centralized architecture (Figure 1a), a single instance of the application executes. The shared window system then distributes output to and collects input from each conference participant.

The base window system agents constitute the window servers of the base window system. For example, with the X Window System, a base window system agent corresponds to an X server. The shared window system agents provide the functionality of the shared window system. Figure 1a shows a system agent per user, however, the topology may also be different as will be discussed in Section 4.2.

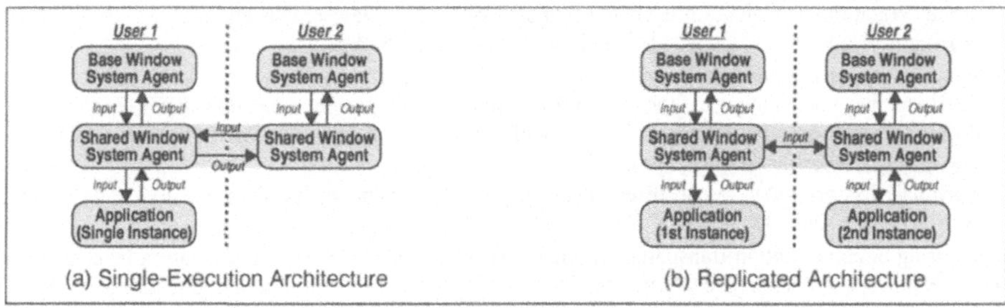

Figure 1: Single-Execution vs. Replicated Architecture

In a replicated architecture (Figure 1b), an instance of the application executes at each conference site. Here, the shared window system distributes only user input to all the other application instances ensuring that each receives the same sequence of input events. As all instances see the same input, their states remain synchronized, yielding identical output on each site. Crowley et al. [5], Ensor et al. [10], as well as Lauwers and Lantz [16] describe systems that are based on a replicated architecture.

Compared to the single-execution approach, the replicated approach tends to offer superior response time and reduced network load as only input events are sent across the transport system. Also, it is easier to accommodate differences in display hardware since each application instance can tailor itself to the local characteristics.

However, these advantages disappear when considering the serious synchronization and consistency problems associated with application replication [1, 17]. First of all, the replicated approach does not work if an application to be shared is not available at all sites or if the installed versions are different. Further, it is almost impossible to fulfill the dynamic participation requirement and thus allow for spontaneous interaction since this requires the ability to create up-to-date replicas of running applications [17].

In a replicated architecture, the shared window system guarantees that the same user input is delivered to all application instances, but it cannot assure the equivalence of input originating from other sources such as data read from files, values of environment variables, or messages from other applications. The general need for data replication constitutes an enormous disadvantage of the replicated architecture.

A related problem is output consistency. Applications may send output to various destinations in the environment, e.g. by writing to a file, sending a document to a printer, or invoking a mailer. When multiple instances of a shared application produce such output, the shared window system should maintain the single-execution semantics. However, this can hardly be achieved without modification of the applications to be shared.

4.2 Centralized vs. Distributed Architecture

The choice of an appropriate topology is also an issue of major impact. With a centralized architecture, all conference activities are mediated by a central component, which may but need not be located at one user's workstation. Figure 2a depicts a scenario with four users, each one sharing an application with the other users. The shared window system agent, which acts as the central mediator, receives application output from these applications and forwards it to the base window system agents of all users. In the opposite direction, it receives application input from the base window system agents and forwards it to the respective application in accordance to the current floor control settings.

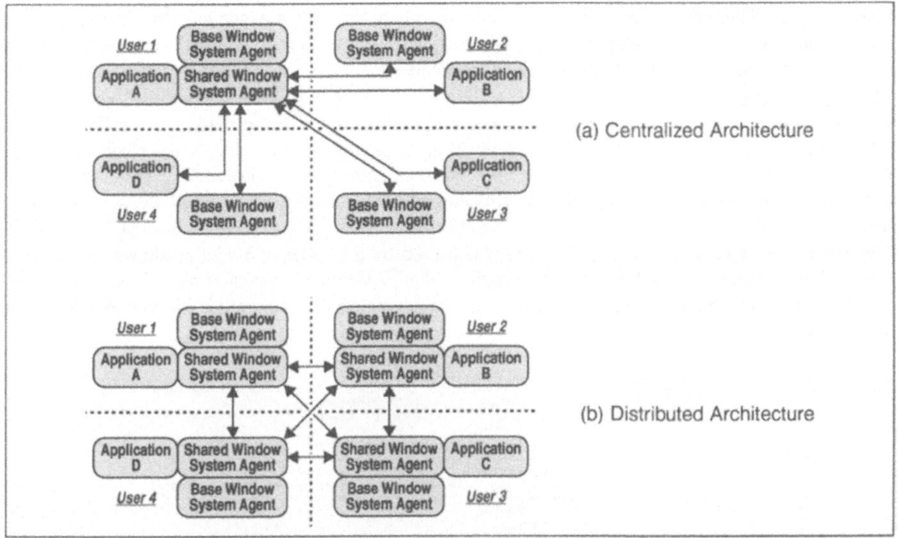

Figure 2: Centralized vs. Distributed Architecture

In contrast, a distributed architecture (Figure 2b) distributes the sharing functionality among all sites that are involved in a conference. Each shared window system agent exchanges application input and output with its user's base window system agent on the one hand and with its user's applications on the other hand. A shared window system agent does not communicate directly with other users' base window system agents and applications, respectively, but only with the other users' shared window system agents.

The principal advantage of the centralized architecture is the fact that is may easily support users working in a heterogeneous workstation environment as long as a network-transparent base window system is used. Here, an implementation for one platwork is sufficient while the distributed approach requires an implementation for each platform to be supported.

However, the centralized architecture is much more vulnerable to failures of either the conference server itself or the communication links connecting to it. The probability of a failure is smaller as compared to the distributed architecture, but when a failure occurs, the damage is more serious. Further, the load of the conference server grows as the number of participants and activities increases. This is an obvious obstacle for scalability. Finally, all conference participants but the one running the conference server suffer from a long communication path which results in unnecessarily bad performance for user interaction with locally executing applications.

Configurability and security aspects also play an important role. As pointed out in Section 3.6, cooperative activities often occur spontaneously and unplanned such that users cannot always anticipate with whom they will be cooperating. In order to be able to share already running applications with any other user at any time, it is necessary to run these applications through a shared window system agent from their beginning. With a centralized architecture, all users that will possibly cooperate with each other should run their applications through the same shared window system agent, i.e., all these users would be required to agree on a shared window system agent to be used cooperation. In any real scenario, however, this approach is not practical. Only a distributed architecture allows for users' independence and hence provides the required flexibility with respect to configuration.

As far as security issues are concerned, the distributed architecture is clearly the preferred architecture since the shared window system has total control over the communication between different user's workstations and hence may employ appropriate security mechanisms.

Finally, the master/slave concept inherent in the centralized architecture hampers user autonomy. It is our strong belief that the concept of independent cooperating entities is more promising for the further development of open systems for cooperative work.

4.3 Separation of Policies from Mechanisms

To support a wide range of cooperative styles, it is recommendable to separate policies from mechanisms [19, 20]. The mechanisms provide the functionality of the shared window system, acting on a low abstraction level in order to be applicable for various purposes. On a more abstract level, policies determine the behaviour of the system as perceived by the users.

The appropriateness of a policy highly depends on the preferred style of cooperative work. Thus, a shared window system should not enforce specific policies, but rather provide the mechanisms that allow various policies to be built on top of them. With floor control, for example, the mechanisms handle the low-level activities of passing the floor and maintaining a synchronized event stream for all users while the policy comprises a set of rules that determine how users request and are granted the floor.

The separation of policies and mechanisms is achieved by a two-layer model as shown in Figure 3: application sharing is carried out by cooperating "Shared Window System Agents" (system agents), which offer the mechanisms, whereas policies are implemented by cooperating "Shared Window Control Agents" (control agents).

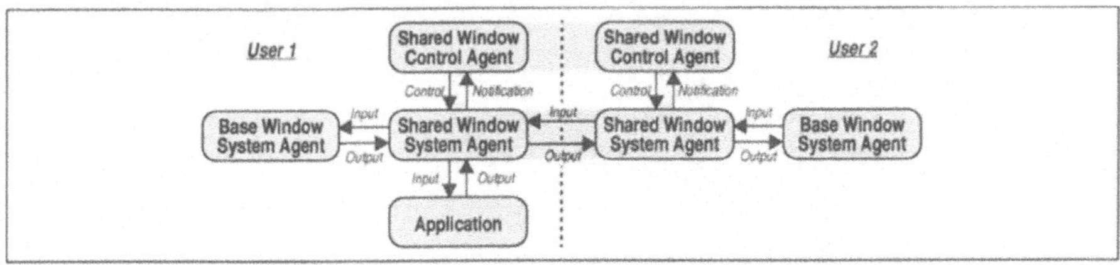

Figure 3: Separation of Control and System Layers

5 System Design and Implementation

Taking into account the issues dealt with in Section 4, we chose a distributed architecture for our shared window system and selected the X Window System as the base. Furthermore, our shared window system follows the single-execution approach, where applications execute only once. The principal reason for this is that the replicated approach suffers from serious synchronization and consistency problems. The only drawback of the single-execution approach is the fact that it requires not only application input but also application output to be distributed. Given the high-speed networks that recently have emerged and the asynchronous nature of the X Network Protocol, we do not take the distribution of application output as a significant disadvantage. Ahuja et al. [1] report that the single-execution approach does not suffer a significant performance loss as compared to the replicated approach.

The system architecture, as present at each user's site, is depicted in Figure 4. For all communications between the shown components, the X protocol is used. It was extended by a proprietary protocol extension called "Xsws", which is understood by the so-called Xwedge agents [13]. The Xsws extension provides the functionality of the shared window system.

Each site runs an X server and a window manager. Both components are part of the base window system and automatically initiated upon start-up of the user's workstation environment. The Xwedge agent is a system agent as introduced in Section 4 that provides the functionality of the shared window system. For the user, the Xwedge agent behaves like an X server.

The Xwedge agent accepts connections from three classes of X clients:

- *The Application Manager:*
  The application manager is a special X client that manages the collaboration-transparent applications running under the shared window system. It constitutes a control agent as introduced in Sec-

tion 4. In order to perform its task, the application manager utilizes elements of the Xsws extension. Each Xwedge agent accepts only one application manager, in the same way as only one window manager may be active for a given X server.

- *Collaboration-Transparent Applications:*
  Collaboration-transparent applications are single-user applications that may be shared with other users. Not being aware of the collaborative situation, these applications do not make use of the Xsws extension. Collaboration-transparent applications are managed by the application manager.

- *Collaboration-Aware Applications:*
  Collaboration-aware applications explicitly handle the collaborative situation by exploiting elements of the Xsws extension. They manage themselves and are therefore hidden from the application manager.

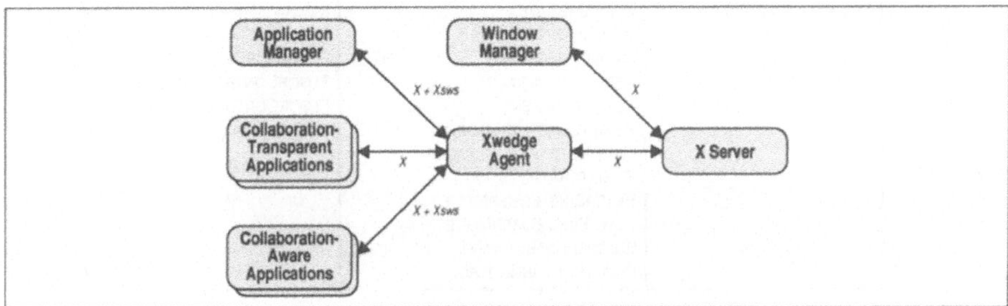

Figure 4: Per-Workstation System Architecture

The Xsws extension provides means for admission control and floor control, as well as miscellaneous supporting functions. The control elements and the notification elements are shown in Table 1, "RTR" denoting round-trip requests, i.e. request/response pairs.

Admission control determines which users are allowed to participate in a cooperative activity as well as how they join. Floor control serves as a concurrency control mechanism that determines at any given point in time which user is allowed to direct input to an application. The category "miscellaneous control" comprises elements for messaging, for resource and event notification, as well as for the support of application managers and collaboration-aware applications.

There are no preferred admission policies. Instead, the Xsws extension offers the concept of an application owner and the concept of attaching/detaching additional users to/from applications. The application owner is defined as the user on whose display an application is displayed when not being shared. Sharing an application with other users is achieved by attaching these users to the application. The user group of an application is the set of users that comprises the application owner as well as all attached users. These concepts provide the flexibility that allows any admission policy to be implemented.

Floor control is applied on a per-application basis. The main concept of the Xsws extension the input group, which is the subset of the user group that comprises all users that are permitted to provide input to a given application.

In order to control an application's user group or input group, respectively, the Xsws extension provides various control elements. The most important requests are "AttachUser" and "DetachUser" serving admission control as well as "EnableInput" and "DisableInput" for floor control.

6 Supporting Collaboration-Awareness

In Section 1, we indicated that the sharing of collaboration-transparent applications might not be the best choice for cooperative work in all situations. Specialized collaboration-aware applications may meet the requirements of a given type of cooperative work much better.

The limitations of application sharing are twofold: Firstly, all users are presented the same set of windows with identical contents, i.e., all users have the same view of the application. Personalized views cannot be provided. Secondly, shared applications only have one input focus and, hence, do not allow multiple users to concurrently follow their respective input focus and to provide input to the application independently of what the other users are doing. Concurrent, independent input is also not possible.

Functionality Class	Control Elements (Request Types)		Notification Elements (Event Types)
Admission Control	ATTACHUSER		APPLICATIONSTARTED
	DETACHUSER		APPLICATIONTERMINATED
	LISTAPPLICATIONS	(RTR)	USERATTACHED
	GETAPPLICATIONNAME	(RTR)	USERDETACHED
	GETAPPLICATIONOWNER	(RTR)	
	GETUSERGROUP	(RTR)	
Floor Control	ENABLEINPUT		INPUTENABLED
	DISABLEINPUT		INPUTDISABLED
	SETINPUTSENSITIVITYMASK		FLOORSHIFTED
	GETINPUTGROUP	(RTR)	FLOORRECEIVED
	GETFLOORHOLDER	(RTR)	FLOORLOST
Miscellaneous Control	SENDMESSAGE		MESSAGERECEIVED
	BROADCASTMESSAGE		RESOURCECREATED
	GETNEXTMESSAGE	(RTR)	RESOURCEDESTROYED
	SETRESOURCEMASK		FLOORCONTROLENABLED
	SETEVENTMASK		FLOORCONTROLDISABLED
	REGISTERAPPLMANAGER	(RTR)	INPUTORIGIN
	UNREGISTERAPPLMANAGER		
	REGISTERAPPLICATION		
	ENTERSINGLEUSERMODE		
	LEAVESINGLEUSERMODE		
	ENABLEFLOORCONTROL		
	DISABLEFLOORCONTROL		

Collaboration-transparent applications are not aware of the fact that they are shared and cannot distinguish one user from the other. They do not care which user generated a particular event. Therefore, each user has the same set of operations available (assumed he/she holds the floor) and is therefore treated exactly the same.

In contrast, collaboration-aware applications explicitly take into account the collaborative situation and hence may take special action. On the one hand, it is possible to present different output to different users. On the other hand, an application may accept input from various users simultaneously and handle it appropriately. This corresponds to the two requirements that we have formulated in Sections 3.8 and 3.9, respectively: the ability to provide personalized views and to allow for concurrent, independent input.

Our shared window system is not restricted to sharing collaboration-transparent applications. We found a way to overcome the limitations of collaboration transparency in traditional shared window systems and also provide support for the construction of collaboration-aware applications. After connecting to the Xwedge agent, collaboration-aware applications have to registers themselves as such with the shared window system.

The shared window system distributes X requests to the X servers of all users attached to a given application. This is why all users are presented the same set of windows with identical contents. However, personalized views require that series of X requests may selectively be sent to a single user's X server only. If X requests are to be sent to one user only, we temporarily enter the so-called "single-user mode". There are two requests that allow a collaboration-aware application to enter and leave this mode: the "EnterSingleUserMode" and the "LeaveSingleUserMode" requests, respectively.

Floor control is incompatible with parallel user interaction, which guarantees only one user to provide input at any given point in time. To overcome this, collaboration-aware applications are given the possibility to switch off floor control such that the floor is not implicitly shifted among the members of the input group any longer. The "DisableFloorControl" and the "EnableFloorControl" requests may be used to have floor control switched off and on, respectively. In order to handle input events originating from various users, a collaboration-aware application must be able to know the origin of such events. Whenever the input origin changes, the Xwedge generates an "InputOrigin" event.

Constructing a graphical user interface based on the X Library (Xlib) requires a considerable effort since it provides the same low-level abstractions as the X Protocol. This has led to the development of user interface toolkits that provide so-called widgets, which are user interface components to be used as building blocks for graphical user interfaces. Xview (Xv) and Motif (Xm) are two prominent examples for such user interface toolkits. These toolkits are themselves based on the X Intrinsics Toolkit (Xt), which offers the generic mechanisms for the creation and administration of widgets. Unfortunately, the user interface toolkits were designed for the construction of single-user applications and do not provide support for multi-user interfaces.

Widgets provide several features that relieve the programmer of handling events on the level of the X Protocol. It is possible to register callback functions for given events that happen to a widget, e.g., the programmer may register a function to be called whenever the user has pressed a given button in the user interface. Also, the programmer need not worry about "X Expose" events generated by the X server, which require a region of a window to be redrawn by the application, because widgets redraw themselves upon receipt of a corresponding event. The Xt library dispatches these events and calls the widget's expose method.

We found a method to combine existing user interface toolkits with our shared window system, such that the development of collaboration-aware applications is sped up significantly. Although we have chosen the widely-used Motif toolkit, other existing toolkits may also be used because our solution is a general one. Collaboration-aware Motif applications are typically composed as shown in Figure 5. Primarily, they use the Motif widget set provided by the Xm library. Furthermore, it uses widget management functions provided by the Xt library, possibly also Xlib functions, and the Xsws library, of course.

Initially, it was not clear how to provide personalized views with a collaboration-unaware widget set, where widgets redraw themselves at unpredictable points in time. Widget redraws are triggered by "X Expose" events whenever previously obscured window areas become visible again. The nasty effect here is that widgets may be replicated to all attached users even if the widgets are private ones.

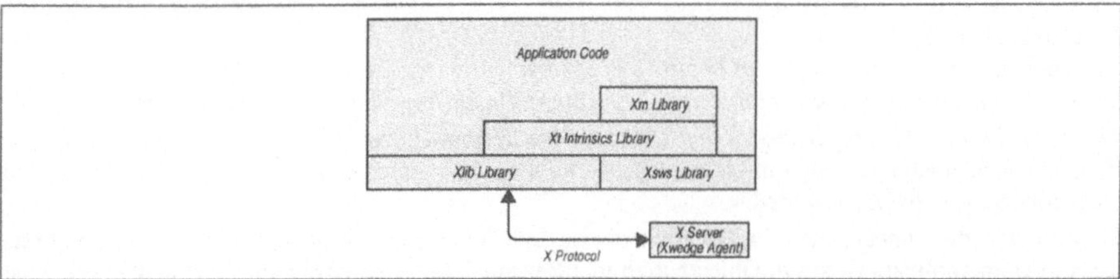

Figure 5: Collaboration-Aware Motif Applications

The key idea, which eventually led to a very elegant solution, is the concept of distinguishing shared and private widgets. A shared widget is a widget that is displayed in the user interfaces of all users of a given application while a private widget is presented to a single user only.

The realization of this concept requires that private widgets are created and redrawn only on a single user's X server. In other words, while creating or redrawing a private widget, the single-user mode should be enabled for the user in question and left afterwards to create or redraw shared widgets. There are no difficulties in achieving this during the widget creation phase. However, things are more complicated for redraws. To achieve redrawing of private widgets performed in single-user mode, two minor modifications had to be applied to the Xt library, which now provides an additional function "XtSingleUserPrivateWidget" to register a widget as private for a given user.

The concept of private and shared widgets made it possible to combine the advantages of the Motif user interface toolkit with the multi-user capabilities of our shared window system. The small set of mechanisms provided by the Xwedge was sufficient to turn the Motif toolkit into a toolkit that allows the construction of multi-user interfaces. Combining the advantages of the Motif user interface toolkit with the multi-user capabilities of our shared window system turned out to be a success. In conjunction, the two tools proved to be valuable. The missing of one of either tools would significantly limit the usefulness of the other tool for the construction of multi-user interfaces.

Having only the Motif toolkit, the programmer would have to write code that opens connections to multiple users' displays, creates windows on these displays, renders to these windows, and processes input events originating from different users. Furthermore, the application would have to deal with the departure of users and the arrival of new ones. Also, it would not be possible to present shared widgets with their special behaviour.

Conversely, if the programmer had the Xwedge only, constructing the user interface on top of Xlib would require a considerable programming effort. There are a few user interface toolkits specifically designed for the construction of multi-user interfaces. With these, the programmer could even do without the Xwedge. These toolkits however, suffer from the fact that the resulting collaboration-aware applications often do not integrate with the "look and feel" to which the users are used.

The concept of private and shared widgets was the key to our approach, which made the synergy of the Xwedge and the Motif toolkit possible at all. Without much effort, the mechanisms to support this concept could be implemented as an add-on to a previous version of our shared window system. The fact that the small set of mechanisms provided by the Xwedge was sufficient to turn the Motif toolkit into a toolkit that allows the construction of multi-user interfaces, is actually a surprising result.

While also being useful for applications that present only private widgets, the benefit of using the Xwedge together with the Motif toolkit is probably biggest for applications that present only shared widgets and for applications with a user interface that combines shared and private widgets.

7 Summary and Conclusions

The previous sections have described our shared window system referred to as Xwedge. It must be admitted that several such systems have been studied and implemented previously. Similar systems are even available commercially. So what is innovative about the Xwedge? The general answer to this question is that our system, in contrast to all shared window systems known to us, addresses fundamental issues that are crucial for a general-purpose shared window system as outlined in Section 3.

Our work shows that it is feasible to build a shared window system that has a distributed architecture, is policy-free, and is even capable of supporting collaboration-transparent as well as collaboration-aware applications in parallel. In particular, the fact that our shared window system supports both collaboration transparency and collaboration awareness makes our approach unique.

With the four conclusions given below, we summarize our contribution to the field of cooperative work.

Conclusion No. 1:

A shared window system should not impose any specific policy for admission and floor control and thus be based on a two-layer model that strictly separates policies from underlying mechanisms.

We introduced the two-layer model that separates the system agents, which provide the mechanisms, from the control agents, which implement a given policy. The strict separation allows a wide range of cooperative styles to be supported.

In particular, the concept of an application owner and the concept of attaching/detaching additional users to/from applications are flexible enough to allow any admission policy to be implemented. Apart from the fact that application owners cannot be detached from their own applications, the provided mechanisms give full control over an application's user group and hence allow any admission policy to be implemented.

Likewise, the concepts of an input group, a floor holder, and an input sensitivity mask are sufficient to implement a wide range of floor control policies. On a per-application basis, the mechanisms provided allow to control the number of users that can concurrently hold a floor, and how the floor is passed. On top of these mechanisms, we implemented several floor control policies for the so-called Joint-Viewing and Tele-Operation Service (JVTOS) [14], three policies with explicit floor passing and one policy with implicit floor passing.

Conclusion No. 2:

The sharing of collaboration-transparent applications and the provision of collaboration-aware applications are not competing but complementary concepts.

Our shared window system may be used for sharing collaboration-transparent applications as well as for supporting collaboration-aware applications, even in parallel. The concurrent use of collaboration-transparent and collaboration-aware applications was made possible by our system architecture, which allows for three classes of X clients as described in Section 5.

The support of collaboration-aware applications constitutes an added value to shared window systems, which makes them more powerful than simple application sharing systems. The fact that only a few changes to our shared window system were necessary in order to support collaboration-aware applications is a clear indication that the concepts of collaboration-awareness and collaboration-transparency are complementary ones.

Conclusion No. 3:

An architecture that distributes the sharing functionality among all involved sites has significant advantages over a centralized architecture.

By its nature, a centralized architecture is much more vulnerable to failures of either the central entity itself or the communication links connecting to it. Of course, the probability of a failure is smaller as compared to the distributed architecture, but when a failure occurs, the damage is more serious. Further, the load of the central entity is an obstacle for scalability. Our shared window system, which has a distributed architecture, has undergone a series of performance tests. Though the relative performance decreases as the number of users increases, at the same time, the performance penality per additional user decreases.

Actually, the configurability aspect is far more essential. Only a distributed architecture allows for users' independence and hence provides the required flexibility with respect to configuration. The reason for this is that with a centralized architecture, all users that can possibly cooperate with each other would be required to agree on a shared window system agent to be used for the cooperative activity. In any real scenario, however, this approach does not appear practical.

Under the security aspect, the distributed architecture is also the preferred architecture since the shared window system has total control over the communication between different user's workstations and hence may employ appropriate security mechanisms.

Conclusion No. 4:

A shared window system that supports collaboration-transparent applications as well as collaboration-aware applications is a powerful piece of support infrastructure for cooperative work.

Many types of cooperative work do not really require the construction of new applications. The sharing of existing single-user applications allows joint usage of unmodified applications. This approach has two considerable advantages. Firstly, existing applications need not be reimplemented in order to be used for cooperative work. Secondly, the users do not have to learn new applications as they can share existing single-user applications, to which they are already used.

There are cases where collaboration-aware applications may meet the requirements of a given type of cooperative work much better. However, for the construction of such applications, there is no need for specialized user interface toolkits designed for the construction of multi-user interfaces. The private widget concept makes it possible to construct such applications with existing user interface toolkits in conjunction with our shared window system. This approach has two considerable advantages. Firstly, the programmer may stick to the programming paradigm known from the existing user interface toolkits, which significantly speeds up application development. Secondly, the resulting collaboration-aware applications integrate with the "look and feel" of single-user applications that were developed with the same user interface toolkit.

Acknowledgements

This paper summarizes the author's Ph.D. thesis, which was awarded the GI/ITG Fachgruppenpreis "Kommunikation und Verteilte Systeme" 1995. The work presented here was performed at the Computer Engineering and Networks Laboratory of ETH Zürich under the supervision of Bernhard Plattner, whom I would like to thank for supporting this work, and for being both a teacher and an example in search for quality. My thanks go also to Hannes P. Lubich for being co-examiner and for his helpful comments on and discussions about many aspects of this work.

I am specially grateful to my colleagues with whom I worked in the CIO/JVTOS project. Many of the ideas put forward were born there. In particular I would like to thank Gabriel Dermler, Konrad Froitzheim, Edgar Ostrowski, Frank Ruge, Michael Weber, and Heiner Wolf. Finally, I wish to express my warmest thanks to the co-implementors of the Xwedge: Daniel Bauer, Marcus Brunner, Germano Caronni, and Hasan.

References

1. S.R. Ahuja, J.R. Ensor, S.E. Lucco: "A Comparison of Application Sharing Mechanisms in Real-Time Desktop Conferencing Systems". Proceedings, ACM Conference on Office Information Systems, pp. 238 - 248. Cambridge, Massachusetts, 1990.

2. E. Baldeschwieler, T. Gutekunst, B. Plattner: "A Survey of X Protocol Multiplexors". ACM Computer Communication Review, Vol. 23, No. 2, pp. 13 - 22. ACM Press, 1993.

3. R. Bentley, T. Rodden, P. Sawyer, I. Sommerville: "Architectural Support for Cooperative Multiuser Interfaces". IEEE Computer, Vol. 27, No. 5, May 1994, pp. 37 - 46.

4. G.S. Blair, T. Rodden: "The Challenges of CSCW for Open Distributed Processing". Proceedings, International Workshop on Open Distributed Processing. Berlin, 1993.

5. T. Crowley, P. Milazzo, E. Baker, H. Forsdick, R. Tomlinson: "MMConf: An Infrastructure for Building Shared Multimedia Applications". Proceedings, ACM 1990 Conference on Computer-Supported Cooperative Work (CSCW '90), pp. 329 - 342. Los Angeles, 1990.

6. P. Dewan, R. Choudhary: "Primitives for Programming Multi-User Interfaces". Proceedings, ACM 1991 Symposium on User Interface Software and Technology (UIST '91), pp. 69 - 78. Hilton Head, South Carolina, 1991.

7. P. Dourish, V. Bellotti: "Awareness and Coordination in Shared Workspaces". Proceedings, ACM 1992 Conference on Computer-Supported Cooperative Work (CSCW '92), pp. 107 - 114. Toronto, 1992.

8. C.A. Ellis, S.J. Gibbs, G.L. Rein: "Groupware: Some Issues and Experiences". Communications of the ACM, Vol. 34, No. 1, pp. 38 - 58. ACM Press, 1991.

9. D.C. Engelbart, W.K. English: "A Research Center for Augmenting Human Intellect". Proceedings, AFIPS Fall Joint Computer Conference, pp. 395 - 410. AFIPS, Reston, Virginia, 1968.

10. J.R. Ensor, S.R. Ahuja, D.N. Horn, S.E. Lucco: "The Rapport Multimedia Conferencing System: A Software Overview". Proceedings, Second IEEE Conference on Computer Workstations, pp. 52 - 58. Santa Clara, 1988.

11. P.F. Fitzgerald, N.Y. Rosson, L. Uljon: "Evaluating Alternative Display Sharing Architectures". Proceedings, IEEE Conference on Communication Software: Communications for Distributed Applications & Systems, pp. 145 - 157. Chapel Hill, North Carolina, 1991.

12. S. Greenberg: "Sharing Views and Interactions with Single-User Applications". Proceedings, ACM Conference on Office Information Systems, pp. 227 - 237. Cambridge, Massachusetts, 1990.

13. T. Gutekunst, D. Bauer, G. Caronni, Hasan, and B. Plattner: "A Distributed and Policy-Free General-Purpose Shared Window System". IEEE/ACM Transactions on Networking, Vol. 3, No. 1, Feb. 1995, pp. 51 - 62.

14. T. Gutekunst: "JVTOS—The Joint Viewing and Tele-Operation Service". Proceedings, 7th World Telecommunication Forum (Telecom 95), Technology Summit. Geneva, 1995.

15. D. Garfinkel, R. Branson: "A Comparison of Application Sharing Architectures in the X Environment". Proceedings, Xhibition '91, pp. 69 - 74. San Jose, 1991.

16. J.C. Lauwers, K.A. Lantz: "Collaboration Awareness in Support of Collaboration Transparency: Requirements for the Next Generation of Shared Window Systems". Proceedings, ACM CHI '90 Conference (Human Factors in Computing Systems), pp. 303 - 311. Seattle, 1990.

17. J.C. Lauwers, T.A. Joseph, K.A. Lantz, A.L. Romanow: "Replicated Architectures for Shared Window Systems: A Critique". Proceedings, ACM Conference on Office Information Systems, pp. 249 - 260. Cambridge, Massachusetts, 1990.

18. H.P. Lubich: "Towards a CSCW Framework for Scientific Cooperation in Europe". Lecture Notes in Computer Science, Vol. 889, Springer, 1995.

19. T. Rodden, J.A. Mariani, G. Blair: "Supporting Cooperative Applications". Computer-Supported Cooperative Work (CSCW), Vol. 1, No. 1 - 2, pp. 41 - 67. Kluwer Academic Publishers, 1992.

20. M. Roseman, S. Greenberg: "GroupKit—A Groupware Toolkit for Building Real-Time Conferencing Applications". Proceedings, ACM 1992 Conference on Computer-Supported Cooperative Work (CSCW '92), pp. 43 - 50. Toronto, 1992.

21. R.W. Scheifler, J. Gettys: "The X Window System". ACM Transactions on Graphics, Vol. 5, No. 2, pp. 79 - 109. ACM Press, 1986.

22. K. Schmidt, L. Bannon, "Taking CSCW Seriously". Computer Supported Cooperative Work (CSCW), Vol. 1, No. 1 - 2, pp. 7 - 40, Kluwer Academic Publishers, 1992.

23. M. Stefik, G. Foster, D.G. Bobrow, K. Kahn, S. Lanning, L. Suchman: "Beyond the Chalkboard: Computer Support for Collaboration and Problem Solving in Meetings". Communications of the ACM, Vol. 30, No. 1, pp. 32 - 47. ACM Press, 1987.

Verkehrssteuerung in ATM-Netzen — Verfahren und verkehrstheoretische Analysen zur Zellpriorisierung und Verbindungsannahme

Hans Kröner[1]
Institut für Nachrichtenvermittlung und Datenverarbeitung
Universität Stuttgart, Seidenstr. 36, D-70174 Stuttgart

Kurzfassung

Die Steuerung der Verkehrsflüsse und die Zuteilung der Netzressourcen ist ein zentrales Thema bei der Standardisierung und Entwicklung von ATM-Netzen. Die vorliegende Veröffentlichung befaßt sich mit zwei Schlüsselkomponenten des dafür vorgesehenen Verkehrsmanagements, der Verbindungsannahmefunktion und der Verlustprioritätsbehandlung. Im ersten Teil werden einige grundlegende verkehrstheoretische Leistungsuntersuchungen beschrieben, welche die Basis für das Verkehrsmanagement bilden. Anschließend wird die Leistungsfähigkeit von verschiedenen Verlustprioritätsmechanismen für büschelförmige Ankunftsverkehre abgeschätzt. Zum Abschluß wird ein in der Arbeit entwickeltes zweistufiges Verbindungsannahmeverfahren vorgestellt und untersucht.

1 Einführung

Der Asynchrone Transfer-Modus hat sich aufgrund seiner flexiblen und effektiven Kapazitätszuteilung als universelles Vermittlungsprinzip für zukünftige Breitband-Netze etabliert. Die zugrundeliegende asynchrone Zeitmultiplextechnik erlaubt eine ökonomische Integration verschiedenster Dienste mit heterogenem und z.T. variablem Bitratenaufkommen, indem die Informationen auf Zellen mit konstanter Größe aufgeteilt wird. Die damit verknüpften hochgradig dynamischen Belastungen der Netzressourcen und die wechselseitige Beeinflussung der Verbindungen führt jedoch bei Überschreitung einer bestimmten zulässigen Netzlast zu einer merklichen Beeinträchtigung der Dienstgüte.

Zur Einhaltung bestimmter Grenzwerte in Bezug auf Zellverluste und -verzögerungen ist daher ein effizientes Verkehrsmanagement notwendig, das in zwei grundlegende Blöcke zerfällt, die nach unterschiedlichen Prinzipien arbeiten [2, 6]:

- Unter dem Oberbegriff Verkehrssteuerung (Traffic Control) wurden verschiedene Mechanismen und Funktionen zusammengefaßt, die auf die *Vermeidung einer Überlastsituation* abzielen.

---

[1]Der Autor ist nun bei Leuze electronic, In der Braike 1, D-73277 Owen/Teck, Telefon +49 7021 573 208, Fax +49 7021 573 199, Email hkroener@leuze-owen.de

- Die Mechanismen zur *Behandlung einer Überlastsituation* (Congestion Control) bilden die zweite Komponente des Verkehrsmanagements, welche die Intensität, Ausbreitung und Dauer einer Überlastsituation begrenzt.

Für das Verkehrsmanagement wurde ein ganzes Bündel von sich ergänzenden Einzelmechanismen spezifiziert, die in Abbildung 1 dargestellt sind. Diese Menge von Funktionen erlaubt die Steuerung und Kontrolle des Verkehrsaufkommens in verschiedenen Zeitmaßstäben, entsprechend den dynamischen Schwankungen des Verkehrsflusses. Damit ist eine effiziente und direkte Steuerung der von unterschiedlichen Ursachen herrührenden statistischen Verkehrsschwankungen möglich. Die zeitliche Staffelung der einzelnen Mechanismen führt auf ein hierarchisches Verkehrsmanagement, bei dem die längerfristigen Steuerungsfunktionen auf der kurzzeitigen Regelung des Verkehrs aufbauen. Alle Mechanismen müssen sorgfältig aufeinander abgestimmt werden, um ein möglichst konsistentes Gesamtkonzept zu erhalten.

Darüber hinaus wurden innerhalb der ATM-Schicht verschiedene Dienstklassen eingeführt, die auf die speziellen Anforderungen der übergelagerten Breitband-Dienste zugeschnitten sind. In den Spezifikationen des ATM-Forums wird zwischen der CBR- (Constant Bit Rate), rt-VBR- (real-time Variable Bit Rate), nrt-VBR- (non-real-time Variable Bit Rate), ABR- (Available Bit Rate) und UBR-Dienstklasse (Unspecified Bit Rate) unterschieden [2]. Da sich diese Dienstklassen im Hinblick auf die Verkehrs- und Dienstgütespezifikationen unterscheiden müssen die einzelnen Funktionen des Verkehrsmanagements an diese Dienstklassen angepaßt werden (vgl. Abschnitt 4).

Die vorliegende Arbeit konzentriert sich auf zwei Teilfunktionen des Verkehrsmanagements — die Zellverlustpriorisierung und die Verbindungsannahme. Im folgenden Kapitel werden zunächst die verkehrstheoretischen Modelle und Methoden vorgestellt, die der

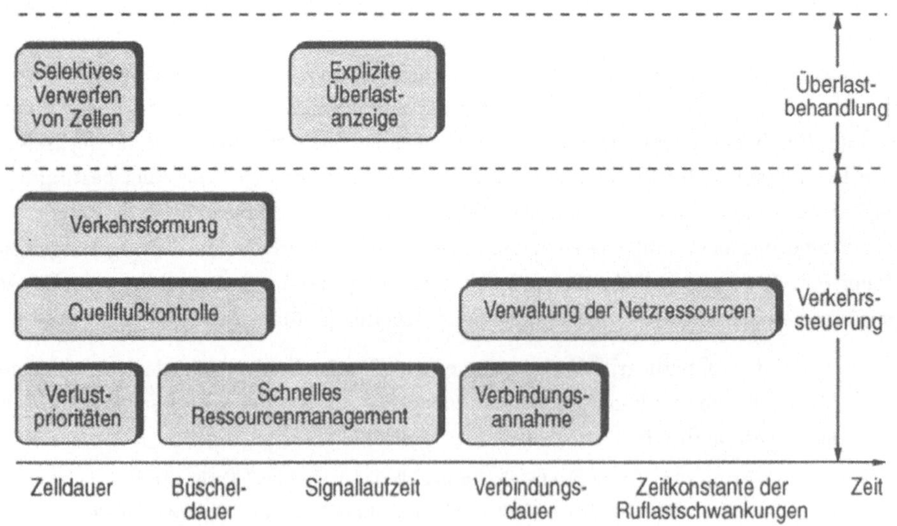

Bild 1: Steuerungsfunktionen und deren Zeitkonstanten

Arbeit zugrundeliegen. Anschließend werden einige grundlegende Ergebnisse beschrieben, die einen tiefen Einblick in das generelle Verhalten eines ATM-Netzes geben. Kapitel 3 behandelt die Ansätze zur Zellverlustpriorisierung und zeigt deren Leistungspotential auf. Im vierten Kapitel wird ein in der Arbeit entwickeltes zweistufiges Verfahren zur Verbindungsannahme vorgestellt, das auf den in den einführenden Kapiteln gewonnenen Erkenntnissen basiert. Abschließend wird ein kurzer Ausblick auf zukünftige Entwicklungen gegeben.

2 Leistungsanalyse von ATM-Netzen

2.1 Hierarchischer Modellierungsansatz

Der realistischen Nachbildung des Nachrichtenverkehrs kommt eine Schlüsselrolle bei der verkehrstheoretischen Modellierung und Analyse von ATM-Netzen zu. In der Regel wird dabei auf den in Bild 2 veranschaulichten hierarchisch strukturierten Modellierungsansatz zurückgegriffen (vgl. z.B. [5, 16]), der zwischen der Verbindungs-, Büschel- und Zellebene unterscheidet. Ähnlich wie in durchschaltevermittelnden Netzen beschreibt die Verbindungsebene das Wechselspiel zwischen Verbindungsauf- und -abbau. Solange die Verbindung besteht findet ein Informationsaustausch statt, wobei die Übertragungsbitrate einen festen oder variablen Wert aufweisen kann. Dies führt zu den in Bild 2 gezeigten Schwankungen des Bitratenbedarfs auf der Büschelebene und der damit einhergehenden „Modulation" des Zellflusses auf der Zellebene.

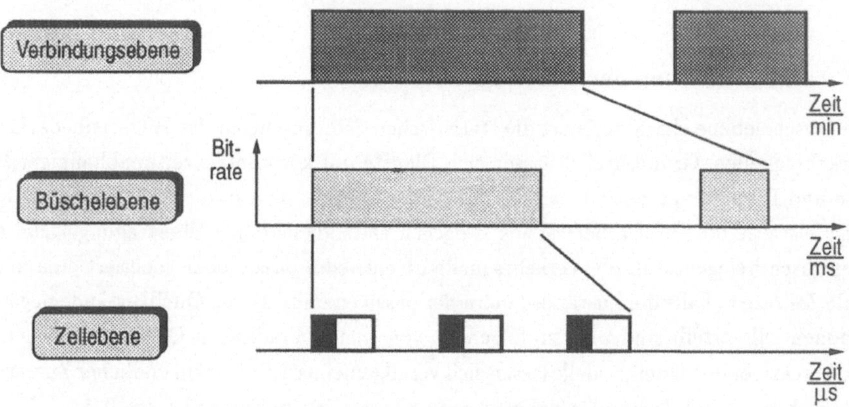

Bild 2: Hierarchische Beschreibung von ATM-Verkehrsströmen

Die statistischen Verkehrsschwankungen auf diesen drei Ebenen werden von verschiedenen Faktoren (Teilnehmerverhalten, Dienst, Protokoll bzw. Codierverfahren) beeinflußt und weisen vielfältige Abhängigkeiten auf. Darüber hinaus ist die zeitliche Dynamik der einzelnen Modellebenen sehr unterschiedlich, womit eine getrennte Betrachtung (Dekomposition) der unterschiedlichen Ebenen möglich wird. Die Verkehrsanalyse kann sich daher auf eine oder zwei Ebenen konzentrieren, wobei der Lastzustand der darüberliegenden Ebenen festgehalten wird und die Lastschwankungen der darunterliegenden Ebenen vernachlässigt werden. Dies führt zu entsprechenden Teilmodellen mit verschiedenen Abstraktionsniveaus, die im folgenden behandelt werden sollen.

2.1.1 Modellierung der Verbindungsebene

Auf der Verbindungsebene verhält sich ein ATM-Netz ähnlich wie ein durchschaltevermittelndes Netz, d.h. es kann als Verlustsystem modelliert werden. Beim Eintreffen eines neuen Verbindungswunsches prüft die Verbindungsannahmefunktion, ob die Verbindung auf dem betrachteten Verbindungsabschnitt zulässig ist oder abgewiesen werden muß und damit verloren geht. Der Ankunftsprozeß der Verbindungswüsnche kann bei ausreichender Teilnehmerzahl durch einen Markoff-Prozeß nachgebildet werden, während die Verbindungsdauer meist durch eine negativ-exponentiell verteilte Zufallsvariable beschrieben wird.

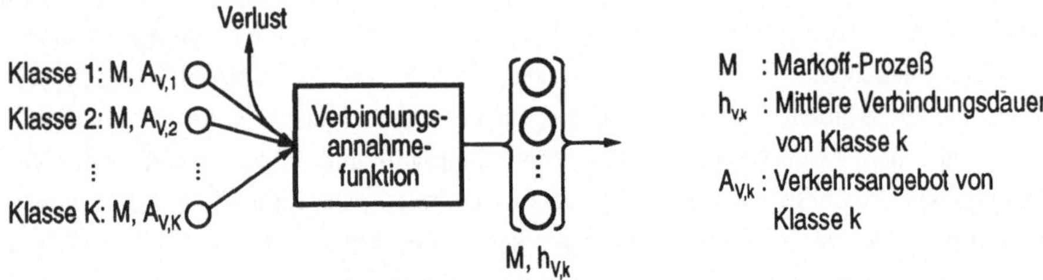

Bild 3: Verkehrsmodell der Verbindungsebene

2.1.2 Modellierung der Büschelebene

Die Büschelebene charakterisiert die statistischen Schwankungen des Bitratenbedarfs der Verkehrsquellen. Grundsätzlich lassen sich Dienste mit konstanter, zeitunabhängiger Bitrate und Dienste mit zeitlich variabler Bitrate unterscheiden. In die erste Kategorie fällt beispielsweise die Sprachübertragung, wogegen Datendienste den Übertragungskanal nur sporadisch belegen, d.h. die Verkehrsquelle ist entweder passiv oder generiert eine maximale Zellrate $\hat{r}$. Falls die Zustandsdauern der passiven und aktiven Quellzustände negativ-exponentiell verteilt sind wird im folgenden von einer sporadischen Quelle gesprochen.

Die beschriebenen Quellmodelle lassen sich verallgemeinern, indem ein endlicher Zustandsautomat mit $L+1$ Zuständen definiert wird bei dem jedem Zustand l, $l = 0, 1, ..., L$, eine bestimmte Zellrate $r(l)$ zugeordnet ist. Die Verweildauern in den einzelnen Zuständen können allgemein verteilt sein; für analytische Betrachtungen werden häufig negativ-exponentiell verteilte Zustandsdauern angenommen.

Innerhalb des ATM-Netzes überlagern sich die Verkehre der einzelnen Verbindungen, wobei der diskrete Charakter der Zellankünfte und -bedienungen auf der Büschelebene nicht sichtbar ist und durch einen kontinuierlichen Fluß von Information ersetzt wird. Diese makroskopische Betrachtungsweise führt auf das sogenannte „Fluid Flow"-Modell [1, 19]. Dabei kann das Grundmodell des statistischen Multiplexers durch das in Bild 4 gezeigte Verkehrsmodell beschrieben werden. Die Zuflußrate ist durch die Summe der Zellraten aller N Verbindungen bestimmt, und die Abflußrate C entspricht dem Zelltakt des Übertragungsabschnitts. Falls die Zuflußrate größer als die Abflußrate ist, steigt der Füllstand des Puffers an, während er im umgekehrten Fall abnimmt. Beim Erreichen des maximalen Pufferfüllstands S geht die Differenz aus Zu- und Abflußrate verloren.

2.1.3 Modellierung der Zellebene

Die Zellebene erlaubt eine detailliertere Nachbildung des Ablaufgeschehens. Aufgrund der getakteten Betriebsweise muß der Quellverkehr durch zeitdiskrete Prozesse nachgebildet werden, die den Ankunftsabstand zweier aufeinanderfolgender Zellen beschreiben. Damit können die von einer CBR-Verkehrsquelle produzierten Zellankünfte durch einen deterministischen Ankunftsprozeß mit einem Zellabstand von d Zeitschlitzen Δt modelliert werden. Die im vorigen Abschnitt eingeführte sporadische Quelle kann durch einen geeigneten Erneuerungsprozeß nachgebildet werden, da sie eine geometrisch verteilte Anzahl von Zellen mit konstantem Zellabstand sendet und anschließend in den passiven Zustand übergeht, der ebenfalls eine geometrisch verteilte Anzahl von Zeitschlitzen umfaßt.

Das auf der Zellebene verwendete Warteschlangenmodell des statistischen Multiplexers ist in Bild 5 dargestellt. Zusätzlich zu den im vorigen Abschnitt definierten Größen muß noch die Bedienreihenfolge der Zellen (FIFO, First In First Out) und die Reihenfolge von zeitgleichen Ankünften und Bedienungen (AF, Arrival First) festgelegt werden.

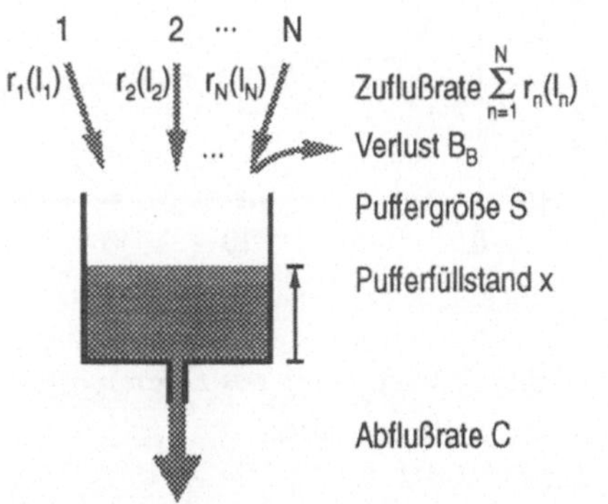

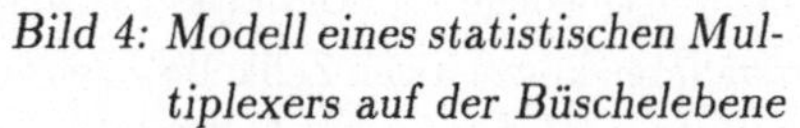

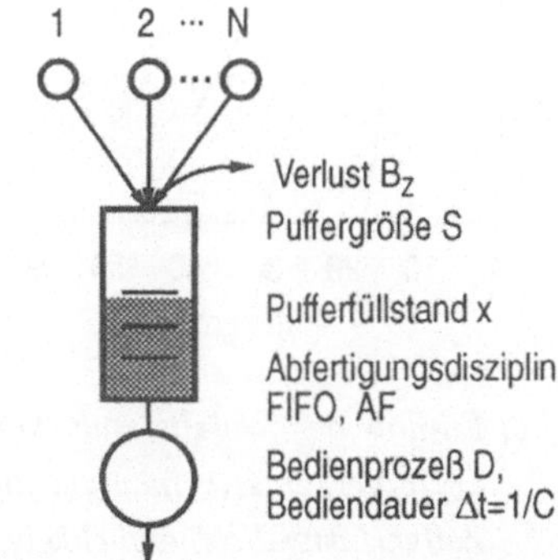

Bild 4: Modell eines statistischen Multiplexers auf der Büschelebene

Bild 5: Modell eines statistischen Multiplexers auf der Zellebene

2.2 Leistungsuntersuchung generischer ATM-Systemmodelle

In diesem Kapitel werden einige charakteristische Ergebnisse der in [9, 10] durchgeführten systematischen Untersuchungen wiedergegeben. Die analytischen Grundlagen dieser Ergebnisse sind in [8, 9, 10] beschrieben.

Einführend soll das asynchrone Multiplexen von CBR-Verkehrsströmen mit unterschiedlichen Zellabständen d betrachtet werden (vgl. Bild 6). Die Verbindungszahl N wurde so gewählt, daß das Verkehrsangebot den konstanten Wert $A_Z = N/d = 0,85$ annimmt.

Obwohl der Übertragungsabschnitt nicht voll ausgelastet ist kommt es durch die Asynchronität der verschiedenen Verbindungen zu kurzzeitigen Überlastsituationen, die zu Zellverlusten führen können. Aus den Ergebnissen ist zu entnehmen, daß die Zellverlustwahrscheinlichkeit mit steigendem Zellabstand d, d.h. sinkender Bitrate der Verkehrsquellen zunimmt. Für den Grenzübergang $N, d \to \infty$ geht der Ankunftsprozeß in einen Poisson-Prozeß über (vgl. [9]), weshalb das $M/D/1/(S+1)$-System eine obere Grenze für die Zellverlustwahrscheinlichkeit von CBR-Verkehren darstellt.

Als zweites Beispiel soll die Überlagerung von $N = 8$ gleichartigen sporadischen Verkehrsströmen betrachtet werden (vgl. Bild 7). Die Verkehrsquellen senden in der aktiven Phase alle $d = 4$ Zeitschlitze eine Zelle. Für den Büschelfaktor Z, d.h. das Verhältnis zwischen maximaler und mittlerer Zellrate, und die mittlere Anzahl von Zellen innerhalb der aktiven Phase (Büschelgröße b) wurden die für Video- und Datendienste repräsentativen Werte von $Z = 5$ bzw. $b = 100$ gewählt.

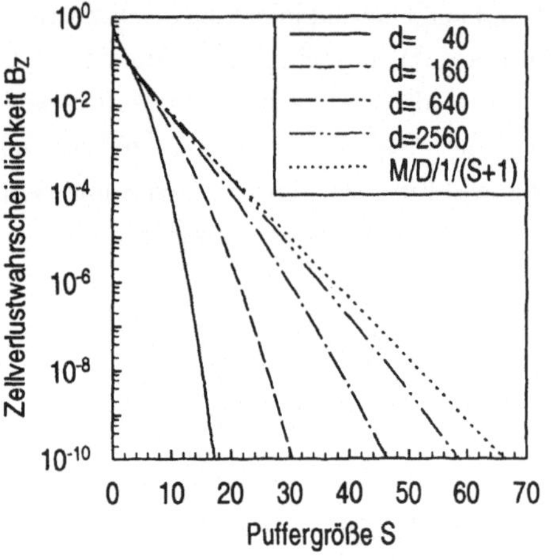

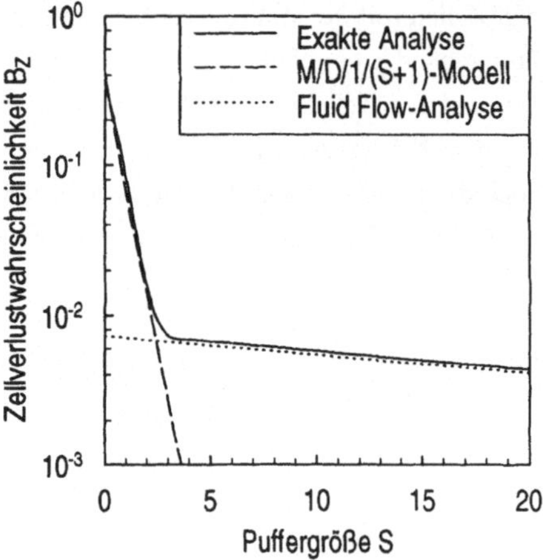

Bild 6: Einfluß des Zellabstands von CBR-Verkehrsströmen auf die Zellverlustwahrscheinlichkeit

Bild 7: Validierung des Dekompositionsansatzes

Unter den genannten Randbedingungen sind zwei verschiedene Blockierungssituationen möglich (vgl. [8, 15]). Einerseits treten die oben erwähnten kurzzeitigen Zellkollisionen auf, falls zu einem Zelltakt mehrere Verbindungen auf die Ausgangsleitung des Multiplexers zugreifen wollen. Andererseits ergeben sich auf der Büschelebene zusätzliche langanhaltende Überlastsituationen, falls die Summenbitrate aller Verbindungen die Übertragungskapazität überschreitet. Diese grundlegenden Blockierungseffekte äußern sich in dem in Bild 7 gezeigten charakteristischen Verlauf der Zellverlustwahrscheinlichkeit in Abhängigkeit von der Puffergröße. Für kleine Puffergrößen resultieren die Zellverluste überwiegend aus den durch die Asynchronität der Zellankünfte verursachten kurzzeitigen Verkehrsschwankungen, die bei einer Vergrößerung des Puffers schnell abklingen. Die von der Büschelebene herrührenden, langanhaltenden Verkehrsschwankungen können dagegen nur durch relativ große Puffer ausgeglichen werden.

Die in Bild 7 gezeigten Ergebnisse zeigen ferner, daß die behandelten Blockierungseffekte durch unterschiedliche Verkehrsmodelle beschrieben werden können. Kurzzeitige Blockierungen können durch das bereits erwähnte $M/D/1/(S + 1)$-System modelliert werden, während das „Fluid Flow"-Modell die von der Büschelebene herrührenden langanhaltenden Überlastsituationen beschreibt.

Im folgenden werden die für sporadischen Quellverkehr erzielten Ergebnisse weiter vertieft. Insbesondere soll die Korrelation der Zellverluste mit Hilfe des oben beschriebenen „Fluid Flow"-Modells bestimmt werden. Bei diesem Modell treten nur dann Verluste auf, wenn der Puffer voll belegt ist und die Ankunftsrate die Bedienrate übersteigt. Die Korrelation der Zellverluste drückt sich dadurch aus, daß das System zwischen Phasen, in denen Verluste auftreten, und Phasen, in denen keine Verluste auftreten, alterniert. Dieses Verhalten kann mit den folgenden Meßgrößen erfaßt werden:

- Mittlere Dauer der Verlustphase

- Mittlerer zeitlicher Abstand zweier Verlustphasen

- Verlustwahrscheinlichkeit innerhalb einer Verlustphase

Die in den Bildern 8 und 9 gezeigten Ergebnisse belegen, daß die durch die Zwischenpufferung erzielte Verringerung der Verlustwahrscheinlichkeit ausschließlich auf eine Vergrößerung des zeitlichen Abstands zweier Verlustphasen zurückzuführen ist. Andererseits äußert sich eine Vergrößerung des Puffers sogar in einer Verlängerung der Verlustphasen (vgl. Bild 8). Ebenso nimmt die innerhalb einer Verlustphase auftretende Verlustwahrscheinlichkeit mit steigender Puffergröße zu [9, 10]. Dieses auf den ersten Blick paradoxe Systemverhalten läßt sich damit erklären, daß nur extreme Überlastsituationen zu einem Pufferüberlauf führen, wogegen kurzzeitige Blockierungen durch den Puffer ausgeglichen werden können. Über ähnliche Ergebnisse wird auch in der Literatur berichtet (siehe z.B.

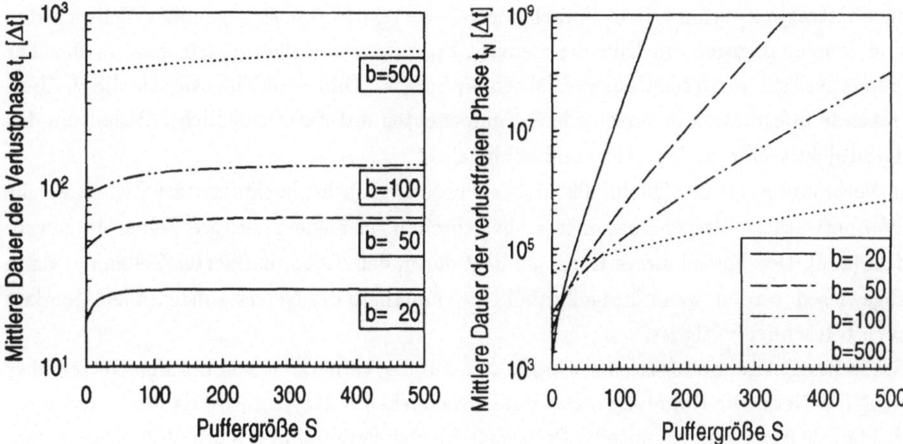

Bild 8: Mittlere Dauer der Verlustphase   Bild 9: Mittlere Dauer der verlustfreien Phase

[12]). Ferner heißt dies, daß die Verbindungsannahmefunktion nur den zeitlichen Abstand zweier Verlustphasen beeinflussen kann, jedoch nicht deren Dauer und Stärke.

Diese Ergebnisse geben nur einen kleinen Teil der in der Arbeit durchgeführten Leistungsstudien wieder. Insbesondere wurden folgende Teilaspekte systematisch untersucht:

- Einfluß der Quellparameter auf die Zellverlustwahrscheinlichkeit [9, 10]

- Untersuchung von heterogenen Verkehrszusammensetzungen [9, 10]

- Untersuchung der Zellverluste und -verzögerungen einer ganzen ATM-Verbindung [9, 11]

3 Untersuchung von Verlustprioritätsmechanismen

Die Ergebnisse des vorigen Kapitels bestätigen, daß die Zellverlustwahrscheinlichkeit der entscheidende Dienstgüteparameter ist, der das zulässige Verkehrsangebot begrenzt. Mit Hilfe von Verlustprioritäten läßt sich dieser Parameter an dienstespezifische Anforderungen anpassen.

3.1 Anwendungsbeispiele und Anforderungen

Verlustprioritäten ermöglichen das selektive Verwerfen unwichtiger Zellen, falls innerhalb des ATM-Netzes eine Überlastsituation auftritt. Mit Hilfe einer entsprechenden Pufferverwaltung können Zellen mit hoher Verlustpriorität vor einer Blockierung durch niederprioritäre Zellen zuverlässig geschützt werden. Diese Eigenschaft ist für eine Reihe von Anwendungen interessant.

Primär ist hierbei die flexible Auswahl eines im Hinblick auf die Dienstgüteanforderungen des Kommunikationsdienstes geeigneten Übermittlungsdienstes zu nennen. Eine hochqualitative Übermittlung ist nur für relativ wenige Anwendungen, wie beispielsweise Videoübertragung, erforderlich. Sprachdienste, die relativ robust gegenüber Zellverlusten sind, können dagegen mit Hilfe der niederen Prioritätsklasse übermittelt werden. Darüber hinaus zerlegen moderne Codierverfahren für Sprach-, Bild- und Videosignale die zu übertragende Information in verschiedene Komponenten mit unterschiedlicher Bedeutung für die subjektiv empfundene Ton- und Bildqualität.

In Verbindung mit der Quellflußkontrolle wurde angedacht, hochprioritäre Zellen, welche die überwachten Verkehrsparameter überschreiten, in niederprioritäre Zellen umzuwandeln [2, 6]. Der Vorteil dieses Konzepts liegt darin, daß die so markierten Zellen nur dann abgewiesen werden, wenn dies aufgrund einer innerhalb des Netzes auftretenden Überlast auch tatsächlich nötig ist.

Ein weiteres Anwendungsszenario ergibt sich aus der Vernetzung von Lokalen Netzen über ein ATM-Netz. Die Kopplung dieser unterschiedlichen Netztypen wird dadurch erschwert, daß Lokale Netze auf den unteren Protokollschichten verbindungslos arbeiten, wogegen das ATM-Netz verbindungsorientiert betrieben wird. Die zur Reservierung der entsprechenden Übertragungskapazität benötigte Zeitdauer kann dadurch überbrückt werden, daß der verbindungslose Verkehr mit niedriger Priorität ins Netz gesendet wird.

3.2 Mechanismen zur Prioritätsbehandlung

In der Literatur wurden verschiedene Verlustprioritätsmechanismen mit einer Vielzahl unterschiedlicher Varianten vorgeschlagen. Bild 10 gibt einen Überblick über die Konzepte, die diesen Ansätzen zugrundeliegen. Die einfachste Möglichkeit, verschiedene Zellverlustwahrscheinlichkeiten zu erzielen, basiert auf der Verwendung *getrennter physikalischer Wege* für die unterschiedlichen Prioritätsklassen [7, 13]. Die für niederprioritäre Zellen reservierten Wege können stärker ausgelastet werden, da eine höhere Zellverlustwahrscheinlichkeit toleriert werden kann. Dieser Ansatz hat den Vorteil, daß kein Eingriff ins Puffermanagement erforderlich ist. Allerdings ist die Flexibilität des Konzepts dadurch stark eingeschränkt, daß keine Betriebsmittelteilung zwischen der hohen und der niederen Prioritätsklasse stattfindet.

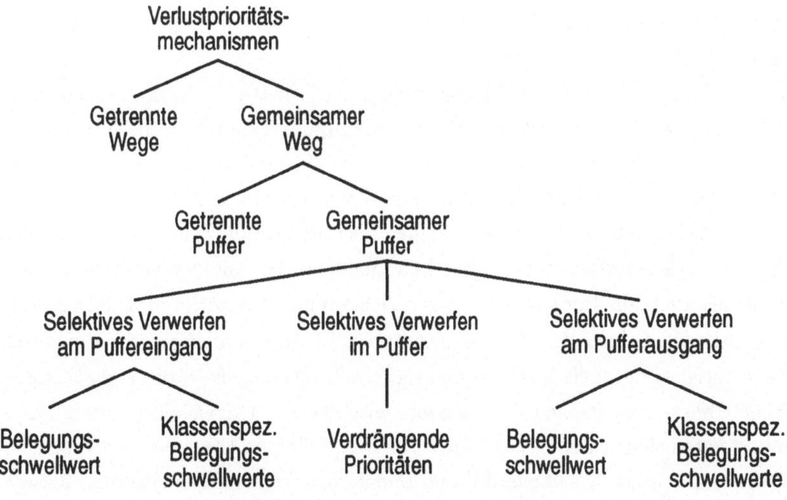

Bild 10: Klassifikation von Verlustprioritätsmechanismen

Bei einem gemeinsam genutzten Weg für beide Prioritätsklassen sind Eingriffe in die Pufferverwaltung unumgänglich. Der Puffer kann beispielsweise in zwei logisch getrennte Teilbereiche unterteilt werden, die jeweils einer Prioritätsklasse fest zugeordnet sind [7, 13]. Bei einer gemeinsamen Nutzung des Pufferspeichers müssen Zellen selektiv, entsprechend ihrer Priorität, verworfen werden. Dies kann sich auf ankommende Zellen, bereits im Puffer befindliche Zellen oder zur Bedienung anstehende Zellen beziehen, d.h. die Priorisierung kann am Eingang, innerhalb oder am Ausgang des Puffers erfolgen. Eingangsseitig können Zellen selektiv verworfen werden, indem eine zusätzliche Zugangsbeschränkung eingeführt wird. Folgende Zugangssteuerungen können unterschieden werden:

- *Klassenspezifische Belegungsschwellwerte* [3]: Eine ankommende Zelle wird abgewiesen, falls die Anzahl der von dieser Prioritätsklasse wartenden Zellen einen bestimmten Maximalwert erreicht hat.

- *Globaler Belegungsschwellwert* [3, 7]: Eine ankommende niederprioritäre Zelle wird abgewiesen, falls der Pufferfüllstand einen vorgegebenen Schwellwert überschreitet.

Qualitative Überlegungen zeigen, daß ein Schwellwertverfahren mit globalem Belegungsschwellwert bessere Ergebnisse erzielt, da eine Zelle mit niederer Priorität unabhängig von der Priorität der im Puffer befindlichen Zellen angenommen bzw. abgewiesen werden sollte [9]. Da es außerdem Implementierungsvorteile aufweist wird nur dieses Verfahren weiter betrachtet.

Eine weitergehende Prioritätskontrolle ergibt sich, wenn auch bereits im Puffer befindliche Zellen selektiv verworfen werden können. Da dies nur dann Sinn macht, wenn Platz für eine neu ankommende Zelle geschaffen werden muß, spricht man auch von *verdrängenden Prioritäten* [17]. Dieses Verdrängungsprinzip gewährleistet, daß eine Zelle mit hoher Priorität nur dann verloren geht, wenn der Puffer ausschließlich mit hochprioritären Zellen belegt ist. Ferner wird auch die Gesamtverlustwahrscheinlichkeit minimiert, da eine Zelle nur bei voll belegtem Puffer verloren geht. Nachteilig wirkt sich der höhere Implementierungsaufwand aus, der dadurch entsteht, daß die Zellreihenfolge auch bei einer Verdrängung erhalten bleiben muß.

Am Ausgang des Puffers wird die Priorisierung der Zellströme dadurch erreicht, daß eine zur Bedienung anstehende niederprioritäre Zelle zugunsten einer nachfolgenden hochprioritären Zelle selektiv verworfen werden kann. Die Entscheidung, ob eine niederprioritäre Zelle verworfen bzw. bedient wird, orientiert sich wiederum am Pufferfüllstand [14] oder an der Anzahl der sich im Puffer befindlichen hochprioritären Zellen [18]. Diese Verfahren sind den Prioritätsmechanismen, die ankommende Zellen selektiv verwerfen, sowohl aus Leistungs- als auch aus Implementierungsgesichtspunkten unterlegen. Die Leistungsfähigkeit der ausgangsseitigen Prioritätssteuerung wird hauptsächlich dadurch eingeschränkt, daß die Priorisierung nicht direkt durch den Ankunftsprozeß — die eigentliche Ursache möglicher Überlastsituationen — gesteuert wird. Ferner tragen die unmittelbar vor der Bedienung verworfenen Zellen zur Belastung des Pufferspeichers bei und erzeugen somit eine gewisse „Blindlast". Aufgrund dieser offensichtlichen Nachteile werden diese Verfahren nicht weiter betrachtet.

3.3 Vergleichende Leistungsbewertung

In diesem Abschnitt wird ein kurzer Auszug der in der Arbeit erzielten Ergebnisse gegeben. Die analytischen Zusammenhänge können in [7, 9] nachgelesen werden. Zunächst werden die Prioritätsmechanismen für Poisson-Ankunftsprozesse verglichen. Beide Verkehrsklassen haben gleiche Ankunftsraten und die zulässigen Zellverlustwahrscheinlichkeiten wurden zu 10^{-6} und 10^{-10} gewählt. Tabelle 1 gibt die für ein vorgegebenes Verkehrsangebot erforderliche Puffergröße wieder. Das Verdrängungsverfahren spart innerhalb des betrachteten Lastbereichs zwischen 37,5% und 42,6% des benötigten Pufferplatzes ein.

Im folgenden soll untersucht werden, wie sich die Prioritätsmechanismen bei büschelförmiger Belastung verhalten. Die in Bild 11 für das Schwellwertverfahren gezeigten Ergebnisse beziehen sich auf den im vorigen Kapitel eingeführten Referenzverkehr. Es werden $N = 8$ Verkehrsquellen mit einem Büschelfaktor $Z = 5$, einer mittleren Büschelgröße von $b = 100$ Zellen und einem minimalen Zellabstand von $d = 4$ Zeitschlitzen überlagert. Dabei senden 6 Verkehrsquellen Zellen mit hoher Priorität, während die verbleibenden Verkehrsquellen niederprioritären Verkehr erzeugen. In allen Beispielen wurden zwei Pufferplätze für die

Angebot A_Z [Erl.] Puffergröße S	0,7	0,75	0,8	0,85	0,9	0,95
Ohne Prioritäten	32	39	50	67	100	197
Schwellwertverfahren	24	29	36	46	65	120
Verdrängungsverfahren	20	24	30	40	59	113

Tabelle 1: Pufferdimensionierung für verschiedene Prioritätsmechanismen

hohe Priorität reserviert.

Die in Bild 11 skizzierten Ergebnisse zeigen, daß die hohe Priorität ($B_{Z,H}$) deutlich weniger Zellverluste erleidet als die niedere Priorität ($B_{Z,L}$). Ferner bestätigt sich das im vorigen Kapitel aufgezeigte typische Systemverhalten. Das M/D/1/(S+1)-Modell spiegelt die für kleine Puffergrößen entscheidenden, kurzzeitigen Zellkollisionen wider, während für große Puffergrößen die durch das „Fluid Flow"-Modell beschriebenen langanhaltenden Überlastsituationen ausschlaggebend sind. Für das Verdrängungsverfahren ergeben sich ähnliche Ergebnisse [9], d.h. beide Verfahren weisen für realistische Puffergrößen eine vergleichbare Leistungsfähigkeit auf.

Anhand eines realistischen Verkehrsszenarios soll die durch das Schwellwertverfahren erzielte Erhöhung der Netzauslastung quantifiziert werden. Dazu wurden die in Tabelle 2 aufgeführten Dienste und Quellparameter aus der Literatur entnommen. Der in Verkehrsklasse 1 gesendete Datenverkehr hat niedrige Priorität, da er im Verlustfall wiederholt werden kann, was bei Videokommunikation aufgrund der Echtzeitbedingungen nicht möglich ist. Der Datenverkehr wird durch das bereits eingeführte sporadische Quellmodell beschrieben, während eine Videoquelle durch die Überlagerung von 20 sporadischen Quellen modelliert wird. Die Puffergröße entspricht S=64 Zellen, wovon 7 Pufferplätze für die hohe Priorität reserviert werden.

In Bild 12 werden verschiedene Strategien zur Verkehrssteuerung verglichen. Bei der *Spitzenbitratenzuweisung* sind nur solche Verbindungszustände erlaubt, bei denen die Summe der Spitzenbitraten unter der zur Verfügung stehenden Übertragungsgeschwindigkeit liegt. Beim *statistischen Multiplexen* muß die Verlustwahrscheinlichkeit für alle Zellen un-

Verkehrs- klasse	Dienst	Anzahl der spor. Quellen	Max. Zellrate [Zellen/s][a]	Büschel- faktor[a]	Mittlere Büschelgröße[a]
1	Datenübertragung	1	26041,7	10	338,5
2	Videoübertragung	20	2520,8	5	809,2

[a] Die Angaben beziehen sich auf eine sporadische Quelle

Tabelle 2: Charakteristische Kenngrößen der gewählten Verkehrsklassen

ter 10^{-10} liegen. Durch die Einführung von Verlustprioritäten erhöht sich dieser Wert auf 10^{-6} für die niedrige Priorität.

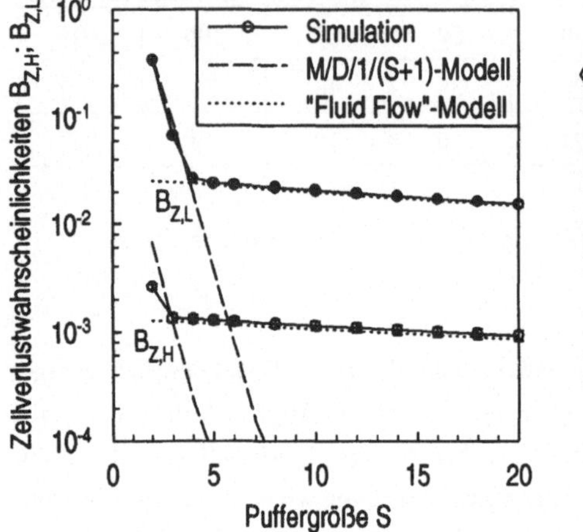

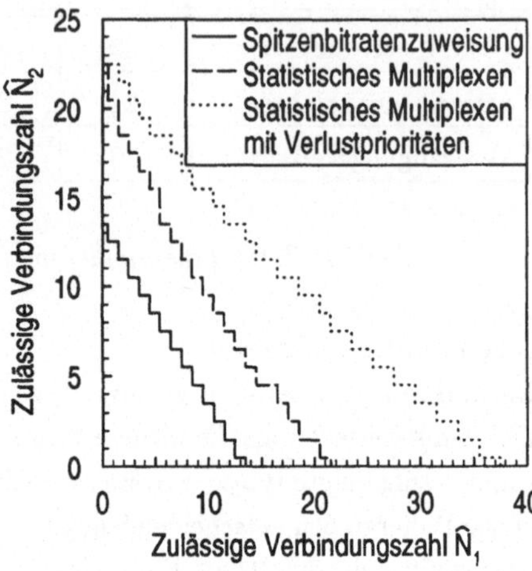

Bild 11: Einfluß des Schwellwertverfahrens auf die Zellverluste bei sporadischem Quellverkehr

Bild 12: Vergleich verschiedener Grundkonzepte zur Verkehrssteuerung

Die Ergebnisse zeigen, daß der durch das statistische Multiplexen erzielte Auslastungsgewinn im vorliegenden Fall signifikant erhöht werden kann, indem zwischen verschiedenen Verlustprioritäten unterschieden wird. Allerdings muß angemerkt werden, daß diese Steigerung der Netzauslastung — ähnlich wie der gewöhnliche Multiplexgewinn — von den Verkehrsparametern der verschiedenen Verbindungen abhängt.

4 Verbindungsannahme in ATM-Netzen

Die Verbindungsannahmefunktion nimmt innerhalb des Verkehrsmanagements eine zentrale Rolle ein. Sie entscheidet über die Annahme bzw. Ablehnung eines Verbindungswunsches anhand der deklarierten Verkehrsparameter, der nachgefragten ATM-Dienstklasse sowie der gewünschten Dienstgüte. Die Gesamtentscheidung basiert auf Einzelentscheidungen für die verschiedenen Verbindungsabschnitte.

4.1 Ansätze zur Verbindungsannahme

Die Verbindungsannahmefunktion hängt entscheidend von der gewählten ATM-Dienstklasse ab. Für CBR-Verkehre kann sich die zugewiesene Übermittlungskapazität an der Spitzenzellrate orientieren, während in den anderen Dienstklassen ein sogenannter Multiplexgewinn angestrebt wird, der sich aus dem statistischen Ausgleich der Bitratenschwankungen verschiedener Verbindungen ergibt. Für die ABR- und UBR-Dienstklasse gestaltet sich die Verbindungsannahme ebenfalls einfach, da die Dienstgüte nicht garantiert werden muß. Bei ABR-Verkehren muß lediglich eine bestimmte minimale Bitrate reserviert werden, während für UBR-Dienste überhaupt keine Ressourcenzuweisungen bestehen und damit theoretisch jeder Verbindungswunsch angenommen werden könnte.

Die folgenden Betrachtungen beschränken sich daher auf VBR-Dienste, für die bestimmte Dienstgütevorgaben eingehalten werden müssen. Aus der Literatur ist eine Vielzahl verschiedener Ansätze bekannt, die sich auf zwei grundlegende Prinzipien stützen:

- *Direkte Verfahren* stellen einen direkten Zusammenhang her zwischen den Verkehrs- und Systemparametern einerseits und den Dienstgüteparametern andererseits. Dieser Zusammenhang wird aus geeigneten analytischen Ansätzen abgeleitet (vgl. z.B. [5]).

- *Indirekte Verfahren* definieren eine effektive, äquivalente oder virtuelle Bedienrate, die eine indirekte Verknüpfung zwischen den Verkehrs- und Dienstgüteparametern schafft. Diese Rate hängt von den Verkehrsparametern der betrachteten Verbindung(en) ab und muß innerhalb des Netzes reserviert werden, damit die vorgeschriebene Dienstgüte eingehalten werden kann (siehe z.B. [4]).

4.2 Zweistufiger Annahmealgorithmus

Der in [9] beschriebene ausführliche Vergleich der verschiedenen Verbindungsannahmealgorithmen zeigt, daß die vergleichsweise komplexen direkten Algorithmen die Dienstgüte sichern können, wogegen es bei den einfachen indirekten Ansätzen zu Verletzungen der Dienstgüte kommt. Daher liegt eine zweistufige Implementierung der Verbindungsannahme nahe. In der ersten Stufe wird ein einfacher Algorithmus eingesetzt, der eine rasche Entscheidung über die Annahme bzw. Ablehnung eines neuen Verbindungswunschs treffen kann. Die von diesem Algorithmus verwendeten effektiven Bedienraten werden durch einen im Hintergrund ablaufenden Algorithmus dynamisch an die aktuelle Verkehrszusammensetzung angepaßt.

Bild 13 verdeutlicht die Funktionsweise des in der Arbeit entwickelten zweistufigen Ansatzes anhand einer Stichprobe des zeitlichen Verlaufs der effektiven Gesamtbedienrate C_E, die zur Sicherung der vorgeschriebenen Dienstgüte zur Verfügung stehen muß. Die effektive Gesamtbedienrate kann sich aufgrund der folgenden Ereignisse ändern:

- *Verbindungsaufbau:* Die effektive Gesamtbedienrate wird durch den in der ersten Stufe ablaufenden Algorithmus um den Wert $C_{S,k}(j)$ erhöht, falls eine Verbindung aus Verkehrsklasse k aufgebaut wird. Die effektive Bedienrate $C_{S,k}(j)$ wird durch den Hintergrundalgorithmus bestimmt und hängt vom betrachteten Zeitintervall $(j \cdot T, (j+1) \cdot T]$ ab. Ein neuer Verbindungswunsch wird abgelehnt, falls die effektive Gesamtbedienrate $C_E + C_{S,k}(j)$ die Zellbedienrate C überschreiten würde.

- *Verbindungsabbau:* Die effektive Gesamtbedienrate wird um den Wert $C_{R,k}(j)$ erniedrigt, falls eine Verbindung aus Verkehrsklasse k abgebaut wird. Im allgemeinen Fall ist die effektive Bedienrate $C_{R,k}(j)$ und die beim Verbindungsaufbau zugewiesene Bedienrate $C_{S,k}(j)$ verschieden. Deshalb wird zusätzlich abgeprüft, ob die effektive Gesamtbedienrate unter der maximalen Zellrate $\hat{r}$ bleibt. Die für den

Verbindungsabbau gültige effektive Bedienrate $C_{R,k}(j)$ wird ebenfalls durch den Hintergrundalgorithmus festgelegt.

- *Parameteranpassung durch den Hintergrundalgorithmus:* Da der in der ersten Stufe ablaufende Algorithmus die effektive Gesamtbedienrate C_E überschätzt, bestimmt der in der zweiten Stufe angesiedelte Hintergrundalgorithmus die Differenz ΔC_E zur tatsächlich benötigten Gesamtbedienrate. Ebenso werden auch die effektiven Bedienraten $C_{S,k}$ und $C_{R,k}$ zu periodischen Zeitpunkten $j \cdot T$, $j = 0, 1, ...$, an die tatsächliche Verkehrszusammensetzung angepaßt.

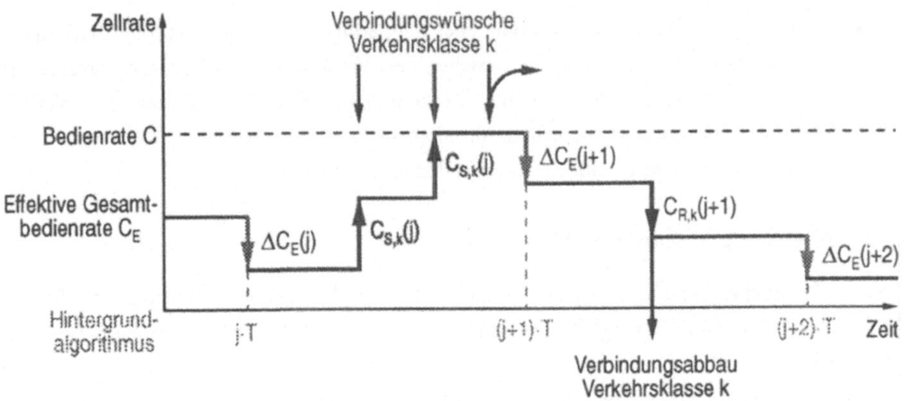

Bild 13: Stichprobe des Zeitverlaufs der effektiven Gesamtbedienrate

Abschließend soll auf den Hintergrundalgorithmus näher eingegangen werden. Die effektive Bedienrate wird mit Hilfe eines pufferlosen „Fluid Flow"-Modells bestimmt, bei dem Verluste auftreten, sobald die Gesamtankunftsrate r über der Bedienrate C liegt (die Verlustrate beträgt $r - C$). Die Gesamtankunftsrate r setzt sich aus den Ankunftsraten r_n aller Verbindungen $n = 1, 2, ..., N$ zusammen und kann nur Vielfache einer bestimmten Grundbitrate Δr betragen. Für statistisch unabhängige Verbindungen ergibt sich die Verteilung $p_R(i) = \mathrm{P}(r = i \cdot \Delta r)$ der Gesamtankunftsrate aus einer Faltung der Bitratenverteilungen $p_{R,n}(i) = \mathrm{P}(r_n = i \cdot \Delta r)$ der einzelnen Verbindungen. Mit diesen Vorbemerkungen ergibt sich die Verlustwahrscheinlichkeit $B_B(C)$ aus dem Verhältnis zwischen der mittleren Verlustrate und der mittleren Ankunftsrate $\bar{r}$.

$$B_B(C) = \frac{\Delta r}{\bar{r}} \sum_{i=C/\Delta r+1}^{\widehat{r}/\Delta r} (i - C/\Delta r) \cdot p_R(i) \tag{1}$$

Für die Bestimmung der effektiven Bedienrate kann der Term $i - C/\Delta r$ durch die Summe $\sum_{j=1}^{i-C/\Delta r} 1$ ersetzt werden. Nach einigen elementaren Umformungen erhält man [9]

$$B_B(C) = B_B(C + \Delta r) + \frac{\Delta r}{\bar{r}}[1 - F_R(C/\Delta r)] , \tag{2}$$

wobei $1 - F_R(j)$ der komplementären Verteilungsfunktion der Ankunftsrate entspricht.

Die effektive Gesamtbedienrate kann durch eine schrittweise Auswertung von Gleichung 2 erfolgen. Diese Auswertung kann abgebrochen werden, wenn $B_B(C)$ den Maximalwert $\widehat{B}_B$ übersteigt. Die gesuchte effektive Gesamtbedienrate C_E^* ergibt sich aus

$$B_B(C_E^*) \leq \widehat{B}_B \quad \text{und} \quad B_B(C_E^* - \Delta r) > \widehat{B}_B \; . \tag{3}$$

In den Aufgabenbereich der zweiten Stufe fällt auch die Anpassung der effektiven Bedienraten $C_{S,k}$ und $C_{R,k}$. Der einfachste denkbare Ansatz weist diesen Kenngrößen einen festen, zeitunabhängigen Wert zu (diese Strategie wird im folgenden mit Variante 1 bezeichnet). Eine Verletzung der Dienstgüte kann ausgeschlossen werden, falls einer neuen Verbindung die maximale Zellrate zugewiesen wird ($C_{S,k} = \widehat{r}_k$). Der Hintergrundalgorithmus paßt diese zugewiesene Bedienrate dynamisch an den tatsächlichen Bedarf an. Um die Einhaltung der Dienstgüte garantieren zu können, darf deshalb beim Verbindungsabbau nur die mittlere Zellrate freigegeben werden, die eine untere Grenze für die tatsächlich benötigte Bedienrate darstellt, d.h. es gilt $C_{R,k} = \overline{r}_k$.

Die Leistungsfähigkeit kann verbessert werden, indem auch die effektiven Bedienraten $C_{S,k}$ und $C_{R,k}$ dynamisch an die aktuelle Verkehrszusammensetzung angepaßt werden (Variante 2). Die für einen Belegungszustand $N = (N_1, N_2, ..., N_K)$ benötigte Gesamtbedienrate wird im folgenden mit $C_E^*(N)$ bezeichnet. Falls alle Verbindungen aus Verkehrsklasse k abgebaut werden, liefert der beschriebene Algorithmus eine reduzierte Bedienrate $C_E^*(N_1, ..., N_{k-1}, 0, N_{k+1}, ..., N_K)$. Die effektive Bedienrate einer Verbindung ergibt sich, indem die Differenz dieser Gesamtbedienraten auf die Anzahl der Verbindungen aus Verkehrsklasse k bezogen wird. Mit einer ähnlichen Überlegung für den Sonderfall $N_k = 0$ erhält man schließlich

$$C_{S,k} = C_{R,k} = \begin{cases} [C_E^*(N) - C_E^*(N_1, ..., N_{k-1}, 0, N_{k+1}, ..., N_K)]/N_k & \text{für } N_k > 0 \\ C_E^*(N_1, ..., N_{k-1}, 1, N_{k+1}, ..., N_K) - C_E^*(N) & \text{für } N_k = 0 \; . \end{cases} \tag{4}$$

4.3 Leistungsuntersuchung

Die Leistungsfähigkeit des zweistufigen Verfahrens wurde mit Hilfe von Simulationen abgeschätzt, wobei das in Abschnitt 2.1.1 beschriebene Verkehrsmodell verwendet wird (vgl. Bild 3). Die Entscheidung über die Annahme bzw. Abweisung eines Verbindungswunsches wird von der Verbindungsannahmefunktion getroffen, wobei eine maximale Verlustwahrscheinlichkeit von 10^{-10} angestrebt wird. Der Verkehr wird von den in Tabelle 2 definierten Verkehrsklassen erzeugt. Um die gesamte Verbindungsannahme-Grenzkurve erfassen zu können, werden jeweils fünf verschiedene Verkehrszusammensetzungen untersucht, die sich hinsichtlich des Verkehrsangebots unterscheiden:

$$A_{V,1} = \frac{10 \cdot (5 - j)}{3} \text{ Erlang} \quad \text{und} \quad A_{V,2} = \frac{10 \cdot (j - 1)}{3} \text{ Erlang} , \quad j = 1, 2, ..., 5. \tag{5}$$

Die Verbindungsdauern sind negativ-exponentiell verteilt und weisen für beide Verkehrsklassen denselben Mittelwert $h = 100$ s auf.

In Bild 14 wird die erste Variante des zweistufigen Algorithmus mit der Spitzenbitratenzuweisung und dem Faltungsalgorithmus verglichen. Der zeitliche Abstand zwischen zwei Parameteranpassungen wurde zu $T = 1$ s gewählt. Für den zweistufigen Algorithmus sind alle Verbindungszustände markiert, bei denen eine Verbindung aus der Verkehrsklasse 2 abgewiesen wurde. Die Ergebnisse bestätigen, daß die Leistungsfähigkeit des zweistufigen Algorithmus zwischen der Spitzenbitratenzuweisung und dem Faltungsalgorithmus liegt und die geforderte Dienstgüte eingehalten wird. Andererseits läßt der zweistufige Algorithmus deutlich weniger Verbindungen zu als der in der zweiten Stufe implementierte Faltungsalgorithmus. Dies ist hauptsächlich auf die innerhalb der ersten Stufe angewandte großzügige Kapazitätszuweisung zurückzuführen.

Durch die dynamische Anpassung der innerhalb der ersten Stufe verwendeten effektiven Bedienraten läßt sich die Effizienz des zweistufigen Annahmeverfahrens deutlich verbessern (Bild 15). Dies wird auch daran deutlich, daß der Zeitabstand zwischen zwei Parameteranpassungen gegenüber dem vorigen Beispiel verzehnfacht wurde, um den erhöhten Rechenaufwand dieser Variante zu berücksichtigen.

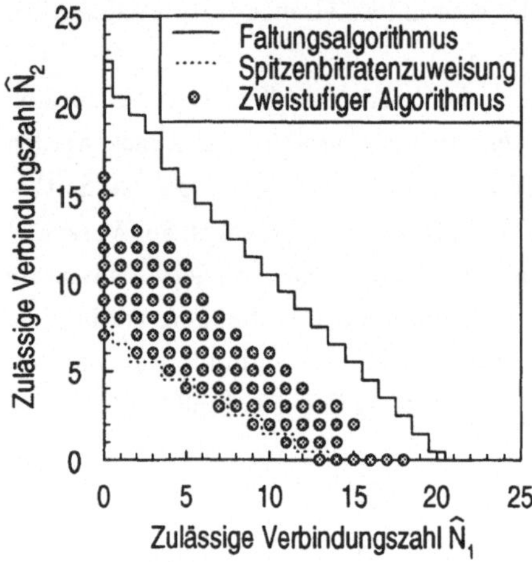

Bild 14: Verbindungsannahme-Grenz-
kurven für die Klassen 1 und
2 (Variante 1, T = 1 s)

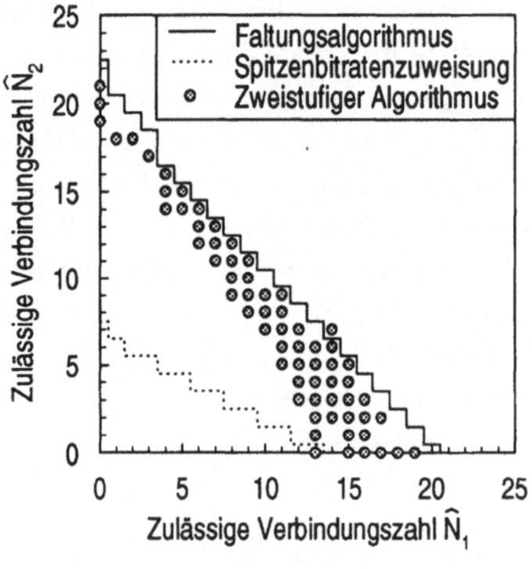

Bild 15: Verbindungsannahme-Grenz-
kurven für die Klassen 1 und
2 (Variante 2, T = 10 s)

5   Zusammenfassung und Ausblick

Im Rahmen dieser Arbeit wurden verschiedene Teilaspekte des für ATM-Netze vorgesehenen Verkehrsmanagements untersucht. Die wichtigsten Ergebnisse können folgendermaßen zusammengefaßt werden:

- In ATM-Netzen treten unterschiedliche charakteristische Blockierungseffekte in verschiedenen Zeitebenen auf, die sowohl bei der Verkehrsmodellierung und -analyse als auch bei der Verkehrssteuerung voneinander getrennt werden können.

- Mit Hilfe von Zellverlustprioritäten kann sowohl eine Verkleinerung der Netzpuffer als auch eine signifikante Erhöhung der Netzauslastung erzielt werden. Das Schwellwertverfahren bietet einen guten Kompromiß zwischen Leistungsfähigkeit und Implementierungsaufwand.

- Mit Hilfe der vorgeschlagenen zweistufigen Realisierung der Verbindungsannahme kann die Genauigkeit von komplexen direkten Verfahren mit der Echtzeitfähigkeit von einfachen indirekten Verfahren kombiniert werden.

Andererseits bleiben viele Fragestellungen offen, die weitergehende Untersuchungen erfordern. Die beschriebenen Ergebnisse basieren auf Modellannahmen, deren Gültigkeit mit Hilfe von Verkehrsmessungen im Rahmen von Feld- und Laborversuchen nachgewiesen werden muß. Besonders problembehaftet ist die Deklaration der von den Steuerungsfunktionen verwendeten Verkehrsparametern beim Verbindungsaufbau [16]. Hier erscheint eine aktive Beeinflussung des Quellverhaltens erfolgversprechend. Beispielsweise kann der Quellverkehr an das beim Verbindungsaufbau vereinbarte Verkehrsaufkommen angepaßt werden, indem die Quellcodierung entsprechend geändert wird. Weitere Verbesserungen können durch die Zwischenpufferung der Zellen am Netzzugang bzw. innerhalb des Netzes erzielt werden. Dabei werden komplexe Pufferungsstrategien nach dem „weighted fair queueing"-Prinzip verwendet, welche die verschiedenen Verkehrsströme bzw. Verbindungen in unterschiedliche logische Warteschlangen einsortieren, deren Bedienrate und Pufferkapazität an die Erfordernisse der jeweiligen ATM-Dienstklasse angepaßt werden.

Danksagung

An dieser Stelle möchte ich vor allem Herrn Professor Dr.-Ing. P. Kühn für die Betreuung der Dissertation und die damit verbundenen Diskussionen und Anregungen ganz herzlich danken. Mein besonderer Dank gilt auch den Kolleginnen und Kollegen vom Institut für Nachrichtenvermittlung und Datenverarbeitung für die gute Zusammenarbeit, die vielen fruchtbaren Diskussionen und ihre tatkräftige Unterstützung.

Literatur

[1] D. ANICK, D. MITRA, M.M. SONDHI: Stochastic theory of a data-handling system with multiple sources. *The Bell System Technical Journal*, vol. 61, no. 8, October 1982, pp. 1871–1894.

[2] ATM FORUM: *Traffic Management Specification, Version 4.0*, AF-TM-0056, ATM Forum Technical Committee, April 1996.

[3] K. BALA, I. CIDON, K. SHORABY: Congestion control for high speed packet switched networks. *Proceedings of the IEEE INFOCOM '90*, San Francisco, June 1990, pp. 520–526.

[4] R. GUÉRIN, H. AHMADI, M. NAGHSHINEH: Equivalent capacity and its applications to bandwidth allocation in high-speed networks. *IEEE JSAC*, vol. 9, no. 7, September 1991, pp. 968–981.

[5] J.Y. HUI: Resource allocation for broadband networks. *IEEE JSAC*, vol. 6, no. 9, December 1988, pp. 1598–1608.

[6] ITU-T: *Traffic and Congestion Control in B ISDN*, ITU-T Draft Recommendation I.371, Geneva, May 1996.

[7] H. KRÖNER: Comparative performance study of space priority mechanisms for ATM networks. *Proceedings of the IEEE INFOCOM '90*, San Francisco, June 1990, pp. 1136–1143.

[8] H. KRÖNER: Statistical multiplexing of sporadic sources — exact and approximate performance analysis. *Proceedings of the 13th ITC*, Copenhagen, June 1991, pp. 787–793.

[9] H. KRÖNER: *Verkehrssteuerung in ATM-Netzen — Verfahren und verkehrstheoretische Analysen zur Zellpriorisierung und Verbindungsannahme.* Dissertationsschrift, Universität Stuttgart, Stuttgart 1995.

[10] H. KRÖNER: A general fluid flow model for an ATM multiplexer — second order characteristics of the arrival and loss processes. *International Journal of Electronics and Communications*, no. 4, vol. 50, July 1996, pp. 261–273.

[11] H. KRÖNER, M. EBERSPÄCHER, T.H. THEIMER, P.J. KÜHN, U. BRIEM: Approximate analysis of the end-to-end delay in ATM networks. *Proceedings of the IEEE Infocom '92*, Florence, May 1992, pp. 978–986.

[12] S.-Q. LI: Study of information loss in packet voice systems. *IEEE Transactions on Communications*, vol. 37, no. 11, November 1989, pp. 1192–1202.

[13] A.Y.M. LIN, J.A. SILVESTER: Priority queueing strategies and buffer allocation protocols for traffic control at an ATM integrated broadband switching system. *IEEE JSAC*, vol. 9, no. 9, December 1991, pp. 1524–1536.

[14] D.M. LUCANTONI, S.P. PAREKH: Selective cell discard mechanisms for a B-ISDN congestion control architecture. *Proceedings of the 7th ITC Seminar*, Morristown, October 1990, paper 10.3.

[15] I. NORROS, J.W. ROBERTS, A. SIMONIAN, J.T. VIRTAMO: The superposition of variable bit rate sources in an ATM multiplexer. *IEEE JSAC*, vol. 9, no. 3, April 1991, pp. 378–387.

[16] E.P. RATHGEB: *Verkehrsflüsse in ATM-Netzen — Modellierung und Analyse von Verkehrsquellen und Quellflußkontrollverfahren*, Dissertationsschrift, Universität Stuttgart, Stuttgart, 1991.

[17] S. SUMITA, T. OZAWA: Achievability of performance objectives in ATM switching nodes. *Proceedings of the International Seminar on Performance of Distributed and Parallel Systems*, Kyoto, December 1988, pp. 45–56.

[18] L. TASSIULAS, Y. HUNG, S.S. PANWAR: Optimal buffer control during congestion in an ATM network node. *Proceedings of IEEE INFOCOM '93*, San Francisco, April 1993, pp. 1059–1066.

[19] R.C.F. TUCKER: Accurate method for analysis of a packet-speech multiplexer with limited delay. *IEEE Transactions on Communications*, vol. 36, no. 4, April 1988, pp. 479–483.

Datenbankzugriff in mobiler Umgebung

Antje Scholler
Technische Universität Dresden, Lehrstuhl Rechnernetze
01062 Dresden

Kurzfassung

In der diesem Aufsatz zugrundeliegenden Diplomarbeit wurden Untersuchungen durchgeführt, die sich mit dem Einsatz von Daten- und Applikationsbeschreibungen im Bereich des Mobile Computing - speziell beim mobilen Datenbankzugriff - beschäftigen. Die Diplomarbeit entstand innerhalb eines gemeinsamen Forschungsprojekts zwischen dem Daimler Benz Forschungszentrum Ulm und der TU Dresden zum Thema Daten- und Lastverteilung in mobilen Rechnersystemen. Schwerpunkt der Untersuchungen ist hier die Fragestellung, ob Applikationsabläufe und Datenzugriffe in mobilen Umgebungen optimiert werden können, wenn explizites Wissen über Applikationen und Daten vorliegt. Weiterhin ist von Interesse, wie dieses Wissen vorgegeben wird bzw. dynamisch ermittelt werden soll. Anhand eines neuen Cache-Kohärenz-Schemas wird die Anwendung von Datenbeschreibungen hinsichtlich eines optimaleren Datenzugriffs in mobilen Umgebungen demonstriert.

1   Einführung

Die Mobilkommunikation hat in der letzten Zeit stark an Bedeutung gewonnen. Aus kaum einem Bereich der Wirtschaft ist sie noch wegzudenken. Auch die mobile Computerkommunikation spielt dabei eine immer größere Rolle. Die rasche Entwicklung auf dem Gebiet der drahtlosen Kommunikation und immer leistungsfähigere portable Endgeräte unterstützen diesen Trend.

Neben mobilen Anwendungen, wie z.B. Electronic Mail, Workflow Management oder Zugriff auf weltweite Informationsdienste, spielt der Datenbankzugriff in mobiler Umgebung eine wichtige Rolle. Bedingt durch die mögliche Mobilität sowohl der Datenbank-Clients als auch der Datenbank-Server beim Datenbankzugriff treten Probleme auf, die mit den Konzepten konventioneller Datenbanksysteme nicht hinreichend behandelt werden können. Im mobilen Bereich können sehr viele DB-Konzepte aus dem Bereich verteilter Datenbanksysteme angewendet werden. Ein Großteil dieser Mechanismen kann aber nicht ohne weiteres zum Einsatz kommen, da in mobilen Umgebungen andere Bedingungen vorherrschen.

So haben mobile Systeme z.B. keine festen Topologien, sowohl Clients als auch Server können mobil sein (sich dynamisch ändernde Lokationen). Verbindungen zwischen Kommunikationspartnern beim mobilen DB-Zugriff können großen Schwankungen unterliegen (in Bezug auf Kommunikationsbandbreite, -kosten, Entfernung). So ist es z.B. möglich, daß ein mobiler Rechner eine DB-Anfrage bei Ankopplung an ein lokales Festnetz (z.B. Ethernet oder ATM) startet und sich danach aus dieser Umgebung fortbewegt, wobei er dann nur noch eine Verbindung per Funk-WAN (z.B. GSM) aufbauen kann. Ein weiterer Aspekt beim DB-Zugriff im mobilen Bereich ist das häufige Auftreten von vorhersehbaren (z.B. gewollte Abkopplung, um Energie zu sparen) und nicht vorhersehbaren (z.B. durch Funkstille) Verbindungsunterbrechungen (Diskonnektivitäten). Ein Problem beim mobilen DB-Zugriff stellt auch die begrenzte Kapazität vieler mobiler Rechner (z.B. Palmtops) dar. Diese Rechner sind durch geringe Rechen- und Speicherkapazität, begrenzte Batterieleistung und kleinere Displays gekennzeichnet. Beim Datenbankzugriff in mobiler Umgebung sind prinzipiell drei Herangehensweisen denkbar:

- Verwendung der herkömmlichen Mechanismen, z.B. Konzepte aktiver Datenbanken [Sch95]
- Erweiterungen bzw. Modifikationen der bestehenden Mechanismen, z.B. erweiterte Transaktionskonzepte [PiB94, JBE95, Nar94, FaZ95]
- neue Konzepte, z.B. semantische Auswahl bei multimedialen Daten [SBH96].

Für alle drei genannten Herangehensweisen sind in [Sch96] Beispiele beschrieben. In dem vorliegenden Papier wird nur ein kleiner Teil der in [Sch96] vorgestellten Datenbankmechanismen in mobiler Umgebung betrachtet. Das heißt, es werden hauptsächlich Erweiterungen von Cache-Kohärenz-Schemata und die Verwendung von Daten- und Anwendungsbeschreibungen im mobilen Umfeld diskutiert.

Das folgende Kapitel beschäftigt sich mit dem Einsatz von Daten- und Anwendungsbeschreibungen beim mobilen Datenbankzugriff. In Kapitel 3 wird dann ein spezielles Cache-Kohärenz-Schema vorgestellt, das für die Verwendung im mobilen Bereich entworfen wurde und bei dem die Verwendung speziell von Datenbeschreibungen beim Datenbankzugriff untersucht wurde. Dieses Cache-Kohärenz-Schema wurde implementiert, und es wurden verschiedene Tests und Messungen durchgeführt, deren Ergebnisse im 4. Kapitel zusammengefaßt werden. Der Beitrag schließt mit einer Zusammenfassung.

2 Daten- und Anwendungsbeschreibungen

Um den Datenbankzugriff im Mobilbereich optimieren und besser an die sich oft ändernden Systembedingungen anpassen zu können, ist es sinnvoll und auch notwendig, daß statische bzw. dynamische Informationen über Daten, Clientapplikationen bzw. die Umgebung bekannt sind. Diese Informationen und zusätzliche Entscheidungskriterien werden in Form von Daten- und Anwendungsbeschreibungen zur Verfügung gestellt bzw. dynamisch ermittelt. Abhängig von diesen Beschreibungen können dann Entscheidungen, z.B. zur Last- und Datenverteilung oder zu Caching- und Prefetching-Strategien, getroffen werden. Unter Daten- und Anwendungsbeschreibungen werden in dieser Arbeit also alle anwendungs- und datenspezifischen Informationen sowie zugehörige Entscheidungskriterien bzw. -mechanismen verstanden, mit deren Hilfe eine Anwendung so gut wie möglich an die aktuellen Systembedingungen angepaßt werden kann.

Für den mobilen DB-Zugriff wichtige Informationen in Anwendungsbeschreibungen sind z.B. die Angabe des konkreten Bedarfs an benötigten Daten. Das bedeutet, daß angegeben werden sollte, auf welche Daten (Datenbanken, Teile von Datenbanken, Datensätze) die Anwendung zugreifen will. Ebenso sollte eine Anwendung spezifizieren, ob Caching bzw. Prefetching von Daten erwünscht ist und ggf. welche Caching- bzw. Prefetching-Strategie angewendet werden soll. Durch diese Angaben könnte z.B. automatisch ein Caching- oder Prefetching-Mechanismus gestartet werden, um eine bevorstehende Diskonnektivität zu unterstützen.

Den Datenbeschreibungen kommt beim mobilen DB-Zugriff eine große Bedeutung zu, da es aufgrund der wechselnden System- und Verbindungscharakteristika besonders darauf ankommt, unterschiedliche Datentypen unterschiedlich zu behandeln. Es ist z.B. ohne Probleme möglich, eine umfangreiche Videodatei zum Client-Rechner zu transferieren, wenn eine LAN-Verbindung zwischen Client und Server besteht. Bei einer GSM-Verbindung zum Server wäre die Übertragung einer Videodatei allerdings weniger angebracht. Neben der Angabe der Informationsart (Video, komprimiertes Video, Bild, Text, etc.) ist es auch sinnvoll, andere Informationen über die Daten, wie z.B. die Änderungshäufigkeit (evtl. Änderungszeiten) oder Relationen zu anderen Daten in den Datenbeschreibungen abzulegen.

Die Verwendung von Datenbeschreibungen beim mobilen Datenbankzugriff wurde im Rahmen dieser Arbeit an einem speziellen Cache-Kohärenz-Schema untersucht, das in Kapitel 3.1 vorgestellt wird. Bei diesem Cache-Kohärenz-Schema werden z.B. Informationen aus den Datenbeschreibungen verwendet, um zu entscheiden, ob Änderungen an bestimmten Daten vom Server an die Clients propagiert werden oder nicht. So werden z.B. Änderungen an Hotspot-Daten nicht an die Clients versendet. Die Clients wissen aufgrund der Datenbeschreibung, daß sie keine Änderungen zu den Hotspot-Daten erhalten und deshalb diese Daten nicht im lokalen Cache ablegen sollten, sondern bei jeder Datenbankanfrage diese Daten erneut vom Server anfordern müssen.

3 Cache-Kohärenz-Schemata

Um auch im abgekoppelten Zustand den Zugriff auf benötigte Daten zu ermöglichen, besteht die Möglichkeit, einen Teil der Daten vor der Verbindungsunterbrechung auf den mobilen Rechner zu kopieren. Das kann durch Caching oder Prefetching erfolgen. Auf das Prefetching soll an dieser Stelle nicht weiter eingegangen werden, siehe dazu [Sch96, LiM94].

Beim Caching wird eine Kopie der entfernten Daten, auf die als letztes zugegriffen wurde, lokal gehalten, so daß ein wiederholter Zugriff auf dieselben Daten lokal abgearbeitet werden kann ohne zusätzliche Netzbelastung [LiM94]. Grundgedanke dafür ist, daß auf Daten, auf die von einem Programm in letzter Zeit zugegriffen wurde, auch in der nächsten Zeit wieder zugegriffen wird (zeitliche Lokalität). Da die Daten (sowohl die Originale als auch Cache-Kopien) geändert werden können, spielt die Erhaltung der Cache-Konsistenz eine wichtige Rolle. Es muß ein Cache-Kohärenz-Schema zum Einsatz kommen.

Aus der Literatur sind verschiedene Arten von Cache-Kohärenz-Schemata bekannt, von denen an dieser Stelle nur zwei genannt werden sollen. Bei einem Cache-Kohärenz-Schema mit Update Propagation propagiert der Server die geänderten Daten an die Clients, was mit einer starken Belastung des Kommunikationsnetzes verbunden ist. Der Vorteil dieser Methode besteht allerdings darin, daß die Clients nach jeder Aktualisierung lokal über die neuen Datenwerte verfügen und keine Anfrage an den Server stellen müssen. Bei Cache-Kohärenz-Schemata mit Invalidation Propagation propagiert der Server bei Änderungen nicht die neuen Datenwerte an die Clients, sondern es werden periodisch oder asynchron (sofort nach der Änderung) lediglich Invalidierungsreports verschickt. Dieser Ansatz erfordert dann zwar ein aktives Anfordern des geänderten Datenobjekts durch den Client; zunächst können aber Kommunikationskosten gespart werden, da nur relativ kleine Invalidierungsreports versendet werden.

Probleme können bei den beschriebenen Cache-Kohärenz-Schemata auftreten, wenn der Client einige Zeit lang abgekoppelt war, da er dann nicht weiß, welche Änderungen in der Zwischenzeit gemeldet wurden. Für synchrone (periodische) Invalidation Propagation wird in [BaI94] vorgeschlagen, daß der Client bei bzw. nach einer Verbindungsunterbrechung nach Ablauf der vordefinierten Periode alle Datenobjekte aus dem Cache entfernt, wenn bis dahin keine Invalidierungsnachricht eingetroffen ist. Das bedeutet, daß der Client bei Wiederankopplung den gesamten Cache-Inhalt neu anfordern muß, auch wenn in der Zwischenzeit nicht alle Datenobjekte aktualisiert wurden. Bei asynchronen Invalidierungsnachrichten (und auch Änderungsnachrichten) gibt es die Variante, den Cache-Inhalt sofort bei Diskonnektivität als ungültig zu kennzeichnen. Da das i.d.R. vermieden werden sollte, wird in [BaI94] empfohlen, in die asynchronen Invalidierungs-Reports zusätzliche Informationen über andere Datenobjekte aufzunehmen, z.B. Kennung und Zeitstempel der letzten Änderungen der sich am häufigsten ändernden Datenobjekte. Der Client kann an diesen Informationen erkennen, welche dieser Datenobjekte in der Zwischenzeit aktualisiert wurden. Generell gibt es für die Behandlung des Cache-Inhaltes bei einer Abkopplung zwei Grenzfälle möglicher Herangehensweisen: die optimistische und die pessimistische Strategie.

Die optimistischen Strategien gehen davon aus, daß während der Verbindungsunterbrechung keine Änderung eintrifft und die Daten bei Wiederankopplung noch gültig sind. Diese Herangehensweise ist zwar durch einen geringen Kommunikationsaufwand gekennzeichnet, aber auch durch eine geringere Sicherheit, mit gültigen Daten zu arbeiten. Tritt während der Verbindungsunterbrechung eine Änderung ein, wird unbewußt mit ungültigen Daten gearbeitet.

Bei den pessimistischen Strategien wird der gesamte Cache-Inhalt sofort bei der Abkopplung invalidiert und muß bei Wiederankopplung bei einem Zugriff erneut vom Server geholt werden, auch wenn nicht alle Daten während der Abkopplung geändert wurden. Der pessimistische Ansatz ist also durch einen hohen Kommunikationsaufwand und durch eine absolute Sicherheit, nicht mit ungültigen Daten zu arbeiten, gekennzeichnet.

Die beiden Fälle sind nur für die Extremsituationen geeignet. So können optimistische Strategien bei kürzeren Abkopplungen eingesetzt werden und pessimistische Strategien bei längeren Abkopplungen. Da wir aber davon ausgehen, daß in der Realität die einzelnen Datenobjekte durch sehr unterschiedliche Änderungszeiten bzw. Änderungshäufigkeiten gekennzeichnet sind, stellt das im folgenden beschriebene Cache-Kohärenz-Schema einen Kompromiß zwischen dem optimistischen und dem pessimistischen Ansatz sowohl in Hinsicht auf Kommunikationsaufwand als auch auf die Aktualität dar.

3.1 Cache-Kohärenz-Schema mit Zeitstempelvergleich (Comparing Timestamps)

Das im folgenden diskutierte Cache-Kohärenz-Schema basiert auf folgenden Überlegungen:

Die mittlere Zeit zwischen zwei Änderungen eines Datenobjekts sei ΔT. Mit einer bestimmten (und relativ hohen) Wahrscheinlichkeit kann man nun davon ausgehen, daß ein Datenobjekt solange aktuell (und damit gültig) ist, bis diese Zeit ΔT für das Datum abgelaufen ist. Dieser Ansatz ist sowohl für synchrone als auch für asynchrone Änderungs- bzw. Invalidierungsnachrichten einsetzbar. Dem folgenden Algorithmus soll eine Art asynchrone Incremental Update Propagation [Cho96] zugrunde gelegt werden.

Greift ein Client auf ein entferntes Datenobjekt zu, wird eine Kopie dieses Datums in seinem Cache abgelegt. Bei einer erstmaligen Anforderung erhält der Client das gesamte Datenobjekt sowie Zeitstempel (TS^S_i) und Änderungsfenster (ΔT_i) dieses Datums:

$$(\text{Datenobjekt},\ TS^S_i,\ \Delta T_i).$$

Sobald beim Server ein Datenobjekt geändert wurde, schickt der Server Änderungsnachrichten an die Clients. Bei der Update Propagation würde in den Änderungsnachrichten das gesamte geänderte Datenobjekt zu den Clients übertragen werden. Wenn der Server keine Client-Liste verwendet, ist diese Vorgehensweise nur bei kleineren Datenobjekten (einzelne kleinere Datensätze, arithmetische Werte, etc.) empfehlenswert. Für größere Datenobjekte (z.B. Spreadsheets, Preistabellen, etc.) ist es besser, das Cache-Kohärenz-Schema dahingehend zu erweitern bzw. zu modifizieren, daß der Server nur Änderungen an Datenobjekten an die Clients übermittelt. Beispiele für Änderungsanweisungen für eine Tabelle sind

Erhöhe alle Einträge in Spalte 5 um 3% oder
Überschreibe Zelle(35,42) mit 6.

Die Anweisungen müssen von den Clients verstanden werden, da sie diese Änderungen auf ihre Cache-Datenobjekte anwenden müssen. Erhält ein Client eine Änderungsnachricht, nachdem er abgekoppelt war, darf er diese Änderung nicht in jedem Fall auf das Datenobjekt in seinem Cache anwenden. Es besteht nämlich die Möglichkeit, daß er während der Abkopplung Änderungsanweisungen nicht erhalten hat. Es sind zwei Möglichkeiten denkbar, dieses Problem zu lösen. Zum einen könnte der Client bei Wiederankopplung beim Server nachfragen, ob während der Diskonnektivität Änderungen an Datenobjekten propagiert wurden. In einem System mit mehreren Servern ist diese Variante allerdings sehr aufwendig. Eine andere Variante besteht darin, daß der Server bei jeder Änderungsnachricht, die er propagiert, zusätzlich den Zeitstempel der vorletzten Änderung des Datums $TS^S_{i,vorletzte}$ zum Client übermittelt. *Änderungsnachrichten* vom Server *für große Datenobjekte* können daher folgendermaßen aussehen:

(Datenobjekt-ID, Änderungsanweisung, TS^S_i, $TS^S_{i,vorletzte}$, ΔT_j).

Der Client kann dann durch einen Vergleich dieses Zeitstempels mit dem Zeitstempel der letzten Version des Datenobjekts in seinem Cache feststellen, ob er Änderungen nicht erhalten hat, und entsprechend reagieren. Um die Kommunikation zwischen Client und Server so gering wie möglich zu halten, ist diese zweite Variante zu empfehlen.

Um den Algorithmus im folgenden so anschaulich wie möglich darzustellen, sollen einige *vereinfachende Annahmen* getroffen werden:

- Schreibzugriffe auf die Daten werden nur beim Server durchgeführt.
- Der Client führt nur Lesezugriffe auf die Daten aus.
- Der Server führt keine Client-Liste, in der die Clients seiner Umgebung verzeichnet sind.
- Die Datenobjekte beim Server sind nur große Datenobjekte, so daß nur Änderungen an den Datenobjekten zu den Clients übermittelt werden.
- Der Fall, daß eine Verbindungsunterbrechung eintritt, nachdem ein Client eine Anfrage an den Server gestellt und bevor er die Antwort erhalten hat, wird hier vernachlässigt.

Unter diesen Voraussetzungen läuft der Zeitstempelvergleich wie folgt ab: Bei einer Verbindungsunterbrechung werden die Daten beim Client nach einer bestimmten Zeit nur als ungültig markiert, aber nicht aus dem Cache entfernt. Voraussetzung dafür ist, daß dem Client Informationen zur Verbindungsbewertung zur Verfügung stehen, d.h. der Client muß feststellen können, ob die Verbindung zum Server unterbrochen ist und er möglicherweise Änderungsnachrichten nicht erhalten hat. Soll nach der Wiederankopplung beim Client auf ein bestimmtes, als ungültig markiertes Datum zugegriffen werden, werden eine Kennung und der Zeitstempel der letzten beim Client verfügbaren Version dieses Datenobjektes zum Server gesendet. Wurde das Datenobjekt während der Verbindungsunterbrechung beim Server nicht geändert, wird nur ein Flag zum Client zurückgeschickt, das anzeigt, daß keine Änderung stattfand. Das Datum wird daraufhin beim Client wieder als gültig markiert. Anderenfalls erhält der Client eine Aktualisierungsnachricht vom Server.

Damit die Möglichkeit besteht, daß auch die Clients, die durch eine Diskonnektivität Änderungsnachrichten „verpaßt" haben, nur die verpaßten Änderungsnachrichten zu dem bestimmten Datenobjekt vom Server erhalten und nicht das gesamte u.U. sehr umfangreiche Datenobjekt, führt der Server eine Änderungsliste. In dieser Liste protokolliert der Server alle per Broadcasting an die Clients versendeten Änderungsnachrichten mit dem Zeitstempel der Änderung. Das Führen einer Änderungsliste ist nur bei nicht zeitkritischen Änderungen sinnvoll (ansonsten können durch zeitabhängige Relationen zwischen Datenobjekten Probleme auftreten). Wieviel Änderungen zu einem Datenobjekt in der Änderungsliste gespeichert werden, hängt von verschiedenen Faktoren (z.B. Änderungshäufigkeit der Daten beim Server, Zugriffshäufigkeit der Clients auf die Daten, Umfang der einzelnen Änderungen, etc.) ab. Beispielsweise könnte die Anzahl der in der Liste abgelegten Änderungsnachrichten entsprechend der Änderungshäufigkeit beim Server variieren oder von vornherein festgelegt sein (beispielsweise Beschränkung auf die letzten 10 Änderungsnachrichten pro Datum).

Der Client erhält in der Aktualisierungsnachricht vom Server somit alle Änderungsanweisungen aus der Änderungsliste für dieses Datenobjekt ab dem vom Client übermittelten Zeitstempel. Er wendet dann diese Änderungen nacheinander auf das Datenobjekt in seinem Cache an und markiert das Datum dann wieder als gültig. Ob die Übermittlung von mehreren Änderungsnachrichten oder die Übertragung des aktuellen Datums kostengünstiger sind, war hier nicht Gegenstand der Untersuchungen.

Mit dieser beschriebenen Herangehensweise kann verhindert werden, daß jedes Datenobjekt nach einer Diskonnektivität vom Client neu angefordert werden muß, auch wenn es nicht geändert wurde. Es kann mit einer hohen Wahrscheinlichkeit entschieden werden, ob die Daten zu einem bestimmten Zeitpunkt gültig oder bereits ungültig sind. Nach einer Verbindungsunterbrechung muß nicht der gesamte Cache-Inhalt neu angefordert werden, sondern nur die Datenobjekte, die sich während der Abkopplung geändert haben. Und selbst dabei muß bei dem vorgestellten Algorithmus nicht das gesamte, u.U. sehr umfangreiche Datum neu übertragen werden, sondern nur die verpaßten Änderungsanweisungen.

Allerdings wurde bisher noch nicht berücksichtigt, wann, wie und durch wen die Daten als ungültig markiert werden. Folgender Ansatz ist denkbar:

Beim Client ist eine Instanz dafür verantwortlich, die entsprechenden Datenobjekte bei bzw. nach einer Verbindungsunterbrechung als ungültig (invalid) zu kennzeichnen. Man könnte alle Datenobjekte nach einer gewissen Zeit nach der letzten Änderungsnachricht gleichzeitig als invalid markieren. Diese Vorgehensweise ist aber in den meisten Fällen nicht angebracht, da die Daten beim Server zu verschiedenen Zeiten und unterschiedlich oft geändert werden. Deshalb wird beim Server für jedes Datenobjekt anhand statistischer Auswertungen z.B. der letzten 100 Änderungsintervalle (bestimmte Verteilungsfunktionen) ein eigenes Änderungsfenster ermittelt. Das Änderungsfenster ΔT_i erhält der Client immer dann, wenn das Datenobjekt bzw. Änderungen vom Server zum Client übertragen werden. Die Informationen über Änderungsfenster und Gültigkeit der Daten sind beim Client in einer Tabelle (siehe Abbildung 1) abgelegt, die für jedes im lokalen Cache des Clients enthaltene Datum neben dem Änderungsfenster (ΔT_i) auch den Zeitstempel der letzten Änderung dieses Datenobjekts (TS^C_i) und ein Flag (Valid-Flag), das anzeigt, ob das Datenobjekt gültig, wahrscheinlich gültig oder ungültig ist, enthält.

Datenobjekt DO_i	Änderungsfenster ΔT_i	Zeitstempel TS^C_i	Valid-Flag
DO_1	150	1531	1
DO_2	35	1590	0
DO_3	70	1590	2
. . .	. . .	. . .	. . .

Valid-Flag = 0 -> DO_i ist *ungültig*
1 -> DO_i ist *gültig*; eine *Verbindungsunterbrechung* fand statt
2 -> DO_i ist *gültig*; keine *Verbindungsunterbrechung* fand statt

Abbildung 1 - Tabelle mit Änderungsfenster und Zeitstempel beim Client

Solange keine Diskonnektivität auftritt, ist das Valid-Flag für jedes Datenobjekt auf 2 gesetzt. Tritt eine Verbindungsunterbrechung ein, werden alle Valid-Flags mit dem Wert 2 auf 1 gesetzt und eine Client-Instanz überprüft nun in bestimmten Abständen (T_{thr}), welche Datenobjekte invalidiert (d.h. Valid-Flags von 1 auf 0 gesetzt) werden müssen.

Das Valid-Flag eines Datums kann wieder auf 2 gesetzt werden,

- wenn für dieses Datum eine Änderungsnachricht vom Server eintrifft und dabei der Zeitstempel der beim Client verfügbaren Version T^C_i mit dem übermittelten Zeitstempel der vorletzten Änderung $T^S_{i,vorletzte}$ übereinstimmt oder
- wenn nach einer Client-Anfrage alle zuvor nicht erhaltenen Änderungsanweisungen auf die Cache-Datenobjekte angewendet wurden oder vom Server signalisiert wird, daß keine Änderung des Datums stattfand (Flag CHANGED=FALSE) oder
- wenn das ganze Datenobjekt neu angefordert wurde.

3.2 Verwendung von Datenbeschreibungen beim Cache-Kohärenz-Schema mit Comparing Timestamps

In diesem Abschnitt soll gezeigt werden, auf welche Art und Weise bei dem vorgestellten Cache-Kohärenz-Schema mittels Datenbeschreibungen der mobile Datenbankzugriff optimiert werden kann. Die Nachrichtenstruktur der Comparing Timestamps-Methode erlaubt es, zusätzliche Informationen über die Datenobjekte vom Server zum Client zu übermitteln. Das Änderungsfenster stellt dabei eine zusätzliche Datenbeschreibung dar. Zum einen kann damit das mittlere Änderungsintervall angegeben werden, das über statistische Auswertungen vom Server ermittelt wird, andererseits kann das Änderungsfenster über statische bzw. dynamische Daten- und Anwendungsbeschreibungen in Abhängigkeit von den aktuellen Systembedingungen vorab festgelegt werden kann. Für die zweite Variante sind folgende Möglichkeiten denkbar (und im Rahmen der Arbeit realisiert worden):

- Steht beim erstmaligen Anfordern eines Datums in der Nachricht vom Server $\Delta T_i = -1$, dann bedeutet das, daß Änderungen an diesem Datenobjekt nicht vom Server propagiert werden (weil es z.B. ein Hotspot-Datum ist und sich deshalb sehr oft ändert). In diesem Fall müssen die Clients die Daten immer wieder vom Server anfordern, ohne irgendwelche Zeitstempelvergleiche durchzuführen.

- Wenn beim erstmaligen Anfordern eines Datums in der Nachricht vom Server $\Delta T_i = -2$ steht, so heißt das, daß dieses Datenobjekt ebenfalls nie in den Änderungsnachrichten enthalten ist, weil es sich nie ändert (z.B. Quartalsabrechnung, etc.). Dieses Datenobjekt bleibt im Cache immer gültig. Das kann z.B. dadurch realisiert werden, daß das Valid-Flag auf 3 gesetzt wird und somit nicht in den Zeitstempelvergleich einbezogen wird.

- Um die beiden gerade beschriebenen Erweiterungs-Varianten zu realisieren, führt der Server eine Liste von Datenobjekten, für die er Änderungen propagiert. Datenobjekte wie Hotspots oder über lange Zeit konstante Daten werden in diese Liste nicht aufgenommen. Die Entscheidung, welche Datenobjekte in die Liste aufgenommen werden und für welche Daten $\Delta T_i = -1$ oder $\Delta T_i = -2$ zum Client übermittelt wird, wird mit Hilfe der Datenbeschreibungen der Datenobjekte getroffen.

4 Implementierung und Messung

Zur Demonstration und Validierung des in Kapitel 3 beschriebenen Algorithmus wurde eine Datenbank-Demonstrationsanwendung implementiert. Die Implementierung erfolgte mit Visual C++, Version 2.2 unter Windows NT 3.51 und nutzt als Grundlage der Client-Server-Kommunikation den Microsoft RPC. Weitere Informationen zur Implementierung und zusätzlichen Messungen sind der Diplomarbeit [Sch96] zu entnehmen.
Um die Eignung des Algorithmus mit unterschiedlichen Parameterkombinationen zu testen, wurden mehrere Messungen durchgeführt. Für die Tests galten folgende Bedingungen:

- Die Testumgebung bestand nur aus einem Client und einem Server
- Die Änderungen an Daten erfolgten im Abstand des Änderungsintervalls und wurden anschließend an den Client propagiert
- Nach jedem Zugriff wurde überprüft, ob das DB-File beim Server gültig oder ungültig ist, um Fehlentscheidungen festzustellen.

Durch die Messungen sollten u.a. folgende Fragen beantwortet werden:

- Können durch den Einsatz dieses Algorithmus die Kommunikationskosten gegenüber einer Strategie, bei der der Cache-Inhalt sofort bei Abkopplung invalidiert wird, gesenkt werden?
- Kann durch die Angabe des Änderungsintervalls mit hoher Wahrscheinlichkeit auf gültig bzw. nicht gültig entschieden werden?
- In welchen Fällen könnte auf die Kenntnis des Änderungsintervalls beim Client verzichtet werden?

Bei den hier vorgestellten Messungen wurde zunächst die Abkopplungsdauer bei ansonsten konstanten Parametern variiert. Diese Meßreihe wurde anschließend für verschiedene Änderungsintervalle durchgeführt. In den Diagrammen in Abbildung 2 ist auf der Abszisse jeweils die Abkopplungsdauer in einem Bereich von 1 bis 100 Sekunden (entspricht 0,1mal bis 10mal der Verbindungsdauer) dargestellt. Auf der Ordinate ist jeweils das Fehlzugriffsverhältnis (in Prozent) abgetragen. Das *Fehlzugriffsverhältnis* ist der Anteil der Zugriffe auf Daten während und nach einer Abkopplung, bei denen beim Client angenommen wird, die Daten seien noch gültig (Valid-Flag = 1), obwohl sie beim Server bereits geändert wurden.

$$\text{Fehlzugriffsverhältnis} = \frac{\text{Anzahl der Zugriffe auf Daten mit Valid-Flag = 1, die aber beim Server bereits ungültig sind}}{\text{Gesamtanzahl der Zugriffe auf Daten mit Valid-Flag = 1}}$$

Aus den Diagrammen in Abbildung 2 ist folgendes ersichtlich: Bei sehr kurzen Verbindungsunterbrechungen ist das Fehlzugriffsverhältnis gering. Das ist damit zu begründen, daß während der kurzen Diskonnektivitäten die Wahrscheinlichkeit sehr gering ist, daß eine Änderung eintrifft. Nach der Verbindungsunterbrechung sind die Daten also mit hoher Wahrscheinlichkeit noch gültig, und eintreffende Änderungen können auf die Daten angewendet werden.

In den Diagrammen der Abbildung 2 ist auch zu sehen, daß das Fehlzugriffsverhältnis mit zunehmendem Änderungsintervall bei ansonsten konstanten Parametern sinkt (vgl. z.B. Unterschied zwischen den Diagrammen 1 und 5). Das ist dadurch zu erklären, daß mit zunehmendem Änderungsintervall die Wahrscheinlichkeit sinkt, daß während der Verbindungsunterbrechung eine Änderung eingetroffen ist.

Die durchgeführten Messungen haben gezeigt, daß das Cache-Kohärenz-Schema mit Comparing Timestamps grundsätzlich für den mobilen DB-Zugriff geeignet ist. Jedoch haben weitere Messungen auch gezeigt [Sch96], daß der Algorithmus in Systemen, in denen die Clients generell nur selten und für kurze Zeit abgekoppelt sind, und in Systemen, in denen die Clients generell oft und sehr lange abgekoppelt sind, einen nicht notwendigen Overhead darstellt und daß in diesen beiden Extremfällen optimistische bzw. pessimistische Strategien angewendet werden könnten. Das vorgestellte Cache-Kohärenz-Schema ist also für solche Systeme, in denen Änderungsintervall und Abkopplungsdauer etwa in derselben Größenordnung liegen, für Systeme, bei denen sich die Änderungsintervalle der einzelnen Datenobjekte stark unterscheiden und für Systeme, wo das Verhältnis zwischen Verbindungsdauer und Abkopplungsdauer der einzelnen Clients sich stark unterscheidet, gut geeignet.

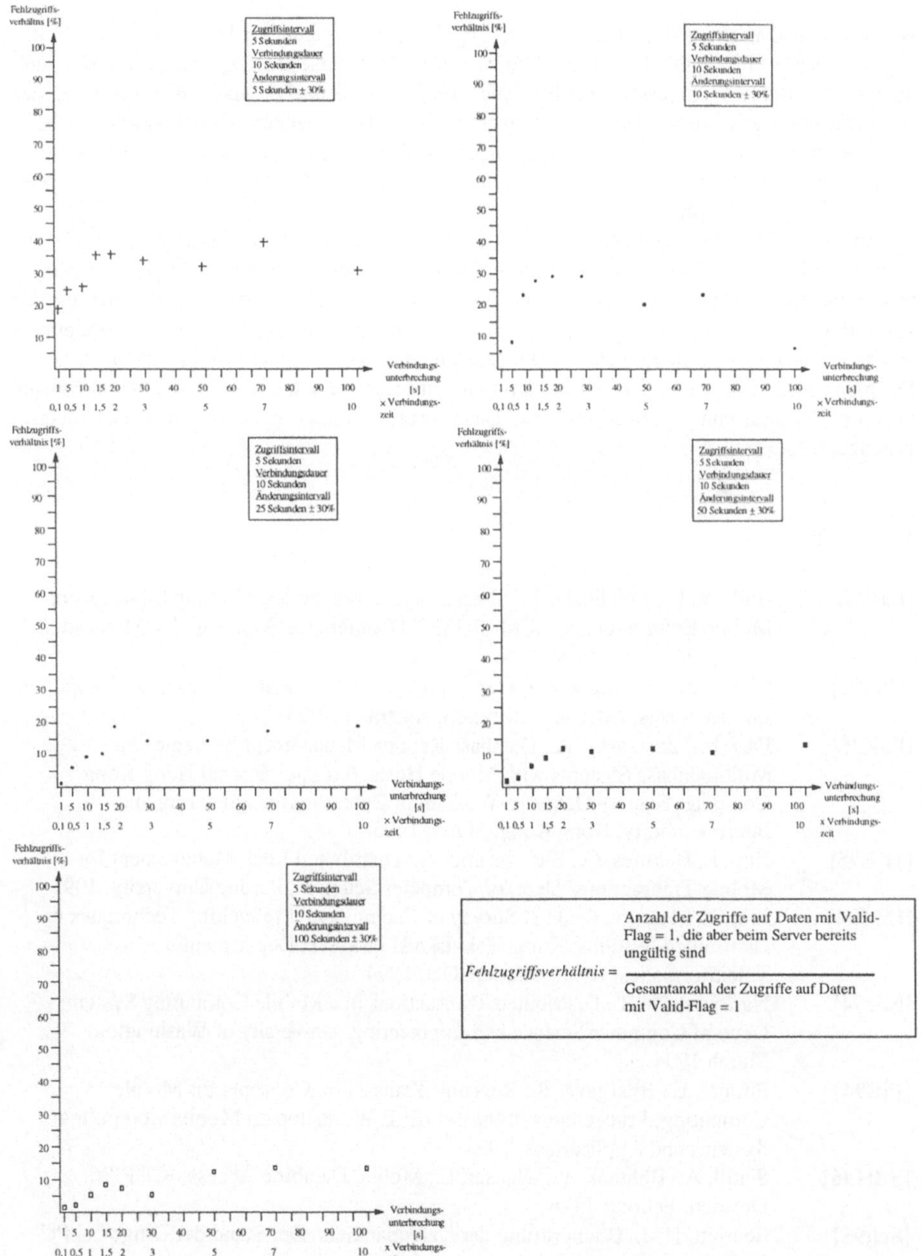

Abbildung 2 - Fehlzugriffsverhältnis

5   Zusammenfassung

Bei den zum Datenbankzugriff in mobiler Umgebung durchgeführten Untersuchungen in der Diplomarbeit wurde deutlich, daß ein Großteil der konventionellen Datenbankkonzepte auch im mobilen Bereich eingesetzt werden kann. Es zeigte sich aber auch, daß für viele der Mechanismen aus dem Bereich konventioneller Datenbanken Modifikationen bzw. Erweiterungen nötig sind, um den Bedingungen mobiler Umgebungen gerecht zu werden. Für einige durch die Mobilität entstehende Probleme sind grundsätzlich neue Konzepte beim Datenbankzugriff notwendig.

Anhand eines weiterentwickelten Cache-Kohärenz-Schemas für mobile Clients wurde die Anwendbarkeit von Datenbeschreibungen untersucht. Die vorgestellte implementierungstechnische Lösung diente zusammen mit den vorgestellten Messungen zur Validierung des Algorithmus. Es wurde nachgewiesen, daß mit Einbeziehung zusätzlicher Beschreibungsmechanismen eine Optimierung des mobilen Datenbankzugriffs erreicht werden kann.

Die hier vorgestellte Arbeit ist Teil der am Lehrstuhl Rechnernetze laufenden Untersuchungen über den Einsatz von Applikations- und Datenbeschreibungen in Algorithmen des mobilen Datenzugriffs.

Literatur

[BaI94]   Barbará, D., Imielinski, T.: Sleepers and Workaholics: Caching Strategies in Mobile Environments; ACM SIGMOD Conference, Minneapolis, Minnesota, May 1994

[Cho96]   Cho: Data Caching with Incremental Update Propagation in Mobile Computing Environments; MCDA96, Monash, Australia, 1996

[FaZ95]   Faiz, M., Zaslavsky, A.: Database Replica Management Strategies in Multidatabase Systems with Mobile Hosts; 6th International Hong Kong Computer Society Database Workshop: Database Reengineering and Interoperability, Hong Kong, March 1995

[JBE95]   Jing, J., Bukhres, O., Elmagarmid, A.: Distributed Lock Management for Mobile Transactions; Dept. of Computer Sciences, Purdue University, 1995

[LiM94]   Liu, G., Maguire, G.Q.: A Survey of Caching and Prefetching Techniques in Distributed Systems; Kungl Tekniska Högskolan, Department of Teleinformatics, Kista, Sweden, Oct. 1994

[Nar94]   Narasayya, V.R.: Distributed Transactions in a Mobile Computing System; Dept. of Computer Science and Engineering, University of Washington, March 1994

[PiB94]   Pitoura, E., Bhargava, B.: Revising Transaction Concepts for Mobile Computing; Proceedings of the 1st IEEE Workshop on Mobile Computing Systems and Applications, 1994

[SBH96]   Schill, A., Böhmak, W., Heuser, L.: Mobile Database Access; ICDP'96, Dresden, Februar 1996

[Sch95]   Schmitt, H.-J.: Buchprüfung der Datenbankiers. Der Stand der Dinge bei PC-SQL-Servern; c't magazin für computer technik 6/95

[Sch96]   Scholler, A.: Datenbankzugriff in mobiler Umgebung; Diplomarbeit; TU Dresden, Lehrstuhl Rechnernetze; 1996

Leistungsuntersuchung photonischer Vermittlungsstufen

Jan Späth

Institut für Nachrichtenvermittlung und Datenverarbeitung
Prof. Dr.-Ing. Dr. h.c. P. Kühn
Seidenstraße 36, 70174 Stuttgart
Tel.: 0711/121-2488; Fax: 0711/121-2477; E-Mail: spaeth@ind.uni-stuttgart.de

1 Einführung

Durch die hohe Übertragungskapazität optischer Faserstrecken und die Fortschritte in der optischen Vermittlungstechnik sind photonische Netze als künftige Transportnetze hervorragend geeignet. Diese Weitverkehrsnetze werden dabei hierarchisch aus optischen und elektronischen Schichten aufgebaut sein. Entscheidende Voraussetzung für einen Erfolg neuer photonischer Technologien ist dabei eine Netzplanung, die zu effizienten und sehr leistungsfähigen Netzen unter Einhaltung der QoS-Anforderungen (*Quality of Service*) führt [2]. Eine wichtige Neuerung stellt dabei das WDM-Verfahren (*Wavelength Division Multiplexing*) dar, bei dem mehrere unterschiedliche Wellenlängen gleichzeitig auf einer Faser geführt werden.

Für mögliche Netzkonzepte ergeben sich zwei grundsätzliche Alternativen: (1) das WP-Verfahren (*Wavelength Path*), bei dem von der Quelle bis zur Senke eine durchgehende Wellenlänge verwendet werden muß, und (2) das VWP-Verfahren (*Virtual Wavelength Path*), bei dem die Wellenlängen den Verbindungen abschnittsweise zugeordnet werden und deshalb für jede Wellenlänge ein Umsetzer (Konverter) erforderlich ist (Bild 1). Diese Konzepte beeinflussen die Architektur der zentralen Elemente künftiger Weitverkehrsnetze, der Vermittlungsknoten mit optischer Cross-Connect-Funktionalität. In dieser Arbeit werden deshalb mögliche Architekturen solcher *Cross-Connects* (CCs) unter besonderer Beachtung der Wellenlängenkonverter vorgestellt und verglichen. Der Schwerpunkt liegt dabei auf einem Analyseverfahren zur Bestimmung der Verlustwahrscheinlichkeit von CCs auf Verbindungsebene.

2 Anforderungen an die Architektur photonischer Vermittlungsknoten

Erste Ideen zur Realisierung photonischer Vermittlungsknoten basierten auf einer opto-elektronischen Wandlung der Signale und anschließender Vermittlung im elektrischen Bereich. Da ein Großteil der Nachrichten vom Knoten meist nur weitergereicht wird, wurden dann Konzepte vorgeschlagen, bei denen ein Teil der Kanäle (d.h. Wellenlängen) rein optisch durchgeschaltet wird. Anfang dieses Jahrzehnts entstanden dann Architekturen, welche optische Vermittlung - allerdings noch ohne Wellenlängenumsetzung - erlaubten. Die Anforderungen an künftige Vermittlungsknoten umfassen u.a.:

- hohe Durchsatzraten durch rein optische Vermittlung einzelner Wellenlängen

- Vermittlung aller im WDM-Verfahren auf einer Faser transportierten Wellenlängen

- Einspeisung bzw. Auskopplung lokalen Verkehrs

- Umwandlung von Signalen in den elektrischen Bereich zur weiteren Signalverarbeitung

Das Ziel ist es, eine wirtschaftliche Alternative zu elektrischen Netzknoten bei vergleichbarem Durchsatz und unter Einhaltung der QoS-Anforderungen zu erhalten. Eine wichtige QoS-Anforderung ist das Erreichen einer geringen Verlustwahrscheinlichkeit. In optischen WDM-Netzen kann es zur Blockierung von Verbindungen kommen, wenn die gleiche Wellenlänge von verschiedenen Eingangsfasern eines Knotens auf dieselbe Ausgangsfaser vermittelt wird, was zu einem sogenannten *Wellenlängenkonflikt* führt. Dies kann durch Wellenlängenkonverter verhindert werden. Sie erlauben die Umsetzung einer ankommenden Wellenlänge auf eine (beliebige) abgehende Wellenlänge. Solche Konverter stellen ein wichtiges Element künftiger optischer (CCs) dar. Da ihre Realisierung sehr aufwendig ist, wurden verschiedene Architekturen für CCs vorgeschlagen, die im folgenden kurz vorgestellt werden.

3 Architekturen photonischer Cross-Connects

Das zentrale Element eines optischen CCs ist die Vermittlungsstufe, die aus zwei Teilen besteht: einer Raumstufe und einer Wellenlängenstufe (Bild 2). λ_1 bis λ_N bezeichnen dabei die N Wellenlängen, die auf einer Faser transportiert und am Eingang der Vermittlungsstufe durch Demultiplexer getrennt werden. Die Architektur kann prinzipiell noch durch eine Zeitstufe als dritte Vermittlungsstufe erweitert werden. Da augenblicklich noch keine überzeugenden Realisierungen einer rein optischen Zeitvermittlung vorliegen, soll diese im folgenden nicht weiter betrachtet werden.

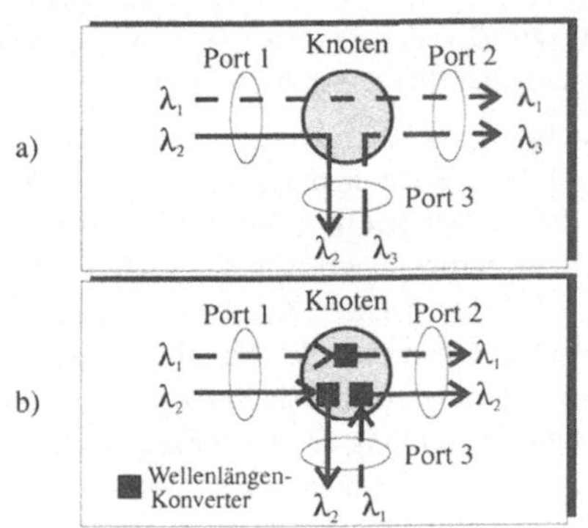

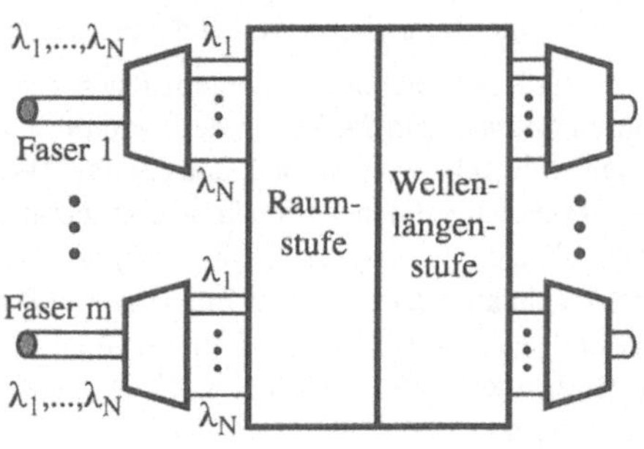

Bild 1: a) WP-Konzept (keine Konverter)
b) VWP-Konzept

Bild 2: Grundarchitektur eines Cross-Connects

Eine Möglichkeit zur Klassifizierung von CCs stellt der Grad der gemeinsamen Nutzung von Ressourcen dar. Da nämlich meist nicht für alle Kanäle gleichzeitig eine Wellenlängenumsetzung in allen Knoten erforderlich ist, können die teuren Konverter durch Konzentration in sogenannten *Pools* gemeinsam genutzt werden. Es lassen sich die folgenden fünf Gruppen unterscheiden (diese Unterteilung ist prinzipiell auch für andere Ressourcen wie z.B. Regeneratoren denkbar):

- CCs mit einem Konverter pro *Kanal* bzw. *Wellenlänge* (VWP-CC)
- CCs mit einem Konverter-Pool für jede *Faser* („Share-per-Fibre"-CC)
- CCs mit einem Pool für jede *Knotenverbindung* (Link), die evtl. mehrere Fasern umfaßt
- CCs mit einem gemeinsamen Pool für *alle Kanäle* („Share-per-Node"-CC)
- Ein Konverter-Pool für *mehrere CCs* oder sogar das ganze Netz

Die Ressourcen könnten bei einer netzweiten, gemeinsamen Nutzung am effizientesten verwendet werden. Allerdings erfordert dieses Konzept nicht nur einen sehr hohen Aufwand für das Netzmanagement, es müssen auch zahlreiche physikalische Randbedingungen wie z.B.

maximale Laufzeiten berücksichtigt werden. Dieser Ansatz scheint daher nur in relativ kleinen Netzen sinnvoll zu sein und wird im folgenden nicht weiter betrachtet.

Bei einem qualitativen Vergleich der unterschiedlichen Architekturen läßt sich feststellen, daß mit steigender Anzahl der Konverter sowohl die Leistungsfähigkeit des Netzes als auch die Kosten zur Realisierung der Knoten steigen. Außerdem wird der Aufwand für das Netzmanagement mit zunehmender Zentralisierung (d.h. gemeinsamer Nutzung) größer. Intern blockierungsfreie CCs können nur dann erreicht werden, wenn für jede Wellenlänge in jedem Knoten ein Konverter zur Verfügung steht. Ein ausführlicherer Vergleich findet sich in [1].

4 Modellierung

Dieser Abschnitt enthält eine kurze Beschreibung der Modellbildung für die Leistungsuntersuchung eines einzelnen CCs mit einer prinzipiellen Architektur gemäß Bild 2. Jeweils m Fasern sind am Ein- und Ausgang des CCs angeschlossen. Ein Demultiplexer trennt die N Wellenlängen, die im WDM-Modus auf jeder Faser transportiert werden. Diese Wellenlängen durchlaufen eine blockierungsfreie Raumvermittlungsstufe. Daran schließt sich eine Stufe mit Wellenlängenvermittlung gemäß dem jeweiligen Pool-Konzept an, ehe Multiplexer die Wellenlängen auf den abgehenden Fasern wieder zusammenfassen. Für die technische Realisierung gibt es jeweils mehrere Möglichkeiten ([1]).

Um die Verlustwahrscheinlichkeit des CCs zu berechnen, ist es ausreichend, die abgehenden Fasern zu betrachten, da nur dort Verluste auftreten können. Es gibt zwei Ursachen für Verluste. Zum einen kann eine abgehende Faser voll belegt sein, so daß die neu ankommende Verbindung abgelehnt werden muß. Zum andern kann ein Wellenlängenkonflikt auftreten, der mangels verfügbarer Konverter nicht aufgelöst werden kann. In beiden Fällen der Blockierung wird die Verbindung abgelehnt, d.h., es wird ein reines Verlustsystem betrachtet.

Für die Modellierung des Verkehrs wird eine unendliche Zahl von Quellen angenommen, die Verbindungswünsche zufällig zu einem beliebigen Knoten des Netzes erzeugen. Dabei wird eine gleichförmige Verteilung des Verkehrs angesetzt, d.h., jeder Knoten wird mit der gleichen Wahrscheinlichkeit als Ziel ausgewählt. Da keine spezielle Routingstrategie vorausgesetzt wird, führen diese Annahmen zu gleichen Wahrscheinlichkeiten für die Verwendung der Ausgangsfasern. Damit sind die m Ausgangsfasern eines Knotens mit Ausnahme der eventuellen gemeinsamen Benutzung von Konvertern unabhängig voneinander.

Darüber hinaus wird angenommen, daß jede der verfügbaren w Wellenlängen mit gleicher Wahrscheinlichkeit benutzt wird. Dies ist durch die Voraussetzung gerechtfertigt, daß jeder Sender bei einer neuen Verbindung und ebenso jeder Konverter beim Umsetzen einer Verbindung eine zufällige aus den verfügbaren Wellenlängen auswählt.

Diese Annahmen führen zu einem Poisson-verteilten Ankunftsprozeß mit Rate μ von Verbindungswünschen für jede Ausgangsfaser eines CCs. Außerdem werden die Verbindungsdauern als negativ-exponentiell verteilt mit Mittelwert ε angesetzt. In realen Netzen werden aufwendigere Routingstrategien als die angenommene zufällige Auswahl angewandt werden. Da dies zu höheren Durchsätzen führen wird, stellt die gemäß obigen Annahmen berechnete Verlustwahrscheinlichkeit eine Obergrenze für die zu erwartenden realen Verlustwahrscheinlichkeiten dar.

5 Analyseverfahren

Im folgenden wird beispielhaft die exakte Analyse eines „Share-per-Fibre"-CCs mit Hilfe einer zweidimensionalen Markoff-Kette gezeigt. Außerdem wird eine Näherungslösung für „Share-per-Link"-und „Share-per-Node"-CCs vorgestellt.

Die Anzahl der verfügbaren Wellenlängen w wird als Variable berücksichtigt, da eine Senkung der Verlustwahrscheinlichkeiten möglich ist, falls mehr Wellenlängen zur Verfügung gestellt werden als gleichzeitig auf einer Faser transportiert werden können ($w > N$). Mit k werde die Anzahl der Konverter des Faser-Pools bezeichnet. Zu jedem Zeitpunkt gibt es eine Anzahl von Kanälen, die keine Konverter verwenden (i, $i \in 0, 1, ..., N$), und eine Anzahl von Kanälen mit Konvertern (j, $j \in 0, 1, ..., k$). Somit läßt sich der Zustandsraum durch (i, j) mit der Randbedingung $i + j \leq N$ beschreiben. Die Verkehrsannahmen aus Abschnitt 4 ergeben ein Angebot $A = \mu/\varepsilon$ pro Faser.

Bild 3 zeigt die resultierende Markoff-Kette mit Übergangsraten. Zustände, in denen neue Verbindungswünsche aufgrund voll belegter Fasern verlorengehen, sind dick umrandet. In den grau unterlegten Zuständen tritt ein Verlust nur dann auf, wenn die Wellenlänge der Verbindung bereits belegt ist, da keine Konverter mehr verfügbar sind.

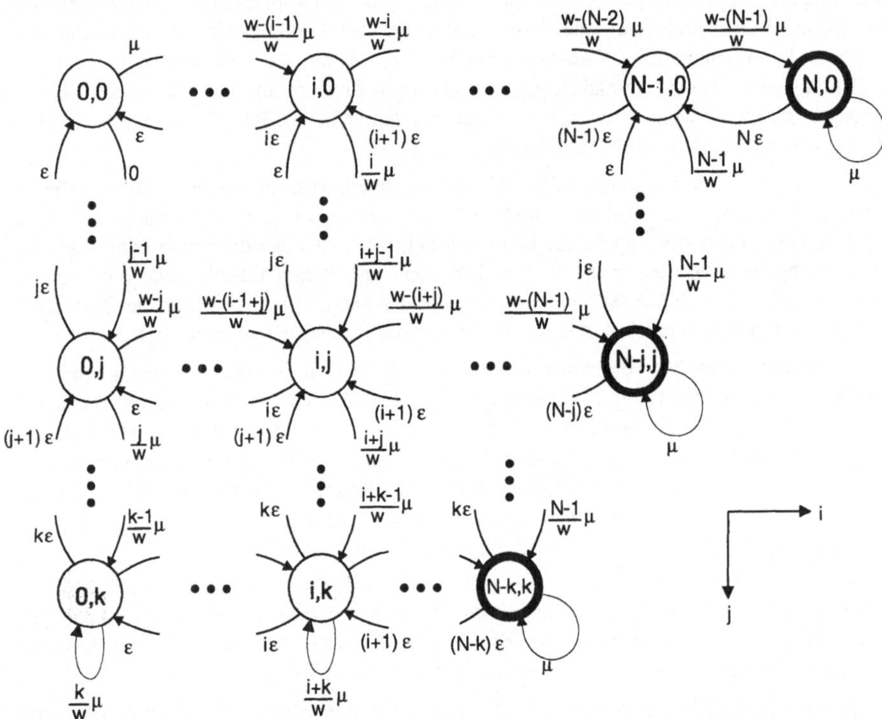

Bild 3: Zustands-Übergangs-Diagramm für eine „Share-per-Fibre"-Architektur

Die Analyse dieses Modells führt auf ein System linearer Gleichungen. Die Gleichgewichtswahrscheinlichkeit $p_{i,j}$ des Zustands (i, j) kann durch diese Gleichungen und die Normie-

rungsbedingung $\sum_{i=0}^{N} \sum_{\substack{j=0 \\ j \leq k}}^{N-i} p_{i,j} = 1$ bestimmt werden. Aus den Werten $p_{i,j}$ ergeben sich

die Wahrscheinlichkeiten für Verluste durch Wellenlängenkonflikte zu

$$B_{konv,\,faser} = \sum_{i=0}^{N-k-1} p_{i,\,k} \cdot \frac{i+k}{w} \quad \text{und zu} \quad B_{voll} = \sum_{j=0}^{k} p_{N-j,\,j} \quad \text{für Verluste durch voll-}$$

ständig gefüllte Fasern. Die Gesamtverlustwahrscheinlichkeit resultiert somit zu $B = B_{konv,\,faser} + B_{voll}$.

Prinzipiell ist es möglich, für alle Architekturen von CCs die Verlustwahrscheinlichkeiten mittels mehrdimensionaler Markoff-Ketten exakt zu berechnen. Da sich aber bereits für einfache Strukturen sehr komplexe und große Zustandsräume ergeben, können exakte Ergebnisse nur für relativ kleine CCs gewonnen werden. Für größere CCs und insbesondere für CCs mit einer beliebigen Anzahl von Fasern und einem Pool pro Link bzw. pro Knoten wurde deshalb ein Näherungsverfahren entwickelt.

Eine Näherung für die Verlustwahrscheinlichkeit aufgrund Konvertermangel (B_{konv}) bei „Share-per-Link"- oder „Share-per-Node"-CCs kann wie folgt gewonnen werden. Zuerst wird eine unbegrenzte Anzahl von Konvertern angenommen (Wellenlängenkonflikte können nicht auftreten) und die sich ergebende Wahrscheinlichkeitsverteilung für die Anzahl belegter Konverter einer Einzelfaser bestimmt. Die Wahrscheinlichkeitsverteilung für die Gesamtzahl belegter Konverter ergibt sich durch eine Faltung der einzelnen Wahrscheinlichkeitsverteilungen. $B_{konv,\,l}$ bezeichne die Wahrscheinlichkeit, daß insgesamt genau l Konverter durch alle Fasern belegt sind. Dann kann B_{konv} durch die Summe der Wahrscheinlichkeiten aller Zustände, in denen mehr als die k verfügbaren Konverter belegt sind, angenähert werden:

$$B_{konv} = \sum_{l \geq k} B_{konv,\,l} \ .$$

Diese Approximation liefert eine Obergrenze der Verlustwahrscheinlichkeiten durch Überschätzung der exakten Ergebnisse. Sie wurde durch einen Vergleich mit der exakten Analyse eines „Share-per-Node"-CCs mit zwei angeschlossenen Fasern mittels einer vierdimensionalen Markoff-Kette überprüft.

6 Ergebnisse

Im folgenden werden einige Ergebnisse vorgestellt, die den Einfluß der Konverterzahl auf die Verlustwahrscheinlichkeit eines CCs zeigen. Diese und weitere Ergebnisse finden sich in [1].

Die Anzahl N der Wellenlängen auf einer Faser wird mit 8 in einer zur Zeit realistischen Größenordnung gewählt, obwohl in einigen Veröffentlichungen auch von wesentlich größeren Werten ausgegangen wird. Außerdem wird die Anzahl der verfügbaren Wellenlängen w gleich N gewählt. Werte für $w > N$ sind zwar möglich, spielen in zur Zeit diskutierten Systemen aber keine wesentliche Rolle.

Bild 4 zeigt die exakt gewonnenen Verlustwahrscheinlichkeiten für einen CC mit „Share-per-Fibre"-Architektur. Die Fälle $k = 0$ bzw. $k = 8$ stellen einen CC für das WP- bzw. VWP-Verfahren dar. Die Ergebnisse zeigen, daß sich die Verlustwahrscheinlichkeiten für die angenommenen dynamischen Verkehrsverhältnisse, ausgehend von einer Faser ohne Konverter, durch Bereitstellung zusätzlicher Konverter deutlich senken läßt. Es zeigt sich aber auch, daß eine Erhöhung der Konverterzahl von z.B. 6 auf 8 kaum mehr eine Verbesserung bringt.

Dies kann durch die Tatsache erklärt werden, daß die Verlustwahrscheinlichkeit aus zwei Komponenten besteht: (1) alle Kanäle einer Faser sind belegt und (2) ein Wellenlängenkonflikt kann nicht aufgelöst werden, da keine Konverter mehr verfügbar sind. Der Einfluß dieser beiden Anteile hängt wesentlich vom Verkehrsangebot und der Architektur des CCs ab.

Bild 5 zeigt die Verlustwahrscheinlichkeit eines „Share-per-Node"-CCs mit $m = 8$ Fasern, wovon jede $N = 8$ Wellenlängen gleichzeitig tragen kann, was insgesamt 64 Kanäle ergibt. CCs in dieser Größenordnung sind mit momentan verfügbaren Technologien realistisch. Die Kurven für $k = 0$ bzw. k = 64 ergeben sich für einen WP- bzw. VWP-CC. Diese Werte, die durch eine exakte Analyse gewonnen wurden, begrenzen den möglichen Bereich für Verlustwahrscheinlichkeiten bei beliebigen Pool-Konzepten.

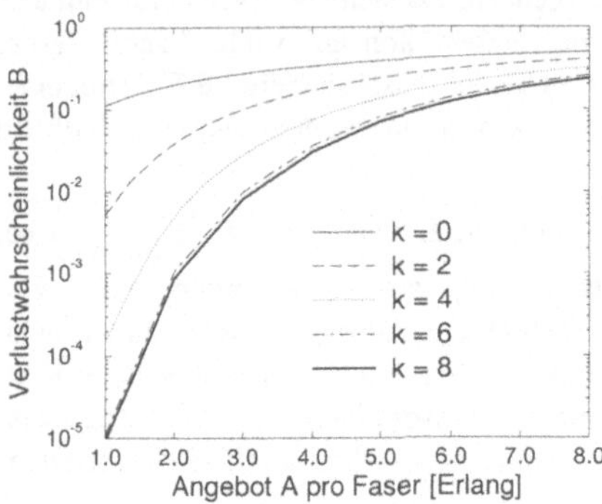

Bild 4: Verlustwahrscheinlichkeit B für „Share-per-Fibre"-CC ($N = 8, w = 8$)

Bild 5: Gesamtverlustwahrscheinlichkeit B und Näherungen für Verluste durch Wellenlängenkonflikte B_{konv} ($m = 8, N = 8, w = 8$)

Wie im vorigen Abschnitt dargestellt, überschätzt die gewählte Approximation (gestrichelte Linien in Bild 5) den exakten Verlauf von B_{konv}. Damit können Bereiche bestimmt werden, in denen die Anzahl von Konvertern bei gegebenem Verkehrsangebot nur noch eine vernachlässigbare Auswirkung auf die Verlustwahrscheinlichkeit hat. Minimale Gesamtverluste werden dann erreicht, wenn für jeden Kanal ein Konverter zur Verfügung steht (im Bild 5 die Kurve für B bei $k = 64$). Die Verringerung der Gesamtverluste durch Hinzufügen weiterer teurer Konverter ist vernachlässigbar, solange B_{konv} unterhalb dieser Untergrenze liegt.

7 Zusammenfassung

In dieser Arbeit wurde ein kurzer Vergleich optischer Cross-Connects mit unterschiedlichen Pool-Konzepten für Wellenlängenkonverter vorgestellt. Für die verschiedenen Architekturen wurden exakte und approximative Verfahren zur Bestimmung der Verlustwahrscheinlichkeiten erarbeitet. Die Näherungsverfahren dienen zur Reduzierung des Rechenaufwandes, der bereits bei relativ einfachen Knotenstrukturen stark ansteigt. Die Ergebnisse zeigen, daß die Verluste bei dynamischen Verkehrsverhältnissen durch Einsatz von Konvertern stark verringert werden können. Ab einem bestimmten Ausstattungsgrad führen zusätzliche Konverter allerdings nur noch zu vernachlässigbar kleinen Verbesserungen. Somit können die Ergebnisse zur Dimensionierung von CCs mit Wellenlängenkonvertern unter Einhaltung einer bestimmten Verlustwahrscheinlichkeit dienen.

Literatur

[1] J. SPÄTH, U. GREMMELMAIER, U. BRIEM, M.N. HUBER, „Architecture and Performance Evaluation of Future Photonic Networks", *Proceedings of the 12th ICCC Conference*, Seoul 1995, Bd. 2, S. 661 - 666

[2] J. SPÄTH, U. GREMMELMAIER, M.N. HUBER, U. BRIEM, „Design and Planning Aspects of Future Photonic Transport Networks", *Proceedings of the 13th EFOC&N Conference*, Brighton 1995, Bd. 2, S. 60 - 63

Index der Autoren